Lisbon Street
Art & Urban Creativity

2014 International Conference

Urbancreatvity.org

Title:
Lisbon Street
Art & Urban Creativity
2014 International Conference

Editors:
Pedro Soares Neves
Daniela V. de Freitas Simões

Graphic Design:
Pedro Soares Neves
Proof reading:
Daniela V. de Freitas Simões

©Authors and Editors
Lisbon, November 2014
ISBN: 978-989-20-5138-3

Support:

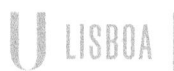

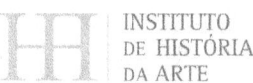

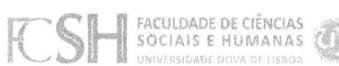

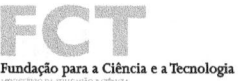

Table of contents

Pedro Soares Neves
Daniela V. de Freitas Simões

Street & Urban Creativity

In the aftermath of the Lisbon Street Art & Urban Creativity International Conference (July, 2014), it became clear due to the large number of contributions from distinctive disciplinary fields that the research methodologies while tackling with 'Street & Urban Creativity' – are in fact unique and transdisciplinary.

Over the past decades, graffiti, street and urban creativity in general have centered the debate around urban art, urban creativity and even public art whether considering them an aggression on the city and its users, whether building them as not only a sociological and anthropological response but also, a creative one to the built environment.

However, and even though a consensus has not been reached (and probably never will), the focus on these practices and their actors has increased considerably, inside and outside the academia. In 2008, the Tate exhibition, Street Art at Tate, re-centered the debate once again, in these practices, being both preceded and followed by other exhibitions in museums, galleries and other institutions.

In the editorial quadrant, several authors have focused their attention and research in Graffiti and Street Art and Urban Creativity in general, ranging from the most renown names and illustrations to the most remote and non-traditional geographies.

On the 15th February 2014, the Call for Papers for the Lisbon Street Art & Urban Creativity International Conference was closed and the overall number of submissions was of 95 abstracts.

Abstracts were submitted by main authors of 18 different nationalities of which 67% were non-Portuguese and therefore, international applications. The percentage distribution was the following:

Australia	2%
Austria	2%
Brazil	4%
Canada	3%
Finland	1%
France	2%
Germany	13%
Greece	3%
Italy	7%
Mexico	1%
New Zeland	1%
Portugal	33%
Spain	5%
Sweden	2%
Switzerland	2%
Turkey	1%
UK	7%
USA	9%

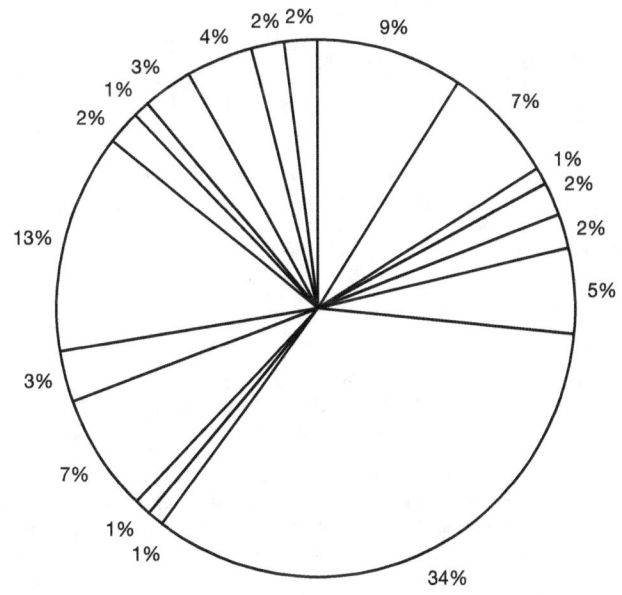

The blind peer review selection process of the abstracts was conducted by the Conference's Scientific Committee and was completed in March 3, 2014 having been accepted in early phase a total of 70 communications. However presentations were reduced to 49, totaling 85 authors (58 speakers) – complemented by four keynote speakers :

- Cedar Lewisohn (Tate Modern) ;
- Martyn Reed curated ± (NUART Festival)
- Marcus Willcocks (Central Saint Martins - University of the Arts London)
- Graça Fonseca (Lisbon City Hall) .

The post-Conference assessment inquiry result was as follows :

Exceptional	20%
Excellent	56%
Very Good	20%
Good	44%
Satisfactory	0%
Shortly Satisfactory	0%
Bad	0%

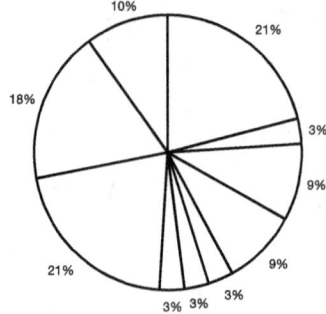

Conference covered various fields of study.
The percentage of delegates per scientific area:

Anthropology	10%
Sociology	18%
Historiography	21%
Museology	3%
Psychology	3%
Philosophy	3%
Design	9%
Architecture	9%
Economy	3%
Other / practice	21%

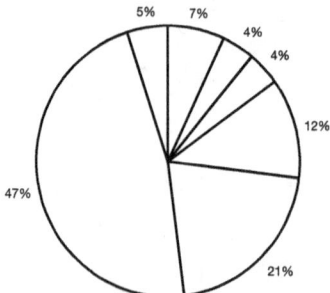

With the following academic levels covered:

Post-Doc	5%
PhD	47%
PhD Candidates	21%
Master's	12%
Ma. Students	4%
Graduates	4%
N/A	7%

Following the Conference experience The Executive Committee intends to promote and foster the existence of broader approaches to the conference outcomes. The Street & Urban Creativity International Research Topic will henceforth develop actions to generate stronger articulations between researchers through collective applications, applied researches and publishing material.

With the purpose of gathering knowledge and serve as reference platform for both academics, practitioners, municipal technicians, cultural agents, and others that need to tackle and be informed as much as possible about the journal subject (Graffiti, Street Art and Urban Creativity in general) in a scientific manner we have decided to launch the "Street & Urban Creativity" Scientific Journal to develop contents in wide cross disciplinary approaches.

The project connects both practice driven knowledge and academic different graduation degrees. The emphasis on the PhD, and PhD candidates as the main group for developing contents positions the top intellectual level of the project. The openness and practical driven, everyday contact from part of the anonymous citizen with the phenomena that are addressed by the journal, also gives a wider approach and positions the intellectual level of the project as being very accessible and relevant for non academics as well.

The Street & Urban Creativity International Research Topic is being constituted as the research base for the work (conferences, journal and other) and support the teaching in the different scientific areas where the contents are approached. We expect that this book will serve as one of many other consulting documents and activities that we will contribute as best as possible for the understanding and decision-making upon the Street & Urban Creativity subjects.

Dra. Catarina Vaz Pinto
Councilwoman for Culture – Municipality of Lisbon

Opening Remarks

I would like to thank the invitation to open this seminar on arts and urban creativity. I know you have an intensive program and must be anxious to listen to this morning's keynote speaker, Cedar Lewisohn, responsible for Tate's Street Art exhibition of 2008. But let me take this opportunity to share with you some ideas about this issue from the perspective of a policy maker, such as I am.

As you all must know, the Lisbon City Council has developed a policy program that gave the support to the Cronos Project in Lisbon and since then is responsible for the Urban Art Gallery. It was, and still is, a policy that addresses or tries to give an assertive response to the issue of graffiti and street art. And this wasn't, and still isn't, a simple question.

The straightforward answer was until then the road of prohibition and criminal prosecution. In some cases, it still is, as derives from the recent approved law concerning graffiti and street art. Street art and graffiti can now be, according to the law, distinguished from vandalic interventions. Once again it is not a simple question or even a matter of taste. Maybe these two 'labels'- art or vandalism - , so to speak, can be considered the defying cornerstones of cultural policy nowadays.

They involve in only one simple line of paint the rights of private property owner's, the regulation of the public space and the need, the right of being seen, of leaving some kind of mark, some kind of statement. Involving in only a simple sticker or tag, different social groups and asymmetric distributions of power and wealth. Involving and convoking the state intervention in mediating this conflict expressed in the communicational walls of the city and the urban cloth. For some, seen as signs of an underlying urban disease (even after Tate's recognition). For others, signs of the artistic vitality of the city.

This other path as proved itself a walk worth walking. Not only gave way to new career paths for a new generation of artists and writers, but also proved itself more democratic, because under the label of street or urban art, one can see the opening of public spaces (and spheres) to these forms of cultural expression.

We are now, once again and in my perspective, in a new crossroad. Can we or should we institutionalize these cultural expressions? If so, to what extent does this institutionalization affects the creative milieu, its members and practitioners? It's an answer I do not have yet.

Urban creativity is nowadays the headline of any economic discourse around smart and entrepreneurial cities, globally competing as platforms for cosmopolitan businesses and creative individuals. A model to project the city that is not fully accepted by researchers.

Not that I reject the economic spill-over effects of cultural and creative activities into industries in the creative economy, but as a policy maker in the field of culture, my core business, is, using the state of the art jargon, the development and educational training of creativity as a fundamental skill to survive in the twenty first century. It's another perspective to convoke culture into the creative economy. And maybe another path worth walking.

Thank you for your attention.

Ema Rocha, independent researcher

'Musealizar por aí'
Graffiti – The Street as Exhibit

In July 2012, Huffington Post publishes a news item about the possibility of graffiti's conservation. Because of a framed stencil and sequent social network discussion, the newspaper asks his readers about the need to preserve certain writer's interventions on walls, which were illegal, and until then ephemeral. Many were the times in which renowned Museums or Cultural Institutions welcomed celebrated international writers. This article does not aim to behold what has the graffiti provided for the museums, but rather what have museums passed on to graffiti. In which ways has the museological model spread on, from inside the galleries to the streets? Graffiti, (and post-graffiti), being the willful, genuine, visual expressionist is, turned into a sign of contemporary urban significance, having the City as his set, transforming it into a wide in the open gallery.

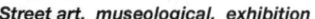

Street art, museological, exhibition

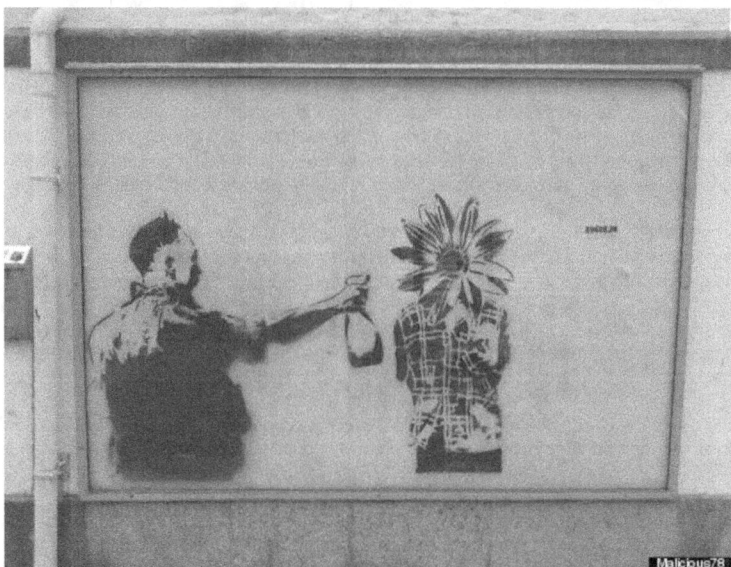

Fig.1 Framed Banksy stencil on Reddit © Malicious78

In July 2012, user Malicious78 posted on Reddit[1] a photo of a framed Banksy stencil covered with Plexiglass. (fig.1)The caption said: "Graffiti becomes art when the artist becomes famous enough. Our city council framed this piece behind Plexiglass." Other users' comments appeared, showing us other cases, in which the landlords of these buildings or the mayors of these towns were the ones trying to preserve these stencils. In the same day, Huffington Post publishes an article entitled "Should Street Art is framed for its own protection? Reddit speaks out. "One of the users from the Reddit discussion wrote:

> "Yeah, but part of the point of street art is that it's temporary and outside of the mainstream art scene. It's not supposed to be displayed in galleries, framed/protected nor talked about by pretentious arseholes. However sad it may be to see an amazing piece of graffiti destroyed, I'm afraid that is part of what graffiti is about... They are taking it out of "the wild" as you put it and surely it can no longer be considered 'street art' in the classic sense. This goes against the anti-establishment principles of street art."

One can tell that street art is behaving exactly as fine arts have behaved for at least one century. Shocking and striking until society gets shocked and outraged with something else. In some other comment, user Dajbman22 wrote:

> "That is the insane beauty of art. No matter how hard an artist tries, in the end, it is the viewing audience and society at large which dictates what is art (or at least art worth viewing/preserving) and what is not."

These news were our motto to take the time to meditate on our new fondness for the streets, on our taste for what used to be the side-line, on why is this a public discussion? We intend to show that we have been 'musealizing' or 'gallerizing' our cities, our walls, as a means of appreciating and perpetuate them.

There are a variety of reasons and events that might explain this street art acceptance and this civil preoccupation with its conservationBottom of Form. First, we need to acknowledge that graffiti, illegal or not, has been exposed to our eyes for decades. As Ricardo Campos wrote in his PhD thesis: "The advertising, graffiti, urban signage, all live in the same scenario, crisscrossing languages and nurturing new forms communication"[2].Half of the world's population lives in urban areas, so the city is half world's landscape, it's our scenery.

On the other hand, we need to keep in mind the role of the museums and gallerists. Let us remember Sidney Janis. His new-York gallery was the home for a very early graffiti exhibition. Organized by Dolores Neumann, art collector and fan of graffiti, in 1983, the exhibition encouraged a number of the young graffiti writers to transfer their work to canvas. It showed tags and canvas paintings by Noc 167 (Melvin Samuels Jr.), Daze (Chris Ellis), Ramm-El-Zee (Stephen Piccirello), Toxic (TorrickAblack), Blade (Steven Ogburn) and Crash (John Matos), besides others. This exhibit allowed Sidney Janis to buy several street paintings. After his death, his heirs donated, in 1999, circa 50 paintings to the Brooklyn Museum, enabling one of the biggest and first exhibitions of this street art. "Graffiti" was the name of the exhibition; it took place in the Brooklyn Museum, between June and September 2006. It explored "how a genre that began as a form of subversive public communication has become legitimate—moving away from the street and into private collections and galleries."[3] Let us now enhance the two exhibitions in Europe that were probably very responsible for the general public street art taste.

First, we had Tate Modern's "Street Art", from 23rd May until 25th August 2008. All of the façade facing the river presented artistic interventions from six of the biggest street artists in the world like BLU, Os Gémeos and JR, which became more noticed than ever for that exhibition. Curated by Cedar Lewisohn, this exhibition also featured a walking tour with a map (fig.2) that we will talk about later on.

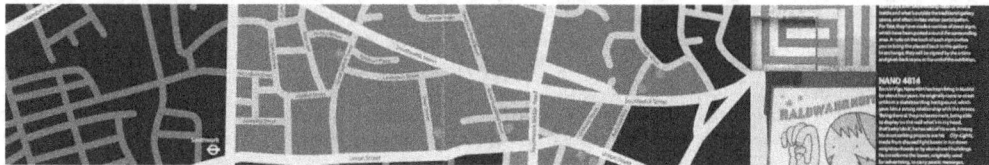

Fig.2 Part of the map from the Walking Tour "Street Art" Tate Modern Exhibition © Tate Modern

Besides this one, we want to mention another exhibit that we consider, for the exclusivity of the institution, to be very symptomatic of the artistic taste for the streets. Untitled "Born in the Streets: Graffiti", curated by Leanne Sacramone and Thomas Delamore and having KetOne as consultant[4], the exhibition took place in Foundation Cartier, in Paris, from July 2009 until January 2010. It was intended to call for the sources of the movement while offering an outlook of the diversity of contemporary graffiti writing. It was a way to recreate the streets inside. Thus, we have the exhibition at Tate, who featured an urban tour of site-specific art from a group of Madrid-based street artists, maybe initializing a way to treat the city as an open-air gallery.

In a try to prove this street 'musealization' we have isolated six key concepts from the ICOM's museum studies glossary that we intend to be the most important roles for a museum[5] to play. Thus, we will present each one of them e look for traces of them in well-known graffiti/street art/urban interventions.

Conservation

According to ICOM[6], Conservation regards to the group of measures that has as a goal the protection of the tangible cultural heritage, ensuring his accessibility to present and future generations.

Therefore, Banksy seems to be the street artist main concern of conservation. Besides what we have already seen in the beginning of this article, about the frames around Banksy's stencil, we have much more to read about the attempt to keep Banky's wall pieces where they belong, and not letting the street ruled as it used to: the orders for cleaning or the graffiti crossing over. Of all, we chose for this article the story about a neighbourhood watch that saved Banksy. After Hurricane Katrina, Banksy executed a lot of stencils in New Orleans, usually showing mournful people because of the natural disaster. One of this stencils, usually called "umbrella girl" or "rain girl", painted on a cinder block, was almost getting stolen when the people from the neighbourhood watch saw someone trying to cut off the wall and called the police[7]. We had already seen what happened when some town mayors and some buildings landlords tried to preserve some stencil pieces in their town walls. We can get in touch with several online opinions that challenge the decision; but, overall, if it is being done, is because most of the lay society believes that that is something for future generations to know, see and, why not, study.

Exhibition

This might be the museological aspect that we can more often find when it comes to treat the street as a canvas. We can first approach the walking tours, which are, by far, the most significant proof of what we wish to demonstrate.

In Brooklyn, the Street Art Walk Tour:

"Brings the walls alive with walking tours in Lower Manhattan, Bushwick, and Williamsburg. Packed in the span of 2 hours you will see an eclectic, ever-evolving mix of art featuring artists from around the world. The tour includes a diverse array of mediums such as paste-ups, stencils, murals, stickers, left objects and graffiti. Artists may include Willow, Roa, Sweettoof, Dain, Dee Dee, Swampy, Invader, Buffmonster, Paul Richard, C215, Over Under, Faile, Bast, HowNosm, Enzoand Nio, Erik Berglin,Stikman, ASVP, Hellbent, KinoQ, Fumero, Sonni, Icy and Sot, Reka, OCMC, El Sol 25, Stik, Never Satisfied, The Yok, Sheryo, FKDL, Ron English, Tristan Eaton, Beau Stanton, Cern, Cekis, Lunar New Year, Gilf, RWK, BD White, Mr. Toll and countless others."[8]

In Berlin, The Street Art Tour and Workshop includes:

"History & origins of this underground global phenomena; Urban art in society & underground circles; Street art vs Graffiti, unwritten rules & codes of conduct; Mural art by Blu, OsGémeos, Ema Jones, ROA and more; Culture jamming, activism in art &adbusting, Futuristic graffiti techniques; Paint inside a former abandoned factory complex and creative space; Talks and demonstrations by local artists and instruction on how to make your own street art & graffiti pieces; All materials and a personally made souvenir to take home![9]*"*

In Portugal, especially in Lisbon, we are fortuned to have a variety of projects that have put us in the map of the essential cities to look for street art and graffiti.

First, let us talk about Museu Efémero (Ephemeral Museum). Sponsored by Pampero Fondación, Museu Efémero "opened his doors" in 2008, admitting to be the first ephemeral museum in the world. Ask can be seen on picture 3, (fig 3.),Museu Efémero consisted of labels applied on walls, with the description of the piece right next to it, including the artist's name and a number for the corresponding podcast. On the website you could easily download not only these podcasts, but also maps of parts of Lisbon where graffiti and street art was prevailing and significant. Museu Efémero had a big part of the project at Bairro Alto (before his cleaning in 2009), but also in Amoreiras and other Lisbon's neighbourhoods. It is necessary to say that this project is prior to Lisbon's placement as one of the most interesting street art cities in Europe. That headline might have come along with CRONO Project, as we will see right away.

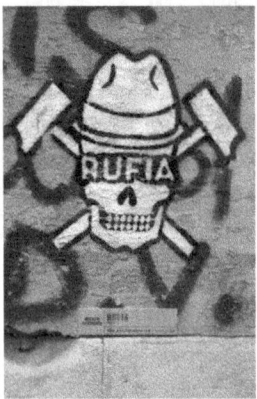

Fig.3 Label at Museu Efémero
© Pampero Fundación

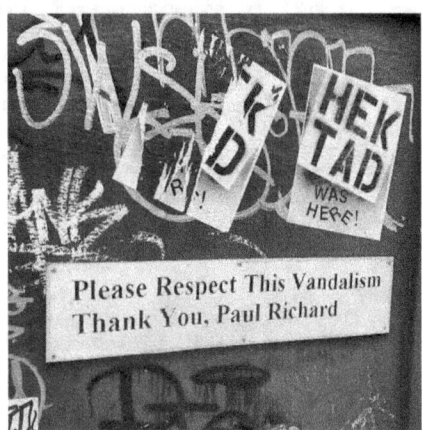

Fig.4 Paul Richard – Designated Art
© Martha Cooper

The CRONO Project is perhaps the most ostentatious of all the urban art projects in Lisbon. With a scheduled agenda, CRONO was developed in four stages between May 2010 and October 2011, with the presence and works of several national and international artists like BLU, Os Gémeos, Sam3 or Vhils. The before unoccupied and wrecked buildings that these artists painted resulted in several articles in the international press. It size and centrality in the capital city drew the social media attention to them, starting the debate if it was a good way of renewing old buildings or a smart way to hide them.

Also in Portugal, but in the countryside, we have the WOOL festival that claims the Covilhã town walls as support for urban interventions in order to get the population in touch with the contemporary and urban aesthetics, arranging the city to change her looks with the intervened places. For something not so completely different, we would like to name an artist who didn't grow as a writer typically does, but made himself into the urban trends, using the streets as sets to his own installations.

Paul Richard, and his line of work "Designated Art", not only draws attention to the objects that are on the streets by transforming them into "ready-mades", adding a label similar to a museum's or gallery's, using the same font and outline, but what is vital for this discussion is that he does it to graffiti, usually to tagging, naming graffiti an integral part of the "vrbe" and treating graffiti's as exhibition. (fig.4)

Study

We believe there are some unique cases of questioning the process of the street intervention itself, that really are cases in which the way the subjects are shown to the public are already an interpretation of the artist's creative process. First, we would like to talk about a book that we believe to be treating the graffiti art as any kind of art. "Urban Illustration Berlin: Street Art City guide" (fig.5), by Benjamin Wolbergs, brings us Berlin as a canvas, documenting more than 500 works in the streets of the city, from anonymous artists to well-known graffiti writers. The book is divided into three parts: in the first one, the author presents to us each piece by artist and technic, including a geographical reference for a map; the second part is composed by artist's interviews; the third and last part refers to a map on which one can find the references from the artist and the technique, that enables this book to be the ultimate guide to a city as gallery. This allows the public to really behave as a visitor in a museum, to have the kind of curiosity for the works that are usually set inside. The second case we want to reflect on is a national artist, Miguel Januário, also known as MaisMenos. He is really not a study case rather than a documentation of the own work case, followed by a theorization of his own creative process.

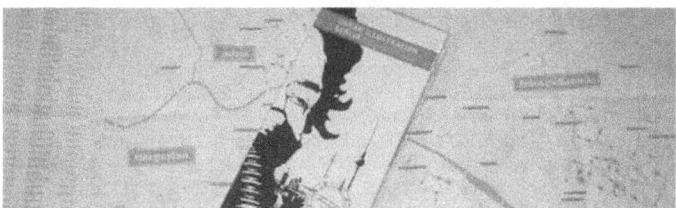

Fig. 5 "Urban Illustration Berlin: Street Art City guide", by Benjamin Wolbergs

With a really long list of sarcastic pun-intended sentences or words, both in English and Portuguese, spread throughout the country, MaisMenos has built a font and style to his work, that is immediately recognizable to the eyes of the streets beholder. However, his puns go beyond walls. MaisMenos has documented in video several of his artistic performances, that don't categorize as street art as in city illustration but still are urban performances. From playing golf with bread instead of balls in front of the Parliament[10], to perpetuate in video his participation in "Guimarães Capital Europeia da Cultura 2012", (where he showed the murder and funeral of the nation), MaisMenos has been offering us a study, a lection about his own interventional projects.

Acquisition

One of the biggest auction houses in Europe, Artcurial, in Paris, did in early 2014, a street art pieces auction for charity, featuring some of the most famous street artists wide world like JR, KoolKrom or Keith Haring. The price of the pieces rose easily to amounts like 30 000€. There is one very explanatory video that not only shows some of the artist's work inside, but also the kind of stressful environment so typical of an auction. We intend to show parts of this video at the conference[11].

Pleasure

Pleasure is, by far, the most generic concept we have introduced in this article. We saved it to talk about the one issue that concerns the undisclosed benefits for a city that lodges its own graffiti: tourism. Street art really can make a difference in the number of young visitors. We do not expect for the senior community to pick a trip on account of the street art available, but a city that shows its walls as canvas is usually a young, hip, trendy place to be in or visit. We know that graffiti has always involved a lot of travelling. Way before graffiti gave birth to street art, and to a kind of urban taste, graffiti writers travelled from one place to next, usually by train, spreading their tag or their crew name, or visiting graffiti jams to paint in partnership with foreign friends. During "Writer's delight", the Portuguese graffiti festival, we can get in touch with several foreign writers who came to Portugal at their own costs to participate in the painting of a "wall of fame", and then usually take some days in the city. We can also realize there are some other writers that come so they can watch the live work piece of long-term graffiti mates. Street art can be very flashy to the young, travelling minds of a generation whose great priority is seeking for the not yet seen. We aim to take on this text as a present-day refection. We believe that in this urban creativity time, there is room for the civil concerns with the appropriation, preservation and exploitation of our urban signs, in which graffiti and all that came along with it forms part.

Notes and References
1 http://www.reddit.com/r/pics/comments/w4lok/grafitti_becomes_art_when_the_artist_becomes/
2 CAMPOS, Ricardo. Pintando a Cidade. Uma Abordagem Antropológica
ao Graffiti Urbano. (Dissertação de Doutoramento em Antropologia.
Universidade Aberta). 2007, p.414;
3 In http://www.brooklynmuseum.org/exhibitions/graffiti/
4 Ket One was born in Jackson Heights, Queens. He is a writer that is a worldwide graffiti consultant;5 We used the term "museums" because we believe museums are the cultural institutions that have a very well determined mission, and that can give us more to work with. However, we do not intend not take into account institutions like galleries or pinakotheken.
6 http://icom.museum/fileadmin/user_upload/pdf/Key_Concepts_of_Museology/Conceitos-ChavedeMuseologia_pt.pdf
7 http://www.sfexaminer.com/sanfrancisco/neighborhood-watch-saves-banksy-painting/Content?oid=2716352
8 http://streetartwalk.com/
9 http://alternativeberlin.com/berlin-graffiti-workshop-and-street-art-tour
10 In 2013, the Portuguese government discussed the proposal of lowering the taxes applied to golf, after they raised the taxes for food.
11 http://vimeo.com/91390255

Sofia Ponte, Faculty of Social Sciences and Humanities (FCSH) / Art History Institute (IHA) and Faculty of Fine Arts, University of Porto (FBAUP); ohsofia@gmail.com

How does street artworks survive in museums?

paraSITE is an artwork by Michael Rakowitz, that consists of a portable shelter for homeless people that has been distributed to over 30 people in several cities in the USA, since 1997, and has been presented in temporary exhibitions since 1999. We are witnessing to an increasing recognition of art institutions of non-traditional artistic practices. The art museum not only helps to recognize the artistic value of such artworks, exhibitions have an important role in both showing and informing its audience of this type of art production. I will use this political artwork to present my current understanding of how complex is the (re)presentation of street artworks at temporary exhibitions.

Introduction

In this paper I explore my interest in the interplay between the urban artistic production taking place outside the conventional space of art and the practice of its display in museums. There is an increasing interest from academia and museum institutions in studying the complex interrelations established between museums and the contexts in which street artworks are created, but there is still much to discuss and understand about the public presentation of these type of artistic production in exhibitions. As Mary Anne Staniszewski suggests in her study about the history of exhibition displays at the Museum of Modern Art (MoMa) in New York, exhibitions are significant rhetoric mediums with the potential to affect the process of interpretation far beyond the work of art in itself in ways which are historically constituted. An artwork when temporarily or permanently displayed in a museum is framed not only among other artworks, but it is integrated in a narrative in accordance to the story curators are trying to convey and in relation to the intentions of the museum when producing a particular exhibition. Many of current street art, urban interventions and social functional art reinforce the concept of public sphere as a controversial area of production, acquisition and transmission of knowledge. These artworks are ephemeral, temporary and sometimes even illegal. How then can its immaterial and symbolic nature be preserved and communicated in art museums? I will underline the need to reflect on what exhibitions may bring into the content and experience of street artworks and urban interventions in art museums since these artworks cannot be fully understood independently from its presentation. Using the example of paraSITE (1998-ongoing), by artist Michael Rakowitz (USA/Iran 1973), I will analyse this artwork conceptual artistic dimension and process of production. I will then discuss the variations of some of its display, and will argue that interactivity, usually a radical behavior to have inside art museums, should be reflected upon when applied to paraSITE. In order to do so, I will sustain that this artwork carries (and produces) in itself an ambiguous contemporary resonance akin to certain definitions of anthropological artefacts.

Street art and other concepts for art in the streets - When evaluating his choices of relevant artworks made between 1986 and 2010, in the publication Defining contemporary art - 25 years in 200 pivotal artworks which aims to provide a comprehensive overview of artistic production since the early twenty-first century, the critic and curator Daniel Birnbaum, citing the artist Marcel Duchamp, refers that today a work signalled as an artwork does not look like an artwork, but consists mostly of "events, spasms, ructions that don't look like art and don't count as art but are somehow electric, energy nodes, attractors, transmitters, conductors of new thinking, new subjectivity and action that visual artwork in the traditional sense is not able to articulate." While this perspective reveals the nonconformity and commitment of some experts to examine and engage with a complex world and to overcome the existing categories of art history, it also addresses the need to invent new terms and vocabulary to describe and translate new and emerging initiatives and ideas. This means that "street art" and "urban intervention" are definitions that coexists with other recent art concepts, such as interventionist art, sustainable art, useful art, operational aesthetic, or social functional art, to mention only a few. Whilst dealing with the public sphere these tendencies share the predisposition to expand the visual language but also to critically question the ideological conditions of institutional narratives. These art concepts easily fit into the group of artworks and art events that overlap with daily life. The artwork paraSITE by artist Michael Rakowitz is one of these works of arts that fits in several definitions and that has been produced by an art practice that allows various descriptions. The scholar Anthony Downey describes the artist Michael Rakowitz, as someone „with a concern for the economies of exchange that inform social, political and historical events, in the contested realm of human experience"[1]; The journalist Nick Stillman depicts the practice of the artist as „symbolic interventions in problematic urban situations"[2]; curator Ann Pasternak in turn refers that Rakowitz's art production is about creating "reflective experience"[3]; journalist Hanae Ko refers to Rakowitz's work as "interventionist"[4]. While curator Jane Simon points out that Rakowitz "is socially and culturally minded, sensitive to needs of a migrant and underrepresented public"[5], curator Stephanie Smith underlines in the practice of this artist the "critical"[6], point of view through which the artist develops conceptual approaches addressing issues of the social sphere, and involving processes and products that relate multiple fields and collaboration strategies.

Michael Rakowitz presents himself as a conceptual artist for whom matters related to the lives of individuals in their day by day are dimensions of concern and creatively motivating. In a conversation with Nick Stillman in 2012 he refers that "working with communities becomes a way for me to better understand a city" and "a fascinating education into how a city presents itself – or even conceals itself". Rakowitz also mentions that he chose to work in the public space out of frustration in art school – "what I didn't like about [it] was that everyone's work ended up in a gallery, so I started to do things that fell into the rubric of site-specific."[7]

paraSITE: the project

ParaSITE explores the relationships in urban spaces between homeless people and the rest of the population. It consists of a portable customized shelter for homeless made from recycled plastic bags and waterproof tape that inflates by absorbing the air from urban buildings' exterior ventilation system. Rakowitz describes it as the "most socially engaged piece" he has made so far, not only because the design of the various prototypes were developed in interaction with some of its first users but because it stands for something politically tangible. This view is reinforced by social practice artist Monel Chang in her article "Rakowitz constructs practical art", were she writes that "through paraSITE project, Rakowitz indirectly gave the homeless he was working with public names and faces; they became visible components of the city."[8] As I mentioned elsewhere[9], not only Rakowitz is calling attention to a matter of social concern, he is also implicating society both in the center of this social problem and in its solution.

I will use the term "social functional art" to describe street artworks such as paraSITE, that are utilitarian in conception and that grew from conceptual art practices developed from institutional critique in the 1970s. This period released art from its "cultural confinement"[10] in art museums and placed the artwork in non-artistic sites. Artistic practices in informal spaces such as the street, are a hybrid reflection of the multidisciplinary strategies grounded in conceptual processes and production. Social functional artworks are part of a practice that simultaneously creates functioning prototypes and addresses social situations while offering an experience of art. As mentioned by curator Jane Simon, it is a practice that "can initiate a discussion about reimagining the world of the future", "encourag[ing] us to think our habits, our desires, and our needs" and "creat[ing] a nexus of appetite and criticism that helps explain[ing] our complicated relationship to capitalism, marketing, and objects."[11] As the art critic Martha Schwendener points out, functionalism is a strategy that is being significantly applied in the arts in recent years, with a particular ruling principle: "rather than choosing functional objects and transforming them, by artistic decree, into dysfunctional objects, artists are more prone to creating objects that accomplish – perhaps as surrogates – the functions that they may not be able to perform in the "real" world."[12]

There are several examples in art history of artworks produced under social and functional tactics. Michael Rakowitz´s paraSITE follows the tradition of the utopian inflatable structures developed by Buckminster Fuller (1895-1983) and also shares some of the ideals of Russian Constructivism, which incorporated artists' interest in intervening in the social field through a functionalist and propagandistic approach. This avant-garde movement developed a particular fusion of art and life, establishing relationships between the inherited artistic culture and the modernization of their contemporaneity. It called for a universal culture founded on reason, collective production and technological usefulness. For this case study it is particularly significant the constructivist notion of „artist - constructor" and the implication of the artist in society. These are two features that inspire many contemporary practices that meet the interest in seeing implemented their artistic grounds in the social life and the everyday. When Aleksandr Rodchenko (1891-1956) temporarily abandoned painting to develop „production art" in order to engage with the objectives of the Russian Revolution, he aimed to create useful objects that served society[13]. Before and after the October 1917 revolution many artists worked for the state administration where they developed several agitation and propagandistic tactics that aim at informing and educating people on the principles and values of socialism. They included agitational poster campaigns but also, vehicles functioning as mobile agitational centers, such as "agit-train" and "agit-ship", disseminating and distributing Bolshevik propaganda to remote areas in Russia during the civil war[14].

Curator Manuel J. Borja-Villel refers to the idealistic intentions of this early 20 century constructivist essence. According to him "these were linked to an aestheticized functionalism, devoid of critical depth and designed to produce utopias, non-places built for a non-existent and universal man."[15] However, in contrast, Rakowitz brings a positive critical dimension to his artistic project. Since the beginning of the project the artist is thinking of a particular social type of homelessness. The project exists in relation to a particular group of individuals that tangibly uses paraSITEs in the public sphere, homeless men, and, whether inside or outside the field of contemporary art, he is implicating everyone else in that process. Therefore, besides having an aesthetic element paraSITE has a social function with immediate impact in the lives of certain individuals.The paraSITE project was developed after a workshop in Kerak, Jordan, in the ambit of a field trip organised by students of the MIT Architecture and Urbanism Department of the School of Architecture and Planning in January of 1997. The workshop aim was to study several abandoned villages in the Dead Sea southeast. It was Rakowitz's task in this field trip to collect statements from the villagers about the precarious buildings abandoned in this region. It was in the ambit of these conversations that Rakowitz learned that some of the villagers belonged to former desert Bedouin nomadic communities. Rakowitz mentions this encounter in his Master dissertation, written in 1998, where he explains that it was after meeting these people that he became interested in the concept of nomadism and in flexible ways of housing. Bedouin tents are built and modified daily depending on the patterns of desert warm wind. Likewise paraSITE as a tangible object, is concerned with the concept of nomadism and flexible dwelling in contemporary cities. Although not all nomads are homeless, all homeless are more or less nomads in urban centers. Rakowitz identified the homeless "as a new kind of nomad everyday"[16] at the end of the twentieth century and increasing its number day by day.

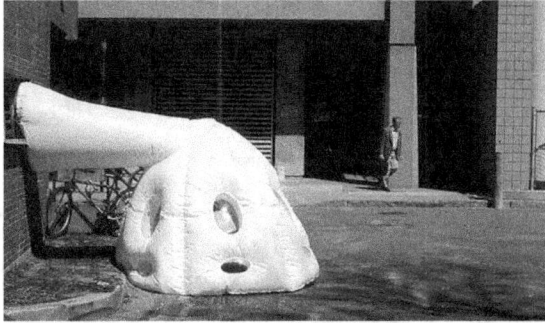

Fig.1 Bill Stone´s paraSITE, Cambridge, MA, USA, 1998 Image © 2014 courtesy Michael Rakowitz.

paraSITE emerged at a time when several "homeless-proof" initiatives where activated by the city council of Cambridge, MA, and other city councils in the USA. Its design especially conforms to New York's anti-homeless laws, which prohibit tents more than three and a half feet tall (approximately one meter and seventeen centimeters tall). Considering both the hard living conditions of street people and the aggressive tactics developed by government authorities to remove them from the city center, the artist established a political and ironical parallelism between a biological parasite and the homeless social group. He explains:

1. PARASITISM IS DESCRIBED AS A RELATIONSHIP IN WHICH A PARASITE TEMPORARILY OR PERMANENTLY EXPLOITS THE ENERGY OF A HOST - paraSITE proposes the appropriation of the exterior ventilation systems on existing architecture as a means for providing temporary shelter for homeless people.

2. PARASITES LIVE ON THE OUTER SURFACE OF A HOST OR INSIDE ITS BODY IN RESPIRATORY ORGANS, DIGESTIVE ORGANS, VENOUS SYSTEMS, AS WELL AS OTHER ORGANS AND TISSUES. The paraSITE units in their idle state exist as small, collapsible packages with handles for transport by hand or on one's back. In employing this device, the user must locate the outtake ducts of a building's HVAC (Heating, Ventilation, Air Conditioning) system.

3. FREQUENTLY A HOST PROVIDES A PARASITE NOT ONLY WITH FOOD, BUT ALSO WITH ENZYMES AND OXYGEN, AND OFFERS FAVOURABLE TEMPERATURE CONDITIONS. The intake tube of the collapsed structure is then attached to the vent. The warm air leaving the building simultaneously inflates and heats the double membrane structure.

4. BUT A HOST IS CERTAINLY NOT INACTIVE AGAINST A PARASITE, AND IT HINDERS THE DEVELOPMENT AND POPULATION GROWTH OF PARASITES WITH DIFFERENT DEFENSE MECHANISMS, SUCH AS THE CLEANING OF SKIN, PERISTALTIC CONTRACTION OF THE DIGESTIVE APARATUS, AND THE DEVELOPMENT OF ANTIBODIES. In April of 1997, I proposed my concept and first prototype to a homeless man named Bill Stone, who regarded the project as a tactical response. At the time, the city of Cambridge had made a series of vents in Harvard Square "homeless-proof" by tilting the metal grates, making them virtually impossible to sleep on[17].

prototypes and "remains": paraSITE in exhibitions

As Rakowitz mentions, paraSITE not only functions as a "temporary place of retreat", it can also be regarded as "a station of dissent and empowerment". It solely depends on the way one looks at it. paraSITE exists in the "real world", it has been distributed to over 30 homeless people in cities such as Baltimore, New York and Boston, since 1997, and has been presented in galleries and museums since 1999, as part of the group show "Temporary Shelters" curated by Bernice Steinbaum at the Here Here Gallery, in Cleveland. In addition to the shelters built in collaboration with homeless individuals, two prototypes have been produced with the cooperation of art institutions, AKSIOMA-Institute for Contemporary Art in Ljubljana, Slovenia (2005) and the Laumeier Sculpture Park in St. Louis, USA (2012).

There are three kinds of paraSITE design prototypes being regularly displayed at contemporary art exhibitions. One is a returned shelter that from now on I will name as "remain" to distinguish it from other paraSITE prototypes. I am naming them differently because each device poses different questions to its exhibition. The main difference between the paraSITE prototype and the paraSITE "remain" is that the first is a working model and the second has been built and used in the streets. As Rakowitz sees no problem in showing the paraSITEs shelter in museums, he recommends that both, the prototypes and the "remains", should be displayed along with its history. For Rakowitz it is extremely important "that the work isn't misunderstood as performance" so adjunct material such as photographs taken by the artist, video documentation and information panels, are frequently displayed alongside the object. In case of displaying a "remain" shelter the artist also sustains that it should "retain the marks of [its] use."[18] I discussed elsewhere that the concept of "remain" helps to distinguish paraSITE from a conventional sculpture or installation. The prototype presented at "Safe Design takes on risk" exhibition in 2005 at the MoMA, at "The Interventionists - art in the social sphere" exhibition, in 2004 at MassMoca and at the Cooper-Hewitt Design Triennial in 2003, was the same working model that helped the artist to develop the initial design of a shelter. This prototype was then later acquired by the MoMA in 2007 by its Department of Architecture and Design and has since then been presented in two other shows at this institution, "Just in: Recent acquisitions from the collection" in 2007, and "Born out of necessity" in 2013. And there is also a second paraSITE prototype being regularly on display.

When artworks enter the institutional art context they partially suffer from dislocation and decontextualization. This happens to any artwork or artefact musealized. In the particular case of paraSITE, that implies being used in the streets of a city, how does its installation in temporary exhibitions affect its meaning?

Since a museum experience takes place at several levels, some more obvious than others, but mediated by various conceptual representations, from the architecture of the space, the exhibition design, the strategies of artworks installation, to the artworks themselves, the apparatus with which an artwork is integrated in a museum absorbs the implicit framework of an exhibition historical, ideological and political representation (Vergo, 1986:54). paraSITE is a relevant artwork to discuss its exhibition processes and musealization because it has been displayed in at least 33 exhibitions that thematically deal with social problematics in various ways and contexts. It has been part of Historical Perspectives temporary exhibitions, i.e. collective shows that gathered artworks, architecture models and design objects created over the twentieth century investigating and questioning our sense of living, adapting and surviving to change in general, and to climate change, in particular; It has been displayed in collective exhibitions that also gathered artworks, architecture models and design objects concerned with Communities and individuals, i.e. temporary group shows envisioning collective and individual social transformation; It has integrated temporary shows specifically dealing with the House and Shelter topic, or collective exhibitions specifically focusing on problems of homelessness or on the contrary, on utopian dwelling; and finally it participated in temporary collective exhibitions dealing with Visionary Objects with social concern, gathering objects representing the latest innovations in art, design and architecture, projecting future scenarios in response to emergencies or new zones of sustainability in contemporaneity life and in its future. Each of these themes and issues allow us to characterize a given time and because of that they frame the boundaries and codes of culture. Most of the initial shows paraSITE was part dealt with change, changing the status of homeless individuals and changing the awareness of museum goers of art and society. This coincided, for example, with western society facing the turn of the century.

In each of these temporary shows paraSITE has been displayed in various ways. Its (re)presentation ranges from the most abstract, attempting to evoke the project historical context, to the most allegedly realistic setting. It has been displayed solely as a sculpture[19], only through visual documentation[20] and through the display of the shelter accompanied with visual documentation [21]. The prototype and the "remain" have been displayed inside galleries directly on the floor, protected by security bars, inside a square drawn on the floor, or simply on the floor such as a minimalist sculpture; It has also been displayed in exteriors such as building facades, parks and sidewalks. Posed by Barbara Kishenblatt-Gimblett in her discussion concerning ethnographic artifacts, my question then is where does this object begin and where does it end?[22]

Please touch: ambiguities in social functional artworks display

Each approach to contextualize paraSITE and its functional use in its various exhibitions has provided a specific background, raised questions and designed a conceptual frame of reference. Its presence within the diverse temporary exhibitions it has integrated has been differently justified. Sometimes it has been considered as a representative of a certain idea about what a work of art is, others as part of a social system, or as a symbol of a culture of a specific age. When displayed as visual documentation it has been presented by means of several photographs and video documentation of the three different shelters design being used; drawings sketches of the shelter; a paraSITE kit with the necessary tools to build a shelter; an instructions manual; signs, labels and wall texts explaining the project. In the "Beyond Green – toward a sustainable art" itinerant exhibition curated by Stephanie Smith at the Smart Museum of Art, University of Chicago, in 2005, several wall texts were produced and placed on the wall nearby the "remain" shelter, displayed together with drawings, photographs, video documentation and the paraSITE kit. An excerpt of one of the wall texts explained how the shelter started to be presented:

> *Rakowitz customizes each shelter for its intended occupant, a process he relates to portraiture.*
> *The shelter that he designed for Bill Stone is presented here; Stone gave it back to Rakowitz*
> *once he no longer needed it, and it retains the stains of use in the streets.*

Recognizing the relevance and the ephemeral nature of artworks such as paraSITE, museums have been presenting it with consequences not yet sufficiently evaluated. Indeed, reflection on the processes of translating this artwork into an institutional framework and the revision of its codes considering its museological presentation, have not yet been properly examined.

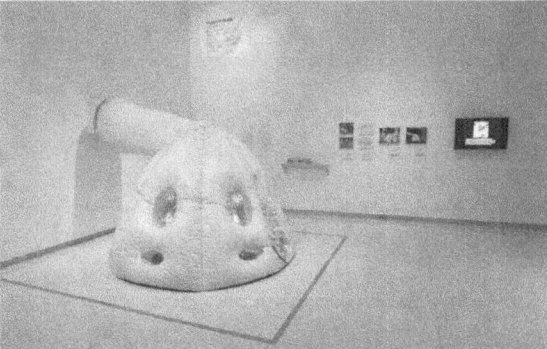

Fig.2 Installation view of paraSITE at Beyond Green: Toward a sustainable art exhibition at Smart Museum of Art, USA, October 6, 2005 - January 15, 2006; The David and Alfred Smart Museum of Art, The University of Chicago; Image © 2014 courtesy of The David and Alfred Smart Museum of Art, The University of Chicago.

The concept of "New museology"[23] developed during the 1980s and 1990s, when the social function of the museum begun to be challenged, is insufficient to respond to social functional art and ways of addressing it to the public, however varied that public might be. The aesthetic presentation of contemporary art nowadays deals with various ephemeral and immaterial aspects, which question the range of installations developed in the past. Exhibition designs, also under great transformation, have welcoming recent artistic values such as the use of innovative technology, the influence of mass communication, such as the acoustic-guides, audiovisuals displays, journals, the concept of site-specificity and interactivity with the viewer to better elucidate them about the nature of the artworks exhibited. Many of these strategies take for granted that viewers are able to follow this additional material. In spite of how radical interactivity towards works of art might seem, there have been several exhibitions in the past[24] offering the possibility of interacting with works of art on display, and some of them included paraSITE.

However, what exactly is added to the visitor experience if the shelter can be tried out? As I mentioned earlier paraSITE, is an artistic object connected to a social context that was conceived to be used. At a first sight it seems ok to invite visitors to go inside the object since its nature is functional. That has occurred in Utopia Now! exhibition curated by Marina McDougall in 2002, where visitors were welcomed to go inside for a "test nap" as mentioned by the curator. And in Camp Out: finding home in an unstable world, in 2012, were the paraSITE prototype could also be tried. Curators installed a text label nearby the object, displayed in the gardens of the museum, indicating this possibility. Besides the fact that visitors are not expecting to be able to touch in artworks, to be able to enter in paraSITE is even a bigger surprise and reinforces, I believe its ambiguity. What will visitors feel like entering the shelter? As curator Marina McDougall remarks, "we know that some people will be tempted to go inside. But they should be warned. It's been, shall I say, used"[25]. Does going inside paraSITE helps to demonstrate the ability of contemporary art in bringing awareness to homeless and their living conditions or just adds an "experience" to the spectacle of culture? paraSITE was made to be used in situations where individuals are in need of it, which is most often not the case with individuals that visit museums. To go inside a "remain" that was someone's shelter, feels like invading what used to be someone's house. On the one hand reinforces the serious discrepancies between individuals' lives, which is Rakowitz intention; but on the other hand, without any immediate need for it, feels like a theatrical experience whose function is merely rhetoric. Does one needs to try paraSITE to understand what it stands for?

Manuel J. Borja-Villel considers some of the limitations of art museums by referring that "organizing exhibitions or collections without taking into account the role of the institution in the society of which it forms part can easily produce the opposite results to those hoped for: rather than transforming our environment,it reinforces the status quo."[26] In the particular case of paraSITE, the excessive educational intentions curators have demonstrated towards the concept of this artwork might be one of the reasons that produce this kind of ambiguities. To try out the shelter might only fit as a strategy to inform visitors on the tangible nature of paraSITE as an example of an avant-garde artwork. Because Rakowitz's main purpose when producing paraSITE was to create a symbolic survival strategy to force the complexity between the homeless and the non-homeless[27]. The artist is careful in explaining that paraSITE shelters are not conceived as a proposal for affordable housing or a solution for homelessness, but as an urban intervention to increase public awareness of a complex contemporaneity condition. Many of Rakowitz's homeless collaborators, in fact see the shelters as "protest devices"[28].

When paraSITE was displayed in Camp out finding home in unstable world, curators Marilu Knode e Dana Turkovic developed other display strategies. The label next to the shelter, which invited visitors to try it, also explained that there was a stack of printed instructions for building ones' own shelter, which visitors could take from the exhibition in the indoor museum space for free. The curators also took out advertisement space in a local magazine to print the instructions Michael Rakowitz developed for building paraSITEs. The instructions manual along with a text describing the project and the exhibition that framed it, written by the Laumeier Curatorial Fellow Ashley Kopp Wenzel, were published in the What's up magazine[29] and explained that "in offering these instructions Rakowitz states "paraSITEs are meant to alarm the public and to have them consider whether or not it is acceptable to use. It is a bandage that brings attention to a societal wound; it doesn't fix the apparatus that caused the wound.""[30]

To summarize, not all interactivity in art museums harm or affect negatively a social functional artwork, on the contrary. The shows dedicated to the work of the Brazilian artist Lygia Clark (1920-1988) at Fundacion Antoni Tapies, in Barcelona, in 1997, and at MoMA, in New York, in 2014, had several replicas of the objects designed by Clark. Replicas of artworks such as "Bichos" [Animals] and "Borrachas" [Rubbers] were displayed in tables and could be handled by visitors and others such as "Máscaras" [Masks] and "Redes" [Nets], made to be manipulated, were destroyed at the end of the show.

Another example is the recent show dedicated to the work of the German artist Franz Erhard Walther (1939), *Eyes closed/Eyes open: recent acquisition in drawings at the MoMA, New York, where on selected dates trained facilitators assisted visitors in using Walther's First Work Set (1963-69),* an artwork composed by a set of interactive elements, which is only complete with the physical interaction of the viewer.

These two examples not only allow the viewer/user to experiment the complexity of the artwork but also show visitors that exhibition norms and conventions vary in relation to the art concept they are in the presence of.

Concluding remarks

Contemporary art museums are sites of historical practice and not solely aimed at aesthetic experiences, either interactive or not. paraSITE' status quo, expresses multifunctionality, which is not so different from certain anthropological artefacts. An artefact can be a "man-made object charged with cultural meaning, which can, if studied carefully offer us information on the society in which it has been created"[31] and in the specific case of paraSITE, also offer us useful information on the homeless, on the artist, on the curator, on the museum enabling one to "read" several layers of meanings. One can relate to paraSITE aesthetically and consider how it disrupts a classical notion of a work of art, artistic practice, authorship; One can relate to it reflexively and analyze how it tries to deconstruct conceptions that structure the field of art, questioning what generally is assumed to be the artist function in society; One can relate to it ethnographically and contextualize the artwork representation of culture and the social conditions that allows a comprehensive study of the people it involves and its society. All of these possibilities can be simultaneously revealed by its public exhibition in the art museum. Ruth B. Phillips argues that

> "the lessons that [ethnographic] objects teach in museums are accomplished not by fixing their
> positions within unitary sequences of temporal change and geographical variation, but by a post-

structuralist recognition that [ethnographic] objects are capable of generating multiple meanings through the interaction of their material traits with diverse individual subjects."[32]

Phillips also argues that to be fair to these ethnographic objects there is a "necessity of re-placing [ethnographic] objects in new kinds of interpretive contexts that draw both on the local knowledge of originating communities and on new theories of historical materiality and visuality." Only then, as I tried to demonstrate in this paper, the exhibition of paraSITE can contribute to a useful debate regarding the artwork theme and also yield insights into the histories of the social relationships it is addressing. Museums are not just about objects they are also about the cultures that produce them. We realize that societies aren't, and never were, neutral states of human coexistence. Cities are spaces where individuals socially engage with each other on many levels. Some of us live in cities with man made infrastructures and communally sharing privileges and problems. On the one hand we can exchange ideas, share natural resources, access to local markets and amenities but on the other hand we are easily exposed to violence, living costs higher than one might afford, pollution, traffic, isolation, surveillance, solitude, and so on and on.

Artists who create social functional art appropriate, intervene and „operate" in real life situations. They treat the streets as a symbolic space that, as argued by Patricia Phillips "derive its "publicness" not from its location, but from the nature of its engagement with the congested cacophonous intersections of personal interests, collective values, social issues, political events, and wider cultural patterns that mark out our civic life"[33]. This notion also includes the museum as we know it today. paraSITE is still being used not only in the streets of the city Michael Rakowitz lives, in Chicago, but in several other cities in the western world. As mentioned by the artist the project continues utopic, "it became clear that the project could be on-going. Homelessness hasn't gone away so why should the project?"[34] So there might be more opportunities to reflect about paraSITE´s relation to contemporary art institutionalization. Artists that operate simultaneously on various disciplines, commonly alter the relationships the tangible often has from the outset, essentially envisioning other points of view. Street artworks and urban interventions such as paraSITE may inform about alternative ways of living, frame our individual and social activity, sense of place and identity, and in the long run, existential sense of living, but also, and primarily contribute to transform the artistic experience to areas not yet explored.

Notes and References

1 Anthony Downey, "From invisible enemy to enemy kitchen. Michael Rakowitz in conversation with Anthony Downey" Ibraaz (March 29, 2013).
2 Nick Stillman, "Conversation with Michael Rakowitz". New York Foundation for the Arts, (2006).
3 Ann Pasternak quoted in Christopher Borrelli article, "The complicated art of Michel Rakowitz", Chicago Tribune, (March 9, 2012).
4 Hanae Ko, "The sweet and bitter road: Michael Rakowitz". ArtAsiaPacific, Issue 78, (May/June 2012).
5 Jane Simon, "A return to function", Return to function, ed. Jane Simon, (Madison: Madison Museum of Contemporary art. 2009), 22.
6 Stephanie Smith, "Beyond Green". Beyond Green: toward a sustainable art, (Chicago: Smart Museum of Art. 200), 6.
7 Ashley Kopp Wenzel, "parasite: a sculpture and a refugee". Camp Out: Finding home in an unstable world, (St.Louis: Laumeier Sculpture Park. 2012), 17.
8 Monel Chang, "Rakowitz constructs political art" in The Williams Record, (November 3, 2010).
9 See Sofia Ponte, "Musealizing functional art" in Sustainable art: facing the need for regeneration, responsibility and relations, (Warclow, Warsow: Institute of Art History, University of Wrocław and Polish Institute of World Art Studies, 2014).
10 Miwon Kwon, "One place after another: notes on site specificity" in Space, site, intervention. Situating installation art. (Ed.) Erika Suderburg, (Minneapolis: University of Minnesota Press, 2000), 43.
11 Jane Simon, "A return to function" in Return to function, ed Jane Simon, (Madison: Madison Museum of Contemporary Art, 2009), 19.
12 Mary Schwendener, "Notes on function" in Return to function ed. Jane Simon, (Madison: Madison Museum of Contemporary Art, 2009), 75.
13 The scholar Victor Margolin argues, however, that constructivist aims and projects were never more than a conceptual outline, suggesting that they were largely an experimental activity with a rhetorical purpose rather than practical one. Artists like Rodchenko were focused on function and how certain objects conceptually allow creatively in relation to the material world and according to the revolutionary model. For more information on this see chapter "Inventing the artist-constructor: Rodchenko 1922-1927" in The struggle for utopia: Rodchenko, Lissitzky, Moholy-Nagy 1917-1946, published by The University of Chicago Press, p.84-85.
14 Michael Rakowitz parasite, (Cambridge: MIT, 1998), 34.
15 Manuel J. Borja-Villel, "Introduction" in Lygia Clark, (Barcelona: Fundacion Tapies, 1997), 13.
16 Monel Chang, "Rakowitz constructs practical art" in The Williams Record, (November 3, 2010).
17 Artist's statement published at http://www.woostercollective.com/post/michael-rakowitzs-parasite
18 Michael Rakowitz in interview with Stephanie Smith in the exhibition catalogue Beyond Green - toward a sustainable art, (Chicago: Smart Museum of Art. 2006), 25.
19 In art exhibitions such as "Get rid of yourself" at ACC Galerie Weimar, Germany (2003), "The interventionists - art in the social sphere" at MassMoca, St. Adams, USA (2005) and "Less - alternative living strategies" at PAC, Milan, Italy (2006).
20 In temporary art exhibitions such as "Temporary Shelters" (1999), "The photographic imagination" (2000) at the Here Here Gallery Cleveland, USA, and "Concerted Compassionism" (2000) at White Columns Gallery New York, USA
21 In temporary art and design exhibitions such as "Living in mobile units" at the Hasselt Museum, Belgium (2004), "Beyond Green: toward a sustainable art" (2006) at the Smart Museum of Art, Chicago, USA and "La Ville mobile" at the Biennale Internationale Design Saint- Étienne, France (2010).
22 Barbara Kishenblatt-Gimblett, "Objects of ethnography" in Exhibiting cultures. The poetics and politics of museum display ed. by Ivan Karp and Steven D. Lavine, (Washington: Smithsonian Books, 1991), 388.
23 "New museology" is a term introduced by Pater Vergo in his edited book The New Museology, published in 1989 by Reaktion Books.
24 For more information on this see "The power of display or the avant-gardes as exhibition" in The power of display. A history of exhibition installations at the Museum of Modern Art by Mary Ann Staniszewski.
25 Marina McDougall interviewed in David Temple article "Future Shock - Utopian visions visit the Sonoma County Museum" metroactive, (February 14, 2002).
26 Manuel Borja-Villel, "The museum questioned" Relational objects: MACBA collection. ed. Jorge Ribalta, (Barcelona: MACBA, 2010).
27 Michael Rakowitz parasite, (Cambridge: MIT, 1998), 19.
28 Marina McDougall, Utopia Now (S.Francisco: CCAC Institute, 2001): 24-25.
29 What's up magazine aims to alleviate poverty and so the vendors keep the proceeds of their sales.
30 Ashely Koop Wenzel, "Camp out: finding home in an unstable world: Laumeier Sculpture Park exhibits Michael Rakowitz – an artist for the homeless" in What's up. Vol. 11 Issue 1, (2012).
31 Miller Keller quoted in Mieke Bal "The discourse of the museum", Thinking about exhibitions ed. Reesa Greenberg et all, (London and New York: Routledge, 1996), 206
32 Ruth B. Phillips, "Re-placing objects: Historical practices for the second museum age", The Canadian Historical Review , Volume 86, Number 1, (March 2005), 87.
33 Patricia Phillips, "Out of order: The public art machine". Artforum, (1988), 93.
34 Rakowitz interview "parasite: a sculpture and a refugee" with Ashley Kopp Wenzel in the exhibition catalogue Camp Out: finding home in an unstable world, organized by the Laumeier Sculpture Park between June 2 and September 6, 2012.

Ulrich Blanché, Institute for European Art History (IEK), University of Heidelberg,
uliblanchet@gmail.com

Banksy vs. Bristol Museum - Street Art or street "flavored" art?

I define street art as self-authorized signs in public space whose authors want to communicate with a broader public. This paper questions the limits of this street art definition in other locations than the "street," i.e. galleries and museums. I formulate my critique or discussion on the basis of thoughts about the "Banksy vs. Bristol Museum" exhibition in 2009. Did British street artist Banksy show in this exhibition street art – or rather street art "flavored" art or street art "souvenirs," as he calls prints of his street art works in 2002.[1]

Street art, Museum, Banksy, Bristol, Urban Art

Introduction

The action or performance of attaching a work of urban art is, analogue to the medium, part of the artwork. Even if the motif of the piece of street art is not political itself – a stenciled rabbit for example – the act of attaching signs to an urban surface without official permission is political. This action itself questions authorities – often big brother or big business: „The difference between sender and receiver, between producer and consumer of signs, must remain total, as within it lies the real form of social power." (Baudrillard, 1975)[2]

My paper for the Art and Urban Creativity conference questions the limits of this street-art-definition in other locations than the "street," i.e. galleries and museums. I shape my critique or discussion on the basis of thoughts about the "Banksy vs. Bristol Museum" Exhibition in 2009. Did British street artist Banksy show in this exhibition street art– according to the mentioned definition or rather street art "flavored" art or street art "souvenirs," as he calls prints of his street art works in 2002 (Carey, 2001).[3]

Numbers, dates, facts

The following passage gives the reader a short background about the "Banksy vs. Bristol Museum" exhibition. The Bristol City Museum and Art Gallery was founded in 1905. It is a universal museum for art, archeology and natural history, which saw "a full-scale infiltration and 'remix'" (Sawyer, 2009)[4] by Banksy.

According to The Guardian Banksy is the most famous graffiti artist of the world.[5]More than 300.000 people, around 4000 a day, saw his "versus Bristol Museum" exhibition in 2009. "Visitors queued come rain or shine for between two and six hours to see more than 100 works by the elusive artist in the exhibition […]."(The Bristol Post, 2009)[6] In just six weeks this provincial museum in the artist's native city became - because of Banksy - one of the 30 most viewed art venues of 2009 according to the Art Newspaper – worldwide (BBC News, 2010).[7] It was the biggest Banksy exhibition to date. The graffiti artist showed around 110 art objects and paid the City of Bristol a symbolic Pound for staging the show. "This is the first show I've ever done where taxpayers' money is being used to hang my pictures up rather than scrape them off" (The Guardian, 2009).[8] "Despite joking about taxpayers' money being used to hang his pictures "rather than scrape them off", Banksy has paid for the lot, from installation to extra security. It is, he says, his thank-you to a city that nurtured him."[9]According to the Bristol Post the exhibition "put £10 million into the city's economy and doubled the turnover of a number of local businesses at the height of the recession" (The Bristol Post, 2009).[10]
Banksy approached the Museum through his Company Pest Control Office and convinced the museum executives to let him stage an exhibition there according to his ideas. During the eight months of preparation the whole plan to do an official expo of Banksy's work was kept secret from Bristol City Council chiefs. The Museum officials had to sign a 37 pages contract to guarantee Banksy and his team anonymity and plenty of rope to realize his concept.[11]

Exhibition concept

The concept of "Banksy versus Bristol Museum" was divided in two parts. One part was the official Banksy exhibition, the obvious part. The other is the hidden part where the visitor could discover Banksy's Remix of Objects from the museum's collection. In the exhibition flyer the obvious part is divided into four areas called "Entrance," "Information," "Art of Banksy" and "Unnatural history". In the Entrance Hall Banksy showed a short form of an installation entitled "Boghenge" he did at Glastonbury festival two years earlier. He erected this portaloo take on Stonehenge next to the museum toilets as you can see on the plan. Banksy carried his street sculpture into a museum to open his exhibition in a music festival-like manner. The information area in the great hall recalls another outdoor location, the street, maybe also a music festival through a burned and vandalized ice cream van or a fun fair through a puppet police officer in riot gear riding a child's mechanical toy horse. Other artworks in the hall evoke an action movie by a Guantanamo prisoner escaping in a reconstruction of a historical Bristol Biplane from a 1960ies movie which is part of the permanent collection or a circus with a lion statue that just ate his tamer. This gypsum statue is part of a series of fake marble statues in the same room all hinting at statues in museums connected with real life, for instance boutique mannequins, or homeless on city streets. Like in most of his street art Banksy reacted to and commented on the location where he places his works, in that case to the neoclassical Bristol museum building dominated by white marble-like classical columns and balustrades.

The "art of Banksy" section contains mostly remixes of flatware, id est classical artworks on canvas and paper and a showroom appearing to be Banksy's studio. Additional sculptures, for instance an ironical Carl-Andre-like brick wall on the floor full of graffiti, camouflage nets on the ceiling, a trash can try to transfer the authenticity of a dark and dirty back street into the gallery. At the same time Banksy heightens the contrast and shows his works in a more arty way than necessary by using big gold frames or defamiliarizations of famous artworks. Banksy lets collide clichés of classical, traditional, stereotypical art with classical traditional forms of vandalism by presenting both in an over-identifying way. The viewer should question his or her classical, traditional and sometimes stereotypical understanding of art, of vandalism, of graffiti and their usual way of presentation in an art context. So far the street artist Banksy creates more or less traditional artworks for a gallery; street flavored art if you wish that lives mostly on the street credibility of the artist. The last part of the obvious Banksy exhibition is less obvious than the already mentioned one. Paying credit to the fact of Bristol Museum being a natural history museum as well Banksy shows in his Unnatural history section a surreal zoological garden of remixed fake animals, so called animatronics or robots looking and behaving like animals. Canned animal sounds from tape, real old cages from zoos or circuses created the illusion of a zoo. This illusion is destroyed once the visitors discovered the swimming fish are actually fish sticks, the crawling snakes are sausages or the leopard is actually a leopard fur coat. "Can street art ever be shown in a gallery?" Banksy was asked in 2010. His answer: "I don't know if street art ever really works indoors. If you domesticate an animal, it goes from being wild and free to sterile, fat and sleepy. So maybe the art should stay outside. Then again, some old people get a lot of comfort from having a pet around the house" (Banksy, 2010).[12] Eight years before Banksy called street art indoor spin offs "souvenirs". Both terms, "pet" or "domesticated animal" and "Souvenir" sounds slightly pejorative without dismissing lock, stock and barrel the concept of street art prints or street art motifs on canvas etc.

Those artworks like the whole obvious part of the Banksy exhibition do not make much sense as single pieces of art; as such they are rather one-line jokes. But they are part of a gesamtkunstwerk, a total work of art, the exhibition itself, which is a kind of all-over art installation. The co-equal opponent of Banksy is the museum per se, in this case Bristol Museum like the title "Banksy versus Bristol Museum" already implies. The fulfillment of this title is basically the second part of the show, the hidden part. In the information area the museum put up a sign with a text from the exhibition flyer: "Please be aware that some of the historic relics now on display throughout the museum are fakes." In a kind of treasure hunt visitors had the chance to see the museum's permanent collection of geology, minerals, porcelain, dinosaurs, wildlife and the art collection in a different way, as Banksy hid objects and his own artworks in every section without obviously tagging or denoting them as his works. "He is celebrating the stuffiness of the institution while teasing it. Either you're offended by his cheek, which is the point, or you love the mischief, which is also the point"(The Guardian, 2009).[13] This led to a rediscovery of other parts of the museum by visitors who in other cases might never have visited a museum or these sections of a province museum. "Upstairs, and you embark on a treasure hunt: Where's the Banksy? Like his previous (unin- vited) infiltrations of art galleries, or his outdoor graffiti work, you find yourself looking carefully, so as not to miss a trick. When you spot a new work, you feel like shouting: Found it!"(The Guardian, 2009)[14]

In the Geology / Minerals Section the visitor could find a Shopping Trolley Hunter on a Rock and a stalactite in the shape of a one- finger salute. In the Egypt Room Banksy tagged a terracotta style soldier with a 'Reduced' price tag, the boring old Plates section hid a bronze sculpture of a Degas-like Ballerina wearing a gas mask and the British Wildlife Section combined the a stuffed fox from the museum with a blood-like red color-spattered "Countryside Alliance pro Fox Hunting" placard. Instead of just being showed history or thinking about the past, the spectator is not only presented some artifacts of the past, but directly confronted with current (political) issues. Therefore Banksy combines a mammoth with consumerism or stuffed animals with a cynical comment on the cruelty of fox hunting, a subject widely debated in Great Britain. On the top floor, in the Art Gallery, Banksy hanged his versions of updated oil paint- ings among those of the museum collection. For instance in the French Art Gallery his version of Jean-François Millets Les Glaneuses from 1857 (the English title is Gleaners) shows one of the Gleaners taking a cigarette break. The figure was cut out of a reproduction of Millet's painting and accurately repainted sitting on the gold frame. The sign next to the Banksy showed the inscription Local Art- ist, the title, Agency Job (Gleaners) and the year 2009. Banksy's painting might appear as a pure joke. Actually it transfers much of Millet's subject matter into the present than the original. Because of paintings like Les Glaneuses Millet's contemporaries thought of him as a kind of revolutionary as he painted the hard rural work of peasant in such a drastic and realistic way. His depiction was interpreted as a critique on the conditions of employment in his time. Especially in the title Banksy recalls that critique as he hints to the problematic status of agency workers or temporary workers nowadays.
Banksy's explanatory signs next to the artworks recall style, layout, color and typography of the original signs Bristol museum uses. Although he provided them with reduced information compared to the signs of the museum - and as well compared to fake signs he used himself from 2003 until 2005 when he started both, to update artworks and to hang them into museums without making his authorship obvious for the viewers at first.

Smuggling art into museums
In October 2003 Banksy smuggled his first - as he called it "Vandalized Oil Painting"(Banksy, 2001)[15] - into a Museum, London's Tate Gallery. Next to his gold framed painting Banksy glued the following text mocking the Tate's sign next to it but also the presentation of art in a museum per se: "Banksy, 1975," (Sawer, 2003)[16] "Crimewatch UK has ruined the Countryside for all of us, 2003, Oil on Canvas

This new acquisition is a beautiful example of the neo post-idiotic style. The Artist has found an unsigned oil painting in a London street market and then stenciled Police incident tape over the top. It can be argued that defacing such an idyllic scene reflects the way our nation has been vandalised by its obsession with crime and paedophilia [sic], where any visit to a secluded beauty spot now feels like it may result in being molested or finding discarded body parts"(Banksy, 2004).[17] Like mocking and subverting billboards or street signs by authorities on the street Banksy produces fake signs in museums: "If you want to survive as a graffiti writer when you go indoors I figured your only option is to carry on painting over things that don't belong to you there, either" (Banksy, 2006).[18] Banksy transferred his institutional critique from the street into the museum. Looked at in a formal way Banksy always comments on the location, the surroundings of his artwork. Smuggling his art into museums is a similar act than spraying illegally on the street, he created art without permission that fits and criticizes its environment.

This is not the case with the "Banksy vs. Bristol exhibition" as Banksy presented his art with permission of the museum, which he still shows as elitist, conservative and backward looking. But by criticizing the museum from within Banksy pointed to a possible solution of an ongoing problem of all museums – how can they stay up-to-date? Manco called Banksy's Vandalized Oil Paintings "updated oil paintings" (Manco, 2002)[19]. How can a Museum be or stay a museum for all, not just the one who with a broad, maybe academic background, but also for those who like shops, circus, fun-fairs or music festivals. Banksy likes the museum, especially Bristol Museum, which he criticizes:

"Art is not like other culture because its success is not made by its audience. The public fill concert halls and cinemas every day, we read novels by the millions and buy records by the billions. We the people, affect the making and the quality of most of our culture, but not our art. The Art we look at is made by only a select few. A small group create, promote, purchase, exhibit and decide the success of Art. Only a few hundred people in the world have any real say. When you go to an Art gallery you are simply a tourist looking at the trophy cabinet of a few millionaires" (Banksy, 2006).[20] His institutional critique of the museum per se is not destructive, rather a call for democracy in art and a call for less commercial interest in art.

Conclusion

Banksy's critique, his art at Bristol Museum is constructive, but it is not street art. It is still art in public spaces and it is inspired by graffiti and street art, it is street 'flavored' art executed by a street artist living from the street credibility of a street artist. Banksy paints Bristol museum in the manner of graffiti, for instance say the sign at the doors appears to be vandalized by Banksy using his trademark pink spray can writing, recalling the hip-hop battle term "versus". He pretends to be illegal to give his purpose, education in art, more credibility like he pretended to put up legal art in 2003 when he smuggled his works into museums. In the case of these actions Banksy's goal was also to become well known, visible as an artist. "Banksy the street artist best known for daubing buildings and dustbins with graffiti outside the Tate Gallery has had his 'art' installed on its walls inside. For a few hours anyway. Artwork being considered for display at Tale Britain usually undergoes a rigorous process of nomination. But under heavy disguise. Banksy bypassed the lengthy process by sneaking his work on the wall of Room 7 when no one was looking. The 'fake' was discovered only when it crashed to the floor hours later" (The Independent, 2003).[21] Banksy painted "Mind the crap" on the Tate's stairs in 2002[22] and "This is not a photo opportunity" on a dustbin outside the Tate, he wanted his art to be in the Tate, but without following the rules of its "rigorous process of nomination" and by criticizing the museum.

The goal of being known as an artist he had already reached for the "versus Bristol" exhibition. Now his institutional critique was more important, equally important and closely connected to the aim to reach an even broader and larger audience, who should acquire each artwork in a museum in a playful, direct approach. Visitors of museums should start a thinking process and "update" art and other objects in a museum in the same way like Banksy updated his oil paintings. Like these oil paintings a museum should become a space, where art can inspire its visitors instead of browbeating them.

Maybe the better classification for the Banksy versus Bristol Museum exhibition would be the umbrella term urban art as it is not as narrow as street art but still applies to a museum as a public space. Therefore I suggest using the term Urban Art as an extended Street Art in other public places than the street, for instance a museum or a gallery.

Notes and References

1 Banksy in an interview with Jim Carey, "Creative Vandalism," Squall Magazine (30 May 2002)
2 Jean Baudrillard, Kool Killer, trans. Hans Joachim Metzger (Berlin: Merve, 1978), 23. Original edition in French, Jean Baudrillard, "Kool Killer ou l'insurrection par les signes," Interférences 3, (1975).
3 See endnote i.
4 Miranda Sawyer, "Take a stuffy old institution. Remix. Add wit. It's Banksy v the museum: Artist's cynical but affectionate return to his home town," The Guardian, June 13, 2009, accessed June 1, 2014, http://www.theguardian.com/artanddesign/2009/jun/13/banksy-bristol-city-museum
5 Sawyer, "Take a stuffy."
6 Anonymus, "Banksy exhibition puts £10m into Bristol's economy," Bristol Post, September 01, 2009, accessed June 1, 2014, http://www.bristolpost.co.uk/Banksy-exhibition-puts-163-10m-Bristol-s-economy/story-11252196-detail/story.html
7 Anonymus, "Banksy graffiti works enter world exhibition top 30," BBC News, March 31, 2010, accessed June 1, 2014, http://news.bbc.co.uk/2/hi/entertainment/8595341.stm
8 Anonymus, "Banksy at Bristol City Museum," The Guardian, June 12, 2009, accessed June 1, 2014, Http://www.theguardian.com/artanddesign/gallery/2009/jun/12/banksy-bristol-art-exhibition
9 Anonymus, "Banksy at Bristol City Museum."
10 Anonymus, "Banksy exhibition puts £10m."
11 Anonymus, "Banksy in secret exhibition stunt," BBC News, June 12, 2009, accessed June 1, 2014, http://news.bbc.co.uk/2/hi/entertainment/arts_and_culture/8094839.stm
12 Ossian Ward, "Banksy Interview – Art," Time Out London, Mar 1, 2010, accessed June 1, 2014, http://www.timeout.com/london/art/banksy-interview-art-time-out-london
13 Guardian, "Banksy at Bristol City Museum."
14 Guardian, "Banksy at Bristol City Museum."
15 Banksy, Banging your Head against a Brick Wall (London: Weapons Of Mass Distruction, 2001), n.pag.
16 Banksy did not quote his name and date of birth together with the rest of the text in Banksy, Wall and Peace (London: Random House, 2006), 68, but an article in the Evening Standard Banksy posted on his website in 2004 quotes the full text. See Patrick Sawer, "How the art world's mystery man came unstuck at the Tate," The Evening Standard, October 18, 2003, 21. Banksy tended to make himself younger, he was rather certainly born in 1973. For a full discussion of his date of birth see Ulrich Blanché, Konsumkunst: Kunst und Kommerz bei Banksy und Damien Hirst, (Bielefeld: Transcript, 2012), 340f.
17 Banksy, Cut it Out (London: Weapons Of Mass Distruction, 2004), n.pag.
18 Banksy, Wall and Peace, 158.
19 Tristan Manco, Stencil Graffiti (London: Thames and Hudson, 2002).
20 Banksy, Wall and Peace, 170.
21 The Independent, October 18, 2003.
22 Banksy, Existencilism, (London: Weapons Of Mass Distruction, 2002), n.pag.

Alice Nogueira Alves / Faculty of Fine Arts (FBA-UL) / (CIEBA); alicenalves@gmail.com

Emerging issues of Street Art valuation as Cultural Heritage

Over the past decades the issues about the contemporary art turning into heritage have been discussed more intensely. Under this context one can identify the artistic manifestations linked to Street Art and, more specifically, to modern murals.

Modern murals, Identity, Preservation, Conservation

Introduction

Among the set of ideas presented in this article, the idea of Street Art is placed in a context of institutional acceptance. Far from the practice of vandalism, that characterizes the emergence of contemporary graffiti, and which still defines it in many contexts, the idea defended here is related to a recognized artistic practice, although it may be, or not, anti- establishment and critical. To distinguish these two factions, we will adopt the expression used in English-speaking countries for the contemporary mural painting – modern murals[1]. After overcoming the outbreaks of regionalist production, we are currently in a global artistic society. This widening, so characteristic of the twentieth century and of the movements of the artists in the different continents, emerged from the context of mobile art, to become part of an immobile one, practiced in urban space. Nowadays, the artists move around, not by political and social reasons, but to practice their creative freedom in different parts of the globe. On the other hand, we also see an enlarged shifting of the public to places where art is and the dissemination of artistic works over the internet.

It is clear that the status of Street art has changed in these past few years, becoming the most popular artistic movement and the closest to society. It's not just considered an act of vandalism anymore since it's a new source of revenue in the art market and for galleries. Now [all over the world], Street art attracts crowds through its artistic demonstrations and its continually growing number of artists. (Marie, 2011 – Transl. Jacqui, 2012)[2].

Our notion of Heritage has been changing in a world increasingly smaller, where there is a dimension of closeness given by the internet itself, new identities emerge and the need to assert a common thread becomes urgent. The local heritage is also returning to a universal idea, this time not by the imposing European values to the world, but by the emergence of a global culture. A new "multicultural" culture as characterized by Lourde Arizpe identified with a new vision of the planet given by its observation from the space, where "Neither political borders nor cultural boundaries are visible…" (Arizpe, 2000; 33). To judge this recent view, we need new global standard measures in a language that will bring us all together (Ibid; 33), where, in addition to the one already established by international institutions in several areas, we will also have art and creativity. The need of the new generations to place themselves at this confluence of the material world with the virtual one, leads to the search for new meanings, creating a space where they can live, far away from the traditional one, and where they will recreate their own sense of place and identity (Arizpe , 2000; 35).

"Emerging Heritage" - Between Heritage and Identity

Cultural heritage is cognitively constructed, as an external expression of identity, operating in a range of ways and levels. It is a social fact, and like all social facts, it is both passive and active. Its passivity rests in its role as an arena of selection: most elements (of whatever kind) do not make it into the heritage zone. Its activeness lies in its influence: once particular elements are established as heritage, they exercise power; they have a life of their own that affects people's minds and that consequently affects their choices. Heritage becomes a representation of beliefs about self and community which nest in with other related belief systems to create a holistic structure that ramifies through all the areas — politics, economics, use of resources — where social life touches us as individuals. (Pearce, 2000; 59)

In the early twentieth century, in a publication about the Modern Cult of Monuments, Alois Riegl, presented his view on the discussion related to the different values of Heritage. This compelling work identifies various types of values, including the art-value of contemporaneity and the relative art-value. By taking this example, we can extrapolate several issues to the current discussion. Leaving the first value to a subsequent chapter, let us give some attention to the second one. According to Riegl, it is the current society who at the present time values certain periods of the past, represented by monuments. They have a value related to our contemporary context, to our knowledge of history itself, defined and limited by cultural, social or even political and ideological issues. In this sense, we begin this theoretical approach by assuming that it is up to us to identify and appreciate certain elements over others. Throughout the twentieth century the notion of heritage has developed, from the identification of an individual element for its intrinsic value, defined by a certain intellectual class, to the one made by the community who benefits from these goods. This "new" heritage is now connected with the notion of identity values, thus being defined by its surrounding community. As such, we see the need for its defense and maintenance by the community as a cohesive whole, which depends on its own preservation as a social group.With this development, we now have a huge variety of elements identifiable as monuments, depending on the values attributed to them.

This aspect is reflected on the most recent and major international regulations, such as The Charter of Krakow 2000 - Principles for Restoration and Conservation of Built Heritage, where we find the following definition:

> *Heritage is that complex of man's works in which a community recognizes its particular and specific values and with which it identifies. Identification and specification of heritage is therefore a process related to the choice of values.* (The Charter of Krakow 2000)

This definition of values, subsequently reflected in the allocation of the value of cultural heritage to a particular object, is dependent on the context on which it is performed and it is essential to decide the elements to be elected to represent us in the future. Therefore, the chosen objects are the most representative of our community, be it local or global, reflecting our daily living and the image that we consider to be more real and exemplary for future generations to know who we were, and to understand the path that has led until their present (Avrami, Mason, Torre, 2000; 10). As the transformations of communities became valued until the present day, and the primacy of the past was abandoned, the number and variety of goods to be considered as World Heritage increased significantly. For this reason the way we deal with it also changed and will change constantly in the future (Avrami, Mason, Torre, 2000; 7). Unlike the classical theories which defended heritage's tightness, the irrefutable fact that we are imprinting our current interpretation on the property on which we intervene is now acceptable. This will be the version that will pass onto our successors, the same way we have inherited it from our predecessors, whether it is one of preservation or degradation (Lowenthal, 2000; 23).

> *This state of affairs is the postmodern context, where today's "lifestyle" is being transmuted into tomorrow's "cultural heritage," and it prompts the identification of a number of interesting themes that are potential sites for the invention of new heritage.* (Pearce, 2000; 63)

Now, we arrogate ourselves to previously define our elements to be safeguarded as the heritage of the future, where in addition to the elements that compose our past and, consequently, our history and culture, one finds our successes and failures in the present moment but, mainly, our achievements, among which we can mention the ones of an artistic nature.

This necessity to safeguard the heritage of the present is probably related to the vertigo of the social and technological developments experienced in the twentieth century. The past has become much closer and the future is tomorrow. We begin to change our notion of time and ourselves, increasing it to a global scale, which affects us all and not just a particular cultural elite. According to François Hartog (2006) this confusion of times, led to the urgency of preserving as much of our present as we can. As if we are afraid of losing our collective or even individual memory in the future, be it a near or distant one and that in this way our life becomes meaningless. "Emerging Heritage" was an expression adopted by Marie Berducou (2013), where heritage includes new elements, such as the industrial, technical and scientific ones. Within this group we should also integrate contemporary art. In the latter field, it is urgent to answer arising issues, so that the answers can reach future generations, as marks of our cultural statements at the present time. This concern with the preservation of contemporary art is not new; it has been present in many artists since the late nineteenth century. A good example was Duchamp himself, whose own reflection around this problem is perceived through his concern on the use of resistant materials and techniques, and which ended up materialized in the ultimate musealization of his pieces in Philadelphia (Pohlad, 2000). However, in general, since the early avant-garde movements of the twentieth century, we have been witnessing a gradual dematerialization of art, where the concept has become more important than the material component. This aspect results in numerous problems when you begin to discuss the preservation of some more recent works, where degradation processes occur very fast and are extremely difficult to control.

To this factor, we can add the nineteenth-century development of ephemeral art. This transience, sought by several artists, opposes itself to musealization, to art "freezing" for the enjoyment of future generations. Despite this fact, we witness the authorization given by many artists for their works to appear in museum collections, causing conservators more and more problems regarding those works' preservation. In the present case of Street Art, we can refer some specific factors that end up valuing the nowadays murals. Following the principles enumerated by David Throsby (2000, 29) we can mention an aesthetic value, which reflects a new taste, specially identified by new generations; a spiritual value, which reflects the symbolic identification of represented elements and their messages; a social value, where a connection towards the "other" is made, causing a sense of identity; and a symbolic value, reflecting a meaning of identity of a generation. Although, apparently, the historical value is kept away from this scenario, we can already attribute this status to the first artistic manifestations of this nature conducted in the last decades of the twentieth century. When the works of Banksy are sold, or the ones of Vhils auctioned, as happened recently, this sort of artistic expression is being economically valued. Despite the fact that economic and cultural values are defined by different factors, and thus somewhat disconnected (Throsby, 2000), there is actually a valuation of the second one that depends on the first, which gives the work a new status.

With the increasing of the transmission of images in a virtual space, this aesthetic taste ultimately prevails, marking the new contemporary art movements, now far from marginality, as they enter the art market, where they reach the status of an art object. However, by achieving this status, the ephemerality of these objects becomes itself a complicated concept. These artistic expressions enter a ranking of "important objects" a process which is characteristic of our current society, and, thus, identity ties start to appear leading to the need for their preservation, and consequently, to our need to leave an imprinting in history stating our contribution towards the development of these expressions. We begin to consider these elements as our heritage, and once they become a symbol of identity they cannot be, in any way, devalued.

The heritage valuation of modern murals
With the legalization of the practice of mural painting in public and private spaces, the aesthetic issue gained a new strength, bringing this kind of language to a long trodden road made by man since ancient times, where the parietal painting was always a constant. The anti-establishment character given to mural painting in the twentieth century, as happened for example with the Mexican muralists in the thirties, remained very present until this day; although we can already find many works where the aesthetic issue is dominant. Leaving behind the question of whether this practice may or may not be considered as graffiti, we are interested in deepening what happens when these manifestations become institutionally accepted, and even commissioned by public or private institutions, when contemporary artists begin to be recognized, not only at a national level but more importantly, in a worldwide manner.

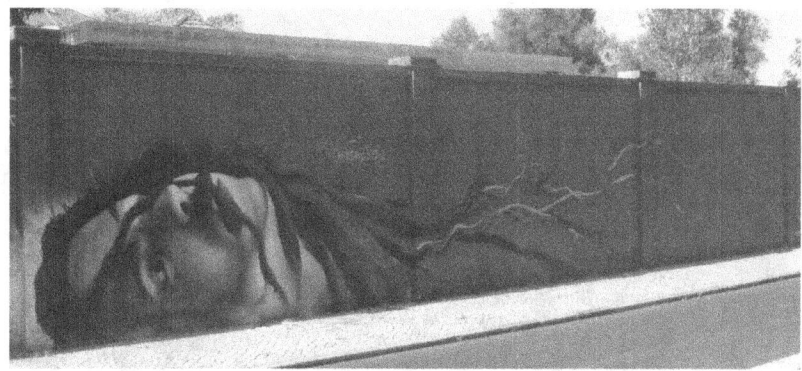

Fig. 1: **Self-portrait,** Marcos Granja (GRANJE), Rua das Murtas, Lisboa - 7th stage of the project "Faces of the Blue Wall" - GAU
(Urban Art Gallery) initiative in collaboration with the CHPL (Lisbon Psychiatric Hospital Center)[3].

The stylistic and identity issues of each country are forgotten, and we find a global art, that moves interested masses across countries, to enjoy the creations of artists currently well identified. A new economy linked to Tourism arises, thoroughly exploring these new expressions. This process is obvious when there are lists of cities to be visited. One example is the recently released list of the 26 cities with the best Street Art, by the American newspaper Huffington Post, where Lisbon occupies ninth place (Brooks, 2014). Among other initiatives of this kind, another great contribution to this worldwide spread is the recent posting of an online collection of Street Art by the Google Cultural Institute where about 5000 pieces all over the world are gathered (https://streetart.withgoogle.com/en/#home). In Portugal, the support for this initiative was provided by the Urban Art Gallery, attached to the Department of Cultural Heritage of the Municipality of Lisbon, which aims to:

> *...raise awareness concerning the richness and diversity of the artistic and cultural heritage of Lisbon and towards the urgency of its safeguard as a legacy to future generations, tracing as a double priority of the Gallery the prevention of vandalism and the disclosure of discourses of graffiti and street art as expressions of urban art.* (Carvalho, 2012, 5)[4]

The first concerns around the preservation of modern murals began to appear in the United States of America, where this artistic practice was common, especially in the seventies. In Los Angeles there is an association, the Mural Conservancy of Los Angeles, which "... is committed to preserving the heritage artists of the Los Angeles one of the mural capitals of the world" (http://www.muralconservancy.org /). In New York, new methods are being studied to lift more recent paintings in a search for the first graffiti / murals for their preservation. Everywhere around the world, the concern of ensuring the continued existence of pieces that were originally ephemeral seems to be increasing.

However, not every case is obvious. When there are other issues involved, the mere preservation initiative can be controversial. A case which led to the transformation of mentalities was the Berlin Wall. In a Europe where a postwar generation still lives, marked by the question of what are the limits of the dehumanization of man, the preservation of the wall, an element against which they fought and which haunted them for so many decades, can be a complicated issue. Moreover, the use of the wall as support for different artistic manifestations, initially with a more confrontational nature, made it a symbolic element, which reflects history and art before and after its fall in 1989. Here, two values come into confrontation: a positive and a negative one. The latter turns out to gain ground when combined with the "progress" that has been frightening theorists since the nineteenth century by threatening the conservation of artistic and historical heritage.In this case, despite the previous restoration of some of its paintings, the wall is in poor condition (http://www.eastsidegallery-berlin.de/data/eng/index-eng.htm). Recently, a large section was destroyed, leading to an appeal to UNESCO in 2013, claiming the World Heritage status to be given to the wall (Williams, 2013). When we go through several entries on the internet, we realize this globalization and the fact that there are already several examples of Street Art classified as heritage at European level, which gives them a special protection status, but also forces the community to keep them as intangible assets. Examples of this are Blek le Rat paintings, titled Madonna in Leipzig, or the work of Klaus Paier, Lovers in Aachen, both in Germany (Schilling, 2012). In England, the works of Banksy, already have the protection of an English Heritage Preservation Order. In 1997, the Alliance for Downtown New York, declared the space of downtown Manhattan open to Street Art (Rayner, 2008).

We think this aspect is interesting and relates to the difference between the European and the North American approaches. In the first case, we always find references to the classification of isolated elements. This is due to the tradition started in the French post-revolutionary period, in the last decade of the eighteenth century. On the other hand, the sense of community is more characteristic of the American continent, making the elements that define the community as a whole, more easily eligible for classification. However, in the European context, despite the special areas of protection provided, these protective measures usually do not extend to places where the paintings were made, making their detachment and consequent loss of meaning and authenticity, a common action (Brajer, 2010; 99). The controversies generated around the removal of Banksy paintings from the walls where they were originally made, have brought into the open many issues related to this kind of problem. The marginal nature of these paintings sought by the author himself prevents him from agreeing with this procedure, and ultimately he refuses to authenticate his paintings detached from their original location. To protect these elements, acrylic plates have been placed in various locations, attached to the wall. This type of procedure, although contributing to the preservation of the element (which is in itself debatable) ends up changing its reading in the set.
However, as stated by Ricardo Campos, the perpetuation of Street Art has been designed in a more virtual universe, through the

dissemination of reproductions (Campos, 2008). In fact, Melbourne's National Library, controversially archived a website related with graffiti (http://www.melbournegraffiti.com). This action was taken under the Program Pandora to preserve websites with heritage value (Mickelburough, 2011). But the most classic question remains: to see a reproduction of a work of art will never be the same as observing the original. Some aspects on the conservation of modern murals

For a conservator, who is predominantly involved in treating the material structure of a work of art, the technical and material aspects are of fundamental significance. Seen in the context of preserving this material substance, one can ask whether the approach to contemporary and modern murals is really so different from murals of the past. In many instances, it is not! However, because modern murals (as also old murals) are not just material objects with specific physical and chemical properties, it is impossible to ignore the intangible aspects, the theoretical issues that focus on the idea or meaning of the work, including those involving diverse functions and values. (Brajer, 2010; 85)

As with all contemporary art, the intangible issue mentioned in the quote above becomes paramount in its conservation. This aspect relates to the fact that these works have been performed in our contemporary society and that many of their authors are still alive. Therefore, the keys for their interpretation are closer to us, and the artist collaboration in the decision-makingprocess, or even in the intervention itself, becomes essential when it comes to the conservation of this conceptual component.
On the other hand, the expectations that we have about the visual aspect of a certain painting or the final outcome of an intervention, also play an important role in these matters. Based on the above mentioned newness value, defined by Riegl in 1903, we may establish here some interesting relationships. When Riegl tried to find a relationship between the main theories of Restoration of the nineteenth century, where the issue of what should be most valued in a monument was discussed, the image or the material that composed it, the author concluded that although the signs of material degradation in ancient art serve as testimonies of its antiquity, in the case of new/contemporary work, we do not accept this natural decay, because we have different expectations depending on the age of the assets.

.. On the one hand is an appreciation of the old for its own sake, a view that condemns any renovation of the old on principle; on the other hand is an appreciation of the new for its own sake, a view that seeks to remove all traces of age as disturbing and displeasing.... (Riegl, 1996; 81) (Riegl, 2013; 51)
Thus, when we approach contemporary art, we always hope that it is as "new" as it was when it left the artist's hands. We are very uncomfortable with its degradation because we consider it as sloppiness. Therefore, the act of "freezing" the works in time, and not accepting their natural degradation, ends up carrying some risks: "... modern murals may be in danger of being permanently caught in the present." (Brajer, 2010; 94)

For this reason, the repaint of modern murals has been a constant, and a major cause of this phenomenon is linked to this issue. Premature aging due to poor quality of materials in conjunction with adverse exposure conditions (climatic factors and vandalism), are accelerating these processes and posing questions about how to preserve these elements a little earlier than it would be expected. The issues related to the need for interventions to be carried out by professionals in the Conservation and Restoration field, suffered a large increment with an international meeting held at the Getty Institute in 2003, Mural Paintings and Conservation in the Americas, from which resulted a Rescue Public Murals project[5], included in the non-governmental organization Heritage Preservation, with members from many different areas, "that has a mission to save the objects that embody our shared and individual pasts.". In this context, some of the fundamental issues relating to this matter have been formulated:

How, for instance, can a conservator best participate in helping to save a mural whose message is no longer relevant to the community? Can he/she contribute technical expertise to the artist and the community, while allowing the content of the painting to change? What are the limits to the Code of Ethics of the American Institute for Conservation (AIC) in these cases? Can 'preservation' be understood to equal, in some cases, simple documentation of a mural whose physical condition can no longer be checked from deterioration? Can collaborations be worked out that will allow all parties concerned to work together in order to make decisions about how best to speak for these little understood works of art and social history? (Shank, Norris; 2008; 13)

With regard to the material issue, the cases we found show a continuity in the technical procedures of conservation and restoration usually adopted in the field of the oldest murals, although there are some variations in the products used. Although more problematic due to the fragility of the materials used by the artists, but also of the state of the support, these paintings often have serious stability problems due to their own fragile nature. However, other values should be taken into account, such as the image to be preserved and the importance of color. These questions are not exclusive of modern murals, in fact they are extensive to all contemporary art. In this particular case, studies on the best practices for making most durable murals have been conducted, including how to avoid certain pigments such as titanium dioxide-based whites, or by applying layers of protection from ultraviolet rays, or even the creation of new products to be applied as protective layers (Shank, Norris, 2008; 14). On the other hand, studies on the materials used, techniques of intervention and protection, are also starting to appear, as well as others issues related with their preservation. In this context, collaboration with universities is already a constant. We can mention the case of the University of Delaware (http://www.heritagepreservation.org/RPM/MuralMaterialsResearch.html), or, in a European context, the University of Valencia.

In order to preserve modern murals, various strategies are being adopted. We can refer the effective transposition of polychromic layers to other supports, such as canvas, and their later musealization (Rayner, 2008) (Brennan, Pons, Sancho, 2012). This sort of procedure, although often the only to ensure the continued existence of many paintings, ends up distorting the very essence of this artistic practice, as it replaces an originally fixed support for a removable one. However, it has been widely practiced throughout the twentieth century in mural and tile panels. Another common practice is the repaint, valuing the image at the expense of the very materiality of the object. This kind of intervention turns out to be very common in the conservation and restoration of contemporary art, due to the conceptual issue and the fragility of the materials used in its production, as well as to the previously mentioned question of our own expectations. However, new methodologies have been developed. In an intervention carried out by the Rescue Public Murals project, on an important painting of Philadelphia, Common Threads by Meg Saligman, only layers of varnish were applied, not only as a protection means but also to revive the existing colors, without having to resort to full repaint of the work (http://www.heritagepreservation.org/RPM/archive7.html).

Another practice taking its first steps is the recreation of missing paintings. An example of this practice was the mural of Keith Haring (1958-1990), originally painted on a wall in New York. To celebrate the fifty years of his birth in 2008, this work was recreated under the initiative of the Deitch Projects Gallery, with the support of the Keith Haring Foundation. Due to the fragility of the paint originally used, the work faded quickly, being covered by the artist himself a few months later. Through photography, and by removing several layers of graffiti performed later at the same site, it became possible to find the original colors (Order, 2008; 1). Shortly after the recreation the mural suffered a new intervention by Nagel Ortiz / LA II - who had formerly worked with the artist - by filling the voids of the painting. This event was considered by some as a creative moment and by others as vandalism (Order, 2008, 2). However, the following year, the city itself covered the wall again, in a gesture that could have been of preservation rather than destruction.

Such cases became common all over the world, when the first walls of the seventies and eighties began disappearing or being vandalized by other graffiti. In some extreme cases, as happened in Los Angeles in 2007, the 1984 Oliympic Murals ended up covered with a layer of an organic material, environmentally friendly, and with a gray ink intended for their protection against degradation caused by natural factors or even by vandalism. Since 2012, a team formed by the aforementioned Mural Conservancy of Los Angeles, has been bringing back to light those works performed on 110 Freeway, creating an open gallery (Joe, 2013), where this kind of heritage of the city is again enjoyed by its residents and outside visitors.

Despite these isolated cases, the long-term preservation of modern murals has been controversial (Shank, 2004). Regardless of the specific intervention of Conservation and Restoration that is required, it is also necessary to keep a maintenance process that public institutions are not, in general, alerted to and able to conduct. This situation can turn even more complicated when considering private property. In fact, the issues related to the walls where the paintings were made, raise questions about who will be responsible for their maintenance. The price of a professional intervention turns out to be a problem too, and that kind of work ends up being held by the original authors or the local community, resulting often in full repainting or aesthetic updates (Shank, Norris, 2008, 12). In these processes the original version of the painting is lost.

Is the objective to stabilize the paint and ground, or is it more appropriate to restore the mural to its original brightness and intensity, erasing its historic value in favor of a fresh appearance? (Rainer, 2003, 5)

This question is itself controversial, for if the communities define a particular object as a heritage element, and determine the kind of intervention it needs, then we have to accept the way this intervention is carried out. On the other hand, if we try to preserve the original work, this may be outdated and no longer framed by the community, which is itself in constant development (Weber, 2004). A discussion where all parties participate and contribute to the final completion of the intervention is required.

The work should be considered not only as a work of art but also as part of a wider social process (Drescher, 2004, 5). It is up to communities to defend their values and to take upon this initiative.

Final remarks and interrogations

The group that identifies the cultural good is no longer confined to a particular region but encompasses a universal culture, which is in itself developing in an increasingly uniform and closer world. Are we losing our identity or creating a new one, based on new technologies that disseminate information and on the increasing mobility across the planet? When becoming institutionalized, Street Art gained an importance in the art world, and in many cases it reached the status of a work of art and inherited all the consequent features involved in that definition. Far from being a forbidden art, this practice is very accepted under the social point of view, and Lisbon is a good example. The fact that it is becoming an international capital in this field, contributes to a new idea of the city, with which its citizens tend to identify themselves more and more every day. This phenomenon is not obviously unique and, in some of the major North American cities, we witnessthe birth of this heritage identification with urban mural art of the twentieth and twenty-first centuries, and the need for its preservation and restoration.

Apart from the ephemeral permanence and subsequent virtual disclosure of Street Art, sought by the authors themselves, the people who benefit culturally or economically from this phenomenon, tend to give it a new value, defining its production as a symbol to be preserved. In some places, the artists themselves elect which previously made elements are to be preserved, by not painting over them and respecting their integrity as identity elements of technical developments of a given place, as happens with some murals in Lisbon. Modern murals have a communicative function, whose key for interpretation is inaccessible to most of their viewers, although they are still a form of public art accessible to everyone. Nevertheless, as it happens with our historic monuments, this common aspect that derives from the daily coexistence with the asset, and the progressive identification of the population with these artistic elements, creates a sense of ownership that will result in this heritage connotation. The assignment of a value to these murals, places their material loss at the same level of the eventual loss of an identity element of the present time. The education of taste has always existed and, in this case, we witness the celebration of certain artists appointed by a cultural elite. Incidentally, when we have Municipalities' offices and other state institutions, not only in Portugal but also in other countries, selecting the worthy specimens to be preserved, we are precisely shaping the taste of the general public based on a set of pre-defined concepts, in the same way the museum institution itself does. When we turn a city into a visitable place by its Street Art, are we not creating an outdoor museum? Even assuming that the works have a transitional nature and will disappear after a short time, soonbeing replaced. Or is this a new system of temporary exhibitions? In this particular case, where the globalization of this practice is becoming clear, are we moving towards a broader community where intervention techniques and preservation attitudes will become uniform in various locations, or will we continue to follow regional procedures?

Notes and References

1 Murals are most commonly defined as wall paintings, works of art integrated into a specific architectural space. (Rainer, 2003;4)

2 Nous l'avons bien constaté, le statut du Street art a changé ces dernières années, devenant le mouvement artistique le plus populaire et le plus proche de la société. Il n'est plus seulement aujourd'hui considéré comme acte de vandalisme, étant une nouvelle source de revenus dans le marché de l'art et les galeries. A la mode, le Street art attire les foules à travers les manifestations artistiques et ses artistes toujours plus nombreux. (Marie, 2011).

3 The author of this article would like to thank Marcos Granja his permission for the publication of this photograph.

4 ...sensibilizar para a riqueza e diversidade do património artístico e cultural de Lisboa e para a premência da sua salvaguarda enquanto herança e legar às gerações vindouras, traçando a Galeria como dupla prioridade, a prevenção ao vandalismo e a divulgação dos discursos do graffiti e da street art enquanto expressões de arte urbana.(Carvalho, 2012,5)

5 RPM is a national effort to bring attention to US public murals, document their unique artistic and historic contributions, and secure the expertise and support to save them. Since its launch in December 2006, RPM has focused on creating a structure for bringing together, and funding the efforts of, conservators and muralists in order to assess the conservation needs of several key murals throughout the USA. The RPM web site allows the public to make recommendations of endangered murals for RPM to consider for assessment. RPM has created a database of more than 800 individuals and organizations crucial to saving murals, while it establishes a nationwide network. (Shank, Norris, 2008, 13)

Arizpe, Lourdes, "Cultural Heritage and Globalization". In Values and Heritage Conservation, Research Report,Los Angeles: The Getty Conservation Institute, 2000, 32-37, accessed May 19, 2014, https://www.getty.edu/conservation/publications_resources/pdf_publications/values_heritage_research_report.html

Avrami, Erica, Mason, Randall, Torre, Marta de la, "Report on Research". In Values and Heritage Conservation, Research Report, Los Angeles: The Getty Conservation Institute, 2000, 3-11, accessed May 10, 2014, https://www.getty.edu/conservation/publications_resources/pdf_publications/values_heritage_research_report.html

Berducou, Marie, "Discussion Group Presentation, Science for Emerging Heritage: Recognizing and Adapting to Changing Cultural Heritage Values". In ICCROM Forum on Conservation Science, 16-18 October 2013, accessed May 8, 2014, http://forum2013.iccrom.org/wp-content/uploads/2013/10/EMERGING_Berducou.pdf

Brajer, Isabelle, "Reflections on the fate of modern murals: values that influence treatment – treatments that influence values". In Theory and Practice in the Conservation of Modern and Contemporary Art – Reflections on the Roots and Perspectives, ed. Ursula Schädler-Saub and Angela Weyer. London: Archetype Publications, 2010, 85-100.

Brooks, Katherine, "The 26 Best Cities in the World to see Street Art", in The Huffington Post, last modified April 17, 2014, accessed May 8, 2014, http://www.huffingtonpost.com/2014/04/17/best-Street-art-cities_n_5155653.html

Campos, Ricardo, "Movimentos da imagem no Graffiti. Das ruas da cidade para os circuitos digitais". In VI Congresso Português de Sociologia. Mundos Sociais: Saberes e Práticas. Lisboa: Universidade Nova de Lisboa, Faculdade de Ciências Sociais e Humanas, 2008, accessed July 1, 2014, http://www.aps.pt/vicongresso/pdfs/98.pdf

Campos, Ricardo, Porque Pintamos a Cidade? Uma Abordagem Etnográfica do Graffiti Urbano. Lisboa: Fim de Século, 2010.

Carvalho, Jorge Ramos de, "Três anos depois...". In Galeria de Arte Urbana 3 anos. Lisboa: Câmara Municipal de Lisboa, 2012, 5, accessed May 8, 2014, http://issuu.com/galeriadearteurbana/docs/livro_gau_3anos_web

Cerejo, Sara Dalila Aguiar, Risco e identidade de género no universo do graffiti. Lisboa: Edições Colibri – SociNova, 2007.

Dias, Fernando Rosa, "Os Graffiti e a Arte Moderna Portuguesa". In Do Graffiti, Passado e Presente de uma Expressão de Risco,coord. José Quaresma. Lisboa: Faculdade de Belas-Artes da Universidade de Lisboa, CIEBA, FCT,2013, ed. CD-ROM, 22-38.

Drescher, Timothy W., "Priorities in Conserving Community Murals". In Mural Painting and Conservation in the Americas (2003). Los Angeles: The J. Paul Getty Trust, 2004, accessed May 13, 2014, https://www.getty.edu/conservation/publications_resources/pdf_publications/pdf/drescher.pdf.

Ferrão, Hugo, "Graffitis e os Rituais Sacrificiais do Estado de Excepção". In Do Graffiti, Passado e Presente de uma Expressão de Risco,coord. José Quaresma. Lisboa: Faculdade de Belas-Artes da Universidade de Lisboa, CIEBA, FCT, 2013, ed. CD-ROM, 51-58.

Ferrão, Hugo, "Grafiti – Mestiçagem Imagética dos Não Lugares". In Arte e Teoria, Revista do CIEBA – Centro de Investigação e de Estudos em Belas-Artes – Secção Francisco de Holanda, 2 (2001), 156-165.

Forero, Josephine Landertinger, "Save the Wall! – East Side Gallery endangered", In The MaG, Human Rigts Magazine, Global Eyes Production, last modified March 20, 2013, accessed October 26, 2014, http://the-mag.net/save-the-wall/

García, Rita Lucía Amor, Pons, Mercedes Sánchez, Sancho, Mª Pilar Soriano, "La conservación de grafitis en el festival de arte urbano Poliniza 2010". In Conservación de Arte Contemporáneo - 13ª Jornada. Madrid: Museo Nacional Centro de Arte Reina Sofía, Departamento de Conservación-Restauración, 2012, 199-208, accessed June 23, 2014, http://www.museoreinasofia.es/sites/default/files/publicaciones/13-jornada-conservacion.pdf

Garfinkle, Ann, "The Legal and Ethical Consideration of Mural Conservation: Issues and Debates". In Mural Painting and Conservation in the Americas (2003). Los Angeles: The J. Paul Getty Trust, 2004, accessed May 13, 2014, https://www.getty.edu/conservation/publications_resources/pdf_publications/pdf/garfinkle.pdf

Golden, Mark, "Mural Paints: Current and Future Formulations". In Mural Painting and Conservation in the Americas (2003). Los Angeles: The J. Paul Getty Trust, 2004, accessed May 13, 2014, https://www.getty.edu/conservation/publications_resources/pdf_publications/pdf/golden.pdf\

Hartog, François, "Tempo e Patrimônio – Temporality and Patrimony ". In VARIA HISTORIA, vol. 22, 36, Jul/Dez 2006. Belo Horizonte: 2006, 261-273, accessed March, 12, 2014, http://www.scielo.br/pdf/vh/v22n36/v22n36a02.pdf

Jacqui, "Conservative Bristol". In FatCap,trad. MARIE, 2011,last modified January 23, 2012, accessed May 8, 2014, http://www.fatcap.com/article/conservative-bristol.html

JAO, Carren, Uncovered Olympic Glories: Murals Restoration on the 101 Freeway, last modified May 23, 2013, accessed May, 12, 2014, http://www.kcet.org/arts/artbound/counties/los-angeles/mural-restoration-101-freeway.html

Laermans, Rudi, "Paradoxes of Patrimonialization". In (No)Memory, 7, (2004), 6-15, accessed July 7, 2014, http://www.skor.nl/_files/Files/OPEN7_P6-15(1).pdf

Lowenthal, David, "Stewarding the Past in a Perplexing Present". In Values and Heritage Conservation, Research Report. Los Angeles: The Getty Conservation Institute, 2000, 18-25, accessed May 19, 2014, https://www.getty.edu/conservation/publications_resources/pdf_publications/values_heritage_research_report.html

Marie, "Bristol Conservatrice". In FatCap, last modified September, 2011, accessed May 8, 2014, http://www.fatcap.org/article/bristol-conservatrice.html

Marques, António Pedro Ferreira, "Mignor". In Do Graffiti, Passado e Presente de uma Expressão de Risco, coord. José Quaresma. Lisboa: Faculdade de Belas-Artes da Universidade de Lisboa, CIEBA, FCT, 2013, ed. CD-ROM, 13-21.

Matta, Paulo Saragoça da, "O Enquadramento Jurídico do Graffiti" (Diálogo sob a forma de entrevista). In Do Graffiti, Passado e Presente de uma Expressão de Risco, coord. José Quaresma. Lisboa: Faculdade de Belas-Artes da Universidade de Lisboa, CIEBA, FCT, 2013, ed. CD-ROM,7-12.

Mickelburough, Peter, "Graffiti site preserved for cultural value". In Herald Sun, August29, 2011, accessed May, 8, 2014,http://www.heraldsun.com.au/archive/news/graffiti-site-preserved-for-cultural-value/story-fn7x8me2-1226124020261#content\

Muñoz Viñas, Salvador, Contemporary Theory of Conservation. Oxford: Elsevier Butterworth-Heinemann, 2005.

Orden, Erica, "A Downtown Icon Is Re-Created". In The New York Sun, April 22, 2008, accessed May 12, 2014, http://www.nysun.com/news/new-york/downtown-icon-re-created

Orden, Erica, "Haring's 'Silent Partner' Speaks". In The New York Sun, August 1, 2008, accessed May 12, 2014, http://www.nysun.com/arts/harings-silent-partner-speaks/83012/

Pounds, Jon, "The Gift of Absence: Mural Restoration in a Policy Void". In Mural Painting and Conservation in the Americas (2003). Los Angeles: The J. Paul Getty Trust, 2004, accessed May, 13, 2014, https://www.getty.edu/conservation/publications_resources/pdf_publications/pdf/pounds.pdf

Pohlad, Mark B., ""Marconi repaired is ready for Thursday…" Marcel Duchamp as Conservator". In Tout-fait – The Marcel Duchamp Studies Online Journal, Vol.1, 3 (December 2000), accessed January 13, 2014, http://www.toutfait.com/issues/issue_3/Articles/pohlad/pohlad.html \

Quaresma, José. "O Graffiti e as exigências da Intersubjectividade". In Do Graffiti, Passado e Presente de uma Expressão de Risco, coord. José Quaresma. Lisboa: Faculdade de Belas-Artes da Universidade de Lisboa, CIEBA, FCT, 2013, ed. CD-ROM, 59-68.

Rainer, Leslie, "The Conservation of Outdoor Contemporary Murals", in Conservation, The GCI Newsletter, Vol. 18, 2 (2003), 4-9, accessed May 15, 2014,.https://www.getty.edu/conservation/
publications_resources/newsletters/18_2/

Rayner, Alex, "Street art: Scribbles behind the wardrobe". In theguardian.com, August 26, 2008, accessed May, 12, 2014, http://www.theguardian.com/artanddesign/2008/aug/26/Street.art

Reis, Jorge dos, "Caligraffiti – De Pompeia a Piccadilly". In Do Graffiti, Passado e Presente de uma Expressão de Risco, coord. José Quaresma. Lisboa: Faculdade de Belas-Artes da Universidade de Lisboa, CIEBA, FCT, 2013, ed. CD-ROM, 39-50.

Riegl, Alois, O Culto Moderno dos Monumentos. Lisboa: Edições 70, 2013.

Riegl, Alois, "The Modern Cult of Monuments: Its Essence and Its Development". In Historical and Philosophical Issues in the Conservation of Cultural Heritage, ed. Nicholas Stanley Price, M. Kirby Talley Jr., Alessandra Melucco Vaccaro. Los Angeles: The Getty Conservation Institute, 1996, 69-83, https://docs.google.com/file/d/0B40gMrq2RJzbOWY0ZTQ3MjItM2JlYS00MjJkLWFmMTMtYjcxZWUwY2Q3OTJh/edit?hl=en#

Shank, Will, "Before the Paint Hits the Wall". In Mural Painting and Conservation in the Americas (2003). Los Angeles: The J. Paul Getty Trust, 2004, accessed May 13, 2014, https://www.getty.edu/
conservation/publications_resources/pdf_publications/pdf/shank.pdf

Shank, Will, Norris, Debbie Hess, "Giving Contemporary Murals a Longer Life: The Challenges for Muralists and Conservators". In IIC congress Conservation and Access. London: September 2008, accessed February 25, 2014, http://www.incca.org/files/pdf/resources/SHANK_W_NORRIS_D_H_Giving_Contemporary_Murals_a_
Longer_Life.pdf

Schilling, Jan, "Preserving art that was never meant to last". In DW – Deutsche Welle, May 7, 2012, accessed May 8, 2014, http://www.dw.de/preserving-art-that-was-never-meant-to-last/a-15933463-1

Throsby, David, "Economic and Cultural Value in the Work of Creative Artists". In Values and Heritage Conservation, Research Report. Los Angeles: The Getty Conservation Institute, 2000, 26-31, accessed May 19, 2014, https://www.getty.edu/conservation/publications_resources/pdf_publications/values_heritage_
research_report.html

Weber, John Pitman, "Politics and Practice of Community. Public Art: Whose Murals Get Saved?".In Mural Painting and Conservation in the Americas (2003). Los Angeles: The J. Paul Getty Trust, 2004, accessed May 13, 2014, https://www.getty.edu/conservation/publications_resources/pdf_publications/pdf/weber.pdf

Williams, Mary Elizabeth , "Part II: UNESCO Forced to Consider Street Art as Cultural Heritage", Center for Art Law, last modified April 29, 2013, accessed   October 26, 2014, http://itsartlaw.com/2013/04/29/part-ii-unesco-forced-to-consider-street-art-as-cultural-heritage/

Yngvason, Hafthor, "The Painted Murals of Cambridge: Maintaining the City's Collection". In Conservation, The GCI Newsletter, Vol. 18, 2 (2003), 4-9, accessed May 15, 2014, https://www.getty.edu/
conservation/publications_resources/newsletters/18_2/

http://www.heritagepreservation.org/RPM/archive7.html

http://www.eastsidegallery-berlin.de/data/eng/index-eng.htm

Cultural Assets

Helena Elias, Escola de Comunicação, Arquitetura, Artes e Tecnologias da Informação (ECATI) / ULHT, CICANT,
hc.elias@gmail.com
Inês Marques, Escola de Comunicação, Arquitetura, Artes e Tecnologias da Informação (ECATI) / ULHT, CICANT,
inesravi@gmail.com
Susana Leonor, Escola de Comunicação, Arquitetura, Artes e Tecnologias da Informação (ECATI) / ULHT, ID+ Aveiro,
susanamleonor@gmail.com

Recent public art interventions in the context of the luso-brazilian cultural relationship: street murals of Os Gémeos in Lisbon and Vhils in Rio de Janeiro*

Over the 20th century public art produced in the context of the luso-brazilian cultural relationships was mainly restricted to statues and busts. Recently, long after democracies have been established in both countries, other art manifestations have come to represent this cultural connection. In the political framework of the Portuguese New State, public art works were produced and commissioned by the state institutions that mostly had the control over the artistic processes and its outcomes. In such condition, the inauguration of a monument was usually attached to events concerning the history and culture of both countries. With democracy, new public art interventions begun to emerge, as a result of the plurality of actors and promoters negotiating public space. Within the luso-brazilian cultural relationship, public interventions regarding historical and cultural contexts of both countries have come to be presented in a variety of artistic expressions and subjects portrayed. Such was as the case of the work Caramuru (2008, Viana do Castelo), the 25 de Abril monument (2001, S. Paulo) or the street mural interventions of Vhils (Rio de Janeiro), whose work was integrated in the Year of Portugal in Brazil (2013). Also other commissioners got involved in partnership such as Metro de Lisboa and Metro de S. Paulo, with the works Brasil-Portugal: 500 anos – A Chegança (1994) and As vias do céu/As vias da água (1994). Later, other organizations such as the Crono Project and the Lisbon City Council joined to support Brazilian street artists Os Gémeos in their graffiti mural intervention (2011). Considering the evolution of public art in the framework of the cultural relationships of both countries, this paper discusses specially the recent interventions of Os Gémeos in Lisbon and Vhils in Rio de Janeiro, since they represent new approaches to public space regarding the cultural exchange of Portugal and Brazil.

public art, luso-brazilian cultural relationships, street interventions

Introduction

Over the twentieth century, much of the public art produced in the context of the Portuguese and Brazilian cultural connections has portrayed the affinities and dissimilarities staged in the cultural and political background of both of the countries (Schiavon 2008, Muller 2010, Costa 2009 John in 2002, Paul 2000). Both countries have faced dictatorships and democracies and in such political agendas, public art has played an important role in the representation of the political and cultural exchanges of both countries. The placement of statues and busts regarding the common historical past of both countries was the main public art practice developed during the Portuguese dictatorship. Later on, after the year 1974, Democracy has opened progressively the range of practices, audiences, sponsors and mediators, impacting as well as in the commission procedures and outcomes of public art works.

Recently, different approaches to public spaces have challenged the traditional ways of promoting public art works concerning the cultural contacts between both countries, namely mural street interventions. The aim of this paper is to contextualize Vhils and Gémeos recent public art interventions in Lisbon (2011) and Rio de Janeiro (2013) in the scope of the cultural relations between Portugal and Brazil.

To exemplify our argument we will discuss first some of the major works of public art that relate the two countries during the Portuguese Estado Novo dictatorship and during the first decades of Democracy. After, we will focus on urban art interventions of Os Gémeos and Alexandre Farto (Vhils), emergent expressions of this relationship, but clearly different from previous works of public art.

We shall see that the commissioned sculptures during the Portuguese dictatorship present a visual coherence and convey a particular message since they obey to the official discourse highlighting the Portuguese colonial empire. The subjects portrayed, the symbols and the media, as well as the celebratory occasions that motivated the orders and the opening speeches, clearly show this ideological argument since they addressed the fundamental question of Portuguese foreign policy: the need to maintain the colonial empire. In this context, Brazil was always seen as proof of the capabilities of the Portuguese colonizers, regarded as a continuance of Portugal, a country of the future, and the successor of the Portuguese glorious past (John 2002 p. 77). The Brazilian receptivity to this approach was particularly relevant, at a time when the colonial policy (Schavion in Muller, 2010 p.4) of the Portuguese Government was being strongly criticized by the United Nations.

In the Portuguese democratic period, a greater diversity of promoters offer a range of opportunities for the presentation of new visual languages and subjects portrayed which impacts as well in the variety of public art orders framed by the Portuguese and Brazilian cultural relations. We will mention some of the actors involved in these works of art from the nineties of the twentieth century to the present, and finally, we will analyze the relevance of this new public art approaches to the presentation of this kind of aesthetic proposals for public spaces. We will discuss these issues while commenting the works of the Os Gémeos and Vhils for the cities of Lisbon and Rio de Janeiro, respectively.

Personalities and historical commemorations represented by statues and bust
During the Portuguese dictatorship the most relevant works were invariably the works of statuary. The commemoration of symbolic occasions and historical events were usually the reason for the State to order a new work. The issues covered mainly the pay of a tribute to a historical or cultural character linking the common history of the two countries (see fig. 1, 2 and 3).

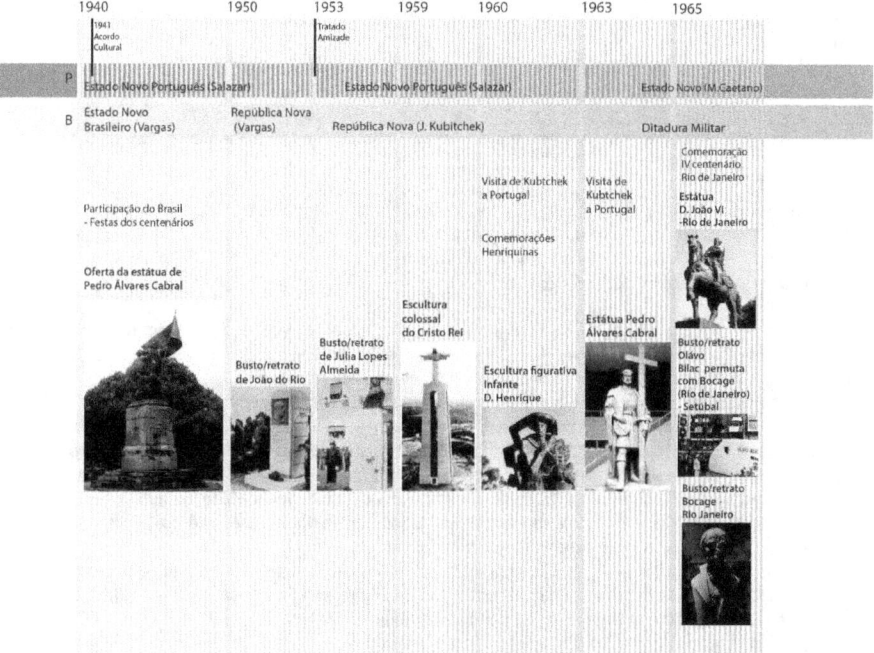

(fg. 1 and 2) – Timeline of the artistic interventions in the context of the cultural interchange of both countries

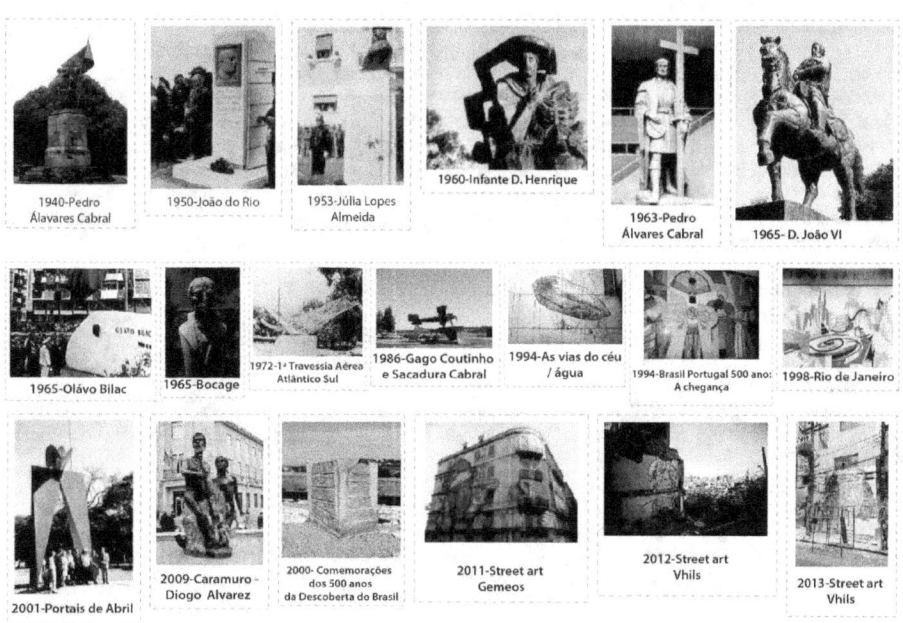

(fig. 3) – Works commissioned in Portugal and placed in Brazil and Brazilian works placed in Portugal – statuary, busts, abstract and figurative sculpture, mural interventions

This is the case of two statues paying tribute to Pedro Álvares Cabral. The first statue, a copy of the statue of Pedro Álvares Cabral created by Rodolfo Bernardelli (1940), was offered by the Brazilian government to Portugal on the occasion of the Celebration of the Double Centenary of the Foundation of the Nationality (1140-1640-1940), where Brazil was the only foreign country invited to the commemorations.

The second statue, of the sculptor Alvaro Brée, was placed in Belmonte as part of the Plan of Statues of the Ministry of Public Works (Elias 2007: 48). The work was expected to be included in the program of the celebrations of the Death of the Prince Henry the Navigator in the year of 1960. However, the work was only installed in 1963, with the presence of Juscelino Kubitschek, who was visiting Portugal (Elias 2010: 140, Elias & Marques 2012: 9).

In 1965, already during the Brazilian military dictatorship, the Commemoration of the Fourth Centenary of the City of Rio de Janeiro Foundation provided the Portuguese government (Ministry of Public Works) the opportunity to offer the equestrian statue of King John VI, sculpted by Barata Feyo. One year later a copy of that statue was installed in the city of Oporto and aligned geographically with the statue of the Brazilian city (Abreu 2005: 203).

There were few exceptions to the models of the statuary imposed by the political regime. Such was the case of the monument to Prince Henry, offered by the Portuguese Government and placed in Brasilia in 1960, on the occasion of the Celebration of the Fifth Centenary of the Death of Prince Henry. A first proposal, following the aesthetic model fostered by the Portuguese regime, had been previously rejected by the Brazilian authorities, with the argument that the statue did not fit the modern image of the city of Brasília. The Portuguese government presented then another work of art which had been designed for a different context: a modernist sculpture by Barata Feyo, which had integrated the winning proposal for the 3rd design contest for the monument to Prince Henry at the Cape of Sagres, Portugal. The contest had been cancelled by the government (Elias 2005: 40) and so the winning sculpture model was available to be ordered and installed in other place. This work was accepted by the Brazilian authorities. The sculpture, while maintaining the usual symbols such as the globe and the cross of Christ, offered a modern interpretation of the subject portrayed, particularly expressive in their angular and textured volumetric surfaces.
It was still the case of the monument to the Aerial Crossing of the South Atlantic, a project developed under the Celebration of the Fiftieth Anniversary of the 1st Air Crossing of the South Atlantic (1972). The winning proposal, by the sculptor Laranjeira Santos and architect António Fernandes, was the first large abstract public sculpture held in Lisbon.

Another significant activity, with respect to public art, was the inauguration of busts which portrayed writers related with the cultural relationships of both countries. In 1950, the bust of the poet João do Rio, who was then considered by the Portuguese Government as a great admirer of Portugal, was placed in Lisbon. In 1953, Brazil offers to the city of Lisbon a copy of the bust of Julia Lopes de Almeida, a work from the Brazilian sculptor Margarida Lopes de Almeida. In 1965, the bicentennial of the birth of the Portuguese poet Bocage is highlighted by the two countries with an exchange of busts between Brazil and Portugal. The Brazilian Academy of Letters offered to the Portuguese government a bust of Olavo Bilac - poet and publisher of the work of Bocage in Brazil. The ceremony took place in Setúbal, the hometown of Bocage. The Portuguese government offered the bust of Bocage which was placed in Rio de Janeiro. This practice is continued after the establishment of democracy in both countries. In the year of 2009 the Councils of Lisbon and Rio de Janeiro exchanged the busts of Father António Vieira and the writer Machado de Assis. However, the democratic context in both countries has brought a much greater variety of promoters, subjects, and outputs. This framework has operated as an effective renewal under the public art practice. While celebratory occasions still motivated the production of works honoring personalities and historical events, a higher range of interventions was also noticeable in the public spaces. Some of these approaches were reinterpretations of History more critical and less apologetic of the colonial past.

Democracy: commemorative works, other subjects and visual languages
In 2000 the council of Belmonte supported ten works of public art by on the occasion of the celebrations of the 500th anniversary of the Portuguese arrival in Brazil. In a variety of forms, the sculptures were entitled with names such as Pedro Álvares Cabral e seus irmãos, A travessia, Dos sonhos e das vontades, Aquele abraço, Mares or Adamastor. These titles suggest the abandon of the exclusive representation of the hero in order to embrace universal ideas.
Another case, despite not exclusively centered on the Portugal-Brazil relationship, was the exchange of art works between the Underground of São Paulo and the Underground of Lisbon, in 1994, when this city was entitled as the European Capital of Culture (Lopes 2007).

The analysis of the works exchanged between Brazil and Portugal shows the continuity of the subjects related to the history of both countries and the meeting of cultures, although with representations that differ greatly from traditional laudatory statuary. For instance, the panel of tiles Brazil-Portugal 500 years: A Chegança created by Brazilian artist Luis Ventura to be installed in the underground station of Restauradores depicts a different portrait of the colonizers and the meeting of cultures on the year of arrival of the Portuguese in Brazil.

The stone panels intervention Vias do Céu, Vias da Água, by the Portuguese artist David Almeida, promoted by the Underground of Lisbon and integrated into the station Conceição of the city of São Paulo suggest poetic visions of human actions of the past of the two countries. Other cultures become part of the representations of Brazil, in Portugal. Such is the case of the monument Caramuru, sponsored by the city of Viana do Castelo in 2009. The work, an authorship of José Rodrigues, honors Diogo Álvares, who was hosted in the indians Tupinambá territory, having married Paraguaçú, the daughter of the chief of the tribe whose history features the origin of the cabocla noblesse. The main part of the work, a sculptural piece in bronze of Paraguaçú, glorifies other aspects of colonization since emphasizes the supposed predisposition of the Portuguese to the miscegenation and easy acceptance to live with other cultures.

Also the practice of commemoration of the historical past relating both countries is less dominant. Other works remembering recent Portuguese historical events present a more contemporary approach. An example of this is the monument Portas de Abril. The work was created by the sculptor José Aurelio to celebrate the revolution of 25th of April of 1974, an historical process that led to the establishment of Democracy in Portugal. The monument was inaugurated in 2001 in São Paulo, Brazil. With seven feet tall, a steel gateway holds in the top the shape of a carnation flower. The work was designed to be a symbol of democracy and freedom and is different from the works of the New State not only because of the ideological discourse attached to the occasion but also because of the choice for more abstract representation of the event. During the ceremony of inauguration José Aurelio stated that the monument stood for which the Portuguese wanted to be reminded today, and regretted that the Portuguese community in Brazil was still attached to the Portuguese image created by the old regime[1]. A number of sponsors and promoters got involved for the construction of the monument: the Centro Cultural 25 de Abril in São Paulo, the Association of Municipalities of Setúbal, Association 25 de Abril in Portugal, and National Commission for the Commemoration of the Portuguese Discoveries, the Camões Institute as well as the Portuguese Parliament.

The Luso-Brazilian relationship in a global context: The case of Os Gémeos and Vihls

Other public art practices began to emerge with the opening of new media, variety of subjects and visual languages as well as the involvement of new promoters. Such is the case of the works of Os Gémeos and Alexandre Farto (Vihls). These works place the Luso-Brazilian cultural relationship in a global context. In both cases we find that there are new agents willing to present a culture of fruition of the city visibly distinct from the previous orders that framed the cultural connections of both countries. The intervention of Os Gémeos was promoted by the CRONO Project and the Council of Lisbon (CML). The municipality of Lisbon created the Urban Art Gallery (GAU) in order to support new approaches since that artistic interventions were still "very much associated with the practices of statuary, the tiles, and other artistic disciplines with aesthetic manifestation in the city." [2] The partnership[3] between the Azafama Citadina Association, the CRONO project[4] and the Gallery of Urban Art of the Council has been developed during the years 2010 and 2011 with the objective of welcoming projects of graffiti and street art in various public spaces in the city. The former idea has been first launched by a group of people aiming to facilitate the presence of an art available to all in the city space.

Although not developed without some constraints (Neves and Lopes 2014), these interventions pursued to conserve the statement of the social identity of the graffiti art groups by maintaining issues and procedures that portrayed them (Neves and Lopes 2014). Considering the public and private institutions and associations involved in the spaces of the city this kind of commission shows us an example of a social process running in a Down / Up basis. The proposal was designed and then the Lisbon Council joined the initiative to support officially the intervention (Neves and Lopes 2014). Apart the Brazilian artists also the Italian and Spanish artists Blu and SAM3 participated with mural interventions in the city of Lisbon. The Brazilian artists Os Gémeos are famous because of their murals conveying political and social messages featured by the yellow characters which label many of their works in various cities of the world. In Lisbon, Os Gémeos have developed their work without predetermination of any assignment or subject. They drew the usual yellow character with a scarf hiding the face. There is a particular detail in the label of the scarf that is to be mentioned. In the place of the brand there is the saying "I love vandalism" (figure 4).

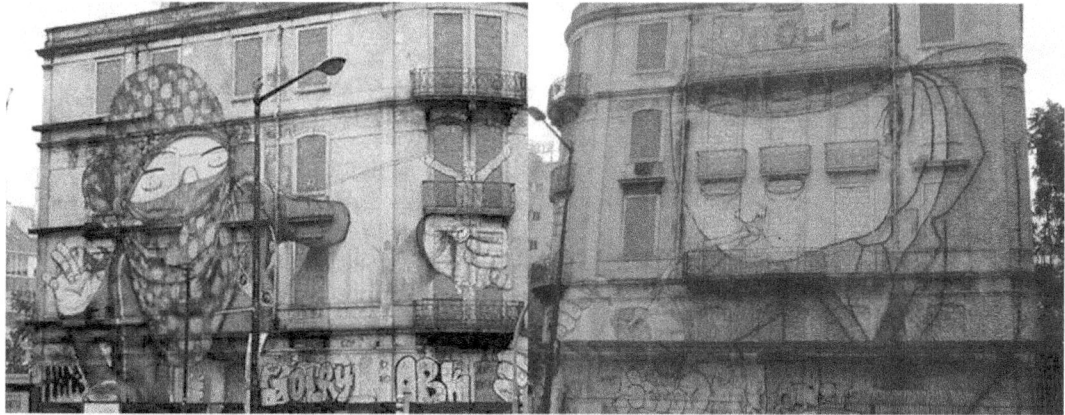

(fig. 4) – works of Os Gémeos and Blu at the Fontes Pereira de Melo Avenue. Source:Authors

Blu´s mural, painted on the same street, marks the same political statement by showing us an opulent character with a crown in which the ornaments are the signs of the multinational oil companies. These works use the intertextuality between the local and the global, which goes beyond the recognition of characters that BLU or Os Gémeos usually create in several metropolitan centers around the world. The works are located in one of the busiest avenues that connect two centers of business, trade and financial areas - Marquês do Pombal and Saldanha Squares and so they have a site-specific context since they address the issues of capitalism and globalization (figure 4). Indeed, after these interventions, the fruition of Saldanha / Marques de Pombal junction cannot be dissociated from these new aesthetic proposals of urban art. The presence of these interventions does not go unnoticed and the works contribute to a new understanding of this space, formerly aesthetically depressed. These street murals with a monumental scale questions the local and global economic powers represented in the cities and thus publicly challenge the citizen through its social and political message.

As a result of the most recent cultural contacts between Portugal and Brazil, there is the work of Alexandre Farto, aka Vhils included on the commemoration schedule for the event Year of Portugal in Brazil. The event sought to provide a contemporary portrait of Portugal, especially emphasizing the historical, cultural production and technological advances today[5]. There were cultural and business activities running in both countries. The main goals were to promote Portuguese culture and products in Brazil, by bringing more tourists and Brazilian enterprises, as well as to get the civil societies involved. In the news that covered the various initiatives[6] it is highlighted the importance of showing to the Brazilians the new image of Portugal[7]. The intervention of Vhils in Brazil covers an extensive process which is not restricted to the work in the hill of Providence, namely the mural intervention. Along with the work of the gallery and the exhibition of Rui Chafes at the Museum of Modern Art (MAM), Vhils intervention was considered a major artistic event presented in Brazil. Indeed, the artist exhibited his work on April 25, 2013 in Rio de Janeiro, following the invitation of the Clark Gallery Art Center in the district of Botafogo, as part of the activities planned for the Year of Portugal in Brazil event. Entitled as Fragmentos, the gallery work was connected to his street art presented in Rio[8]. However, this show was also linked with previous work developed in in 2012 for the Morro da Providência. This project was developed with and for the local community. The purpose was to leave a record of the faces of people who lived in Morro da Providência and moved to other parts of the city due to the works to improve the transport infrastructure of the World Cup 2014. The urban plan included the construction of a lift, tilt and plan new roads, but did not considered the needs of most inhabitants of the hill. The artist spent a month in contact with the people who have seen their homes demolished and being expropriated, and recorded their portraits in the walls of demolished houses as a way of preserving the memory of those people who lived in this community over 30 years[9].

The opening of the exhibition at Clark Gallery Art Center was attended by the Commissioner of the event The Year of Portugal in Brazil and Portugal's ambassador in Brazil. The community of Tabajaras, represented by the artist with a series of new portraits in the urban context also attended the exhibition. Besides the exhibition Fragmentos, Alexandre Farto intervened in three areas of the Rio de Janeiro, namely the Community Tabajaras (fig. 5), a building next to the Siqueira Campos metro station and Arcos do Túnel Velho.

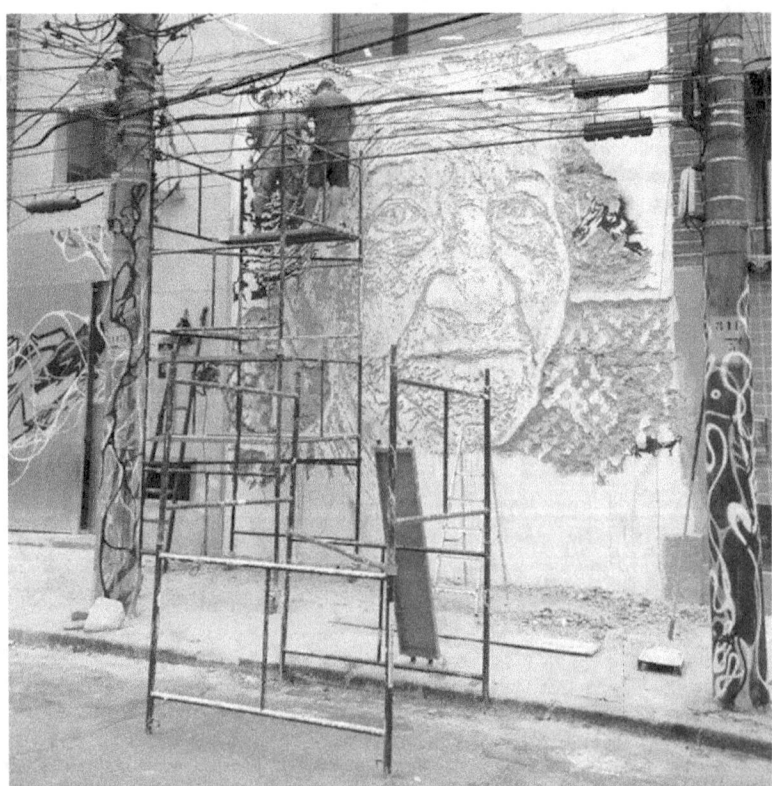

(fig. 5) – work of Vhils in the community of Tabajaras - Clark Art Center 2013 source: http://www.alexandrefarto.com/

According to Miguel Moore, Fragmentos and the external interventions in the public spaces of Rio connect the issues that Vhils has been developing lately in his practice in several cities. The artist draws attention to the places transformed by processes of expropriation and gentrification that have marginalized the original populations and have removed them from the possibility of involvement in the urban transformations of the sites that were part of their communities. Alexandre Farto explores a metaphor of the human condition, through the layers produced by scratching the walls as way of exposing what exists beyond the surface of things[10]. The artist draws sculpted textures in the walls highlighting the layers of building materials of the house. The portraits reveal the memories and stories of the houses and also of the inhabitants. Also this intervention is seen as a perceptive metaphor about how the destruction of the building material properties also entails a process of annihilation of the social dimension of these neighborhoods, characterized by a strong sense of community, in a city that often that they feel as a hostile environment[11]. The exhibition also shows the faces of the people drawn in the materials which usually form part of the construction of houses (wooden doors, brick or cement), creating interactivity with the intervention carried out within the community, connecting to a site-specific relationship with the work in the urban environment. Indeed, Fragmentos are, in a sense, the shortcut icons that invite the audience to go through the actual space where the event is.

Conclusions: expressions of public art between Portugal and Brazil

The Portuguese democratic context opened a set of diverse public art works that represent the country at the present times. With the new generations of artists, the relations between the two countries, in what concerns the issue of Public Art, reached far beyond the nature of the diplomatic connections established in the past decades, especially in the Portuguese context, which seeks now to bring a contemporary approach to the art produced in order to update the cultural image of the country. The official speeches that marked celebrations and events such as the April 25 or the Year of Portugal in Brazil clearly emphasize the strong cultural relationship between the two countries and what both share. A common feature of these events is the wish to upgrade the image of Portugal in Brazil. For example, the assertion for the existence of a democratic country at the inauguration speech of the monument to the 25th of April clearly disconnected the event and the work of art from the image produced by the propaganda of the Portuguese dictatorship. More recently, in the framing of the Year of Portugal in Brazil, the Portuguese image is based on concepts such as innovation, technology and new cultural trends, such as the presentation of contemporary visual artists with art proposals as the case of Farto and Chafes.

Regarding the sort of works usually presented in public art framed by this cultural exchange, we identify that the statues and busts represent significantly less the cultural relations between the two countries than before. Especially, new artistic approaches begin to characterize this relation, namely the mural interventions of Os Gémeos and Vihls. Another interesting point, concerning the performativity of the public art works, is that the most recent contacts provide direct intervention of the artists in the space while connecting to the environment, ie, both the Os Gémeos as Alexandre Farto worked on the place until the completion of the work, creating specific works (site-specific), addressing social criticism issues. In these cases, it is the artist (and not the work) that moves itself to the site, remaining there until the work is completed. Finally, it is important to say that these works involve processes that imply a new fruition of the city. Especially in the context of creation and dissemination these works now assume a global dimension through the social networks, rather than being just framed by the Portuguese and Brazilian cultural relationships.

* The authors are investigators of the research project Public Art in the context of the luso-brazilian cultural relationships, supported by CICANT-CIC DIGITAL, Lusofona University, Lisbon. http://artepublica.ulusofona.pt/

Notes and references

1 JL 16 de Maio de 2001
2 http://gau-lisboa.blogspot.pt/2010/05/crono-um-roteiro-de-arte-urbana-em.html
3 http://cargocollective.com/Crono/Global-EBOOK-Final
4 According to Pedro Neves, a group of independent people created the Azafama Citadina association in order to make easier the partnesips with other state intituitioins." See NEVES, Pedro, "Plataforma de arte urbana, prenúncio de uma mudança em Lisboa", Arte & Sociedade, Actas de Conferência, 2011
5 The president of the Luso-Brazilian Foundation recalled that the idea was discussed at the Luso-Brazilian congress. The celebrations started in the 7th of Septembre 2012 and close in the 10th of June 2013, Day of Portugal. The event involved the
Cultural State area, developed by the ministry of economy and the ministry for education and science.
6 http://www.camaraportuguesa-rj.com.br/ano-de-portugal-no-brasil-apresenta-arte-portuguesa-em-duas-exposicoes-no-rio/, http://www.jb.com.br/anna-ramalho/noticias/2013/04/24/alexandre-farto-inaugura-mostra-e-intervencoes-urbanas-na-zona-sul/, http://anodeportugalnobrasil.pt/o-ano/galeria-multimedia
7 The organizing committee has pointed out that the idea of the Portuguese as the baker or grocer, in result of the emigration in the early twentieth century, "has been changed at least twice": Following the emigration of Portuguese elite in the post-25 of April, and especially after the purchase of Telesp Celular by Portugal Telecom in 1998. However, "these changes reached a certain social and technocratic class" and one of the objectives of the program is to "go further and provide visibility into what is now Portugal throughout Brazil," he said. It is "a new Portugal that is taken to Brazil."
8 Already in other cities such as San Diego, the artist had been invited to exhibit his work. In the exhibition Viva la revolucion: a dialogue with the urban landscape, in MOCASD in 2010, the artist presented Scratching the Surface and acted in a specific area of the city. The Os Gèmeos also were presented in the event. See: https://www.mcasd.org/exhibitions/viva-la-revolucion-dialogue-urban-landscape
9 The process was documented in the film of João Pedro Moreira.
10 https://www.facebook.com/events/442532442501174/?ref=5
11 https://www.facebook.com/events/442532442501174/?ref=5

Abreu, José. A Escultura no Espaço Público do Porto no Século XX: Inventário, História e Perspectivas de Interpretação. Pub. de la Universitat de Barcelona, 2005.

Almeida, Adjovanes. Brasil e Portugal no Sesquicentenário da independência brasileira (1972). Anais electrónicos do XIII encontro de História, anpuh-rio, 2008, disponível em: http://encontro2008.rj.anpuh.org/site/anaiscomplementares

Costa, Maria. Travessias: afinidades eletivas da censura no Brasil e em Portugal na primeira metade do século xx. Anais do XXXII Congresso Brasileiro de Ciências da Comunicação – Curitiba, PR – 4 a 7 de setembro de 2009, disponível em: http://www.intercom.org.br/papers/nacionais/2009/resumos/R4-2559-2.pdf

FCG Anos 70 Atravessar Fronteiras, CAM, 2009

Elias, Helena. Lisboa, Sagres, Brasília in Revista História, nº 79, Set. 2005, pp. 36-39.

Elias, Helena & Marques, Inês As última encomendas de arte pública do Estado Novo (1965_1985) On the w@terfront Public art: from dictatorship to democracy 2012: Núm.: 23 pp. 1-25 disponível em: http://www.raco.cat/index.php/Waterfront/article/view/254755/341703

Elias, Helena & Leonor, Susana. Intervenções artísticas nos espaços públicos nos anos 70 em Portugal. Congresso SOPCOM/LUSOCOM, ISCSP, Setembro de 2012

Elias, Helena (2007) A Statue for each Town: Public Sculpture under the New State (1955 – 1965). On the Waterfronts, nr 9, May 2007, pp. 42-68, http://www.raco.cat/index.php/Waterfront/issue/view/16384/showToc

Elias, Helena (2007a) Arte Pública das Administrações Central e Local do Estado Novo em Lisboa: Sistemas de encomenda da CML e do MOPC/MOP (1938-1960), Tese de Doutoramento, Universidade de Barcelona, disponível em: http://diposit.ub.edu/dspace/handle/2445/35438

Elias, Helena Sistemas de arte pública do Estado Novo em Lisboa. Actas das Conferências Arte e Sociedade, Faculdade de Belas Artes da Universidade de Lisboa, Dezembro 2010, pp.136-151

João, Maria Memória e Império, Comemorações em Portugal (1880-1960) Lisboa: Fundação Calouste Gubenkian e Fundação para a Ciência e Tecnologia

Lopes, Telmo Arte Pública em Lisboa 94 Capital Europeia da Cultura. Intenções e oportunidades. On the waterfronts, Nr9, may 2007, ,pp.94-102

Mendes, M. Sobre a estátua equestre de D. João VI da autoria de Barata Feyo, in Colóquio Artes, nº 34, Junho de 1965, pp. 12-16

Marques, Inês Arte e habitação em Lisboa - Cruzamentos entre desenho urbano, arquitectura e arte pública, Tese de Doutoramento, Universidade de Barcelona, 2012

Moreira, Rocha & Martins. História e tecnologia: preservação do património estatuário como identidade cultural luso-brasileira, Projecto História São Paulo, n.34, jun. 2007, p. 69-84

Müller, Fernanda (2008) A imagem de um Brasil ideal ou uma re-colonização às avessas. XI Congresso Internacional da ABRALIC, 2008, USP – São Paulo

Müller, Fernanda (2008a) Brasil e Portugal em revista : a imprensa periódica na fronteira entre cultura e política. Amerika, 3 , 2010 disp. http://amerika.revues.org/1408

Neves, Pedro & Lopes, Telmo (2014) Graffiti, o caso de "Os Gémeos", Picoas, Lisboa 2011, Actas do Seminário de Arte Pública e Educação: Memória e cidadania, Universidade Lusófona, ISBN 978-989-757-021-6.

Paulo, Heloisa Aqui também é Portugal : A colónia Portuguesa do Brasil e o salazarismo Coimbra: Quarteto Editora, 2000

Schavion, Carmem, O Estado Novo no Brasil e as relações culturais luso-brasileiras no período, IX Encontro Estadual de História, 2008, disponível em: http://eeh2008.anpuhrs.org.br/resources/content/anais/1210897420_ARQUIVO_TextoANPUH.pdf

Ronald Kramer, University of Auckland, Department of Sociology,
r.kramer@auckland.ac.nz

"The thing about walls is they became big murals": The rise of legal graffiti writing cultures

Drawing from interviews conducted with 20 New York City graffiti writers and from unobtrusive observations, this paper seeks to rethink contemporary graffiti writing culture in two important respects. On the one hand, previous scholars have tended to explore graffiti writing as an illegal and criminalized (sub)culture. On the other, they have found it to be a practice that embodies a "critical" stance towards society. This paper shows that since 1990 a subset of graffiti writers who paint with permission has emerged, and that those who produce legal graffiti tend to lead lives and espouse values that most would not hesitate to recognize as "conventional." I conclude by suggesting that graffiti writing needs to be acknowledged as a multifaceted and historically fluid culture.

Ethnography, Legal graffiti, Culture

> *I can take two, three, four days, a week, a month to do a piece on a wall. On the walls you get to do your piece a fairly nice size and then if you want to add background and characters and all that stuff you could. On the train, your piece was constricted because of the next guy's piece. Now, the thing about walls is they became big murals. In the early to mid-90s you had a lot of people going from one aesthetic to another (NIC ONE)*

Introduction

By the mid 1970s a particular form of graffiti, distinguished by its emphasis on highly stylizing an individual's name, emerged as the dominant form of public writing in New York City. Referred to over the years as "subway art" (Cooper and Chalfant, 1984; Stewart, 1989), "spray can art" (Chalfant and Prigoff, 1987), and "hip-hop graffiti" (Phillips, 1999), this variant of graffiti has been analyzed by academic discourse in more ways than one. On the one hand, there is a tendency to situate what I will call "graffiti writing culture"[i] as a small fragment within broader cultural formations, such as "hip-hop" (Hager, 1984; Rose, 1994; George, 1998; Chang, 2005) or gang culture (Phillips, 1999). On the other hand, some accounts treat graffiti writing culture as demanding study in its own right. In these cases, analysts have tended to focus on graffiti as it existed in New York City during the 1970s and 1980s (Lachmann, 1988; Austin, 2001; Miller, 2002) or on emergent graffiti writing cultures that, although in different geographic regions, took their inspiration from what was happening in New York City (Ferrell, 1993; Macdonald, 2001; Rahn, 2002).

Although this latter approach has innumerable strengths and has contributed greatly to our understanding, it tends to prioritize illegal graffiti. In doing so, it generates an image of graffiti writing culture that is no longer complete. Drawing from over 5 years of ethnographic fieldwork incorporating interviews, observations and document analysis, I explore the post-1989 era of graffiti, a time in which many graffiti writers not only turned to legal modes of graffiti production, but also sought social acceptance for their practice and creative outputs.

Graffiti as "generalized lawlessness" and an "art of rebellion"

Most accounts of graffiti tend to take its illegality for granted (Mailer, 1974; Castleman, 1982; Stewart, 1987; Lachmann, 1988; Spitz, 1991; Ferrell, 1993; Austin, 2001). Given that graffiti is often produced in direct violation of the law and accompanied by auxiliary criminal activities, such as the stealing of spray paint and breaking into train yards, this is not surprising. In many accounts, especially those with a tendency to romanticize the practice, the focus often turns towards how graffiti is over criminalized. Such criminalization is usually motivated by political and economic ends, and occurs by investing "graffiti" with negative meanings and via the introduction of stricter legislation (see especially Castleman, 1982; Ferrell, 1993; and Austin, 2001 on this point).

In other accounts, illegality functions as an essential element in theorizing graffiti writing culture. According to Nancy Macdonald (2001: 126), the illegality of graffiti constitutes "the subculture's backbone" because it allows for the construction of a masculine identity or character. As she puts it

> *This subculture must be acknowledged for what it is... an illegal confine where danger, opposition and the exclusion of women is used to nourish, amplify and salvage notions of masculinity (2001: 149).*

For Janice Rahn (2002) illegality does not so much ensure a space in which a sense of masculinity can be developed, but one in which "autonomy" from dominant social groups can be found. Insofar as this autonomy is achieved through illegality, the latter becomes an "ethic" amongst graffiti writers and needs to be preserved

> *The community's ethics concerning graffiti's illegal status ensures that it cannot be entirely co-opted. As it becomes popularized, writers seem to push their art back to the margins of a clearly distinguishable underground culture. Members are dedicated to their own code of ethics ... (Rahn, 2002: 162).*

The illegality of graffiti often paves the way for further explorations of how graffiti writers violate the law in other respects. When, for example, Castleman explored graffiti writing culture in the early 1980s, theft was so common amongst writers that it could be said to constitute a "tradition" (1982: 46). On occasion, this proclivity for theft even led to the commission of burglary

> Another spectacular rack-up ... was not the result of chance discovery ... [T]hree writers carefully planned and executed a late-night robbery at a warehouse in the Bronx, getting away with more than 2000 cans of spray paint. Only Rustoleum and Red Devil paint, the brands most preferred by writers, were taken (Castleman, 1982: 47).

In Austin's account the theft that constitutes a "tradition" for Castleman becomes a "virtue" that, if followed dutifully, establishes a writers "street cred" and commitment to the subculture's "ethical code"

> Since the quantity of paint needed for a piece was beyond the economic means of most writers, necessity was made a virtue, and theft or swapping were considered the only ethical means of acquiring paint (2001: 65).

Alongside the focus on graffiti writing's illegal aspects, one is also likely to find the notion that it embodies a critical or oppositional stance towards the dominant society in which it is located. Based on an analysis of the graffiti scene in Denver, Colorado during the late 1980s and early 1990s, Ferrell (1993: 172) finds that "the politics of graffiti writing are those of anarchism." As he ultimately concludes, graffiti "stands as a sort of decentralized and decentered insubordination, a mysterious resistance to conformity and control, a stylish counterpunch to the belly of authority" (1993: 197).[ii]

More circumspect in his approach, Ivor Miller (2002) draws from research conducted on New York City's graffiti writing culture during the 1970s and 1980s to argue that graffiti is an "intrinsically rebellious" public art that addresses "race" and class tensions. In relation to the former, Miller argues that graffiti constitutes a cultural response to "the imposition of the European colonial masters' culture" upon those of non-European descent (2002: 33). In relation to class tensions, Miller claims that graffiti writers "combat the impositions of a consumer society" by "reshaping the alphabet to redefine their own identities and their environment" (2002: 85). Furthermore, insofar as graffiti writers make their art free to the public, Miller argues that writing culture defies a "system that put[s] a price tag on everything" (2002: 154).[iii]

Following the cultural turn, Janice Rahn (2002) finds that graffiti is an "adolescent obsession" (2002: 210) that speaks less to class and "race" tensions than to regimes of "knowledge and power" (2002: 137). For Rahn, the specific power/knowledge regimes in question are those that surround adulthood. In this context, graffiti is said to afford adolescents an opportunity to express disdain for the normalization and disciplinary processes that can be associated with one's teenage years and presuppose the transition to adulthood (Rahn, 2002: 143).

Finally, Nancy Macdonald (2001: 154) refrains from framing graffiti writing as resistance altogether. Instead, she finds it to represent a deliberate quest for social and cultural isolation. By creating a gulf between themselves and the broader society, graffiti writers can confound and frighten outsiders - a pastime from which they supposedly derive great pleasure

> The greatest satisfaction comes when graffiti does not just confound, it frightens. To many, graffiti is sinister and threatening and this gives writers something of an upper hand (2001: 158).

This brief analysis reveals the existence of a diversity of findings concerning the relationship between graffiti writing culture and the society in which it is embedded. Yet these differing interpretations all emphasize illegality and suggest that the relationship between graffiti writing culture and society is one marked by discordance. For the most part, graffiti writing culture is postulated as a critical force that challenges society.

In the post-1989 era, however, graffiti writing experienced a profound transformation in its norms and practices. Due to prolonged state opposition in New York City, graffiti writers were squeezed out of the subway system and went above ground. Those interested in painting elaborate graffiti works started seeking out permission from property owners to paint their walls. This occasionally led to opportunities to paint commissioned works for private and business clients (e.g., business owners requesting store fronts to be painted in graffiti style fonts).

To be sure, commercial and legal graffiti did exist prior to 1990, but it was much less common than it is today. After 1989, the production of legal graffiti quickly came to dominate the subculture. And, although some graffiti writers continue to paint illegally or work on both sides of the fence (MacDiarmid and Downing, 2012), the most prominent graffiti writers in the world focus overwhelmingly on legal work. While it is difficult to quantify these changes, my fieldwork suggests that the "career" of the illegal graffiti writer, especially when compared to writers of earlier eras and those who paint with permission, is generally one of short duration. After a year or two, perhaps after as little as six months, the majority of those who paint illegally either retire or, if they are committed to the aesthetics of graffiti, begin to pursue legal domains in which to paint. There are, of course, some exceptions to this rule, such as JA, who are known for painting illegally for well over a decade. Nevertheless, beyond a small handful of writers, there are not too many in New York City that could be recognized for painting illegally for a prolonged period of time. In light of such transformations, the portrayal of graffiti writers as outlaws and revolutionaries may be historically accurate, but it only provides a partial image of contemporary graffiti writing culture.

The production of legal graffiti in New York City

Throughout the 1970s and 1980s, the location most favored by graffiti writers in New York City for plying their craft was the subway system. Although it was present throughout this period, the city also waged an aggressive 20-year war against graffiti that ended in 1989 with the declaration of a "graffiti free" subway system (Schmidlapp and Phase2, 1996: 112). Since the early 1970s, the city has spent millions of dollars each year eradicating graffiti and portraying it as a sinister force. Amongst many other strategies, the city has built mechanical train washes ("the buff"), fenced off train yards with razor wire, institutionalized anti-graffiti police squads, and eventually enacted a policy of withdrawing trains from service if they have graffiti on them (Austin, 2001; Kramer, 2009; Stewart, 1989). Despite all these efforts, the city seems to have simply extracted graffiti writers from their subterranean urban existence and propelled them into the streets. In this new domain, graffiti writers have adapted to new conditions in three main ways. First, and to be a sure, some remain committed to the subway, choosing to document and share their train painting exploits even if the image quality isn't always the best. Second, a portion of writers work "above ground" and focus their energy on buildings, highway embankments, signs, storefront gates, freight trains, and anything else they can possibly write on. Third, many writers seek out legal avenues in which to pursue their craft. This third adaptation is an important, albeit often overlooked, development within graffiti writing culture. It could easily be said that enough graffiti writers have crossed the line that distinguishes illegal from legal graffiti, such that it is possible to categorize legal graffiti artists as a distinct coterie within graffiti writing culture. To put it another way, if during the 1970s and 1980s graffiti writers painted subway trains and, at best, occasionally ventured out to produce legal graffiti, since 1989 a portion of writers have focused exclusively on the production of legal graffiti. This shift in the "mode of production" seems to have paved the way for the development of a new ideological standpoint amongst those who produce graffiti with permission.

The vast majority of legal graffiti in New York City is found on the exterior sidewalls of small businesses, large factory walls in the outer boroughs, schoolyard walls, and sometimes on vans and trucks. In order to produce legal graffiti murals, graffiti writers must seek out and obtain written consent from property owners. For the most part, writers simply ask property owners if they will grant permission to paint murals on their wall space. These negotiations are often facilitated by the graffiti writers leaving business cards and, sometimes, portfolios of their work with property owners.

Most legal graffiti writers do not seek financial rewards from property owners and most will paint for free provided they are able to retain control over the creative process. The shunning of material rewards does not necessarily reflect the belief that to exchange creative services for money somehow compromises the artist and renders what they produce inauthentic. Rather, money is shunned because graffiti writers ultimately seek a Hegelian mutual recognition from their peers, most of whom will view the work on the Internet or perhaps in magazines after it has been documented (cf. Snyder, 2009 and Halsey and Young, 2006: 279-280 who report similar findings). In this context, it is not money that is necessary, but wall space, which affords the opportunity to paint on a large scale. A single artist or many artists working in collaboration may produce legal works of graffiti. Occasionally, graffiti writers acquire permission to paint on surfaces that can accommodate up to, if not in excess of, 20 artists. But more often than not, murals are painted by three to five artists. The amount of time spent working on a mural varies. Not taking into account weather conditions, artists capable of painting fast can cover relatively large walls in a single day; but sometimes walls take months to complete due to the detailed work involved. Generally speaking, however, most large-scale murals are completed over the course of two to four days.

Most works of legal graffiti contain "pieces," which emphasize through highly stylized lettering the tag names of artists, and a "background," which usually takes the form of some kind of visual scenery. A work that incorporates pieces and a background is referred to as a "production" (Snyder, 2009). Prior to and during painting the artists working on a mural will discuss in great detail. The themes and concepts to be explored in the background, the composition and location of "pieces," the size of imagery and letters, the colors to be used, the style in which things are to be painted ("photo-real" versus "illustrative" for example), will all be discussed at length. Graffiti writers will also work out who is doing what and when. Occasionally, detailed sketches are produced in advance and then reproduced on the wall. More often than not, however, the artists will be accustomed to working as a group and will develop a set of creative ideas during the painting process.

The seriousness with which graffiti writers approach their aesthetic production is further reflected in the concern they display with the materials they use. Much in the same way a fine artist primes a canvas, legal graffiti writers will use regular household paint to roll or "buff" the surfaces on which they will be producing murals. They may spend anywhere from 20 to 100 dollars on the paint required to prepare a wall in this manner. Some, in order to make the process of priming walls much more time efficient and less labor-intensive, have invested several hundred dollars in air compressors and spray guns. Graffiti writers, however, are most fussy when it comes to the aerosol spray paint cans that they use. Since the early 1990s, graffiti writers in European cities have worked with spray paint manufacturers to create an aerosol can specifically designed to meet their needs. In fact, it could easily be said that there now exists something of a "graffiti industry." Aside from the well over 1500 colors supplied by new companies, the most important development in terms of aerosol paint was the introduction of low-pressure cans. These aerosol cans release paint at a much slower and softer rate, which allows graffiti writers to shade in ways almost impossible with the technology that was available during the 1970s and 1980s. But it is not only the cans that have advanced. There is also an extensive market for the caps that dispense the paint from the spray can when depressed. Caps allow a writer to vary the width of spray. By the mid-1990s, technology along these lines had advanced so far that a writer could make lines the width of a pencil to lines three inches thick.

For a variety of reasons, such as new anti-theft technologies, these products cannot be stolen and therefore cost money. A good quality can of aerosol spray paint costs approximately eight US dollars. Any given cap costs about 50 cents and, given that some caps clog fairly easily, it is not unlikely that an artist will need to use three to four caps per can. This means that every high quality can of spray paint used comes at a cost of approximately 10 dollars. In light of this booming graffiti industry, the American paint brands that Castleman's graffiti heroes evidently held in high esteem, and which presently cost less than half as much as the new paints available, have been disavowed by legal graffiti writers. Today's legal graffiti artists not only refrain from stealing their paint, they also insist on spending more than twice as much in order to work with the best materials. To be sure, all these costs add up. A legal graffiti writer is not unlikely to use at least five cans of paint in order to produce a decent piece.[iv] The amount of paint required for the background of a legal mural, although it varies depending on the kind of detail involved, will require at least another five to ten cans of spray paint. Thus, a work of legal graffiti that includes five pieces and a background involves an expenditure of several gallons of house paint and at least 30 cans of spray paint. In short, stealing relatively cheap American brands of spray paint and then illegally painting subway trains is no longer the only method that is available and perceived as acceptable for the production of graffiti. A portion of today's graffiti writers actively seek permission from property owners in order to spend close to, if not more than, 350 dollars on murals that will appear on walls and other publicly visible surfaces that they do not own, and from which they will not derive any direct material advantages.

Take a walk on the tame side

Contrary to popular (and academic) belief, much contemporary graffiti is not produced by youth. To be sure – and this consistent with the findings of Snyder (2009) – many of the legal graffiti writers that I have met over the years did start their "careers" during their teenage years by painting illegally. However, as they began to reach their 20s and as the trains were no longer viable as surfaces to paint, they transitioned to legal graffiti work. Once they had made this transition, they tended to remain on the permissible side of the border that divides legal from illegal graffiti. It would seem that with the occupying of a financially rewarding position within the economic structure, mortgage payments, family, and other responsibilities, illegal graffiti quickly comes to be seen as an unnecessary risk to one's career and lifestyle.

Legal graffiti writers range in age from 12 to 50 years of age. Although the majority of graffiti writers are men, they come from a variety of class and ethnic backgrounds. They display great occupational diversity and may work as graduate students, corporate employees, teachers, fine artists, professional graphic designers, or pursue creative careers, such as interior design. Ironically perhaps, I met several writers in New York who work for the Metropolitan Transport Authority (MTA) or other city agencies. A handful even work in various branches of law enforcement. Many of the older graffiti writers that I have met are in stable family environments, often raising children with their partners. This relatively "conventional" material existence is often accompanied by an embracing of hegemonic values and a desire to participate in society. Arguably a little unexpected, many of the graffiti writers I have spoken to voice support for the sanctity of private property and oppose "vandalism"

> The vandalism, if you get caught, you got caught man. Don't bitch and moan about it… You got caught doing something you weren't supposed to do - you painted somebody's property (BEEN3)….you have the new guys that are out there and they don't know what they're doing. They're writing on people's garages, they're writing on people's cars and vans and they're writing on people's gates. I don't appreciate that. If you're gonna get into graffiti, you better learn the rules of graffiti… (SONIC). …it's against the law to write on someone's door. You don't ask for permission so you have to deal with the consequences. And that's something I'm really surprised with graffiti writers sometimes because they don't accept that (EMA).

Graffiti writers also tend to accept the notion that individuals are entitled to free speech even if this means having to extend tolerance towards political elites and those in powerful social positions who voice opposition towards graffiti. This is especially striking in a place such as New York City where political elites and the major print media routinely denounce graffiti writing culture

> RK: Do you think political leaders are right to oppose graffiti?
> BISC: They have a right… Every one has a right to any opinion.
> CEY: I don't know if I would say they are right, but I can certainly understand the point of view if they decided that they didn't have any appreciation for it.
> RK: How do you feel about the way graffiti is spoken about in the mass media? Say for example the New York Times…
> NIC ONE: With the news media, their job is to run with the news like any other self-respecting news or media organization. So I don't have any hate or any ill will towards them. I don't have any disgust towards them. Whoever is doing the [article] writing will go with the information they are getting at that very moment.

Alongside this embracing of dominant values, to which several further examples could easily have been added, many graffiti writers express a strong desire to participate in society. At an everyday, local level, graffiti writers often see themselves as enhancing the community areas in which they produce murals. BEEN3, a graffiti artist who paints with a "crew" that are particularly renowned for their murals in the borough of Queens and who call themselves THE WALLNUTS, offers a concise summary of how graffiti artists can contribute to public spaces in ways that are beneficial

[With] the walls, we are not doing anything illegal. We are asking for permission. We are paying for all our own supplies, which is helping the city because we are paying taxes on it of course. Everything they [the city] need is being done: They don't have to pay to maintain it because we're maintaining it. They don't have to worry about cleaning it anymore. And a couple of other things: It makes the neighborhood look better than just having it destroyed.

If the words of other graffiti writers are anything to go by, it would seem that the general public do indeed appreciate the work. Although, admittedly, I have heard one or two stories in which some members of the public do not appreciate legal graffiti art, legal graffiti writers overwhelmingly report positive feedback from the public

We have never had a bad comment from the general public ever… In fact, we were doing a wall with a big demon on it and he's coming out of the ground… We didn't realize it, but this was across the street from a church. We were doing the wall and we turn around and a nun comes walking across the street. Me and MUSE are just like: 'Oh man, she's just gonna lay into us'. She came over and said: 'I see your guys work around. I love it. Could I have one of your cards in case we ever need anything done?' … So that's the type of thing we get from the public (DEMER). I have had mostly really beautiful encounters with the public in New York City and all over the world. People are often very thankful for the work we do. They offer food, music, drinks… (CERN). You know, I've never had so much flattery in my life. I don't consider myself a talented guy or anything like that. I just do what I like to do. And the response I've gotten has been really, really positive (JUSE ONE).

One of the ways in which the relationship between contemporary graffiti writers and the society that surrounds them can be understood involves asking writers how they feel about officially sanctioned public arts projects, such as the "Arts for Transit" program in New York City. The Arts for Transit program, in an effort to improve by aesthetic means a relatively drab underground environment, works towards placing officially approved art throughout the subway system. I have not come across a single graffiti writer who opposes public arts projects. If anything, they all want to see more art – of whatever kind – in the public square. Moreover, many express an active desire to participate in public art programs, especially Arts for Transit. The following are illustrative examples

The Arts for Transit program is cool. I wish they would try to find a balance with [graffiti] writers … I hope the generations that take control of these institutions aren't so closed minded (CERN). I myself can adapt to different mediums. I could deal with something like [the Arts for Transit] program, especially if there is a little money involved or some exposure. It's just another outlet (PART).

Finally, utilizing the increasing use of graffiti within advertising as a pretext, I have often asked graffiti writers to reflect on the nexus firmly solidified during the early to mid 1990s between the aesthetics associated with graffiti writing culture and the sphere of commodity exchange. While several scholars, most notably Hebdige (1979: 92-99; but see also Spitz, 1991: 34), have suggested that the absorption of emergent cultural forms by the realm of commercial exchange signifies the dissolution of their critical potential, my fieldwork suggests a strikingly dissimilar view is warranted. Amongst the graffiti writers with whom I have spoken, the issue is not one of maintaining a position that is independent of consumer culture and therefore one from which a resistant standpoint can somehow be secured, but a matter of establishing connections with those who control capital in order to ensure that any possible economic gains go to graffiti writers and/or graffiti writing culture

I think it's a real good thing when we can get in and work with people outside of the culture. The problem is that outside entities come into our culture, they look at the way we do certain things, then they go paying some other people top dollar and they cut us out. You'll see a lot of computer generated illustration and graphics that are graffiti based. And if you're from the graffiti world, you'll sit there and say: 'Yo, a graffiti writer had to have something to do with that'. And, yeah, a graffiti writer had something to do with that, but not necessarily created it for them (NIC ONE).

When it comes to having real graffiti writers do these advertisements and getting paid good money for it, it's all great. I'm happy to see graffiti writers make money for it. [Advertisements show that] graffiti is a big part of America. And they use it to advertise their multi-million dollar business and their products… [But] for someone who never did graffiti, yet actually take the style and use it and make money of it, there's a problem there … I don't dig that too much (SONIC).

When you have a graphic designer trying to imitate graffiti I think it's wrong. If graffiti writers can get paid and be involved in it, then I'm definitely all for it. People say it's 'selling out'… I think that's a ridiculous term. If you love what you're doing and you can get paid to do it, there's nothing better than that (DEMER).

It would seem, then, that producers of legal graffiti lead lifestyles and hold to values that many people would consider "conventional." Many of them are career and family oriented individuals who spend their spare time creating paintings within the urban environment. More often than not, the artists absorb the costs involved in producing legal graffiti. The writers see themselves and their art as contributing to communities in ways that are beneficial and it would appear that portions of the general public are appreciative of the work that they do. (To be sure, much of the general public enjoy the more elaborate forms of illegal graffiti too.) When possible, graffiti writers try to work not against, but as NIC ONE might well put it, "with people outside the culture." Almost needless to say, this is not the type of imagery that comes to mind when one usually thinks of anarchists, rebels, or those who revel in their outlaw status.

Conclusion

Drawing from ethnographic fieldwork, I have suggested that a portion of graffiti writers in New York City do not reflect, at least in two important respects, the image created of them in previous academic accounts. Whereas previous research tended to focus on illegal graffiti and often saw in this illegality some form of resistance, it would appear that since 1990 some graffiti writers have not only become adamant about seeking out and acquiring permission in order to produce graffiti, but have also attempted, in various ways and at various levels, to become a part of the society in which they find themselves embedded. Of course, this should not be taken to mean that we can go too far in the opposite direction and begin to imagine graffiti writing culture as something that always operates on the permissible side of legality. Nor should we simply imagine graffiti writers as philanthropic altruists free from egoistic impulses. To do so would amount to over emphasizing a particular segment or region of graffiti writing culture at the expense of others.

However, in light of how graffiti has adapted to a shifting political context, it is clear that writing culture cannot be reduced to a singular entity that is united through a shared disregard for the law. To be sure, previous scholars did explore tensions amongst graffiti writers, but they did not explore the differences (and/or similarities) between those who produce graffiti with and without permission in much detail. This, of course, did not generally occur because, until the 1990s, such a tension was difficult to discern given the ways in which the painting of graffiti was historically practiced. It is, however, becoming apparent that graffiti writing needs to be recognized as a culture that has expanded and become more complex, and is likely to continue to do so with time. I suspect that this is due to a variety of reasons, such as the movement of its practitioners through the life course, and through times and spaces regulated in fluid ways by powerful actors such as the state. Our understanding of graffiti would be enhanced by further research that consults a greater diversity of graffiti writers, that is, those who paint with and without permission, and works towards the development of a descriptive account that more adequately reflects the heterogeneity of contemporary graffiti writing cultures. Future research could also address explanatory and policy concerns. In relation to the former, one important question revolves around the causes and mechanisms that shape the choices of individual graffiti writers in terms of how and what type of graffiti they will want to produce. In relation to the latter, future research could explore the policy implications of legal graffiti at the city level. Should urban political elites, for example, reconsider current policies that attempt to suppress graffiti and, instead, work to incorporate legal graffiti writers into civic life?

Notes and References

[i] I prefer the term "graffiti writing culture" over "aerosol art" and "hip-hop graffiti" as this appears to be the convention used most widely amongst graffiti writers. While this type of graffiti was firmly established by the early to mid 1970s, it is important to note that it has its origins in the late 1960s (Powers, 1999). It then appeared throughout New York City's subway system during the 1970s and 1980s before finding new spaces in which to exist during the 1990s (Murray and Murray, 2002; Ganz, 2004). Although slightly anachronistic, it is generally acknowledged to consist of three main forms: "Tags," "throw-ups" and "pieces." In my view, on the basis of the (sub)cultural context in which it is produced and its stylistic regularity, this type of graffiti is to be sharply distinguished from political graffiti, racist graffiti, and so on. In what follows, I am not concerned with these latter forms, but only with "graffiti writing culture."
[ii] For variations on the graffiti-as-resistance theme that take their lead from psychoanalytic perspectives, see the brief essays of Spitz (1991: 44, 55) and Mailer (1974: np).
[iii] For a comparable view concerning the relationship between graffiti and consumer society, see the brief analysis offered by Stewart (1987: 174-176).
[iv] Halsey and Young (2006: 278, 290) also found that graffiti writers – even those who paint illegally – will spend approximately fifty dollars to produce a "piece."
Austin, Joe. (2001) Taking the Train: How Graffiti Art Became an Urban Crisis in New York City. New York: Columbia University Press.
Castleman, Craig. (1982) Getting Up: Subway Graffiti in New York. Cambridge, Mass.: MIT Press.
Chalfant, Henry and James Prigoff. (1987) Spraycan Art. London: Thames and Hudson.
Chang, Jeff. (2005) Can't Stop Won't Stop: A History of the Hip-Hop Culture. New York: St. Martin's Press.
Cooper, Martha and Henry Chalfant. (1984) Subway Art. London: Thames and Hudson.
Ferrell, Jeff. (1993) Crimes of Style: Urban Graffiti and the Politics of Criminality. Boston: Northeastern University Press.
Ganz, Nicholas. (2004) Graffiti World: Street Art From Five Continents. New York: H.N. Abrams.
George, Nelson. (1998) Hip Hop America. New York: Viking.
Hager, Steven. (1984) Hip Hop: The Illustrated History of Break Dancing, Rap Music, and Graffiti. New York: St. Martin's Press.
Halsey, Mark and Alison Young. (2006) 'Our Desires are Ungovernable': Writing Graffiti in Urban Space', Theoretical Criminology 10 (3): 275-306.
Hebdige, Dick. (1979) Subculture: The Meaning of Style. London: Routledge.
Kramer, Ronald. (2009) A Social History of Graffiti Writing in New York City, 1990–2005. PhD dissertation, Yale University: Department of Sociology.
Lachmann, Richard. (1988) 'Graffiti as Career and Ideology', American Journal of Sociology 94 (2): 229-250.
MacDiarmid, Laura and Steven Downing. (2012) 'A Rough Aging out: Graffiti Writers and Subcultural Drift', International Journal of Criminal Justice Sciences 7 (2): 605-617.
Macdonald, Nancy. (2001) The Graffiti Subculture: Youth, Masculinity and Identity in London and New York. Hampshire: Palgrave Macmillan.
Mailer, Norman., with photographs by Mervyn Kurlansky and Jon Naar. (1974) The Faith of Graffiti. New York: Praeger.
Miller, Ivor L. (2002) Aerosol Kingdom: Subway Painters of New York City. Jackson: University Press of Mississippi. \
Murray, James and Karla Murray. (2002) Broken Windows. Corte Madera, CA: Gingko Press.
Phillips, Susan A. (1999) Wallbangin': Graffiti and Gangs in L.A. Chicago: University of Chicago Press.
Powers, Stephen. (1999) The Art of Getting Over: Graffiti at the Millennium. New York: St. Martin's Press.
Rahn, Janice. (2002) Painting Without Permission: Hip-Hop Graffiti Subculture. Connecticut: Bergin and Garvey.
Rose, Tricia. (1994) Black Noise: Rap Music and Black Culture in Contemporary America. Hanover, NH: Wesleyan University Press.
Schmidlapp, David and Phase2. (1996) Style Writing from the Underground: (R)evolution of Aerosol Linguistics. Terni, Italy: Stampa Alternativa/IGTimes.
Snyder, Gregory J. (2009) Graffiti Lives: Beyond the 'Tag' in New York's Urban Underground. New York: New York University Press.
Spitz, Ellen H. (1991) Image and Insight: Essays in Psychoanalysis and the Arts. New York: Columbia University Press.
Stewart, Jack. (1989) 'Subway Graffiti: An Aesthetic Study of Graffiti on the Subway System of New York City, 1970-1978'. Unpublished doctoral dissertation, New York University.
Stewart, Susan. (1987) 'Ceci Tuera Cela: Graffiti as Crime and Art', in J. Fekete (ed) Life After Postmodernism: Essays on Value and Culture. New York: St. Martin's.

Daniel J. D'Amico, The William Barnett and The Joseph A. Butt S.J. College of Business at Loyola University New Orleans, danieljdamico@gmail.com

Lessons from Mardi Gras: Fostered Culture Between New Orleans and an Online Learning Community

This paper summarizes and comments upon a series of short films produced in conjunction with the Institute for Humane Studies' Learn Liberty online video program, to communicate and educate audiences regarding social science, political economy, and the cultural history of the city of New Orleans. When viewed together, the video clips provide material for an online learning module. The videos were supplemented with a discussion forum, live question and answer sessions with directing faculty members, and online access to additional reading and research materials. The content aimed to investigate how individuals and groups within the various civil society networks of the city utilize and interact within their unique geographic, social, economic and cultural space. Viewers learn about the key ideas of social capital, spontaneous order, and how various individuals and groups within the city face unique forms of knowledge, incentives, and personal experiences throughout history - especially the recovery process surrounding hurricane Katrina. This paper summarizes the pedagogical experience of the online learning program created by the short films, it briefly summarizes the content therein, and offers additional commentary upon their theoretical and empirical substance, last it identifies potential areas for future application of similar research and educational models.

Introduction

"The mission of the Institute for Humane Studies (IHS) is to support the achievement of a freer society by discovering and facilitating the development of talented students, scholars, and other intellectuals who share an interest in liberty and in advancing the principles and practices of freedom."[1]

In pursuit of this goal, LearnLiberty.org (LL) is an online portal of educational videos and supplemental content aimed to communicate and encourage interest into the ideas of freedom and the social science theories and research surrounding liberty. Preceding the 2014 New Orleans Mardi Gras carnival season, LL sought to produce a topically themed series of videos investigating some of the unique cultural phenomena and processes of socially-relevant political economy common throughout the city of New Orleans and its history. Videos would analyze a variety of unique cultural practices and contemporary historical episodes of New Orleans all via the analytical toolkit and social theories of classical liberal political economy. By highlighting distinctively New Orleanian practices, the videos aimed to portray and provide an engaging and appealing way of educating and communicating basic theories and concepts of economics, political science, and sociology to a broad base of perhaps otherwise uninterested online viewers. The complete video series, access to supplementary research materials, login availability for the private Facebook group with forum discussion, and an hour long question and answer session are compiled and labeled, "Lessons from Mardi Gras: What New Orleans Can Tell Us About Society," and accessible via the Learn Liberty Academy (LLA) online portal.[2] This paper is intended to give a brief summary of the intentions and production processes behind the video series. It will also provide some further details regarding the theoretical and academic inspirations behind some of the themes and ideas found therein. This essay will also describe the pedagogical effects that the video series invoked and give commentary upon how such programs might be adopted by other educators seeking unique methods for exposing students to diverse and distant cultural experiences. Strategies for improvement will also be touched upon.

Lastly, this paper aims to draw attention to the symbiotic relationship between urban space, artistic cultural processes, social science, digital video technologies, and online social media. In this vein, the Learn Liberty Academy program and the learning processes it fostered serve as a sort of case study to provide further evidence of the complex and emergent features of human social orders. Such complex emergent results stemming from digital media forums, parallels the relationship from urban spaces and the complex processes of economic and social development they foster as explained by Jane Jacobs (1961). In so far as urban environments lower the transaction costs of trade and communication between entrepreneurial actors, they also foster communication, learning and innovation. Drawing upon Jacobs' insight, Virgil Storr (2008) suggests market economies be recognized as a social space, for they serve as a fertile hosting ground for unique, often larger and more diverse social contacts, interactions and lasting relationships than is often feasible in non-market environments. McCloskey (2007) boldly suggests, this observation is not only true, but argues market processes represent the ultimate and essential foundations for the vast majority of qualitative social and cultural networks today. Dutton (2009) has recently noted the heightened technological capacity of the Internet to foster social networks traversing more diverse geographies and interconnecting larger groups of more diverse individuals. The Internet operates as a sort of digital urban space. In this case, users participated online in a sort of distinctive digital urban space, in which such space was explicitly focused upon and dedicated to investigating and discussing the urban space and social history of the city of New Orleans. In result, the online community was in a way infused by New Orleans culture, and at least reportedly served to inspire an appreciation and wantonness of the digital participants to spend real time in New Orleans, personally consume its cultural products, and participate in its social networks. The remainder of this paper is organized as follows. Section II is a brief description of the documentary production process and how the online learning program operated. Section III summarizes some pedagogical insights garnered from participating in the program. Section IV

Lessons from Mardi Gras: What New Orleans Can Tell Us about Society, Program Description

Five short documentary films were produced entitled, "How Eating Babies Strengthens New Orleans," "Bars and Brass Bands in the Big Easy," "How to Make a Criminal Cocktail," "The Gumbo Recipe that Works for Everybody," and "Virtue and Vice at Mardi

Gras." Each video was scripted and edited to be approximately 5 minutes in length and aimed to briefly communicate some basic theme of social science, highlight the unique cultural practices of the city of New Orleans, and were released and disseminated via the websites LearnLiberty.org and its appendage YouTube channel. Social science theories covered and touched upon within the series included but were not necessarily limited to: spontaneous order theory, social capital, deep play, the law of unintended consequences, and economic freedom. Within a week of release, each of the short films had garnered several thousand views, hundreds of shares and dozens of likes and comments on both YouTube and other social media outlets such as facebook and twitter.

In addition to each film's individual release and comment threads hosted on YouTube, they were also combined and released as an online guided educational program entitled, "Lessons from Mardi Gras: What New Orleans Can Tell Us About Society," coordinated by the Learn Liberty Academy. The program lasted 6 days. Interested viewers from around the world were instructed to online pre-register for the program. Registrants were emailed a log in for access to the video material upon its immediate release. Videos were also paired with supplemental reading materials, including relevant pieces of investigative journalism, public policy analysis and academic research. Participants also had access to a private Facebook group with forum discussions moderated by experienced researchers whom prompted each days interactions with motivating discussion threads. On the second to last day of the program, Eileen Norcross, a public policy researcher with The Mercatus Center of George Mason University (a sister organization to IHS) and myself, participated in a live online question and answer session. All of the materials from the class, including a recorded version of the live question and answer session, all of the associated reading materials, any extra online content links, and the comment feeds from the Facebook forum discussions are stored in the online programs archive so that registered members can perpetually access them. Faculty and student participants were continually asked to share comments and feedback throughout the process, all such reactions were overwhelmingly positive. As the program faculty member, primary video performer, designer of the series, and key facilitator of the online discussions I would like to speak briefly to how beneficial and enjoyable my personal experience and participation was. The most obvious base line of comparison for me as an Assistant Professor of Economics at Loyola University New Orleans, within a college of business hosted at a mid sized liberal arts university, was that of the conventional course work and traditional class room experience. In no uncertain terms this format seemed more economical, meaning that we accomplished far more substantive progress in less time and at the expense of fewer resources than is often feasible in a conventional university setting. There are still obviously advantages to a formal university experience in real time and space, but the ease and depth of material covered in this online format is worthy of note.

Pedagogical Performance, Outcomes and Room for Improvement
First, it should be noted that the Learn Liberty Academy, as an online educational program dedicated to fostering learning about the theoretical foundations and implications of a free society, tends to attract a relatively biased sample of students. In this context, such a bias is not necessarily problematic, and in many ways proved beneficial throughout the program. Students who follow the online programs of the IHS, make use of its digital resources, attend summer conferences, and enroll in LLA programs, tend to be more often self-identified libertarians, meaning they tend to support economic and civic liberty but hold a variety of personal attitudes regarding individual morality. Participant samples tend to have a larger population of undergraduates primarily interested in economics and related social sciences. Because of these impassioned interests students tend to be more well-read than the modal undergraduate, especially within these topic areas. They also tend to share a common familiarity of some seminal works in the classical liberal corpus.

This sorting contributed to a significantly different culture of communication and interaction amongst the participants and program guides relative to conventional university course work. For example, at several instances I was inspired to make notes of references and questions posted by students, as they were particularly relevant and value added for my own research and publishing interests. Given that Facebook's formatting of likes and comment shares seamlessly organized this exchange, while allowing and encouraging members to share additional links, pdfs, and video content from their own investigations and research, I developed the impression that the medium had serious potential for collaborative learning and research efforts if focused upon well suited topics and further supported by samples of students with significant motivation. Compared to my traditional course work in which I often service in person lecture courses comprised of 80-100 undergraduates from various majors on campus, enrolled members of the LLA program appeared to draw upon a deeper and more relevant body of previous knowledge and reading, had more often performed the suggested reading, and asked more targeted and critically engaged questions. Online discussions between participants developed spontaneously without significant effort from the program instructors, again more so than I am accustomed to witnessing in the conventional class room setting.

The Videos and the Theories Therein.

A. How Eating Babies Strengthens New Orleans,
Despite its sensationalist and perhaps crude title, this video was produced with the intent to educate viewers about the basic concept of social capital. King Cakes are a common pastry popular in New Orleans, traditionally prepared and consumed throughout the Carnival season. The dish consists of twisted dough, typically filled with different flavors of custard, cream cheese and or jelly, covered in colored icing and confectionary sugar. While the dish is simple enough, eating and sharing King Cake has become a common cultural practice throughout the New Orleans area, largely because of the unique symbolism and customary norms surrounding its consumption. Like most things Mardi Gras, King Cakes are thoroughly infused with historic, religious, and cultural symbolism. Like most decor throughout the carnival season, King Cakes are decorated in the traditional festival colors: Purple, Green and Gold. Such supposedly originated as the "official colors" of Mardi Gras in 1892, by Rex a fictitious character, leader of the Rex Krewe, and proverbial king of the Mardi Gras parade. Founded in 1872 The Rex Organization, themed its Tuesday morning 1892

parade, "The Symbolism of Colors," thus selecting purple to represent justice, green for faith and gold power (Hardy 2014).

King cake is originally a popular Catholic European custom prepared and eaten during the Epiphany. In its contemporary New Orleans form, the dish itself draws upon both French and Danish pastry styles and is prepared and consumed prior to the Lenten season during the Mardi Gras carnival. It's key and most unique ingredient is a small plastic and or porcelain baby figurine, symbolizing Jesus, hidden within the knotted folds of the dough. Once the cake is sliced and eaten, the person who finds the baby in their slice is thought to gain good fortune, sometimes considered the king or queen for the duration of the party and traditionally responsible for bringing the next king cake and or hosting the next party. As is seen throughout many traditionally New Orleans dishes, King Cake is less typically served in restaurants but more so bought in local bakeries and served amongst small communities of families, friends, neighbors and co-workers. As one example, my own office adheres rigidly to the tradition wherein there is a King Cake in the common area every Friday during the carnival season. Who ever finds the baby in one week is responsible for bringing the cake the next week. Our faculty secretaries and longest standing New Orleans locals, enforce compliance via mild but good-hearted shaming. Hence in both cooperation and defection, sharing and consuming king cake appears to carry the effect of fostering the qualitative feature of our office's social capital. Individuals reflect upon their own experiences of learning about the custom, finding the baby, complying with the norm and shaping their preferences for favorite bakeries throughout the city. Such conversations and practices tend to foster group camaraderie and a unique solidarity with New Orleans heritage. The origins of King Cake, and the baby practice in particular are uncertain. Though some speculation and folklore links the practice to pre-christian rituals wherein royal authorities were selected by such processes though sacrificed for the hopes of a good harvest the year after; hence the bittersweet practice of holding the responsibility for bringing future cakes.[3]

If truly influential for shaping King Cake customs, such ancient practices reflect a common feature of several phenomena observed throughout the video series. Mainly, many New Orleans cultural practices appear to serve as informal mechanisms to pre-empt and or mitigate inter-group and political conflicts. Historically selecting authority by random variables protects against corruption. Whereas enforced term limits guide preferable outcomes during tenure. Similar cases have been made regarding the broader practices of Mardi Gras parades more generally. The expenditure of public resources for the sake of present consumption, at first appears financially unsound and or even irrational. Though such customs may have proved effective to mitigate conflict amidst competing potential authorities, of which any individual or group interest may harbor corrupt interests relative to other groups. Spending public wealth on consumptive parades may be suboptimal for the financial vitality of the city, though sufficient for gaining collective approval (Levy 1989 and Gudeman 2001).

B. Virtue and Vice at Mardi Gras

This video links the idea of Deep Play, popularized by social anthropologist Clifford Geertz (1973) to some of the cultural aspects of the Mardi Gras carnival festivities. Geertz first borrowed the concept of Deep Play from classical political economist Jeremy Bentham (1789), who described it as a sort of game wherein given the incentives faced by individual participants no rational person would voluntarily chose to participate. Geertz described his observations of cock fighting rings in Bali as an apparent form of Deep Play, because he noticed a large gap between the low levels of wealth possessed by cock-fight gamblers compared to the seemingly high and intense wagers placed upon the individual cock-fight matches. At first glance the wagers seem financially unreasonable. Bentham saw deep play as a form of irrationality and even a dangerous behavioral phenomenon, wherein individuals were consumed with personal moral emotions to the expense and detriment of their more sober and rational calculations. Given one's rational preferences they would not chose to play a high stakes wager with an uncertain or unlikely outcome, but in the presence of such emotive zeal, the player does in fact participate. Geertz saw Deep Play, within the context of Balinese cock-fighting as less problematic and perhaps even socially enhancing. Geertz observed that not only were the wagers relatively high and uncertain, but they seemed to correlate in size and uncertainty particularly when historical legacies of inter-group and inter-personal conflict ran deepest. Much like long-standing rivalries in contemporary professional sports, showmanship and competitive jeering were most vocalized when competing individuals represented broader social groups and tensions. In this vein, Geertz recommended viewing the patterns of high wagers and risks as proxies for the level of investment and commitment to the participants respective groups and tribes. As such, cockfighting and its associated prohibition actually served to form bonds of cooperative interest across groups and individuals whose interests were otherwise at odds. Competing groups work together if only in the limited context of the cock-fight but learn tacit information about each other, and crucial to their limited levels of coordination nonetheless. Forms of Deep Play such as cockfighting in a way served as a sort of public good and peace-making spectacle for the general long run peace and stability of the community. Hence Bentham was perhaps correct in his description that no rational individuals would voluntarily choose to contribute to public good provisions. From a modern vantage wherein public good provision is presumed to require formally governmental techniques of coercive redistribution to maintain provision, Geertz's comments on Deep Play seem to suggest a greater potential for alternative informal processes to maintain sufficiency.

In short, participants value the game, for the sake of playing thus participation can sustain itself beyond the expected pecuniary returns of winning. Similar patterns wherein Deep Play practices pre-empt and mitigate otherwise potentially violent conflict scenarios have been observed throughout tribal dance customs (deMarrais et al. 1992 and Niehaus and Stadler 2004), modern rap music culture (Lee 2009), and the rural Cajun Mardi Gras (Ancelet 2001 and Sexton 2001). By providing a venue in both space and time for the outlet of animosity and competitive rivalry, these examples of cultural performance arguably provide a potential substitute route away from the behavioral processes of violence (Royce 1980). I suggest the entire cultural phenomena of Mardi Gras be seen through the lens of Deep Play. At first impression, a city such as New Orleans with its long legacies of crime, poverty and infrastructural decline should perhaps not expend such significant resources for the sake of celebration and consumption. Upon closer inspection one can see that many of the individuals and groups who participate the most in coordinating Mardi Gras are actually nested within processes of competitive rivalry that actually help maintain and progress the broader event. Individuals and families vie for space on the parade routes and contest each other for beads and Mardi Gras Krewes compete for the prestige of best floats, famous guests and formal balls.

C. The Gumbo Recipe that Works for Everybody

Spontaneous Order as a concept originated amidst the Scottish enlightenment as writers such as Adam Ferguson (1767, 119) described social institutions such as language and effective forms of law and governance as "the product of human action but not human design." Adam Smith (1776) popularized and extrapolated the idea to explain the self-regulating tendencies of the market economy as guided by an "invisible hand." Amidst the mid 20th century F.A. Hayek (1945, 1967, 1973) and Michael Polanyi (1962, 1975) formalized the terminology of spontaneous orders. Surveying across the idea's intellectual history Barry (1982) defines them as such:

> The simplest way of expressing the major thesis of the theory of spontaneous order is to say that it is concerned with those regularities in society, or orders of events, which are neither (1) the product of deliberate human contrivance (such as a statutory code of law or a dirigiste economic plan) nor (2) akin to purely natural phenomena (such as the weather, which exists quite independently of human intervention). While the words conventional and natural refer, respectively, to these two regularities, the 'third realm,' that of social regularities, consists of those institutions and practices which are the result of human action but not the result of some specific human intention (7-8).

In short, this video suggests that the long, decentralized and evolutionary qualities of folk recipes be recognized as a form of spontaneous order. Tyler Cowen (2000, 2012) and Virginia Postrel (1998, 2003) have argued similarly regarding cultural and artistic production processes more generally. In the context of New Orleans culture, no single piece of culture seems more parallel to the idea of spontaneous order than gumbo. Anecdotally, New Orleans residents commonly refer to the cultural identity of the city as gumbo akin to how the United States is often referred to as a melting pot. First, gumbo is literally an evolved combination of individual parts which contribute to a combined flavor greater and more complex than any of its constituent components. Second, the historical legacy of gumbo's relationship to Mardi Gras celebrations also reinforces the link between cultural processes and social capital discussed earlier. In the rural surrounding areas of New Orleans, during the Cajun Mardi Gras, individuals will travel from home to home, and request contributions for the collective gumbo. Different homes contribute different ingredients from vegetables to meats, beans and fishes. The complete recipe of the particular gumbo is unplanned and only discovered throughout the cooking process. Gumbo is shared throughout the community regardless of contribution type or quality though informal social pressures help affirm contributions and deter excessive extraction (Sexton 2001).

D. How to Make a Criminal Cocktail

Hosting a variety of locally invented and popularized cocktails, New Orleans serves as an ideal cultural setting to reflect upon the legacy of prohibition in America and the implications for political economy therein. This video comments upon the apparent irony of the contemporary cultural appreciation surrounding craft cocktails, as cocktails themselves were largely adaptive ways of coping with many of the inefficient challenges and problematic quality features associated with prohibition policies.

During America's prohibition period in the early twentieth century, New Orleans and other major port cities held a comparative advantage in both smuggling alcohol from outside of the country as well as hosting speak easies and venues for consuming contraband directly. Travelers tended to drink closer to smuggling centers as the likelihood of detection was lower than transporting spirits throughout the states. In recent years, economic historians and applied economists have noticed and explained the disruptive effects that prohibition enforcement can and has had upon the qualitative features of alcohol production and distribution markets. First, is a unique manifestation of the Alchian and Allen effect and or third law of demand. With a constant transaction cost across different quality types of goods, individuals will tend to prefer a higher quality version, because the opportunity costs associated with high quality are lower in the face of transactions costs. If you risk jail time for making, distributing, selling or consuming both weak and potent spirits alike there is good reason to specialize more intently on more potent spirits. Stronger liquor is also more easier to smuggle and distribute per once of potency than beer and wine for example. Hence during prohibition beer and wine consumption were deterred yet harder alcohol consumption increased. Here lay many of the unintended consequences to prohibition. More potent liquor is preferred on the quality margins of stealth and potency but suffers on others. "Bathtub" gin was certainly not a marketing ploy. Harder spirits were also harsher in both health consequences and flavor. Hence cocktails and mixed drinks were innovated and expanded in market share for their abilities to mask the flavor and cut the severity of black market alcohols. In the wake of alcohol liberalization the city of New Orleans today fosters a vibrant craft cocktail culture. Various bars throughout the city inform customers of the long histories and diverse varieties of signature drinks. Non-prohibited markets tend to evolve and diversify as sellers manipulate production processes to service the preferences of consumers in lower cost and more satisfying ways. Quality craftsmanship and connoisseur demanders are the byproducts of the process.

E. Bars and Brass Bands in the Big Easy

Needless to say, New Orleans hosts a variety of distinctive musical genres uniquely linked to the cities unique cultural location and history. Jazz and cajun zydeco are perhaps the most obvious examples as their improvisational essences complement New Orleans's diversity and gumbo melting pot identity. One such unique variety thereof, New Orleans's Brass Bands have in the latter 20th century become a critical component to the musical identity of the city. Leading and comprising almost every Mardi Gras parade are the representative marching bands of the local public and private schools throughout the city. Such performances provide a tangible and reliable way for local school systems to finance and operate high quality music and fine arts performance programs, perhaps unaffordable otherwise. Young New Orleanian student musicians are throughout their adolescence trained and offered vast opportunities to musically perform and participate throughout different venues and spaces in the city. Hence overtime, the city has benefitted culturally from hosting and fostering this unique human capital asset. Marching brass bands or second lines are a common fixture throughout various New Orleans civil society processions, weddings, and funerals. For some ensembles, popularity has translated to national audiences and formal recording contracts. For poorer communities, music performance provided a significant opportunity for class and economic mobility but also a robust human capital asset that helped in processes of recovery and resilience surrounding hurricane Katrina (D'Amico 2010).

F. The Relationship Between Commerce and Crime

This video aims to relate Jane Jacobs theory termed the "eyes on the street" model of crime, wherein crime rates in urban neighborhoods are inversely related to the level of economic and commercial activity at play in said neighborhood, the Marigny and Bywater neighborhoods of New Orleans. In the wake of hurricane Katrina the small, mostly residential area between the French Quarter and the Mississippi River experienced a major degree of rejuvenation. One significant influence was the laissez faire attitude taken towards business licensure, zoning enforcement, and alcohol regulation in the because of administrative and high opportunity costs after the storm. Several new eateries, music venues and storefronts opened throughout the neighborhood and especially along Frenchmen Street. While said neighborhoods are still within the city's relatively high crime setting they foster significantly lower rates, post Katrina, than their immediate and surrounding neighborhoods which amount to some the highest in the country let alone the city. Hence it is my suggestion that crime rate quality like property values has been bolstered by increased commerce and activity. Individuals throughout the area take marginal steps and actions to secure space, report criminal activity and maintain the safety of the families, friends, neighbors, workers, employees and customers.

Conclusion

The city of New Orleans has historically fostered individuals, groups and communities in such ways that they have produced and contributed to its distinctive and iconic cultural identity and diverse array of cultural products. Such networks and the cultural content therein were shaped by the geographic, demographic, political, and economic features of the city through time. New Orleans music, cuisine, art, fashion, communities, etc. are the adaptive and evolutionary results of the city's residents participations through history. In a minor and impossibly imperfect attempt these videos capture, identify and assess such trends. In many ways the internet fosters similar patterns of social coordination as does urban space though at even lower transactions costs on a variety of margins. Students across international boundaries were able to access and interact with relevant material and similarly interested peers. Content and collaboration opportunities are available and amenable in perpetuity.

Notes and References

1 http://www.theihs.org/history-mission
2 http://www.learnliberty.org/course_details/lessons-from-mardi-gras/
3 See Mcinnis (2007) and Sottek and Button (2014).
Ancelet, B. (2001). "Falling Apart to Stay Together: Deep Play in the Grand Marais Mardi Gras," The Journal of American Folklore. 114(452): 144-153.
Barry, N. (1982). "The Tradition of Spontaneous Order," Literature of Liberty, v(2): 7-58.
Bentham, J. (1789). Introduction to Principles of Morals and Legislation. T. Payne and Son.
Cowen, T. (2000). In Praise of Commercial Culture. Harvard University Press.(2012).
An Economist Gets Lunch: New Rules for Everyday Foodies. Penguin.
D'Amico, D. (2010). "Rock Me Like a Hurricane! How Music Communities Promote Social
Capital Adept for Recovery," in E. Chamlee-Wright and V. Storr (eds.) After Katrina: The Political
Economy of Disaster and Community Rebound. deMarrais, K., Nelson, P. and Baker, J. (1992).
"Meaning in Mud: Yup'ik Eskimo Girls at Play," Anthropology & Education Quarterly.23(2):120-44.
Dutton, W. (2009). "The Fifth Estate Emerging Through the Network of Networks,"Prometheus.27(1): 1-15.
Ferguson, A. (1767 [2001]). An Essay on the History of Civil Society, Cambridge University Press.
Geertz, C. (1973). "Deep Play: Notes on the Balinese Cockfight," in The Interpretation of CulturesBasic Books.
Gudeman, S. (2001). The Anthropology of Economy: Community, Market, and Culture. Blackwell.
Hardy, A. (2014). "The History of Mardi Gras," Available at: http://www.mardigrasguide.com
Hayek, F. (1945). "The Use of Knowledge in Society," American Economic Review, 35(4): 519-30.(1967).
Studies in Philosophy, Politics and Economics, Simon and Schuster. (1973). Law Legislation and Liberty Volume 1: Rules and Order, University of Chicago Press.
Jacobs, J. (1961). The Death and Life of Great American Cities. Random House.
Lee, Jooyoung (2009). "Battlin' on the Corner: Techniques for Sustaining Play," Social Problems.56(3): 578-98.
Levy, D. (1989). "The Statistical Basis of Athenian-American Constitutional Theory," Journal of Legal Studies. 18(1): 79-103.
McCloskey, D. (2008). The Bourgeois Virtues: Ethics for an Age of Commerce. University of Chicago Press.
McInnis, A. (2007). "Cake Carnage and Making Babies," First You Make a Roux. at: http://www.killerrubboard.com/magazine/magbabystory.html
Niehaus, I. and Stadler, J. (2004). "Muchongolo Dance Contests: Deep Play in the South African Lowveld," Ethnology. 43(4): 363-80.
Polanyi, M. (1962). "The Republic of Science: Its Political and Economic Theory," Minerva, 1: 54-74 (1975). Meaning, University of Chicago Press.
Postrel, V. (1998). The Future and Its Enemies: The Growing Conflict Over Creativity, Enterprise and Progress. Free Press.
(2003). The Substance of Style: How the Rise of Aesthetic Value is Remaking Commerce, Culture, and Consciousness. HarperCollins.
Royce, J. (1980). "Play in Violent and Non-Violent Cultures," Anthropos. 75(5/6): 799-822.
Sexton, R. (2001). "Ritualized Inebriation, Violence, and Social Control in Cajun Mardi Gras,"Anthropological Quarterly. 74(1): 28-38.
Smith, A. (1776 [1904]). An Inquiry into the Nature and Causes of the Wealth of Nations, Liberty Fund.
Sottek, M. and Button, G. (2014). "King Cake: A Rich Tradition," Mardi Gras Traditions. Availablen at: http://mardigrastraditions.com/king-cake-history/
Storr, V. (2008). "The Market as a Social Space: On the Meaningful Extra-Economic Conversations that Can Occur in Markets," The Review of Austrian Economics. 21(2&3):135-50.

Carlos Alcobia, Student and guest researcher at the artistic studies research center (CIEBA)

Largo da Batata
Video Art and São Paulo's forthcoming arenas of protest

Through the critical analysis of the events surrounding the "Passe Livre" manifestations, we track the importance and use of large scale video during the São Paulo protests. This paper follows the stepstaken bythe seven individualsthat organized avideo intervention during thepolitical gatheringof the 17th of July 2013 at Largo da Batata (São Paulo) where operatingfrom an improvised media HQ they projectedpolitical slogansagainst a building while thecrowd roaredand cheered below. From the initial preparations to the aftermath of those actions, we aim to understand the constraints and possibilities offered by new visual Medias and scrutinize what implications they bring in terms of the "realization" of the public spacewithinthe urban landscape. We also analyze these events under the view of the temporary hegemonies concept (Mouffe, 2000; Mouffe, 2005) arguing thatlarge scale urban projectionsare responsible for adding a new layer in terms of temporality, as we focus on discussing the impact of these new strategies for the creationof "instantaneous" arenas of political contest.

Agonism, São Paulo, Video Art, Passe Livre, Largo da Batata

SÃO PAULO - A CRITICAL APPRAISAL

> *"It's a beautiful thing, the destruction of words."* – George Orwell, 1984

For me, an outsider, São Paulo somehow resemblesto a paper wrapped city. I can't really see its insides. But it is where the edges start ripping the paper, that I (the outsider) am able to peekjust enough to start guessing more about its contents.

For several reasons in the last couple of years I've been trying to follow more closely the socio-political agenda of São Paulo, as I became fascinated by its strong political consciousness.But unfortunately so far I was only able towitness on how theefforts and struggle to eliminate social asymmetrieswerecontinuously frustrated within the same Society as it reacts against itself in order to maintainthe status quo.While not capable of understanding the mechanisms underlying this behavior, São Paulo still appeals to me for being a living laboratory where the political is enacted within the city daily life. This diligentand somehowparanoid collective identity, that keeps ripping and weaving an anthropophagic narrative, simultaneously builds and consumes on its own self.

Taking into consideration the contributions given by some authors like Jacques Rancière, Rosalind Deutsch, or Chantal Mouffe which explain the constitution of the political as something only possible through an act of struggle for the redistribution of visibility(Rancière, 2010; Mouffe, 2005; Deutsch, 1998), we propose yet another perspective regarding the recent social and political convulsions on São Paulo under the scope of political actions taken by a generation of counter-publics- from which a state of continuous dissensus emerges. Mainly for that reason the current reflectionnot only aims to document the chain of events behind the 2013 Brazilian protests, but by focusing our analysis in the actions led by some of the protagonistsof the Largo da Batata gathering[1], we also aim to produce a critical inquiry about the new nature of São Paulo's counter publics. This nature - that derives from the unprecedented capabilities of using the urban landscape as the platform for discourse - also enables a vision from what the concept of Agonistic Arenas can be built upon.

FOR A DEMOCRATIC POLITICAL SPACE

> *"Social space is produced and structured by conflicts. With this recognition, spatial democratic politics begins "*- Rosalyn Deutsche

Physical space refers to the built infrastructure of the organization and architecture environment, which may or may not be restricted within the urban context. Social space, on the other hand, refers to a space within the scenic sense - a stage for acts and actions where people interpret their social roles and assume the negotiation, appropriation and interpretation of ideas and visions that are external to them. Thereby the social space reflects the social order and its institutions with regard to specific forms of interaction and communication, but it is still a discursive space that indicates the ideas of city and urbanity in which later actions are taken upon. So only through the dialectical connection between the construction material, social practice, discourse, and representation is that public spaces are first created (Wildner, s.d).

The public space by being thesum of these relations between forms and practicesremains always full of power and ideology (Deutsch, 1998), often becoming an arena for confrontation and intersection of individuals and their different expectations. But not only can we argue that it is within the urban space that the physical, social and discursive references are brought together in order for the debate to occur, but we should also understand the importance of action to trigger the enabling conditions. This means that in order to truly constitute itself the public space requiresto be created and recreated again and again precisely from result of the debate between conflicting expectations and also the fight for the possession of the same rights (and even on the extension of these rights) to other groups within the same community (Deutsch, 1998).This opinion clearly diverges from the view of Habermas (Habermas, 1989) from which the concept of the Public Sphere originated and to whom it is impregnated by a speech free of dominance and that always seeks a final consensus. Instead Agonist theory argues that it is precisely when the conflict for hegemonyerupts that the Public Sphere can be constituted without aiming to any sort ofconsensual resolution.It is only during Totalitarianism rule that public spaces are emptied of their contents as there is the need to deny the opportunity forconfrontations that could question the very foundations of the political system. In order to preserve the existence of a common ground where conflicting positions can stand together and rights can be either acquired or sustained, it becomes crucial that the compound of conflictual society, politics, and ultimately public space, is not overshadowed or suppressed, as argued by the political models of consensus.

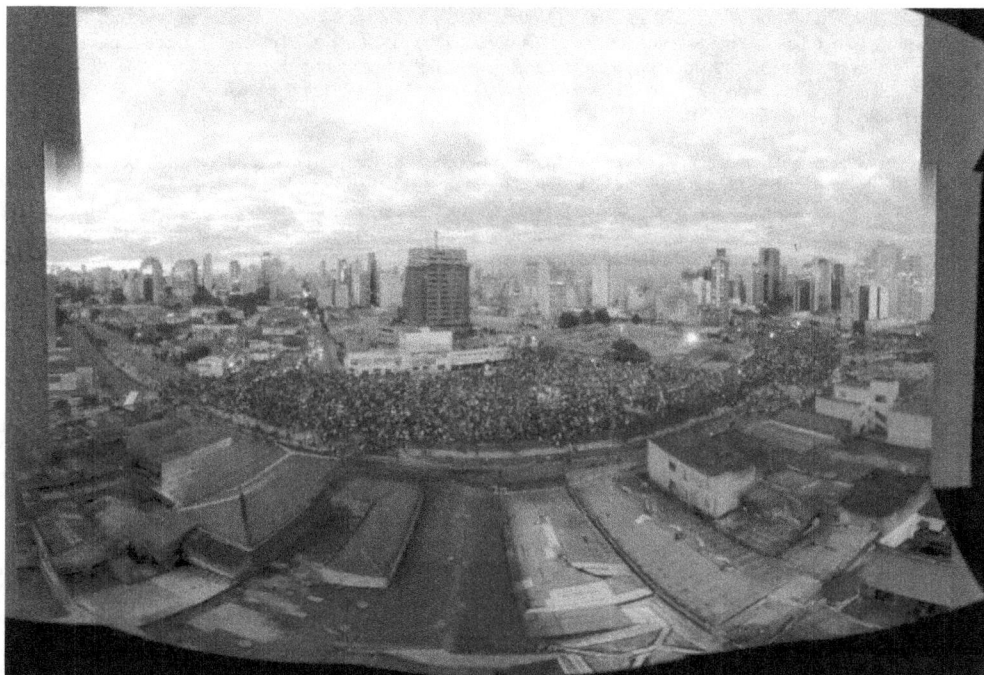

Fig. 1 - Overview of Largo da Batata in the beginning of the protest (Source: Eduardo Fernandes)

What seemed to emerge from a continuum of protests overthe reduction in Public Transport fees (Movimento Passe Livre), rapidly escalated to violent disturbances in São Paulo, originated bygroups of citizens that also demanded for social and political change. Since the overly privatized São Paulo does not offer its population the necessary use of public space required to enact the confrontation of opposites,this ended up by acting like a pressure cooker kept under control just by means of police and social repression. Yet, and after a crescendo of events (some of which that preceded but at some point intersected the Passe Livre manifestations), the 13th of July that marked the Battle of Consolação was the major outburst that resulted from the accumulated pressure. The high degree of repression used by the military police combined with the sophisticated and tactical use of social networks by the protesters – with the prominent role of NINJA (Narrativas Independentes, Jornalismo e Ação) responsible forvideo-streaming and documenting the insides of the Consolação protests - became a game changer as it set the conditions for the promoted thediscourse of São Paulo's counterpublics directly to the central stage of visibility. NINJA was letting the World see what happened under the paper wrapped city, as nowthe previously absent Mass Media was forced to acknowledge and disseminatethe repression held against the protesters by the military police. This fueled a very negative reaction in the public opinionas the vivid images of meaningless violence leaped the margins into the center andthustriggering the events of the 17th of July.

The protests of the 17th of Julywere meant not only to be a signal of reaction against the repression of Consolação but it also intended tobe the carrier of other contents to a wider audience that now followthem at the television and even joined in the rallies. As the protest now revealed a far more ambitious agenda, it started stretching beyond the initial Passe Livre pleasant embracing more structural demands: the need to endthe military police;the need to end its means of repression; the right of the overall population to better living conditions; the urgencyof giving more importance to the reduction of the social inequalities.

This protest also marked the start of thedissemination process of the protests to other Brazilian cities thatdecided to organize their own rallies as an act ofsolidarity with the protesters of Consolação. The 17th of July went on to became the vehicle that brought the impregnated dissensus from within the inner layers of the city up to its superficial skin previouslyhomogenously occupied by the forces of centraldiscourse.

TEMPORARY ARENAS OF DISCOURSE

"War is both father of all and king of all: it reveals the gods on the one hand and humans on the
other, makes slaves on the one hand, the free on the other" - Heraclitus

We can understand transgression as a synthesis of the concept of territoryas it is inherent to the movement that existingbetween territoriescontributes to establish the territory delimitations and its understandings. Since the precursor work of Naim Jung Paik that artists were able to restructure the artificial language that emanated from video and provoke adisruption in thepreviously linear relation established between the work of art and the environment around it. Video art now enabled the author to address the viewers in new and simultaneous forms, crossingand through transgression setting boundaries for new spaces and uncharted territories. The "Messages to the Public", a series of media-based interventions commissioned by the Public Art Funds is fundamental for this understanding. From 1982 and until 1990, every month a different visual artist were invited to make use of the Spectacolor central screen of Times Square New York with a message that infiltrated the 15-20 minutes set of passing by commercials. This meant the possibility for the artists to use one of the prime spaces of the consumerist market to denounceand criticize aspects of that same consumer society. It was somewhat of a Trojan horse behind enemy lines, and some of the works presented there later became iconic and hugely influential to the following generations of artists - Jenny Holzer "Truisms" (1982); Barbara Kruger "I am not trying to sell you anything' (1983); or Martha Rosler ""If You Lived Here…" (1989).

A more proximate work to the intervention of Largo da Batata came from artist Krzysztof Wodiczko and his action titled "Reagan Hand Shake" (1984) where the hand of the then presidential candidate Ronald Reagan was projected over the AT&T building located near Wall Street, denouncingthe pledge for allegiance between those who aim the political power with those who possess the financial power. Again the transgression - channeled to an unprepared viewer and triggered by a provocative confrontation–and that announced the emergence of new arenas of political discourse in this emergent Media City.

The action in São Paulo came neither as the result of an arts grant program nor as an artistic gesture of protest. Instead it was the outcome of a challenge placed by a militant that while having access to the necessary equipment (as the result of also being a professional VJ), suggested that this sort of political action had the conditions to be accomplished byhim and a handful of his friends that shared both his professional and ideological backgrounds. The plan for implementation was rather straightforward but rather complex in terms of logisticsasit included carrying two large projectors (each weighting over 60 Kgs) to the 20th floor apartment that was made available by a common friend. Once there they would still need to secure access to a 2200 Watts and 19 amperes of stable electric supply in order to be able to project at a distance of 230 meters to an abandoned building that stood on the other side of the square (Largo da Batata). They had previously decided that they would only project simple and unambiguousslogans, directly related with the protest as it was crucial to keep the crowd focused before starting the march. But in reality, present conditions revealed to be so precarious that there wasn't even certainty that they could accomplish the video action. Due to long the curriculum of military repression[2], all precautions had to be taken by the participants of this action in order to maintain its total secrecy, namely restricting the access to mobile 3G in the room during the projections and this meant no direct communication with the protesters that were gathered below. Alsothe organizers of the protesters had scheduled the beginning of the march from Largo da Batata while there was still sunlight, which rendered impossible any projection. All this meant thatthey had to rely on a combination of factors that they could not control, and even inbest case scenariosthey would only have a rather narrow window of opportunity to operate from.

Although all the individuals that were present in the improvised "HQ" were hard seasoned Video artists, this was the first act of political protest developed by them, so when the moment of the projection actually came, their initial relief added tothe surprise that came from witnessing the roaring reaction from the crowd down below. As Eduardo Fernandes, one of the interviewed protesters stated "When we turned on the projection the crowd roared. We never had this before with a projection (…) it was a rock star moment!"
The projection that occupied the whole building façadewas available for everyone to see (protesters or not), thus becoming the ultimate transgression,crossing boundaries that not only questioned the nature and use ofthe city landscape as communication device, but also allowed that an external action coordinated the reactions of thousands of spectators that spontaneously assimilated and appropriated its contents.It was an action that bridged to a collective political moment of dissent at a scale never experienced before. The projectionwas transforming the urban landscape in anarena for political contest, acting as mediatorbetween the intimate space of the individual and the public space for the collective dissensus.It is true that it remained only as a temporary occupations, but the political has no claim to last - its only purpose it to create a disruption in the system, and thus materialize a sense of urgencyand redistribution of visibility (Mouffe, 2005;Rancière, 2010).

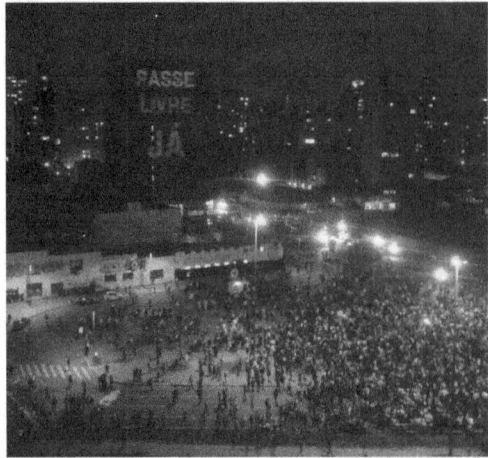

Fig. 2 - Image of Largo da Batata towards the end of the video action
(Source: Eduardo Fernandes)

ON POLITICAL ART AND AGONISM

"I do not believe that the function of art is to be nice. "Art is not democratic. It is not for the people." - Richard Serra

What Eduardo Fernandes and his group have intelligentlyproducedwasthe manipulation of signs used by the central discourse itself, decontextualizing or deflating their significance, in order to maintain the crowd focused on the main arguments of the protest. This strategy proved successful in keeping the protestersfocused and able to bring forward a cohesive and coherent body of communication through means of a new symbolic symbiosis between the protest slogans and the discursive strategies traditionally held by the police state to which they opposed.

The intentionality of the act itself raises questions about if this meant to make art politically instead of making political art.I believe the difference lies in the act itself, in the action.The political element is not only a part of the social structure or an element inside the production process. Instead it configures itself primarily as a supplement to the distribution of powers, spaces, functions and identities that make up Society, and thus leading to the redistribution of capacity. In other words, the political element is a catalyst for the individual's struggle for visibility that is denied to him within the system to which he belongs. With the purpose of achieving this supplementation in distribution, the political discourse is based on the confrontation of different perspectives to which art can contribute by creating visibility within the ideological nuances and transforming the public space into a pedagogical space. It is this pedagogical space to which Richard Serra refers to as "where the citizens can become students" (Estevez, 1996). A space for conflict mediation, necessary to ensure that no one has afterwards the need for transgression of the private borders of other individuals.

We can identify this ambition in the actions held of Largo da Batata, as São Paulo is the pressure cooker previously referred from which violent outbursts can emanate (as we also discussed before) if no relief is made available. But for art to become political it becomesequally important that the foundingantagonism always prevails from something taken from the perspective of the institution and the dominant ideology. Because of its ability to disrupt regulated and regulatory processes, responsibilities and hierarchies, political art has the capability to expose the system outside of its dominant position but for that need to appropriates some of its conditions – and this could also been identified in video action of Largo da Batata.

The aftermaths of the events in Largo da Batata can be seen as the normalization forces taking place after the climax. On the following day to the protest, the municipality council was vandalized under the permissiveness of the police. Eduardo Fernandes believes that this was in fact the result of a reaction plan that sought to stimulate and explore the fears of amiddle class towards criminality. By providing space and even contributing to forms of vandalism the police aimed toregain the support of the public opinion for the maintenance of a repressing apparatus. Besides that, on the 20th of July the left wing protesters was expelled from the streets by middle class and right wing individuals that saw in newly found media attentionfor the protests as an opportunity to start heading attacks against the Brazilian president Dilma Rousseff. President Rousseff, which after a decline in her approval rates, decided to join forces with the conservative lobby in order to contain the protests.
And as the Brazilian society was being supplied with the scapegoats from which it could exorcize the general fear (i.e. Black Bloc stereotyping phenomenon), the return to a state of social numbness ultimately led to a complete retreat from the space then conquered by the early protests that culminated in 17th of July action.
As Eduardo recalls it "(at the end) the only think maintained was the police violence. First as a tragedy, then as a farce".We can see this in the eyes of what Jacques Derrida named "the stabilization of the system of meaning" (Derrida, 1976; Deutsch, 1998) by whichDerridaconsidered that since agonism and conflict refers to something that cannot fully bring under control (and thus become stable) it draws a long term stabilization course in the action-reaction dialect relation between opposing forces. Stabilization is thus a post-structural concept, referring to a relational system that can never be seen as completed, formed or closed, and that meantthat the temporality surrounding the existence of an Arena of dissensus is a consequence of the stabilization forces thatemerge and vanish according to the confrontation and overlap of the opposing forces that constitute the public space.
According to Eduardo we can conclude by drawing three main conclusions from these experiments:

"Demand the impossible but refuse to take part of the solution – as part of the civil society my job is to demand and your job (the government) is to answer to these requests";

"Military police is out of control as even the civil government is unable to control its own police";
"We again witnessed the classic left-wing split, that only convenes itself again when inside prison"

After conducting a few other actions in the follow up of Largo da Batata, Eduardo Fernandes (and the others that occupied with him thatapartment on the 17th of July), eventually ceased their activitiesas result of the widespreaddisilusion with the turn of events, and till today only the collective Projeção of Rio de Janeiro still keepsresorting to large scale city projections toconvene politicized messages.

Nevertheless, and after recent contacts with some colleagues in São Paulo, it became clear to me that the disillusionperiod was already giving place to new stage oflearning and struggle, as persons reorganized for the next set of actions.This leads me to conclude that as the city diligently keeps wrapping and weaving around itself, protecting and hiding its social fractures, the São Paulo counter-publics are alwayspresent. Although sometimes hiding somewhere underneaththe paper wrapped city, they keepthoroughlyscanning and identifying its inner fragilities, as to prepare the next big opportunity to emerge from its within.

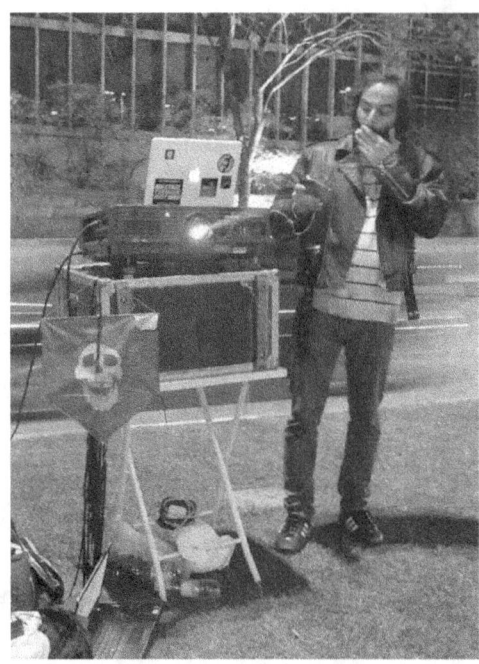

Fig. 3 - One of the protesters during a subsequent video action
(Source: Eduardo Fernandes)

The author would like to thank the collaboration of Eduardo Fernandes (Edu Zal) for the interviews, discussions and documentationprovided during the research process.

Notes and References

1 A national rally day organized by independent organizations to protest against police brutality and held simultaneously on the 17th of July in several Brazilian cities
2 In Brazil the national security is still on the hands of the Military Police as it was in the time of the Dictatorship
Acampora, C. (2003). Nietzsche's Agonal Wisdom. International studies in Philosophy, pp. 205-222.
Acampora, C. D. (2002). Of Dangerous Games and Dastardly Deeds: A Typology of Nietzsche's Contests. International studies in Philosophy, pp. 135-151
Balkin, J. M. (1996). Deconstruction.
Benjamin, W. (s.d.). Unpacking my library - a talk about book collecting. In H. Arendt, Walter Benjamin - Illuminations (pp. 59-67). NY Schocken Books
Bishop, C. (2004). Antagonism and Relational Aesthetics. October, pp. 51-79.
Bishop, C. (2006). The Social turn: Collaboration and its discontents. ArtForum, pp. 179-185.
Chambers, S. A., & Carver, T. (2008). Democracy, pluralism and political theory. Nova Iorque: Routledge.
Derrida, J. (1976). Of Grammatology. Baltimore: The Johns Hopkins University Press.
Deutsche, R. (1998). Evictions: Art and spatial politics. Cambridge: MIT Press.
Deveaux, M. (Vol 25 nº4 de 1999). Agonism and pluralism. Philosophy Social Criticism, pp. 1-22.
Dryzek, J. S. (2003). Deliberative democracy in divided societies: alternatives to agonism and analgesia. Social and Political Theory Program.
Estevez, M. (1996). Theorizing Public/Pedagogic Space: Richard Serra's Critique of Private Property. Postmodern Culture.
Finnegan, C. A. (2003). Elastic, agonistic publics: John Dewey's call for a third party. Argumentation and Advocacy.
Foster, H. (1998). The anti-aesthetic. Nova Iorque: The new Press.
Fraser, N. (1990). Rethinking the Public Sphere. Social Text, pp. 56-80.
Fritsch, M. (2008). Antagonism and Democratic Citizenship (Schmitt, Mouffe, Derrida). Research in Phenomenology, pp. 174-197.
Habermas, J. (1989). The Structural Transformation of the Public Sphere: An Inquiry into a Category of Bourgeois Society.
Jordan, M., & Miles, M. (2008). Art and Theory After Socialism. Bristol: Intellect Books.
Karppinen, K., Moe, H., & Svensson, J. (2008). Habermas, Mouffe and political communication. Javnost - the public, pp. 5-22.
Kearney, R. (1999). Questioning Ethics: Contemporary debates in philosophy. Nova Iorque: Routledge.
Lind, M. (2009). The Curatorial. ArtForum.
Lind, M. (2010). Complications; On Collaboration, Agency and Contemporary Art.
Martin, R. W. (2005). Between consensus and conflict: Habermas, post-modern agonism and the early American public sphere . Polity.
Mouffe, C. (1996). Deconstruction and Pragmatism. Londres: Routledge.
Mouffe, C. (1999). Deliberative Democracy or Agonistic Pluralism? Social Research.
Mouffe, C. (2000). For an agonistic model of democracy. In C. Mouffe, The Democratic Paradox (pp. 80-107). Verso.
Mouffe, C. (2005). On the Political. Nova Iorque: Routledge.
Mouffe, C. (2007). Artistic Activism and Agonistic Spaces. Art and Research, p. Volume 1 Nº2.
Mouffe, C. (s.d.). Deliberative Democracy or Agonistic Pluralism. Reihe Politikwissenschaft.
Nietzsche, F. (1996). "A Disputa de Homero". In F. Nietzsche, Cinco Prefácios para cinco livros não escritos. Rio de Janeiro: Sette Letras.
Nietzsche, F. (2001). Ecce Homo – como alguém se torna o que se é. São Paulo: Companhia das Letras.
Osten, M. v. (2011). Producing Publics – Making Worlds! On Curating.
Rancière, J. (2010). Dissensus - On politics and aesthetics. Nova Iorque: Continuum International Publishing Group.
Rancière, J. (2011). The Thinking of Dissensus: Politics and Aesthetics. In P. Bowman, & R. Stamp, Reading Rancière (pp. 1-17). Londres: Continuum International Publishing Group.
Sheikh, S. (2004). Public Spheres and the Functions of Progressive Art Institutions. Republicart: http://www.republicart.net
Wildner, K. (s.d.). La Plaza: Public Space as Space of Negotiation. Republicart: http://www.republicart.net
Yamamoto, K. (s.d.). Beyond the Dichotomy of Agonism and Deliberation: The Impasse of Contemporary Democratic Theory.

Maria Domenica Arcuri, Indipendent Researcher

"Utopia on Walls":
The Collective Political Artworking of Felice Pignataro

The essay centres on the artworking of the social activist Felice Pignataro, presented as acts of political practice performed among the streets and on the walls of the Neapolitan periphery between 1982 and 2003. The first section focuses on his actions in Scampìa, a peripheral area that is sadly infamous for being a 'modernist ghetto'. As I contend in the second section, the actions in this peculiar dystopic space – as well as in other areas I mention – unfold his 'utopia on walls' – with murals being a strategy to nourish the imagination and evoke the possibility of 'another world'. In the last section, I explain in details the ways in which Pignataro's artworking configures a political practice that is always situated and collectively created.

Pignataro, murals, collective artworking

Introduction

> *"Utopia has been discredited, it is necesary to rehabilitate it. Utopia is never realised and yet it is indispensable to stimulate change"* (Lefebvre, qtd. In Latour and Combes 1991, 18-19).

L'Utopia sui Muri (Utopia on Walls) is the title of a book collecting some experiences of painting workshops and murals by Felice Pignataro and the Gridas, a cultural association of Scampìa, in the north-west outskirts of Naples (Pignataro 1993).[2] Gridas means 'Gruppo Risveglio dal Sonno', group of awakening from slumber, and was founded in 1981 by Felice Pignataro and his wife Mirella in order to awaken the sleeping consciousness.

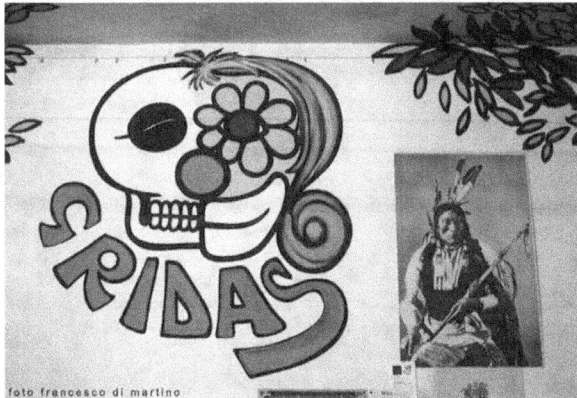

Fig. 1 – The logo of Gridas

The logo of Gridas (Fig. 1) depicts half face of a clown and half a skull and clearly reminds the Mexican iconography of the skulls of Dia de los muertos, a symbol celebrating death and rebirth.[3]

A recurring image in the murals by Pignataro is the sun with a human face often surrounded by a ring-a-ring-o'-roses of kids, as if evoking another world, showing a glimmer of it. In fact, as it says on the official website "the value of experience lies in its unfolding, in the temporary escape from everyday life's dreariness – to affect imagination, to foster the development of everyday struggle from the vivid image of a potential aim to achieve".[4] The utopia the title of the book refers to is the one Eduardo Galeano talks about, "Utopia lies at the horizon. When I draw nearer by two steps, it retreats two steps. If I proceed ten steps forward, it swiftly slips ten steps ahead. No matter how far I go, I can never reach it. What, then, is the purpose of utopia? It is to cause us to advance" (Galeano 1993).[5]

Taking inspiration from Galeano, Pignataro expresses his personal vision of painting on the walls and of murals as an art form that discloses and announces change: "by covering the miserable walls of our every day prison with images, a depressing landscape becomes the colourful harbinger of our future society" (Pignataro, qtd. in Esposito 2005; my translation).[6] This is Felice's journey, who is fully aware of the aberrance and the cultural marginalisation of the urban space where he decides to live. His journey starts from the walls of Scampìa, a suburban neighbourhood of Naples sadly known for its decay and camorra feuds. It runs through the walls of other often forgotten and neglected towns of the Neapolitan hinterland. It embeds his utopia in vivid images, expressing the urgency of change and of a more just society and transforming the ugliness and greyness of the everyday life built space. In short, it is a journey that leads us towards an elsewhere, where we can catch a glimpse of another possible future, a world where it is possible to have a better life.

Scampìa

Scampìa. At the exit of line 1 of Naples underground, an imposing and excessive sign informs passengers that they have reached Scampìa. You feel a bit lost. You take a bus and start the tour of areas where you would not walk through – unless you want to visit a friend. You wander around ugly concrete blocks, some of them surrounded by tall gates, some other with an inner courtyard accessible through disturbing passages, disclosing labyrinthine paths. In some areas, there are no shops, no squares, no places where you can meet up.

Right in the middle of the residential area, you face the aggressiveness of huge fast flowing roads – often dark and resembling go-kart tracks. Viale della Resistenza, an evocative name, skirts an urban park that gives the impression of an oasis. Actually, the entrance looks like a sort of turnstile, a physical and psychological barrier that seems to be there in order to discourage people. The outer edges of the park are the gathering point of people who come not only from other neighbourhoods of Naples but also from far away towns, seeking a quiet place where they can inject themselves the dose of heroine just bought. For this reason, it is common to be witness to splatter scenes, with blood staining hands and clothes. Walking there becomes impossible because of the huge amount of left over needles. If you are arrive before five, that is closing time, and get over the deterrent entrance of the park, you will discover a set of prohibitions and unfinished things and a vast space, with a neglected or, even worse, tortured vegetation. The other meeting point is Piazza dei Grandi Eventi, a huge empty space – sun-drenched and dispersive – whose architecture does not encourage citizens to use it so that it is left abandoned there. Spaces and walls turn out to be dystopic.

To better understand these architectural 'ravings', it is necessary to go back to 1964, when Scampìa was born after a cheap council-house building programme, in accordance with the infamous Law 167 of 1962 (see Di Martino 2010, 54; Pignataro in Antonelli and Klain 2006).[7] Its purpose was to build a residential neighbourhood to face the growing demad of flats – and as Felice Pignataro states "to let the community benefit from the surplus value of the building areas", by using this surplus to build recreation facilities (Pignataro in Antonelli and Klain 2006; my translation). In fact, no facilities were created and houses were built following principles closer to the requirements of land speculation, irrespective of the inhabitants' needs. Moreover, quoting Pignataro again, "the fact that it is a quite new built neighbourhood compared to the rest of Naples makes it a neighbourhood of rootless and displaced people, who came from totally different environments, such as small towns or working-class neighbourhoods in Naples, where sharing life was the main quality" (Ibid.; my translation). The architectural choices, which seem to split the area into two blocks of buildings, together with the almost total shortage of facilities and meeting places strengthen the feeling of uprootedness and disintegration. To add to all this, some areas are unfinished and some facilities – such as the urban park and Piazza Grandi Eventi – are so huge that it is impossible to manage them and they remain closed and neglected.

The dystopic urban space of Scampìa, a peculiarity of the urban phenomenon that can be defined as 'the modernist ghetto', actualizes Henri Lefebvre's insight on the 'abstract space' produced by capitalism and neocapitalism, that is to say the form in which space – always social because it "implies, contains and dissimulates social relationships" – has been 'forced' (Lefebvre 2008, 82).[8] Lefebvre thinks that abstract space depends on consent, which is to say on cultural hegemony, according to which a dominant group is able to set up a complex system of control that affects all aspects of life and it is not exercized through repressive violence rather through the regulation of opinion (Gramsci 1975, 10).[9] However, this kind of space remains in Lefebvre's account the result of violence and aims at erasing the differences existing in the social space:

> As a product of violence and war, it [abstract space] is political; instituted by a state, it is institutional. On first inspection it appears homogeneous; and indeed it serves those forces which make a tabula rasa of whatever stands in their way, of whatever threatens them – in short, of differences. These forces seem to grind down and crush everything before them, with space performing the function of a plane, a bulldozer or a tank. (Lefebvre 2008, 285)

Therefore, space is functional to power in organising and setting a system. Abstract space, dominant space, establishes a hierarchy, it excludes and includes, it is the space of prohibitions and limitations and aims at erasing all contradictions and at creating the impression of homogeneity. According to Lefebvre, with the birth of the city in the XVI century, the urban space becomes a tool of power and control is exercized through the work of architects and city planners, who follow the dominant representation of the space (ivi, 38, 269).

> In their pre-eminence, buildings, the homogeneous matrix of capitalistic space, successfully combine the object of control by power with the object of commercial exchange. The building effects a brutal condensation of social relationships, [...] It embraces, and in so doing reduces, the whole paradigm of space: space as domination/appropriation (where it emphasizes technological domination); space as work and product (where it emphasizes the product); and space as immediacy and mediation (where it emphasizes mediations and mediators, from technical matériel to the financial 'promoters' of construction projects). It reduces significant oppositions and values, among them pleasure and suffering, use, and labour. (ivi, 227)

Seen from this standpoint, the building of Scampìa, background to Felice Pignataro's utopia on walls, is the construction of an abstract space, saturated by the violence of power. The inhabitants – coming from different places, with different habits and ways of thinking – are crammed in rational and modular housing units (as conceived by the Bauhaus and Le Corbusier) and deprived of places where they can meet, in a space that does not integrate moments of social practice, rather on the contrary it reduces drastically the threshold of sociability (Lewisohn 2008, 87):[10]

> The nature of the administration, of the government, of the state is evident in unrealistic interventions without rhyme or reason, carried out at different times, which seem not to follow any plan or are the realisation of many uncoordinated projects that form a tight tangle. Very broad roads, like landing strips, end nowhere, after incredible windings around improbable traffic islands. Futuristic buildings that were built and abandoned, a sort of chamber of the new metropolitan horrors. (Pignataro 1993; my translation)

The concealed violence of dominant space and the tendency to homogenize is stressed out by Pignataro when he talks about the building of Scampìa: "And then this bomb of the 167 (law) exploded, that is this huge concentration of identical flats, which is a sort of symbol of contemporary society. Homologation against the chance of creativity and imagination for a greater liveability" (Pignataro in Antonelli e Klein 2006; my translation). Gary Shove, who curated Untitled – catalogue on global street art, reflects on the built environment we live in and on the fact that not everyone can take part and contribute to the city planning. Shove criticizes city planners and architects, the so-called visionaries, which produce a considerable discrepancy between theories and their actualization, with the result of often creating an ugly and unpleasant 'built environment':

> The thing about the built environments that we live in is this. We didn't build them. All the ideas that went into creating the plans and the buildings and the streets come from elsewhere. We were not at the planning meetings. How could we have been?
>
> Nobody really figured out that the city would become an environment in and of itself. It just grew that way, and the field of architecture, for all its grand designs was always, really, just running to catch up with urban overpopulation. Those visionaries who tried to make our environment a thing where a whole life could be lived, they were undermined by conditions and circumstance, well that is to say – they were undermined by profit margins.
>
> For these reasons the city came to remain an ugly environment (it always was) in spite of attempts to humanise it after the Second World War. (Shove 2008, 48)[11]

Utopia on walls is then an answer to the failure of the architectural utopia. The discrepancy Shove refers to is embodied in the infamous 'Vele' of Scampìa. Designed by the architect Franz Di Salvo, these buildings, that reach fortyfive metres height, had the purpose to readdress the idea of old city and re-create the memory of the alley with all its relations. Actually, they became places of decay and danger instead. To the imposition of the urban plan, one has to add that central power is bound to profit. In many occasions, this fosters land speculation and often results in selling to private customers, mainly corporations and brands, and in the privatisation of the city, with people being deprived of the space they inhabit and with a constant advertising bombing and overload.

> Who are the council? Have you ever seen these people? What do they actually do? Well the council are for one thing, the people who sell all the space to advertisers ensuring that you cannot turn your head a centimetre without being reminded that your life is not as good as it could be with product X on your side. (Ibid.)

Dynamics intrinsic to space are at work not only in Scampìa, but in the whole built space (Lefebvre identifies in the city the favourite tool of power) of each city, in New York as well as London. They show themselves in the barriers – both the temporary ones, those built for the world leaders' meetings in order to ensure their safety and control protesters, and the permanent ones, as in the case of the wall segregating the Palestinian Territories. Neverthless, referring to Lefebvre again, abstract space, which subsumes and draws together fragments or elements by force, turns out to be a fractured space, since it produces divisions according to work, functions and needs through dispersion, separation and isolation. Hence, it harbours specific inconsistencies and engenders the idea of a new space, which originates from the intensification of those same differences it wants to annihilate and erase (Lefebvre 2008, 52).

> Differences endure or arise on the margins of the homogenized realm, either in the form of resistances or in the form of externalities (lateral, heterotopical, heterological). What is different is, to begin with, what is excluded: the edges of the city, shanty towns, the spaces of forbidden games, of guerrilla war, of war. (ivi, 373)

The never appeased differences try to re-appropriate, even if temporarily, the denied space through forms of resistance that, as Viviana Gravano states, sneak "in all the interstices free from the 'perfect' construction of power", thus producing new space (Gravano 2008, 48).[12] This idea is connected to a new perception of the landscape, started by Walter Benjamin with the flânerie and the city seen as the place of transience and improvisation (Benjamin [1927-1940] 1986, 34-35, 47).[13] Situationists pursued it with their practices of psychogeographical drift and the new urbanism, which associate political issues related to everyday life and urban culture to the city planning (Internazionale Situazionista [1958-1969] 1994, 19, 16).[14] Therefore, the contemporary landscape is no longer understood as an aesthetic object, not as the place of contemplation. Rather, it becomes a mobile landscape, a morphing-landscape, endlessly changing thanks to an activistic attitude, closely linked to vision, perception and action (ivi, 9, 12, 53; Lefebvre 2008, 125).

Utopia on Walls

In these interstices, in the dystopic spaces of Scampìa and other suburbs, Felice Pignataro unfolds his 'utopia on walls', carrying out a sort of 'cultural resistance'. This is not a direct protest against dominant power, rather an attempt to create an alternative structure of empowerment in order to refuse the passive reception of what is imposed and to renegotiate the terms of the discourse concerning space, culture, economic and social relations. Felice's words explain this aim to fight homologation and feed the imagery by preserving differences. They also illustrate his choice of talking of 'utopia on walls' and strongly stress out the importance of collective experience:

> We address especially those who have not yet conformed and are not integrated in the society of greyness and conformism and keep their will to oppose and struggle together with other people to rebel, to build a better and juster world. We try to work on the imagery, in order to preserve this inner gnawing, to strengthen it, to cover it with the colours of life and urge it to explode. Our purpose is to tell the colours of dreams, collective dreams, which are the beginning of a new reality. That is where the title "Utopia on walls" comes from, it is the painted prefiguration of a journey to undertake to reach a better life, so that day after day we can compare everyday life with the goal and get a constant drive to go on. (Pignataro 1993; my translation)

The concept of utopia deployed here is not the one we find in Thomas Moore's Utopia. It is not the imagined projection of a new place; it does not refer to an ideal and sanitized world where all that is considered bad/evil/negative, in short every antagonism, is driven out and the population is regimented in a perfect mechanism. On the contrary, Pignataro seems to focus on the function of utopia as a tool for political and social criticism, in order to question and satirize the present, and as a display of collective desires and a spur for thought. His utopia, which actualizes itself through the re-appropriation of the interstitial spaces with his murals, fractures the dominant assumptions, opening up some 'windows' of reflection to identify possible futures, which are qualitatively different from the present. This utopia recalls the type David Pinder defines potentially subversive:

> The very break with the present that they [utopias] enact can help to disrupt dominant assumptions about the organisation of society, and to point to other possibilities or desires. They can thus be subversive, forcing recognition that particular social arrangements are not natural or eternal but that they could be different, and they can play an important role in opening up new ways of thinking about possible futures, stimulating demands for action and informing political practice. (Pinder 2005, 17)[15]

Pignataro is a committed artist. For him, the political lies in the action itself of painting a wall, of symbolically appropriating the neglected spaces to make them meaningful, starting from modifying the space where we live in order to aim at a more significant intervention. The political also lies in the attempt to work together towards a solution to mutual problems, seeking and putting into practice a better system to live together. He therefore questions the role of the artist as an enlightened being, almost surrounded by a mystical and superior aura, to which he prefers the collective participation to the making of the artwork. Thus, he decides to express himself through murals, as a collective form of creation.

The mural is a painting technique originated in South America as well as a form of horizontal communication. In Mexico, it was used by students to communicate and after the Mexican Revolution (1910-17) it became known thanks to famous artists such as Diego Rivera and José Clemente Orozco and with monumental works depicting social struggles or events of Mexican history. In Chile, Allende's party, Unidad Popular, used murals to communicate in order to politically rise citizens' social awareness and especially to get to illiterate people (Pignataro, qtd. in Di Martino 2010, 60). Another essential feature of the mural is that it belongs to the street; hence, it is a form of art belonging to the people, always enjoyable and free, since it is not shut in a museum and it is not necessary to pay to view it. All these aspects catch Felice's interest, and he chooses the mural in an attempt to communicate in an alternative and broader way, addressing both those people who cannot read and hasty and self-absorbed passers-by.

'Utopia on walls' starts in the schools. Pignataro organises workshops and works predominantly with youths, with the purpose of helping them perceive the school as a place that belongs to them and painting as the tool to re-appropriate it. Through creativity, he tries to draw kids closer to the school and make the latter more aware of the surrounding world and at the same time experimenting with new languages and media. Works represent a moment of freedom, since they are created outside the 'enclosure' of the classroom, and above all since students and teachers work together – often switching roles. Moreover, he believes this kind of collective experience is essential because youths can experience a different way of drawing and painting and, spurred to look through their eyes instead of the standardised 'eyes' of television, they can give free play to their imagination, moving away from predominant models and symbols and inventing new images.

The projects in schools are numerous and they address several themes. Only to mention a few (all with very evocative and explanatory titles), these include: 'Sconfiggere il mostro dell'ignoranza' (Defeating the monster of ignorance) in 1983 in Mugnano (Fig. 2); 'Un treno per cambiare il futuro' (A train to change our future) made in 1985 with classes of Frattaminore primary school ('The locomotive school'); 'La via verso la fratellanza' (The path towards brotherhood) in 1986 at IPSIA of Miano; 'La scuola, luogo di progettazione e costruzione di un uomo nuovo' (The school, place for planning and building a new man) in 1987 at the Liceo Scientifico "F. Brunelleschi" in Afragola; 'La città sognata contro quella reale' (The dreamt city against the real one) in 1989 at the junior high school "M. D'Azeglio" in Marano; 'Il riciclaggio delle idee' (Recycling ideas) in 1992 with the junior high school "Virgilio I" in Scampia.

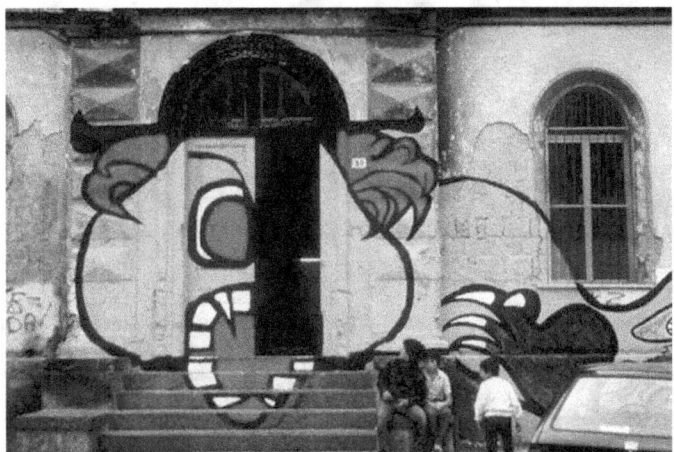

Fig. 2 – 'Sconfiggere il mostro dell'ignoranza'. School entrance. Mugnano (Naples). 1983

The projects begin with the projection of slides of the Gridas and then they tackle with the theme of wall painting and painting as a "means of communication-persuasion and pre-television mass medium" (Pignataro 1993; my translation). This is a sort of brainstorming session, held before the kids formulate their proposals both through images and words. Afterword, it follows a discussion to evaluate both positive and negative implications and consider all possible developments – included the graphic ones – of the chosen themes and their symbolic meanings.

The treated subjects are various and not always a direct reference to current issues. They can have a strong political and social emphasis: brotherhood, peace, wars and migrations, nuclear power, recycling and respect for the environment, work and exploitation, injustice and social justice, housing rights, camorra, imperialism and consumism. The colourful images through which these subjects are expressed seem simple. However, they hide complex and refined cultural references, ranging from Leonardo's Vitruvius man to Far East cosmologies, the Bible or a homage to the painter Marc Chagall – as the artist himself explains in detail in the explanatory notes accompanying many of his murals.

Apart from the murals in the schools, Felice draws his 'utopia on walls' in other interstitial spaces of Scampia, Naples and other cities. He mainly creates collective works that highlight and show his social and political commitment, both through the choice of contents and themes and through the choice of places – such as the mental hospital 'Santa Maria Maddalena' of Aversa in 1996 (Fig. 3) or the prison of Secondigliano in 1997, and particularly the special section for drug abusers where with seven prisoners he paints 'subjects' chosen by them.

The mural on the façade of the mental hospital is called "Escape from lunacy" and is ispired by the ship of fools by Sebastian Brant, on which the fools of the land of Cockaigne are embarked towards Mattagonia (Brant [1494] 1984).[16] On board of Felice's ship there are instead the 'real' fools, those who cause madness – "repressive authorities, people abusing power, a magistrate, a bovine and horned capitalist, a policeman, a bishop, a soldier, a king and a queen, a high-and-mighty politician, such as Andreotti" (Pignataro 1993; my translation). Above the ship there is a purple head – called 'ectoplasm of lunacy' – whose eyes are two windows; in the middle there is the moon, a reference to both popular beliefs according to which the moon is the cause of madness and the Poema dei Lunatici by Ermanno Cavazzoni (Cavazzoni 1987).[17] The funnel-shaped nose is a further cultural reference, this time to Hieronymus Bosch and his painting The Cure of Folly. On the sheets there are quotations from the "letters to humanity", written by Michele and other guests of the hospital, and drawings by Ernesto. This monster splits on the back to let the 'fools' of Aversa free: they are depicted while flying away in their colourful butterfly wings. Even if this mural was not created with the direct collaboration of the 'fools', it is still a collective artwork, since it implied the establishment of human relations, made of little everyday acts, of exchanges and discoveries, and of joyful moments arising from a simple musical stroll with cymbals and drums.

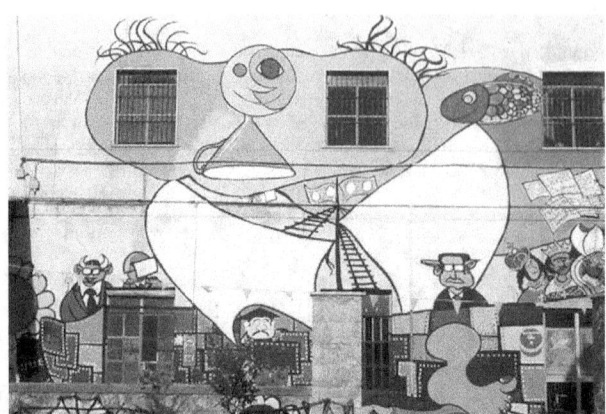

Fig. 3 – Escape from lunacy. Mental hospital "Santa Maria Maddalena". Aversa (Caserta). 1996.

Felice Pignataro is not afraid to openly and publicly express his views, as when he shows support to the Movimento di Lotta per il lavoro (Movement to struggle for work), the Palestian cause and Intifada or the student movement of the Panther in 1990, or challenging the G7 in Naples in 1994 and the G8 in Genoa in 2001. One more interesting example is the mural in solidarity with the resistance to the colonization of Latin America and against the proliferation of arms trafficking – entitled 'Caravels went…aircraft carriers come back' (Fig. 4), realized at the Quadrivio of Arzano in 1982 in collaboration with the Salvador Allende Brigade – a group of Chilean muralists exhiled in Milan. The work is made of two parts connecting with each other at the wall's corner. An eagle with stars and stripes feathers and a crown refers to the excessive power of money and to American imperialism, based on consent achieved through missiles and bombs. The images of the conquistadores underline that the so-called 'discovery of America' was actually a conquest, an act of colonization. Other Chilean historical events, contemporary misfortunes until Pinochet and a sentence by Salvador Allende are depicted. Capitalism's negative outcomes are also represented, such as persecutions and police repressions, unemployment and consumeristic obsessions and in the end there is an opening on to hope with a little bird flying out of an open cage, towards a tree laden with fruit and a rainbow.

In 1992, a mobilization – prompting collaboration between European and Latin American artists – was launched to realize murals in ten European cities, so that another narration should oppose the official celebration of the 'discovery of America': a narration telling of natives' resistance to conquest, oppression and exploitation. Felice decided to partecipate and asked the Regional Culture Department of Campania to sponsor him, but he was given a refusal. Afterwards, he resolved to restore the previous mural, involving the kids of the junior high school "Virgilio I". On the right and left sides of the mural, they added three caravels and an aircraft carrier and the slogan of the 1992 carnival – "caravels went…aircraft carriers come back" – to synthetize the story of export and imposition of capitalism, from the beginning of the European colonialism towards America to the contemporary US war policies, disguised as 'exporting democracy'.

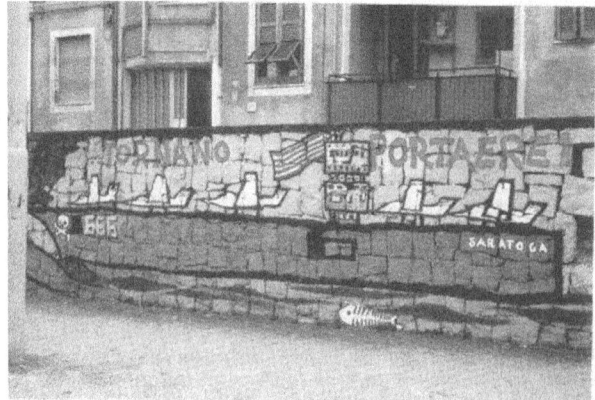

Fig. 4 – Caravels went…aircraft carriers come back. Quadrivio di Arzano (Naples). 1982-1992.

Other interventions show a direct action on the fabric and design of the urban space and their transformation. This is the case of a gate on which he painted parts of the trunk and branches of the trees hidden behind it in order to make nature visible again (Fig. 5). Or again, a bus shelter, where he painted people waiting for their bus and a bench with the figure of a man and a woman who are sitting, while more figures are caught in everyday activities on the wall behind them.

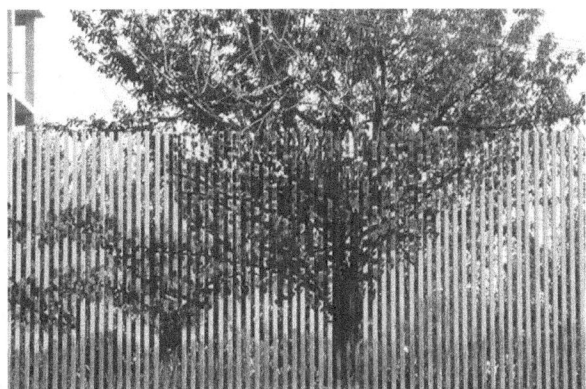

Fig. 5 – The power of painting. Real trees and painted trees (detail). Marano (Naples). 1990

Collective artworking

After this short journey through the images and themes of a series of murals, some remarks are still necessary to appreciate the efficacy of Felice Pignataro's "utopia on walls" – addressing both the ways in which to relate to and include the support and the collective dimension of the works. Before realizing a mural, the artist carries out an inspection of the existing space and its surfaces: the unevenness in the texture can be deployed to obtain chiaroscuro; windows, holes and protrusions can and should be incorporated to enhance the work. Windows become eyes or also train windows; doors become mouths (Fig. 2) or a locomotive; a huge window on top of an entrance door becomes part of a windshield.

Pignataro does not conceive murals as an overlapping of drawings and colors to a support; rather, the surface is an integral part of the work, which should be embedded and transfigured to make the wall 'talk' (Pignataro 1993). This trasfiguration can be read as a situationist détournement: 'built' and imposed elements become temporary signs of communication, which intervene in the visual landscape and become active and subversive elements, able to encourage a possible liberation of space. In this way, Pignataro performs an act of re-appropriation, which temporarily interrupts the domain of 'abstract space'.[18]

This is not a purely aesthetic act. The aim is not merely to embellish gray and decaying walls; rather, as the artist himself underlines, the aim is to communicate and foster a reaction and a reflection, to awake consciousness – no matter how late the message reaches people or how faded the images are – to point towards utopia.

> No matter how faded or hidden they are, images keep their power to question and suggest a different chance – a concealed thought waiting to be rediscovered and brought back to light by a less distracted observer, who can re-start a dialogue with them and go on questioning. This witness to the fact that there has been – or maybe there still is – a glimpse of consciousness, a will to life that is worth being recuperated and nurtured. It is like a sediment, a seed buried deep into a seemingly asleep consciousness, which will nonetheless sprout one day to carry out and practice painted utopia. (Pignataro 1993; my translation)

The détournement through murals changes the wall into a means of communication, "a technological device that comes to mediate communication and information sharing between people" – a definition used by Anna Feigenbaum to provocatively refer to the communicative function of fences, when they become contestation sites (Feigenbaum 2010, 128).[19] The wall, as a mean of communication, partakes in an alternative narration and a critical point of view than those imposed by official media. It tells stories that are often forgotten or ignored; it talks of close and far, daily as well as historical acts of resistance – such as those of the Neapolitan unemployed or Palestinian people or again the slaves in the colonies; it recalls myths and legends; it speaks of mutual hopes and shared dreams, while drawing a possible world. It also witness to the stories of those who collaborate with Felice to realize murals – such as schools kids from decaying or difficult areas – and to the stories of places that have been neglected and the people who live them – as with the mental hospital or the prison and their 'guests'.

A remark should also be made on the collective dimension of the works, which – as already explained – are the outcome of workshops and collaboration directly involving youths or indirectly engaging passers-by and by-standers, who stop by to have a look and occasionally venture into opinions and suggestions. Although unaware of this, Felice Pignataro creates a 'situation' in his painting workshops – a strategy of engagement that is characteristic of the Situationist International. He creates an 'engaged encounter' and a creative moment in the urban fabric, which is able to engender a transformation in the city (see Lefebvre 1996, 12).[20] Walls and murals become the site of collective actions, which help create and experiment human relations – beyond the urgent need to express dissent. They are testimony to the possibility of a change and the feasibility of alternative projects, through those spaces that Lefebvre defines as "representational spaces" – that is to say, living spaces, charged with passion and action and imbued with imaginary and symbolic elements (Lefebvre 2008, 41-42).

At the same time, as Pignataro claims, "art adds an emotional and enthralling value to truth and beliefs. It is a way of knowing, of socializing, of engaging with others" (Pignataro, in Antonelli and Klain 2006; my translation). By encouraging a series of actions and activating perceptions and affects, the realization of a mural turns into that 'event' Maurizio Lazzarato writes about: it points out the unbearable (in an epoch or a space) and lets one catch a glimpse of the new possibilities of life it can express (Lazzarato 2004, 6).[21] Pignataro's murals embody a confrontation between everyday reality and utopia, to verify that one is following the chosen path towards the aim. The temporary escape from a doom and sad everyday life allows nurturing the imaginary, keeping alive those differences that 'abstract space' tries to erase and harbouring resistance. It could be claimed that Felice's collective murals represent Lefebvre's 'differential space' – that news space coming out from interstices, from resistance and differences that persist in 'dominant space', where new relations are produced (Lefebvre 2008, 52).

Felice Pignataro's 'Utopia on walls' lies in the 'making', in the collective realisation of a work, when a new way of being together, sharing, learning and acting is experienced. With its phantasmagorias, 'utopia on walls' aims to intrigue, upset, cause uneasiness, modify perceptions to disclose a possibility of change and leave traces in one's memory – as with those kids who used to work with Felice and now, as adults, still fondly remember that man who used to 'to pick them up out of the gutter', and the experience they shared.

> There is a memory that lasts longer than neglected walls and fading colors. It lies in people's consciousness. We are confident that, as the kids we fleetingly painted with remember us after so many year, the fading images are still clear in their consciousness, waiting to become real. With this hope, we still paint on the walls – as long as there is someone asking us to, as long as a sense of humanity exists. (Pignataro 1993; my translation)

This is how art can maybe 'change the world', being a place and a moment of reflection, discussion and exchange and contributing to change the perception of the world. In this sense, Felice Pignataro's 'utopia on walls' seems to herald the utopia of a possible world, through an alternative form of communication that is made of the same fabric of dreams:

> This communication springs from dreams. With dreams, it shares the contempt for official art's artifices and for the syntax of discourse – inaudible cries, slaps or strokes that the official sensory apparatus cannot feel. We are in the territory of dreams – a dream that comes out scratching a wall. (Origlia 1994, 25)[22]

Notes and References

1 Latour, Patricia and Combes, Francis. Conversation avec Henri Lefebvre (Paris: Messidor, 1991).
2 Pignataro, Felice. 1993. L'utopia sui muri. Napoli: L.A.N. s.r.l. Accessed May 30, 2014. http://www.felicepignataro.org/home.php?mod=pubblicazioni&sub=lib001_ita.
3 All the images in this essay are freely accessible on the web.
4 More information on Felice Pignataro and the Gridas at "Felice Pignataro". Accessed May 30, 2014. http://www.felicepignataro.org/home.php. My translation of the quote from the website.
5 Eduardo Galeano, qtd. at Goodreads. Accessed May 30, 2014. http://www.goodreads.com/quotes/33846-utopia-lies-at-the-horizon-when-i-draw-nearer-by.
6 Pignataro, qtd. in Luigi Esposito, 2005. Accessed May 31, 2014. http://www.felicepignataro.org/home.php?mod=bio&sub=e_002_ita1.
7 See: Di Martino, Francesco e il Gridas. Sulle tracce di Felice Pignataro (Napoli: Marotta&Cafiero, 2010); Felice!, directed by Matteo Antonelli and Rosaria Désirée Klain, produced by Associazione 'Periferie del Mondo – Periferia Immaginaria', Digitalchroma srl, 2006, color, 55'.
8 Lefebvre, Henri. The Production of Space (Oxford: Blackwell Publishing, 2008).
9 Gramsci, Antonio. Quaderni dal carcere (Torino: Einaudi, 1975).
10 Lewisohn, Cedar. Street Art. The Graffiti Revolution (London: Tate Publishing, 2008).
11 Shove, Gary (ed). Untitled. Street art in the Counter Culture (Darlington: Pro-Actif Communications, 2008).
12 Gravano, Viviana. Paesaggi attivi. Saggio contro la contemplazione. L'arte contemporanea e il paesaggio metropolitano (Milano: Costa & Nolan, 2008).
13 Benjamin, Walter. Parigi, capitale del XIX secolo. I «Passages» di Parigi (Torino: Giulio Einaudi Editore, [1927-1940] 1986).
14 Internazionale Situazionista. Internazionale Situazionista (1958-1969) (Torino: Nautilus, [1958-1969] 1994).
15 Pinder, David. Visions of the City. Utopianism, Power and Politics in Twentieth-Century Urbanism (Edimburgh: Edimburgh University Press, 2005).
16 Brant, Sebastian. La nave dei folli (Milano: Spirali Edizioni, [1494] 1984).
17 Cavazzoni, Ermanno. Il poema dei lunatici (Torino: Bollati Boringhieri, 1987).
18 According to Raul Vaneigem, space is occupied by the enemy, who has domesticated it through rules, jurisdiction and geometry, but it is possible to materialize freedom and reappropriate some parts of this surface" (qtd., in Internazionale Situazionista, op.cit., vol. 1, 18; vol. 6, 35).
19 Feigenbaum, Anna. "Concrete needs no metaphor: Globalized fences as sites of political struggle". Ephemera: theory and politics in organization. Vol. 10 (2), 2010: 128. Accessed May 31, 2014. http://www.ephemerajournal.org/contribution/concrete-needs-no-metaphor-globalized-fences-sites-political-struggle.
20 Lefebvre, Henri. Writings on Cities (Oxford & Malden MA: Blackwell, 1996).
21 Lazzarato, Maurizio. La politica dell'evento (Cosenza: Rubbettino, 2004).
22 Origlia, Dino. "Il sogno che graffia". In Graffiti Metropolitani. Arte sui muri della città, edited by Ivo Balderi and Livio Senigalliesi (Genova: Costa & Nolan, 1994).

Kristopher Murray, Concordia University

Rethinking political subjectivity in the urban context through the lens of graffiti and street art.

Graffiti and street art are argued as approaching the qualifications for what Isin terms 'acts of citizenship' possessing creative, inventive, and performative elements that traverse actual and symbolic frontiers. In doing so, they call into question given assumptions about equality, fairness, justice, and the diminishing public sphere. Contrasted against Boltanksi's sociology of critique, the potential that graffiti and street art have to reveal the contradictions of institutional authority in the everyday is explored through examples in Montreal, the United States, and the Middle East. Ultimately, graffiti and street art are argued as original positions where radical uncertainties can prevail over some institutional forms of domination.

Graffiti, street art, rupture, injustice, political subjectivity

Contested and ambiguous, urban graffiti and street art seemingly inhabit an uncertain grey area that is neither legal nor illegal, art nor vandalism. Celebrated yet abhorred, criminalized yet commodified, both are often the topic of contentious debate. In short, they are uncertain objects that have oscillated historically between these dichotomies. This paper aims to emancipate these phenomena from their uncertainty and rethink the idea of political subjectivity in the urban context. In searching for a grammar and language to accomplish this task it needs to be established that graffiti and street art can be understood as being politically subjective in the first place. Following Engin Isin's work on citizenship, graffiti and street art can be understood as acts of civil disobedience possessing creative, inventive, and performative elements that call into question given assumptions about equality, fairness, and justice in the world. Graffiti writers and street artists are engaged in purposive acts that challenge the use of public space and rupture normative practices surrounding legal and institutional authority. How and for what purposes are these phenomena being mobilized by politically oriented actors in the everyday and what sort of injustices are these acts calling out in the world, if any? Furthermore, if these acts do call attention to injustice in the world then they need to be more than just what Luc Boltanski calls "socially-rooted, contextual forms of criticism," (2011: 5) they need to unmask the domination and immanent contradictions behind the injustices that they call out or direct our attention to. Like Isin, Boltanski argues for a shift in perspective focusing on actors in situ to acquire better and thicker descriptions of their activities as reflexive and autonomous individuals. This shift demands attention to the deed rather than the doer to characterize what is happening and how it is creating new possibilities for politically subjective orientations. More so, the justifications that ordinary actors provide for these deeds, including their competencies and narratives, are to be taken seriously to reveal the contradictions with institutional ideals. Societies are not homogenous constructs; they are pluralities composed of multiple and differentiating worldviews and opinions that necessitate the need for constant justification. Boltanksi argues that this justification has not only become an essential component to politics, but that it is done so in the public domain. Isin takes this a step further by investigating how activist citizens enact claims to rights and call out injustices by crossing both symbolic (legal, political, social, or cultural) and physical (private or state) boundaries. In this sense, graffiti and street art can be understood as emergent radical positions where political consciousness is intimately tied to one's actions as much as to challenging institutional and state authorities.

Citizenship and activism through the challenge to institutional authority

Boltanski (2011), Isin (2012), Simmel (1971), and Weber (1978) offer useful insights into the complexities of how politically subjective individuals both interact with and subvert institutional authority. Boltanski draws out the "hermeneutic contradictions" inherent in "the intersection of semantic controls and physical constraints" of institutions where "we find tests and rules" (2011: 80) challenged and qualified by actors in the everyday. He proposes that this tension is a contradiction at the heart of social life that abandons institutional authority that states the 'whatness of what is' and replaces it with "an exchange of points of view" (2011: 86). On the one hand this enables actors in the everyday to challenge and qualify institutional rules and authority, but on the other, risks leaving these exchanges or challenges open ended and without resolution. Moreover, the uncertainty revolving around any basis for effective or constitutive action threatens to create fragmentation which could lead to violence. This contradiction is not merely a theoretical or analytical device; it is active in the minds of everyday actors and is psychologically experienced.

Isin's approach to political subjectivity is squarely situated in open and deliberate challenges to institutional authority where activist citizens traverse symbolic and physical boundaries through purposive acts. He defines citizenship as a process involving creative, inventive, and autonomous ways of becoming politically subjective by expressing "the right to claim rights" that "articulates an injustice and demands or claims its redress" (2012: 109). It is the enactment of a claim or a demand that is essential for political subjectivity to be realized –it must be exercised in order to be recognized. In positing citizenship as something enacted, Isin approaches political subjectivity primarily through acts. He is interested in "how people constitute themselves as political subjects by the things they do, their deeds" and particularly how these deeds break away from their habitual norms, expectations, routines, and rituals to "claim rights that they may not have" (2012: 10-11). He argues that by allowing for moments of rupture and accounting for those actions that fall outside the general scope legal definitions of citizenship practices, the complex qualities that constitute acts can be more readily appreciated. Specifically, he points to the importance of accounting for civil disobedience to draw out the paradoxes of "legality and illegality, responsibility and answerability, intentionality and purposiveness, acts and actions, and rupture and change" (2012: 12).

The full meaning of an act can only be revealed after it has ended; therefore the full scope of a deed can only be appreciated by the event that it creates. Thus, acts of citizenship are only realized after they have occurred. Isin clearly differentiates between peformativity and enactment to distinguish actions from acts, where the former is used to indicate "citation, repetition, and iteration of forms, repertoires, and descriptions under which political subjectivity is produced", while the latter brings about "events as rupture in the order of things in a given site where political subjectivity is constituted" (2012: 126). In other words, the performance of citizenship is a participative process involving practicing subjects while the enactment of citizenship involves the creation of subjects through deliberate acts. Important to this formulation is the purposiveness of acts that separate them from the intentionality of descriptive actions. On the one hand, intentionality is a means to an end that involves a calculated motivation by the subject who performs according to an existing normative or behavioral script. On the other hand, the purposiveness of acts involves bodies in situ, "caught in the act" that "often do not have the possibility for such calculations but orient themselves towards a scene" (2012: 129). These acting bodies implicate themselves in breaking the codified rules, regulations, and norms that demand citational, repetitive, and iterational practiced action. The purposiveness of acts is found in this irresponsibility to normative conventions and in the justifications that actors are made answerable for through the ruptures they create. Isin says that "our acts may contravene our responsibilities but are answerable to the principles for their enactment" (2012: 130). If acts are found to be in breach of our responsibilities to these normative and practiced conventions then they need to be equally, if not more justifiably reasoned.

In shifting his discussion from actions to acts and from intentionality to purposive irresponsibility, rule breaking, and challenging conventional forms of citizenship, Isin is also calling attention to how bodies are acting in ways that are redefining their relationships with institutional authority (the sovereign state and the borders that separate them). Specifically, he is speaking about citizens who are compelled to act in ways that take them across physical and symbolic borders or frontiers and challenge the narratives of sovereign states. He posits that active citizenship involves scripts of regulative behaviors and modes of conduct that governments have co-opted into strategies "that articulate various aims" and where "creativity, inventiveness, and autonomy" are only valuable "insofar as they can be harnessed for calibrating conduct" (2012: 148). Indeed, he argues that these regulated modes of active citizenship can be nothing more than 'programmes of political subjectivation': citizens made active through prescribed strategies of cultivation articulated by the governing authorities. Conversely, activist citizenship involves the relentless pursuit of new scripts in the struggle against perceived injustice, "for equality and for identification" (2012: 148) and does not stifle creativity, inventiveness, or autonomy, but instead harnesses them.

Both Weber (1978) and Simmel (1971) remind us, however, that domination is still an interactive process. Simmel helped to illuminate the sociological relevance of conflict and domination as forms of sociation and that as much as "the desire for domination is designed to break the internal resistance over the subjugated…even the desire for domination has some interest in the other person, who constitutes a value for it" (1971: 96-97). That is, domination is not a one-way street; it is full of "variegated and contradictory oscillations" (1971: 77); of conflicts and disputes at all social, economic, and political levels that continually challenge the imposition of any dominant order. Weber most certainly agreed when he put forth that domination is legitimated through rational, traditional, and charismatic grounds, and that "the scope of determination of social relationships and cultural phenomena by virtue of domination is considerably broader than appears at first sight" (1978: 215). Domination must be legitimated for it to have any basis, and this legitimation is to be found in the interactive process between those who have the power and those who do not. Domination is never absolute; it must be constantly reinforced, performed, qualified, validated, and justified. Where Weber does fall short is in locating what Simmel identifies as the antagonistic aspects of this process. Weber most certainly agrees that those who are in power, particularly in legal-rational bureaucratic types, are as much subject to the rules and laws as those they dominate, but he fails to explicate the problems of maintaining this form of rule. Simmel points to the 'antagonistic games' played by both sides in the legitimation process and that "where the law is not forceful or broad enough a person is necessary, and where the person is inadequate, the law is required" (1971: 116). Contemporary legal bureaucratic forms of neo-liberalism are dependent on this oscillating mixture of legal and charismatic authority in order to maintain a state of rule amid disputes and conflicts over social, economic, and political issues. It is a game where stakeholders present qualifications for truth, fairness, entitlement, and justice, in the everyday or in principle, in order to maintain power or to reconcile it.

Boltanski's second hermeneutic contradiction expands on his issue that Simmel and Weber raise concerning the difficult and delicate balancing between legal and charismatic authority in contemporary neo-liberal systems. He looks to the unease that is created between the bodiless being that is the institution and the "corporeal being that gives it a voice" (2011: 87) as an issue of language. Essentially the manner in which institutional representatives communicate the functions and edicts of the administrative, coordinating, and regulative bodies they speak for. Moreover, it is the tension created by representative voices in sustaining ritualized functions through the perceived –or imagined –power of institutional authorities that can help us to see the gaps between "reality and the world, but also of the relative fragility of reality as constructed reality" (2011: 91). These hermeneutics can also help us to grasp not only the contradictions inherent in how institutions communicate and administer authority generally, but how subcultures (or the marginalized and disenfranchised) are represented by these authorities, as well as by subcultural members from within and related (interested) parties. Each make their own claims to their respective authoritative domains and knowledge and in doing so look to fill the gaps made by institutional representatives, between reality and the world: voices to a fragile, fragmented, and constructed reality. Graffiti and street art are here positioned as engaging in what Boltanski calls "interpretive games" that are "paving the way for a challenge to, or at least, a relativization of, institutional qualifications" (2011: 93) Importantly, what happens when these claims come into contact? How can subcultural representatives effectively re-interpret official formulations to effect any productive interrogation of these official formulations and/or injustices in the world?

Graffiti, Street Art, and Political Subjectivity
Graffiti and street art are a contemporary manifestation of the antagonistic games that Simmel speaks of, an indignation towards and general lack of faith in institutional and political authority. Graffiti writers and street artists are engaged in what Boltanski describes as a process of how to act "and above all what is possible to do –that is to say, the issue of the ability to act" (2011: 86). By assessing the limits of these institutional constraints, graffiti writers and street artists are actively exploring alternate or lateral possibilities for action; and in their relationship to this action are defining the city as a site of antagonism and contestation. In general, they counter the idealistic portrayal of society by calling out its inadequacies and revealing some of its perceived absurdities. As disobedient rule breakers, graffiti writers and street artists rupture the normative framework of the everyday by creating events or scenes where the types of possibilities for a claim to rights can emerge. These scenes possess creative, inventive, and performative elements, that help graffiti writers and street artists traverse actual and symbolic frontiers. In doing so, they call into question given assumptions about equality, fairness, and justice that surround everyday life in the city and the diminishing public sphere. Graffiti and street art, however, interact with political subjectivity in different ways that situate them uniquely yet not exclusively in the framework of activist citizenship.

For the most part, graffiti writers seem to operate on what Weber (1978) called a value-rational basis: they are compelled to paint; they simply do it for the sake of doing it; they seek out a more profound experience to identify with that will bring them closer to some transcendental level of personal understanding in the world. Conversely, street artists are more instrumentally-rational: it is a means to an end, meant to get a message across, and to illicit a response from a generalized other. As well, they are no less compelled to act in ways that call out injustices that they perceive in the world, however, there is an instrumental undercurrent that is still central to their motivations. Certainly, both graffiti writers and street artists have an affective component that permeates their motivation: the emotional, physiological, and kinetic energies that are captured in doing illegal acts, particularly the adrenaline rush associated with painting high risk locations or making a quick getaway. Indeed, for many graffiti writers the essence of what they do is in the act itself and not so much as the lasting image, that, appreciated of and of value, is not as prized as the experience itself.

Alain Badiou posited that something is an act "only if it is revolutionary in the sense of bringing about a radical transformation" and that "every rupture begins, for those engaged in it, through a rupture with oneself" (2005: 125). I think he succinctly sums up the existential project that graffiti writers are pursuing: self-rupture. Graffiti writers do not look to call out an injustice in the world, so to speak, but rather aim to fill a void in their lives. It infuses them with an energy or adrenalin rush and snaps them out of what they perceive to be a repressive, repetitive, and generally monotonous daily life, that they argue, stifles their creative spirit. They do not aim to force recognition from any generalized other through the rupture that their work embodies, rather, as the rupture they seek to transcend their everyday and find recognition in themselves. For many writers, the act of graffiti liberates them from the pressures of everyday conformity giving them an outlet to channel their discontent into a creative and subversive practice. It represents a form of free speech and creativity invigorating them with energy and life that they find is otherwise wasted in the machinations of everyday labor. Doing graffiti gives them the opportunity to be who they want to be rather than who they have to be. Graffiti writers may borrow –or poach –from the cultural and symbolic capital available to them, but they do so with the intent to use it for their own projects of self-identification and re-inscription. Generally, they do not intend to call out any sort of injustice in the world. If there is an injustice they are confronting it is a personal one, an existential crisis that is somehow remedied through graffiti and identification with the subcultural lifestyle.

Isin and Boltanski both argue that critical interventions need to be collectively recognized to be successful. Collective recognition takes individually held opinions or positions and makes them 'common knowledge.' Street artists look to call out an injustice and provoke a response from others, to get others to recognize this injustice due to their intervention. They look to force transcendence in a generalized other through the rupture created in or through their work to help make something more commonly known or understood. Their messages are recognized because they are created from the cultural and symbolic capital of the system they seek to subvert. Street art needs to be generally recognizable if it is to be successful, otherwise it might fade into the background of audio and visual noise in the city. Moreover, as Anna Waclawek explains in Graffiti and Street Art, most seek highly visible and trafficked locations to ensure the maximum exposure of their work allowing "street artists to communicate ideas at street level as opposed to talking down citizenry from billboards" (2011:32). Graffiti, on the other hand, is purposefully enigmatic, clandestine, and secretive because it is meant to be recognized only by other similarly oriented individuals. Although a great deal of graffiti is found at the street level there is also much that is not accessible, hidden in back alleys, rooftops, rail way tunnels, and abandoned locales. So much as graffiti writers are the rupture, street artists are the embodiment of critique. Their work is capable of translating a message through the subverted cultural capital. In calling out injustices, street artists are trying to sanction the acknowledgement of injustices that, until their acts of transgression and disobedience, had remained largely unacknowledged.

The concept of rupture is further explored in Butler's (2004) contention that the capacity to develop a critical position presupposes a distance from the social norms constituting our everyday existence. This is no simple affair as "our individual personhood is fundamentally dependant on these social norms" (2004: 2) and intimately attached to the shared rules, laws, and conventions that govern them in the everyday:

> If I am someone who cannot be without doing, then the conditions of my doing are, in part, the conditions of my existence. If my doing is dependent on what is done to me or, rather, the ways in which I am done by norms, then the possibility of my persistence as an "I" depends on my being able to do something with what is done with me...If I have any agency, it is opened up by the fact that I am constituted by a social world I never chose. That my agency is riven with paradox does not mean it is impossible. It means only that paradox is the condition of its possibility. (2004: 3)

Although Butler's argument is situated in terms of gender and the struggle in asserting individuality in the face of instituionalized norms, the paradox of existence is no less different in terms of political subjectivity. Indeed, as Isin argues, it is the enactment of a claim to rights that is the basis of political subjectivity itself –being is recognized though the act of doing. Graffiti writers constitute their identities by doing graffiti, that is, a writer cannot be without doing graffiti. Moreover, the "I" of this identity can only be fully constituted when it is affirmed through the other, in this case by other writers or, through media coverage of some form. At the same time, the "I" that seeks this affirmation through a critical and transformative relation to these constitutive norms, laws, and conventions –even if by breaking them –threatens to undo the very essence of the individual because of the fundamentally dependant relationship it has with them. Thus, the "I" becomes unrecognizable and so a departure from what constitutes being a person –a human being –begins to take place as life becomes untenable, unlivable even. This, Butler argues, is where the critical juncture occurs and from where critique emerges. This is the rupture with the self that Badiou (2012) speaks of, and from where acts can begin to inhabit the revolutionary and bring about radical transformation. By interrogating the constraints of our everyday lives we "open up the possibility of different modes of living" and "establish more inclusive conditions for sheltering and maintaining life that resists models of assimilation" (2004: 3-4).

This precariousness of our existence –this vulnerability of self –that accompanies the act of self-rupture both defines and is defined by graffiti writers and their acts of civil disobedience. As the embodiment of rupture graffiti writers exist on the edge of precariousness, inhabiting an uneasy yet critical position in relation to their own self, a process that Mead (1934) argues allows for pure self-consciousness to arise though social experience when the individual becomes an object unto himself. This is what Butler is referring to when she says "that a new psychic topography is required" (2004: 14). It emerges through the struggles with restrictive languages of everyday norms, laws, and conventions that find articulation through the utterance, the image, and through disobedient acts.

Street Art and the Traversing of Symbolic and Physical Boundaries

In late 2001, the Montreal based the stencil artist Roadsworth began painting cyclist symbols on roads in the Plateau neighborhood in protest of the lack of paths and lanes for bikers in the city. His campaign of subversion developed "into increasingly symbolic displays of civic and environmental critique"[1] where he re-designed or added stenciled animals, flowers, screws, cameras, and other sorts of images to existent road lines, pedestrian cross walks, and parking lots in the Plateau. He turned crosswalks into giant footprints, rows of candles or outlined them with garlands of flowers or barbed wire. He made dividing lines on roads into heart beat pulses, zippers, and plugs; parking lot spaces into on/off switches, placed thinking monkey's and watchful owls across lines of shadow from light poles, made can opener tops of man hole covers, and various other types of images all playing on the space that they inhabited. His intention was to disrupt the regulated code of the city streets not to cause harm, but instead to play with the images, to re-employ them in such a way as to communicate something abstract and humorous rather than something regulative, cold, and calculative. As Waclawek points out, his stenciled imagery offered "a unique opportunity for a dialogue between citizens and the structure of the city" (2011: 34) to occur, that, prior to his intervention, was largely ignored.

Roadsworth called attention not only to the auto-centricity of urban planning and the need to incorporate a multi-modal approach to urban design (for automobile, bike, pedestrian, and those with special needs). His stencil campaign also provoked a public debate over street art and artistic expression after his arrest in September of 2004[2]. His work not only traversed symbolic boundaries by playing on the official signage of city streets and traffic systems, it also represents an important example of how subcultures can provide an environment for the exchange of alternate points of view that challenge institutional authority and legal structures. In particular, street art provides a powerfully fertile milieu namely because of the creative potential of its messages to traverse not only visual boundaries, but social, economic, and political ones as well. The playful imagery that Roadsworth painted on the streets of the Plateau in Montreal was accessible to anyone because it was simple and left much to the imagination of the viewer. In this way it was also antagonistic and interactive creating a multiplicity of possible interpretations with regards to how place and space was experienced by Montreal citizens. His case and the decision to dramatically reduce his punishment was also an important reality test that helped to qualify not only his work but street art in general in Montreal. The subsequent public support campaign and victory were instrumental in establishing greater public and private interest in street art in the city and no doubt influenced a number of other street artists in their endeavors. Nearly a decade later, in 2013, Montreal was host to one of the largest international street art festivals in Canadian history taking place in the Plateau over the course of several days and involving artists from across the country, the United States, Europe, and South America.

There are also a number of street artists from the United States that have been engaging the public with their work to call attention to social, political, economic, corporate, and environmental injustices since the 1970s and 1980s. The Billboard Liberation Front (BLF), a collective of street artists who have been modifying billboard advertisements along United States highways and in cities for well over two decades, believe that corporations should not be the only ones with access to these spaces.[3] Ron English is another prolific billboard painter who has been engaging in culture jamming and uses posters and wheat paste to deliver his own brand of subversive social and political commentary concerning consumption culture since the 1980s. A self named 'pop iconoclast', English has painted numerous billboard locations across the globe and his work has been featured in museums, books, on film, and in television[4]. His unique form of 'propaganda' is a subversive and playful take on existent brands that he depicts on billboards and other places. For instance, English's billboard mock up of Camel Cigarettes, "Camel Jr's" depicts the cigarette company's iconic figure re-imagined as a child in diapers happily smoking a cigarette, wide eyed and waving to the public. His poster "Abraham Obama," was "an image widely discussed in the media as directly impacting the 2008 election"[5] and was a poster image perhaps matched only by that created by a fellow American street artist named Sheppard Fairey.

Fairey first came to prominence in the 1980s for his OBEY stickers and stencils featuring the portrait Andre the Giant in Washington D.C., Boston, Baltimore, and New York City. He became better and more widely known after he created the red and blue poster image of Barrack Obama's face with the word HOPE beneath it in 2008. That poster quickly became one of the most recognizable images associated with the Obama campaign, and after the election won, the image was acquired by the Smithsonian Institute for its national portrait gallery collection[6]. Although he gained popularity for its use in this campaign, a legal copyright battle over the original image[7] later ensued with the Associated Press that tarnished his reputation[8]. Regardless, Fairey's OBEY Giant campaign is considered a cornerstone of street art's evolution in United States that many street artists have used to publicly convey their messages. The iconic symbolism, branding, and simple messages in Fairey's work are also important aspects of how his imagery has managed to connect with the wider public and gain mass appeal.

Some street artists go the world over to provoke awareness of an injustice that they perceive and to help provide a voice for those who may not have the means to do so themselves. The British born street artist Banksy was the first to paint on the West Bank Wall in Israel in 2005 spurring a call to action and awareness to its oppressive and illegal nature. Several of the images have since been painted over or modified by Israelis, Palestinians, or others; however, a few still remain. Like much of his street art, the nine pieces he originally painted were a mixture of provocative and satirical imagery and were meant to expose the contradictory nature of the wall as a defense barrier that, in his opinion, "essentially turns Palestine into the world's largest open prison."[9] Isin remarks how Banksy's act effectively turned a site of oppression into a site of contestation by symbolic and cultural capital that was not available to those who are engaged in the struggle itself. It is an act of solidarity traversing frontiers, which calls into question the borders that are being erected (2012: 56).

Banksy's act carried transformative properties that translated his imagination into action capable of interrupting –or rupturing –at that point, the 425 mile long grey concrete walls and razor-wire fencing bring attention to what he, and many others, consider to be a terrible injustice to the people of Palestine and the West Bank.

Two years later Banksy returned the Palestinian West Bank along with seven other international street artists to paint more pictures on the wall and to hold an exhibition in Bethlehem to draw attention to the poverty in the area and to help attract tourism[10]. Since then, a number of artists have traveled to the West Bank and Palestine to add their messages and art to the wall and voice their concerns over the same issues. The wall also hosts countless messages from Palestinians and other locals voicing their opposition to the wall and the oppression by the Israeli government. Taken together, the West Bank wall is home to possibly the largest collection of protest messages concerning the Israeli-Palestinian conflict, and it is ongoing.

Discussion & Conclusion

The importance of these street artists is not what they are doing singularly so much as what they represent as a collective of multiple and exchanging points of view that challenge corporate and institutional truths and authority. In a 2009 interview with Sheppard

Fairey, journalist Antonio D'Amrosio of The Progressive[11] called him a "citizen artist" to reflect both the shift in his message from "Obey" to "Hope" and the urgency he embraces in the production and dissemination of his work. Indeed, all of the above mentioned are citizen artists in their own right. More so, each of the above street artists can be considered as citizen artists in their own way, actively engaged in traversing symbolic boundaries, challenging –even smashing at times –the fragility of the corporately constructed reality emitted from advertisements and officially designed messages. Their satirical and antagonistic acts of subversion are a reminder that domination is certainly not a one sided affair: the imposition of institutional and corporate power in the public sphere is always an interactive process; domination is neither absolute nor is it ever without opposition.

These street artists provide an interesting and important point of examination with concern to performance-driven acts of citizenship that traverse both symbolic and physical borders. Not only do they turn sites of oppression into sites of contestation through events or ruptures, they show others that anyone can do this so long as they are willing to pay the price associated with such action. They also offer dynamic, vibrant, and self-motivated examples of the hermeneutic contradictions that, as Boltankski argues, challenge the institutional tests and rules that dictate the 'whatness of what is' proving that this tension is indeed a contradiction at the heart of social life dependant on this continued exchange of multiple points of view.

When these points of view and claims comes into contact with each other, however, the real risks of these open ended and uncertain exchanges comes into full view: fragmentation, disagreement, discord, and even violence are all real possibilities –as are threats the bodies or lives of those willing to pay the price of taking that action. Sometimes that price is legal troubles or jail time while other times it is the threat of physical harm. According to The Guardian, when Banksy was painting on the West Bank wall in 2005, an elderly man approached him and said that his painting beautified the wall. When Banksy thanked him, the man replied: "We don't want it to be beautiful, we hate this wall. Go home."[12] Banksy was also quoted by his spokesperson as having been intimidated by Israeli soldiers who fired warning shots into the air and made it clear that they were pointing their guns at him[13] while he was doing his work. The artist Niels Bakkerus was confronted by an angry and violent group of school children, screaming and throwing stones at him while he painted at a section of the wall that cut through their playground. Apparently just two weeks prior a little girl had been shot and the grounds had been left covered in stones and the empty shells of tear gas bombs. At one point he had to leave as the situation getting out of hand: he could not understand what was being shouted at him, except that he knew it was not pleasant –the whole situation left him extremely agitated, nervous, and he felt threatened[14]. Paul Insect also spoke about how intense and volatile the environment was in the West Bank in describing his work with the artist Blu that was interrupted by Israeli gunfire about 200 yards down the road from where they were painting. When armored vehicles rolled by their location declaring that a special forces unit had shot a 'Palestinian soldier' they decided to get down off of their ladders and return to "right side of the barbwire fence"[15] where they would be safer from the threat of possible gunfire.

As William Parry points out in Against the Wall: The Art of Resistance in Palestine when the artists were painting at the West Bank wall there was a great deal of excitement from the youth in the areas. Many of the elders were worried, however, that the children would grow up with the wrong impression of what the wall represented, as "they don't necessarily want the kids to start viewing that area positively, and so they see the work as a thing of beauty, but in a place where beauty shouldn't be" (2011: 10). The people who live day to day in the West Bank in the oppressive shadow of this eighty foot tall wall do not see the same value that these international street artists do in creating international symbols to broadcast around the world. Although these artists believed that their pieces could help to bring attention and help to the plight of the Palestinians –like the sentiments of the elderly man who approached Banksy, many do not appreciate attempts to beautify it or change what it represents: the "aggressive prison Wall" (2011: 10) that it is in the context of everyday life of Palestinians.

On the other hand, as some of these testimonials show, even amid the frustration, fragmentation, and violence, there is room and hope for unity and collective action. As Simmel argued, it is through conflict that agreements are made between opposing parties, and it is through their interaction that this unison is made –but each side must be willing to pay the price to reach this unity. If not, then it may become too costly for one side to make the leap of faith necessary to see change realized. Although the sentiments from many of the elders were negative, a number of the artists had positive and uplifting interactions with the local population. Artists from the Gouda Group in the Netherlands, for instance, went with a group of Dutch youth to Palestine to spend two weeks not just painting at the wall but to get to know "Palestinian youth on a personal level [and] to learn about their lives and stories and to communicate this to other people in The Netherlands later on."[16]

Whether graffiti and street art truly unmask the domination and immanent contradictions behind the injustices that they direct our attention to is still yet to be seen. As Boltanski reminds us, the risk of these exchanges and challenges being left open ended and without resolution persists and begs the question: how can either street art or graffiti unmask domination or immanent contradictions if they are left unresolved or ignored? On the one hand, street art creatively breaks the distraction that some people have under the spectacle of the everyday and forces cognition of some kind of contradiction or injustice in the world. On the other hand, graffiti offers an avenue for individuals to pursue existential projects that can lead them towards what could be called a position of self-rupture where possibilities for engaging injustices outside of their projects could be realized. Although not overtly political, Banksy's nine pieces on the West Bank Wall did draw attention to the oppression of the people of Palestine. Similarly Roadsworth's stencil campaign in the Plateau of Montreal did not overturn the autocentricity of western car culture, but it did provoke creative thought about the use of public space and a public outcry to the freedom of artistic expression. Here it can be argued that street art, more than graffiti, is approaching this level of critique. These creative, inventive, and autonomous acts of citizenship enacted by these writers and artists have provided the possibilities or potentialities to break not only their static and habitual modes of everyday behavioral activity but those of others. In doing so they are both involved in actively critiquing the dominant institutional order and contributing to the repertoire of collective activism and memory, even if they are left unresolved and are ignored by the institutional authorities they are meant to critique. Graffiti writers, however, are mostly in it for themselves, but are happy to critique the perceived contradictions inherent in a system where they feel dominated by neo-liberal corporatized policies that value property and capital over the welfare of the masses. This critique, however, remains with them alone.

The 'interpretive games' that these street artists are playing have certainly helped to pave the way in challenging institutional qualifications for who deserving of, at the very least, of basic human rights and dignities. Though, whether they truly believe their work is making a difference in the lager scope of things is arguable given some of their testimonials. Many of the street artists who participated with Banksy on his West Bank wall project stated that they hoped their work was helping to raise awareness of the glaring oppression of the Palestinian people. Whether painting their messages on the massive 'prison wall' would do anything to deter Israeli government from further construction was another matter entirely; one they mostly felt was something beyond the scope of their capacities, even as popular international artists and activists. Moreover, that the United Nations[17] and other international humanitarian agencies[18] have deemed the construction of the wall illegal and yet the government of Israel continues to build it which leaves many of these artists feeling powerless in the face of such a sovereign military power. Regardless, many of the artists commented that even if they could break the feeling of oppression for one moment in a person's daily life through their work, then they had been successful, even if only momentary.

The feeling of powerlessness is a shared one then. Though street artists and those they seek to represent by calling out perceived injustices are not in the same life circumstances, both are just as powerless to stop the sovereign beast of Israel from continuing its oppressive regime. The Palestinian people are certainly in more of a precarious position than those international artists who visit the West Bank and must deal with physical as well the symbolic violence on a daily basis. As evidenced by some of the testimonials of the participating artists, the threat of bodily harm was shared with the Palestinian people to a degree, and that this threat could have become a very real is not entirely impossible, though it is more than likely that these artists would have been detained rather than shot or killed –a luxury that the people of the West Bank unfortunately do not share. Still, these artists took courageous leaps of faith in attempting to build a new and transformative "psychic topography" (2004: 14) that Butler could certainly appreciate. It is also a topography that the younger generations of Palestinian people are increasingly recognizing as having the potential to not only transform old and habituated attitudes but imaginations as well.

Ultimately, as Isin reminds us, the full meaning of an act can only understood after it is finished, and we must remember to pay the deed more attention than the doer if we are to have any success in such critical projects. As much as this paper has shown that the deeds of graffiti writers and street artists have had an impact in how we view such acts, we are still very much obsessed with the doers –vandals and artists –rather than their deeds. As much as Banksy, Fairey, BLF, Roadsworth, or Ron English had made significant steps towards articulating a radical voice of resistance, they are still the main attractions of the events they create and the news stories that circulate them. Still, the projects that graffiti writers and street artists are involved in –be it existential or representative of some larger injustice –are still ongoing. As this paper has shown, the meaning of some of their acts of citizenship have been realized, though the true extent of how they have made truly important and long term effects are yet still to be seen. As well, graffiti writers and street artists continue to define new ways in which citizenship can be enacted through the events created through deliberate acts. Importantly, we need to recognize the events that these deeds create and how they can be used to empower others. Finally, we need to be willing to pay the price for these challenges and interventions to make the difference we hope to see in the world; otherwise we will continue to see the paradox of our existence as holding us back, rather than truly being the condition of its possibility.

Notes and References

1 Boudreau, Laura, Spacing. 2006.
2 Local police charged him with 83 counts of mischief (spanning over three years, though it was eventually dropped to 51 counts), $250,000 in fines, jail time, and a permanent record. A local gallery owner and several members of the arts community in Montreal and abroad came to his defense and set him up with legal counsel. They also started up a "Save Roadsworth" campaign and reached out to the media to publicize his case and street art. The public response was outstanding: countless letters were written, petitions were signed, and several public figures spoke out in his defense. After 16 months of legal hearings amid public outcry and protest and the continued efforts of his supporters, the City of Montreal settled out of court. Roadsworth was fined $250 and forty hours of community service (painting and stencil work at a public elementary school) in the same borough he was accused of vandalizing.
3 Examples of some of their "clients" include McDonalds, Phillip Morris, Wachovia Bank, AT&T and the NSA, and Johnny Walker. The BLF manifesto can be found on their website (http://www.billboardliberation.com) that outlines the philosophy behind the subversive culture jamming this organization represents. The website also includes several articles from participating members concerning the imposition of public space by corporations and advertisers. As well, an 18 page document is available for download, aptly named "The Art and Science of Billboard Improvement: A Comprehensive Guide to the Alteration of Outdoor Advertising", that provides an outline and step-by-step instructions on how to go about "improving" billboards and other forms of "outdoor advertising" for anyone interested in pursuing such activities.
4 https://www.popaganda.com is Ron English's main site that provides information concerning his history, mission, and work.
5 https://www.popaganda.com/about
6 http://en.wikipedia.org/wiki/Barack_Obama_%22Hope%22_poster
7 The original photograph was taken by freelance photographer Mannie Garcia.
8 Fairey sued the Associated Press in 2009 claiming that the image was used in fair use after being approached for compensation which ended in a out of court settlement in 2011. In February 2012, Fairey pleaded guilty to fabricating and destroying documents related to his 2009 court battle with the Associated Press and admitted to being in error regarding his original claim that the photograph was used in fair use and had attempted to cover it up. He was sentenced to two years probation, fined $25 000, and ordered to 300 hours of community service.
9 This statement was purportedly provided on his website or by his spokesperson and reproduced by The Guardian in an article dated August 5, 2005. The full statement and article can be viewed on the news agency's official site at http://www.theguardian.com/world/2005/aug/05/israel.artsnews
10 The seven participating artists were Swoon, Blu, Paul Insect, Faile, Sam3, Ericailcane, and Ron English. The exhibition was named Santa's Ghetto in Bethlehem 2007
11 http://www.progressive.org/dambrosio0609.html
12 http://www.theguardian.com/world/2005/aug/05/israel.artsnews
13 http://www.theguardian.com/world/2005/aug/05/israel.artsnews
14 Krohn & Lagerweij (2010: 85)
15 Krohn & Lagerweij (2010: 97)
16 Krohn & Lagerweij (2010: 47)
17 In 2004 a Palestinian initiated U.N. resolution led the International Court of Justice to declare the construction of the wall to be contrary to international law.
18 Red Cross declared the wall to be in violation of the Geneva Convention in 2004. Other groups and agencies include, Human Rights Watch, Amnesty International, Machsom Watch, The World Council of Churches.

Badiou, Alain. (2005) Metapolitics. Translated by Jason Barker. Verso.
Boltanski, Luc. (2011) On Critique: A Sociology of Emancipation. London: Polity Press.
Brown, Wendy. (2013) Civilizational Delusions. Secularism, Tolerance, Equality. In Revealing Democracy: Religion and Secularism in Liberal Democracy. Eds. C. Maille, G. Nielsen, D. Salee. Brussels: Peter Lang.
Brown, Wendy. (2006) Regulating Aversion. Princeton University Press.
Butler, Judith. (2004) Undoing Gender. Routledge.
Gibson, Bethany & Roadsworth. (2011) Roadsworth. Goose Lane Editions.
Isin, Engin F. (2012) Citizens Without Frontiers. London: Bloomsbury.
Krohn, Zia & Lagerweij, Joyce. (2010) Concrete Messages: Street Art on the Israeli-Palestinian Separation Barrier. Dokument Press.
Mead, George Herbert. (1934) Mind Self and Society. Ed. By C. Morris. University of Chicago Press.
Parry, William. (2011) Against the Wall: The Art of Resistance in Palestine. Chicago Review Press.
Simmel, Georg. (1971) On Individuality and Social Norms. Ed. by Donald N. Levine. The University of Chicago Press.
Waclawek, Anna. (2011) Graffiti and Street Art. Thames & Hudson: London.
Weber, Max. (1978) Economy and Society. Ed. by G. Roth and C. Wittch. University of California Press.

Luis Menor Ruiz, Institut de Govern I Polítiques Públiques de la Universitat Autònoma de Barcelona (IGOP-UAB); luismenorruiz@gmail.com

Street Art and Urban Space: a Problem or an Opportunity For local Governments? Barcelona as a Case Study

The one thing that artistic expressions, under the Street Art label, have in common is the treatment they receive from the local government, who consider this type of expression as a problematic phenomenon. The most commonly found policy is that of a "schizophrenic" logic: on the one hand, Street Art is criminalized through punitive municipal regulations, yet on the other hand, it is accepted through the organization of different recreational activities. This, therefore, makes the institutionalization of Street Art a fundamental matter of study. Here, we will analyse the city of Barcelona as our case study.

Street art, institutionalization, public policies

Introduction

Street art has become one of the most notable cultural phenomena of our time. Many artists have opted to operate on the street because of the immediacy and freedom of action that it provides, avoiding the mediation of traditional display institutions, i.e. art galleries and museums, secularly involved in the process of communication between artists and viewers. In its purest version, these 'street' interventions are executed without "permission" of the local authority which renders the artist free of any bureaucratic formality, institutional "suggestion" or eventual official imposition. However, in turn, the artist is doomed because of their illegality. This condition would be determined by the type of legislation, and the public policies that implement each local government in this instance. The margins in which urban artists work depends on the way the public authorities deal with unregulated artistic activity. In the vast majority of cases, this approach adopts a "problematic" perspective where the light is shone on the "damage" caused in this public space by such artistic manifestations, ignoring all cultural and social potential of this phenomenon. In parallel to the stigmatization of unregulated public art, it can be confirmed that, paradoxically, urban culture is increasingly attractive both for public authorities and commercial advertising businesses. This motivates the adoption of ambivalent policies by local governments where, on one hand, non-regulated art, such as street art or graffiti, is criminalized, prosecuted and then punished and, on the other hand, is stimulated and encouraged through different recreational and cultural initiatives. A clear example of this type of public policy, which in this paper is referred to as "schizoid", is overseen by the City Council of Barcelona. Until they were forced to adhere to entry last municipal regulations of 2004, the so-called Municipal Ordinance of the Urban Landscape Uses of the City of Barcelona, the Mediterranean capital had been one of the most prominent international centres of urban culture.

With that legislation, punishment for any intervention in a public space has amounted to fines of up to 6,000 €. Moreover, eradicating non-regulated works on the street was systematic. Since then, those artists who work on the street without the authorization of the City Council are doomed to illegality and the punitive consequences established by municipal ordinance. But in contrast, the punitive treatment that advocates street art and graffiti is accompanied by policies to stimulate and promote them through the organization of various events and cultural initiatives. Among recent initiatives supported by the council, we can highlight activities such as audio-visual series held in the MACBA (Museum of Contemporary Art of Barcelona), urban culture festivals like Festival Hypnotic or supporting initiatives like Murs Lliures conducted by the cultural association Rebobinart. In addition to this, it is important to note that public policy in relation to street art in Barcelona have been ineffective, since they have not eradicated it as intended, and inefficient, as public spending on cleaning graffiti has only increased in recent years. All this calls for a profound reflection on the adequacy of current public policy of the City of Barcelona to address non-regulated artistic expressions such as street art or graffiti. The complexity of this issue makes its analysis very difficult but, on the other hand, its growing importance makes a multidimensional analysis fundamental. This paper aims to contribute to this analysis paying special attention to the study case of Barcelona. The structure of this paper will be as follows: first of all, the differentiating factors between street art and graffiti will be highlighted. Secondly, a typology which broadly reflects those existing public policies in regard to street art and graffiti will be defined. Thirdly, this paper will focus on the study case of Barcelona as a paradigm of ambivalence in designing and implementing public policies as well as the inefficiency and ineffectiveness in addressing the phenomenon. Finally, the main conclusions will be addressed.

Street art or graffiti?

One of the most recurrent issues in addressing non-regulated artistic expressions such as street art and graffiti has to do with the nature of their categories. Can street art and graffiti be considered the same artistic expression? Can they be framed in the same category or are they distinct phenomena? If so, what are the factors that differentiate them? As usual with all complex questions answers are neither unequivocal nor final. Abarca (2010), seeking to create definitions that could fit more closely to their characteristics, coined the term "independent public art". This term refers to all "artistic action that takes place in the public space at the sole initiative of artists and that it is free from any external control, which responds to non-trade concerns, and whose physical fruit, when available, are abandoned to their fate." This category includes, therefore, both graffiti and street art. First of all, contemporary graffiti must be considered as a main category. Its definition could be: these artistic expressions which emit unofficial messages as a response to economic, political or cultural powers, and urgent wish of communication (Ramirez, 1992). They originate from the late sixties in cities like New York and Philadelphia resulting in a rich urban visual culture. Although this term is often used in its individual form, it is actually the plural of the Italian term graffito, meaning image or text on a wall (Lewisohn, 2008). One of the main features of graffiti is its illegality, since its means, goals and strategies are strongly opposed to institutional power.

On the other hand, the street art label is more difficult to establish given the multiplicity of actions that may fall within that category. In most cases, it refers to independent art forms of action in the public space beyond graffiti (Abarca, 2010). The origins of the name are difficult to establish. Its use was already widespread in the late 1970's. One of its earliest printed uses was in 1985 included in the book 'Street Art' by Allan Schwartzman (Lewisohn, 2008).

The biggest mistakes are not only terminological but conceptual. The most frequent one is to assume that the same label can be assigned to any independent artistic performance. The general point of view, and mostly expressed in the mass media, assumes that all work done on the street without official permission is classified as graffiti. Unfortunately, this confusion concerns not only the media but also public opinion and, in particular, many local governments. Through their policies local administrations give the same treatment to tags, murals or interventions as they do to any piece of street 'furniture'. Although links between street art and graffiti are obvious, it is necessary to emphasize that neither the technical implements, nor the purpose, the audience, the form nor intention (Lewisohn, 2008) are the same.

The first issue to consider has to do with techniques. While graffiti writers use a very narrow range and always aggressive technical means, such as pen or spray, street artists use much broader resources and are not necessarily considered aggressive. These urban artists can use a wide range of techniques such as spray, conventional painting materials, stencil, stickers, pastes, chalks and even three-dimensional elements. All this makes street art a non-legal art form more so than an illegal one since the effects of these resources are less harmful and lasting on the bases where they are applied. This means that these actions do not cause incensed reactions from the authorities.

Secondly, another distinguishing factor is the type audience being targeted. Graffiti writers aim to address an expert audience that fully understands the codes used in each signature while urban artists are interested in reaching a much wider audience. The concepts of style, location and "getting up" are fundamental to understand the implications that graffiti has among its practitioners and, therefore, among its viewers. Depending on one's spray skills and the difficulty of execution and location, as well as the number of times you repeat your own signature, you will have more respect from your peers (Abarca, 2010). Therefore, these graffiti writers' ultimate goal is to bomb urban space with their own signature as much as they can. In the case of the street artist this issue is very different. There is no need to gain the respect of their peers; their intention is to connect with general public. Moreover, street artists do not seek to saturate the visual space; they choose spaces that enable them to establish a relationship of intimacy and complicity with the viewer.

Finally, another differential factor that I would like to highlight is the profile of its 'artistes'. Although graffiti writers tend to be young, many are in their thirties or even forties. Their social background is very heterogeneous. Despite the current social heterogeneity, the phenomenon sinks its roots into the most humble strata of where it originated (Castleman, 1982). The references to popular visual culture are very common in the case of graffiti. Comics, cartoons or advertising are usually recurring motifs. Despite the use of motifs from popular culture, street artists tend to make common references to the so-called "high" culture. While iconographic references of graffiti artists are often intuitive, street artists use a higher degree of sophistication.

All these factors have to be regarded with caution. As noted at the beginning of this paper, the phenomenon of independent public art, both in the case of street art and graffiti, is very complex and does not fit too well within strict categorizations. Nowadays, the boundaries are very blurred and we sometimes encounter graffiti writers-cum-street artists and also street artists who alternate their artistic practice with graffiti. The issue of age is also relative since many graffiti writers who have practiced graffiti for many years continue to exercise as such. It is wrong to understand this group as if it were composed entirely of teenagers. On the one hand, it may be worthless making sweeping generalisations to pigeon whole these artists but, on the other hand, some cautiously adopted classifications may contribute to understand the reality of the phenomenon.

Public Policies Typology

In spite of everything I have described in the previous section, local governments still give, in most cases, the same treatment to graffiti and to street art. Although the criminalization of both phenomena is systematical, we must emphasize that in not all geographical cases is the same answer found. Focusing specifically on urban policies, one can observe the varying degrees of intolerance: in the form of fines and penalties. One question remains: since the answer is not the same in all cases, would it be possible to design a classification that portrays the various ways in which local governments are approaching the phenomenon? The answer is yes but, again, this categorization should be used with extreme caution.

This classification could be grouped into three broad categories: 1) zero tolerance or prohibition;2) participatory, and 3) schizoid. It is essential to emphasize that these categories are neither pure nor fixed. Not pure because, except in the case of the prohibitionist policies, where we do find a more homogeneous and clear policy against any unregulated art, it is almost impossible to find a complete homogeneity in the response those local governments give to independent public art.

On the other hand, these are not fixed categories because recent experience shows that such policies, adopted by local governments in most cases experience an evolution (or involution) which is totally unpredictable. Policies can evolve from "tough" to "controlled permissiveness" as may be the case in Lisbon. Others, on the contrary, experience and involution from a very high tolerance to severe punitive regime. A good example of this, as discussed below, is Stockholm. While others actually combine punitive and penalty regime to promote independent public art through the organization of various activities (audio-visual series, festivals, etc...), as is the case in Barcelona. Therefore, it must be kept in mind that the categorization or typology drawn here presents an open and somewhat unpredictable fluid nature, according to the complexity of the phenomenon itself.

The prohibitionist category is characterized by a policy of zero tolerance to any artistic unregulated public space. The clearest example of this type of policy is Stockholm. In recent years, the Swedish capital has been implementing a policy that not only criminalizes, prosecutes and punishes the practitioners of these activities, but also prohibits any visual reference in its public space that may refer to the culture of graffiti[1]. This policy, implemented in 2007, operates mainly through two axes: repression (surveillance and punishment in the form of fines or imprisonment of up to one year) and immediate cleaning (conducted through "24 hours policy" consisting of a cleaning system that runs on a maximum within 24 hours). As presumably, the economic and social costs of these policies are considerable. The policy of "zero tolerance" has a cost the coffers of the Swedish capital around 200 million kronor a year (almost 23 million euros). This amount does not include the work of private security companies[2]. The case study of Stockholm is significant because of the evolution of their policies from the emergence of the phenomenon in the 1980s to the current prohibitionist policy. During the last 20 years, since the mid-1990s, the Council has moved from a policy of tolerance and development, enabling walls for the development of interventions, to an increasingly restrictive policy. The current policy of zero tolerance is the culmination of that process.

Secondly, in the collaborative category, initiatives have been implemented whereby the local government proposes specific projets to urban artists in order to improve the appearance to certain degraded urban areas. The clearest example of this category is Lisbon. In recent years, the city of Lisbon has been taking a collaborative process between the Government of the Portuguese capital, through its Department of Cultural Heritage, and street artists whose workings are spread throughout Lisbon. The initiatives of the City Council are developed through a municipal agency called Urban Art Gallery (GAU). This agency has undertaken projects such as Cronos[34], developed by the initiative of several artists in the city between 2010 and 2011. During the course of twelve months, various local and international artists were invited to intervene in various degraded city buildings. The thematic requirement was simple: allude to the four seasons of the year. The participating artists were not confined to show their work on simple walls but to do display their craft on broad facades of buildings that were abandoned. The aim was to achieve a dual purpose by local authorities: an aesthetical regeneration of the degraded urban areas in Lisbon, whilst channeling unregulated artistic interventions into activities under municipal control.

These last two objectives have initiated the work created by GAU recent years. This initiative has not only had the participation of expert artists and street art expert but with the public itself. Through various council decisions, residents have agreed to the various sketches of these street artists... One of these initiatives was the open call to redecorate the recycling bins for glass. The result has not only given the city a much friendlier appearance but also increased opportunities for citizen participation[5]. All this has meant that Lisbon is at the forefront of street art tourism. Go Urban is a journey that links the main creations of each street artist with each other. Guided tours round the various displays of street art are organised by the City Council.

Barcelona as case of study

In this section I will address the description and review of existing public policies in the city of Barcelona in order to define the most relevant stakeholders and analyse the existing public programs and data associated with them. It should be pointed out that these policies are characterized by the way of tackling street art as a problematic and essentially negative phenomenon, which requires initiatives to combat it discernibly. Following the broken windows theory (Wilson and Kelling, 1982), which will be discussed later, the vast majority of local authorities, and Barcelona is no exception, have criminalized graffiti assuming that the best way to fight major crime is through the elimination of minor offenses. This has resulted in an overly restrictive and punitive municipal regulation in relation to all those unregulated plastic manifestations in the public space.

The stakeholders are grouped into three groups: artists, merchants and politicians. To these three groups, a fourth collective could be added: civilians. The uncertainty of such collective and the complexity that would entail its analysis has prompted us to leave this aside for future studies. At first glance, it might seem that all these groups have conflicting interests and, therefore, there is an inherent conflict between them. But recent facts belie this assertion. It is true that many traders have expressed their dissatisfaction with the graffiti found on the walls of their businesses. However, many others have found ways to avoid unwanted painted by hiring street artists to decorate their shutters. Such initiatives have been fought particularly ferociously by the City Council. Late 2010, the local government banned merchants to decorate their businesses with graffiti. Marc Garcia, co-founder of the collective Persanas Lliures stated: "The City tries to curb this demand [for graffiti by traders] and that is why the owners are now being fined in order to stop this insurgency against the ordinance." In George Lobell's own words, spokesman for the Enroller's initiative, when the City Council prohibit merchants hiring graffiti artists to decorate shutters: "It's like the council's heavy fist has banged on the table, they are overwhelmed with disfavoured proposals from not just artists, but traders."[6]

Meanwhile, the spokesman of the Institute of Urban Landscape and Quality of Life, the regulatory body of the urban aesthetics of Barcelona, stated: "The ordinances interpret graffiti painting in the public space as fouling behaviour that not only devalues the public or private equity but also causes a visual degradation of the environment, affecting the quality of life for residents and tourists. Therefore, the merchants who hire or allow a graffiti artist to paint the exterior of theirs shop are exposed to penalties."[7]

The consequences of such action by the City Council merely instigate conflict between the parties rather than mitigate it. The prohibition of street artists working for merchants and traders in order to decorate the facades of their businesses is actually encouraging a proliferation of uncontrollable tags. This fact is clearly conveyed by what happened with the Municipal Ordinance in 1999, and in the opinion of Llobel "Now graffiti writers do faster scribbles so as not be caught by the police. Part of the graffiti will always be anarchic, because its essence is freedom, but all who prefer to avoid the risk of a fine would paint on legal sites"[8].

In relation to public programs of the City of Barcelona, three axes can be found: prohibition, eradication and promotion. The prohibition is explicit both in its rules[9] and in the rigour of its application. The removal of graffiti and other artistic expressions is articulated by the City Council through two initiatives: 1) giving economic aid to merchants to eliminate graffiti relieving them of the financial burden of its eradication and 2) collaboration with third sector organisations. These organisations carry out social actions in order to reintegrate groups at risk of social exclusion by employing them to erase such graffiti.

In the case of the aid given to traders, it was developed in two phases. First, the City Council facilitated a list of companies that both met the technical requirements for the initial cleaning and would commit to performing the maintenance, for the traders. The objective of this first intervention was mainly to remove all of graffiti and stickers. The second phase of the campaign urged participating merchants to sign a maintenance contract for a period of four years with the company who had initiated the cleaning. To promote this program, the City Council subsidized 50% of the cost of the initial cleaning and the contract for the maintenance of painted surfaces. The remaining 50% had to be paid by the traders themselves enrolled in support programs. In total, for the council, it was a financial investment of € 900,000, which was included in the municipal budgets for the years 2009 and 2010.[10] Moreover, as discussed, the City Council has also implemented initiatives to erase graffiti through collaboration with third sector organizations. These organizations carried out socio laboral actions with groups of young people at risk of social exclusion[11]. The Comtal Foundation launched the project "Colour in the shutters" in which a group of 15 young people between 19 and 25 years old were asked to clean and paint a hundred shopfront shutters after a specific training.

The third axis clearly contradicts the previous two: the promotion of street art through various publications and leisure and cultural activities. This publication is specifically the catalogue "141 days in Barcelona. The Fòrumat your hands" It's a compilation of pictures and testimonials about the Forum of Cultures held in Barcelona in 2004. This cultural event resulted in the signing of the Agenda 21 for culture.[12] Agenda 21 argued for encouraging the active participation of society in public affairs through culture by promoting the diversity of cultural expressions. Amongst the concerns of the publication "141 days in Barcelona" graffiti is a fundamental part of the cultural heritage of the city and, therefore, deserves a prominent place.

In reference to certain activities, it is important to note that the organization of audio-visual series and Hip-hop festivals in which graffiti has an outlined presence. From 27 to 30 November 2008 the first edition of NOW Documentary Minifest was held in which seven current issues were addressed from "new approaches and perspectives". Among these seven issues, graffiti was tackled in "The Reverse Graffiti Project" category in which the documentary 3'23", directed by Doug Pray in 2008, was projected. Moreover, in September 2012 the 9th edition of the Hipnotik Hip Hop Festival took place where, once again, graffiti had a strong presence along with other manifestations of Hip Hop culture, such as Rap or Break dance. Both events were held at the Centre of Contemporary Culture of Barcelona (CCCB), one of the flagships of the cultural institutions in the city of Barcelona, next to MACBA.

Finally, emphasizing these contradictions, the City Council has undertaken collaborations with affiliations of street art with the purpose of facilitating walls whereby artists can channel their art. One of the pioneering efforts, in this regard, is Murs Lliures conducted by the collective Rebobinart. As stated on the project website: "Murs lliures born from the need to unleash creativity spaces for urban artists from Barcelona, a city that had turned its back on this art, and which many artists of great quality, had fled to paint on walls in other locations, where they had more time to do their more elaborate work, and not be fined for doing so." Also, "Murs Lliures works in each district to allocate spaces, which have become a meeting point for the creativity of the neighbourhood. The spaces assigned for each district are managed by a panel, who basically seek the widest possible participation." Only time will tell whether support for this initiative by the Consistory is a real turning point in the politics of local government with respect to street art or, on the contrary, if it is actually full of contradictions, and still miles away from reaching an ideal.

It is time to deal with the data relating to the public expenditure of the Council of Barcelona[13] in reference to street art. It must be pointed out that no specific data could be found in relation to the spending of promotional activities of street art. So in this current analysis we will address only the expenditure relating to public spending of graffiti removal in the last five years:

from 2007 to 2012. These are very eloquent as we can see that the spending has only increased since the obligatory latest update from the 2006 municipal ordinance regulating landscape uses. We note that this upward trend has some ups and downs. Between the years 2008 (3,346 €) and 2010 (3,704 €) there is a slight decrease in spending over previous years. Yet, altogether, it is clear that there is an absolute increase in the spending on cleaning graffiti that goes from 3,634 € in 2007 to 4,014€ in 2012 with an accumulated expenditure during such period (2007-2012) of 22,785€. The local government is hence, not only opposing one of the most genuine artistic and cultural expressions of our cities, but is also making policies that are both ineffective in dealing with such expressions, and has become ineffective when rationalizing public expenditure within these urban locations. Other budget items must be added to this data, items that have been used to combat graffiti, for example the financial aid given to traders for cleaning facades and shutters. As already noted such aid was distributed within the 2009 and 2010 budgets[14].

Explanatory factors
At this point, one needs to raise the question of the factors that explain the classification categories in which this paper is based on (prohibitionist, collaborative and schizoid). These can be classified into two factors: the ideological factor and the market factor. The ideological factor has its roots in the theory of broken windows by James Q. Wilson and George L. Kelling (1982). This theory establishes a causal link between public orders, or rather the lack of them, and criminal acts (Thacher, 2004). Based on the work of psychologist Philip Zimbardo, the theory is constructed with the metaphor of a broken window. If any broken window remains unrepaired in a community long enough it can lead to other broken windows. The fact that the window remains unrepaired in any neighbourhood is a sure sign that no one cares about it and, therefore, is issuing a clear message: breaking the windows has no ramifications (Wilson and Kelling, 1982) and thus eventually encourages criminal people to threaten the order of any community by breaking more windows and thereby wreaking havoc.

The aim of this theory is to note any (in the words of its authors) "unattended" behaviour as the culprit in the breakdown or collapse of community control. Such a bankruptcy would inexorably lead to crime and consequently to the consummation of crimes and major offenses. In other words, excessive permissiveness, with minor offenses like drinking, urinating, obscene behaviour or sleeping on the street, can lead to crimes of greater importance, for example: assault, theft or even murder. As might be expected the authors do not hesitate to also target the graffiti as undesirable and "unattended" behaviour. In the author's words, quoting Nathan Glazer, the proliferation of graffiti, even when not obscene, confronts the subway rider with the "inescapable knowledge that the environment he must endure for an hour or more a day is uncontrolled and uncontrollable, and that anyone can invade it to do whatever damage and mischief the mind suggests."

The strong causal link established by the theory of Wilson and Kelling has subsequently been challenged by criminology experts like Thatcher (2004). This author highlights other issues that go far beyond those identified in the Broken Windows Theory and where the role of public policy and long-term strategy is essential. Moreover, he states that the relationship between disorder and serious crime is modest and that other social forces play a role in this junction. But despite all the above, the ideology of the Broken Windows Theory has not only had profound implications on the mode of governance of many local governments, and therefore strongly influences the way they address all artistic expression unregulated in the public space (either in the form of graffiti or street art), but also the way in which certain sectors of civil society perceive this phenomenon.

On the other hand, the market factor correlates with type of city management that we have nowadays. The current economic paradigm motivates cities to compete with each other to attract flows of offshore capital. The objective of big cities would therefore be to locate these flows on its territory. This management gets closer and closer to business management (Cocola, 2009). This change in the model of management has resulted in the promotion of public service, public users are now considered as if they were customers. From this approach, the use of marketing in urban management aims to satisfy the needs of each different user group, not only visitor sand tourists but also retail distribution companies (Elizagárate, 2007). Such satisfaction is based on the adequacy of the urban scene to the need of each customer in the city.

Consistent with urban marketing is the development of a communication strategy, in which the concept of "city brand" occupies a prominent place. The promise of 'value' in cities increases with an organized advertising campaign in which the characteristics of both its value and its brand image (Cocola, 2009) would be exposed. This is to way; culture plays a prominent place in the city brand promotion. Contemporary art museums are often the cornerstone of such promotion processes. This is due to their ability of attracting visitors of both a medium and high socioeconomic status. In many occasions, such as the MACBA in Barcelona or Bilbao's Guggenheim, museums are built expressly to attract tourists. Although, instead of having a permanent collection, these museums have temporary exhibitions to generate a renewed interest in these possible visitors (Cocola, 2009). This reinforces their status as contender and, therefore, the emptiness of their nature.

Because of the mercantilist approach to culture and to threats, it is not surprising that the reis and ambivalence towards the schizoid models since every cultural event should serve to promote the brand of each city whilst avoiding any problematic artistic expression. In this sense, the phenomenon of street art and graffiti fits poorly within this management model as their own free and untamable nature makes it unmanageable for local governments, and therefore contradicts the interests of urban marketing.

Conclusion

As addressed in this article, the phenomenon of street art and graffiti is an issue that is generating a lot of controversy in our cities. Several factors converge to explain this situation. First, the ideological factor, with its origin at the Broken Windows Theory, which considers petty crime as the embryo from which other larger crimes are generated, such as theft or even murder. Independent public art falls into this category as the "degradation" that it would provoke would thereby encourage the performance of serious crimes. On the other hand, the market factor makes the current management of cities and their public spaces limited to a commercial logic. It is therefore understandable that a phenomenon whose manifestations are unassimilable by a system that only cares about profitability are considered proscribed, and therefore should be banned, prosecuted and punished.

Through the various categories of public policies drawn up here, it has been confirmed that independent public art can be managed with different approaches, having a range from zero tolerance to permissiveness controlled by public authorities. Not forgetting the schizoid approach. There are, therefore, different ways of managing conflict based on the legal frame work applied, and the public policies implemented. The social and cultural costs vary considerably in each case because whilst in Stockholm there is an almost total absence of independent public art, in Lisbon there is a rich artistic life on the street which motivates not only the participation of local artists but attracts many foreign artists, and even tourists.

The case of Barcelona, whose public policies have been included in the "schizoid" category, is one of the most interesting cases of study given its paradoxical characteristics. This case serves to access an increasingly common way of dealing with these phenomenons. This approach is based on both the criminalization and promotion of street art and graffiti. It is the most interesting case to analyze because it exposes the contradictions of public authorities in their approach to cultural phenomenon, which is operated by institutional logic. In this research, I have addressed the supposedly democratic and inclusive but false discourse of many public institutions. This is evident in negotiating phenomenons that do not conform to the demands made by official agents. Hence, the way in which they promote the phenomenon is superficial and disrespectful to its essence. The clear fact that current public policy of the Council of Barcelona has been ineffective has been shown by its failure to eradicate graffiti, and its inefficiency, given the increase in public spending in reference to graffiti removal, incentivizes a rethinking of the "problematizing" approach as the best way to deal with the phenomenon.

Some questions should be raised beyond institutional logic of economic efficiency: How best can the cultural and social potential of a city like Barcelona are displayed through its current public policies? Should another approach be considered to combat the inherent conflict of the independent artistic practice? Should mere criminalization and vacuous promotion of the phenomenon be overcome? Could cultural citizen participation be incentivized through other policies? Could street art and graffiti be a possible "solution" rather than being a problem? It is not easy to answer these questions but it seems both obvious and important to note that in order to address independent public art it is necessary to breakdown the current mercantilist and ideologically biased logic of local governments. Policies should be created differently, changing economic criteria, and establishing other parameters where the real value focuses on the social, participatory and truly cultural criteria.

Notes and References

1 "Zero tolerance for street art in Stockholm", Polis blog, August 20, 2011, http://www.thepolisblog.org/2011/08/zero-tolerance-for-street-art-in.html
2 "Stockholm graffiti – beating the ban", The Local, September 2, 2011, http://www.thelocal.se/35918/20110902/
3 "Interview Crono Project", Fatcap, July 31, 2012, http://www.fatcap.com:8081/article/interview-crono-project-1.html
4 "Cronos 2010-2011", Issuu, 2011, http://issuu.com/unidade/docs/crono_lisboa_2010-2011
5 Abraham de Vicente, "El arte urbano mundial en Lisboa," Are-ezine, March 12, 2012, http://www.are-ezine.com/arte-urbano-mundial-en-lisboa/
6 Meritexel M. Pauné "Los comerciantes de Barcelona serán multados si encargan graffiti para su persiana", La Vanguardia, December 27, 2010, http://www.lavanguardia.com/vida/20101227/54092822960/los-comerciantes-de-barcelona-seran-multados-si-encargan-graffiti-para-su-persiana.html
7 "Barcelona pagará la limpieza de 2.500 persianas con graffitis a cambio de su mantenimiento", La Vanguardia, March 13, 2013 http://www.lavanguardia.com/local/barcelona/20130313/54368346410/barcelona-pagara-la-limpieza-de-2-500-persianas-con-graffitis-a-cambio-de-su-mantenimiento.html
8 Ibidem
9 "Ordenanza de los Usos del Paisaje Urbano de la ciudad de Barcelona publicada en el BOP 146 con fecha 19/06/1999", Updated April 1, (2006)
10 "Nova campanya de neteja i manteniment de persianes", Suplement Barris de Ciutat Vella, July, 2009
11 Jessica Mouzo Quintáns, "Lavado de antigrafitos", El País, November 6, 2012, http://ccaa.elpais.com/ccaa/2012/11/05/catalunya/1352150547_545184.html
12 "Agenda 21 de la Cultura. Ciudades y Gobiernos locales unidos". Culture comission, Barcelona, 2004, http://www.agenda21culture.net/index.php/es/documentacion-oficial/agenda-21-de-la-cultura
13 Anuari Estadístic de la Ciutat de Barcelona (2012)
14 Suplement Barris de Ciutat Vella (2009)

Agustín Cocola Gant, "El MACBA y su función en la marca Barcelona", Ciudad y territorio. Estudios Territoriales, XLI (159) (2009): 87
Ana Ávila, "Los viejos y los nuevos museos", in El sistema del arte en España, J.A. Ramírez et al. (Madrid: Cátedra, 2010).
Banksy, "Wall and Piece", (London: Random House, 2005)
Cedar Lewisohn, "Street art, the graffiti revolution", (London: Thames and Hudson, 2008)
Craig Castleman, "Getting up. Hacerse ver. El graffiti metropolitano en Nueva York", (Madrid: Capitán Swing, 2012)
David Thatcher, "Order maintenance reconsidered: moving beyond strong causal reasoning", The Journal of Criminal Law & Criminology, 94, 2, (2004): 381
George L. Kelling, James Q. Wilson, "Broken Windows. The police and neighborhood safety". The Atlantic, March 1, (1982)
Javier Abarca, "El postgraffiti, su escenario y sus raíces: graffiti, punk, skate y contrapublicidad" (Ph.D diss., Universidad Complutense, 2010)
Juan Antonio Ramírez, "¿Arte o delito? Los graffiti, entre la comisaría y la galería" in Arte y arquitectura en la época del capitalismo triunfante. Ed. Juan Antonio Ramírez (Madrid: Visor, 1992)
M. Sharon Jeanotte, "Singing alone? The contribution of cultural capital to social cohesión and sustanaible communities", The International Journal of Culture Policy, Vol. 9 (1), (2003): 35-49
Nancy Duxbury, "CulturalCitizenship and Community Indicator Projects: Aproaches and Challenges in the Local/Municipal Context", Canadian Cultural Observatory, (2005)
Rosalyn Deutsche, R., Cara Gendel Ryan, (1984) "The Fine Art of Gentrification", October [Published by The MIT Press], Vol. 31, Winter, (1984): 91-111.
Victoria de Elizagárate, "Comercio y ciudad. La misión del marketing de ciudades en el desarrollo de la competitividad del comercio urbano." Colección Mediterráneo económico. Vol. 11, (2007): 299

Manuel García y Ruiz van Hoben, Faculdade de Letras – Universidade de Lisboa

Art(s) in the City. Chronicles of a Spray Can

We can understand cities as a cultural object, which can be consumed in different ways in base of some cultural patterns. We present here how these different experience acts mediate on the conception and perception of the city and how urban art is affected by rules that are intimately related to this deciphering of the reality. We make a first approach to some of the urban art terminology and some of the constraints that writers have to confront on the exercise of their work.

cities, graffiti, acts of experience, urban consumer, homocontrol, heterocontrol

Mental town

You are in a big city. You are walking through one of the main streets of the city. Now, stop. Observe. What do you see? Apparently a simple exercise, however, lot of variables comes into play that affects our perception of "reality". Urban life is complex, as are the cities and the systems that shape them. Each city responds to different models of territorial organization and these are influenced by certain factors: whether natural (land adaptation and environmental factors such as rivers, cliffs, hills, etc.), or social (borders, temporary settlements, migration flows, etc.). Obviously, we did not find such an exact dichotomy in reality, with "social" factors being a sea of possibilities that alter and modify the organization and delimitation of the city. Urban planning must take into account the polyphony of these elements and be flexible, as the city is a being in constant change.

Michel de Certeau argued for a construction of reality from an active exercise, "the walk". In his book The Practice of Everyday Life he presents a way of reading the city, a way to consume from its praxis and usage. This influential author subverts the traditional idea that the ordinary citizen is a passive subject, a constant consumer unable to decide freely. He introduced the concept of strategy, which refers to the ability of an organization, institution or agency to manage, influence and lead a group of people under certain circumstances, prestablished and conventionalized; this would be the case of governments (regardless of reach), corporations and even associations. In contrast to this concept, he suggests the tactics that would refer to those forms in which citizens subvert the limits imposed and adapt their pattern of use or consumption. An example of a strategy, focused on the urban world, could be the formal design of the city: streets, crosswalks, vertical signals, etc. which set "maps". Behind them there are some decisions taken by an authority that promotes a series of practices, hoping that they are met and respected. On the other hand, citizens walk through the city the way they deem appropriate, not respecting the preset itineraries designed to meet such city. Thus creating their own "geography" formed on the basis of their own experience and desires. Citizens' experiences mediate their choices in different aspects of urban life. Continuing with the previous case, citizens will subconsciously choose a route to reach different destinations, then the sum of these pathways could be understood from a particular citizen as a mental city set. One of the great contributions of the architect and researcher Kevin Lynch is the notion of mental map. Although this concept already existed, it was developed and evolved in his work The Image Of The City, where he tried to figure out the dominant forms (elements) in the construction and articulation of the city in the memory of the citizens. This author delimited sensitive elements from the experience with volunteer participants who were required to draw a (their own) city sketch for a visitor who did not know the place. Five categories which we consider interesting to better understand urban design were identified: nodes, stable elements that due to attendance of people -or activities- bear a particular relevance such as subway stations and intermodal stations; limits, establish and differentiate areas; districts, where a certain homogeneity is perceived; roads, pathways or popular familiar communication-ways; landmarks, areas of high interest or high rate of recall for historical reasons, dimensions, design, etc. such as churches, monuments and parks. These categories seem to be recurring in creating a personal city, but are they perceived alike?

The Urban Consumer

We have used the term citizen so far to appoint any person who travels the city, but we believe that this term does not really fit with the reality of today. Many people in the cities do not have the status of "citizen", however, because of this they are denied the opportunity to build certain relations –deeper or superficial- towards the city. The term citizen refers to any person who is by birth or naturalization in possession of full rights and obligations, with respect to the place where they belong or where they live; therefore we find many people who do not meet those prerequisites on our streets. We can meet tourists in our cities who simply visit them and consume the goods and services they have to offer; we can meet with immigrants in the naturalization process, with limited rights and countless obligations; we can find illegal immigrants, the so-called paperless, who do not have rights, but are somehow subscribed to the obligations of the place... along with other variables this make us question the citizen term for those who build the city, not from a constructive perspective, but from a compositional perspective.

As we said earlier, we spoke about the Decerteurien tactics, which describe how individuals break strategic impositions set by institutions or agencies in the performance of their daily life, assuming that they are able to reinvent and adapt spaces for themselves. We see here that they become something more than a simple user, guided and with no decision, to turn into a consumer-creator with his own choice, able to discern what is better, more interesting and more convenient for them. The city, thus, is understood as a cultural element or cultural object to be consumed (and created) by a set of heterogeneous individuals whose uses and needs differ; but nevertheless maintaining closed relationships – in variable degrees - with a common physical and legal frames that dictates certain limits of action and reaction. Therefore, the city may be wholly or partially consumed, we mean that it can be more than walked -in Decerteurian terms-, because that would only describe some of the natures of the city. We understand as city the sum of natural offers and the sum of intangible assets that a specific place can offer to those who are traversing their perceptible perimeters. Here, elements that were described by Lynch to demarcate areas and establish boundaries are somehow able to differentiate the start and end of an urban area, based on experience and not on the strategic regulation.

The designation of urban consumer allows us to cover a wider range of options and also to set the different cities that make up the plural city. The city as a whole set of experiences (mental cities) of urban consumers will be referred to as Urban Polyhedron[1], because of its polyphony and multiple conception. For proper city management we see that we should include all target groups that circulate through it, regardless of their status or (un)regulated situation. These urban consumers have specific characteristics that define and individualise according to a fixed set of variables based on their emotional, legal, cultural and physical relationship with respect to where they are; by knowing them better, we could create strategies that could satisfy the needs of the people that "run" in the city.

In previous work we defined five types of acts of experience (2013:25), which give us the keys to better understand spatial geography based on usage and cultural practices of the people in our cities. These acts of experience refer to the articulation of the above variables in a given consumer, and are differentiated by the degree of participation that they manifest. Within these previous works we opted for an explanation and analysis of the city following a textual model in which the different parts fit as described by Lynch as part of a sintagmatic model, for this study we chose a less abstract and more focused approach in a traditional urban perspective. To this end, the macrostructural and microstructural categories will simply be considered as a set of signs (places and spaces). Acts of experience outlined below will allow us to understand the public who live in our cities and the needs that they may have.
At first we would find the Native Experience Act (NEA) where the consumer is fully aware of the sign system of the city, ie they know -or they are familiar- with all elements: compositional and organizational of the territory that set up the urban design. This individual demonstrates a thorough knowledge of the interpretive code (local culture) and the constraints of the place (laws). They are able to "commute" between spaces and places with full knowledge, although they are not aware of this situation. They know their role in the urban polyhedron even if they are not conscious of it.

Next would be the Guest Experience Act (GEA) which would refer to an urban consumer who does not know the sign system of the city. This type of consumer reads the urban system through comparisons, exclusions and value judgments in base of their own AEN. They are unable to fully understand the system but they do show interest in it. Because of their lack of familiarity and / or contact they proceed with superficial readings, nevertheless, they are able to identify common forms of urban consumption. Here we could mention, for example, an Asian tourist in a western city. The tourist ignores the language, culture, history, legal system, architecture, etc. however, they participate of the city as a consumer (cultural, goods and services...). They satisfy their cultural appetite through visiting different spaces, recognizing different places; they indulge their interests by tasting different cuisines, etc. but fail to see the place through the eyes of native consumer. Just watch and compare their cultural framework where shape is temporary. Their vision and participation in urban polyhedron is superficial. This tourist travels the city and after their stay, sometimes, the "experience" ends. It is also possible to pass to another level of urban consumption if they are introduced or they pass through a learning process (AEA).

The Biphasic Experience Act (BEA) presents a highly knowledgeable urban consumer with very similar skills to the ones presented by the native urban consumer in what we refer to as the signic decoding urban system. Their knowledge of the interpretive system and local constraints are excellent even though they are not native. They can function as locals but they will always keep their alien nature. This type of consumer has an important component of evaluation, because although they behave like a local, they compare their experience in contrast to their native cultural framework or NEA. We could say that they are individuals that commute between different urban experiences: physical, emotional, experimental etc. but tied to some references that are not native to the area. As an example, we might talk of Chinese residents in the city of Lisbon or the first generation of immigrants in any city. These residents are able to read and participate on the construction of the urban polyhedron, supplying different interventions: acting as locals or foreigners. They are involved on different scales of the urban life and are able to cope with perfect ease between communities and groups.

One of the most interesting is the Acquired Experience Act (AEA): the urban consumer intimately knows the sign system. Their relationship with the interpretive system and constraints is the same as a native. Here we could find a transited individual, ie someone who has been initiated, educated and trained in a liminal urban context. Unlike BEA these individuals neither judge, nor compare, they just switch between acts of experience, according to the time and situation. They are able to enjoy the urban act equally as a foreigner and as a local. We could find this situation in the first generation of translocated consumers, or young dislocated individuals who were introduced in other urban universes at an early age, such as children of immigrants (second generation). These individuals are able to commute between acts of experience by obtaining and reaching balance of an equal benefit.

The difference between BEA and AEA appears to be in a situation of a feeling of belonging. Individuals feel different degrees of belonging according to the relationship and the settlement of other subjects who share their NEA in the area and with whom they establish deeper or superficial relationships. In this situation we could detach the construction of the cultural and urban alien areas inside of the general urban picture. In other words, we could find other foreign cities within our cities. To quote one case, we could reference the different China Towns around the world where, upon entering, we quickly realize that we crossed an urban and cultural border, within a particular city.

Similarly, we could find an urban consumer who is never present, ie someone who knows the sign system of the city, the cultural system and the limitations as a resident but who has never established direct contact with the place. The so-called Virtual Experience Act (VEA) occurs in situations in which individuals learn and internally incorporate into their persona, as an urban consumer, compositional elements and cultural traits of a place that is beyond their physical contact. We could talk about those people that have "walk" through a city via computer simulation, or those who have memorized the city before their -eventual- arrival to the place, such as military or individuals who have been trained through video games.

The urban consumer therefore is highly pluriform. We could even expand the urban experience acts to regional, national, transnational, etc. experience acts. In this type of spatial jumps we would find common points that would increase to a larger scale. These jumps also denote different degrees of subject involvement. An individual could read a country in accordance with national and local basis, in the same way that an individual reads two different cities. This cultural and spatial expansion would still be more than a rise or distancing urban act.

Urban Art

Knowing the people who walk in our streets, knowing how these people manage to understand the world around them and how they create in base of their emotions, their cultures, their beliefs... we can start talking about street art as a reflection of an urban consciousness.

Before starting we should ask the question, what is art? It is a question that many have attempted to answer but that seems to have an unclear definition. For some "art" is in relation to an idea of "aesthetics", of what is beautiful; for others it is in relation to a concept of "know-how" or technical knowledge; this difference is reflected in the popular assessment of the pieces exhibited in museums and galleries. The dichotomy between ars-artis in latin, meaning on one side the concept of creation and on the other side the concept of work, has led to a clear conception of artistic activity, whose effects move in the same evaluation of the pieces.

Nowadays, we talk about arts. The definition of which may also be inherited from the past but is no longer applicable in our world today. When speaking of urban art we find very different types of art, referring to different artistic natures. Here are some concepts that we consider as important. There have been several attempts to categorize public art. The most prominent grouping encompasses works, typically modernist, abstract sculptures that have been placed outdoors to decorate the plazas fronting governmental or corporate buildings. (Waclawek, 2005: 66)

The above definition refers to the so-called plop art, a common trend that projects the occupation of available spaces by pieces of art, of varying cultural value. Such pieces serve as a representative function, sometimes they are a metaphor of the institution that raises them, and other times they are a merely decorative form that fills space. Those pieces may be present, as the author tells us, in public and private spaces, with varying visibility and visitability.

Then we find a new category called art-in-the-public-interest, which introduces a management or cultural policy that seems highly interesting because of the authority granted (choice) to the urban consumer. These pieces respond to the call of public or private institutions for projects to elicit the public participation of the resident[2] urban consumers. Thus giving them the ability to choose, or participate in the election of the pieces to be lifted into public space, and even sometimes in private spaces (pieces in foundations, private gardens open to the public, etc.). Here, the participatory effect of choice creates an illusion of true democratization of space and art. We must not forget that the institution that promotes the action has the last word, creating a paradox of authority between the parties.

Within urban art we could find heritage-art. This would be understandable as the set of pieces that have come down to us as a legacy of earlier times. They might be equestrian statues, monuments, fountains, etc. but always respond to a historical meaning and their value within a given context. These pieces are usually encompassed in property records and are generally included in tourists' itineraries, and are protected by public authorities, as they are points of public interest.

These definitions lead us to talk about art on display, which can be public or private depending on the location of the pieces and the regulations that control its visibility and visitability. We understand, as public art on display, those pieces that are easily accessible, free to consume, and have good visibility for the urban consumers. Those whose consumption would have -implicit or explicit- economic or spatial constraint (a private garden, payment of tickets...) would come to be called private art on display.

We prefer the term art on display, which would transform the city into a museum of magna dimensions. The act of circulating in the city becomes the act of consuming art, of deciphering the passions that lurk around every corner, admiring the history and soaking up the culture. The art on display describes all those pieces that are within sight of the urban consumer and this would include graffiti as an available visual and artistic item in town. For many, graffiti is criticized and not considered as art. It responds to a double nature: firstly evoking elements of design (art), then communication elements reminiscent to advertising (text-claims). Here we might ask whether the mere fact of using artistic elements and concepts elevates graffiti as "art". In the same way, and due to its communicational components, we wonder if it should be called "information". In 2008, the Tate Gallery in London and in 2009 the Cartier Foundation in Paris transported this "art of making" to the showrooms, raising this form of painting the formal status of "art". The institutionalization of graffiti-art, therefore, has begun. With this rise begins its study; not only from an anthropological perspective -somehow associated to studies on urban tribes- but as a form of art with styles, techniques and exclusive ways of doing.

The current graffiti, known as post-graffiti, is successor to the hip-hop tradition, but today is not restricted to any particular social or identity group. There are many writers (graffiti artist) who come from social and identity groups, who are not traditionally associated with this urban "art of the spray", as a consequence of certain openness to professionals coming from the faculties of fine arts, academies of design and advertising agencies, among others. This phenomenon of intergroup acculturation allows us to imagine how techniques from one discipline intersect with each other to enrich the design in the streets, making it not only an art but a form of dialogue.

Traditionally, the process of learning the techniques of spray was given by the adscription of an amateur writer in an already consolidated group (crew) in which, typically, one or more senior members share their knowledge and exercise the role of leader. Today, with the height of new technologies many writers learn these techniques through the mass media, including video tutorials available on the internet. Learning techniques can also come from the aforementioned schools, workshops organized by public government bodies, private schools and even by way of meetings or events of different sizes, where curious and uninitiated amateurs can contact "masters" and develop a network.

In general, it all starts with the tag. Then, works evolve into more complicated designs, more elaborate patterns, which lead to research; of surfaces to cover, time and materials to be used, among other constraints. But, it is not all spray-graffiti, we could also find yarn-graffiti, which consists of covering different surfaces with complex webs of tricot, among other knitting techniques. We could find areas that have been seeded with plants to create new shapes with sufficient capacity to communicate in what is called guerrilla gardening. We could say that under the umbrella term urban graffiti art, an innumerable set of techniques and art forms are reunited. They have common elements but they are all different; on the one hand, they are considered as illegal (affecting the property of others with no permission) and on the other hand they have the sufficient expressive and aesthetic capacity to draw the attention of urban consumer in performing their daily activities.

Control of Graffiti Activity

It is hard to get known in a city as a graffiti artist. It is difficult due to the overabundance of visual impacts that urban consumers receive daily. Street art must fight against advertising, traditional forms of urban art; against time and against the cleanups. Graffiti is ephemeral; it is done to last a short time. During this short lifespan they should have a real impact, both within the graffiti artist community, and more broadly, into the stroller consumer. It all starts with the tag, as mentioned; an amateur must sow the city with his signature. Amateurs must raise their notoriety as a prolific artist, being present in all possible corners. They must build a name for themselves. Here the local community, those already initiated into the art of graffiti, can choose -or not- accept the candidate. In case of acceptance, the amateur can get a place in the streets without the fear of being erased, or overwritten (covered by other pieces by other writers). This becomes a real competition to be seen, a form of struggle to ensure the best places to showcase their talent and work. Becoming a King of graffiti is difficult, it is not enough to be a good artist, other factors also come into play such as notoriety, respect, etc.

We found that the activity of the spray art is heavily regulated. On one hand we would find outside elements in the production of works that regulate its creation, implemented by institutions or government regulators; on the other hand we would find other internal control systems that interact and restrict its execution. We could say that this ephemeral art is under strict control. At first we should talk about self-control, that is, the ability of an artist to work within a set of guidelines or standard prescribed within their community and be able to add their own personal flair. Within these guidelines we find the imposition of respect to other artists (local or international); acceptance of a certain hierarchy in base of experience or the role performed within the community; the use of available spots, and in some cases, even the use of certain colors. This would be the more personal control of artistic activity, since it depends only on the artists themselves (ethics); they may choose to comply with the rules or act freely, knowing in advance the impact that these decisions may have amongst each other (except for the community, marginalization...). The second level of control could be called homocontrol. This refers to the exercise of control a collective of artists performed on the production of pieces in a given location. We can talk about a certain spirit of an urban artists guild where through influential relationships and personal relationships the best practices of graffiti are managed. While the breadth and strengths of these groups of homocontrol are questioned, they are certainly present in every city and they practice different forms of censorship on the participants who do not accept local norms. We could see this type of action, for example, applied to an artist who decided to work on a wall independently and completely disengaged from the local "norm". Any member of the "guild" in their duty of correction, and with intent to remind to the artist how to work in the area, could (must) overwrite the work with another piece, or sometimes make alterations or simply erase it. The initial artist, thus, receives a notice, which may be frequently repeated as punishment, to the point that their paintings would never be displayed. While this seems extreme, it is rare for a case to reach such heights. Occasionally, if the piece does not follow local standards, because the name of the artist or the value and quality of the piece, it may receive a pardon, or may simply be welcomed as an addition to the city museum, influencing post local creation.

Finally, we should mention heterocontrol. This form of control is external to the writers' community, and is marked by the bodies of institutional control. The heterocontrol, therefore, include all legal or governing codes that regulate the artistic activity in the street. In most Western countries there is no clear direction on the practice of graffiti, although the vast majority is an offense or an attack on the property of a third party. Generally, we see that local governments are usually those who end up dictating the best practices as forms of prevention, cleanup and recovery of the affected areas. The heterocontrol is the most feared by urban artists, resulting in the formal prohibition of the artistic activity. Those who are caught in the exercise thereof may suffer very severe penalties, depending on the damage caused and charges against them. Overall, graffiti is reported as vandalism but it may be raised as destruction or damageability of public or private property; it may even be considered as assault on identity or violation of private property. Penalties vary and there is no unity, so we detect a situation of ambiguity and lack of control within their own legal system. This situation is mediated, in part, under the premise of freedom of expression and right of manifestation of the inhabitants of a place.Graffiti meets an illegal nature, when practiced "spontaneously" on a surface without the express consent of an owner, but we may find some exceptions such as the professionalized graffiti. In contrast to the sauvage graffiti of which we were speaking, we can also find works relating to a contract for the provision of services, where a homeowner requests the work of a writer. The owner (recruiter) informs the artist of the purposes for which they want the work, ensuring that they complies with all local regulations. The artist (service provider) after the briefing would be responsible for the execution of the service after acceptance of the sketch or suggestions submitted to the owner. For this work, the artist would be paid based on the difficulty of implementation, time spent, materials, etc. to be agreed between respective parties. A "recruiter" can also be a public or private entity that wants to include specific aspects to better approach a specific audience, enhance their brand, corporate image, with a new target group, etc. by exercising this type of pieces. On the other hand we have cases like the GAU (Urban Art Gallery of Lisbon), in which local governance become aware of the reality of graffiti, its positive opportunities and negative impacts and they decided to promote good practices in order to avoid vandalism through institutionalized urban art. The Department of Cultural Heritage of the Municipal Chamber of Lisbon promotes academic research in reference to urban art in its broadest sense; as much as it works for the greater visibility of these artistic forms in the street, always respecting rules that guarantee respect for the property of third parties. They also have undertaken an excellent job of cataloging pieces and promoting training actions such as workshops or public seminars. Institutionalization of urban art is seen as a way to prevent the vandalism and deterioration of public space. An optimistic vision that has drawn the attention of the whole world turning the Portuguese capital into one of the foci of creation and reinvention of urban space and urban design and culture.

Among the many projects undertaken by this department we find the implementation of zones of free-style execution. Located on the Calçada da Gloria, in the heart of the city, we find a series of walls where the training, implementation and achievement of urban pieces are accepted freely and legally. This initiative allows artists, both amateurs and experienced, to work in the knowledge of security, and it offers the possibility of being publicly viewed. Also in the vicinity, we can find large panels where national and international artists who are invited, and scheduled, to perform their works referring to a specific topic or agenda. This initiative has managed to stabilize prominent names as well as open dialogue with other major graffiti artists, with the street acting as a gallery or museum, where all urban consumers can see a selection of high quality pieces for free. Similarly, this selection may have influenced styles, formats and themes for many other artists, both local and visitors. It is a form of creation and elevation of urban art (institutionalized) at the height of art, a way to break taboos and educate the public. One other project that caught our attention is the "Reciclar o Olhar" (Recycle the look), which participated in the concept of art-in-the-public-interest. Pieces forming this project are submitted for evaluation, as concepts by individuals who want to perform or set a public installation, in other words are interventions from the people living in the city. Final pieces are elected by public vote and are legally produced and displayed in glass containers scattered throughout the city. These containers are pre-selected and are included in the strategic design of the space, promoting the visibility of urban art in all areas of the city.

Verb-iconic Geography

The urban consumer, regardless of their type, their way of understanding or filtering of the world, can compose a verb-iconic map from capturing pieces of urban art. As is the case with advertising, urban art must fight for the attention of the urban consumer since many visual stimuli reach each individual daily, therefore the positioning of the pieces is very important.

Places are disputed between local artists as we explained above, and only the best, the most daring sometimes, receives the attention of the urban consumer. A graffiti, a piece of urban art, is seen a few minutes; it might be removed and never been seen again, but for the short time it has been exposed it may have produced thousands of impacts with a high rate of recall in a certain population. Also, they may have managed to be photographed, immortalized and very likely spread on the internet, becoming viral thus gaining notoriety and winning the battle of its ephemeral nature. Artists should be familiar with the best places to exhibit their work. No wonder that many are trained in specialized areas, such as in the premises of the GAU, or in liminal places where surveillance and heterocontrol force is less noticeable, before they leap into mainstream space. Liminal spaces are undoubtedly true urban schools and art museums. They are places within the city boundaries, not frequented by the general population and generally in between processes of change. We understand liminal places as all those that respond to a process between states but do not fall into marginalization. Bridges, abandoned buildings, factories etc. are examples of the liminal spaces that urban artists use while developing their skills.

We also appreciate that the city may have zones of saturation. We understand these areas as hot spots where urban-graffiti-works mainly develops intensely. Usually given by proximity to settlements of depressed populations, where heterocontrol forces are not present or they seem to be almost non-existent. Artists, therefore, have easy access to large surfaces and also enough time for the production of their works. In this type of area native authors tend to flourish with motivation to report a situation, which they judge as balanced, or fair. We find equally low saturation areas in the city, which calls to our attention that they generally correspond to places with greater vigilance, or places with a more pronounced foot-traffic. Saturation zones may be those areas that due to high visibility become targets of attention. They are easily visible places that effortlessly catch the attention of the urban consumer. They would compete with advertising panels, though often attacked (adbusting), which ends with the victor holding pieces of local authors (usually young) who try to make a name for themselves in the public space. Recently, our attention goes to the capacity of urban art turning liminal places into part of the mainstream space. Graffiti attracts a new crowd of onlookers and fans of this type of pop art, subverting the aforementioned space (liminal) into a place of pilgrimage, helping to reactivate unfrequented places and promoting new economic, touristic flows and revaluing the real estate.

Urban Arts and Urban Consumers

Urban consumers are a challenge for public and private management as they are plural. It is difficult to foresee all the needs they may require and even more difficult to imagine their reactions to any decision concerning them. Many of these reactions can see them materialized in associative movements or protest marches. The plurality of approaches and interests makes difficult to satisfy everyone. For a visitor (VEA), a fully decorated building with graffiti may be an attraction that would motivate them to return to town; the same building may be offensive to a native consumer, seeing an element of his past invaded or attacked. Street art by its physical adhesion to urban surfaces and their direct contact with the past, raises both passions and misgivings. Here is where the institutionalization of urban art is imposed. Education and appropriateness of messages are composed, as essential, in such situations where obscene messages, or political, etc. may offend the sensibilities of other consumers, raising unexpected movements. Programming and designing strategies is imposed as a step to be taken by all municipalities opting for a model that helps the evolution and education of this art, rather than oppressors models that subscribes zero tolerance. Similarly, we advocate urban art as a vehicle for bringing together consumers, a way of approaching others and learning from their experiences and their understanding of the city. Certainly, art can be used as a facilitator between cultures and can help build bridges of mutual understanding as we have seen on the actions taken in the Lisboan neighborhoods of Mouraria and Graça. Now, open your eyes. What do you see?

Notes and References

1 García y Ruiz, M. (2013). Steps Towards an Urban Speech. Unpublished Master, Universidade de Lisboa, Lisbon.
2 The resident urban consumer refers to those consumers whose usual location is in a particular place and with whom they maintain high participation rates.
Associação Renovar a Mouraria. (2013). renovaramouraria.pt. Retrieved 08/09/2013, from http://www.renovaramouraria.pt/
Camara Municipal de Lisboa. (2012). GAU - Galeria de Arte Urbana. Retrieved 23/03/13, from http://galeriaurbana.com.pt/
Campos, R. M. d. O., Spinelli, L., & Mubi Brighenti, A. (2011). Uma cidade de imagens : produções e consumos visuais em meio urbano. Lisboa: Mundos Sociais.
Certeau, M. d., Giard, L., Mayol, P., & Pescador, A. (2010). La invención de lo cotidiano (A. Pescador, Trans. 1a ed.). México, D.F.: Universidad Iberoamericana Instituto Tecnológico y de Estudios Superiores de Occidente.
Chandès, H., & contemporain, F. C. p. l. a. (2009). Né dans la rue, graffiti [exposition, Paris, Fondation Cartier pour l'art contemporain, 7 juillet-29 novembre 2009]. Paris: Fondation Cartier pour l'art contemporain.
Dicks, B. (2004). Culture on display the production of contemporary visitability. Berkshire, England: Open University Press.
García y Ruiz, M. (2013). Steps Towards an Urban Speech. Unpublished Master, Universidade de Lisboa, Lisbon.
Heinich, N. (2004). La sociologie de l'art (Nouv. éd. ed.). Paris: Éd. la Découverte.
Lynch, K. (1960). The image of the city. Cambridge Mass.: Technology Press.
Raven, A. (1989). Art in the public interest. Ann Arbor: UMI Research Press.
Rodríguez, R., & Mora, K. (2002). Frankenstein y el cirujano plástico una guía multimedia de semiótica de la publicidad, Textos docentes / Universidad de Alicante.
Tate. (2008). Urban Art Exhibition : 23 May – 25 August 2008. Retrieved 13/06/2013, from http://www.tate.org.uk/whats-on/tate-modern/exhibition/street-art
Waclawek, A. (2011). Graffiti and street art. New York, NY: Thames & Hudson, Inc.

Maria do Mar Fazenda, PhD Artistic Studies – Art and Mediations, Faculty of Social Sciences and Humanities (FCSH)/NOVA University (UNL) mar.fazenda@gmail.com

Urban Acupuncture,
artistic interventions in a deactivated shop window in Lisbon

Applying the term Urban Acupuncture, borrowed from social and environmental theories, to an ongoing project that uses a shop window of an insolvent shop as an art gallery. This program of exhibitions tackles a symptom of the financial crisis that is well inscribed in the city. For one year, an artist is invited each month to occupy this deactivated space-in-between of a Lisbon street. Activating what is no longer run strictly by commercial interests; punctuating the street with small-scale gestures, each artist's contribution participates in the city's renewal as well as engaging a wider social, political and aesthetic urban context.

City, Artistic Urban Intervention, Urban Acupuncture

Introduction

If we dismantle the conference's title, Lisbon Street Art & Urban Creativity, we get the set of keywords: Street; Art; Urban; Creativity. By adjoining and pairing them, we get the opposites: Street/Art; Urban/Creativity. From those we produce the broader dichotomies: Public/Private; Anonymous/Personal. During the last century, artistic interventions in the urban context have permeated these pairs of distinctive realms with streams of representation and alterity. Those opposites no longer represent paradoxes. Based on this reassessment of the concepts in question, this paper aims to map artistic intervention in the city - Rewriting the city -, identify its main driving impulses and typologies of intervention - Reenacting the city - in order to provide context - Responding to the city - for the exhibition series in a deactivated shop window in Lisbon, organized by Arte Ilimitada, an art school that operates in the same building as the shop window/gallery. A Montra [The Shop Window] located at Calçada da Estrela, a street in downtown Lisbon, is occupied, each month, by an artist who produces a specific art piece for that location of particular characteristics; As it is a device that favors the observation of the pieces through a window, by passers-by, at any time of the day or night, the project will function as a subtle action of intervention in the city - Repairing the city -, creating an urban rumor that comments and touches pins up . The project appears as a consequence of the current economic situation, as described in the first article about the project, published in the Ipsílon supplement of Público newspaper, in October 2013:

> *A vacant window shop as an art gallery*
>
> *They are everywhere, in downtown Lisbon and throughout the country: dark, empty and covered with dust, or closed up with paper and cardboard. They gradually appear, faster by the day. A sort of void in the life of neighborhoods that shocks us at first, and whose presence (actually the trace of an absence...) we have become accustomed to ignore.* [1]

This paper proposes to explore the idea that perceiving the urgent symptoms of the current crisis in the urban landscape and intervening on those specific tense spots corresponds to a gesture of renewal and repair of a certain condition. A practice similar to that defined in urbanism as Urban Acupuncture.

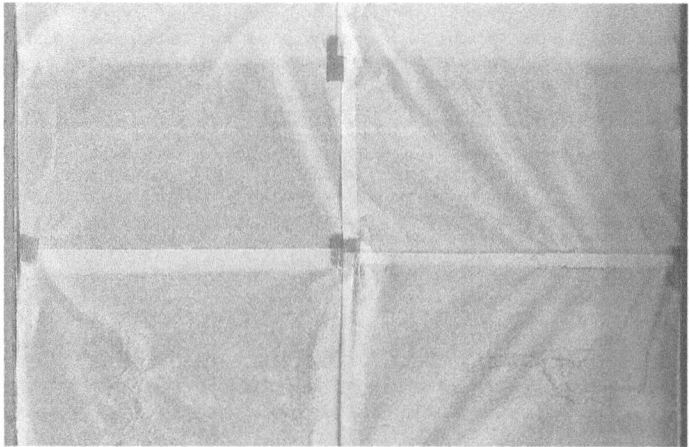

Fig. 1: Luisa Cunha, I'll be Back, 2013. Photograph on satin paper on PVC. 137 x 197cm. First intervention for the A Montra project in October 2013. Courtesy of Arte Ilimitada.

Rewriting the city: Cities of Affection, some references of their expression[2]

The contemporary artist lives, works and maneuvers in cities. Since Modernity, the artist's encounter with urban territory is a source for creative expression. Artistic practices have been inscribing their own map into urban contexts. A map that overlaps the pre-existent geography, and unfurls the original map into multiple images of thought. A possible historical outline of an interpretation of the city is anchored in and generated from the figure of the Flâneur set up by Charles Baudelaire in Le Peintre de la Vie Moderne (1863) and later reprised by Walter Benjamin (the romantic vision) and by Georg Simmel (the man in the crowd). In 1913, the Futurist painters Mayakovsky and Burliuk strolled around the streets of Saint Petersburg dressed in vibrant colours to promote their revolutionary theatre productions. In 1921, Tristan Tzara and Paul Éluard began a series of expeditions into areas of Paris that were unknown, little frequented or "with no reason to exist". In 1954, Guy Debord coins the term Psychogeography, to designate the poetics of urban drifting as a strategy for incorporating a new experience of urban space supported by constructed situations.

During the military dictatorship regime, Brazilian artist Hélio Oiticica (b.1937; d.1980, Rio de Janeiro, Brazil) developed his artistic practice based on the art-life dialectic. It is within the "experimental exercise of freedom" that Oiticica moves to the Morro da Mangueira (one of the first slums of Rio de Janeiro) in the 1960s, where he develops a series of works out of living in, experiencing and interacting with that community. One of the impulses that drove Oiticica's work was to understand how that struggling, precarious and jagged "grey area" could survive and still overcome the geographical, social and political representation that was attributed to it. Samba, the rhythm and expression of the body as interruption/suspension/encounter with life, was the vehicle of energy that Oiticica appropriated for his oeuvre. The capes, flags or banners that the artist named as "Parangolés" were activated by those wearing them and by the free movement of those dancing. It was in the movement of discovering their "skin" that each revealed the colors, textures and language: I Incorporate Revolt; From adversity we live; I am possessed; We are starving: are some of the sayings in the parangolés. In 1965, between the modernist struts of the architecture of the Rio de Janeiro Museum of Modern Art (MAM), Oiticica presented "Parangolé" as a performance in collaboration with the Mangueira Samba group: moving worlds, combining ways of being, causing a reorganization of the social space.

In the turn of the 60s to the 70s, the Site-Specific practice, particularly strong in the New York art scene, led artists to move from inside the galleries or establishment to the streets (Richard Serra), the countryside (Walter de Maria) or to the frontier territory in between (Robert Smithson). The intent of working in a different scale, with different materials and from other contingencies takes place alongside the city's own transformation; namely, it is in this period that new lifestyles, artists and galleries occupy certain areas of New York, such as SoHo and Chelsea that would later be targeted by tremendous real estate speculation. It was within this urban dynamic that Gordon Matta-Clark (b. 1943; d. 1978, New York, U.S.A.) dropped out of Architecture school to develop an artistic practice around what he called Anarchitecture. Along with the drawings-cutouts-interventions in architectural structures, for which he became known in his short career, Matta-Clark produced a series of film-essays on the urban experience, dealing with different political arenas, such as ecology, social engagement or economic criticism, towards a presentation of an alternative way of living within the urban context. "Tree Dance" (1971) records the first performative action triggered by Matta-Clark, where a number of people are invited to climb trees and occupy mesh nests; of the various actions that took place in the difficult areas of Brooklyn we can cite "Fire Child" (1971) or "Roast Pig" (1971) where the artist would work in the abandoned streets populated by homeless people, drug addicts, or other displaced people of the city; the distribution of oxygen in the streets of Manhattan in "Fresh Air" (1972); the witnessing of life in the restaurant that Matt-Clark opened along with other artists in "Food" (1973); the recording of a Keatonesque gag in "Clockshower" (1974), in which the artist climbed a public clock tower and showered; or the recent archaeology of cities' undergrounds "Substrait (Underground Dailies)" (1976) filmed in New York and "Paris Sous-Sols" (1977) filmed in Paris, while he had been working on the "Conical Intersection" piece at the Centre Georges Pompidou construction site. The Centre also marks a new era in Parisian urbanism. Finally, "Office Baroque" (1977) documents his last project, conducted in Antwerp, in a building located in a transitional area of occupation of retail commerce by an area of touristic interest (known today as gentrification).

In 1987, Belgian artist Francis Alÿs (b. 1959, Antwerp, Belgium) moved to Mexico City as an architect. However, the living conditions in that megalopolis showed Alÿs that architecture was not an sufficiently effective instrument for socio-political intervention. He has since been devoted to research on the articulation of the body in the complex and conflictual urban context of Mexico City, from which resulted the walk as his main artistic device.

"The Collector" (1991) is the first action made public by the artist: for a period of time, Alÿs walked the streets of Mexico City, pulling a toy cart made of recycled materials. Inside was a magnet that drew every metallic debris left along the route, and the stroll was complete when the dog was completely covered with urban debris. It invokes the figure of the "Rag picker", fundamental in Benjamin's own understanding of the flâneur and his interaction with the city. In 1994 Alÿs redid this piece for the Havana Biennial but in the streets of Havana the artist replaced the toy with his shoes covered in magnets. The stroll, or the act of strolling, was consubstantiated into a subtle strategy for observing, analyzing and intervening in urban realities. Alÿs, who simultaneously developed other forms of expression, has been conducting several strolls in different urban identities. Through the astute reading of a certain place, the artist draws an intervention itinerary that results in a critical analysis - to which he adds an intelligent sense of humor - of the urban environment in question. In "The Leak" (1996) he went across the neighborhoods of São Paulo, leaking a can of blue paint; "Narcotourism" (1996) consisted of walks through Copenhagen during the course of seven days, each day under the influence of a different drug; in "Paradox of Practice" (1997) the artist pushed a large block of ice along the streets of Mexico City between 9:15 AM and 6:47 PM, the time at which the block of ice had completely melted; In "The Loser/The Winner" (1998) he took a walk in the city of Stockholm wearing a woolen sweater that would unstitch as the body travelled across the city; "Reenactment" (2000) witnesses Alÿs' stroll across the streets of Mexico City holding a gun, being arrested twelve minutes after his itinerary began; in "Sometimes doing something poetic can become political and sometimes doing something political can become poetic"(2004) the artist moved along the Gaza Strip (Palestine-Israel) leaking/drawing a green paint line on the asphalt across both territories. Whether it is through the will of introducing poetry into the street life experience (Hélio Oiticica), the intention of disturbing the texture, or the text, of a city (Gordon Matta-Clark), the delimitation of sensible territories in the fragile map of urban spaces (Francis Alÿs), the affective interpretation of the city contributes to its reading while simultaneously rewriting it.

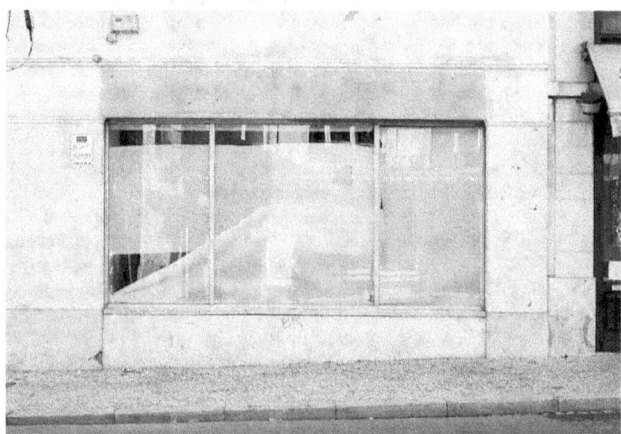

Fig. 2: Catarina Botelho, Inventário, 2013. 24 ink jet prints on cotton paper, 22,5x30cm (each photograph). Intervention for the A Montra project in December 2013. Courtesy of the Artist.

Re-enacting the city: Passages, spaces of transformation

Nowadays, neither is the Street is totally Public nor is Art ever Private – the sense of Urban has become an agent as well as a place of hospitality where an economy of affections and tensions interact. As we have said before, there is a well defined genealogy of the inscription of the relation between the individual and the urban that is, in the European context, anchored in the literary figure of the Flâneur, as activated by Benjamin through his own experience in the city of Paris, found both in the shock with Modernity – "Paris – Capital of the Nineteenth Century" or adopting the vision of the angel of history that looks at the ruins of his past in Berlin – "One-Way Street". Within the field of Visuality, the social construct of the visual, we find photographer Eugène Atget, Benjamin's contemporary, and his immense documental archive of the urban transformations of the turning siècle, with Baron Haussmann's redrawing of the city of Paris. Atget that did not consider himself a visual artist but a technician (a photographer) who worked for other artists: he would sell his pictures of Parisian houses, interiors, streets, people, etc., to painters who would work from them. It was not until the publication, on the cover of the ultimate Surrealist magazine of the time, of a portrait of a group of people in a square in Paris observing an eclipse, that a re-evaluation of his work would actually occur, along with the rescue, by Man Ray, of the massive photographic archive from Atget's abandoned studio. In an intimate dialogue with literature, it is also not surprising to find in André Breton's novels, such as Nadja or L'Amour fou, the chance encounter with poetic situations in the quotidian causality of the urban experience, like the ones registered in Atget's pictures of the fortifications of Paris: the laminar frontier between the city and the village, the marking division between the centre and periphery and its inhabitants – the zoniers as they were called. Also rich in possible social associations and readings is his series of photographs of different street professions, such as the Rag picker, the Hat seller or the Prostitute that would occupy a position in between the inside and outside. Such a state of "in-betweeness" would gain its corpus in the shop window, another device and symptom of Modernity well documented by Atget: "Hats, umbrellas, gloves, and cloth mantles were displayed in shop windows and vitrines as if they were antiquated objects in a natural history museum"(Friedberg, 1993)[3]. It was also absorbed by Benjamin's major and unfinished project Passagenwerk, about the then recent commercial architectural project, the Parisian Arcades - also part of the Haussmann's urban reconfiguration of Paris. The same streets where the 'Mai 68' would take place, reenacting the city itself by intense student and popular political demonstrations and organizations, within the framework of Psychogeography, delineated some years before by the Situationist International. After an emotional and conceptual divorce from the Situationists, Henri Lefebvre proposes in his urban study La Production de l'espace (1974) the favoring of space over time in three dimensions: Social practices (bureaucratic and power spaces), the representation of space (the social organization of space) and the space of representation (space of habitation, imagination and experience). All these forms of representation are interconnected and relate to the development of the city, and by consequence or intercorrelation, to creative and intellectual production. Lefebvre synthesizes his theory in the social appropriation of space, where each individual assigns their own meaning to space. Between individuality and the notion of belonging to a whole; the living organism of the city, language and thought develops in a constant exchange. Each inhabitant finds a meaning and a place for their existence in the interchange of the various spaces that produce the city.

In these two artistic gestures of rewriting and reenacting the cities, there seems to be a common driving force: urban transformation and the impulse to document it (e.g. Haussmann's new Paris by Atget), react to it (e.g. the gentrification process of NYC by Matta-Clark) and comment on it (e.g. the Palestinian/Israeli conflict by Alÿs). It is in the streets of these urban contexts in transformation that artists inscribe their commentary, frequently by appropriating "grey areas" of the city (the "margins" of the city, abandoned buildings, empty sites, common land, etc.); Turning visible what had become invisible – by neglect or from various impasses of bureaucratic, financial, historical or social nature – and with this shift producing a new space of representation.

In the specific context of the art project A Montra [The Shop Window], the "void" in the city that is being discussed is an insolvent shop, more precisely its window. "The new life of a Lisbon shop", as it has been described in the magazine Time Out Lisboa[4], "if commerce is dying, then let it be art to take its place [...] a new meaning for 'window shopping', just go to Calçada da Estrela." Recalling the moment when commodity culture was still not an actual estrangement within the city, as in the first Paris arcade (1780s), and constituted a social arena for new figures of representation to play out. One century later the investment of the shop window display headed a democratic impact in society. As in A Montra's interventions, it is about catching the eyes of passers-by, in this case drawing attention to a symptom of our society's problems. On the first intervention by Luisa Cunha (Fig.1), a photograph of a deactivated window shop covered with papers, which coincided dimensionally with the shop window in Calçada da Estrela: "During the day the window seems to merge with the other dying shops... at night it becomes a lightbox" (Matos, 2013). The art critic was unaware of Miguel Palma's forthcoming intervention in A Montra where he used a lightbox, referencing the medical device used to analyze x-rays (Fig. 5). The conversion of the "illusion window" from a commodity to an artistic space is highlighted by the transformation of the display into a lightbox.

The space of the shop window has been used exhaustively by artists, resorting mainly to two approaches: 1) as an approximation of the museum vitrine, which defined the modern device of display and visibility; 2) as a form of statement about or criticism of consumption society. This kind of art display demands another genealogy, that will not be addressed here, but a signal of its pertinence is the anthology of essays edited by John C. Welchman[5], The Sculpture and the Vitrine, that dedicates a chapter to this specific vitrine – the shop window – from which we quote a fragment of the art history and theoretical map that it is followed in the study:

> The [exam of] some of the points of origin of the vitrine and the various relations it brokers with sculpture, first in the Wunderkammer and cabinet of curiosities and then in dialog with the development of glazed architecture beginning with Paxton's Crystal Palace (1851) [...] offers close discussions of the role of the vitrine and shop window in the rise of commodity culture and their apposition with Constructivist design in the work of Frederick Kiesler; as well as original readings of the use of vitrines in Surrealism and Fluxus, and in work by Joseph Beuys, Paul Thek, Claes Oldenburg and his collaborators, Jeff Koons, Mike Kelley, Dan Graham, Vito Acconci, Damien Hirst and Josephine Meckseper, among others. Sculpture and the Vitrine also raises key questions about the nature and implications of vitrinous space, including its fronts onto desire and the spectacle; transparency and legibility; and onto ideas and practices associated with the archive: collecting, preserving and ordering.

On what concerns this paper - A Montra and its ongoing program of site specific artistic interventions - different key elements of this genealogy come into play, that will be mapped out in the following section. A Montra is taken by its formal characteristics (enclosed space, transparent, reflector, etc.) both as a vitrinous space and as a commodity culture display device par excellence – that tells a story that starts in the Wunderkammer and follows its implications onto desire and the spectacle up to the Cinema experience. These approaches, proportionally relevant to each of the different works presented at A Montra, seem to merge and produce another layer of discussion, as the vitrinous space of a shop that no longer produces or reclaims consumption is used. This has so far been most directly addressed by Fernando J. Ribeiro's intervention (Fig.3). "A Montra project reminds us of the social, cultural and economic importance of shops in a city, and of the void that can be found in a scenario of daily bankruptcies"[6], as art critic Miguel Matos would rephrase in a second article on the project in Time Out Lisboa. This art project, grown out of the specific urban context where it happens, revises the concept of urban intervention, as it creates an idea of a counter-shop window, that more than trying to catch our eye and depend on our mobility, asks for a participative position in the city (as well as one of citizenship).

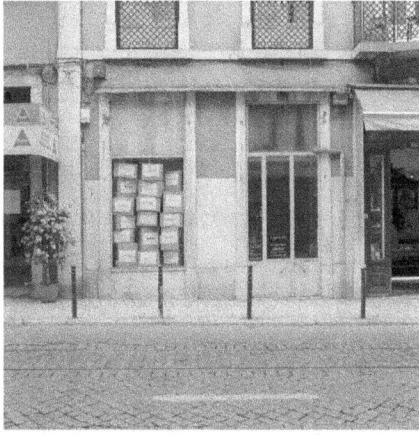

Fig. 3: Fernando J. Ribeiro, Untitled (Thank You, Danke, Xie Xie), 2013. Card boxes, paper. Variable dimensions. Intervention for the A Montra project in November, 2013. Courtesy of Arte Ilimitada.

Responding to the City: Artistic interventions in a deactivated shop window in Lisbon

The Belgian (former) architect Francis Alÿs decided to become an artist when he moved to Mexico City driven by what would represent the central axis of his work: the urban myths. Such an idea suggests that the City has a memory that narrates and constructs its own appearance, also conveying the idea of body. The city as a living organism that opens up to artistic interventions and responses is a concept tightly correlated with a moment of transformation and simultaneously of a counter-moment, of social, political or economic nature. The specific Portuguese moment of the financial crisis, both inscribed and created the project A Montra, as stated in the Press Release that presented the launch of the project:

> A Montra is a project that appears as a consequence of the current situation, where we can observe a growing number of spaces being vacated here and there on every neighborhood of our city. Wherever we go we can find yet another shop closing, with papers covering the shop windows. For sale or for rent. The country?

> In a segment of Calçada da Estrela, the shops that had been settled there for several decades: the drugstore, the clothing store, the appliance store or the grocery with candied fruit, all closed. The pharmacy and the pastry-shop resist. It is there, between these two spaces, that we find the A Montra, which is ironic, as it might occur us that this is precisely how the country survives: between the Pastry and the Pill.[7]

For one year, an artist – from a group of heterogeneous age, experience and recognition – was invited each month to occupy the deactivated space-in-between in a Lisbon street. Marking the map of Lisbon; the project A Montra created an urban rumor. The artists responded to the City, a mute city, as described by one of the participant artists, André Sousa, or reacted to the city closed upon itself, as sensed by another participant in the project, Catarina Botelho:

> "When I was asked to exhibit in a shop window, of an also bankrupt shop, I wanted to reflect on that issue and on the way people relate to the public space, how they keep - or not - proximity relations", says Catarina Botelho. An idea and a daily practice were determinant in the work: the collection and the strolling through streets and avenues. "I walked around the city and accumulated, gathered images, but I did not make a map of Lisbon. I wanted to 'collect' the spaces that were closed to the eyes of passers-by. I was interested in the idea of blockage that is very present. The city is closing up upon itself", she highlights. [...] "Some allow us to see something of the interior, others don't", she commented.[8]

The project A Montra, located at number 132 of Calçada da Estrela, in the historical neighborhood of Estrela, started in October 13 with the intervention I'll be Back (Fig. 1) by Luisa Cunha (b. 1949, Lisbon, Portugal), that in a sense condenses the double (formal and conceptual) approach to this particular exhibition display, referred before, in the mise en abyme created by the photograph of a shop window displayed in the shop window. Luisa Cunha described her intervention in the shop window paper (the press release that each artist wrote as a presentation of the work in display), in a poetic, minimalistic, Gertrude Stein-like way:

> a shop window display that displays what is displays what the window displays and what it doesn't[9]

An economic gesture that diagnoses an urban symptom felt in a common ground (a City) within a period of time, and that is interrelated with the accompaniment of a certain reality and landscape. This moment relates to the Public debt of a Country and its aftermath, felt in the urban context. November's intervention Untitled (Thank You, Danke, Xie Xie) (Fig. 3) by Fernando J. Ribeiro (b. Lisbon, Portugal), was a direct comment on what capitalist logic produces and how it maps today's world:

> The invisibility of the products ensures its privacy. The feeling of possession towards transacted products is fostered by the appropriation of their logos. The logos sum up the scale of the world into psychoaffective atmospheres. A commercial space acquires intimacy by the exchange of gratifications expressed with the logos' fragrances.[10] (emphasis added)

Fernando J. Ribeiro's occupation of A Montra was an assumed political statement, specifically addressing commodities that are produced and transacted based on value, status and financial profit. The following intervention, by Catarina Botelho, presented in December, also questioned the present social and financial context of the city. For Inventário [Inventory] (Fig.2), the artist collected photographs of "deceased shops that she displayed in a live shop window (...) the set reminds us of a real estate (or funeral home) display panel" (Matos, 2013). The logic instituted by the artist for this series of photographs extraverted the punctual presentation in A Montra project. For the artist it also a way of keeping in touch and participating actively in the documentation of the transformations felt in the urban, social, affective arenas of her city:

> I walk through my city – Baixa, Avenida, Cais do Sodré, Santos, Chiado, Alfama, Saldanha, Intendente, Avenidas Novas – I go from one place to another and along the way I see dozens, no, hundreds of closed shops (and since I started this inventory, each day I see another one).

Their windows look like paintings to me. These places, where once people came in and out, are now closed upon themselves as if they were boxes with no openings, from which the air refuses to come out.[11] (Emphasis added)

The same sense of blockage, both formal and conceptual, was tackled by Mafalda Santos (b. 1980, Oporto, Portugal) in her sculptural installation entitled Alvará [Permit] that involved the construction of a wall made of used paper, of various nature, stacked near the glass, as to completely cover the shop window. The result had a painting-like quality, and simultaneously dealt with the "reality" and causes of the bankruptcy of many of the shops in the streets of Lisbon.

The intervention deals with issues such as accumulation, obsolescence and abandonment of so many spaces like this closed shop, whose story can be told by layers of documents and dead bureaucracy. Like a longitudinal section made in order to analyze the different strata of a rock, it seeks to enable in the observer that ability to read the history of a place from the marks and residues that it accumulates throughout time.[12] (emphasis added)

This sense of passage of time has been particularly well grasped in the representational strata proposed by Mafalda Santos' intervention, but also by the continuity of the project A Montra that has been inscribing and concentrating the city's representational time; the city as an organism that has been redirected to this program punctuating moments of reflection. The possibility of observation, by passers-by, at any time of the day or night, was the main force in the February project. The work of Miguel Palma (b. 1964, Lisbon, Portugal) often approaches the technological/spiritual and machine/body dichotomies. For the shop window, Palma applied the relation diagnosis/symptom to the pair city/body with his installation Dentro de nós só Deus sabe [Inside us only God knows] (Fig. 5), as described in the presentation of his work:

The artist was inspired by the interior of the shop's architectonic space, alike to many spaces in Lisbon, that are these days abandoned and degraded. It highlights a current problem of the city of Lisbon, the abandonment of its historic centre, the aging of the city and of its population, the bankruptcy of traditional local commerce. The religious nature of the title, in contrast with the reference of scientific instruments of diagnosis, can be taken with a certain irony. We have the means for diagnosing reality but we prefer to delegate this role to a mythological figure, and to accept with resignation a certain idea of fate and fatality. A certain praise to suffering, confirmed by the contemplation of disease and of the frailty of the human condition. [13] (emphasis added)

The two interventions that followed privileged performance actions relating to the shop window; it is interesting to consider how each occupation also reacts to both the update of the city's history and to the history that the project itself is producing. It could be argued that each artist rescues, integrates some element from the preceding one; A possible example of this kind of progression and handover of testimony can be found in the way the human body invoked in Palma's work lead to the personal and delicate Levantamento [Survey] performed by Armanda Duarte (b. 1961, Praia do Ribatejo, Portugal),

In the common place,/ the city,/ a vacant shop./ In face of the window, I decide to empathise the empty space/ I have a possible gesture, my body and elementary tools./ Hidden by the quietness of the city, I pull out from the floor, the element that the shop window, in its complete transparency and reflexive ability, reveals as most represented, constant and, apparently, even: in this place, a rock. / Elevated and placed in symmetry with the cavity opened by its absence, the rock will carefully be restituted.[14] (emphasis added)

The rock that was removed from the pavement and restituted to the street in the end of her occupation also played an essential role in André Sousa's (b. 1980, Oporto, Portugal) installation and performance in April's shop window. In Sousa's installation A Montra (Fig. 4), a pavement rock is said to have broken the window: "Mrs. Benedita, the kid broke your window. Will you take my services? I am a good glazier and for this price you won't get another artist." was the plot drawn by the artist for the puppet street theater presented in the first day of his exhibition:

With no reed filtering the voice, we are far from a real Dom Roberto show. In the interest of this gag I must tell the story of how we got here, and evoke the figure of João Barbelas (Raul Solnado) combining Lisbon with his Robertos [puppets] or Chaplin in survival games in the mute city.[15]

The regularity of the changes in the same area of intervention (autonomous, delimited: a public vitrine, the shop window) with different projections coming out of each intervention reflecting the changing urban landscape. The urban rumor or myths (alternative narratives) that begin to propagate from this space and its interventions, as suggested by the sculpture presented inside the shop by Raquel Melgue (b. 1985, Oporto, Portugal) that permeates this urban space with an open dialogue with the city:

Do you hear me? I'm here! To cherish your mind, to sustain your ego, to be your new reality. [16]

Repairing the city: Urban Acupuncture

The sense of Polis as defined by Hannah Arendt has become an agent as well as a place of hospitality where affections, tensions and creativity interact. Such an idea suggests that the City has a memory that narrates and constructs its own appearance, also conveying the notion of body: the city as a living organism is far more approachable. This paper regards the project A Montra as a practice of Urban Acupuncture in a stressed Lisbon – "Just as the practice of acupuncture is aimed at relieving stress in the human body, the goal of urban acupuncture is to relieve stress in the built environment."[17]

By choosing to use a window of an insolvent shop as an art gallery, but mainly, due to each artist's intervention and response to the current city, the A Montra project invokes Urban Acupuncture; punctuating the street with small-scale gestures, that both diagnoses and relieves the symptoms.

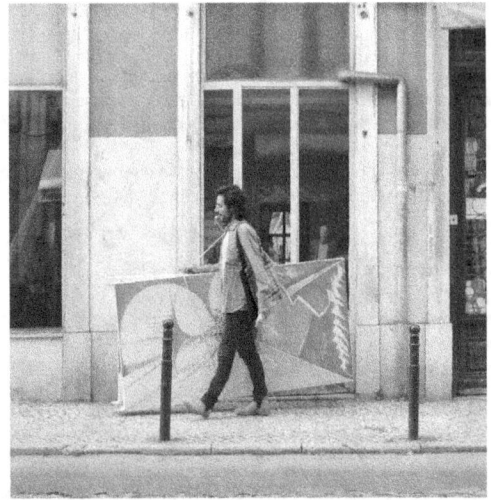 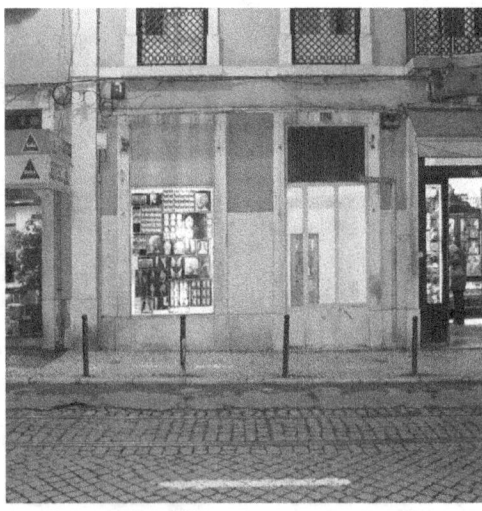

Fig. 4: André Sousa, A Montra. Performance on April 11, 2014. Courtesy of Arte Ilimitada.

Fig. 5: Miguel Palma. Dentro de nós só Deus sabe, 2014. Intervention for the A Montra project February 2014. Courtesy of Arte Ilimitada.

Acknowledgments Translated by João André Abreu

Notes and References

1 A Montra [The Shop Window] is a project coordinated by Benedita Pestana, the director of the Arte Ilimitada art school, whose cooperation and complicity in the exchange of ideas, along with her willingness to provide materials and information on the project I must thank. This exhibition program, for 132 Calçada da Estrela, invited a different artist each month, for the course of one year, from October 2013 to September 2014. The artists mentioned in the text, who have occupied the shop window so far, are: Luisa Cunha, Fernando J. Ribeiro, Catarina Botelho, Mafalda Santos, Miguel Palma, Armanda Duarte, André Sousa and Raquel Melgue; From June to September 2014, the participants will be: António Filipe (Carla Filipe and António Bolota), Ana Perez Quiroga, Tiago Baptista and Ricardo Jacinto. Further information on each intervention and on the A Montra project is available on www.a-montra.com. in Ípsilon supplement of Público newspaper, October 2013.

2 In this part of the text, where I intend to historically map urban artistic interventions, I closely follow an article I authored entitled Cities of Affection: some references of their expression, published in Arquitectura 21 magazine, No. 3, April 2009, pp. 54, 55.
3 Anne Friedberg, Window Shopping. Cinema and the Postmodern (Berkeley: University of California Press, 1993).
4 Miguel Matos in Time Out Lisboa, October 2013.
5 Edited by John C. Welchman, Sculpture and the Vitrine (San Diego: University of California Press, 2013).
6 Miguel Matos in Time Out Lisboa, January 2014.
7 in A Montra project Press Release, October 2013.
8 in "The places and people of Catarina Botelho", Text by José Marmeleira, Ípsilon supplement
of Público newspaper, 20.12.2013.
9 in Luisa Cunha's Folha de montra [Shop window paper], October 2013.
10 in Fernando J. Ribeiro's Folha de montra [Shop window paper], November 2013.
11 in Catarina Botelho's Folha de montra [Shop window paper], December 2013.
12 in Mafalda Santos' Folha de montra [Shop window paper], January 2014.
13 in Miguel Palma's Folha de montra [Shop window paper], February 2014.
14 in Armanda Duarte's Folha de montra [Shop window paper], March 2014.
15 in André Sousa's Folha de montra [Shop window paper], April 2014.
16 in Raquel Melgue's Folha de montra [Shop window paper], May 2014.
17 Wikipedia contributors (2013). 'Urban Acupuncture.' In Wikipedia, The Free Encyclopedia [Consult. 2014-06-06]. <URL: >http://en.wikipedia.org/wiki/ Urban_Acupuncture.

Lara Seixo Rodrigues, WOOL – Covilhã Urban Art Festival (lara@woolfest.org)

The WOOL - Covilhã Urban Art Festival
as an instrument of (community) transformation

Being the direct result of two great passions, one for Graffiti / Street Art and other for Covilhã and its history, closely linked to the textile industry, WOOL- Covilhã Urban Art Festival, appeared in 2011 as the first event of these characteristics in the interior of Portugal, under a specific and unique format and modus operandi, aiming to introduce these new expressions of Contemporary Art, as tools capable of enormous social, cultural, economic and urban transformations in a community.
Today, it is possible to observe a huge number of parallel actions, in new geographies and formats, targeting different (and unusual) age groups, confirming the value of Urban Art as a tool for rehabilitation (and recovery) of citizenship.

Urban Art, Covilhã, rehabilitation, citizenship

WOOL – PASSION, WILLS, FORMAT AND ACHIEVEMENTS

The WOOL – Covilhã Urban Art Festival[1], presented itself in 2011, as the first event in the interior of Portugal and one of the first in the all country[2], regarding these new expressions of Contemporary Art.

At the time, arose as a direct result of two great passions[3]: one by Graffiti and Urban Art and the other by Covilhã and its history, closely linked to the textile Industry; summarized in a whole and important secular past, ranging from exploration of the wool, through production of yarn and fabric, to the abundant exportations throughout Europe, which earned it the title of "the Portuguese Manchester", a portrait reflected in the more than 200 factories and 8,000 workers who labored until the Revolution of 1974.

It would be precisely the tribute to this historical past, unknown by so many and so often forgotten by the local population itself, now transformed into a huge, however, admirable heritage doomed to abandonment (Fig. 1), one of the primary objectives of WOOL. The demand for this reunion with 'our' identity', would be accompanied by other specific ambitions and objectives, such as:

- awake the interest of the community for culture and Contemporary Art, in this particular case, Street Art;
- rehabilitate degraded urban areas (facades) through Art making, while making it accessible to everyone and anyone, as a clear democratization of Art and informal learning;
- building a Urban Art Tour in the city, capable to generate and foster a specialized tourism;
- involve the community in all interventions and actions, to assume it as theirs.

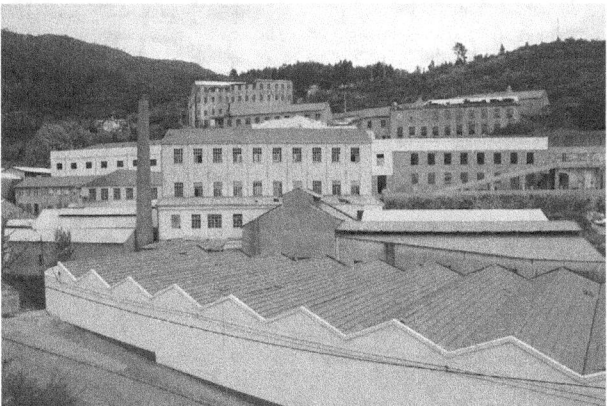

Fig. 1 – Photograph of numerous abandoned factories, located along the Ribeira da Carpinteira in Covilhã.
(credits - Pedro Seixo Rodrigues / WOOL)

To achieve all these goals (and desires), we studied and designed a format and modus operandi, in accordance with the characteristics of the section of the town that we choose as the first stage of action, the historical center of Covilhã, here describe, very briefly, as an urban and architectural neglected area but also socially forgotten, where the residents are mostly an aging population.

The festival WOOL was configured as a sequence of four events isolated in time (one week length), bringing to the city a total of four[4] artists, two Portuguese and two foreigners, capable to present to the community four concepts and / or distinct techniques of 'street work'. In addition to the execution of a mural, which could be extensively followed by all the local community (and virtual, through the various social networks and our own media), each artist also assumes the role of a trainer in a workshop or the role of speaker in a lecture, where would unveil its artistic journey and concepts associated with it. In a pretty virgin territory regarding to Graffiti or Urban Art, where preconceptions and prejudices towards these artistic expressions are immense and sometimes a bit (or a lot) wrong, the option of only an artist intervene in the city in each event and join to this presence, an educational and / or training activity, was related to the opportunity to generate and foster strong and close relations, empathy and involvement between the community, the artist and the intervention itself. It would be according to this ambitious and expectant format and unprecedented objectives, that in September 2011, we would observe the concrete emergence of WOOL, with a wide intervention over four facades near the most emblematic heritage and tourist symbol of the city, the Church Santa Maria [5] (Fig. 2).

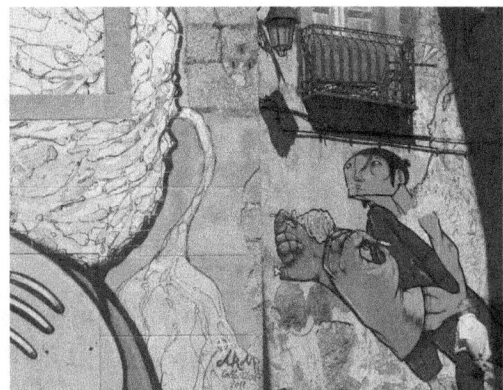

Fig. 2 – Partial view of the intervention by ARM COLLECTIVE, near the Church of Santa Maria, Covilhã.
(credits – Pedro Seixo Rodrigues / WOOL)

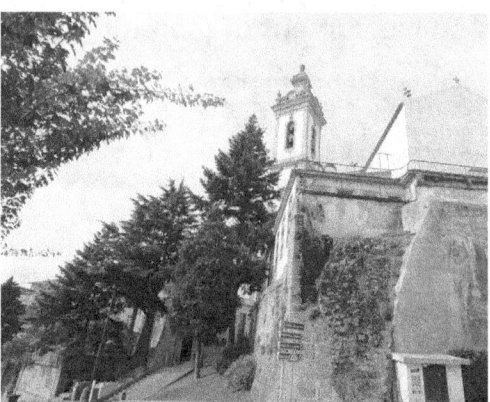

Fig. 3 – View of the intervention of the artist VHILS, located at Rua Visconde da Coriscada, Covilhã.
(credits - Pedro Seixo Rodrigues / WOOL)

The task would be responsibility of the ARM COLLECTIVE, a duo composed by two 'veterans' and renowned national artists, Mar (Gonçalo Ribeiro) and Ram (Miguel Caeiro), whose work we could feature as a perfect symbiosis between a style quite figurative and another full of abstraction. It would be this symbiosis and an enormous talent in the work with aerosol paint (spray), they would use to portray what they described as "the actual state of the textile industry," a clear look at the (almost extinct) professions of shepherd or guarantor, the industrial heritage...; a portrait captured, either by analyzing the packet of information[6] that is provided for each artist that has accepted the invitation to participate in the WOOL, as by a in loco observation, during the tour with which we receive the artists in the city[7].

And if the ambition of a good artistic result, capable to add value and cultural potential to the city, was quickly perceived by us, what completely exceeded our expectations, was the interest of the whole community. The initial suspicion and awkwardness common to all who passed by, only occasionally broken by the question "but, what will they do?". We started to observe pilgrimage of elderly, formed door to door, to come and watch, not the usual Sunday-Mass, but the progress of the paintings, day after day. Instead of answering "we invited a few artists to paint these damaged walls and give a little more color to the city" we started listening to the bets on what were the drawings: a skeleton, a sheep, paws, factories, that head is a ball of wool. We were often amazed at the creativity and assertiveness of these bets and become proud of the all process when a deserted square, became the stage of conviviality during nights and days, and forever. In only seven days, we observed, delighted, to the awakening to (one) Art, the growing interest for it, and the changes of simple but striking, routines and ways of living. Alexandre Farto aka[8] VHILS, the most international of all the Portuguese urban artists and holder of an unique and worldwide art technique, as he himself describes as sculptural stencil, was the second artist invited to intervene in Covilhã[9].

What we were able to follow throughout their stay, was the transformation, through the use of pneumatic hammers and chisels, of a retaining wall completely invisible to the city, into a piece that seeks to portray aging and gloom of the interior of the country (Fig . 3). A message of criticism and intervention in the city, the common exercise in the whole body of the artist's work, something he unveiled during the lecture performed to the community[10]. The third event of WOOL[11], welcomed the Catalan artist BTOY[12], recognized expert in the use of the stencil technique, that left us a facade on the historical centre of the city, offered by a resident (constant presence in the previously actions), a the reinterpretation of a postcard from the early XX century, the image of a shepherd (Fig. 4).

As a reminder, of this extremely rainy week and the need to repeat for three times the all painting, is the gratitude of a nearby resident, who had won a new companion to her window and today she feels a little bit more secure and guarded in her daily solitude. The artist BTOY, is best known for the posters that she leaves, in an more or less random way, on the streets of the cities she visit and Covilhã was no exception (as it was not Lisbon). A total of six posters (Fig. 5), can be found nowadays throughout the city and it should be noted that, although more than two years have passed by, they remain fully intact. This is another example and striking confirmation of the construction of a community heritage, which is taken care by all. Similar attention is observed with the pieces made in the workshop that the artist gave during her stay[13] [14].

For the fourth and final event of the first edition of WOOL[15], we proposed ourselves to make an action for the global project INSIDE OUT PROJECT (IOP)[16], by the French artist JR, who intends by using black and white portraits extended to a larger format, to discover, to collect and to share stories hidden throughout the world. The story that "we set out to tell" was the one of the former workers and entrepreneurs of the almost extinct textile industry, and from a population of almost 8,000 individuals registered in these roles only a few decades ago, from contacts with institutions and professional associations in the area, only 44 people made available to be portrayed.This observation amplified our interest "in this story" and beyond a simple photograph, we interviewed the 44 workers and entrepreneurs aged between 34 and 92 years, "Writing" (for four long months) how was the work and way of living in the heyday of "the Portuguese Manchester" The D-Day of the IOP action, the collage of the portraits on a façade of one of the many abandoned factories of the city (Fig. 6), was held in authentic festive atmosphere, with reunion between workers, employees and employers, with many smiles and some tears involved, a true exaltation of the local identity[ ].

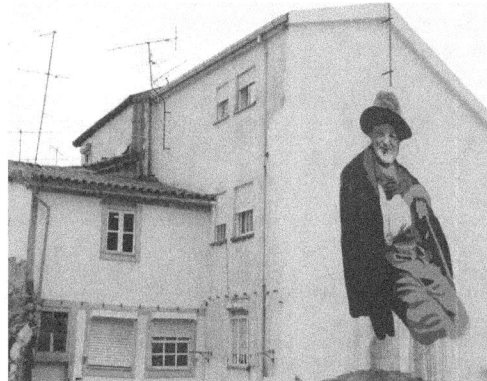

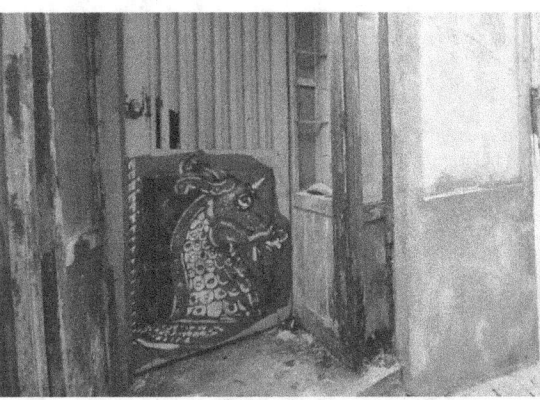

Fig. 4 View of the intervention of the Catalan artist BTOY, located in Largo Sr. do Rosário, Covilhã. (credits - Pedro Seixo Rodrigues / WOOL)

Fig. 5 – Example of one of the paste up that the Catalan artist BTOY left scattered throughout the city of Covilhã. (credits Pedro Seixo Rodrigues / WOOL)

Finished this action, we completed the first edition of WOOL, recognizing that our ambitions had been largely overcome, witnessing a total and growing interest of the local population on Urban Art in general and specifically on all interventions made, nurturing a sense of esteem for all of them, including the smaller ones, left in the streets by Portuguese and foreign artists who were watching and visited the festival, which we labelled OFF FEST[18] [19].

We also witnessed the emergence of tourists who travelled to the city, to see and photograph the pieces. The recognition of the work on promoting the Urban Arts was also expressed by numerous artists and institutions.

Unfortunately, for various reasons beyond our control, the WOOL didn't get more support or funding for a second edition at Covilhã[20], so naturally we searched for other geographies, for new projects and new formats.

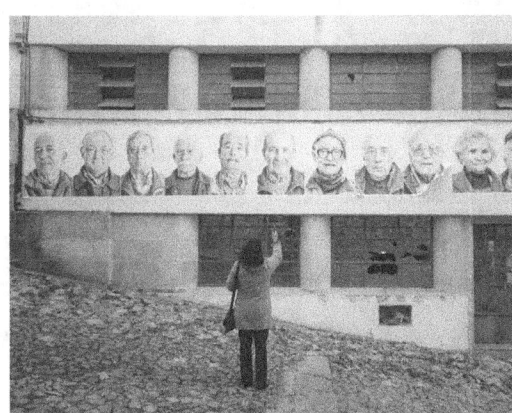

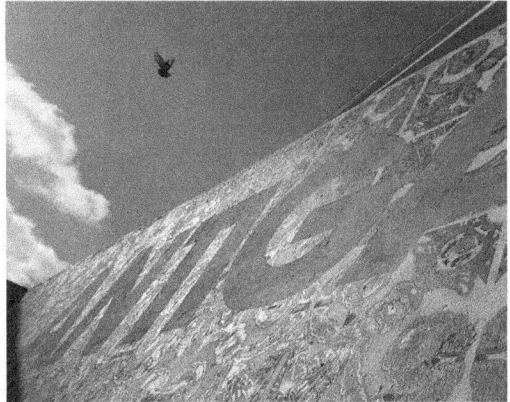

Fig. 6 – Partial view of the action INSIDE OUT PROJECT, global project by French artist JR, a collage held on the factory Amândio Saraiva, located on the Calçada de Santa Cruz, Covilhã. (credits - Pedro Seixo Rodrigues / WOOL)

Fig. 8 – Partial view of the intervention of the artist ADD FUEL, 'Antiga Mente Nova' (meaning 'Old Mind New'), for the 2nd edition of WOOL ON TOUR, at LXFactory, Rua Rodrigues Faria, Lisbon. (credits – Pedro Seixo Rodrigues / WOOL)

WOOL ON TOUR

The first place that welcomed us was the LX Factory[21], undeniably the most creative and artistic center of the capital, which was installed in an old flour mill and later printer industry, a place filled with old and gray facades. The first edition of the actions baptized as WOOL ON TOUR, held in May 2012 and the format designed was to challenge a set of artists from different backgrounds and professional experiences, to work side by side for a week, sharing a whole variety of practices and techniques.

In this first edition, we were able to see working side by side, an artist with a Fine Arts[22] training, whose career has been cemented in Art galleries, one writer[23] (whose learning has been done through the streets of Lisbon), a young illustrator[24], an artist that uses waste as a base to his work[25] and also an artistic join between an illustrator[26] and a tattoo artist[27] (Fig. 7), who ventured in their first and a very large wall. The result of this action can only be read as a wash of colour over the gray walls of LXFactory, as a new life and soul, enjoyed and appreciated by all residents and visitors.In November of 2012, we would repeat the action WOOL ON TOUR[28], with six more of the best and / or most promising artists of the Portuguese Street Art scene, among which we can highlight: ADD FUEL[29] (Fig. 8), with a new and first proposal of reinterpretation and reinvention of the Portuguese tiles tradition and CAOS aka Miguel Januário, holder of a unique graphics and theme, more recognized by his project MaisMenos[30].

In May[31] and November of 2013[32], we could watch two more editions of WOOL ON TOUR at LXFactory, with a total of 11 new artists, invited under the same purpose of intersection and union between artistic courses, careers, trainings and / or different languages. The highlight in the 3rd edition goes to the 'open call for artists', for one of the available walls, which was win by MR. TRAZO[33], a foreign artist, that came purposely to Lisbon to do the mural[34] (Fig. 9).

The last edition[35] held (Fig. 10)[36] in the past month of May, and by the temporal distance between the first and 5th edition, for all experiences and actions taken (making a total of 26 murals to date), we can say nowadays, that the WOOL ON TOUR, became a tradition of the 'Open Day' and of the everyday of this creative complex. A presence and constant action of innovation and renewal, expected and accompanied by the many residents and visitors, many of them foreign tourists.

At LXFactory, we are also visited by numerous foreign journalists[37], who seek to know more about the Portuguese Urban Art and its artists, in this context and scenario. For the existence of numerous pieces in a so small and confined area, by some of the most recognised Portuguese artists in Portugal and abroad, some of them even launched by WOOL, I usually say that the WOOL ON TOUR at LX Factory, turned into a kind of 'catalogue' of the Portuguese Urban Art.

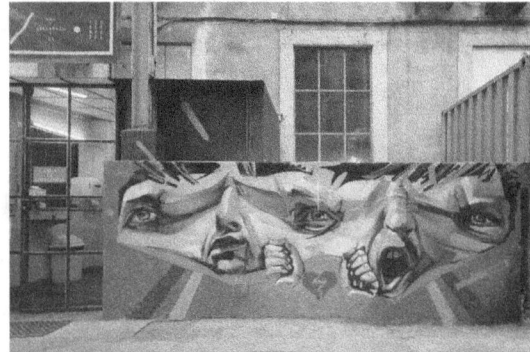 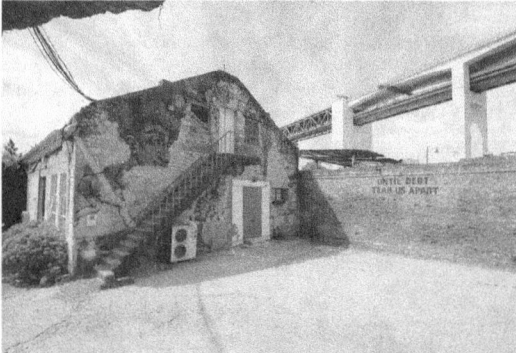

Fig. 9 – Partial view of the intervention of the Spanish artist MR. TRAZO, 'Bipolar love', for the 3rd edition of WOOL ON TOUR in LXFactory, Rua Rodrigues Faria, Lisbon. (credits – Pedro Seixo Rodrigues / WOOL))

Fig. 10 – Intervention of the artist MARIANA DIAS COUTINHO, for the 5th edition of WOOL ON TOUR, at LXFactory, Rua Rodrigues Faria, Lisbon. (credits – Pedro Seixo Rodrigues / WOOL)

THE REQUESTS

The ever-ready and steady disclosure of the various actions of WOOL, in our own means of dissemination[38], and also by the use of several social networks[39], has provided a great proximity between the community, this one understood by artists or simply lovers of Urban Art, who can and do contact us freely, with the most varied requests. One of these, came from the other side of the Atlantic, by Brazilian artist NILO ZACH[40] that was preparing he's passage through Covilhã in the exchange program with UBI[0] and contacted us with the intention of "doing something" with WOOL. A few months later, with his arrival for a period for (only) four months, the "something" would turn into a mural, a Urban Art workshop at the School Quinta das Palmeiras[42], a mural in the "still secret space " (Fig. 11) of WOOL and a collective exhibition at Thirty-Three gallery at Guarda[43]. Between all the actions developed with this artist, we must highlight the always enriching and constant exchange of experiences and ideas around the theme of Urban Art, but above all, the exchange and the testimony of the differences between studies and daily life in Covilhã and Belo Horizonte, hometown of NILO ZACK.

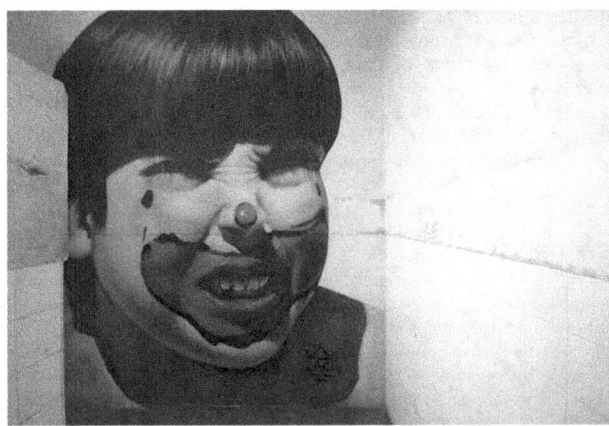

Fig. 11 – View of the intervention of the Brazilian artist NILO ZACH held in the 'still secret space of WOOL, located in Covilhã.
(credits – Pedro Seixo Rodrigues / WOOL)

Other of the recurring requests, has been to conduct training actions, for simple Urban Art lovers, who are curious to learn a bit more and in detail, how to "make" this type of Art. The offer has fallen in stencil workshops[44], where, after a brief presentation of the history and portfolio of the artists who have dedicated their work to this technique, are taught to the participants the basics of the technique of cutting a stencil, reinforcing its importance in the artwork process. All this training, trying to portray and reflect the whole experience and working steps of an urban artist, is completed with a painting on the street[45]. Also due to the communication and dissemination of our work abroad, in September 2012, we received a curious request of a foreign artist. The French artist C215[46], affectionately described by us as one of the "stencil dinosaurs", someone whose work we are following for many years, wanted to make a mural in Lisbon and asked if we could help him with all the legal, bureaucratic and practical aspects, so that he could fulfilled his dream. The result (Fig. 12) that took a vast demand on hours to find the ideal wall, a great deal of practical and bureaucratic work, 4 days of intense work[47], always closely followed by many curious, simple passers and other (old and new) lovers of this Art, can be seen today in a corner of Lisbon, in various publications of the work of C215, and also in small pieces that can be found in some corners of Lisbon.

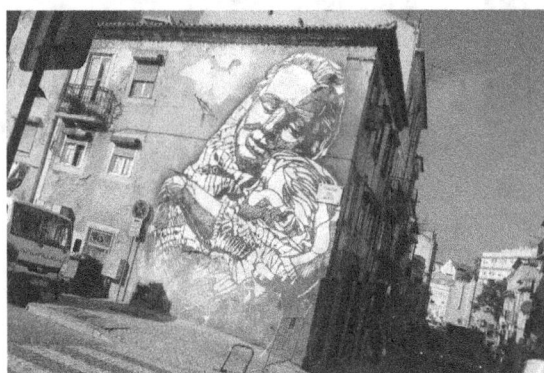

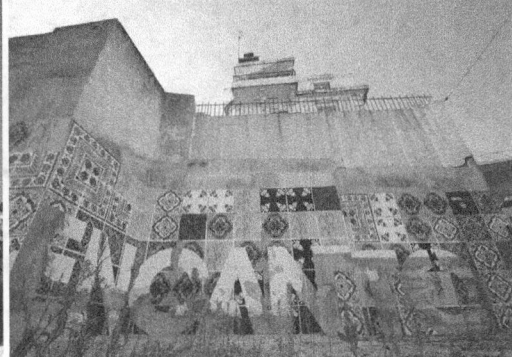

Fig. 12– View of the intervention 'Saudade' that the French artist C215 held in Lisbon in November 2012
(credits - Lara Seixo Rodrigues / WOOL).

Fig. 13 – Partial view of the intervention of the artist ADD FUEL, 'Tem sempre encanto', at Coimbra,
(credits – Pedro Seixo Rodrigues / WOOL)

THE YEAR 2013
The year 2013 would be one of the busiest and most productive years of WOOL, expanding into new geographies, seeking to respond the growing and challenging requests that businesses, cultural associations, municipal entities or private addresses us. Our passage through Coimbra[48] is one of the projects that we have to emphasize in this point of reading. Not only because it resulted of the invitation of the city council itself, specifically from the Office of Social Action and Family, which previously had went to Covilhã, in order to know in person and detail the WOOL work, but also by the underlying objective, of bringing their local community into their own city and mostly, because they intended us to work directly with a small community of homeless people, on the requalification of an area highly degraded and abandoned of Coimbra.

The result, imagined by artist ADD FUEL, was an huge mural (Fig. 13), which been reflection of the continuity of his work, on the reinterpretation and reinvention of the Portuguese tiles, intended to revive the message of the charm of the city, with a pun with a local fado in which the description of the city of Coimbra, is of only being charming in the farewell hour[49]. Coimbra would be followed by Abrantes, where we joined the group of "artists" invited to the 2nd edition of 180 Creative Camp[50] from Canal 180[51]. We took with us two Portuguese urban artists, CORLEONE[52] and SAMINA[53], attempting to reveal and portray two artistic courses, academic backgrounds, techniques, languages and distinct styles, something that characterizes the universe of Urban Art. During 7 days, we performed with more than 50 participants on the field, two workshops, one of 'cut of stencil' and the other of illustration, an collaborative urban art action and a total of five author murals, always with the aid and assistance by participants and the local population. August 2013, place us back on the interior of Portugal and between many of the actions undertaken, we must highlight two. The participation in the Festival Cale (Fundão), a festival of street Arts that runs for two days on the extensive Cale Street, in the historic city center. For this action, the first Urban Art event happening on these city, we invited PANTÓNIO[54], who chose freely three spaces to perform 3 murals (Fig. 14), under the watchful eye of all visitors and residents[55], arousing interest for this Art, but in general for Culture and Contemporary Art, one of our main goals for these territories on the Interior, which have such limited access to events / cultural activities.Other of the many actions taken place in the interior of the country, took place on the outskirts of Covilhã. By invitation of the Association of Local Development _ Beira-Serra, we held an Urban Art workshop in a local social housing for the project named "Youth in Action". The group of 10 young people aged between 10 and 14 years, was under the direction of the urban artist Mar. During five days, these young people learned all about the history of Graffiti and Urban Art, about the techniques, materials, artists, questioning without limits and finally putting it all into practice, in action, re-qualifying a degraded urban area[56].

The month of August also marks the date that WOOL debuted[57] at Figueira da Foz, curating and producing all Urban Art actions to integrate the festival Fusing Culture Experience[58], an unique event in Portugal, joining in a single space, extended to the city, Music, Art, Sports and Food. It also marks the debut of Urban Art activities in this city, which, in general and from past experience, means long months of preparation, conversations and negotiations with all governments and private entities, in order to demystify many of the preconceptions around these artistic expressions, reaffirming and reinforcing the idea that this Art, when well designed and built, are a huge gain in capital for the city, at numerous levels, which I will later present. On the plot of actions taken to the city of Figueira da Foz, we highlight 5 (five) author murals and a stencil workshop[59], as being a reflection of our constant concern to promote understanding and production of this Art. Among the murals made[60], I must highlight the ones by artists ADD FUEL and MÁRIO BELÉM (Fig. 15) because of the 'portugality' and 'local tradition', themes that are always approached on their work , essentials for searching empathy and identification with and throughout the local community and therefore, to safeguard them[].

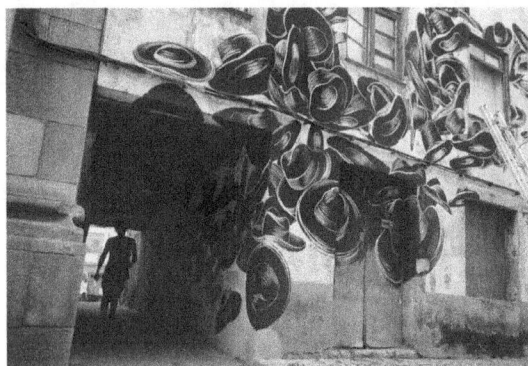 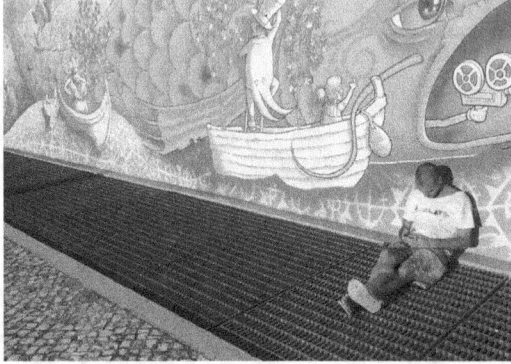

Fig. 14 – Partial view of one of the interventions that artist PANTÓNIO held in Fundão, for the Festical Cale. (credits - Pedro Seixo Rodrigues / WOOL)

Fig. 15 – Partial view of the intervention (100m2) of artist MÁRIO BELÉM held at the 1st edition of Fusing Culture Experience, Figueira da Foz (credits – Lara Seixo Rodrigues / WOOL)

In "our" year of 2013, also marks presence a special project. Especial for being the first held outside the national territory, special since this is the first one where we promoted Portuguese talent beyond the Portuguese-border and in loco, special for all the concept around it, the experience itself and the results obtained in the short and medium term.

The invitation to form a entourage of Portuguese urban artists to participate in what was promised to be the 'largest exhibition ever held, of Urban Art', emerged in mid-January. Named Tour of Paris 13[62], a project by the Mairie du 13e Paris, coordinated by Mehdi Ben Cheikh, Director of Galerie Itinerrance[63] that promotes Urban Artists for many years now, would count with an all-volunteer effort of all participants that during many months, would work inside the tower (and occasionally beyond) in the most absolute secret; only to be revealed to the public during the 30 days of October. We are talking about a total of 4.500m2, divided by 10 floors (36 flats) that compose this tower, located in one of the most dynamic neighbourhoods in Paris[64], that being simply waiting its destruction, as part of a project to modernize the municipal housing park , became a colossal temporary museum of Street Art, open to all for free and without any commercial approach, as a tribute to this type of Art.

The selection of artists, to whom would be given complete freedom of action in walls, ceilings and floors, in complete harmony with the essence of the Urban Art movement, fell mainly on emerging countries in the international arena of Street Art, particularly Latin America and the Middle East and at the European level Italy and Portugal.

The invitation, resulted in challenging a group of artists, which intended to aggregate several generations and souls of the national Street Art and portrait from Graffiti to the stencil, going throughout all the languages, and / or techniques commonly referred to post-graffiti, with contemporary influences of figurative illustration. Accepted the challenge, it would take four 'pilgrimages'[65] to the number 5 Rue Fulton, where gradually the interventions of (and alphabetically) ADD FUEL, CORLEONE (Fig. 16), EIME, KRUELLA D'ENFER, MAISMENOS, MAR, MÁRIO BELÉM, PANTÓNIO (Fig. 17), PAULO ARRAIANO, SAMINA and VHILS would occupy fully and strategically, according to stylistic criteria to guarantee the legitimacy of its legend, the 2nd floor of the Tour Paris 13. The "floor of the Portuguese" as affectionately dubbed, would be "the hinge point in order to achieve the success of this project", as stated still today by the mentor Mehdi Ben Cheikh, shared the tower with other interventions of major international artists such as: C215, INTI CASTRO, ALEXÖNE, ORTICANOODLES, DAVID WALKER, BAGLIONE, STINKFISH, SEAN HART or SPETO, among so many others.

The Tour Paris 13, would become more than a mere object or simple exhibition experience. It was assumed from the zero point, as a complex process and a rare creative experience, that should (and would) be the field to a documentary[66], depicting the arrival, the appropriation of spaces, ideas and questions and especially the determination of the artists in making a giant ephemeral universe[67]. Analyzing this action, with this (more or less short) temporal distance, assuming that initially this challenge presented itself as an extremely positive opportunity, because of the mere fact that this was the first time a group of Portuguese urban artists joined an international event of this magnitude, we would come to realize with great satisfaction, that the participation of the Portuguese group would receive special attention from visitors and from the media all over the world. Greater satisfaction came, and being curators and producers of the Portuguese participation, when the artists started to receive invitations with the purpose of exhibition and / or murals in several places in France and other countries. Renewed satisfaction, with the recent call to form a new group of urban artists to join the new project of Galerie Itinerrance, which will take to a village in Djerba, in the coming months of July and August, a group of 150 artists from 30 different nationalities. Returning to our country and after enumerating some of others requests usually addresses us and that we complete, as. participating in seminars and lectures discussing the theme of Urban Art, conducting lectures in secondary schools, assisting in the performance of master's theses and studies, guided tours at WOOLⒼs interventions in Covilhã and Lisbon or scheduling interviews with Portuguese artists for interviews and / or documentaries; is assumed as mandatory to expose, as a justification for all our actions, that our understanding of what is Urban Art, goes far beyond simple painted walls. We understand (and experience it daily) that Art encapsulates an enormous transformation power:

- at a urban level, as a way of dialogue with the city and its buildings; for the capacity for rehabilitation and regeneration of degraded and / or the ability to recreate sections / routes of city areas that have been forgotten.
- at a economic level, by the ability to create a new model of attraction, new forms of tourism and residence;
- at a cultural level, because this form of Contemporary Art is democratically accessible to anyone, being also a form of non-formal education;
- at a social level, by the way it interacts directly with a community, recreating and creating new forms of citizenship.

This last point, would assume a considerable importance and notoriety in one of the last actions produced by WOOL[68], the Urban Art workshop for elderly: LATA 65[69] (Lata means can, spray can).

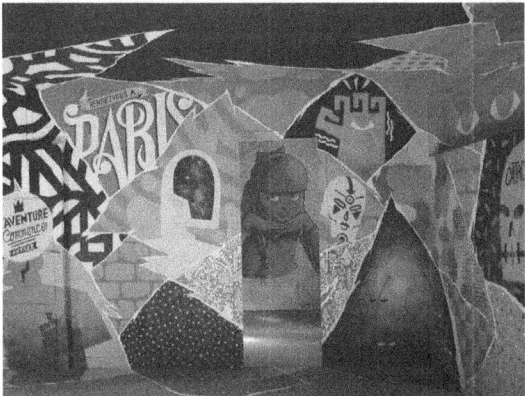

Fig. 16 – Intervention of the artists CORLEONE, KRUELLA D'ENFER and MÁRIO BELÉM (background) in the project TOUR PARIS 13, Paris. (credits - Lara Seixo Rodrigues / WOOL)

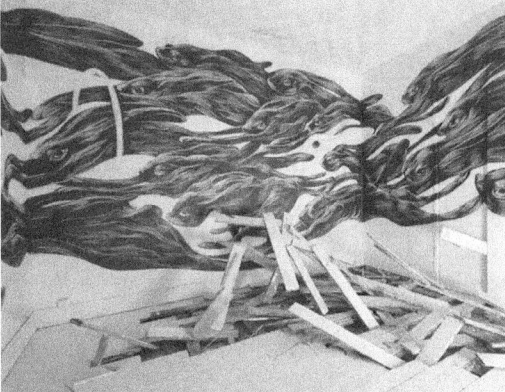

Fig. 17 – Intervention of the artist PANTÓNIO at TOUR PARIS 13, Paris. This intervention would be the cover of the catalogue given to the press in the public presentation of the project. (credits Pedro Seixo Rodrigues / WOOL)

LATA 65 - URBAN ART WORKSHOP FOR ELDERLY

With each new intervention performed by WOOL, we were able to observe the simplicity and naturalness which with Urban Art reached the various age groups, particularly the older 'inhabitants' of our performance areas and especially in Covilhã. Were these 'locals' that became our companions and spectators of all hours. Every day we witnessed daily and nightly elderly people pilgrimages who left their homes, not to go to Mass or a usual cards game, but to follow all details of the making off of the paintings. We heard a thousand stories about what might be emerging on the walls and it moved us hearing things like 'my city regains its colour.' The LATA 65 was assumed, therefore, as a challenge[70] to take this interest shown by Urban Art beyond, with the objective wills to:
- *prove that concepts such as active aging and solidarity between generations make more sense every day;*
- *bring the not so young population closer to a form of artistic expression usually associated with younger adults;*
- *demonstrate that age is just a number.*

The model designed to 'verify these wills' was simple: gather small groups of people who have passed the age of retirement and assisted them with some of the most respected urban artists[71] nowadays, participants learned the history of Graffiti and Urban Art, the various technical 'terms ', the various intervention techniques in the street and finally, go to the street, share with the world their ideas, a mural in the city.

The result was a week of intense activity (Fig. 18), of many surprises and energetic learning, making it look like this project, of real collaboration and sharing, wakes up a forgotten creative spirit, and above all, brings the feeling of pure fun essential at any age. And if there were many doubts (and expectations) about the interest or capacities, including physical, from the learners for the required actions (with an average age of around 84 years in the first edition of LATA 65), really fast and daily were being completely dispelled, confirmed by the participants themselves and by the managers of the Social Centre, on the following testimony:

"... This is an innovative way to show society that the elderly are not people to forget." Dr. Isabel Brito (technical director CSPA)
"... They come with a youthful spirit that fascinates me...", Dr. Isabel Brito (technical director CSPA)
"... Extremely motivated." Dr. Isabel Brito (technical director CSPA)
"... Now I look at the walls with different eyes, I know what is ahead of me on the street.", D. Lurdes Aka Armando.
"... While I'm here, I'm not thinking about the hours and days left for me to die." Mr. Manuel aka Balé
"I found something to live for ..." Luísa Cortesão[72] (Fig. 19)

At this point allow ourselves to state that:

- *it is possible and desirable to awaken, motivate and enthuse the elderly through the Urban Art;*
- *it is desirable to show these generations, new activities, new techniques, as a way to escape and break from their routines, generating quality, youthfulness and well-being in their lives[73].*

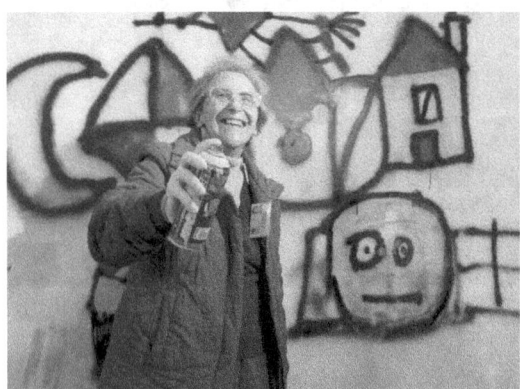

Fig. 18 – Registration for the 3rd day of the workshop of urban art LATA 65, dated November 2012 (credits - Fernando Mendes / LATA 65).

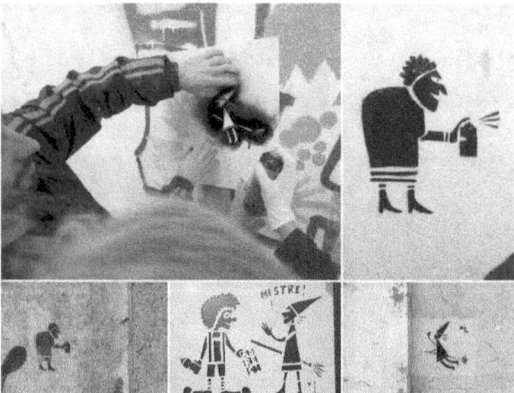

Fig. 19 – Registration of the route of LUÍSA CORTESÃO (L is not an artist): Records found in the streets of Lisbon. At the center, the stencil offered to the former. (credits - WOOL)

These findings could lead us to many others, and the findings can become confirmations, but what stands out, as a great learning throughout the way taken by WOOL[74], that stands today, primarily as a platform for promoting Portuguese Urban Art and Portuguese urban artists[75], as a brand capable of generating a new view over these new artistic expression, is that Urban art manifests and is recommended as a unique tool in the ability to foster, promote and enhance the democratization of Contemporary Art and assumes itself as a unique instrument in the formation and / or transformation of a community, as an unique tool for rehabilitation (and recovery) of citizenship in its broader definitions. It is with this tool, with immensurable results, that WOOL intends to continue to tread new geographies under concepts, with always unique and original operation modes, like unique is each site or community, never forgetting the objectives and mainly, the wills and initial passion that brought us here[76].

NOTES AND REFERENCES

1 more information at: www.facebook.com www.woolfest.org + / + woolfest www.instagram.com / woolfest www.pinterest.com + / + woolfest www.twitter.com / woolfest + www.vimeo.com / woolfest
2 to the date of release of WOOL, will only occurred the project Crono Lisboa, 2010.
3 passions shared by the three founders of WOOL: Lara Seixo Rodrigues , Pedro Seixo Rodrigues and Elisabet Carceller.
4 or collective of artists.
5 event 01 - took place between the 29th September and the 4th October of 2011, at the Church of Santa Maria, Covilhã.
6 the packet of information given to the artists, about the city of Covilhã, contains information and documents about the history of the city, images and pictures, old and current.
7 link to view the complete photo report of the event 01: https://www.facebook.com/media/set/?set=a.236131239768511.56644.217600194954949&type=3
8 aka means "also known as" (translation in Portuguese: "também conhecido como").
9 event 02 - took place between the 22th and 25th October 2011, at Rua Visconde da Coriscada, Covilhã.
10 link to view the complete photo report of the event 02: https://www.facebook.com/media/set/?set=a.236132649768370.56645.217600194954949&type=3
11 event 03 – took place between the 7th and 13th November 2011, at Largo Srª do Rosário (at the top of Rua Alexandre Herculano).
12 Andrea Michaelsson aka Btoy
13 stencil workshop level 01, a total of 16h (2 days), attended by 20 participants, locals and Lisbon, which made the trip across to Covilhã.
14 link to view the complete photo report of the event 03: https://www.facebook.com/media/set/?set=a.236133343101634.56647.217600194954949&type=3
15 event 04 🞏 the photographic and video recording took place between December 2011 and April 2012. The collage of portraits on the facade of the factory Amândio Saraiva, located in the Calçada de Santa Cruz, was held on November 10, 2012 (the request for authorization. the collage of posters took about six months to get).
16 www.insideoutproject.net.
17 link to view the complete photo report of the event 04: https://www.facebook.com/media/set/?set=a.310834825631485.70934.217600194954949&type=3
18 artists WOOL OFF FEST - URIGINAL (ES), ADRES (PT), TARGET (PT), ADD FUEL (PT), MÁRIO BELÉM (PT), NILO ZACK (BR), REGG + VIOLANT (PT) and PFFF (NL).
19 link to complete photo report of all interventions WOOL OFF FEST: https://www.facebook.com/media/set/?set=a.252001958181439.60731.217600194954949&type=3
20 in April 2012, we made one more action in Covilhã, labelled EXTRA WOOL, with the Catalan artist KRAM, coming from Barcelona.
21 at Rua Rodrigues Faria, 103; Lisbon _ www.lxfactory.com.
22 Pedro Zamith - www.pedrozamith.com
23 Barbedo aka THE CAVER - http://cargocollective.com/nunobarbedo
24 Peter Campiche aka CORLEONE - www.akacorleone.com
25 Artur Silva aka BORDALO II - www.bordalosegundo.com
26 MÁRIO BELÉM 🞏 www.mariobelem.com
27 Hugo MAKAROV - www.facebook.com / HugoMakarov
28 artists who joined the 2nd edition of WOOL ON TOUR - Diogo Machado aka ADD FUEL, Paulo Ferreira aka TOSCO, Angela Ferreira aka KRUELLA D🞏ENFER, GEMENIANO CRUZ, Miguel Januário aka CAOS and ANDRÉ FERNANDES TRINDADE.
29 Diogo Machado aka ADD FUEL - www.addfuel.com
30 Miguel Januário aka MaisMenos - http://maismenos.net/
31 artists who joined the 3rd edition of WOOL ON TOUR - SAMINA, COLORBLIND, BOARD BROTHERS, RAM, JOÃO CRUZ and MR. TRAZO (from Spain and winner of the open call for artists).
32 artists who joined the 4th edition of WOOL ON TOUR - KLIT, REGG, GO MES and GUILLERMO DE LLERA.
33 Mário Rodriguez aka MR.TRAZO - www.mistertrazo.com
34 from this exchange of experiences between artists and the organization itself, emergence a partnership between WOOL and ZARAJOS DELUXE (www.zarajosdeluxe.es), a festival founded by the artist Mr. Trazo. During the months of July and September, we will present two artists in the 2nd edition of the festival.
35 artists who joined the 3rd edition of WOOL ON TOUR - NEBERRA, TAMARA ALVES, MARIANA DIAS COUTINHO, DAVID ANTUNES, TINTA CRUA and UIVO.
36 links for complete photo reports of the interventions of the 5th edition of WOOL ON TOUR: Neberra - https://www.facebook.com/media/set/?set=a.6672808566 53545.1073741862.217600194954949&type=3; Tamara Alves - https://www.facebook.com/media/set/?set=a.668467609868203.1073741866.217600194954949&t ype=3; Mariana Dias Coutinho - https://www.facebook.com/media/set/?set=a.668466289868335.1073741865.217600194954949&type=3; David Antunes - https:// www.facebook.com/media/set/?set=a.668464406535190.1073741864.217600194954949&type=3; Tinta Crua - https://www.facebook.com/media/set/?set=a.67038 7176342913.1073741867.217600194954949&type=3 and Uivo - https://www.facebook.com/media/set/?set=a.666646660050298.1073741860 .217600194954949 & type = 3.
37 interviews, reports and the others, can be found here: https://www.facebook.com/media/set/?set=a.236694026378899.56771.217600194954949&type=3.
38 www.woolfest.org
39 www.facebook.com / woolfest www.instagram.com + / + woolfest www.pinterest.com / woolfest + www.twitter.com / woolfest + www.vimeo.com / woolfest
40 NILO ZACK _ www.pinterest.com / byzulu / nilo-zack.
41 UBI - University of Beira Interior, Covilhã
42 Urban art workshop level 01, took place between the 4th and 9th of February 2013.
43 collective exhibition 'The circus factory', Trinta e Três Gallery, Guarda. Took place between the 19th January and 19th of February 2013.
44 stencil workshop level 01, a total of 10h (2 days), given by urban artist EIME. Held in February and November 2012 in Lisbon. In August 2014, in Figueira da Foz And in July 2014, in Águeda.
45 link to view the complete photo report of the workshop held in November 2012: https://www.facebook.com/media/set/?set=a.436674993047467.96356.21760019 4954949&type=3
46 Christian Guemy aka C215 - www.c215.fr.
47 intervention of C215 dated of November 2012 and is located at Travessa dos Brunos, Lisbon.
48 project in July 2013. Located at Avenida Fernão Magalhães (near the Citizen's Shop), Coimbra.
49 link to view the photo report of the implementation of this intervention in Coimbra: https://www.facebook.com/media/set/?set=a.537800739601558.1073741841.2 17600194954949&type=3
50 180 Creative Camp is a unique concept of Channel 180 that intends to take to Abrantes, Portugal, some of the most innovative national and international designers in the areas of video, music, photography, design, film, architecture, installation and fine arts.
51 Canal 180 is the first Portuguese television channel "Open Source" entirely dedicated to culture, arts and creativity. Presents the most innovative content produced by an international network of creators, being recognized and awarded internationally.
52 Pedro Campiche aka CORLEONE - www.akacorleone.com
53 João Samina aka SAMINA - www.behance.net / JSAMINA
54 António Correia aka PANTÓNIO - www.pantonio.net
55 link to view complete photo report from interventions in Fundão: https://www.facebook.com/media/set/?set=a.543977055650593.1073741843.217600194954949 &type=3
56 link to view photo report of all the action: https://www.facebook.com/media/set/?set=a.542250249156607.1073741842.217600194954949&type=3
57 will be present again in the 2nd edition of Fusing Experience Culture, curated and production of all actions of Urban Art.
58 more information: www.fusing.pt
59 workshop taught by artist Eime.
60 aArtists invited to the 1st edition of Fusing (2013) - MÁRIO BELÉM, ADD FUEL, KRUELLA D'ENFER, SAMINA and EIME.
61 link to view photo report of all the action: https://www.facebook.com/media/set/?set=a.522629474452018.1073741835.217600194954949&type=3
62 more information www.tourparis13.fr. The Tour Paris 13 was also an unprecedented, visual and audio, engaging and collaborative transmedia project, which gave power to netizens, through the website dedicated to the project of perpetuating this ephemeral adventure of Street Art, which completely disappeared under the rubble of demolition.
63 more information: http://itinerrance.fr/
64 Tour to Paris 13, had neighborhood as the National Library of France and Les Docks - Cité de la Mode et du Design.
65 took place from April to August 2013.
66 directed by Thomas Lallier for France Ô in co-production with La Blogotheque. Recording began in March 2013 and ended with the capture of the demolition of the tower, being release in October 2014.
67 link to view the full photo report of the Portuguese participation in the project PARIS TOUR 13: https://www.facebook.com/media/set/?set=a.562383053809993.10 73741845.217600194954949&type=3
68 the first edition of Lata 65 held between 12th and 16th of November, 2012 at Cowork Lisboa, Lxfactory, Lisbon.
69 more information and complete photo report at: /www.facebook.com/Lata65
70 launched by Fernando Mendes' Cowork Lisboa (http://coworklisboa.pt/).
71 forming artists of the 1st edition of LATA 65 - ADRES, MIGUEL JANUÁRIO and TOSCO.
72 one of the participants of the 1st group, Luisa Cortesão, still does stencil. She continues to apply it in the streets of Lisbon. The project logo was created and donated by Luisa. In the 2nd action of Lata 65 she took the role of former. Her homepage with the work: www.facebook.com / osstenceisdal
73 after 1st edition of Lata 65 (November 2012), were made 2 more actions. In October 2013, after the project candidature to the Participatory Budget of Lisbon, celebrated ourselves as one of the winners, we will perform with the support of the Municipality of Lisbon, 24 actions across the city. Promotional video of the project: https://vimeo.com/76711510
74 all interventions by WOOL, can be found at: https://maps.google.com/maps/ms?msid=213433614628918665172.0004c6b4f652c100ea4be&msa=0&dg=feature
75 to date (end June 2014), are more than 40, the number of Portuguese and foreign artists supported / promoted by WOOL.
76 during the year 2014, we will promote actions in Cascais, Covilhã, Aveiro, Figueira da Foz and Djerba (Tunisia), among others. In 2015, we have scheduled activities for the interior of the country.

Jacob Kimvall, PhD candidate, Department of Art History at Stockholm University
jacob.kimvall@arthistory.su.se

Mapping an Institutional Story of Graffiti and Street Art

The majority of the works in graffiti and street art has always been produced outside of the institutional art system with its galleries and museums, curators and art critics, collectors and dealers. But considering the activities of actors such as United Graffiti Artists during the early 1970s; recent exhibitions at museums and street artists such as Swoon and Banksy whose work often are exhibited at high end galleries and/or sold at international auction houses – it is obvious that graffiti and street art also have an institutional history. This paper is an attempt to take this institutional history into serious consideration.

Graffiti, Street Art, Institution

Introduction

> *Ephemeral, secretive, illegal. Rebellious, provocative, competitive. This is America's newest folk art [...] developed from crude graffiti writing to a highly sophisticated calligraphy Quote from jacket blurb on Subway art (1984)[1]*
> *Street Art is a phenomenon that takes place on the street, in full public view, far from all the galleries and on the margins of the law. [...] this controversial art is produced by people who want to create non-academic images, to convey messages.*
> *Quote from jacket blurb on Street Art (2009)[2]*

Both popular and scholarly descriptions and analysis of graffiti and street art tend to solely focus on various unacademic, uninstitutional or illegal aspects, and it has for example been described as folk art, subcultural art, popular art, and outsider art. Such descriptions might very well be accurate regarding the many of the objects referred to as belonging to the realms of graffiti and street art, but I would claim that this focus also has marginalized important and significant aspects of institutional agency. If one considers the activities of UGA (United Graffiti Artists) and NoGA (Nation of Graffiti Artists) in New York during the early 1970s; graffiti as a part of the post-modernist art-scene in the mid 1980s; recent exhibitions at prestigious museums (such as Art in the Streets at MoCA in Los Angeles, 2011), and street artists such as Swoon and Banksy whose work often are exhibited at high end galleries and/or sold at international auction houses – it is obvious that graffiti and street art also have an art institutional history.

The often highly opinionated debate within graffiti and street art communities regarding the institutional activities indicate a complex relationship between the non-institutional artistic production and institutions. Many rule out any such activity as fake or based on pure exploitation, and that the results are lame in comparision with the real. Artist and art teacher Jack Stewart was one of the first scholars who commented on the differences of graffiti on walls and on canvas, and he saw the latter mainly as a loss:

> *"These graffitiists didn't realize that when they moved from public walls to their own canvases in a studio environment they ceased to make graffiti and began making paintings of graffiti. Graffiti simply became their subject [...] The first loss in their work was freshness and the highly charged sense of excitement that became characteristic of subway graffiti.[3]*

Others hail it, e.g. as an acknowledgement of the movements' artistic legacies. But very few have considered it as a history in its own right, with its own complex logics. It seems deemed to play the role of the Other, in the real – non-institutional – history of street art. This paper thus departs from the ambition to take the institutional history into serious and non-judgmental consideration, and argues that the role of institutional endeavors goes well beyond the limits of mere exploitation, or a simply confirming acknowledgement. It does so by specifically looking at the relation between the art institutional system and graffiti in New York City during the 1970s and 1980s.[4] But lets begin with a brief discussion on the term institution, and its implications in the present field.

The different concepts of institution
Merriam Webster's Collegiate Dictionary presents the following definition of institution:

1 : an act of instituting : establishment

2a : a significant practice, relationship, or organization in a society or culture <the institution of marriage>; also : something or someone firmly associated with a place or thing <she has become an institution in the theater>

2b : an established organization or corporation (as a bank or university) especially of a public character; : asylum 4 [5]

As obvious in this definition, the term may refer to several different but interrelated concepts. Of main interest in this discussion are both of the second concept (marked 2a and 2b), that could summed up as on one hand referring to a set of formalized conventions (exemplified with the institution of marriage), and on the other hand an established organization (exemplified with a bank and university). So which actual institutions and institutional activities with links to graffiti and street art is it possible to identify?

With this first concept – institution as a set of formalized conventions – graffiti and street art actually could be described as two internationalized institutions, since the very recognition of an object as belonging to graffiti or street art is based upon certain criteria, which in turn are dependent on various conventions. This is however not the aspect that is of main interest here.

Different institutions with relations to graffiti and street art

When discussing graffiti and street art exhibited at galleries and museums, the most obvious would be to consider the art institutions, and the so-called Institutional Theory of Art.[6] Put simply, within this theory, art is produced by being recognized as art by the institutions of art and their residents such as art museums and art galleries; curators, collectors and critics. These could be said being institutions in both sense of the definition, both a network of particular organizations and places (specific art museums and galleries) and significant practices (art exhibitions, art criticism). As mentioned already in the introduction, graffiti and street art has been considered and at times recognized as art within this network of art institutions. I shall return to this relation below, but it is also worth mentioning that it, there are several other institutions, with a similar structure of being both a set of conventions and particular organizations, that have an intricate relationship to graffiti and street art. One such institution is the police and the various law enforcement agencies. For example, many cities have instigated special police forces investigating illegally performed graffiti (e.g. the so-called Vandal Squad in New York City) and some countries have instituted specific laws regarding these matters.[7] Another, with a more commercial agenda, is the institution that I would like to refer to as the anti-graffiti industry: the joint endeavors of various graffiti removal companies and organizations that include development of different strategies, technologies, tools and materials. Other institutions that in various ways and degrees engage in graffiti and street art include the media industry (newspapers, magazines and publishing houses as well as specialized webpages and applications), transit authorities and property owners. And last but not least, something that this conference is a living testament to, the institutions of research and higher education displays an increasing interest in these phenomena. These are all examples of institutions that in various ways and with different interests and methods describe, define, frame and intervene into graffiti and street art, and thus to a large extent produce the context where these (artistic) practices takes place.[8]

But since the interest in this case is graffiti and street art as art, I would here like to return to the art institutions, by looking at the interaction between graffiti and the art institutions in New York during the roughly 15 years of 1972-1987. I am looking at this in order to discuss what results these institutional activities may have had on the understanding of graffiti and street art among both practitioners and a wider public.

The art institutions relations to graffiti art in the 1970s and 1980s

In Art Today Edward Lucie-Smith describes graffiti as a "teenage craze" that "disturbed the authorities", but also points out that: "In the 1970s and early 1980s there was a short lived but hectic fashion in the New York art world for subway graffiti".[9] Even if Lucie-Smiths description might appear patronizing, his account is actually one of the more informative on graffiti in any of the over a dozen general art historical survey that I have examined. Lucie-Smith describes graffiti both as a youth subculture and an art movement with institutional connections, if short lived. Lucie-Smith mentions that Razor Gallery has the first graffiti art exhibition in September 1973 (however without naming any of the participating artists). When summing up the graffiti movement as art, he concludes that: "Very few of these young artists showed any stamina in the New York art world", but appoints Jean-Michel Basquiat as the "conspicuous exception".[10]

The exhibition at Razor gallery pointed out by Lucie-Smith is also within the more specialized literature commonly referred to as the first gallery exhibition. It was curated by Hugo Martinez, at the time a sociology student, who got interested in graffiti while teaching at a summer school.[11] Martinez founded United Graffiti Artists (UGA) after meeting the two graffiti writers Stitch I and Snake 1, and by this creating the first organization for graffiti.[12] The majority of members were young Caribbean and African-American males from areas such as Harlem, Washington Heights, and the South Bronx. While the ambition of Martinez seem to have been that UGA should be an exclusive group restricted to the most important graffiti writers, it is probably at the same time best understood as an self organized artist collective, with members varying over time, but with twelve writers as its core members: Stitch I, Snake I, Cat 87, Coco 144, Amrl (Bama), Flint 707, Lee 163, Mico, Phase 2, SJK 171, T-Rex 131 and WG (Wicked Gary).[13]

UGA made its first appearance in December of 1972, with an exhibition at City Collage of New York, and in March 1973, UGA were invited to contribute to a performance with the dance company The Joffrey Ballet. The choreography Deuce Coupe was by Twyla Tharp, and UGA participated by painting live on stage while the dancers performed.[14] Thus, when the show at Razor Gallery opens in September 1973 UGA had already been an active group of artists for almost a year, and in the next few years, their activities resulted in several exhibitions in different locations. The most thouroughly documented of these exhibitions took place in September 1975, when UGA open the autumn season at Artist Space in Soho. In the mid-1970s, Artist Space was an avant-garde artist run venue where art students, artists, critics and scholars are deeply involved in discussions soon to become labeled as the postmodern turn in art and art theory. Barbara Kruger is one of the last artists to exhibit during the spring season of 1975. A few weeks after UGA's exhibition Artist Space host a discussion on "Critics' Responsibility to the Artist", with a panel including prominent postmodern art theorists Rosalind Krauss and Douglas Crimp (who soon would work closely together in the early stages of the journal October). Other involved in the programming of Artist Space during the autumn of 1975 include Hans Haacke and Robert Morris.[15] The exhibition, United Graffiti Artists 1975, was curated by Edit deAK from Artist Space, and the renowned art critic Peter Schjeldahl.[16] UGA also produced a catalogue for this exhibition with essays by Hugo Martinez and Peter Schjeldahl.[17] UGA's early shows primarily took place at non profit driven at artist run or alternative spaces, and could thus be interpreted as part of an experimental and a kind of avant-garde movement, and at least in the case of Artist Space part of a context where the concept of fine art where partly redefined.

UGA-member Snake One says that the UGA openings always attracted large crowds, but not so many of the visitors were graffiti writers, and that it probably "…mostly [was] people involved in the art world who came to the shows".[18] The apparent lack of interest from the graffiti community does not necessarily imply a lack of impact. Sociologist Craig Castleman devotes much space to UGA in Getting Up, the first academic study of New York subway graffiti. According to Castleman, the group was important for the artistic self-confidence of its members: "The UGA writers grew as artists – not only in their painting skills but in their confidence and sense of being serious artists".[19] But even if several UGA members, perhaps most notably Phase 2 and Coco 144, continues to produce and exhibit works up until this day, none of them have pursued with art as a full time profession.[20]

It might also be important to mention that UGA not was the only attempt to institutionally organize graffiti in the 1970's. In July 1974 NOGA (Nation of Graffiti Artists) was founded. The instigator, Jack Pelsinger, had followed UGA since 1972, and was inspired by their work, but he stated to Craig Castleman that the organization should be seen as an alternative to Martinez' and UGA's manifest elitism, and NOGA welcomed everyone as a member.[21] Despite this, the organization had an activity similar to UGA's – with meetings, a collective workshop and group exhibitions. But the more open access also seems to have made NOGA less relevant as a strict graffiti organization. Cultural historian Joe Austin claim that the organization was important as a meeting ground but "more like a community youth art program" where the participants where free to use whatever medium or style they preferred.[22] One of the members of NOGA, Scorpio, is by Castleman referred to as a street artist, which is the earliest example of the use this term in the material I have gone through, and might indicate a distinction similar to the one in contemporary parlance.

Neither UGA's or NOGA's activities surveyed above really fit into a description of a hectic teenage craze in the art world, but more suited to be described as grass rooted, experimental, and tentative attempts to organize graffiti in an institutional art context. They also seem to have been insufficiently funded, and if not completely lacking, at least not gaining sustainable institutional support.[23] In the first half of the 1980s this relation between graffiti and institutional art world seems to have changed, with many new exhibitions and events. Now there were also other types of interests and institutions active – more resourceful with potential to bring artists abroad as well as into more prestigious contexts, and several with a commercial agenda.

All of the documented exhibitions in the 1970s are group shows, but from 1982 and onwards there are a large number of solo exhibitions with graffiti writers, often at galleries more or less specialized in graffiti, with Fun Gallery in New York and Yaki Kornblit Gallery in Amsterdam as the most noticeable examples. But the shift from also coincide with a changes in the New York art scene as a whole, were the 1980s often are referred to as an art boom, partly a commercially one fuelled by president Ronald Reagan's tax cuts.[24] There are only two years – 1977 and 1978 – without any documented graffiti related exhibitions. Considering that both UGA and NOGA were non-profit organizations, who was exhibiting in alternative spaces and the little economic resources they had seems to have been from grants and public funds, it is very possible that the famous fiscal crisis in New York in the mid- to late 1970s is the primary cause behind the lack of exhibitions. And it is possible to also see certain continuity: when Castleman writes his dissertation in the late 1970s, NOGA is still operating, albeit with limited resources;[25] one of the twelve core members of UGA – Phase 2 – is a part of many of the exhibitions in the 1980s;[26] and several of the graffiti writers that are to become central in the institutional graffiti of the early 1980s – such as Dondi, Futura 2000 and Quik – are already in 1979 organized in a group called Soul Artists (also referred in some sources as Soul Artists of Zoo York) that seem to have had a structure very similar to UGA and NOGA.[27]

The first exhibitions in the 1980s are also group exhibitions taking place alternative, artist run, and non-profit spaces, and thus both in format and context similar to the exhibitions in the 1970s. And in spite of the existence of solo exhibitions at specialized galleries, the group show is the format that continues to dominate throughout the 1980s and into the 1990s, often with a curatorial focus on the participants' identities as graffiti writers, or their works as graffiti related.[28] In the early 1980 there are also several successful and influential exhibitions where the a group of graffiti writers are exhibited together with an avant-garde of often likewise young collage-educated artists, where all exhibits as individuals, instead of as in the 1970s as a part of a collective. The most renown of these is probably "New York/New Wave", an enormous exhibit curated by Diego Cortez at the alternative art center PS1, and that opened in February 1981.[29] In this group exhibition, graffiti writers such as Blade, Dondi, Futura 2000, Haze, Lady Pink and Lee were exhibited together with young graffiti inspired artists such as Jean-Michel Basquiat and Keith Haring, as well iconic artists and poets such as William Borroughs, Nan Goldin, Joseph Kosuth, Lydia Lunch, Robert Mapplethorpe, and AndyWarhol.[30]

Another change is that the group exhibitions are move from the alternative spaces in New York into museums in Europe and other places outside of the United States. The exhibition that is referred to as the first with graffiti in a museum context opens in October 1983 at Museum Boijmans Van Beuningen, in Rotterdam. This is a group exhibition including Blade, Crash, Dondi, Futura 2000, Lee (Quinones), Noc 167, Phase 2, Quik, Rammellzee, Seen and Zephyr.[31] The museum group exhibitions often appears to be touring exhibitions built on private collections, and they continue to exist throughout the decade and into the 1990s.[32]

The art institutions role?
So what results may these institutional activities have had on the non-institutional production, in terms of understanding of graffiti and street art among both practitioners and a wider public?

Considering the Craig Castleman's claim that the members of UGA gained a confidence and a sense of being serious artists by exhibiting in galleries, one could assume that UGA's activity in this institutional context confirmed perhaps not only their own, but many graffiti writers' identity as artists, as well as it might opened for that graffiti could be considered art among a general public. This does not imply that every graffiti writer necessarily has needed to identify him/herself as an artist, but rather confirming an possibility.

Nor am I implying the opposite – that the early graffiti writers could not have developed an artist identity and self-understanding of their activity as art without the art institutional system. [33] But this could be understood as a complicated dual process where the exhibitions on one hand may have helped to establish the idea of graffiti's potentiality as contemporary art, as something to be taken into serious consideration within in the art institutions and to some extent among a wider public; and that these exhibitions on the other hand functioned to confirm an notion among the graffiti writers, and later street artists, that their activities should be considered fine art. This was obviously never been an unchallenged notion, and both from within the art institutional system and from within other institutions, especially such as the police and transit authorities, there are often objections raised when graffiti and street art are displayed inside the white cube. And as we have seen, also from within the contexts of graffiti and street art. Thus such exhibitions have been, and remain controversial, but they prevail nonetheless – and this whatever one thinks of this – it should be acknowledged and put under further consideration.

Notes and References

1 Martha Cooper and Henry Chalfant, Subway Art (London: Thames and Hudson, 1984)
2 Johannes Stahl, Street Art. (Potsdam: H.F. Üllmann, 2009)
3 Jack Stewart, Subway Graffiti - an aestetic study of graffiti on the subway system of New York City, 1970-1978. (Diss, New York University, 1989)
4 For my forthcoming dissertation, I have compiled a list of art exhibitions, and other institutional activities regarding New York graffiti during the years 1972-1992, either in New York, or outside of the city but with artists referred to as graffiti artists from New York. The list is derived from exhibition catalogues, artist monographs, books on graffiti, and from interviews with various graffiti writers. The following forthcoming reasoning will largely be based on this work.
5 "Institution." Merriam-Webster.com. Merriam-Webster, n.d. Web. 1 June 2014. <http://www.merriam-webster.com/dictionary/institution>
6 For a concise survey of this theory see Garry L. Hagberg, "The Institutional Theory of Art:Theory and Antitheory", in Companion to Art Theory, edited by Paul Smith, Carolyn Wilde (Oxford: Blackwell, 2002).
7 For a description regarding the objectives and organization of the new York City Vandal Squad (officially Citywide Vandals Task Force) see: http://www.nyc.gov/html/nypd/html/crime_prevention/citywide_vandals_taskforce.shtml [retrieved 2014-06-01]
8 One early example of bringing these aspects to the fore could be found in Susan Stewart's "Ceci Tuera Cela: Graffiti as Crime and Art", published in Life after postmodernism: essays on value and culture, edited by Jon Fekete (Basingstoke: Macmillan Education, 1988). I discuss these aspects more extensively in my forthcoming dissertation The G-Word – Negotiations and Transformations of graffiti. I have published a paper regarding the anti-graffiti industry in the specific context of Scandinavian zero tolerance on graffiti in Kontrolle öffentlicher Räume. Unterstützen Unterdrücken Unterhalten Unterwandern, edited by E.T. Bertuzzo, E.B. Gantner, J. Niewöhner, H. Oevermann (ed.) (Berlin: LIT Verlag, 2013).
9 Edward Lucie-Smith, (1995). Art Today. London: Phaidon p. xx
10 Ibid.
11 Craig Castleman, Getting up: subway graffiti in New York, (Cambridge, Mass.: MIT Press, 1982), p. 117.
12 I have previously published an article on UGA in graffiti specialized magazine UP, some of the shorter elements of reasoning and occasional quotes may be familiar to anyone who reads both texts. See Jacob Kimvall, "The Creation of Graffiti as Art", UP No. 40, June 2009.
13 Castleman (1982), p. 119.
14 ibid.
15 Claudia Gould & Valerie Smith (1998), 5000 Artists Return to Artist Space: 25 Years, New York, Artist Space, p. 68. Peter Schjeldahl claim that this was his one and only attempt to curate an exhibition, and that the experience have given him "a lifelong respect for mediocre curators".
16 Ibid.
17 Catalogue "United Graffiti Artists 1975", published by United Graffiti Artists Inc., 29 Jumel Place, New York, N.Y. 10032.
18 Jacob Kimvall, "The Creation of Graffiti as Art", UP No. 40, June 2009.
19 Castleman (1982), p. 125.
20 Names of more or less all of the members of UGA show up in my material during all of the decades. Phase 2 is a central part of the internationalization of graffiti in the 1980s and early 1990s.
21 Castleman (1982), p. 127.
22 Joe Austin (2001), Taking the train: how graffiti art became an urban crisis in New York city, (New York: Columbia University Press, 2001)p. 72
23 Castleman (1982), p. 119 (regarding UGA) and p. 133 (regarding NoGA).
24 Eleanor Heartney, Postmodernism, (London: Tate Gallery Publishing, 2001), p. 23-24.
25 Castleman (1982), p. 133.
26 See Phase 2's list of exhibitions in Hoekstra Froukje & Haks, Frans, Coming from the subway: New York graffiti art : Geschichte und Entwicklung eine aussergewöhnlichen Bewegung.(Erlangen: Karl Müller Verlag, 1992).
27 Austin (2001), p. 187-188. It is worth mentioning that Soul Artists was a more traditional graffiti crew in the early 1970s. Soul Artists is also mentioned by Keith Haring see Keith Haring & John Gruen, Keith Haring: the authorized biography, (London: Thames and Hudson, 1991) p. 73.
28 This tendency of superficially lumping together graffiti writers from different generations and artistic agendas has been brought to the fore by Zephyr, criticizing the art institutions of being "...unwilling or unable to present those artists as individuals with a distinct vision." His account is specifically regarding Crash and Futura 2000, but I interpret is as critique of the whole phenomenon of group exhibitions. See Jeff Chang, Can't stop won't stop: a history of the hip-hop generation. (New York: St. Martin's Press, 2005) p. 181
29 PS1 has undergone several transformations since 1981, and is today known as an established contemporary art institution that under the name MoMA PS1 closely affiliated with The Museum of Modern Art in New York. For more information see http://momaps1.org/about/affiliation/ [retrieved 2014-03-14]
30 For a full list of the more than 100 participants of "New York/ New Wave" see MoMA:s web resources: http://www.moma.org/learn/resources/archives/ps1_exhibitions/exhibitions_1981 [retrieved 2014-03-14]
31 Witten, Andrew & White, Michael (2001). Style master general: the life of graffiti artist Dondi White. (New York: ReganBooks, 2001) p. 170
32 In my material there are (between 1984 and 1992) are documented graffiti related exhibitions at Louisiana, Humlebaek, Denmark; Groninger Museum, Groningen, Holland (two times, 1984 and 1992); Mittelrheinisches Landesmuseum, Mainz, Germany; Nordjyllands Kunstmuseum, Aalborg, Denmark; Heine-Önstad Kunstsenter, Høviksodden, Norway; Liljevalchs konsthall, Stockholm; Leopold-Hoesch Museum, Düren, Germany; Musée National des Monuments Français, Paris, France
33 Joe Austin suggests that this early recognition of graffiti in the art press played "an important role in the general conceptualization of writing as art among writers". See Austin (2001), p. 72. Some of my informants expressed a firm conviction that an outspoken artist identity existed among graffiti writers previous to the recognition of the institutional art world, and I settle with the an assumption that this played a role.

Susan A. Phillips, Associate Professor of Environmental Analysis, Pitzer College, susan_phillips@pitzer.edu

Bomb the Canon: Rewriting the History of Graffiti in Los Angeles

Graffiti—long an outsider, illicit medium—is currently attempting to write itself into an artistic canon already struggling with the tension between Western conventions and the global circulation of images. In the process of gaining entrance to the Western canon, graffiti practitioners and scholars have begun to cement the narrative about what counts as its history. It's as if the graffiti world has created its own canon of value and acceptability and is leaving much out in the process. Contemporary treatments of graffiti are limited in topical scope, skipping eras, neglecting graffiti-rich communities, failing to trace broader histories, and missing the richness of the moments in-between. By focusing on a one hundred-year span of graffiti in Los Angeles, my work attempts to expand what has become a narrow view of graffiti's inception in the contemporary world—metaphorically to bomb the canon. I examine three instances of writing—a wall of hobo monikers dated 1914-1921, cholo writing from the 1970s, and graffiti at the Los Angeles harbor from 1950-1999.

Introduction

2014 was a critical year for my study of Los Angeles graffiti. First, 2014 was the 100-year birthday of the oldest dated graffiti I have yet found in Los Angeles: a wall of hobo writing from 1914-21. For the past 25 years, I have studied mostly the graffiti of gangs—violent, marginal social groups with deeply totemic forms of body and wall marking (Phillips 1999). While documenting the writing of gangs, I soon became interested in much older genres of graffiti and with the recovery, documentation, and conservation of graffiti dated before 1965. One hundred years might not seem so significant in places like Lisbon or Rome. But Los Angeles is a much newer landscape, with a tradition of erasing, neglecting, and undervaluing its own history (Klein 1997). As of this writing, Los Angeles is also place on graffiti lock-down. The city has declared various wars on graffiti through time. Under certain conditions, vandalism can be charged as a felony, which carries a prison sentence. City officials have spared no expense in painting out the entire Los Angeles River, a paved river people rarely go to, can barely see, and over half of L.A. doesn't even know exists. Something from 1914 that remains on a wall is remarkable in a city that has been defined by rapid change. The hundred-year mark of the hobo graffiti seemed a landmark moment in my work. The second reason that 2014 was important was that it finalized a movement to cement L.A. graffiti's place within the Western canon of art. This canonical invitation was brainchild of Ed Sweeny, owner of ESMoA (formerly the El Segundo Museum of Art). Sweeny had wanted to do a project with graffiti around the black books that writers use. He decided to bring a group of artists to view rare books at the Getty Research Institute, and their visit was facilitated by rare books curator David Brafman. The artists found strongest resonance with a 15th century liber amicorum—a "book of friends" that noblemen would fill with the signatures, crests, and insignia of their associates. In 2014 Brafman curated the resulting ESMoA exhibition, Scratch, which celebrated newfound ability to juxtapose the work of contemporary graffiti writers with compositions by Albrecht Dürer and the like. As the daughter of a Renaissance art historian, I could relate. I fell in love with graffiti because I was already in love with early Christian art and the Northern Renaissance. I was captivated by the Northwest Coast and by ancient Greece and Rome. My sense of wonderment at being inside an Etruscan tomb at age thirteen was not so different from the feeling I had in L.A.'s storm drains years later. The graffiti that most interested me carried a visceral connection to social life, to religion, and to work of both licit and illicit natures. And then there was the focus on script. I had a well-worn copy of Oscar Ogg's *Three Classics of Italian Calligraphy* that my mother had given me (Ogg 1957). I treasured Sally and Jerry Romotsky's (1976) *Barrio Calligraphy*, which reviewed the ornate lettering of 1970s Chicano gang members. Later, François Chastanet (2009) would trace the script of Chicano gang writing against classic lettering forms. In bringing contemporary writers together with their 15th century counterparts, the Getty and ESMoA had created a public forum for graffiti that garnered international attention. Graffiti had entered the Western canon of art.

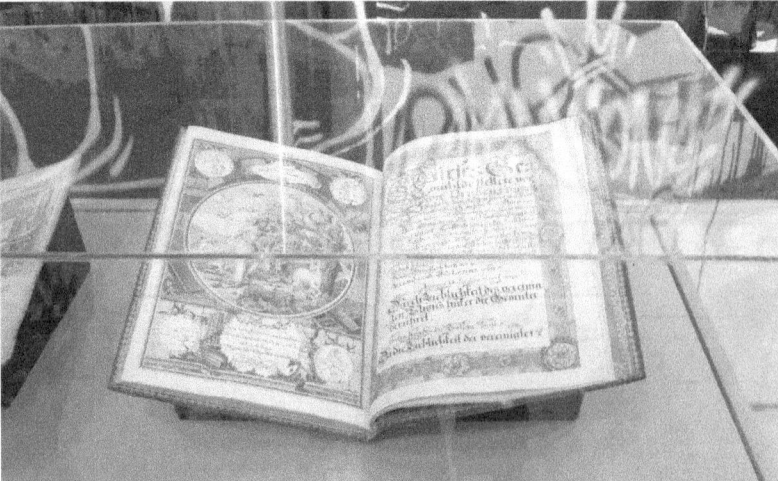

Fig. 1. Rare book from Scratch exhibition at ESMoA with graffiti reflected in background. Photo and permission by author, 2014.

The Scratch show and the production of the L.A. Liber Amicorum made me wonder if this were the right comparison. 15th century noblemen and their networks occupied a far different social space than did many writers in the room. The two did share the fellowship of common production, the idea of a roll call—another gang concept—and the notion of memento or keepsake. They shared attention to lettering, to the balance of composition, and to form.

This paper's title, Bomb the Canon, carries multiple meanings. To "bomb," in the graffiti sense of the word, is to write and it has two key points of relevance. Bombing the Canon in one sense means to write graffiti into it, where bombing is a creative process of inclusion even if you have to take down doors to get there. Another connotation of bombing is destruction. In the sense of this paper bombing can also be read as responding to or questioning the new doors being erected—in short responding to graffiti's inclusion in the canon as a construct. Canonical conventions are about what kinds of objects count and in what style, and about how works are valued and devalued as a result. In the process of attempting to gain entrance to the Western canon, the graffiti world has begun to cement its own narrative about what counts as its history. What counts seems to have shrunk in inverse proportion to the global spread of the graffiti and street art phenomenon. It's as if the graffiti world has created its own canon of value and acceptability, and is leaving much out in the process. The year 2014 is the year that two graffiti threads—one historical and one canonical—converged in my work. Through projects like the L.A. Liber Amicorum, graffiti practitioners, curators, and scholars are currently attempting to write graffiti into a canon already struggling with the tension between Western tradition and the global circulation of images. This chapter aims to explore some of the genres of graffiti being left out of, and their interconnections to, canonical conversations. Studying older graffiti is challenging. Through time I have documented graffiti from every decade of the 20th century from communities ranging from teen lovers in the 1930s to container ship sailors in the 1990s. This one hundred-year span of Los Angeles graffiti has afforded me a vision outside of normative graffiti trajectories. Part of presenting this work is to expand what has become a narrow vision of graffiti's inception in the contemporary world. I wish to draw attention to the current narrative as a construct, and to chart the navigation of insider-outsider designations in the production of illicit images.

Normative Graffiti Narratives

Very little work engages graffiti genres outside of the history, lineage, and sometimes interconnections between 1970s New York and contemporary street art. Most chapters in this volume reflect this trajectory, which has grown in tandem with graffiti and street art's growing importance in the global art scene. Contemporary documentation of historical graffiti dated before 1970 is rare. Writing and analysis of any graffiti genre outside of the 1970s New York-to-street art trajectory are equally rare.

In 2011, the Museum of Contemporary Art (MoCA) in Los Angeles mounted the first large-scale graffiti-based museum exhibition that garnered international attention. MoCA's Art in the Streets included a small section on hobo and railway traditions, and carried a small section on gang graffiti that included the work of Los Angeles Crips. The show's published timeline begins with 1940s "Kilroy Was Here" and very quickly expands 1970s of New York graffiti (Deitch, Gastman, and Rose 2011). Gastman and Neelon's (2011) ambitiously titled The History of American Graffiti carries an almost identical trajectory: beginning with Kilroy, hobos and trainmen in the initial pages, with lip service to gangs, and the remainder devoted to New York and Philadelphia style graffiti beginning in the 1970s. The work in the above and in other books and exhibitions has provided considerable nuance to knowledge of graffiti art from 1970 to the present. Despite its nuance, this view of graffiti remains so focused in its topical scope that it skips entire eras, neglects graffiti-rich communities, fails to trace broader histories, and in general misses the richness of the moments in-between.

Graffiti is sometimes esoteric and solitary, but more often it carries the richness of social connection and group belonging. That latter part is what has drawn me deeper into graffiti's study over a twenty-five year period during which I have been lucky enough to capture writing that spans one hundred years. This article attempts to add to conversations about the canon by exploring three case studies from Los Angeles.

The problem of documentation and conservation accompanies these case studies. With the explosion of large-scale graffiti and street art, smaller-scale local traditions of graffiti are being compromised or lost. Little is intentional about this—graffiti and street art are attractive artistic traditions that people want to be part of. But I worry whether kids in Northern Ireland still write their names in lines one on top of the other, or do they write in tags exclusively? Has Italy's relationship to political graffiti been diminished in waves of street art? The sheer spatial scope of street art and its subsequent erasure is taking out older markings wholesale, at incredible speed. Smaller writing in pencil, chalk or charcoal simply cannot compete with the blanket coverage of large-scale pieces and productions. Part of the point of this chapter is to encourage graffiti scholars and practitioners to look underneath their own work to smaller scales, different communities, and earlier eras. The time is now to document and present the history of what alternative genres remain, and to examine more critically what stands outside graffiti's own developing canon.

Three Case Studies in Los Angeles

For the past 100 years, an alternative written record has been tied to the underbelly of Los Angeles' built environment. The infrastructure of railroads, bridges, storm drain tunnels, harbors, and rivers has given shelter to discrete but overlapping communities whose messages are inscribed with rocks, chalk, crayon, charcoal, pencil, paint, and sometimes railroad tar. The work of these writers offers a vision of the city from below, where authors have constructed a fragile ecology of writing dating back a century. If the places are forsaken, the writers are just as marginal. They write a chronology of presence—mostly of names and dates. Some of their work has been preserved due to flukes of infrastructural design. Older marks survive because they find themselves in odd places, protected from the elements and momentarily out of reach.

This chapter reviews three genres of graffiti that have varying relationships to contemporary graffiti narratives: the work of hobos, cholos, and both fisherman and sailors at the Los Angeles Harbor. Each of these genres carries a different lesson for the concept of the canon. Hobo writing is the oft-cited primum mobile of contemporary graffiti. Cholos are 1970s gang members from Los Angeles whose elegant script lettering is the subject of a nostalgic graffiti gaze, and some links to which have been incorporated into global art worlds. Graffiti at the harbor are the most disconnected from conventional graffiti discourses. The writing of fishermen and containership sailors has its own local and global circulation that is almost completely unknown outside of those particular communities.

Hobos

Hobos have a history and written tradition that dates back to the end of the Civil War. Men who no longer fit the changing industrial landscape of the United States took to the rails, moving from town to town, looking for seasonal work, sleeping where they could, and leaving written marks in their wake. The general framework of wandering travel, taking on monikers, and writing graffiti had its start in the hobo community, which is why many authors cite this tradition in introductory materials. According to Bill Daniels, who has studied hobo writing most extensively, little documentation exists of actual hobo graffiti aside from compedia of hobo signs that have mostly been constructed post hoc (Daniels 2008). Graffiti writing afforded hobos the ability to connect with one another, both remotely and physically, in a time before most people had telephones. People would their write names on walls, along with dates and arrows to indicate the direction they were headed and when (Livingston 1910). Through this system, friends could track one another and meet up at "jungles" or other places. Jungles were camps of largely male individuals devoted to the hobo lifestyle, which was as much about freedom and resourcefulness as it was about danger and degeneracy.

In Los Angeles hobo graffiti from the early 20th Century is rare. An exception is one wall dated 1914-1921 on the Arroyo Seco, a small Los Angeles waterway. The markings on this wall are nearly undisturbed after 100 years. They were protected by river paving, which lowered the river bottom by twenty feet leaving the marks unreachable. The bridge overhead sheltered the writing from the elements, although some later water damage occurred from dripping pipes, which calcified some marks, washed them away, or covered them in moss.

The 80-foot hobo wall mostly consists of names and dates rendered in chalk, with charcoal from fires, in pencil, or with a waxy substance that could be crayon. Some writers lightly inscribed words with railroad spikes. Hobos wrote now-classic monikers as Kid Bill, Kid Smith, Winey Pete, Oakland Red, and Overland Mike. These writers occasionally used stylized scripts, some of which were related to typeface styles of the late 1800s and others to handwriting traditions of the era. The fletching—feathers—of the arrows intertwined into the names and dates were stylized into characteristic heart shapes.

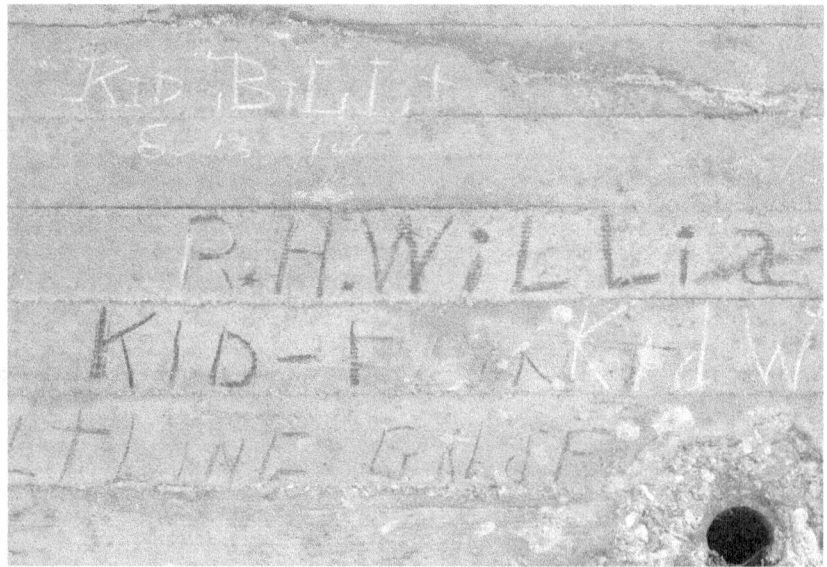

Fig. 2. Kid Bill 8-13-14, R.H. Williamson, Kid Flint and other hobos write in chalk and charcoal in the early 20th Century.
Photo and permission by author.

On this wall are connections to a Civil War camp (Camp 507), to a labor union (Local 70 Teamsters), and to hobo sexual practices. Iconic images of the West include a cowboy and bucking bronco. The mainstays are simpler: names and dates are graffiti's constant companions.

The association of a written tradition with a marginalized social group has a recognizable start in hobo communities in early 20th Century United States. There is clearly room for more scholarly attention to how hobos used writing to construct social space. Some residual aspects of this process remain in marks that still survive. This wall of early writings is unique in its ability to communicate the history of marginalized people in urban space. I have begun conversations with various people and institutions about the conservation of this wall as a cultural heritage site. The association of graffiti with museums or municipal entities may open a space for recognizing graffiti's particular manner of re-writing conventional histories—including the history of itself.

Cholos

In Los Angeles, basic nicknaming and written conventions begin with hobos. Subsequent generations of youth were exposed to hobo traditions along the Los Angeles River, which through time became a place of significant graffiti production and innovation. Just as 19th century typeface influenced the style of hobo writing, hobo writing in turn influenced the practice of Chicano gang writing and naming conventions—in particular in their attention to lettering styles.

Today, writers and street artists continue to distinguish Los Angeles in the graffiti world because of their attention to script. The focus on script sets L.A. apart, and provides a distinct combination of local and global influences. One of those influences originates with gangs. A sub-genre of Los Angeles gang graffiti, "cholo writing," is Chicano/Latino gang writing from the 1970s. Cholo writing is part of a much longer tradition dating back to the 1930s and 40s and dating forward into the present day. By the 1940s, early gang writers had already established stylistic conventions, including the use of quotes to frame compositions, and the frequent use of crosses and rays, which mostly likely stemmed from connections to the Catholic Church. Some of these conventions are still in use and have become incorporated into graffiti-based art production for commercial sale and collection.

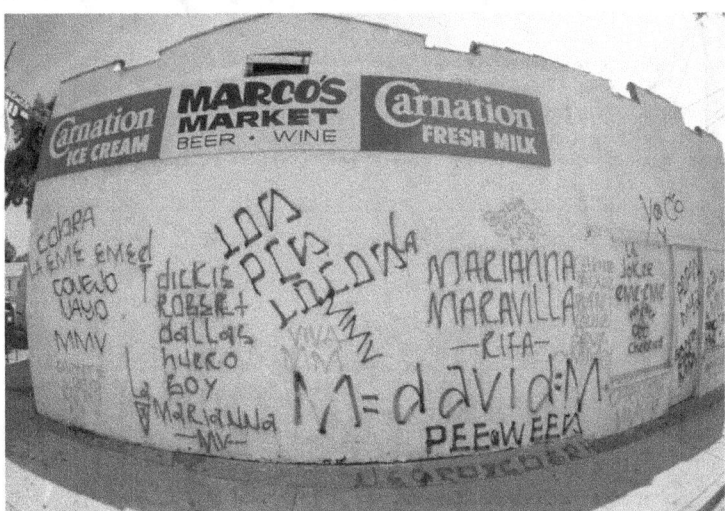

Fig. 3. 1970s gang writing from the Marianna Maravilla neighborhood of East Los Angeles.
Photo by Leonard Nadel, 1974; permission by author.

Cholo writing in 1970s is notable because of the florescence of single-line scripts, which were rendered in spraypaint, pencil, and pen. Youth created intricate scripts as part of gang subculture, with accompanying kinds of dress, speech, gesture, and car culture (Cesaretti 1975; Romotsky and Romotsky 1976). Some graffiti practitioners as well as authors have nostalgic feelings toward the 1970s era (Grody 2006; Chastanet 2009). Today's references to "cholos" as opposed to "gang members" seem safe because cholos pre-date the explosion of lethal violence that occurred in the 1980s and beyond.

This moment of 1970s gang writing is traceable through conversations about the canon because some artists also participate in global art markets. Script-oriented artists have shown their work all over the world. Elements of cholo writing and so-called "handstyles" have been incorporated into the L.A. Liber Amicorum and Scratch projects as a result.

If one were to ask these artists about how their work related to "gangs," they would extremely cautious in their answers. Artists and curators are playing with fire when they draw any lines toward more contemporary gangs. One gallery show called "Alphabet Soup" claimed not to be gang related, yet the work of some artists carried connections to generations of gang writing, some of which were contemporary. Another show called "Con Safos" attempted to celebrate the interconnections between gangs and the graffiti art world in a more open, holistic way. Con Safos—literally "with safety"—references the 1970s practice of protecting work by creating a reflection back onto would-be vandals. The show was supposed to be a representation of the artistic contributions of marginal cultural actors that used gang-related fonts in their work. The pushback from law enforcement and the venue's board was significant and caused the show's cancellation. Both gallery shows demonstrate artists' collective unwillingness to associate with contemporary gang writing, or to use the word "gang" in association with stylistic elements in their work. In Los Angeles, reference to "cholos" represents looking back to a time before gangs were transnational, before they had guns, before they were so violent, and before prison gangs took control over street and prison illicit economies.

In 2014 Los Angeles and the decade leading up to it, artists, curators, and writers have tended to erase gangs as a social group from script-oriented lettering traditions even though gang members were key in establishing them. Words like "cholo" or "handstyles" are signals of that erasure. Part of me wants to embrace that narrative, because the representational risks are clear. But something about the erasure of a community already erased by society rankles me, especially as a person who has studied gang graffiti for the past twenty-five years. For now I am content to draw attention to the narrative as a construct. That narrative eschews the violence of gangs while inviting some gang-related stylistic traditions to the table.

Critical at this juncture is the protection and public presentation of existing photographs from the 1970s era. Several photo collections from the 1970s and earlier are under private ownership; none to my knowledge is in a library although some are available in internet venues. These collections need to be made accessible to the public through the careful inventory and curation of graffiti-related archives.

Harbor

In terms of the three case studied discussed here, the graffiti of the Los Angeles harbor is the most removed from conventional graffiti art practices and discourses. Two distinct genres have existed at the L.A. harbor through time that mimic the United States' shift from a production to a consumption economy. On one side of the port is the graffiti of commercial fishermen and pleasure boaters, who painted boat names on a 200-foot long wooden fence at a local boat works. On the other side of the harbor came the writing of generations of container ship sailors—international seamen who painted the names of their vessels along the "bull-rail" next to where they docked. The fence of boat names is deeply local, whereas container ship graffiti carries ties to international trade and international people. There seems to be little interaction between the two genres, which I describe in turn.

L.A.'s containership graffiti comes in lengthy horizontals, layered in the paint used to touch up docked vessels. Seamen from Russia to Israel have written out the names of their ships, sometimes their own names, and sometimes the date in port. Their graffiti comes in multiple languages, and in alphabets that include Aramaic, Cyrillic, Hebrew, Japanese, and Chinese. I was lucky enough to document some of this writing in the mid-1990s. The port had a policy of not erasing sailor graffiti, some of which dated back to the 1950s. Today, much if not all of this graffiti has been destroyed by port expansion, which compromised the original harbor infrastructure. I have as yet been unable to revisit the harbor to document what is left or to note new writing due to post 9-11 security restrictions.

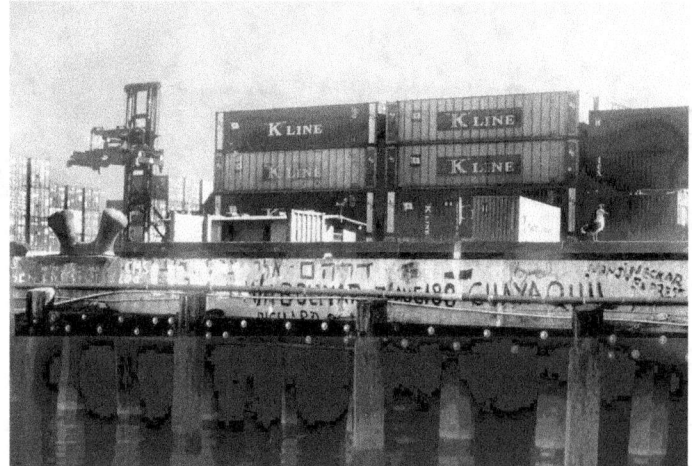

Fig. 4. Container ship in the Los Angeles Harbor, circa 1996. Photo and permission by author.

Seamen tend to follow basic conventions for writing ship's names. M/V is the most common prefix, meaning "Motor Vessel," but others include CMS for Canadian Maritime Shipping, HMS for Her Majesty's Ship, or MSC for Mediterranean Shipping Company. These simple conventions represent a complex social, economic, and political sphere. Tracing particular ship names is difficult. Ships can be named after other ships or can change names through time. Different kinds of cargo ships visit the port, and each can carry different acronyms, codes, and specialized language. Most ships have hidden provenance and sail under flags of convenience. M/V Sparto, for example, may be a crude oil tanker that currently sails under the flag of Cyprus. M/V Bolivar took the name of another ship that sank in the 1940s. The "Neckar Express" built in 1972 is currently operating as the MSC Arabia and sails under the flag of Malta. That particular ship began as the Aristarcos and has had nine names in total, of which Neckar Express was the second.

The frequent changing of ship names makes each instance of sailor graffiti representative of a particular moment in time. I am just beginning research into the shipping context and the written marks container ship sailors have left behind. Their collective work represent another male-centered community tied through labor, identity, and writing. Seamen represented aspects of this identity along the dock with the materials that surrounded them. The graffiti of container ship sailors likely exists in every ports of call around the globe. To my knowledge none of it has been documented or studied.

On the other side of the harbor, a 300-foot long wooden fence of boat names dated 1966-1999, was the work of commercial fisherman and pleasure-craft owners. who brought their boats to the San Pedro Boat Works (SPBW) for painting and other repairs. The graffiti of boat and place names on SPBW's wall—Timm's Landing, the Lusty Wench, Sea Moon, Le Dauphin, and others—covers the entirety of the fence. The boat works' fence represents a selective history of the Los Angeles that includes the heyday and decline of commercial fishing on this side of the harbor.

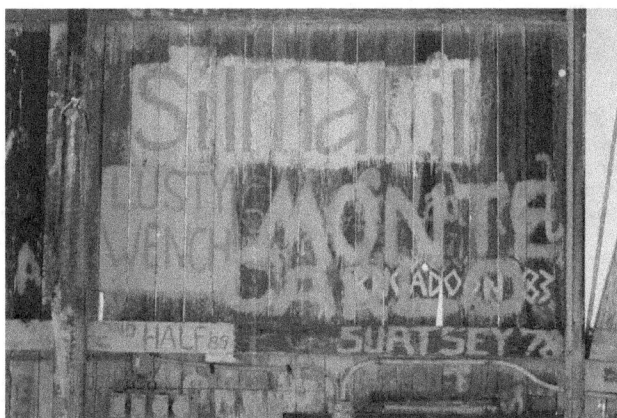

Fig. 5. Fence of boat names, including Silmaril, Lusty Wench, Monte Carlo, 2nd Half '89, Surtsey 78 and others.
Photo and permission by author.

This fence at the now-defunct San Pedro Boat Works will eventually be torn down, as the site was closed amidst an environmental scandal. I have begun conversations with several museums around conserving this fence. Whether or not it is preserved physically, the digital documentation of sites like this is critical and mimics current impulses of graffiti and street art practitioners to document and post their work digitally.

Conclusion

This chapter is meant to offer missing counter threads to what has become a narrow view of graffiti in the contemporary world. By bringing the lineage back 100 years, I wanted to profile three local traditions of writing that are lesser known. I also wanted to connect these genres to graffiti lineages that have now become somewhat standardized, if hotly debated.

The work presented here, most of which remains in situ in Los Angeles' built environment, forms a parallel geography of value. If there is a canon here it is one of male marginalia. My own sensibility in thinking about hobos is that I am thinking about gang members and about sailors or migrants. Through writing, mostly male individuals are occupying spaces they are not supposed to be occupying, and writing where they should not be. This is what Timothy Cresswell calls being "out of place" (Cresswell 1996). Through writing, the groups referenced here construct new notions of place tied to Los Angeles landscapes. They write a story that coexists with dominant narratives, carving out their own social worlds on the underbelly of conventional history. With names and dates as anchors, these writers inscribe themselves into a history that they've fallen out of, or whose intersections force them into largely male circumstances. The main thing with graffiti is whose name is on the wall. The name is graffiti's main stem—the "faith" of graffiti, as Norman Mailer reminds us (Kurlanski, Naar, and Mailer 1974).

L.A. graffiti's invitation to join the Western canon of art traces a particular stylistic and person-centered lineage. My interest is in diversifying what could potentially be included in this canon, and to explore the question of possible connections that may have been overlooked. Graffiti as a rule tends to defy attempts of containment, which is one of the things that makes graffiti-related conversations about the canon so unexpected and rich.

I'm left wondering what it means to look to other forms during this highpoint for graffiti and street art. My sense is that interconnections here need more exploration, that tracings between styles might be fruitful. This chapter has intended to look at the interstices of conventional timelines, and to pay attention to people disconnected from current trends. Most of this work remains undocumented and is at risk. In that sense, conversations about graffiti must be about inclusion and exclusion—canon and its opposite. They also need to be about cultural preservation. My own struggle with the famed ephemerality of this medium is ongoing.

What is not ephemeral—and what may be graffiti's true canon—is the visceral tie between writing, communities, and the built environment. If older graffiti remains at risk, the robust way that writers infuse art and community into landscape shows few signs of flagging.

References
Chastanet, F. (2009) Cholo Writing: Latino Gang Graffiti in Los Angeles. (Stockholm: Dokument Press).
Cesaretti, G. (1975) Street Writers: A Guided Tour of Chicano Graffiti. (Venice, CA: Acrobat Books).
Cresswell, T. (1996) In Place/Out of Place: Geography, Ideology, and Transgression (Minneapolis: University of Minnesota Press).
Daniels, B. (2008) Mostly True: The Story of Bozo Texino. (Portland, OR: Microcosm Publishing)
Deitch, J., R. Gastman, and A. Rose (2011) Art in the Streets (New York: Skira Rizzoli).
Gastman, R. and C. Neelon (2011) The History of American Graffiti (New York: HarperCollins).
Grody, S. (2006) Graffiti L.A.: Street Styles and Art (New York: Abrams).
Klein, N. (1997) The History of Forgetting: Los Angeles and the Erasure of Memory (London: Verso).
Livingston, L. (1910) Life and Adventures of A-No. 1, America's Most Celebrated Tramp (Cambridge Springs, PA: The A-No. 1 Publishing Co.)
Kurlansky, I, Naar, J., and Mailer, N. (1974) The Faith of Graffiti (New York: Praeger).
Ogg, O. (1957) Three Classics of Italian Calligraphy (New York: Dover).
Phillips, S. (1999) Wallbangin: Graffiti and Gangs in L.A. (Chicago: University of Chicago Press).
Romotsky, J. and S. Romotsky (1976) Barrio Calligraphy (Los Angeles: Dawson's Books).

Julia Tulke, independent researcher,
aestheticsofcrisis.org

Aesthetics of Crisis.
Street Art, Austerity Urbanism and the Right to the City

In the context of the European crisis a wave of new urban social movements has transformed cities all over the region into dynamic laboratories of a new spatial activism. Street Art and other forms of Urban Intervention have become important political practices in these struggles constituting a new aesthetics and culture of protest committed to the Lefebvrian claim to the Right to the City. Based on my own empirical research on political street art in Athens, this paper examines how street art, particularly in the European periphery, forms part of a larger project of reimagining and re-appropriating cities in crisis.

Street Art, Social Movements, Crisis

Introduction

In the wake of the complex state of crisis Europe has been experiencing in the past five years, a wave of new urban social movements has erupted and transformed cities all over the region into dynamic laboratories of a new creative spatial activism. Street art and other forms of urban intervention have become important political practices in these struggles constituting a new aesthetics and culture of protest committed to the Lefebvrian claim to the Right to the City – the right of urban citizens to actively participate in the creation and reinvention of cities according to their own human needs and desires[1]. The preoccupation with urban space and its reappropriation that is so characteristic of these contemporary social movements is not surprising given the symbolic significance of cities in the current crisis. On the one hand, they represent key sites for the production of the crisis – both as centers of political administration and financial accumulation, and as sites of megaprojects of neoliberal restructuring, commodification, and speculative investment. On the other hand, cities have been most severely affected by the effects of the crisis and particularly the austerity apparatus implemented most harshly in the Southern and Eastern peripheries of Europe. "[M]any cities [bear] the physical scars of disinvestment, disuse and decline . . . [opening up] spatial cracks . . . in what had been a fairly unbroken field of accelerated development" (Tonkiss, 2013)[2]. These cracks in the urban landscapes – such as abandoned buildings and structures – are now being occupied by a panoply of activists for conceptualizing and living new urbanisms that question and point beyond capitalism as the sole organizing principle of urban public space.

I examined this dynamic empirically in the context of a research project on political street art and urban activism in Athens that I conducted in 2013. Relating materials from this case study to some theoretical reflections I will describe the ways in which, particularly in the European periphery, street art has become part of a larger political project of reimagining, transforming and reappropriating urban space in the context of the crisis. Consequently I argue that profound analyses of street art – its iconographies and vocabularies, the actors engaged in the field, its dialectic oscillation between local and global dimensions, the spaces occupied etc. – are crucial for understanding the interrelation of the crisis, urban space and social and political movements. In order to do so I will first engage in some theoretical observations about the relationship of the crisis, austerity politics, urban space, and social movements. Building upon the established theoretical vocabulary, I will proceed to describe the spatial transformation that Athens has experienced in the course of the crisis and the impact it has had on the street art scene. Subsequently, I will describe some of the strategies of subverting and processing the crisis that street artists in Athens employ to eventually propose some potential trajectories and questions for further research.

Crisis Cities and Austerity Urbanism: Some Theoretical Reflections

The associations evoked by the term crisis could hardly be any more numerous, diverse and complex. It has been used to mobilize discourses about economics, politics, societies, and culture on global, regional, national, and local levels. It has been used for capitalist critique and nationalist propaganda; by politicians, activists, journalists, scholars, citizens. It is thus all the more crucial to establish a critical approach to the term. The understanding of the crisis that my work is based upon recognizes it as both a series of connected empirical effects – such as mass youth unemployment and the dismantling of welfare states in southern Europe – as well as a discursive formation deeply permeated by regional power asymmetries and national agendas. Furthermore the crisis constitutes an asymmetrical system of knowledge production. Specifically in the case of Europe the crisis is discussed as a phenomenon that takes place in and affects the periphery and has to be described and regulated from the relatively stable centre. In the contemporary context the term crisis is most commonly used to describe the global financial crisis and simultaneous deep recession in mainly North-America and Europe since 2007/08. At least two competing meta-narratives circulate about the origins of the crisis, the more conservative one focusing on the events that lead to and followed the bankruptcy of the US-American bank Lehmann Brothers in 2008. The problem is here located in certain faulty institutions and actors (e.g. bad banks and corrupt governments) that subvert the otherwise unproblematic economic and political system. Following this discourse austerity has been established and justified as a punitive political strategy to sanction supposedly deviant governments and put them on a path towards fiscal discipline[3]. A more progressive approach sees the basis of the crisis in the system of neoliberal capitalism itself and assumes that the origins of the present crisis go as far back as the 1970s and an escalation has since been delayed. Most critical theoretical reflections on the matter, share the idea that the crisis is structural, multidimensional and transformative for politics, economics, as well as the material quality of everyday life. The multidimensional crisis operates on several interdependent levels – social reproduction and political representations to just name two – and manifests a series of interconnected empirical effects. As a prolonged state of exception the crisis ultimately creates a situation in which existing modes of action cannot be continued, opening spaces for new practices both repressive and emancipatory[4].

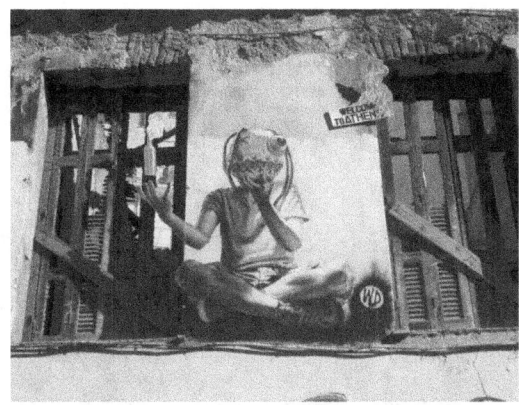

Fig. 1 Welcome to Athens artwork by WD, photo: Julia Tulke

The concept of austerity urbanism is perhaps the closest theoretical approximation currently available to conceptualize how this dynamic plays out in urban space. The aforementioned disinvestment and deregulation cities are experiencing in the wake of increasingly austere governance have devastated urban landscapes and biographies profoundly and lead to some disastrous social effects such as the drastic deterioration of public health[5] and the production of a whole new class of urban poverty[6]. Simultaneously, the same dynamic has liberated urban spaces and surfaces for creative and political appropriation such as occupations or creative interventions. Even though it has been pointed out that such practices may easily be reintroduced into the exclusionary circuits of commodification and gentrification[7] the crisis has produced some remarkable opportunities for subversive spatial activism.

Athens: A City Transformed by Crisis

The drastic welfare cuts enforced in Greece in accordance with the austerity apparatus have paved the road for an accelerated social meltdown, manifesting among other things a general health decline, growing unemployment, and increasing suicide rates (Dalakoglou 2012)[8]. This has also lead to extreme changes in the physical and social fabric of the city: homelessness, increased unsafe drug abuse, prostitution, vacant shops and houses – often nailed shut to prevent people from living in there – abandoned construction sites and an increased presence of police surveillance. Urban space in crisis is thus at the same time deregulated and militarized. Particularly revealing is the new class of the nouveau poor, often people who formerly belonged to the ranks of the aspiring middle classes but have fallen through the ever-expanding gaps in the grid of social welfare. The nouveau poor cut across lines of ethnicity, age, gender, and education and do not directly participate in political and social movements. As the city of Athens has never faced such extreme amounts of people in need, there are hardly any institutions fit to deal with homeless people or drug users. Instead the problems are visibly laid bare in the streets of the urban centre. Many of the political mobilizations that have formed against the backdrop of the crisis are deeply embedded urban space. Perhaps the most meaningful practices therein are the uncounted protests and riots that have startled Athens since 2008. By temporarily claiming and transforming public space, protests provide an opportunity to explore common grievances, negotiate and represent concerns and issues in an inclusive manner. "By creating a march in the midst of the city space, the protestors achieve a subversion of the hegemonic uses of space" (Tsilimpounidi 2012, 548)[9]. While the destructive and aggressive character of riots may not find general approval, they inscribe the spatial claims expressed in protests into the cities physical surface therein permanently transforming urban space. Micheal Herzfeld (2011) observes:

> After the demonstrations were over, the jagged edges of marble facings in the centre of Athens offered expressive testimony to the rampaging demonstrators. These young people, clearly unimpressed by the neo-classical pretensions on display in these extravagances, but perhaps with fine historical sensibility associating them with both wealth and Western domination, had torn off chunks of the stonework and hurled them at the police (23)[10].

The peak of the crisis-induced protest movement can probably be seen in the occupation of Syntagma square in June 2011. For almost a month the square was claimed for both traditional strategies of protest and confrontations and new experiments of cultural expression and direct democracy (Leontidou 2012)[11]. Similarly the anti-austerity movement is not – and was never – restricted to the practice of protest and occupation. There are growing numbers of projects attempting to address the needs of a city in austerity in a more pragmatic fashion – including non-monetary exchange systems such as most prominently time banks, direct consumer-producer networks, neighborhood initiatives, community gardens, and attempts at establishing autonomous institutions such as health clinics (Dalakoglou 2011)[12]. Furthermore artistic expression – mainly street art and graffiti – has become as crucial an aspect of dealing with the realities of the austerity city.

Crisis and Street Art

When taking a stroll through contemporary Athens it is hard not to note the overwhelming force that graffiti and street art has turned into. Particularly in central districts such as Exarcheia or Kerameikos – neighborhoods where a lot of students, marginalized migrants and left-leaning people live – the densely written painted on walls form an integral part of the physical appearance of public space. By now there is a general understanding that the Athens street art scene is one of the most upcoming ones in all of Europe and it has been receiving specific attention regarding its connections with the crisis, which has repeatedly been a topic in widely recognized international media such as The New York Times, Time Magazine and The Guardian.

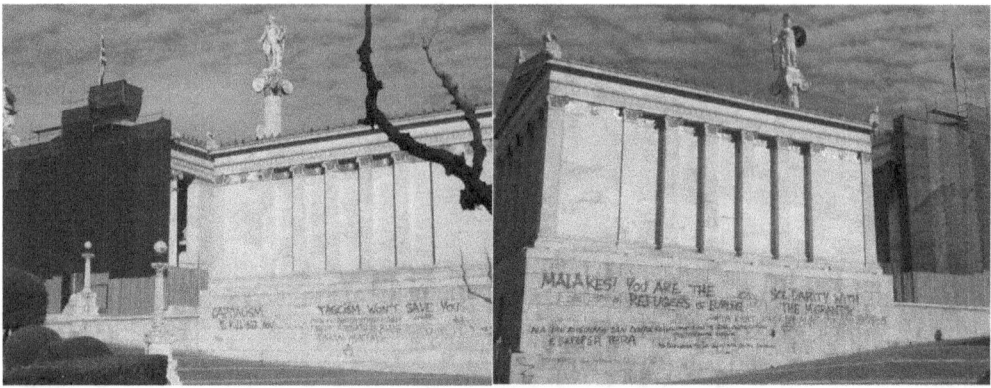
Fig. 2 Two views of the Trilogy, photo: Julia Tulke

The current boom in both quantity and quality of street art in Athens has an obvious connection to the spatial transformations incited by the crisis. For one, due to an increasing lack of capacities in the public sector, artworks on the walls even of public buildings are not regularly removed or painted over anymore. A very drastic illustration is the trilogy, a set of three neo-classical buildings – the National Library, the Academy and the original Athens University – set along the central Eleftheriou Venizelou street. Probably due to its specific location – the street connects the central squares Syntagma and Omonoia and is thus an essential vein in demonstrations – and high visibility the sides and pillars of the buildings have been a popular site for slogan writing in the past years (Fig.). Most of them are removed eventually but stay around for considerable amounts of time. This specific deregulation thus means that artworks and slogans stay around longer and in larger quantities, which simultaneously enables more of a dialogue to unfold on the walls. Additionally artists can often work more freely and invest more time into their artworks. On a more general level the transformations of the city in the course of the crisis produce an abundance of surfaces that are potentially intriguing for artists, such as empty shop windows, houses nailed shut, and abandoned construction sites. Yet another argument that resurfaced in multiple conversations and interviews is that the crisis itself stimulates artistic expression of all kinds and released enormous potentials of creativity as well as a newfound appreciation for art and culture. Artist Refur describes this dynamic as follows:

> And through all this crisis I think we all actually should feel lucky – in quotation marks – because it makes us more creative. I was talking with Lathos [another artist] yesterday and we were talking exactly about that thing, we are creative now because if we were in a period that everything is calm and nothing really happened...you know...we wouldn't have the motivation to express ourselves. It's not a good situation to be in, I'm not saying that, but I think it makes you creative.[13]

Another artist, Sonke, describes a similar shift in the awareness of the general public:

> I think people are more focused now on the simple things, not so much on the cars and style as before. We had a period that lifestyle was really promoted in Greece because the government told us we have a lot of money and we are doing the Olympic Games so at this time the society, the media and the newspapers were very lifestyle with cars and pools and nice homes. And now the people turn back to the basics. So art I think is something that...now I think that people in Athens are more interested in, in art, in music, in the simple things, in the things you don't have to pay to have.[14]

The dense activity on the streets that is characteristic of contemporary Athens – particularly regarding its politicization – has only really started since the events of December 2008. The massive riots that succeeded the murder of 15-year-old Alexis Grigoropoulos by two police back then mark the point at which especially slogan writing started being used as a systematic political strategy. French street artist describes this in contrast with his home country:

> About aesthetic and political issues, the big difference is how, since the murder of Alexis by the police in December 2008, graffiti and street art became like a weapon for the youth to express what they feel about this society. And with the collapse of the economy, that matter grows. I think the Greek scene is much more political than France, definitely.[15]

While the riots of 2008 and 2009 eventually declined – paving the way for a new anti-austerity movement – street art remained a powerful new means of political expression. Simultaneously the political circumstances that gave birth to this new idea of public expression permanently shape the contents and forms that the public expression takes, constituting a specific aesthetics of crisis as I will argue and elaborate upon later.

The Artists
The circle of currently active artists in the growing Athenian scene is made up of roughly three groups. Firstly there are large numbers of anonymous political activists who engage in the omnipresent slogan writing. In fact, learning how to handle a spray can, even if

just for the sake of spreading the anarchy-a or the squatters-n symbols, seems to be an integral part of the political socialization of teenagers. For those activists, slogan writing does not constitute a distinct identity but is rather seen as a part of the wider political struggle. The repetitive writing of simple, recurring slogans – kill fascists, we are all immigrants, acab (acronym for all cops are bastards) – and recognizable symbols often follows a logic of territorial marking and can be found on buildings of political and economic meaning, as on the trilogy, monuments, bank branches or shop windows, and along the three main streets for demonstrations and marches. Secondly, there is the community of people who identify themselves as street artists and are motivated by artistic expression. A small group of them has been active since the early 1990s, but most have only started in the past seven years. As for their professional and economic backgrounds there is a rather wide dispersion. Some manage to support themselves working as artists, some have quite plain daytime jobs or study, and others are unemployed trying to make ends meet by taking smaller jobs. The majority comes from an educated middle-class background but is currently in a more or less precarious situation. When it comes to artistic influences, many state that comic books, graphic design, art, and illustration have played a big role for them, mostly in a mixture of international and Greek origins. Frequently international study and work experiences brought the artists in contact with street art culture elsewhere – mainly Great Britain and the USA – and inspired them to get involved themselves. Even though these artists don't consider themselves explicitly political, many deal with socio-political issues. Artist Cacao Rocks describes his aesthetic politics as follows:

> All graffiti and street art is a political action and an effort for communication. Some artists try to do propaganda with their work and I'm not one of them, I just try to change our environment and the city landscape. I try to do it without the permission of the authorities and of course by breaking some rules. My work is more like telling a story without trying to change the ideas of the spectators if this is possible. I just want to make them feel other things than just waking by a grey wall in the city.[16]

Thirdly, there is yet another group of street artists that are highly politicized and motivated by their desire for political expression. Despite not being permanently active members in political groups, those artists solidarize and associate themselves with the anarchist and antifascist cause and aim to support it the best way they can. The artworks they produce often send out clear political messages and are meant to form a sort of counter-propaganda undermining dominant political and media discourses. An example for this is the issue of the κουκουλοφόροι (hoodie-wearers) which have become the symbolic emblem of the deviant urban rioter in media and politics – up to even a factual criminalization and likening to terrorists. Some artworks try to subvert this discourse in an ironic way or by redefining the responsibility for the extensive riots in the past five years as responses to political decision making. A frequent slogan states the state is the only terrorist while a more elaborate work by political artist Pol shows the face of a κουκουλοφόρος and the caption terrorism is the eight o'clock news. Other topics that can frequently be found in political street art are social justice, antifascism, consumerism, the right to the city, surveillance and militarization, protest and riots in general as well as media critique. The participation in demonstration and direct actions has a formative effect on many of those artists, as stencilist Mapet describes "The 2008 riots gave me a boost because at the time I participated many squats, actions, assemblies and stuff so I was, I spent many hours of my time there so I had more ideas, I became more politicized, all of this with the anarchists mostly, so I produced more stuff" (Interview with Mapet, 4 April 2013). At times this involvement also resulted in workshops, for example to teach activist in squat projects how to make their own stencils. When asked about the influence the crisis has had on their work as street artists, most artists talk about being influenced by the current situation in both direct and indirect ways while often rejecting the notion of the crisis as represented by political and media discourses. Mapet, for example, calls the crisis a brand name, while artist D! strongly rejects the idea of crisis as a whole:

> Firstly I'd like to clarify Greece is not having the so called "crisis". The word denotes an unplanned situation that can often be out of control and against the will of those who handle it, often a truly unexpected situation. The situation in Greece is planned and controlled by state officials who pretend to be incapable of handling what they present as the "crisis". You have to be very naive to believe what the political parties tell the media to tell the world, I believe in facts, not in irrational press releases and absurd statements. The correct "word" for what happens here is Gradual Degradation Scheme of Greece or GDSG.[17]

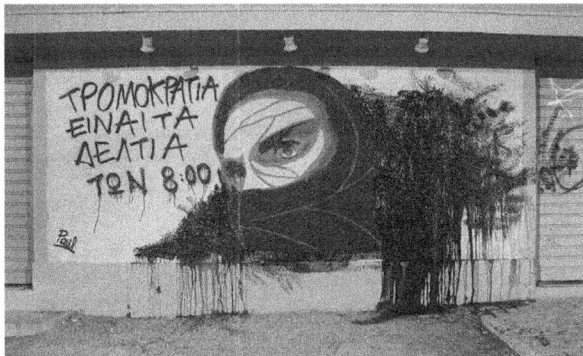

Fig. 3 Terrorism is the eight o' clock News artwork by Paul, photo: Kostas Kallergis

Aesthetics of Crisis

After having laid out the ways in which the crisis impacts urban space and activism in general and having explored the specific case of Athens, the following section will examine what I term aesthetics of crisis, the qualitative transformations of iconography and forms of expression brought about in the context of the crisis. Aesthetics herein denotes not a normative judgment of the visual representation of the city, but the sum of the sensory and symbolic qualities of the artworks and their relationship with the material and mental landscapes of crisis as a whole. While this analysis is exclusively concerned with street art, the aesthetics of crisis potentially include all material and visual changes that occur in the urban fabric within the context of the crisis: abandoned and decaying houses, riot police, homeless. The underlying logic is to approach, explore and come to know the crisis through its manifestations and artifacts. Attempting to clarify the analytical properties of this approach, I will propose and describe the three aesthetic clusters that came to evolve prominently out of my research as ways of representing the crisis: representation of iconography and personifications of the crisis, the representation of the crisis as a lived reality and quality of everyday life, and the representation of the crisis as a political struggle. All three overlap in multiple ways and are certainly not meant to be fixed or exhaustive. However, they do all exhibit specific symbolic and iconographic vocabularies.

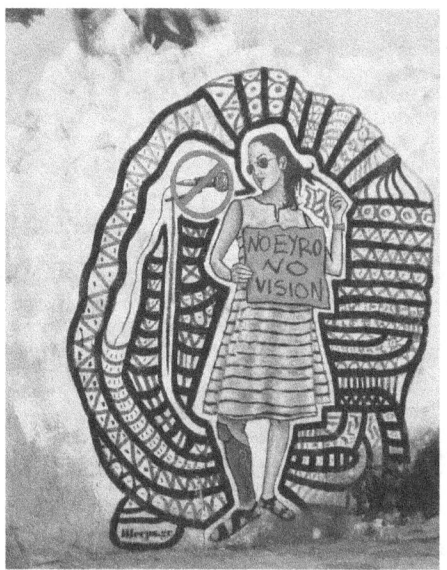

Fig. 4 No Euro, No Vision artwork by bleeps, photo: Julia Tulke

The smallest group of artworks is concerned with the crisis directly[18]. They can be found all over town with no particular point of spatial concentration. The most frequently used references are the EU – often in the € symbol or the characteristic yellow stars of the flag and the faces of different Greek politicians and public figures such as current prime minister Antonis Samaras or former Athens mayor Nikitas Kaklamanis. Occasionally artworks incorporate the Greek flag, refer to international institutions such as the IMF, or revolve around the very word crisis. The tone underlying the consistently negative depictions of crisis is always either dystopian or ironic. Even though as an aesthetic cluster the images directly engaging with the crisis are perhaps the least cohesive, there are two often recurring symbolic discourses and strategies within: the subversive linguistic manipulation of terms, and the use of a pictorial vocabulary quoting from imaginations of ancient Greece. There are countless examples for the first tendency: a large depiction of the IMF logo lined with the words irrational monetary fund in a pedestrian street in Exarcheia, a recurring stencil just plainly stating catastroika or a paste-up of a coin, modeled after the Greek version of the Euro, saying ελευθερία, freedom. What these works share is a deep mistrust in the institutions involved in managing the crisis in Greece. Instead of just accepting them as the given partners of cooperation the artists conceive and represent them as part of the crisis and its repercussions. The messages entailed are accordingly communicated in a simple and direct manner. A more complex artwork that also utilizes this kind of wordplay can be seen in Figure 4. In it a woman in a striped blue dress holds a sign stating No Euro, No Vision, evoking at the same time a reference to the European entertainment spectacle of the Eurovision Song Contest – which was in fact hosted by Athens in the year 2006 – and a criticism of the lack of creativity in dealing with the crisis which is hardly ever discussed publicly without the overpowering frame of reference of the European Union. This is further reverberated in the bits of ancient Greek foot and leg wear the woman sports.

Far more common than direct engagements with the crisis are its representations as a lived reality. Spread all over the neighborhoods of the city, these works are quite often paste-ups of drawings or hand-painted murals suggesting a more personal and artistic character. The overwhelming majority of artworks display realistic and expressive portrayals of human form. One important exception represents the crisis tag βασανίζομαι, meaning I am tormented, that can be found written all over the city in all sizes and styles imaginable. The walls of Athens are covered in faces and bodies bruised and broken by the crisis and its austerity imperative, pale faces with hollow cheeks and tired eyes in expressions of fear and despair, emaciated bodies hanging flaccidly in urban space.

Often these bodies and faces belong to children and young adults, who are thereby constructed as the ones most affected by the consequences of austerity and crisis. A sequential series of paste-ups created by the artist Dimitris Taxis powerfully illustrates this tendency. The paintings pasted to the walls of different neighborhoods show young boys that despite their bodies bear no signs of childhood but instead hold on to guns in terror, hide in tree logs, or sit motionless in between huge stacks of books. The displacement of temporalities seems to play a crucial role, particularly in the last artwork (Fig. 4). Socrates, Plato and Democracy is written on the spines of the book stack he is sitting on, the ones pressing on him from the top read Athens means Luxury, No Future, and Survival Guide. The hunched boy is stuck in time between past and present with, literally, no future in sight, evoking a feeling of standstill that Athenians express quite often in crisis-related conversations. A similar symbolism can be found in another series of pasted drawings by WD. Faceless people of all kinds – men with hats, children, and mothers – are captured in a moment of liminality. The wings on their backs are broken, yet they still remain afloat in the air for the time being, the inevitable downfall always present. One striking characteristic found in most artworks is the isolation of the humans depicted, almost none of them showing larger groups in interaction. Similarly, expressions of optimism or solidarity are rare. An exception can be found in the work of art student STMTS, whose paste-ups of children show both the negative impacts of the crisis but also elude a general sense of hope, the laughing faces of children becoming again beacons of hope for the future. In sum, the many artworks showing the everyday life under crisis represent the recent situation not as a political or economic problem but as a lived reality with grave consequences for the city's population. The overwhelming majority emphasizes humanity in emotional expression and physical vulnerability – frequently projected on the bodies and faces of children and young adults. Depictions of skulls and wounded bodies further mark the crisis as essentially a struggle of life and death. In their realistic portrayal of the humanitarian crisis that Athens has been experiencing in the past three years they claim the walls of the city as a space for emotionally processing the situation. Therein they undermine popular media representations and political discourses externalizing the urban crisis by placing the blame for it on certain groups of urban others. In contrast, the related pieces of street art make visible how universally the crisis permeates the life of every single inhabitant of the city. In fact, one particular project even lays bare the wounds that have been inflicted on the very city of Athens. The anonymous artist uses a virtual pen to draw attention to the cracks urban decay and almost five years of intense protesting have left in the urban surface.

Fig. 5 I wish you could learn something useful from the past
artwork by Dimitris Taxis, photo: Julia Tulke

By far the largest amount of artworks on the walls of Athens relate to the aesthetics of protest or display specific political statements. Unsurprisingly, the overwhelming majority of them can be found in the politicized neighborhood of Exarcheia. The most frequent technique employed is stenciling, followed by freehand graffiti and sprayed or painted slogans, proposing a slightly more aggressive stance on reclaiming space. Stencils particularly enable a simple and quick repetition of an artwork or slogan with a relatively small effort so that they prove particularly effective for spreading political messages. Further they enable people with little artistic skill or patience to participate in the street art scene as well. Tellingly, the three most productive stencil artists in Athens all have explicitly political motivations. More than in any other aesthetic cluster discussed here symbolic elements play a role, most prominently gas masks, molotov cocktails, fists but also televisions and signs of specific social and political movements. A large number of artworks depict either realistic scenes of protest – at times clearly referencing certain photographs that have circulated prominently in mass media – or portraits of protesters, their faces usually hidden behind gas masks or scarves. The depictions of protest usually show larger groups of people marching in dynamic action carrying flags assigning them to a certain group and weapons like stones and petrol bombs. The image of the burning city, either in depiction or in the slogan Athens burns, recurs quite commonly. In contrast, the portraits of protesters are often rather static and expressionless. In the case of the faceless masses of heads in gas masks that seem to appear around every corner, the symbolism is meaningful on two levels. On the one hand they relate to the actual reality of protest where a gas mask has become an obligatory accessory, on the other hand they become emblematic of the increasing militarization, violence and social polarization of the city. Both the depictions of scenes and actors transform the specific temporality of protest as a momentary eruption of political sentiments by permanently inscribing it into the surface of the city. In this way protest is not only manifested and present around every corner of the city, it becomes a part of it claiming urban space as a canvas for subversive political practices. This fundamentally displaces the narrative disseminated by media and politics, where protest particularly the riots they tend to turn into are externalized and attributed to a disruptive group of mayhem-loving hoodie-wearers and anarchists. Generally the artworks revolving around protest and politics hold a rather critical stance on mass media – some of the artists even explicitly name counter-propaganda as their motivation – which at times even becomes the central topic of concern. Usually juxtaposed with simple depictions of television sets, they read slogans such as the television will not be revolutionized or bash it. A small yet notable number of the protest-related artworks examine a completely different aspect: romance. As I was told by several people the long hours of standing around waiting for a protest to take off are quite popularly used by participants to approach one another. The walls of the city bear testimony to this romantic potentiality of political action with phrases like anarchy is for lovers or as the fires burn our hearts will unite. Though some of the politicized artworks stand for themselves, a large amount is clearly associated with political and social groups. Most frequently this association is with the anarchists, the antifascist action, and the squatters' movement. The messages are often quite simple, promoting solidarity – e.g. with migrants or threatened squats – and resistance – e.g. against authority, police, capitalism, nationalism and fascism.

Conclusion: Chronicling the Crisis through Street Art?

As indicated by the Athenian case depicted above there is a clear connection between the variables crisis and austerity, urban space, social movements and street art. However, the ways in which they intersect are just as complex and fluid as the phenomenon of the crisis itself. Closely examining the walls of Athens as artifacts of the crisis helped me understand how urban space is claimed as a democratic medium of communication, expression and subversive political speech – both on an individual and a collective level. Whether the actual artwork follows a logic of confrontation or beautification, dialogue or propaganda, it encourages the passersby to engage with their surroundings and to consider certain power relations inscribed in them. Additionally, the walls of Athens provide a variety of insights about the social movements and political groups strategically claiming them. Even though there are millions of images of uncontextualized crisis street art floating around on the internet, there is a distinct lack of qualitative research in this area. In order to deeply engage with the topic it is crucial to explore the particular political geographies of the respective cities and the ways in which artworks tie into it. Some potential questions for guiding such research are: How are the present states of crisis reflected on the walls of crisis cities? Which iconographies and discourses do they mobilize and how do they relate to the narratives and images of the crisis circulated in mainstream media and politics? Who are the actors involved, what conflicts occur and which alliances do they forge? How do they oscillate between local and global contexts and how do they create transnational networks? As for a more theoretical question it might be interesting to look at the issue of temporality and temporal displacement in the crisis and how it resurfaces in the artworks. Another promising field is affect, particularly the study of the crisis as both an affective regime and a ground for affective politicization. Such an analysis would greatly profit from a comparative perspective. In the European crisis context one might investigate other Mediterranean crisis and austerity cities such as Lisbon or Madrid. Recent events also suggest a broader look at the South-East margin of Europe – cities such as Istanbul, Sofia or Tuzla. Specifically the crisis revolving around the Occupy Gezi protests and its immediate adaption and representation in street art display a variety of remarkable similarities with Athens. Investigating further into any of these connections will not only potentially sharpen an understanding of how street art works as a means of protest and social movements but also open new perspectives through which to read the complex issue of the crisis.

Notes and References
1 See Harvey, David. Rebel Cities. From the Right to the City to the Urban Revolution (London: Verso, 2012).
2 Tonkiss, Fran. Austerity Urbanism and the Makeshift City. City 17.3 (2013): 312-324.
3 The term austerity derives from the latin austeritas and can be translated as rigor, discipline. In financial politics austerity describes a strategy in which government spending – typically social welfare – are radically reduced in order to achieve fiscal balance. Austerity measures have been prominently employed in the European crisis with a particularly harsh regime implemented in Greece. Here the so called Troika – an institution consisting of the European Central Bank, the European Commission, and the International Monetary Fund – negotiated a contract offering loans to the bankrupt Greek state in exchange for the implementation of harsh budget cuts. Since the signing of the first Memorandum in 2010, representatives of the Troika have periodically returned to Greece to monitor the execution of the agreement. For an analysis of the moral ramifications of the austerity regime see Graeber, David. The Greek Debt Crisis in Almost Unimaginably Long-Term Historical Perspective. in Revolt and Crisis in Greece. Between a Present Yet To Pass and a Future Still To Come. edited by Antonis Vradis and Dimitris Dalakoglou (Oakland: AK Press, 2011).
4 For a critical analysis of the current crisis see Aftermath. The Cultures of the Economic Crisis. edited by Manuel Castells, João Caraça, and Gustavo Cardoso (Oxford: Oxford University Press, 2012).
5 For a detailed study of the Greek case see Alexander Kentikelenis, Marina Karanikolos, Aaron Reeves, Martin McKee, and David Stuckler. Greece's health crisis: from austerity to denialism. The Lancet 383 (2014): 748-753.
6 For an account of Athens see Kaika, Maria. The Economic Crisis Seen from the Everyday. Europe's Nouveau Poor and the Global Affective Implications of a 'Local' Debt Crisis. City 16.4 (2012): 422-430.
7 For a critical account see Mayer, Margit. First world urban activism. Beyond austerity urbanism and creative city politics. City 17.1 (2013): 5-19.
8 Dalakoglou, Dimitris. The Crisis before 'The Crisis': Violence and Urban Neoliberalization in Athens. Social Justice 19.1 (2012): 24-42.
9 Tsilimpounidi, Myrto. Athens 2012. Performances 'in Crisis' or What Happens When a City Goes Soft. City 16.5 (2012): 546-556.
10 Herzfeld, Michael. Crisis Attack: Impromptu Ethnography in the Greek Maelstrom. Anthropology Today 27.5 (2011): 22-26.
11 Leontidou, Lila. Athens in the Mediterranean 'Movement of the Piazzas'. Spontaneity in Material and Virtual Public Spaces. City 16.3 (2012): 299-312.
12 Dalakoglou, Dimitris. Beyond Spontaneity. Crisis, Violence and Collective Action in Athens. City 16.5 (2011): 535-545.
13 Refur (street artist and design student), interviewed by the author, April 2013.
14 Sonke (street artist and graphic designer), interviewed by the author, June 2013.
15 Oré (street artist), interviewed by the author, June 2013.
16 Cacao Rocks (street artist), interviewed by the author, July 2013.
17 DI (street artist and visual artist), interviewed by the author, June 2013.
18 All quantitative judgements of the Athenian street art scene are based upon an extensive photo archive of 850 artworks that I compiled during my research in Athens. All photographs were geotagged and coded using the scientific software MAXQDA.

Susan Hansen, Middlesex University, London; s.hansen@mdx.ac.uk
Danny Flynn, London Metropolitan University; dannyamosflynn@hotmail.co.uk

"This is not a Banksy!":
Street art and the transformation of public space

This paper examines the dialogue and transformation of public space that occurred after Banksy's Slave Labour was removed without notice from a wall in North London, transported to Miami and listed for auction. The explosion of new works provoked by its extraction were for the most part simply erased as they appeared. We argue that the excision of Slave Labour provided a 'gap in the sensible' (Rancière, 2004[i]) and the conditions of possibility for the emergence of a lively local intertextual visual dialogue, which transformed this otherwise apparently unremarkable London side street into an arena for ongoing social exchange.

Street art removal; Aesthetic protest; Visual dialogue

Introduction

"Its very destruction causes one to remember." (Schacter, 2008, p.47 [ii])

In London alone, one hundred million pounds per year is spent wiping the walls clean using various solvents and painting over unsanctioned images and writing deemed not to 'add value' to an area (Greater London Authority, 2002[iii]). This is a relentless and ongoing everyday practice of surveillance, judgment and erasure, and in consequence the anti-graffiti industry is worth multi-billions (Brighenti, 2010[iv]). There are several forms of erasure that check the wanton proliferation of street art and graffiti. These include the mundane and indeed expectable lawful removal, or 'buffing', of work by agents of the local council or by private residents. This practice of removal is predicated on the judgment of such work as diminishing the symbolic capital of an area. Islington Council (2014: n.p.[v]) warns that, "it can be the catalyst for a downward spiral of neglect in an area, and encourage other more serious criminal activity." Such aesthetic socio-moral judgments are based on long-held associations between graffiti and criminal activity, as a visible index of social deprivation and urban decay, and as a form of abjection and territory marking akin to public urination, as dirt or filth, or "matter out of place" (Douglas, 2002, p. 36[vi]). Street art may also 'disappear' over time, via the natural processes of degradation and decay; or may be willfully destroyed by being written over, or 'capped', by others. This is usually a marker of blatant disrespect towards the original work and/or artist. A more exceptional and historically recent form of erasure is through the careful excision of street art for exploitation by capital.

Paradoxically, the removal of street art for profit appears to occur only after efforts to preserve and protect the work have been implemented by local councils and residents. This 'protection' is usually accomplished by fixing a Perspex shield over the work, which marks it as being 'of value' and worthy of conservation. This is presumably designed to guard against overwriting, accidental erasure or 'defacement' by others, and to preserve the work against the processes of degradation and decay. This form of protective practice is thus predicated on a judgment of such work as augmenting symbolic capital (Bourdieu, 1984[vii]) or in the local government's terms, 'adding value' to an area. However marking work as 'valuable' to the community and attempting to protect it from harm may have the unintended effect of visibly commodifying the work, which in turn may make it vulnerable to removal for auction on the art market, where work by successful street artists such as Banksy is highly lucrative, even in the absence of provenance, and can reach in excess of a million pounds per piece (Frigerio & Khakimova, 2013[viii]). Indeed, the Sincura Group, who facilitated the recent removal of Banksy's iconic No Ball Games from a wall in the socioeconomically deprived area of Tottenham, London, drew on this very rhetoric of protection by claiming that the work was being salvaged for restoration (BBC, 2013[ix]). However, their further claim that the work was not being appreciated in situ by the local community proved more contentious. Conservation and appreciation are established practices traditionally associated with the recognition of, and duty of care towards fine art and cultural heritage. Sincura's assertion that the excised work was not being appreciated in situ, and the implication that proper appreciation could only occur in a sanctioned gallery space or museum seems extraordinary, given that street art's very existence, as such, has been argued to be dependent on its in situ nature, and ongoing dynamic relationship with the community it exists within (Young, 2014[x]). Street art as a self-consciously indexical and situated practice positions itself in relation to particular aspects of the urban environment, often with socio-political intent evident, in part, through its site of dissemination. In this sense, Dovey et al (2010[xi]) argue, street art and graffiti strives to 'erode' the distance between art and viewer, and to resist ready 'incorporation' into the formalized field of 'art'. However, Burroughs (1988[xii]) suggests that it is the very 'disruption' of accepted categories that, paradoxically, constitutes 'art' itself. Irvine (2012[xiii]) further asserts that a defining feature of what we come to recognize as 'high art' is the work's deautomisatisation of established categories. Thus the very resistance of street art to established categories may render it vulnerable to appropriation and commodification as 'high art'.

We focus here on the transformation of public space provoked by the ephemeral dialogue of a series of relatively unknown artists/writers, over a period of 16 months (February 2013 – June 2014) post the removal of a high profile piece of work by a recognized artist from the same site. While the 'invaluable' work in question – Banksy's Slave Labour – received international media coverage when it first appeared in May 2012, the new works incited by its removal in February 2013 were for the most part simply erased as they appeared at the site of extraction, and were not reproduced in any of the extensive media, community, or local government commentary. However, the excision of Slave Labour provided the conditions of possibility for the emergence of a local intertextual dialogue that marks these practices as participatory, political and performative, and which transformed this otherwise apparently unremarkable London side street into a public space. Slave Labour's removal was the catalyst for a series of often self-consciously egalitarian works of aesthetic protest. Rancière (2004[xiv]) asserts that aesthetic protest can create 'dissensus', or ruptures in common sense, and a gap in the sensible, which works ultimately to show that what we see, according to our usual 'division of the sensible', could be otherwise - thus demonstrating the "contingency of the entire perceptual and conceptual order" (May, 2011, n.p.[xv]). Rancière extends the reach of aesthetics to encompass all those practices that make possible new commonalities of sense, and sense-making practices, created by ruptures in common sense itself. This is political, he argues, as politics is located in "disputes about the division of what is perceptible to the senses." (Rancière, 1998: 176[xvi]). Thus, as May (2011: n.p. [xvii]) explains, "politics is itself aesthetic in that it requires a sharing of sense in common; art is not the exemplary site of sensory pleasure or the sublime but a critical break with common sense." According to Rancière (1998) the division of the sensible takes institutional form in the police as the "symbolic constitution of the social", in encouraging the people not to stop and look at that which should not be seen:

> The police say there is nothing to see, nothing happening, nothing to be done, but to keep moving, circulating; they say that the space of circulation is nothing but the space of circulation. Politics consists in transforming that space of circulation into the space of the manifestation of a subject: be it the people, workers, citizens. It consists in reconfiguring that space, what there is to do there, what there is to see or name. It is a dispute about the division of what is perceptible to the senses. (Rancière, 1998: 176-177 [xviii])

This injunction takes institutional form here in the material practices associated with the division of the sensible: in the local authority's buffing or erasure of work that is not to be seen; in the protection of authorized work permitted to remain; and in the relocation of work that is apparently too valuable to be seen and appreciated 'in situ' by the people.

Slave Labour
Slave Labour (Figure 1, below) was produced during the lead up to the 2012 London Olympics, and at the height of the UK's nationwide celebration of the Queen's Diamond Jubilee, marking 50 years of her reign as monarch. However, and despite the abundance of Jubilee related paraphernalia, advertising and street decorations in London at the time of the work's materialization, most of the media commentary was not overly concerned with what the work may have been intended to critique or signify but was rather initially restricted to a discussion as to whether or not it was 'a genuine Banksy'. The BBC (2012: n.p.[xix]) interviewed a range of 'people on the street' and academic experts and concluded that, "the image has all the hallmarks of a genuine Banksy." Similarly, the media coverage of the later 'theft' of this work was largely contained to canvassing the community's protest at its removal for auction in America and speculation as to the agents responsible for the work's removal.

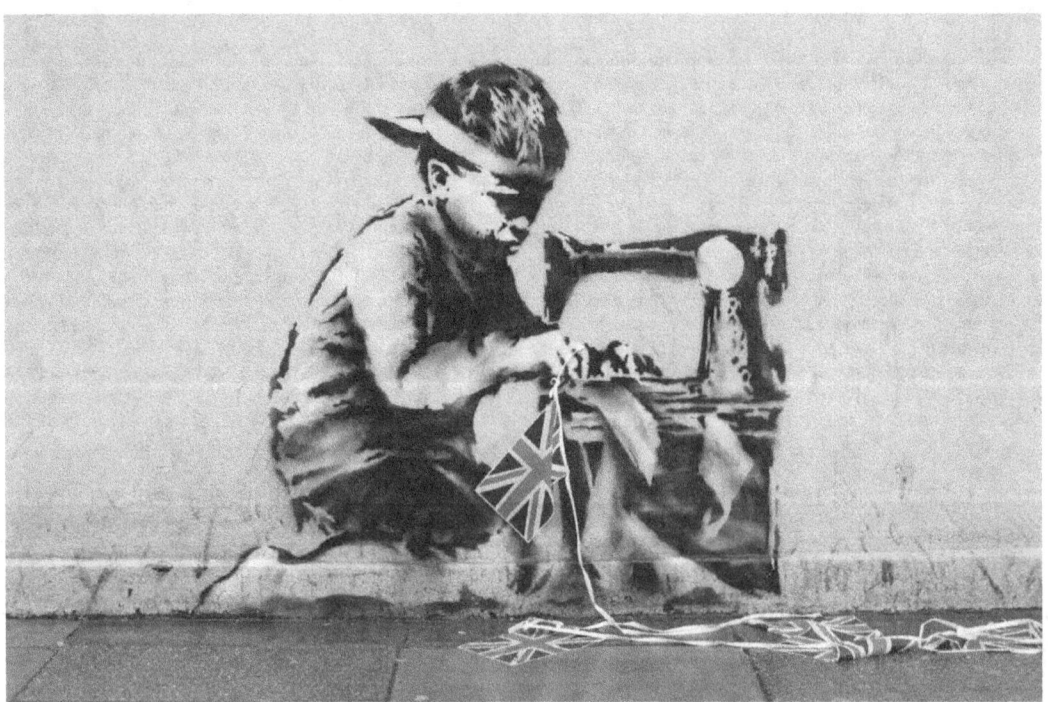

Fig. 1. May 2012. Photograph © Jon Deptford.

When Slave Labour was removed from the wall for private auction, the local community, represented by MP Lynne Featherstone, was vocal in asserting community 'ownership' of, and 'rights to', the work. It was described as a 'gift' to the community to whom, and where, it should be considered to 'rightfully belong' – though this was phrased in terms of social capital and the moral good, rather than in terms of authorial rights and intellectual property:

> *You have deprived a community of an asset that was given to us for free and greatly enhanced an*
> *area that needed it...I call on you, and your consciences, to pull the piece from both potential sales*
> *and return it to its rightful place (Tottenham Journal, 2013: n.p.* [xx]*).*

Local crowds gathered to protest at the site of removal, brandishing signs that read 'Bring back our Banksy'. Here the protesters assert ownership, but not of the particular work, Slave Labour, but the work as 'a Banksy', or rather 'our Banksy' – an asset with a recognisible currency – and demand its restitution. This protest was grounded in the community's originally recognized claim over the work as belonging in – and to – its community of origin. However, as Young (2014: 128[xxi]) points out, while communities' experiences of, and belief in, 'public space' persists, the reality is that in many cities, apparently public spaces are legally comprised of a grid of privately owned spaces. This community protest, which attracted significant media coverage, was initially successful, and on February 23rd, 2013 Slave Labour was withdrawn from auction in Miami, but the work eventually resurfaced in London where it was auctioned on June 1st, 2013 by the Sincura group, representing the Poundland building's owners, for £750,000.

As with much street art, the positioning of the work is a crucial element in its (intended) signification, now largely lost through its abstraction from context. Slave Labour was originally placed on the side of a Poundland discount store building in North London that at the time was heavily stocked with Jubilee merchandise, some of which – the plastic Union Jack 'bunting' emerging from the boy's sewing machine – formed part of the original piece, before the local residents stripped it bare. This 'product placement' draws attention to the conditions of production of these disposable nationalistic icons. It is unambiguously a depiction of abuse, a declaration by the artist, and a reminder that one poorer culture is forced to produce a cheap commodity for another economically superior culture – reducing the very symbol of the British nation to a cheap ornamentation.[1] Slave Labour's in situ location, and three dimensional bunting, implicates the Poundland store and its customers. The precise placement of the work recalls a high profile public scandal over Poundland's involvement in child sweatshop labour after a boy of seven was found to be working 100 hours a week, for just 7p an hour, in an Indian sweatshop that produced goods for the store. He also slept at the factory (Daily Mail, 2010 [xxii]). Children are a vehicle often used by Banksy to deliver a message about the inherent inhumanity of deprivation, subjugation and violence – for instance, a child embracing a bomb in Bomb Hugger (2003); a child frisking a soldier in Stop and Search (2007). These works juxtapose two images that clearly 'do not belong' together, but once joined connote something both innocent and sinister – thus delivering a political message in a comical or surprising manner. Although Slave Labour also depicts a child, it would appear that it departs from this established design logic. The significance in this stylistic break perhaps marks the seriousness of the subject. Unlike the child frisking a soldier in Stop and Search, the child depicted in kneeling servitude in Slave Labour is representative of a multitude of children who exist under such conditions. The life-sized figure of the boy gives human form to the otherwise invisible 215 million child labourers aged between 5 and 17 years old worldwide (ILO, 2010 [xxiii]). The juxtaposition of the figure of a child with the activity of enforced labour should be as surprising, ridiculous and arresting as the depiction of a child embracing a bomb, or stop and searching a soldier. That it is not – that the viewer does not, at first, see the boy as anything other than a veridical representation of a fixed and determinate socio-political reality – is the shameful source of the work's power. We are all implicated in his subjugation.

Initial visual responses: protest and loss
The community protest against Slave Labour's removal was also registered on the wall itself, with an explosion of graffiti, stencils and paste ups marking the site of removal, which was at that time visible as an unpainted and apparently still damp and freshly cemented section of the wall. These initial responses provide a visual cacophony of protest and loss (Figure 2, below).

Much of this work is an index of community grief at the loss of Slave Labour. A large paste up of a weeping nun was positioned directly over the site of extraction; and a red heart was spray painted on the right hand corner of the site, dripping/bleeding red paint onto the wounded wall. Other pieces mark the level of community outrage at the 'theft' of the work for private auction, and the commodification of Banksy's 'gift' to the community. A stenciled paste up reading "Caution: Thieves at Work" abuts the left side of the space left by the extracted work; and printed 'street art' style US dollar notes have been pasted around the perimeters of the site of extraction, along with a single pound note. There are also pieces that reference Banksy's other work, and that of associated artists. To the left of the wall is a small stenciled rat in the style of Banky's influential French precursor, Blek le Rat, holding a tiny spray can and reading the sign it has apparently just painted. In red Banksy style font, the sign repeats the demand on the placards of the community protesters: "Bring back Banksy". Another stenciled rat in similar proportion, but in the recognisible style of Banksy, sits at the same level to the right of the site of extraction. This rat holds a placard with a single word protest – "Why?"

This is a democratic multiparty conversation. Unlike curated gallery space, which offers the public a relatively passive position as viewer (though viewing is arguably always an active process) the extramural space of the city wall positions the public as interlocutors with the right to speak. As with any 'public' conversation with multiple contributors, some of the 'talk' appears 'off topic' and made for the sheer sake of being a part of the conversation and making one's mark; some delight in being ostentatious or crude and shocking (one writer's contribution was a giant penis spray painted in lurid pink); some are hurried and scrawled; others are planned and articulate. However, the vast majority of marks on the wall made here appear site and topic specific, and designed to be received as evidence of the force of the community's outrage at the removal of Slave Labour.

This is not a Banksy

After these initial visual protests had been whitewashed over by the local council, the wall remained blank for several months. The only piece that remained was the small stenciled rat to the right of the site of extraction, which having been attributed to Banksy, was protected from erasure by a Perspex shield. However, on the 17th of April 2013, another monochrome stencil appeared, positioned directly over the original site of extraction (see Figure 3, below). This new stencil is a variation of the iconic Bad Panda stencil, often attributed to Banksy, but which Banksy, via his website, has categorically stated that he is not responsible for. The original Bad Panda was produced in 2005 by the French designer Julien d'Andon, who designed the panda for French brand KULTE. The panda stands on the recognizable logotype of Banksy's name thus apparently identifying Banksy as the author of this work, however the panda also wears a signboard that declares "This is not a Banksy", thus presenting contradictory claims regarding authorship to the viewer. Whereas street art is increasingly considered as an index of the process of gentrification, tags, when they appear in isolation from more aesthetically palatable street art, are considered by the graffiti removal industry to be a high priority for erasure – as self-evidently aesthetically and morally repellent and as an abject sign of urban decay. However, contemporary street art is not always signed or tagged and indeed for 'iconic' street artists like Banksy, tags are no longer necessary for the recognition of 'a Banksy' (or a candidate Banksy). Indeed, Bansky's original tag has been appropriated and recirculated in both popular culture (via prints and branded merchandise) and via the work of other street artists (as points of critique, intertextual reference and dialogue) to such a degree that any new appearance of Banksy's tag in public space is likely to be questioned as being genuine, especially as Banksy himself has largely ceased signing his work, instead providing assurance of authorship, or provenance, through his company 'Pest Control'.

The panda's signboard is a reworked stenciled element borrowed from another of Banksy's iconic stencils, Laugh Now (2003). The text on the panda's signboard, "This is not a Banksy" operates both to contradict the claim to authorship provided by Banksy's tag and also to arrest the potential polysemy, or other possible connotations, of the pipe dangling from the panda's mouth. The text provides a reference to the inscription, "Ceci n'est pas une pipe" (trans: This is not a pipe) from Magritte's The Treachery of Images (1928 - 1929). Magritte's pipe both is, and is not, a pipe, in that it is a representation of a pipe – i.e., not a 'real' pipe. The panda provides the viewer with a similar puzzle, in that it appears to represent/be presented as a Banksy, but is simultaneously, by its own admission, not a 'real' Banksy.

If located within the context of gallery space, the image of the pipe alone may have effectively provided a reference to Magritte's work (although it would lose the site specificity of the signification). However, as street art located in public space, this overdetermination of signifiers (the image of the pipe in addition to the text on the signboard) makes this intertextual reference to Magritte's observations on the treachery of images, or the persuasiveness of representation (or what we count as 'real', or authentic) more available to a community likely not versed in art history, creating a democratic ripple in the division of the sensible (Rancière, 2004[xxiv]). It is perhaps of note that Bansky himself has previously produced a playful museum located work referencing The Treachery of Images, by framing a 'real' working pipe integral to the museum, and adding an inverted variant of Magritte's inscription, which observes that, "This is a pipe" (and not, as in Magritte's work, a representation of a pipe).

The panda's guns, which on a proliferation of faithful reproductions of d'Andon's Bad Panda stencil point upwards, indicating guns blazing, are now in remission, and point down, the overall feel of readiness to defend (perhaps against removal for auction?) rather than being depicted mid-battle. In addition to these stenciled elements, someone has scribbled "Take me to America" in a speech bubble above the Panda's head – a plea, or perhaps a challenge, added hurriedly to the stencil by a passerby. Later additions to the stencil include a single question mark linked with a stroke of ink to the panda's head, marking uncertainty as to the panda's identity; a tiny starred halo drawn between the panda's ears, mocking its status as a work to be revered; and the block-lettered demand, "FREE ART NOW!" along the length of the panda's right arm, adopting the form of a political slogan to refer to both to the wrongfully 'captured' Banksy and the unethical commodification of the 'free gift' of street art.

This piece introduces a note of uncertainty as to the certainty with which 'a Banksy' can be identified and problematises the objectified, commodifed notion of 'a Banksy'. It presents the viewer with a puzzle: It is a representation of a Banksy. It is signed by Banksy. Yet it claims it is not a Banksy. These claims mark the potential repercussions of attributions of authorship to the survival of work in situ. If it were a Bansky, it would be immediately marked as of value (through the protection provided by a Perspex shield) and would be thus vulnerable to removal for profit. If it were not a Banksy, it would, along with other works by less recognized street artists, likely be subject to removal via buffing by the local council.

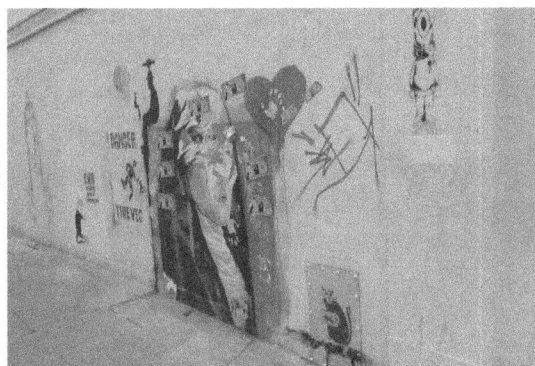

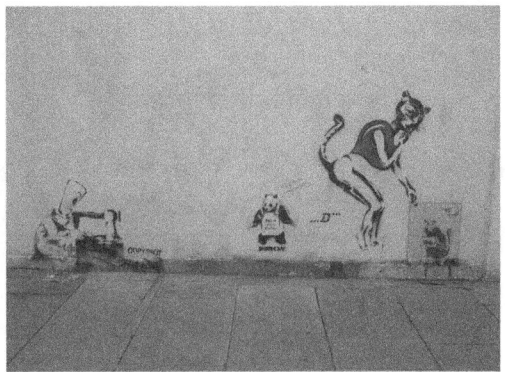

Fig. 2. February 2013. Photograph © Camilla Turner.   Fig. 3. April 2013. Photograph © Susan Hansen.

Selling out

Another stencil, this time emulating the design of Slave Labour, was added to the wall the following week. However, instead of producing cut-price jubilee bunting, the figure at the sewing machine now produces an abundance of American dollars, which spew out from the machine onto the pavement in a three dimensional pasted paper overflow (which recalls the dollar notes initially pasted around the site of extraction). The only major difference between Slave Labour and this new stencil is that the boy's head has been replaced by an oversized nozzle of a spray can onto which a cartoon face has been applied, which identifies the piece as being work by the local street artist Cap Head. This work appears to provide further commentary on the complicit nature of commercially successful street artists in 'selling out' in producing work destined for the profit economy.

A week later, a large humanoid female cat standing upright, statuesque on two shapely human hind legs was stenciled on the wall. The cat has a bright red sleeveless bodice that echoes the red heart that was sprayed free hand in relatively the same position beneath it as part of the works produced in initial response to the removal of Slave Labour, since whitewashed over. The red heart also recalls the red balloon which escapes the child in Banksy's There is Always Hope (2007). The work's tag consists of an ellipsis, resting on the baseline in front of an italicized capital 'D', and an additional ellipsis raised to the cap height.

That the cat stencil appears to contain elements of, or references to, other works by Banksy is perhaps further commentary on Banksy's apparent complicity in creating an appetite for street art that now renders work vulnerable to theft for profit. With a curious bent forward stance, the cat looms over the incarcerated Banksy rat trapped beneath its protective Perspex sheet. The cat holds her index finger to her lips and catches the viewers' gaze directly with a defiant, exaggerated 'shhhh!' as she appears to be about to remove either the stenciled rat's protective Perspex shield, thus exposing it to the brutality of the elements, or perhaps to seize and consume the rat itself.

The addition of the cat stencil to the wall creates a triangular composition linking the three works closest to the site of extraction. With tail raised, the cat appears to be spraying or defecating on the panda stencil that is now dwarfed in proportion to the cat. The panda's scribbled speech bubble now forms an abject arc emanating from the cat that serves to link the two pieces, while the third piece is connected via the cat's left hand plucking at the corner of the rat's Perspex cover. The cat stencil thus enacts a creative reworking of existing elements on the wall in an apparent insult to the pre-existing works – both the officially recognized Banksy rat stencil, and the avowedly fake Banksy panda stencil – further highlighting and subverting established notions of authorship, status, reverence and worth. Two weeks after the appearance of the cat stencil, all of the pieces then on the wall (save Banksy's rat) were whitewashed over by the council.

The boy in a panda suit

The wall remained blank for three weeks after the council had painted over the prior works, then a new stenciled piece appeared directly over the original site of extraction (see Figure 4, below). It depicts a boy wearing a panda suit, and is tagged with double ellipsis and an italicized letter D. The open face of a panda costume is flung back to reveal a human face with lowered brows and a pensive expression. In the panda suit, the boy sits cross-legged as he levitates above the street meditatively, with one hand on his knee while the other is raised to rest his chin on the back of his fingers. Unlike D's prior stenciled cat, which challenged the viewer with her direct gaze, the downward gaze of the boy in the panda suit adds to the sense of sorrow and contemplation he embodies. The trajectory of his gaze, although apparently unfocused, falls across Banksy's rat which is located to the lower right of the piece at the base of the wall.

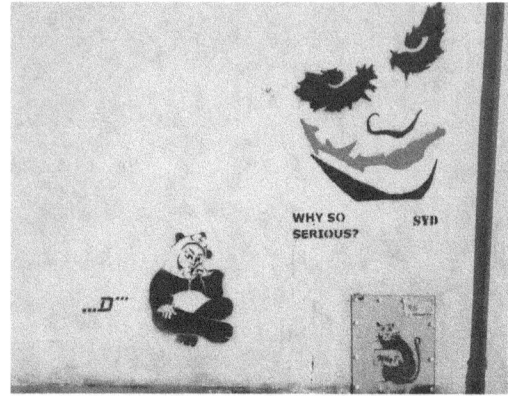
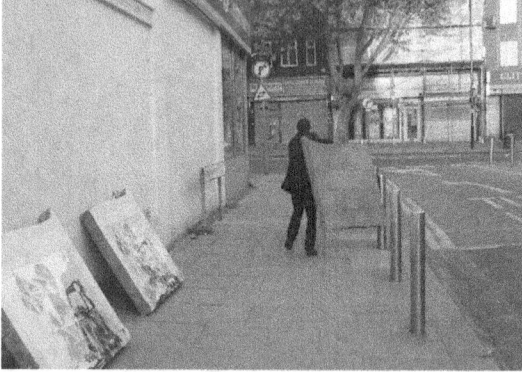

Fig. 4. May 2013. Photograph © Susan Hansen.   Fig. 5. June 2013. Photograph © Laura Keeble.

The boy's panda suit appears to provide a reference to the panda stencil that previously occupied the same position on the wall. That this is revealed to be a panda costume, or disguise, with a human figure concealed within, adds a further dimension to the ongoing visual exchange regarding authenticity, identity, authorship, and worth. It seems to hint at the layering of what is original and counterfeit, and thus seemingly worth something and not worth something, at least purely in financial terms. It is a layer, which echoes the layers within the whitewashed transient communications of postings. The use of a boy in a panda costume represents what is hidden, like the earlier panda that also professed to be not what it seemed. That it appears to be the face of a despondent boy that is revealed is perhaps a reference to the forgotten boy depicted in servitude in Banksy's original Slave Labour.

Five polystyrene replicas of Slave Labour were placed in a row against the site of extraction at 5.30am on June 1, 2013, the morning of the London auction of Slave Labour, temporarily obscuring D's boy in a panda suit stencil (see Figure 5, below). These new pieces are the work of Essex-based artist Laura Keeble, and are entitled Supply & Demand (After Banksy's Slave Labour). These three dimensional pieces have been produced in the exact proportions of Banksy's original Slave Labour. The slightly irregular square of the cut out section of wall has been reproduced, as has the work's plastic Union Jack bunting and the Perspex shield secured over the original to protect it. However these pieces were carried away, presumably by opportunistic passersby, just hours after they were placed against the wall.

This work is both site and temporally specific. It was timed to appear as a concrete form of dissensus or aesthetic protest against the removal and commodification of street art, on the very morning of the auction of Slave Labour. The title of the work, Supply & Demand, is an inversion of the usual form of the idiomatic microeconomic logic of demand and supply, thus providing another reference to the creation of demand or acquisitive greed, which is given further resonance by the swiftness with which the works were claimed and taken from the site.

The boy in a panda suit remained untouched alone on the wall for eight weeks. It was only removed after several other large stenciled pieces were added to the wall. These new works were created with crude mass produced stencils and accompanying slogans. A stencil placed immediately above the boy in a panda suit depicted Batman's The Joker, with his catch phrase, "why so serious?" and a further stock stencil of Imagine Lennon, to the far left of the wall were presumably regarded by the council as objectionable, or as not 'adding value' to the area, as their appearance saw the entire site (including the boy in a panda suit) swiftly painted over, restoring the blank wall.

Cut here

The stenciled piece currently on the wall has outlasted all of the other prior works, and at the time of writing, has been in position for six months (see Figure 6, below). It has survived roadworks; a series of adjacently scribbled tags by other writers; and it continues to resist removal by the council. The tags sprayed elsewhere on the wall over this period were promptly buffed, but this minimal stenciled work persists. The iconic scissors and dashed lines offer an invitation to 'cut here' of the kind more commonly seen on 'cut out and keep' sections of magazines and consumer packaging. This is a clear reference to the removal for profit of Slave Labour, which was, quite literally, cut off the wall. This new stencil positions this act of removal within the sphere of consumption and the profit economy. However, its consumer friendly design also provides a link to the apparent 'gift' or 'bonus' (to the keeper) of a 'cut out and keep' coupon – an unexpected supplement which operates to expose the 'lack' in the completeness or satisfaction provided by the original item. The consumer/viewer is positioned as wanting what they didn't know they lacked until they received the 'gift' of something for nothing. Although this piece references acquisitive consumer culture, it also presents a puzzle – why would one wish to remove a blank section of wall? Is the artist suggesting that an arbitrary section of a whitewashed city wall is equivalent in worth to a Banksy removed for profit? Is a reference to the production of want and acquisitive greed in the viewer/consumer in the commodification of the 'gift' of street art? Does it allude to the fable of the Emperor's New Clothes, by presenting an essentially invisible work (the blank wall framed by the dashed lines) as being of value, as something that one should want to 'cut out and keep'? Is it a memorial to all of the works – of monetary value or not – that have been removed from the wall?

Although the piece is approximately the same dimensions as Slave Labour, it is positioned slightly to the right of the site of extraction, immediately adjacent to Banksy's rat, over the section of the wall previously occupied by D's humanoid cat. It thus references both the extraction of Slave Labour, and by its positioning, the removal of the other works that fleetingly occupied the site beneath – though unlike Slave Labour, these pieces were whitewashed over, and not 'cut out and kept'. This effects a sense of palimpsest, of the layers of work beneath the cut out and keep stencil, which frames a square of apparently blank white wall. In common with many of the other pieces that appeared on this site, the cut here stencil also references prior popular works by Banksy. A series of stenciled pieces of a similar scale appeared on various city walls in London, and in other European cities, in 2005. Perhaps the most widely disseminated of Banksy's variants on the cut here stencil was the giant version stenciled on the West Bank Barrier which received worldwide media attention when it appeared in 2005. Many of Banksy's works placed in Palestine a decade ago were extracted for private auction in 2010, despite Bansky protesting against their removal. Paradoxically, given its injunction to 'cut here', the work continues to resist removal. Its simplicity in design and mimicry of the form of a recognisable Banksy appears to protect it from buffing by the council, although it has not, as yet, been placed under Perspex in official recognition of its worth or potential authorship. As such, it occupies a precarious position, protected from whitewashing via aesthetic judgement of its symbolic capital, but not from the elements or from potential destruction by others. The absence of a protective Perspex shield protects the cut here piece from efforts to remove the work for profit, while its minimal design and replication of the form of 'a Banksy' appear to accord it a measure of temporary protection against erasure.

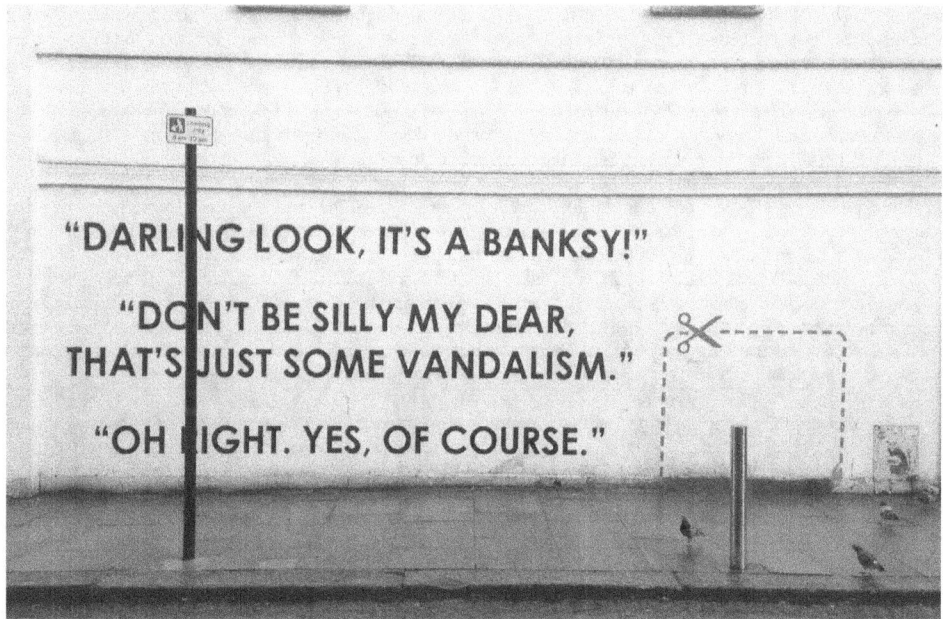

Fig. 6. June 2014. Photograph © Susan Hansen.

Darling look, it's a Banksy!

The most recent work added to the wall, in May 2014, is by the street artist Mobstr, produced in advance of his first solo gallery show in East London. Discussion of the work on Twitter now describes the location simply as "the wall where a banksy was." This very large piece covers the entire stretch of wall with painted lettering that animates the public's imagined reactions to the work on the wall, though which of the works it references – the authentic Banksy rat, the Banksy-style cut here stencil, or Mobstr's own piece – is undetermined. This work does not obscure Banksy's rat, which remains fixed under Perspex to the wall, nor does it interfere with the cut here stencil, which at six months old is beginning to flake without any level of protection against the elements.

The text on the wall arrests the viewer, with an exclamation and an injunction to look: "Darling look, it's a Banksy!" However, this is followed by the dismissive and downgrading retort, "Don't be silly my dear, that's just some vandalism", to which the first speaker concedes, "Oh right. Yes, of course." This work provides a satirically banal commentary on mundane evaluations of the status, or worth, of street art. Like the prior works on the wall, it offers a critique of the objectification and commodification of street art, however unlike prior works, it effects a sharp division between "a Banksy" worth exclaiming over and looking at, and "some vandalism" not worthy of viewers' attention. This is accomplished by adopting the perspective of the imagined consumer-viewers of the work, who, as it turns out, are not looking at the work at all, but are simply concerned with categorizing it crudely as "a Bansky" or as "vandalism", in order to determine if it is worth looking at. Mobstr thus creates a rupture in common sense by making visible the workings of the very consensus that holds together the 'division of the sensible' (Rancière, 2004[xxv]) that informs our practices of looking.

Conclusion

Most of the works discussed here were erased, without protest, presumably by agents of the Haringey council, shortly after they appeared, however they retain traces of already erased and apparently forgotten work in their intertextual references, and they provide a rich source of performative yet transitory collaborative dialogue and critical social commentary. Unlike Slave Labour, most of these works were not appropriated or reproduced, circulated or otherwise recognised or commented upon publicly in the media, save when questions of authorship and potential worth (as possibly created by Banksy) were raised. The only viewers of these lesser known materially ephemeral works – and the only parties to this ongoing correspondence – were the anonymous or pseudonymous street artists themselves, and people who happened to be passing Poundland, although it should be noted that some of the participating street artists circulated images via social media and the internet to those that follow their work.

These works appear, on the whole, designed to be democratically accessible to, and readable by – and indeed to encourage the participation of – a 'non-artistic' community. This is achieved through various means, including the overdetermination of otherwise potentially exclusionary signifiers; via visual and textual references to Banksy, who has come to stand for the commodification of street art as 'art of value'; and via references to signs from pop or consumer culture, as with the invitation provided by the cut here stencil. However it would appear that the latter strategy should not entail too literal a reproduction – like the short-lived Joker/Imagine stencils – or they may be categorized as 'not-art' and promptly removed.

The division of the sensible (Rancière, 2004[xxvi]) takes form here in the material practices associated with the 'policing' of that which should and should not be seen: in the council's whitewashing of objectionable work; in the protection accorded to work of value; and in the excision of work too valuable to be seen and appreciated 'in situ', for conservation and appreciation (BBC, 2013[xxvii]). However, the dissensus invoked by this prolific series of unruly works unsettles this division of the sensible, in that they urge the viewer to stop, to look, and to interrogate the practices of looking that they are engaged in, which may even encourage some to respond by leaving their own marks on the wall. These often self-consciously democratic works of aesthetic protest thus create ruptures in common sense which show that what we see, according to our usual 'division of the sensible', could be otherwise.

Street art that captures the attention of the public may inspire others – from within and without this community of practice – to contribute work of their own. Some of this work will eventually prove objectionable to other members of the public; to the wall's 'owners', and/or to those responsible for the removal of graffiti from the borough. At this point, entire walls may be whitewashed, providing a clean slate for future work. Although we would resist an overly simplistic and deterministic reading of the inevitable commodification and 'death' of street art via its removal from the gift economy (De Certeau, 1984[xxviii]) and incorporation into the profit economy (or more colloquially, "selling out", CDH, 2013[xxix]) concerns with the commodification of street art do seem to inform the rhetoric of the works on the wall. The following crude hierarchy of worth appears to have been applied in mundane evaluations of this work, as indexed by the length of time that work was permitted to remain before being whitewashed:

> Not-art > Graffiti/Vandalism – work received as an unwanted gift that takes away value/symbolic capital from the community and as such is promptly removed, often along with other work on the wall;
> Street art > Gift – work recognized as an ephemeral gift to the community, that may be granted a period of reprieve from removal by authorities, but is always open to erasure and destruction by the elements;
> Street art > Art – work recognized as a gift to the community that is also of value within the profit economy; protected by Perspex shields, but vulnerable to being removed for profit.

The removal of Banksy's Slave Labour for private auction was the catalyst for a transformation of public space, in generating a site for ongoing correspondence, and aesthetic protest, in the series of works that have appeared in its wake. Initial responses to the 'theft' of Slave Labour gave a forceful visual presence to the grief and outrage of the community, while later works provide a critical commentary on the circulation of street art as a commodity, but also highlight that these locally produced works are not part of this system of circulation, which in turn draws attention to the hierarchy of value imposed on works on the street. Any references to the intended site-specific signification of Slave Labour appear largely lost in subsequent work. Thus, the site is now not defined by its proximity to Poundland as a source of goods produced by child labour as originally signified by Banksy's Slave Labour when located in situ, yet it remains indelibly marked by the fleeting presence of the work, as "the wall where a Banksy was."

The practices of removal that street art and graffiti are commonly subject to – whether concerned with 'restoring value' to a community, by its destruction and erasure, or with 'recognising value' by its preservation, protection, and ultimately removal for private profit – yield divergent and differently recognized conditions of possibility for the public spaces they (re)generate. Removal may be ultimately productive and generative in that it provides a 'clean slate' for future work, and may give rise to a proliferation of new images that provoke and foster visual dialogue and correspondence. The ephemerality and material impermanence of street art is thus a necessary if paradoxical condition for it to survive and persist, as such (Young, 2014[xxx]) however much its recent incorporation into the category of high art, and removal for profit, may appear to threaten this foundational 'in situ' definition. If erasure is necessary for graffiti and street art to thrive, perhaps this historically recent form of removal may also prove productive, rather than stultifying. Despite the removal of Banksy's Slave Labour from its original site, and its consequent commodification and depoliticization, the work arguably continues to serve as a catalyst for further work, via the aesthetic protest and dissensus generated by its very absence.

Notes and References

Although the original bunting was removed shortly after the appearance of the work, close inspection of photographs showing the intact bunting shows that the Union Jack flags have been stitched in upside down, which is an historical nautical signifier of distress, or an act of deliberate insult - though this inversion may be inadvertent, as this is a common error, particularly on mass produced products.

i. Rancière, J. (2004) The Politics of Aesthetics. London: Continuum.
ii. Schacter, R. (2008) An ethnography of iconoclash: An investigation into the production, consumption and destruction of street-art in London. Journal of Material Culture, 13, 35-61.
iii. Greater London Authority. (2002) Graffiti in London: Report of the London Assembly Graffiti Investigative Committee, Greater London Authority.
iv. Brighenti, A. (2010) At the wall: Graffiti writers, urban territoriality, and the public domain. Space and Culture, 13 (3), 315-322.
v. Islington Council (2014) Cleaner Islington: Graffiti. http://www.islington.gov.uk/services/parks-environment/cleanerislington/Pages/graffiti.aspx
vi. Douglas, M. (2002) Purity and Danger: An Analysis of Concepts of Pollution and Taboo. London: Routledge
vii. Bourdieu, P. (1984) Distinction: A social critique of the judgement of taste. Cambridge, MA: Harvard University Press.
viii. Frigerio, A. & Khakimova, E. (2013) Shaping the street art legal framework: The clash between private and public interests in the Banksy "Slave Labour" case. Aedon, No. 2.
ix. BBC (2013) Banksy's No Ball Games mural removed from Tottenham wall. BBC News London. July 26, 2013. http://www.bbc.co.uk/news/uk-england-london-23461396
x. Young, A. (2014) Street Art, Public City: Law, Crime and the Urban Imagination. London: Routledge.
xi. Dovey, K., Wollan, S. & Ian Woodcock, I. (2010) Placing Graffiti: Creating and Contesting Character in Inner-city Melbourne. Journal of Urban Design, 17, 1, 21-41.
xii. Burroughs, W. (1988) Introduction. p 3. In. K. Haring & W. Burroughs. Apocalypse. New York: George Mulder Fine Arts.
xiii. Irvine (2012) The work on the street: Street art and visual culture. The Handbook of Visual Culture, ed. Barry Sandywell and Ian Heywood. London & New York: Berg, pp. 235-278.
xiv. Rancière, J. (2004) Ibid.
xv. May, J. (2011) Rancière: Politics, Art & Sense. Editorial. Transformations: No. 19.
xvi. Rancière, J. (1998) May '68 and its afterlives. Chicago: University of Chicago Press.
xvii. May, J. (2011) Ibid.
xviii. Rancière, J. (1998) Ibid.
xix. BBC (2012) 'Banksy' boy worker image on Poundland shop wall. BBC News London, May 16, 2012. http://www.bbc.co.uk/news/uk-england-london-18075620
xx. Tottenham Journal (2013) Banksy art owners have 'last chance to do the right thing', says Wood Green MP. May 29, 2013.
xxi. Young, A. (2004) Ibid.
xxii. Daily Mail (2010) Poundland launches enquiry over boy, 7, paid 7p an hour in Indian sweatshop. July 11, 2010. De Certeau, M. (1984) The Practice of Everyday Life. Berkeley: University of California Press.
xxiii. ILO (2010) Child labour. http://www.antislavery.org/english/slavery_today/child_labour.aspx
xxiv. Rancière, J. (2004) The Politics of Aesthetics. London: Continuum.
xxv. Rancière, J. (2004) Ibid.
xxvi. Rancière, J. (2004) Ibid.
xxvii. BBC (2013) Ibid.
xxviii. De Certeau, M. (1984) Ibid.
xxix. CDH (2013) Notes on the commodification of street art. Art Monthly Australia, 263, 42-44.
xxx. Young, A. (2014) Ibid.

Ágata Dourado Sequeira, ISCTE-IUL / Dinâmia'CET (agata.sequeira@gmail.com)

Out in the Streets: The possibilities and implications of making art in the city's public space

This paper is the result of an ongoing PhD thesis project[1] about the relations between art, urban space and the city, namely through the ephemeral forms of art that are present in the city's public spaces. It is considered here that these relations are never neutral but, instead, very expressive of configurations of power and identity, being street art, both a reflex and a critical approach to those configurations and constraints. Therefore, and from a sociological perspective, the current processes of production of street art in the urban metropolitan context of Lisbon are the focus of this article.

Public Space, Street Art, Urban Sociology.

Street art and change: An ongoing research project

In the last few years, and following a global urban tendency, the subject of street art in Lisbon has been a rapidly growing phenomenon. And as such, the several stakeholders at play – populations, artists/creatives, the art world, academia, media, private entities and public institutions – are trying to understand what street art is and what potential rests upon it, and how they will position themselves in the flow of the events. Therefore, one must add, it is also an exciting field for the social sciences to study.

In this paper I will approach some of the reflections that have been the result of a research project about the transformative potential of art in the public space, in what concerns the populations, the institutions and the people who create.

Once the ephemeral pieces are the ones that can reveal a more immediate potential for transforming the public space – the act of making the piece, the interactions with the passer-bys, and even the planning of the piece (from a single individual's decisions about place to choose and techniques to use, to a myriad of contacts between several agents such as street art producers, public institutions and private stakeholders or owners of buildings) take place in a different time frame than more perennial forms of public art, the object of this research is street art, in the particular case of the metropolitan area of Lisbon.

At the present time, and particularly in the last 6 years, Lisbon is stage to a diverse set of manifestations of street art, which imply a set of changes at several levels. These changes are manifest already in the very expressive basic act of painting a wall in the street (of placing a stencil, sticker or poster, the plastic possibilities are immense) to make a message pass, sometimes a subversive one and with strong social critique, others a more ambiguous message that leaves interrogations to the public, and at the same time the opportunity to turn this act in an opportunity to build or add something to a career in the creative and artistic field. The interpretations of what it means to make street art are as diverse as are the individuals who make it, but what seems transversal to all is the notion that street art, although having its roots in the political mural art and the graffiti writings, no longer confines itself to the meanings and ways of making that these expressions usually implied, but it actually at times seems to blend with other expressive forms – from non-artistic fields to the gallery-oriented field of contemporary art. As a field that is building itself right now, with aesthetic languages that are very current, this phenomenon also seems to be seen as an opportunity for entities that feel the need to incorporate these aesthetic languages in their communication, for marketing and PR purposes. This might be an opportunity for some of the artists and creatives that make street art, but also reveals a latent conflict in the sense it might imply appropriation of a form of artistic expression that other creators and artists feel should be free from all the constraints but their own artistic intention.

Also being subject to a very strong movement of change is the institutional approach towards the possibility of these citizen-artists to use the walls of the public urban space as their own canvas. From what has always been (and seen as) an act of illegality, a rebellious form of appropriation of the public space, to a new paradigm in which street art constitutes itself as an exceptional opportunity to value that same space, allowing the artists and creators to have the possibility to show their work, while at the same time the promotion of the city of Lisbon as a markedly modern and contemporary tourist destination is attempted.

Power, Communication and Creative Paths

At this point, it is paramount to state the two main aspects from which this research stems.

First of all, street art, being of ephemeral nature and such a direct form of interaction with the public space, is a strong reflection of a fluid set of relationships of power within public space. It illustrates (both figuratively and literally) the struggle for a space of communication, of visibility, among competitors such as advertising and institutional powers. If, as Lefebvre famously stated, public space is a stage of intense sociability and diverse meanings (Lefebvre, 2000), it is also a space of social contrasts that might be explicit in its very planning – hence comes the notion of the city as a bureaucratic and class map whose disparities are intended to be suppressed through culture and art (Zukin, 1993). However, the very use of culture and art can in the end reveal these same contrasts, constituting a way of control and domination, given its capacity to produce symbols and establish place. It is argued here that such effects of art in the public place are also visible in the current production of street art in the context of Lisbon.

Therefore, and since the public space is also a powerful mean of communication (Lofland, 1998), the art it features, as is the case with street art, can be read not only in terms of what all the involved have to say through it, but also in terms of how the way it is produced and promoted can speak to us about the mechanisms behind making public space in an urban context: «(...) Space not only structures how communication will occur and who will communicate, it also has consequences for the content of that communication.» (Lofland, 1998:186). So street art instigates a debate on what actually means 'public space', in a time when the city might seem at times overpowered by huge advertising billboards, that might as well depend on a net of bureaucratic procedures and licences, or in a simple authorization from a private owner of an exterior façade, with the connivance of the city hall. At what point private decisions can interfere with public space and what can the practice of street art show us in that matter? This is too big a question to give some sort of answer at this point of my research, but there are a lot of important aspects I'll approach in this paper. Secondly, an aspect that I will not be working thoroughly in the context of this paper, but that is also an important part of this project, is the assumption that street art can also be a strategic element in the construction of an individual creative path. As a specific communicational space (Campos, 2010), street art is expression of identities, lifestyles and discourses from who produces it. As it uses public space as canvas for its artistic manifestations and also as a vehicle for communication, it seems to make a commentary on the visual and artistic forms that are more conventional and institutional, reclaiming for itself its very own space. This is also an undoubtedly political and ideological statement. The fact that so many street art initiatives are being promoted – from the public initiatives to the private ones – all contribute to the fact that there are possibilities for the artists to have their work visible in a way that is possible today as maybe never before. Also, the quickness inherent to making an illegal artwork in a wall is so many times not necessary through these initiatives or intermediaries, so there are more and more complex artworks appearing, that allow the creators and artists to develop their techniques and imagery in what might be a more fluid way. Visibility might come with compromise, and the discourses of the makers of street art are as diverse as themselves. As important as street art as a form of building an individual path is also the reflection about what is artistic work as an activity in this field and what are the agents around it, in a particular context where these considerations seem yet so diffuse.

The social meanings of Street Art
In terms of the methodological approach that underlies this project, it is a qualitative research, including a set of interviews to several stakeholders – from creators of really diverse profiles to associations, institutions and collectives – within the street art that takes place in the streets of Lisbon. Being this object such an inextricably visual one, it is equally important the construction and analysis of a set of images resulting from the field work that document or attempt to illustrate the several aspects that will be subject to reflection. And of course, a solid anchoring in a theoretical support resulting from a transversal bibliographical research is also fundamental for this project – as it is for any attempt of adding knowledge to a field of research.

In this paper in particular, I chose to approach the several meanings of 'making street art'[2], from the more independent initiatives to the ones that are part of institutional actions. The first being usually connected with a certain anonymity and/or peer-recognition of the artist, where the act of making an artistic mark in the public space assumes a political role of appropriation, the claiming of a place for communication that counterpoints the advertising and the institucional marks that dominate the communication in the public space. The second relating to the collaborations in artistic projects commissioned by institutions, where the artist is no longer semi-anonimous but a recognized creative, being the act of intervening artistically in the street not as much an individual political claim to a space for communication but almost an act of construction of an artistic persona that is recognizable in the broader field of the contemporary art world, with all the opportunities that might come as a result. Both of these aspects being equally very rich in terms of what they say politically about the powers that intervene in the public space and the several meanings that derive from these actions.

Who makes urban art? A diversity of profiles
Lisbon is currently, and from the last 6 years approximately, an urban stage for a diverse set of manifestations of what conventionally is called 'street art' or 'urban art' – though these designations are not free of a certain degree of polemic, which I will not approach in this particular paper for the sake of brevity.

The root of this artistic form is as ancient as is the act of drawing or writing something in a wall and make it therefore public. In the contemporary age, it may be in the events of May 1968 in Paris and in the birth of graffiti within north-American hip hop culture that lays the origin of street art. In what concerns the Portuguese context, this origin might be related to the political mural paintings and writings on the walls as political statements in the period around the revolution of April 1974. These are contexts of social agitation, where freedom is the focus and propeller of experimentation in the public space.

Later, graffiti also had expression in Portugal, with several writers making their mark known in the city walls, trains, etc. The quickness of the act of painting that the spray cans allowed these writers, a certain aesthetic and even a specific ethos are still to be found within street art in a broader sense, as there is an intimate relation between street art and graffiti culture, as several individual paths of street artists can attest.

Street art has grown in the last few years and it is no longer at all strictly related to graffiti, though it might include its techniques, as well as stencils, posters and other less formatted expressions under unexpected forms that show once more how rich in terms of plastic experimentation this field can be. There are elements of graphic design, contemporary painting, comic book universe, that also derive from the actual diversity of profiles of the people who make it: some with a background in 'traditional' graffiti, others in several branches of design, many contemporary plastic artists (that 'come from the gallery', so to say) that try the street as a new canvas for their work, self-taught creatives, among others.

It can be said that street art has been penetrating other universes, being the processes of artistic recognition (Heinich, 1993) a reality in several cases, and mixing itself with other «social worlds of art» (Becker, 2010), such as the contemporary art circuit.

Simultaneously, other relationships are inevitable, as the process of making street art many times involves a relatively vast network of agents, curators, public and private entities – which I will refer to in detail in the following section.

Making street art in Lisbon: artists, agents, associations, public and private entities

The attention to street art, and it's visibility is a global phenomenon that also takes place in Lisbon. There have been taking place several actions that reveal distinct forms of producing street art in this metropolitan context. These several initiatives span from the individual will to intervene in the city's public space, to the promotion of street art events from public and private entities in different molds. The different forms of production and making street art are eloquent in terms of what are the powers and the people involved, and what relationships between street art, its artists and the public space are being experimented in Lisbon at the present time.

In a previous stage of this research, I tried to build a relatively rigid systematization of the different types of production of street art – but of course this effort proved not to be precise, because the inter-relations between all of them are present, when it's not the case of an individual artist's initiative. Nonetheless, and bearing in mind the presence of this tendency for the interdependency of the several actors involved, there are in fact strong differences and motivations between them.

Therefore, in order to attempt a characterization of these different forms of production, it might be useful to arrange them according to their more or less institutionally planned character, in an ideal-type way. Consequently we have, on one side, the absolutely non-institutional initiatives, and, on the other side, the projects of institutional initiative, namely the public ones, which in the case of Lisbon, are promoted by GAU (Galeria de Arte Urbana – Urban Art Gallery), an organism of the city's municipality. Between these two poles are other types of production of urban art that result from processes of mediation between the institutional and the artists, through agents – namely associations or collectives that assume the role of promoting street art. Let us now approach each of these types of processes of production of street art individually and in more detail.

As for the non-institutional ones – let's refer to those as individual initiatives - they basically translate in the will of an artist or a small collective or artists to intervene in the street, sometimes - but not necessarily - without any kind of mediation or concerns towards legality, much like traditional graffiti, if not in the content or intention, in the form, or ways of making. These might be relatively spontaneous; with of course the amount of planning that is necessary to pass from the idea to the realization. Most of the times, these are not authorized interventions, but the result of the initiative of the artists, who find in the walls of the city a canvas for their work and will to self-expression. These pieces can have a rawer and even subversive intention in them. It is totally untamed street art, while meaning in a very clear way the willingness to reclaim their space within the city's public spaces. If on the one hand there might be a risk in the moment of making the piece in the street and not getting caught, on the other, there is a certain feeling of surprise for the alert users of the public space when discovering that a new piece of art just 'appeared' in a wall or tree or sign in the street they are passing by. This is certainly a stimulating effect of communication between artist and passer-by that contributes to a sense of communal belonging in relation to the city.

In what concerns public initiatives of street art in the context of Lisbon, GAU (Urban Art Gallery) is inescapable. It is an organ of Lisbon Municipality that aims to promote several street art initiatives around the city, while claiming an important role in displaying the works of street artists in this city but also in mediating the obtaining of permits for the artists to intervene in privately own exterior spaces (such as a building's façade, or a surrounding wall, for instances).

The work of GAU started in 2008 with localized interventions in Largo da Oliveirinha and Calçada da Glória, with the purpose of rehabilitating the Bairro Alto area by cleaning the profusion of tagging that could be seen there (and still can), while at the same time creating a space for quality street art that could be on display. Of course the idea is polemic in several ways and raises a lot of tremendously interesting questions, but those will be approached later on the paper.

Gau is a very active institutional branch that promotes several distinct interventions and an opportunity for the artists to showcase their works in legal walls with considerable dimension. This might not only mean no stress while painting and the offering of a budget for the materials for doing so, but also the visibility and further opportunities for paid work, mainly from companies who want to incorporate some of the aesthetic options these artists take, in their products or image. One example of the work of GAU is 'Rostos do Muro Azul' (Faces of the Blue Wall), an initiative with several editions in which several artists were invited to send their projects for painting sections of the wall that surrounds a psychiatric hospital in Lisbon. Another GAU project is the one called 'Reciclar o olhar' (Recycle the look), where public glass containers for recycling bottles are painted by basically anyone who is willing to send a project - not only street artists, though many do too. Simultaneously, the place where the initiatives by GAU started (Largo da Oliveirinha / Calçada da Glória) is still, from time to time, subject to interventions, as well as many other sporadic projects that this entity promotes a bit all over the city.

An increasingly important work is the one being developed by the mediation agents. These appear mainly in the form of collectives or associations of people who propose to promote street art events or initiatives. These might be collectives of artists (either former or in the active) or cultural associations, being, again, the profiles of the individuals within it, diverse. The work of these agents is important, as it's often them who bring the knowledge of the process of planning a street art initiative – from the idea of the artist to the bureaucratic net of authorizations that will be necessary to accomplish it. The mediation process can be between the several stakeholders involved, such as the artists or collectives of artists, the municipality (through GAU), associations of cultural intends, and the owners of private property where there is an interest (from either side or both) in making a street art intervention. There are several associations or collectives that play the role of mediation agents for the production of street art in the context of Lisbon. One of them is the project Wool, that in collaboration with Lx Factory, a privately own deactivated factory complex that now welcomes several cultural initiatives but also a lot of small companies and their offices, fashion and interior design stores, galleries, restaurants and bars. This place, from time to time, accommodates editions of Wool on Tour, that brings street artists to Lx Factory, to intervene in the former factory's walls. Another privately held former factory also promotes street art initiatives for their inner walls – Fábrica Braço de Prata. This is an extensive building that used to serve as a gun and ammunition factory and now is the home of several cultural activities: it accommodates theater and cinema sessions, dance lessons, concerts, a book store, art exhibitions, a restaurant and bar, among other facilities. Walls surround this building, and from time to time street artists are invited to submit a project to paint sections of these walls, forming an open air gallery of street art.

Other examples - although not extensively listed - of associations that mediate urban art initiatives include APAURB (Portuguese Association for Urban Art) – which collaborated in projects such as «40 anos, 40 murais» («40 years, 40 murals»), a celebration of the 40 years of the revolution of 25th of April 1974, or the interventions in the Alcântara tunnel; Ébano Collective, that proposed the recent series of pieces that took place in the Graça neighbourhood, «Passeio Literário da Graça» («Graça's Literary Walk»); also to be mentioned is Project Crono, which programmed several initiatives, including what may be one of the most recognizable urban art projects in Lisbon – the painting of the façades of a set of derelict buildings in the centre of Lisbon, under permit of the city hall. I'd also like to mention Underdogs, a platform for both Portuguese and international street artists that, working in partnership with the city hall, allows the artists to be able to create street art in large scale in Lisbon, while also stimulating the exchange of ideas, graphic languages and artistic concepts.

Questions and dilemmas around Street Art
There are also an increasing amount of companies or brands that see in street art an opportunity to promote commercial intentions, and it's not uncommon for partnerships or sponsorships to happen between brands, associations and the public institution, in street art events.

But apart from all these initiatives for the promotion and production of street art, there are also appearing small companies that revolve around it, mainly in what concerns tourism. Street art guided tours are already a reality, side-by-side with online street art city guides that pinpoint what pieces to look for, destined to a specific niche of tourism that seems to be growing. In fact, the global visibility of street art and the profusion of images from street art pieces that everyday can be found online, is becoming a powerful tool for the marketing of cities as a tourist destination. Lisbon is no exception, being often featured in quick lists of 'the best street art cities' – as a simple google search can atest[3]. While this mediatic attention is by no means a reliable indicator of the comparative quality and quantity of pieces or street art in each city, it does show how 'street art' as imagery is currently being used a powerful tool for marketing cities as tourist destinations, in a tough competition among urban destinies that aim to pass an image of trendiness and 'now' that certain tourist segments might look for in their travel consumptions.

A parallel aspect that derives from all the interest and visibility or street art is the commercial appropriation of its visual languages for the purpose of selling things: artists are invited to decorate store windows, for instances, or to decorate cars or clothing items. Which might for some constitute a valid opportunity for paid work, while for others an unthinkable activity.

This brings up a very interesting question – with the profusion of events and street art initiatives programmed and promoted by private and public entities, at what point the artistic and creative work that is implied in the painting of a considerably large wall, for example, will be consistently and fully be considered work in its self right – and therefore systematically paid accordingly? Maybe the fact that this aspect is so diffuse at the moment and in this context lies within the fact that this is a new field that is constituting itself, but while there starts to have a consistent response from the several stakeholders – public and private entities – and new agents start to emerge and have a fundamental role in the promotion and establishment of a systematic way of doing things, this specific artistic production, when inserted in this net of relations and influences, might just have to be paid for the work it represents and not a sort of highly elaborate and technically specific 'hobby'. While that isn't the case, street artists who make this activity their main focus, will continue to develop their own strategies of sustainability, such as working with brands when possible, for some, or making pieces in canvas that might be more immediately sellable.

From this also stems another relevant aspect: globally, there is a certain movement of recognition of some street artists by the more conventional and 'gallery-oriented' contemporary artistic spheres. There are several examples of street artists that have seen their work recognized in a broad scale, with their art pieces being exhibited in galleries (both indoor and outdoors), festivals, retrospectives, published in monographies and catalogues, etc. Others might form collectives and organize street art events themselves, or even feel comfortable putting together galleries – in the 'white cube' sense of the word – to showcase their works. So as some street artists move from the street walls towards the gallery space, other ones move from the gallery towards the street, since opportunities in that sense have appeared and this way they can experiment new plastic approaches to their work. This reveals the different backgrounds of the diverse set of people that make street art. Some initiated their artistic path within traditional graffiti culture and eventually gained interest in experimenting with different graphic languages, or exploring other frames of artistic production. Others initiated their street art incursions as result of a will to further stretch the boundaries of the career they were already developing, be it in the context of design or in the field of contemporary art in a stricter sense«.

But always transversal to street art are questions on why the control of public space is not in fact responsibility of everyone but the entities that organize it, or advertise in it, or that build in it, or simply own it; the use of walls in the public space as the medium for several forms of street art, that appropriates itself of them, so many times illegally, others not, might be seen as evident symbolic expression of confrontation and dispute of urban space, reflecting relations of power and tensions that relate to the life in the city on a daily basis. The feeling of exclusion provoked by domination and public communication by media and advertising is on the root of that appropriation of the street walls as a mean of communication – that is also, undoubtedly, public. It can be argued that street art, in its most spontaneous and unprogrammed forms, being of ephemeral nature and in the global current contexts, has the potential to accomplish the promises of public art (Hayden, 1995) in a more direct way. Because it is more immediate and unexpected, it can also be very critical, posing by its mere existence questions about the legitimacy (or lack thereof) of the state, local institutions and the capital of occupying what is in fact called 'public' space. It origins a debate about these issues, fueled by situations where the competition for public visual space is sometimes blatantly aggressive, such as the recent covering up of two well-known big scale façade artworks by Portuguese street artists in Lisbon, by huge billboards advertising a shopping center (that has since been taken down by the company, following intense polemic within digital social networks).

Facing such events, it is particularly appropriate to finalize with the reference to the work of Sharon Zukin: «The look and feel of cities reflect decisions about what – or who – should be visible and what should not, on concepts of order and disorder, and on uses of aesthetic power. » (Zukin, 1995:7). Street art is therefore constituting itself as a powerful way to debate and critically think these issues revolving around the making of the city's public space.

Notes and References

1 Funded by FCT with the reference SFRH/BD/82506/2011
2 Referring to the activity itself and not to the meanings that might be inherent to the artistic intention.
3 For instances: «The 26 Best Cities in the World to see Street Art», http://www.huffingtonpost.com/2014/04/17/best-street-art-cities_n_5155653.html

«20 of the best cities to see Street Art», http://www.boredpanda.com/best-street-art-cities/
«Berlin, Cuba: Best cities in the world for street art», http://www.news.com.au/travel/world-travel/berlin-cuba-best-cities-in-the-world-for-street-art/story-e6frfqai-1226857697272
Becker, Howard S. (2010), Mundos da Arte, Lisboa, Livros Horizonte.
Campos, Ricardo (2010), Porque pintamos a cidade? Uma abordagem etnográfica do Graffiti Urbano, Lisboa, Fim de Século.
Campos, Ricardo; Brighenti, Andrea Mubi; Spinelli, Luciano (orgs.) (2011), Uma Cidade de Imagens, Lisboa, Editora Mundos Sociais.
Choay, Françoise (2006), A Alegoria do Património, Lisboa, Edições 70.
Delgado, Manuel (2011) , El espacio público como ideología, Madrid, Catarata.
Ferro, Lígia (2011) Da rua para o Mundo: Configurações do graffiti e do parkour e campos de possibilidades urbanas, Tese de Doutoramento em Antropologia, Lisboa, ISCTE/ FCT
Hayden, Dolores (1995), The Power of Place: Urban Landscape as Public History, Cambridge, The MIT Press.
Heinich, Nathalie (1993), Du peintre à l'artiste. Artisans et académiciens à l'âge classique, Paris, Éditions de Minuit.
Lefebvre, Henri (2000), La production de l'espace, Paris, Anthropos.
Lofland, Lyn (1998), The Public Realm, New York, Aldine de Gruyter.
Low, Setha (2000) On the Plaza: The politics of Public Space and Culture, Austin, The University of Texas Press
Stahl, Johannes (2009), Street Art, s/l, Ullmann Publishing.
Zukin, Sharon (1993), Landscapes of Power, Berkeley, University of California Press.
Zukin, Sharon (1995) The Culture of Cities, Oxford, Blackwell.

Theodore Kuttner, M.A., Universität-Hamburg, Department of Art History

Os Gêmeos & São Paulo:
Reappropriating Public Space in a "City of Walls"

São Paulo has emerged as one of the major focal points for international street art culture and Os Gêmeos have become known as the international face of grafite in São Paulo. This paper aims to explore the complex relationship between São Paulo grafiteiros and the urban space, using selected works by Os Gêmeos as visual evidence. Os Gêmeos' street art will be explored as a method of restoring humanity to spaces which had been rendered void of cultural interaction, thereby counteracting the proliferation of the non-place caused by urban planning as well as socio-economic and political forces.

Street Art, Reappropriation, Non-Places

Introduction

The twin brothers Otávio and Gustavo Pandolfo, better known by the pseudonym Os Gêmeos, have recently gained recognition on the international art scene and have become the de facto representatives of street art in São Paulo. Having begun their artistic career on the streets of São Paulo as young grafiteiros, or graffiti artists, they steadily built their reputation in the street art scene for their innovative style and fantastical characters. Over the past decade, they have also increasingly been involved in painting commissioned walls and have more frequently taken their art into and onto museum and gallery walls. Although their work represents an intriguing case study for the intersection between the "art world" and the street art scene, this analysis will focus on the art which they have created in the streets. In particular, certain aspects of their work will be placed in the context of the urban structure and sociopolitical dynamic of the city of São Paulo. The visual analysis of selected works by Os Gêmeos will integrate aspects of spatial theory in order to explore the complex relationship between the street artist and his urban environment.

The concept of site-specificity will be examined in the context of Os Gêmeos' street art, with a particular focus on a handful of their São Paulo works. However, here the term "specificity" is used liberally to mean "specific to a type of space" rather than a clearly delineated, unique, and identifiable site. In a general sense, the location of street art is, by definition, in the streets of major metropolises. Although there are many such cities and each one has its own history and specific shape and contours, the characteristics of the contemporary urban landscape serving as the canvas for street artists are more strongly defined by their homogeneity than by their differences. The places where graffiti is generally found – the concrete walls, pillars for bridges and overpasses, trains and train tunnels – can all be considered a particular subgroup within the category of the non-place, as theorized by Marc Augé. Due to the rapid hyper-urbanization of São Paulo, these transitory areas of passage and delineation, demarcation, boundary, and border have come to overshadow the traditional concept of public space as one of culture and interaction. However, it is from this seemingly arid land, the cultural void of the non-place, that the countercultural movement of street art and graffiti sprouted and blossomed. Thus, the idea of location, space, and site-specificity in Os Gêmeos' street art can be conceptualized in three different ways: first, the site as a unique location, second, the urban landscape of São Paulo (or other metropolises such as New York City) as a catalyst for street art, and thirdly, street art as the reaction to the proliferation of the non-place.

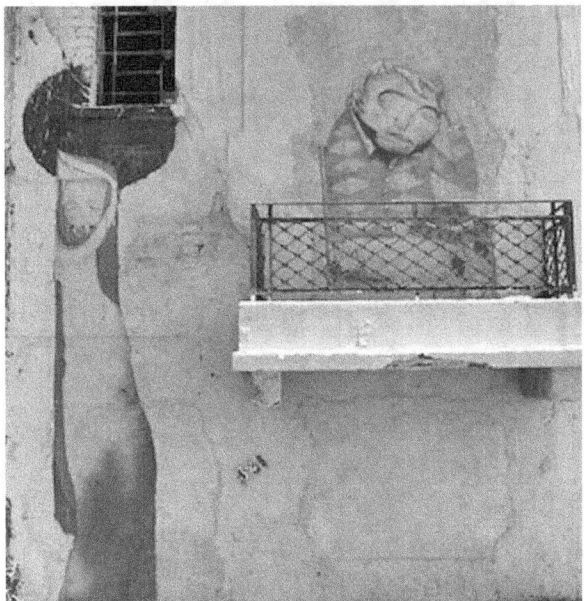

Figure 1: Os Gêmeos - Untitled (Balcony), Brazil, undated,
Source: Lost Art Website, URL: <http://www.lost.art.br/osgemeos_02_97.htm>

A comparison of the urban conditions within São Paulo during Os Gêmeos' formative years (the first Brazilian graffiti boom) and the conditions which had spawned the larger New York City graffiti movement in the previous decade may help reevaluate some of the early theoretical positions on the significance of graffiti within visual culture, with a particular focus on Jean Baudrillard. Additionally, the research of Teresa Caldeira as presented in her book, City of Walls: Crime, Segregation, and Citizenship in São Paulo, will be used to gain insight into the socio-economic conditions and civic development of São Paulo during this period. Furthermore, by placing the analysis of street art culture and the work of Os Gêmeos into the context of spatial theory and Marc Augé's concepts of supermodernity and non-places, the perception of graffiti as an anti-discourse can be reexamined using Os Gêmeos' unsanctioned Brazilian works as visual evidence. In doing so, interpretations of Os Gêmeos' work by certain Brazilian art and cultural theorists who follow similar lines of analysis will also be taken into consideration, specifically those of Charbelly Estrella expressed in her 2006 text "A visualidade de São Paulo e o vocabulário popular do graffiti - a poética dos Gêmeos"[1] which appeared in the analysis of Brazilian graffiti titled "O Graffiti na cidade de São Paulo e sua vertente no Brasil – estéticas e estilos"[2] and edited by Sérgio Poato.

Spatial Theory: Degrees of Site-specificity

Street art varies in its degree of site-specificity. Certain works reference the immediate surroundings and context of the image, contain a message that is directed towards those most likely to view the work, or interact with nearby objects or architectonic elements. This is the case for at least one of Os Gêmeos' works created near the municipal agency for issuing identification numbers, called "R.G." (registro geral), a basic necessity for performing a wide variety of functions when living in Brazil, such as buying a cell phone SIM card. In this piece, Os Gêmeos painted a figure with the caption "Não tenho um R.G." (I don't have an R.G.)[3] bringing attention to the potential exclusion and marginalization of the disenfranchised. Other works function with the surroundings on an aesthetic level rather than within a contextual framework. In figure 1, one sees how the images can interact with the surrounding architectonic elements. The concrete protrusion is given back its original function as a balcony by placing a seated figure above it.

However, even when street art is executed in a way that neither specifically references the exact location of the work nor interacts with the surrounding elements, when simply an arbitrary wall is selected in an area where the grafiteiro believes he can complete the work without being arrested (regardless of the actual risk), more often than not, these surfaces share certain characteristics. First of all, the main support for the pieces, especially in Brazil, is the blank concrete wall. Secondly, graffiti movements worldwide share the characteristic of being distinctly urban, with much higher concentrations in dense metropolises. The third aspect, which is not always the case, but more often than not, is that these surfaces tend to be public structures such as bridges, underpasses, subway stations, highway barriers – products of civil engineering and infrastructure considered critical to the flow of people within highly-populated areas. So even when street art is not decidedly site-specific in the traditional sense, it is still site-specific in that it is designed to exist within a certain type of space.

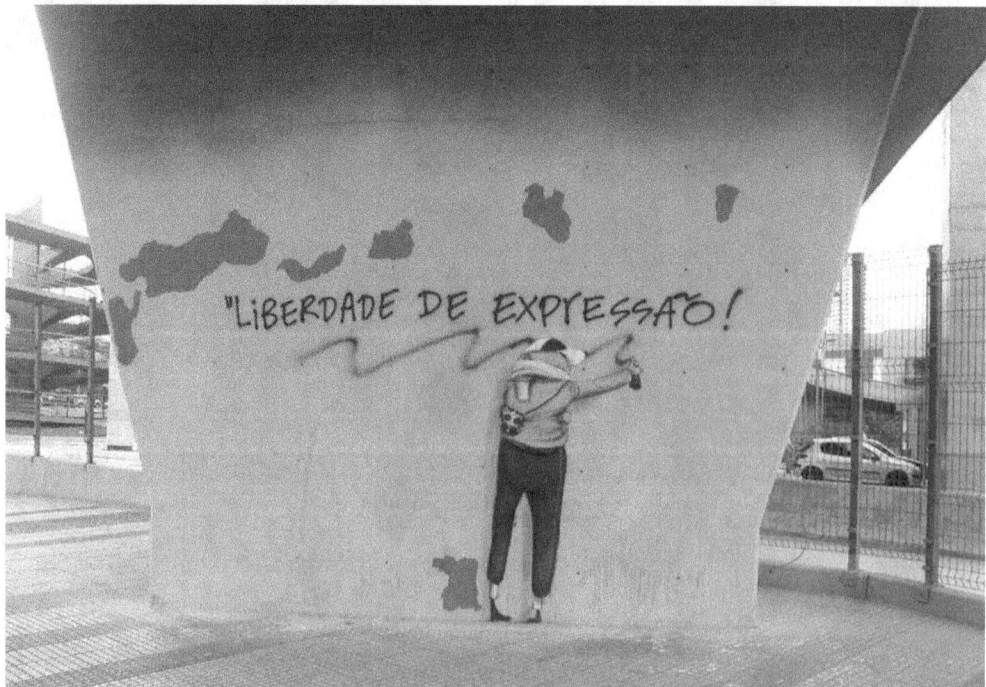

Fig. 2: Os Gêmeos - Untitled (Liberdade de Expressão), São Paulo, undated, ca. 2010,
Source: <http://www.osgemeos.com.br/page/12/>

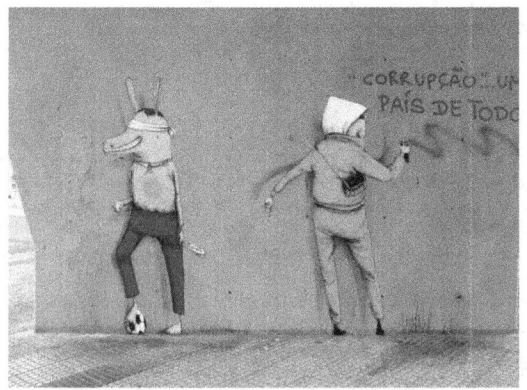

Fig. 3: Os Gêmeos - Untitled (Corrupção... Um País de Todos), São Paulo, undated, ca. 2010, Source: <http://www.osgemeos.com.br/page/12/>

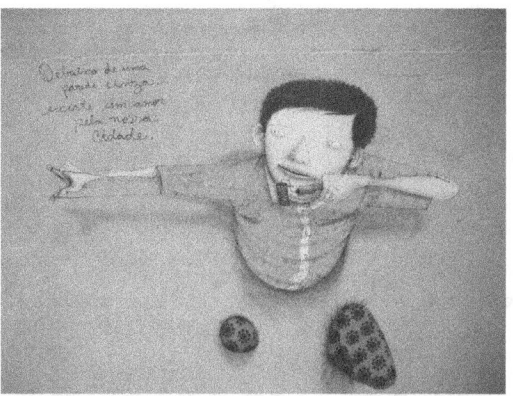

Fig. 4: Os Gêmeos - Untitled (Parede Cinza), São Paulo, undated, Source: <http://www.flickr.com/photos/caioguima/3215701135/>

Figures 2 ,3, and 4 present examples of Os Gemeos' street art that are not site-specific in the traditional sense but nevertheless have implications relevant to location and spatial theory. These works, untitled of course, shall be referred to by the text they contain. In figure 2, we see one of Os Gêmeos' hallmark yellow figures from the back, wearing a green and yellow shirt, a soccer ball pouch on his back, a baseball cap, and a white scarf which appears to also cover his face. The figure holds a spray can and is finishing a flourish to underline the words "LIBERDADE DE EXPRESSÃO!" or freedom of expression. The figure and the text are placed on a structure supporting a bridge which appears to be analogous to the surface for the work Corrupção, um País de Todos (Fig. 3), which translates to "corruption...one nation for all." This self-referential image of the grafiteiro in action also features a blindfolded figure with a grinning donkey-like head and one foot on a soccer ball, representing those citizens whose love of soccer blinds them to the socio-political problems which their country faces. In figure 4, a yellow figure is depicted emerging from the wall using trompe l'oeil, with small cracks painted around where the figure's torso and bent knees appear to be coming out from the surface. Shading techniques reinforce this impression. The figure holds a slingshot out to the left side of the image, tense and ready to release. Yet instead of a stone in the slingshot, he holds a small paint roller. Above the figure's outstretched arm, the text reads "Debaixo de uma parede cinza... existe um amor pela nossa cidade." This translates to: "Underneath a gray wall... there is a love for our city." None of these works reference or interact with the individual characteristics of the wall on which they are painted, nor do they directly refer to the surrounding area or history thereof. Nevertheless, the location of these works is not irrelevant, especially if the concept of location is broadened or redefined. In the case of Parede Cinza (Fig. 4), the work dialogues with the entire urban landscape, which, as Manco et al. describe, is defined by the omnipresence of concrete: "On the outskirts of Brazil's sprawling cities, concrete stretches for as far as the eye can see[.]"[4]

Baudrillard's "Semiocracy" and Graffiti as Anti-Discourse

When considering the location of these works of street art in the most general sense, that is, the city as a canvas, theories about the urban conditions which led to the development of modern graffiti go back to the late 1970s. In Jean Baudrillard's 1975 work "Kool Killer, or The Insurrection of Signs," he conceptualizes the urban space as one that is dominated by a system of codes, stating: "The city is no longer the politico-industrial zone that it was in the nineteenth century, it is the zone of signs, the media and the code."[5] In Baudrillard's concept of the city, which he describes as a „semiocracy," control is exerted upon its residents through this complex system of signs. Thus, the only true form of rebellion is one that comes in semiotic form, a coded attack against the hegemony of codes: fighting fire with fire so to speak. Graffiti, according to Baudrillard, is precisely this kind of semiotic attack and must be seen as a revolt against the power structures that separate the sender from the receiver. In the words of Baudrillard: „Whatever attacks contemporary semiocracy, this new form of value, is therefore politically essential: graffiti for example."[6]

Baudrillard describes how the city paradoxically acts to neutralize and homogenize but at the same time to separate and segregate. Through this process, minority groups are marginalized and disenfranchised, and according to Baudrillard, graffiti is a way to combat this symbolic marginalization and proclaim one's existence within a semiotic system that otherwise stifles these groups' channels of expression. In this sense, graffiti can be seen as the re-appropriation of the urban landscape by the disenfranchised and victims of gentrification. The act of writing one's tag, signature, or piece on a public wall is then inherently political, not only because of its illegality, but also because the very proclamation of one's identity is radical, whether or not that identity is „real." In fact, the use of a pseudonym is furthermore a rejection of the concept of identity being defined by society and an affirmation of one's right to determine his or her own identity or to become anonymous on one's own terms:

Under these conditions, radical revolt effectively consists in saying 'I exist, I am so and so, I live on such and such street, I am alive here and now.' This would still be an identitarian revolt however, combating anonymity by demanding a proper name and a reality. The graffitists went further in that they opposed pseudonyms rather than names to anonymity. [...] Retaliation, reversion of the code according to its own logic, on its own terrain, gaining victory over it because it exceeds semiocracy's own non-referentiality.[7]

Transferring this line of analysis to São Paulo a few decades later, when Os Gêmeos tag a wall or put up a piece on a concrete wall in São Paulo, from a semiotic point of view, they are attacking a system that marginalizes certain sections of society and actively creating an identity for themselves and reinforcing the existence of this identity through action. When they write "Liberdade de expressão" (freedom of expression) accompanied by a caricature of a grafiteiro, it is a quite literal and direct reference to the politics of graffiti and the processes that Baudrillard describes in more detail. With this piece, Os Gêmeos acknowledge the repression of self-expression by the dominant culture and they not only present an affront to that system with this statement, but using self-referentiality, they also visually represent the only suitable political response according to Baudrillard, a semiotic attack by means of graffiti. The concept of graffiti as an identity-forming statement is a position which Os Gêmeos themselves have been quoted as supporting in several sources. Pedro Alonzo writes in Os Gêmeos' most recent exhibition catalogue: "Os Gemeos approach painting in the urban landscape with defiance and vitality: 'When you go on the street and change something, you are saying that you are alive.'"[8] The affirmation of existence is thus given as a main impetus for their street art. The question remains, however, whether the conditions in New York City in the 1970s as described by Baudrillard are analogous to those in São Paulo during its initial graffiti boom in the early 1980s.

Reappropriating Public Space in a "City of Walls"
Since Os Gêmeos were immersed in hip-hop culture and began writing graffiti at a very early age, they grew up as part of the first generation of São Paulo grafiteiros in the eighties, even though they did not gain recognition beyond that scene until after the first wave of São Paulo grafite had passed. Thus, the characteristics of São Paulo during this period, both the socio-economic situation as well as the physical, concrete, structural aspects of the city as a result of urban planning and civil engineering are integral building blocks for the analysis because they provide the context for the graffiti movement during Os Gêmeos' formative years and for the reception of cultural elements from New York City. When mentioned in passing in sources on Brazilian graffiti culture and the work of Os Gêmeos, both similarities and differences between São Paulo and New York are acknowledged: Wivian Weller writes in her essay "Hip Hop in São Paulo and Berlin" for an exhibition catalogue on Brazilian art:

> *In Brazil, the development of Hip Hop culture began in the mid-1980s – in the metropolis São Paulo in the southwestern part of the country. The similarities between the socio-economic and socio-political situations of the black communities in big cities such as New York and São Paulo were apparently the reason the young people in São Paulo embraced Hip Hop culture.[9]*

Aside from the fact that the graffiti movement in both cities was more racially diverse than the Weller implies, the socio-economic and political similarities are valid. In contrast, Pedro Alonzo notes: "Unique characteristics make São Paulo an ideal setting for urban art. The city has over 18,000 buildings, and estimates put the number of abandoned buildings downtown at over 400."[10] However, Alonzo does not compare these figures to other graffiti hubs like New York. These statements alone do not give us true insight into the Paulista's relationship to his or her urban space and the implications thereof in the interpretation of Os Gêmeos and the São Paulo graffiti movement. For that purpose, key points from an extensive analysis by Theresa P.R. Caldeira titled City of Walls: Crime, Segregation, and Citizenship in São Paulo (2000) will be extracted and used to shed light upon the role of the wall and public space in São Paulo graffiti with a focus on Os Gêmeos' work.

In Caldeira's City of Walls, she constructs a compelling argument based on hard data that inequality, separation, and control are not only facilitated by but are also a function of the physical, structural, urban developments within the city of São Paulo over the course of the several decades. She connects the physical and architectural characteristics of the city directly to the social dynamics and modes of interaction among its residents. Although Caldeira does not address graffiti in this particular publication, these aspects are critical to understanding the fundamental relationship between the São Paulo grafiteiros (i.e. Os Gêmeos and their compatriots) and the city that functions as the site for their work. When dealing with socio-political aspects of urban development such as segregation, gentrification, and social inequality, the typical model involves a center-periphery dichotomy in which marginalized groups are gradually forced further outwards with the expansion of the city. However, Caldeira argues that this model does not adequately describe the situation in São Paulo.[11] Instead, she describes a different dynamic in which the spatial organization occurs through physical barriers, typified by the concrete wall. "It is no longer a city providing conditions for inattention to class differences, but rather a city of walls, with a population obsessed by security and social discrimination."[12] She bases her analysis of the urban space on an extensive investigation on the fear of criminality in the city, or at least perceived criminality, which she hypothesizes has a major impact on the physical characteristics of São Paulo's architecture and urban planning.

> *Moreover, in the context of increased suspicion and fear of crime, and the preoccupation with social decay, residents show no tolerance for people from different social groups or interest in finding common solutions to their urban problems. Rather, they engage in increasingly sophisticated techniques of social separation and the creation of distance. Thus, the fortified enclaves— apartment high-rises, closed condominiums, peripheral office complexes, and shopping*

centers—constitute the core of a new way of organizing segregation, social discrimination, and economic restructuring in São Paulo. Different social classes live closer to each other in some areas but are kept apart by physical barriers and systems of identification and control.[13]

Caldeira takes what would traditionally be seen as indicators of economic progress and development, i.e. the large-scale construction projects mentioned, and rereads them as symbols of deep-rooted sociopolitical issues in Brazilian culture that were not solved by the country's relatively recent transition to a representative democracy.

In consequence, not only is São Paulo more unequal than it used to be [...] but this inequality has also become more explicit and visible as rich and poor residents live in closer proximity in the newly expanded areas of the city and metropolitan region. [...] It is also a metropolitan area in which the physical distances that used to separate different social groups may have shrunk, but the walls around properties are higher and the systems of surveillance more obvious.[14]

These statements have several major implications for the analysis of São Paulo graffiti. First of all, the social inequality and the marginalization of underprivileged groups creates a situation analogous to that of New York City during its initial graffiti boom, and also provides the necessary catalyst for the kind of semiotic revolt described by Baudrillard. Secondly, as São Paulo becomes a "city of walls," the architects and civil engineers unwittingly also create a city of canvasses for graffiti artists, providing a seemingly limitless amount of monochrome vertical planes for grafiteiros to fill with paint. Thirdly, due to the proximity of the social classes, there is no district of São Paulo which is immune to the street artist's hand; grafite, pichação, and arte da rua are not only limited to the periphery – the favelas or ghettos – but instead permeate the entirety of sprawling São Paulo. Therefore, the wall itself has a unique combination of sociopolitical and cultural implications in Brazil, and particularly in the city of São Paulo. Depending on one's individual perspective, which in part is shaped by one's social status and upbringing, the wall could symbolize economic development, modernity, progress, and security, or on the other hand, segregation, inequality, limitations, and boundaries. Moreover, for the grafiteiro, it could represent an opportunity for intervention and expression. For the São Paulo grafiteiro, the physical barriers which are used for division simultaneously become the canvas for street art and an opportunity for the exposure of these barriers as such. In Parede Cinza, Os Gêmeos draw attention to the ambivalent attitude which Paulistas have towards the walls which separate them. The act of transgression appears in two distinct forms, legal and physical. The act of illegally writing graffiti on a wall and the mischievous use of a slingshot represent transgression in the sense of rebellion, whereas the figure literally transgresses in the sense of the word's Latin root, "to step across," by stepping across the boundary, the wall which separates the viewer from the unknown, the protected, and the forbidden. Yet these acts of transgression are not laden with the undertones of violent revolt which Baudrillard would prefer, but instead by a sense of playfulness and youthful innocence, as represented by the figure's childlike features and weapon of choice, the slingshot associated with a kind of troublemaking that is ultimately not as threatening as, for instance, a Molotov cocktail would be. These connotations are combined with a distinct tone of Brazilian saudade, or longing, for a city without boundaries. The Paulista's love, not hate, for their city is described, and the wall is shown to be an obstacle for the expression and perception of this love. Fittingly, the character is not shooting a rock from his slingshot, but rather a paint roller, he is not in the act of destroying, but creating.

The systems of identification and control referenced by Caldeira are dealt with in the previously mentioned work about the Brazilian "R.G." numbers, but also in the giant that Os Gêmeos painted on the façade of the Tate Modern as part of their exhibition titled "Street Art." The bundle of CCTV cameras dangling from the giant's right hand calls attention to the panopticism of the London streets. Yet this is a condition which is similarly pronounced in the artists' city of birth, as the obsession with security described by Caldeira leads middle-class residents to flock to high-rise apartment buildings with extensive surveillance systems. Furthermore, the figure's ironic combination of the exposed body and covered face can be seen as a critique of contradictory attitudes towards the desire for both security and privacy. The image of the face is traditionally used as a means of identification, thus by covering it the figure presents an act of defiance and an attempt to preserve anonymity. Yet due to his nudity, the figure is nonetheless fully exposed to the world. The blatant disconnect between these two aspects of the image visualizes the urbanite's conflicting feelings about issues of identification and anonymity, privacy and security: an ambivalence which has complex socio-political implications in the Brazilian megacity due to the factors outlined in Caldeira's City of Walls. Caldeira also specifically addresses the symbolic and even aesthetic role which the security camera plays in São Paulo. The object goes beyond its original functionality as a deterrent to crime and additionally serves to symbolize and hence reinforce social divisions. "All the elements associated with security become part of a new code for the expression of distinction, a code I call the 'aesthetics of security.'"[15] Through a detailed analysis of these aesthetics, Caldeira makes a strong case that the perception of security plays an essential role in forming identity and expressing one's social status as a middle or upper-class Paulista. Because the image is just as critical as the security itself, if not more so, the mechanisms thereof are accentuated and aestheticized in São Paulo culture. In this context, Os Gêmeos' depiction of a giant who has seized security cameras must be seen as an attempt to counteract the aesthetics of security and a criticism of the role surveillance plays in hindering social equity. Due to the omnipresence of the aesthetics of security in São Paulo, the artists' perception of this phenomenon is filtered through the lens of their experience with these issues and manifests itself even in their work produced abroad.

One might assume that the downfall of the military dictatorship in Brazil in 1985 and the ensuing democratization of the country would have alleviated some concerns about oppression, civil rights violations, and social inequity. However, Caldeira argues that this was not the case, as physical and political methods of separation and control were replaced by symbolic (although no less effective) methods. Furthermore, according to Caldeira, the potential for social equality through democracy posed a threat to the dominant culture, causing it to adapt and intensify new methods of exclusion in the form of the organization of the urban landscape. Thus, these systems of control are not in spite of democratization, but because of it:

> In fact, the segregation and the model of obvious separation put in place in recent decades may be seen as a reaction to the expansion of this very process of democratization, since it functions to stigmatize, control, and exclude those who had just forced their recognition as citizens[.][16]

Therefore, as the strategies and characteristics of hegemonic culture become more coded and symbolic – or semiotic – so too do the methods of critique, dissent, and revolt. Not coincidentally, that political process was concurrent with the initial rise of graffiti in São Paulo in the 1980s. So as the Baudrillardian semiocracy was emerging in the form of fortified enclaves and the aesthetics of security, methods of semiotic revolt –grafite and pichação – were being adopted by the working class residents of São Paulo such as the young Pandolfo twins. For the development of graffiti in São Paulo and the particular works at hand, what is perhaps even more significant than the social divisions and symbols of control is the changing role of public space, or more specifically, the decimation of public space as a location for interaction and social exchange. In Trespass: A History of Uncommissioned Urban Art, Marc and Sara Schiller, the two founders of the Wooster Collective, address this as a recurring theme in street art, stating: "Street artists bemoan the rapid disappearance of public space."[17] Furthermore, they not only see street art as a statement, but a direct action or intervention in the public realm to counteract this trend. "With each piece of public art, they reclaim a part of the city that has been sold off to advertisers."[18] In Trespass, the Wooster Collective notes that "it is vital to understand how the uncommissioned intervention is a reflex against the hegemony of public space by the interests of the few over the psychological well-being of the many."[19]

If graffiti is, in fact, a method of reclaiming public space for the people, then it is easy to see why the graffiti and street art scene in São Paulo flourished so extensively over the past three decades, and how it became the perfect setting for Os Gêmeos to repopulate the streets with their parallel society of yellow characters. As a result of the same socio-political forces cited from Caldeira's research, the area which had once been considered public has increasingly turned into a void. According to Caldeira: "As the elites retreat to their enclaves and abandon public spaces to the homeless and the poor, the number of spaces for public encounters between different social groups shrinks considerably."[20] Over the course of four decades, from 1950 to 1991, the population of São Paulo rapidly increased from 2.2 million to 9.6 million residents, with annual growth rates ranging between 3 and 6 % during this phase, before the growth began to taper off in the 1990s. The result was a sort of hyper-urbanization in which buildings and infrastructure were erected quickly and without careful consideration of the consequences for public life. The medium of choice was, of course, concrete. Therefore, the literal "concretization" of São Paulo distinctly changed the urban landscape and the modes of interaction which take place in public space. The primary result for the graffiti artist, as Manco et al. observe, is that "São Paulo and many other cities, expanding without urban planning, are a patchwork of decay and construction that is the undercoat for graffiti artists' interventions."[21] However, the implications for the São Paulo grafiteiro go beyond merely the creation of suitable surfaces for graffiti, since the formation of the urban space and the specific modes of interaction which take place in the streets have a critical influence on the Paulista's visual experience and thus also affect the grafiteiro's ability to dialogue with and within that space.

According to Caldeira, the modernist architecture in Brazil, which was based on egalitarian ideals, had unintended consequences on Brazilian metropolises such as Brasilia and São Paulo. As she describes it, "a solid mass of contiguous private buildings frames and contains the void of public streets."[22] The space in between becomes a void in that it is decreasingly a space for cultural exchange and social interaction. "In destroying the street as the space for public life, modernist city planning has also undermined urban diversity and the possibility of the coexistence of differences."[23] Thus, the disappearance of public space, which street artists attempt to counteract, is intensified in São Paulo by both social and infrastructural factors. The mere existence of cultural creation and exchange within the void of public space is in itself an act of defiance against the system which negates it. So when Os Gêmeos paint "Liberdade de Expressão" on a concrete wall in Brazil, accompanied by a figure of a grafiteiro, they are not referring to a government that directly stifles expression by imprisoning journalists or political opposition, but instead it can be read as a counter to a system that represses the individual's ability to express himself in a public, social, and cultural sphere. As Caldeira continues her critique of the unintended consequences of modernist architecture and urban planning in Brazil, the indictment becomes increasingly scathing:

> The surviving elements of modernist architecture and city planning in the new urban form are those that destroy modern public space and social life: dead streets transformed into highways, sculptural buildings separated by voids and disregarding street alignments, walls and technologies of security framing public space as residual, enclaves turned inward, separation of functions, and destruction of heterogeneous and diverse spaces. [...] Instead of creating a space in which the distinctions between public and private disappear—making all the space public, as the modernists intended—the enclaves use modernist conventions to create spaces in which the private quality is enhanced beyond any doubt and in which the public, a shapeless void treated as residual, is deemed irrelevant.[24]

Yet it is precisely this residual void of public space described by Caldeira that became the location of graffiti culture in São Paulo. The fenced off areas beneath bridges and overpasses, such as those seen in the works Liberdade and Corrupção, may in fact have been residual shapeless, cultureless voids until Os Gêmeos crossed the threshold and placed their characters and their statements on those walls. The concrete wall that serves as the support and subject for Parede Cinza is representative of the system which destroys "heterogeneous and diverse spaces," however, through the act of painting this wall and identifying it as such, the effects of that system are negated by de-homogenizing the space, reclaiming it for the public and restoring individuality to it, thus salvaging it from the void.

Countering the Proliferation of the Non-Place

Although Caldeira does not reference the work directly, her language is strongly connected to the spatial theories of Marc Augé presented in his book Non-Places: An Introduction to Supermodernity. The specific form of hyper-urbanization in São Paulo that renders public space a void, as described by Caldeira, is analogous to the proliferation of the non-place as theorized by Augé. The non-place lacks key characteristics that we as a human society ascribe to places to define their significance, such as history, culture, identity. In an anthropocentric view of space, a location is defined by the kind of human interaction which takes place within that location, and those spaces which do not house cultural or social exchange, nor are affected by them, can be described as non-places. More succinctly: "The non-place is the opposite of Utopia: it exists, and it does not contain any organic society."[25]

When one considers the location of street art in the modern urban environment, the main tendency is that it occurs in infrastructural elements such as railway systems, bridges, motorway barricades, underpasses, subway stations, and even on modes of transportation such as subways and trains, all of which fit Augé's description of the non-place. This is distinctly the case in the images Liberdade, Corrupção, and Parede Cinza, yet the Tate Giant represents a different scenario.

However, since the non-place is defined by a lack of concern with identity and cultural exchange, then these sites can no longer be regarded as non-places after they are approached by the grafiteiros as a location for street art, which in itself is not only a form of culture (be it subculture or counterculture), but moreover a method for individual expression that is intensely concerned with the construction of identity. According to Augé, "The space of non-place creates neither singular identity nor relations; only solitude and similitude."[26] The similitude of the non-place is eliminated by the presence of a unique work of art on that site. Its solitude is disrupted by the exchange which takes place at the site among the group of artists who claim it for their work. This is perfectly symbolized in Os Gêmeos' work Parede Cinza, in which the mischievous grafiteiro emerges, disrupting the gray homogeneity of the concrete and communicating with the viewer with the verbal statement referring to the site itself. Here, not only does the figure appear to break through the wall, but also break down the non-place. Augé acknowledges that the non-place is not an absolute, but instead part of a more fluid relation. Furthermore, he recognizes the opportunity to counter the effects of supermodernity through critical intervention on a cultural level.

> Since non-places are the space of supermodernity, supermodernity cannot aspire to the same ambitions as modernity. When individuals come together, they engender the social and organize places.[27]

The contrast between the ambitions of modernity and the actual effects of supermodernity corresponds to the indirect consequences of modernist architecture in São Paulo which were described by Caldeira. By creating a void out of what had previously been considered public space, the congregation of individuals is hindered, thus making it even more difficult to create anthropological places among the rapidly spreading non-places. This makes it all the more relevant that Os Gêmeos work in symbiotic cooperation, in that the action of creating a work such as Parede Cinza together is itself a social interaction that counteracts the solitude and isolation of the non-place. This is compounded when they collaborate with other grafiteiros in São Paulo on larger projects, as is the case with the Avenida 23 de Maio underpass (Fig. 5), where they worked together with Nina, Nunca, Ise, Finok, and Zefix on a massive mural in December 2008. Here, and in many other pieces of uncommissioned street art, the creation of a collaborative work engenders the social in a place where no other organic form of cultural interaction would otherwise take place, thus restoring culture to the non-place, turning it back into an anthropological place.

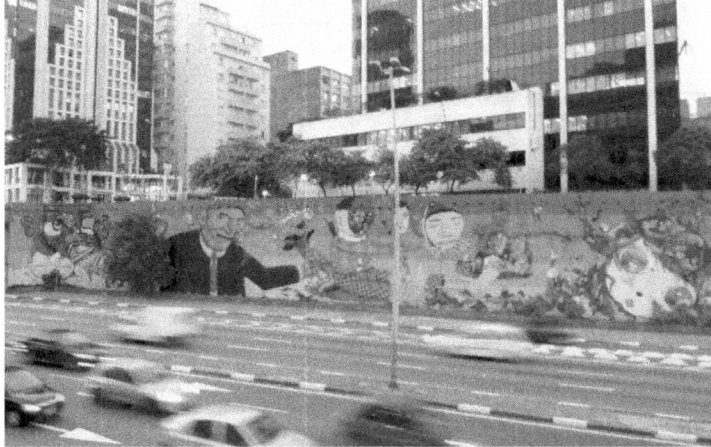

Fig. 5: Os Gêmeos, Nunca, Nina, Ise, Finok, and Zefix - Untitled collaborative work, Avenida 23 de Maio, São Paulo, 2008, Source: Theodore Kuttner, May 2012

The connection between Augé's theories and grafite in São Paulo, particular that of Os Gêmeos, was also made by Charbelly Estrella in her contribution to "O Graffiti na cidade de São Paulo e sua vertente no Brasil – estéticas e estilos"[28] edited by Ségio Poato. Estrella's chapter is titled "A visualidade de São Paulo e o vocabulário popular do graffiti - a poética dos Gêmeos"[29] and in it she describes the work of Os Gêmeos in the context of sociopolitical factors in São Paulo and touches upon aspects such as supermodernity and non-places:

> É uma contra-racionalidade que se inscreve em oposição ao tempo de produção mundializado, em oposição ao tempo das tecnologias, em oposição a esse hipermodernidade.[30]
> [It is a counter-rationality that locates itself in opposition to the era of globalized production, in opposition to the age of technology, in opposition to this supermodernity.]

Estrella describes Os Gêmeos' work as a form of visual poetry[31] (poética visual) based on the folkloric influence and fantastic or surrealistic flourishes in their compositions, and furthermore she posits that these are essential elements for an art form designed to counteract the effects of rapid post-industrial urban expansion, modernist architecture, and non-places. Yet ironically, the object of opposition is simultaneously the source of inspiration, according to Estrella "O ato de grafitar na cidade é uma estratégia poética para manter o diálogo constante com a origem. A cidade concreta é a essência da imaginação do grafiteiro."[32] [The act of writing graffiti in the city is a poetic strategy to maintain a constant dialogue with the origin. The concrete city is the essence of the grafiteiro's imagination.] Once again, these strongly conflicting feelings towards the physical concretization of São Paulo are summarized in Os Gêmeos' work Parede Cinza, where the gray wall is both an object of impediment and the source of creativity.

According to Estrella, the three essential elements in Os Gêmeos work are polyphony, abstraction, and imagination, mainly because these contrast directly with the homogeneity of the concrete landscape and the cold logic of modernist architecture. She uses the term polyphony to refers to the rainbow palette and psychedelic patterns that Os Gêmeos employ in their work, especially for textile elements and often applied using stencils.

> O colorido psicodélico menciona a humanização do cinza impessoal dos muros. Esta é a batalha cotidiana do graffiti - uma espécie de cruzada visual para lembrar à cidade a sua humanidade.[33]
> [The psychedelic palette indicates the humanization of the impersonal gray of the walls. This is graffiti's daily battle - a kind of visual crusade to remind the city of its humanity.]

The visual crusade is not only a reminder of humanity, but also an attempt to restore humanity and life to spaces which have been rendered void of social and cultural interaction, to create an anthropological place out of that which had been turned into a non-place through urban planning and socio-economic and political forces. By repopulating the streets of São Paulo or other urban centers with a society of fantastical people, Os Gêmeos not only counteract the depletion of human social interaction in that space, but also generate a sort of parallel society. The fact that this space had been rendered a void, using Caldeira's description, or a non-place in Augé's terms, gives Os Gêmeos a blank slate (figuratively and literally) to create a world with their own rules and by their own alternative logic. This is a world in which the only rule is to break the rules and express oneself, as embodied by the themes of rebellion previously mentioned in the context of their works Liberdade, Parede Cinza, Corrupção, as well as their Giants. Their logic is a poetic and fantastic anti-logic in contrast to the analytical rigidity of urban infrastructure and modernist architecture. Thus the surface, the gray concrete wall, is transformed from a limiting to a liminal structure, a threshold rather than a barrier, or, as Estrella describes it, a bridge to another world.

> [...] na produção do graffiti está enunciada a imaginação de uma outra cidade - uma ponte entre a cidade material e a visual. Essa conexão baseia-se na estrutura graffiti (imagem visual), no muro (a superfície de concreto) e na cidade (paisagem).[34]
>
> [in the production of graffiti, the imagination of another city is expressed – a bridge between the material city and the visual. This connection is based on the structure of graffiti (visual image), the wall (the concrete surface) and the city (landscape).]

However, this effect is not necessarily unique to Os Gêmeos' grafite in São Paulo. The sentiment is echoed in Marc and Sara Schiller's analysis of street art worldwide in the book Trespass:

> The first moment you notice a stencil on the pavement, a sticker on the back of a mailbox, or a metal sculpture attached to a street sign, you are suddenly transported into another world – to a vibrant subculture that infiltrates and eradicates the monotony of daily life.[35]

Yet there are several elements which particularly strengthen these effects in the case of Os Gêmeos' work in the streets. Firstly, there is the diversity of their characters, which when spread throughout a city with enough density, can give the impression of a living, breathing parallel society. Secondly, as Estrella notes, their bright palette contrasts strongly with the drab gray of the concrete city of walls. Thirdly, the influence of folklore and the fantastic or surrealistic elements make it clear that the artists' goal is not merely to hold a mirror to society, but to offer an alternative in which creativity, expression, cultural participation, and human interaction are not stifled, confined, or barricaded off by social, political, or economic forces. In the mind of Os Gêmeos, their street art represents scenes from an alternative world that they describe as "a magic and real place that lives inside us, a real dream, the scene of our own universe, a place called 'Tritrez.'"[36] Perhaps the irony of the situation is that for many street artists, graffiti culture is exactly that alternative world, this quasi-utopia for which Os Gêmeos' works represent a silent longing. Manco et al. write: "This alternative culture provides a voice for a systematically neglected section of society[.]"[37] This form of alternative culture not only exists, interacts, communicates, and expresses itself within public spaces where other modes of exchange have become obsolete or repressed, but in doing so it transforms the fundamental nature of those spaces.

Notes and References

1 Translation: "The imagery of São Paulo and the popular vocabulary of graffiti - the poetry of Os Gêmeos." 2 Translation: "Graffiti in the city of São Paulo and its development in Brasil - aesthetics and styles."
3 Tristan Manco, Lost Art, Caleb Neelson, Graffiti Brasil (London: Thames & Hudson, 2005) 63. (This work is described in Manco et al. but no image available.)
4 Manco et al. 10.
5 Jean Baudrillard, Symbolic Exchange and Death (London: Sage Publications Ltd, 1993), 77.
6 Ibid. 78.
7 Ibid. 78.
8 Pedro Alonzo, Catalogue: Os Gemeos, The Institute of Contemporary Art/Boston. (Berkeley: Gingko Press, 2012) 114.
9 Wivian Weller, "Hip Hop in São Paulo and Berlin" in: Elke Aus dem Moore, Giorgio Ronna (Ed.), Entre Pindorama (Nürnberg: Verlag für moderne Kunst Nürnberg, 2005) 158.
10 Alonzo, 114.
11 Teresa Caldeira, City of Walls: Crime, Segregation, and Citizenship in São Paulo (Berkeley and Los Angeles, California: University of California Press, 2000) 231.
12 Ibid. 232.
13 Ibid. 254.
14 Ibid. 254.
15 Ibid. 291.
16 Ibid. 255.
17 Marc & Sara Schiller, "City View" in: Ethel Seno (Ed.), Carlo McCormick, Marc Schiller, Sara Schiller, Wooster Collective, Trespass: A History of Uncommissioned Urban Art (Cologne: Taschen, 2010) 11.
18 Ibid.
19 Seno et al. 22.
20 Caldeira, 297.
21 Manco et al. 10.
22 Caldeira, 306.
23 Ibid.
24 Ibid. 308.
25 Marc Augé, Non-Places: An Introduction to Supermodernity (London, New York: Verso, 1995) 90.
26 Ibid. 83.
27 Ibid. 89.
28 Translation: "Graffiti in the city of São Paulo and its development in Brasil - aesthetics and styles."
29 Translation: "The imagery of São Paulo and the popular vocabulary of graffiti - the poetry of Os Gêmeos."
30 Charbelly Estrella "A visualidade de São Paulo e o vocabulário popular do graffiti - a poética dos Gêmeos" in: Sérgio Poato (Ed.), O Graffiti na Cidade de São Paulo e sua Vertente no Brasil – Estéticas e Estilos. Coleção Imaginário (São Paulo: Núcleo Interdisciplinar do Imaginário e Memória – NIME, Laboratório de Estudos do Imaginário – LABI, Instituto de Psicologia da Universidade de São Paulo, 2006) 13.
31 Ibid. 13.
32 Ibid. 14.
33 Ibid. 14.
34 Ibid. 17.
35 Marc & Sara Schiller, "City View" in: Seno et al. 10
36 Os Gêmeos, "Os Gemêos (The Twins)" Interview in: Art Crimes, 2000. URL: http://www.graffiti.org/osgemeos/index.html (Accessed May 7th, 2012) 3.
37 Tristan Manco et al. 10.

Graeme Evans, School of Art & Design, Middlesex University g.evans@mdx.ac.uk

Graffiti Art & the City: from Pariah to Place-Making

The reception and place of graffiti and street art in the city has become more nuanced since its modern origins in US black urban culture. No longer confined to particular ethnic or territorially-defined groups, street art has gained both an aesthetic and place-making dimension, whilst it's local and sub-cultural currency has continued its role and representation as an act of protest and opposition to the mainstream and a visual statement of the artist/tagger's identity. The paper explores this evolution and tension in the context of city place-making and branding through examples from several cities and neighbourhoods.

Graffiti Art, Place-Making, City Branding

Introduction

'Graffiti' and 'Street Art' have received varying research treatment from artist, sub-cultural and crimogenic perspectives which are reflected in the literature - predominantly from/on the USA - on individual graffiti artists, gangs and genres, commonly in art books and coffee table style pictorials. As Irvine observes: 'street art is…defined more by real-time practice than by any sense of unified theory, movement, or message'[1]The production's dialectic between graffiti as vandalism ("criminals") and as "art" (including in galleries, e.g.Basquiat, New York; Banksy, UK) has not considered the wider aspects of the role and place of graffiti art in the city; responses from city authorities, local communities, visitors and property owners; and how different places and city cultures receive and react in different ways, including graffiti now used in place-making, branding and destination strategies. This includes the growth of graffiti commissioning agencies and organisations, often established by former graffiti artists employed by clients (e.g. retail, advertising firms, and local authorities) and legitimatised spaces and walls for safe experimentation. The cultural content of graffiti also reflects local conditions and contexts, whether protest/political, territorial, vernacular (e.g. local events, history), or playful in nature.

The tour bus picked us up outside of the designer-hotel in Manhattan. Commuting office and shop workers, tourists, police and road diggers mingled in the chaos of downtown traffic. Across the Williamsburg Bridge we stopped to pick up our tour guide for the day, Angel Rodriguez, from an insalubrious building covered in layers of posters, graffiti and grit. He was a Latino musician, a salsa drummer from the Bronx who proceeded to give the tour group the background to the area – "Bronx is burning" (arson attacks on tenement blocks by landlords), old jazz and dance club haunts, Fort Apache - "the movie" - the now rebuilt district police station self-styled to defend itself against the "natives", (i.e. black/Hispanics), graffiti art of local rap stars (Fig. 1), the massive American Mint building covering 4 blocks, where two thirds of all US dollar notes were once printed and now housing 2 community schools, artist studios and employment schemes; the local penitentiary with 12 year olds kept in shackles - before arriving at our destination, The Point. Here the graffiti boys' operation base - once the crew that covered the New York subway trains and led to the mayor's zero tolerance regime - have now gone "legit", working for large advertising firms and department stores in Manhattan on large-scale shop displays and billboard art[2]

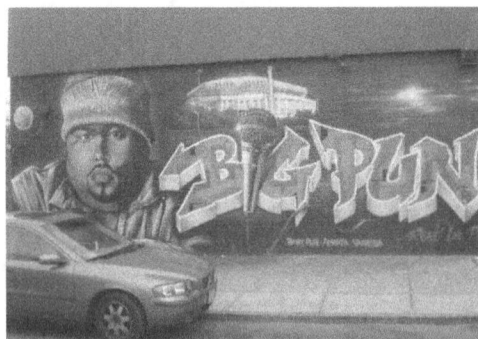

Fig.1: Big Pun memorial, The Bronx, New York

Graffiti has thus come a long way from its modern roots in the 1960s ethnic ghettoes of New York and Los Angeles, signalling perhaps a commodification of this activity, as well as a widening of graffiti into other cultural forms such as music (e.g. rap/hip hop), film (e.g. animation, pop videos) and architecture/urban design, which together have extended its shelf life. Early forays of artists who first worked 'on the street' and in 'street style' into art galleries such as the late Basquiat, has had less success, despite the rapid valorisation of particular artists work in recent years, notably Banksy, whose distinctive stencil murals have fetched over $500,000 (often to US buyers and celebrities). Here however, the work has been first validated in situ (a fundamental element in its value and authenticity), and then removed, much like a historic mural, into a (private) collection. Graffiti has therefore largely resisted (art) museum-ification and thrives primarily in a museum-without-walls - but very much on a city's walls.

Stowers[3] considers graffiti an art form, distinguishing between simple tags and more complex pieces that require planning and contain artistic elements (colour, composition) and calligraphic skills. Alonso[4] uses a taxonomy of graffiti in the case of Los Angeles, starting with the most historic, Political. Here the most open of forms communicable to a wide audience are placed in high profile viewpoints. They often coincide with critical social events and conflicts, including elections and legislative changes that negatively affect a host community. The most common form is Existential or Expressive graffiti, also open depicting racial, sexual, religious or personal commentaries (e.g. in public toilets) and can be prejudice-based or humorous (or both!).Tagging or signatures are also ubiquitous and cause the greatest cost to local authorities and property owners. Described as 'dirty, obscene, and disease-like'[5] and as an epidemic or plague, but as Alonso notes, tagging can be part of the elaborate subculture of Hip-Hop culture alongside its own fashion of dress, music and art. Gang graffiti also exhibits similar elements to tagging, as a territorial statement (and in some respects political graffiti). More elaborate graffiti art is seen in Piecing (or bombing) - larger scale expressions that demand higher levels of artistic skill and spray paint control. Closer to mural art and larger scale art works, Piece graffiti also finds its place in commissioned urban landscapes and art galleries (above), but as already noted: 'Dealers reduced the art to a more restricted and physically smaller space, the canvas, taking away for some writers the magnificence and grandeur of a piece done without restrictions'[6]. This ignores, however, the other restrictions that exist in executing street art in public spaces, not least surveillance and risk of prosecution, and the need to work very quickly as a result.

Whilst the New York subway was successfully cleaned-up, transport still remains a key site for graffiti - attractive form its wide availability and high audience potential. Despite the advent of CCTV and other surveillance, stations and bus stops receive both unwanted as well as commissioned artworks and tagging. For example Stockholm 'art on the underground' (Fig. 2)

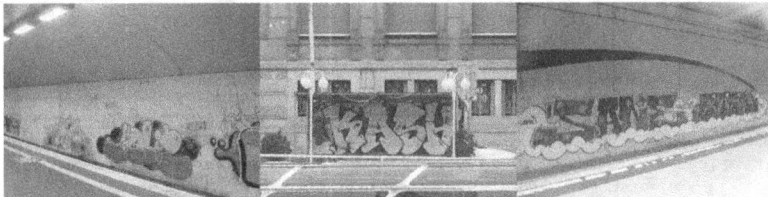

Fig. 2: Art on the Underground, Stockholm; Bus stop, Amsterdam; Underground, Madrid

Graffiti as Vandalism

Official responses to graffiti place it squarely in the criminal 'vandalism' sphere. Indeed commentators fuel this view: 'graffiti disrespects private property and official notions of order and aesthetics'[7] . Early responses to the graffiti 'epidemic' in New York and Los Angeles saw criminal sentences increase and special tasks forces established, claiming that the order of the landscape had been disrupted, and clean-up costs were rising: $50+m a year in both cities by the late-1980s. Today in the UK, clean-up of graffiti is estimated to cost £1 million per year and in Chicago alone $6m – see graffitihurts.org). English Heritage estimates that 70,000 heritage buildings and monuments are vandalised and defaced by graffiti. In 1960s/70s New York, gang graffiti-ists were also enabled by the subway system that took their tags across all of the city's boroughs and away from their local territories, with large 'pieces' covering whole carriages. Graffiti and Street 'art' have therefore been faced with a dual onslaught from different dominant cultures (police/city politicians and art curators/galleries) to remove or restrict its practice and impact. However, despite this, or perhaps fuelled by this marginalisation, counter-hegemonic discourses have emerged which in some senses have kept graffiti alive as a both a cultural concept and a practice that is now evident in many forms internationally –that is, graffiti is now global cultural force. Lachman's observation in 1988 is therefore still valid today: 'Graffiti in some forms can challenge hegemony by drawing on particular experiences and customs of their communities, ethnic groups and age cohorts, thereby demonstrating that social life can be constructed in ways different from the dominant conceptions of reality'[8]. This challenge is evident in artists response to the art market itself, in the case of Banksy's 'mockumentary' film Exit Through the Gift Shop (2010). Here a fictional film-maker pursues the underground art scene in Los Angeles, New York, London and Paris, assuming the role of self-styled street artist hyping his avant-garde 'show' in LA and creating an art world/underground 'buzz' for the lucky few who could take part. Banksy thus 'pokes fun at the contemporary art world and its hunt to unearth and exploit underground art scenes. The willingness to validate recycled art and popular cultural symbols, which are rendered empty if not meaningless, is revealed as undiscerning and opportunistic. Whereby social critique is downplayed in the pursuit of print, poster, and postcard sales'[9]. The mobile value of his own street art has however fuelled a destructive market which sees 'public' works cut from walls to disappear then reappear via auction. These sites continue to attract viewers, and place branding can therefore persist (including in memory) despite the 'absence' of the artwork itself (Fig.3).

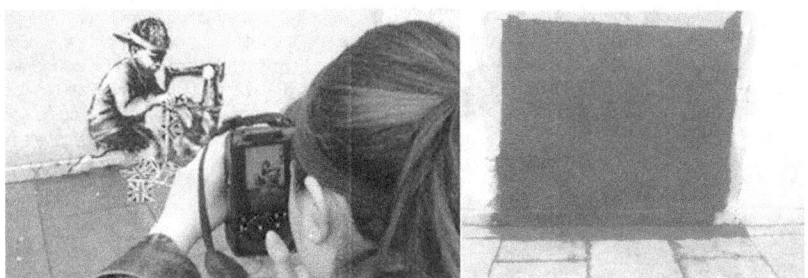

Fig.3: Bansky 'before and after', Wood Green, north London

Mixed messages

Today, this duality (vandalism or art) continues, reflected in prohibitory sentences – in the UK up to 10 years imprisonment where criminal damage by an adult (18+) exceeds £5,000, and detention/training order of up to 2 years for 12-17 year olds. For 'minor offences', sentences are much lower and fixed penalty charges can also be issued (£80) without court proceedings, so there is some discretion over the response if found guilty/'caught in the act'. At the same time, art museums and galleries engage with graffiti as an international art form, for example Tate Modern's 2008 Street Art commission and exhibition which brought together six 'internationally-acclaimed' artists whose work is linked to the urban environment. Sponsored by the Japanese car firm Nissan, this was the first major public display of Street Art in London. In order to give it artistic validation, 'good' street art in this case was distinguished from the more 'low-brow' text-based graffiti and tagging, thus seeking to 'insert graffiti into its proper place and rob it of its denaturalizing power'[10].The link with sponsor Nissan was also significant since the Qashqai car it launched the year before utilised striking street art in its adverts. This also provides a clue to the current ambiguous place and relationship between graffiti/art and the city. In one sense this reflects the consumption and visual culture prevalent in the contemporary city environment - the merger of commerce and culture in highly visualised form. As Chang maintains: 'saturated by images, the contemporary city has been theorized as a site legislated by the eyes'[11].Street art today in Irvine's view 'is a paradigm of hybridity in global visual culture'[12]. Lombard goes further in response to the question, has the governance of graffiti changed since it's more reactive origins? She uses the concept of governmentality[13] ('conduct of conduct'[14]) to analyse how graffiti is currently controlled, arguing that whilst there appears to be a softening of policy and responses towards graffiti, this does not mean that there is less governance, but that this signals a greater acceptance of graffiti due to the effects of a neo-liberal form of governance[15]. Chang also notes the emergence of the countervailing terms: post-graffiti and neo-graffiti, 'signalling some kind of qualitative and stylistic shift in modes of inscribing the city. Encompassing multiple forms or urban inscription like murals, postering and sculpture that move beyond written text..(which) mark the spectacular nature of urban space'[16]. Here she critiques the work of artist Blu, who painstakingly paints and photographs over existing graffiti (representing a single film frame) then turns these into remarkable street life animations (see blublu.org). This is one example of graffiti being transformed into moving image whist drawing and building on its everyday street art nature. This also represents an important cultural practice of capturing as well as creating graffiti art in a different non-ephemeral form - important with so much street art being time-limited and subject to clean-up, defacing, and deterioration due to the weather etc. Archives of graffiti art also seek to document this work alongside publications and films, for example see DeNotto[17] and street art is 'intentionally ephemeral...documented almost obsessively with digital photography for the Web'[18].

A governmental response to the 'demand' for graffiti by young people is also seen in various schemes which seek to offer a safe (from prosecution) opportunity for budding Banksy's to 'practice their art' with impunity. For example in Wales The Heritage Graffiti Project helps young offenders 'learn valuable lessons from their heritage'[19] by introducing them to archaeological artefacts and explaining what they mean to the people who used them (e.g. Roman soldiers, miners, canal boaters). A mural was created: 'Our Wales', by the young people depicting their interpretation and experience which was documented and opened to the public. In the DPM Park in Dundee, Scotland, the longest legal graffiti wall in the UK (110 metres) is open for all to use, at any time and the council-run project runs workshops for local kids.

City attitudes towards graffiti and street art are also changing and variable. These not surprisingly also vary within cities, with some neighbourhoods, sites and buildings treated differently in terms of surveillance, prosecution, protection - and celebration. For example in the Colombian capital, Bogota, following the death of a young street artist shot by police in 2011, a new tolerance of street art has emerged. The city took an 'if you can't beat them, join them' approach. The mayor issued a decree to promote the practice of graffiti as a form of artistic and cultural expression while at the same time defining surfaces that are off limits, including monuments and public buildings. City grants are available for selected artists with 2,3 and 7-storey walls provided along the main thoroughfares as their canvases. The result is colourful displays with political and social messages. Everyday graffiti has also spread under this liberal regime including on buildings prohibited from writing. This indicates the difficulty of controlling graffiti in this way without rules being observed, and the appeal to marking untouched surfaces and public spaces.

Elsewhere, commissioning of young artists to adorn corporate buildings presents an alternative to the usual 'public art' installation. In Frankfurt, the European Central Bank HQ 45-storey building under construction is surrounded by a high protective fence. A local social worker approached the bank who agreed to allow him and the'troubled' young children he works with, to spray paint a wooden fence which they erected around the site (costing €10,000). The graffiti depicts caricatures of ECB President and Chancellor Merkel (60% of the works reflect the Eurozone crisis), to fighting cocks which will be displayed within the building when it opens this year. Several of the graffiti artworks have been purchased (via the 'Under Art Construction' programme), ironically by bankers, although remaining works are not, apparently, for sale. The city mayor has called on other construction sites to emulate this project. Other 'meanwhile' sites are also the subject of sanctioned graffiti since these can on the one hand animate otherwise ugly hoardings and also prevent/dissuade opportunistic graffiti, as well as divert attention from permanent structures. For example in Madrid and in Amsterdam (Fig. 4below) where the former Royal Dutch Shell European HQ building awaits redevelopment and temporary occupation by dance and event's organisers. This area of Amsterdam Noordalso represents a new creative quarter, served by frequent free ferries from behind the main station, where a cluster of digital media workshops and arts and entertainment venues has replaced this industrial complex and working class district. In this case graffiti art signifies transition, fun, creativity – rather than degradation and social unrest, as it would have done in the past.

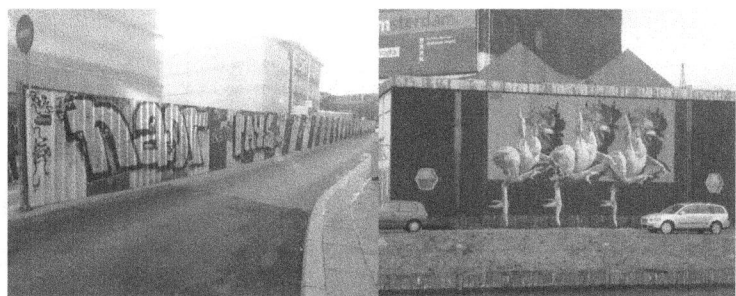

Fig.4: Construction hoarding, Madrid; Graffiti art on the base of former Shell HQ, AmsterdamNoord

The dichotomies between, crime-art, control-tolerate in practice are therefore played out in a continuum along which city authorities, the public and graffiti artists move, as taste (Bourdieu), opinion (including local and national media), city branding and development shift over time. This can represent a hardening as well as a softening and instrumental use of street art, as we have seen, increasingly used in city branding and place-making efforts and strategies. The public is of course no longer homogenous as major cosmopolitan cities and historic towns mix tourists and a range of business, education and leisure visitors with residents and commuting workers from many countries with differing aesthetic and moral positions. The perspective of a say, an overseas tourist to street art/graffiti may be one of attraction, branded image, signifier of a cool place - or one of unsafety ('broken windows syndrome'), decline and poor aesthetic value/appeal. To a resident, the same images may form part of their everyday experience, represent local identity (theirs or others - good, bad or indifferent) or even align with the visitors view. It is more likely however that the local will engage in a deeper, knowing way, depending on the length of time the graffiti has been there, where it is placed (i.e. on what type of building/structure) and its meaning to them (if any). Graffiti art is certainly increasingly identified with a 'sense of place' than was the case before - aside from the previous tags and territorial/gang variety which are more likely to be cleaned up by city authorities. The attraction of place to graffiti artists is reciprocal. Cities in flux such as post-reunification Berlin are perceived as a 'graffiti Mecca of the urban art world… the most "bombed" city on Europe[20]. Here it's acceptance/condonement is associated with Berlin's designation as UNESCO City of Design and as a growing cultural tourist destination, which is in part fuelled by this urban image of street creativity. This includes international artists, including graffiti artists whose work moves from street to gallery to street.

From product to place-branding

Models of city and place branding generally draw their references from product and corporate branding as an extension of marketing strategies that address the product life cycle decline-renewal challenge[21]. In this sense, towns and cities, and specific areas in need of 'regeneration and renewal' that face post-industrial or other structural socio-economic change, have been presented with the branding option as a response to the competitive-authentic city dialectic. How this is achieved and sustained is the stuff of city branding literature with results reflected in proprietorial branding and related indices, league tables and measurement formula. Here the various models attempt to disaggregate or 'reverse engineer' the key factors and variables that provide the brand (marketing) mix – the elements that together present the brand value and power of a place. These combine hard and soft infrastructure with historical and cultural amenities and qualities – which themselves are hard to quantify and ascribe values to – values that also vary according to the viewpoint of resident, visitor, investor, media and politician. As Zenker maintains[22], place identity (a wider concept than the "brand") influences the perception of the target audience, however prior perceptions (and their historic and contemporary sources) also influence the identity of a place as seen both internally and externally, and these are often reinforced through marketing images of cityscapes, including graffiti. In urban space, and therefore in place-making efforts, the 'social production' that Lefebvre observed[23] also stresses the essential experiential nature of the relationship with our everyday environment, and our identification with discrete places and spaces. In this sense we do not "use" space or our urban environment as "consumers" (e.g. of branded products), but we experience it individually, productively (i.e. work) and collectively, albeit with diminishing influence over the (re) construction of the public spaces we inhabit - including the presence of graffiti.

In city branding models, the cityscape (or 'urban landscape') is characterised in several ways: as 'place physics'[24]; and 'spatial picture', as distinct from specific amenities and historical and cultural facilities such as theatres, museums and parks[25]. Kotler et al.[26] prioritise design ('place as character') as distinct from 'infrastructure' and 'attractions' in their place marketing approach, whilst Ashworth and Voogd[27] first proposed a 'geographical marketing mix' to capture the 'whole entity of the place-products'[28] with 'spatial-functional' measures one of four instruments in this mix. However, despite the physical imagery and changing cityscapes strongly associated with city and place branding and destination marketing[29], it is interesting to note that in Zenker's analysis of 18 place branding studies between 2005-10, architecture, buildings and city spaces were largely absent in the brand elements cited. The surveys on which these studies were based tended to focus on generalised or intangible associations (culture, historical, 'buzz' etc.) rather than specific physical or spatial attributes. This is in part self-fulfilling however, since the survey methods used were all text-based questionnaires with no use of visual aids or images as prompts or references, or any ranking of specific buildings and images, e.g. graffiti art[30]. An example of a newly-branded creative quarter is described here, as a case of street art which both defines this district and reveals its importance in playing host to a range of street artists.

Digital Shoreditch, London

The pattern of technology districts adopting the prefix 'Silicon' has accelerated over the last decade. On the one hand this is a case of place and 'hard branding'[31] through the hope value associated with emulating Silicon Valley or 'Silicon Somewhere'[32], on the other, a shorthand for what is primarily a 'soft-hardware' version of information and technology production originally represented by hi-tech manufacturing and related R&D. Clusters that have evolved more organically, to those envisioned through government investment and development areas can be seen at various scales, both regional and highly concentrated spatial geographies. Examples include Digital Corridors (Malaysia, S.Korea), Silicon 'triangles' (Alpine), the sub-regional Silicon Fen (Cambridge, UK) and Silicon Glen (Scotland), to local hubs where ICT and digital firms often co-locate with creative and other advanced producer and financial services. Examples of the latter include Silicon Sentier, Paris; Silicon Allee, Berlin; Silicon Alley, New York - and Silicon Roundabout or Digital Shoreditch, in East London. This latter creative-digital district[33] presents an interesting city branding case, located in a city fringe area historically non-descript, with a low income/deprived resident community, essentially a working area of the city untouched by the visitor economy or more conspicuous cultural consumption. Its cultural workspace tradition dates back several centuries to crafts (jewellery, metalwork), fashion and textile sweatshops, printing and publishing, with an established artist community occupying cheaper studio spaces. This low cost cultural economy provided crucial elements in the area's transformation to one of the most vibrant creative and 'tech city' quarters in the world. This now contains a high concentration of new media and digital firms, alternative clubs and venues for music, art and independent retail outlets and a high concentration of "black collar" workers – an update of the black collar mine/oil worker, now representing the digital/designers and the fashion of wearing black. This profile and reputation has created a demand for hosting key design and digital events and festivals from the London Design Festival to the week-long Digital Shoreditch Festival whichwasfirstheldin2011attracting2,000 participants/visitors rising to 15,000in2013. What is of particular significance is that this network of over 1,000 creative-digital firms and growing annual festival is self-organised, with no public subsidy. In this sense, the quarter 'brand' is owned and has been created 'bottom-up', leaving local and city authorities in an enabling role and ensuring through planning and zoning that the character and socio-economic mix of uses is retained. The image of this neighbourhood combines post-industrial use of industrial workshops and factories, small crafts and retail outlets, social and warehouse 'loft' apartments, and extensive graffiti art on this mix of buildings and walls. This has offered an effective graffiti street laboratory within which aspiring artists such as Banksy and Stik have first experimented (Fig. 5).

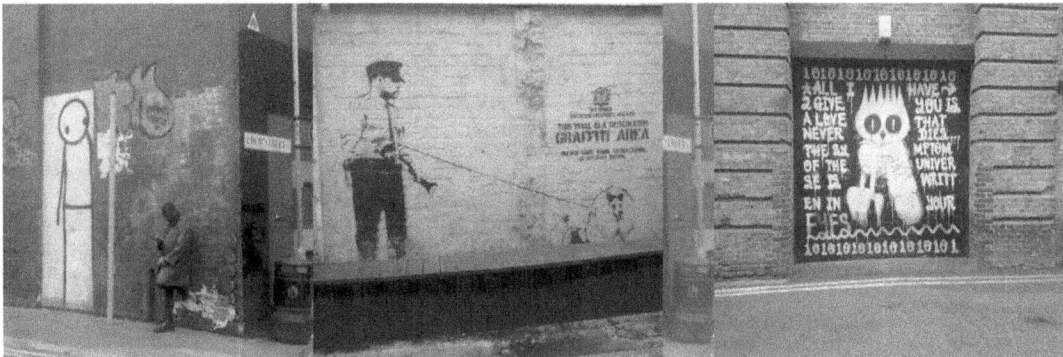

Fig.5: 'Digital Shoreditch' – Stik, Banksy and anonymous street art

A new "destination" has thus been created - several boutique hotels have opened in recent years including the ACE hotel, the first outside of the USA, designed with materials produced locally from specialist bricks, tiles to lighting, and with photographic references in bedrooms to the building's music hall past. As an indication of the importance of street art, several companies provide guided Shoreditch Street Art tours, with online galleries and listing of artist/artwork profiles. Specialist galleries and agencies also provide commissioning services for clients wishing to hire graffiti artists for temporary or permanent work – such as Graffiti Life and Graffiti Kings. The emergence of the professional graffiti artist has therefore arrived. The strategic importance attached to this sub-regional cluster and its role in the new digital industries was also recognised in 2010 when the UK government designated the wider area anchored in the city fringe by this creative industries quarter, as 'Tech City' - a swathe connecting this quarter further east to the Olympic Park, representing the physical the legacy from the London2012 Summer Games. However, this top-down intervention in city branding through high tech economic development, runs counter to the organic and cultural evolution that has created the Shoreditch distinctive quarter of the city - primarily a small firm, creative entrepreneur and informal network phenomenon. The same risks and fears that undermine established cultural and heritage quarters are present here - gentrification effects though rapid rent and property valuation; the import of large firm and institutional organisations and venues; and a decline in the mixed use and diversity of the area, including embracing street art/artists. These are, of course, the key elements that created the attraction of these creative production quarters and that have contributed to their distinctive brand.

Conclusion

Street art and variants of graffiti have a complex and ambiguous place in the city. Cleary a duality now exists between 'high street art' and '(un)popular' graffiti. Technically an illegal activity unless fully commissioned and authorised by property owners and other stakeholders (e.g. transport and local authorities), condonement of street art is evident in cities and areas of a city where either control has diminished or a general laissez faire situation exists. This is evident currently in cities where economic decline and socio-political fragmentation has reduced the power and resources for clean-up or enforcement, for example in cities such as Athens and Madrid. Here the vacuum this has created is also fuelled by political response/resistance to the governance deficit and economic impacts, e.g. unemployment, debt, cuts in services. In other cities, areas such as Amsterdam's university district is subject to extensive graffiti, indicating a combination of tolerance, complacency and 'place-making' by its student residents. Elsewhere, street art is seen in commercially-driven commissioning, installations and 'interventions' (a contemporary art concept) in downtown, retail and in other sites undergoing regeneration (e.g. Dumbo, Brooklyn, New York), particularly in temporary, 'meanwhile' sites. Graffiti still emerges as a dominant image in derelict sites and in accessible transport facilities, and is still associated in this case with decline and redundancy. In other areas, street art reflects a creative 'quarterisation' of a neighbourhood and effectively helps to add value to its image and distinctive brand. In this sense graffiti and street art is 'socially produced', as Lefebvre observed, we do not "use" a sculpture or work of art (or piece of graffiti art), we live and experience it. Street art has thus on the one hand joined the canon of contemporary art and the art market and been appropriated in commercial advertising and media, and on the other hand graffiti in its basic form, continues to inhabit the everyday city environment as a low level 'noise' and nuisance for many, as well as an endless canvas for its producers.

Notes and References

1 Irvine, M. (2012) 'The Work on the Street, Street Art and Visual Culture'. In: B.Sandywell and M.Heywood, The Handbook of Visual Culture. New York: Berg, 235-278.
2 Evans, G.L. (2007) 'Tourism, Creativity and the City'. In: Richards, G. and Wilson, J. (eds) Tourism Creativity & Development. London: Routledge, 35-48.
3 http://www.graffiti.org/faq/stowers.html
4 Alonso, A. (1998) Urban Graffiti on the City Landscape, Western Geography Gradate Conference, San Diego State University, 14 February: 5
5 Creswell, T. (1992) 'The Crucial 'Where' of Graffiti: A Geographical Analysis of Reactions to Graffiti in New York'. Environment & Planning D: Society and Space, 10: 329-344
6 Alonso, A. (1998) Urban Graffiti on the City Landscape, Western Geography Gradate Conference, San Diego State University, 14 February: 11.
7 Ferrell, J. (1993) Crimes of style: Urban graffiti and the politics of criminality. New York: Garland.
8 Lachmann, R. (1988) 'Graffiti as career and ideology'.American Journal of Sociology, 94(2): 231-2.
9 Birdsall, C. (2013) '(In)audible Frequencies: Sounding out the Contemporary Branded City'. In: C.Lindner, C. and H.Hussey (eds) Paris-Amsterdam Underground. Amsterdam: Amsterdam University Press: 116
10 Creswell, T. (1996) In Place/Out of Place: Geography, Ideology and Transgression. Minneapolis: University of Minnesota Press: 55.
11 Chang , V. (2013) 'Animating the City: Street Art, Blu and the Poetics of Visual Encounter'.Animation,8: 216
12 Irvine, M. (2012) 'The Work on the Street, Street Art and Visual Culture'. In: B.Sandywell and M.Heywood, The Handbook of Visual Culture. New York: Berg: 235-278.
13 Foucault, M. (1991) 'Governmentality', in Burchell, G., Gordon, C., and Miller, P. (eds) The Foucault effect: Studies in Governmentality(pp. 87-104). London: Harvester Wheatsheaf.
14 Gordon, C. (1991) 'Governmental Rationality: An Introduction'. In: G.Burchill, C.Gordon, and P.Miller (eds) The Foucault Effect: Studies in Governmentality. London: Harvester Wheatsheaf.
15 Lombard, K-J. (2013) 'Art Crimes: The Governance of Hip Hop Graffiti'.Journal of Cultural Research, 17(3): 255-278
16 Chang , V. (2013) 'Animating the City: Street Art, Blu and the Poetics of Visual Encounter'.Animation,8: 217
17 DeNotto, M. (2014) Street art and graffiti.Resources for online study. C&RL News, April: 208-211.
18 Irvine, M. (2012) 'The Work on the Street, Street Art and Visual Culture'. In: B.Sandywell and M.Heywood, The Handbook of Visual Culture. New York: Berg: 235-278.
19 Heritage Graffiti Project http://cadw.wales.gov.uk accessed 18 May 2014 http://cadw.wales.gov.uk/learning/communityarchaeology/heritage-graffiti-project/?lang=en
20 Arms, S. (2011) The Heritage of Berlin Street Art and Graffiti Scene. Art, Inspiration, Legacy, Smashing Magazine
21 Butler, R.W. (1980) 'The Concept of the tourism area life cycle of evolution: implications for management of resources'.Canadian Geographer, 24(1): 5-12.
22 Zenker, S. (2011) 'How to catch a city? The concept and measurement of place brands 'Journal of Place Management and Development, 4(1): 40-52.
23 Lefebvre,H. (1974) TheProductionofSpace(trans.Nicholson-Smith,D.). Oxford: Blackwell.
24 Anholt, S. (2006) Anholt City Brand Index: "How the World Views Its Cities", Global Market Insight.Bellvue, WA.
25 Grabow, B.(1998)'Stadtmarketing: EineKritischeZwischenbilanz'.DifuBerichte,98(1): 2-5.
26 Kotler, P., et al.(1999)MarketingPlacesEurope: Attracting Investments, Industries,ResidentsandVisitorsto European Cities,Communities,Regionsand Nations. London: Pearson Education.
27 Ashworth, G.J.andVoogd, H. (1990)'Sellingthe City: Marketing ApproachesinPublicSector Urban Planning'. London: BelhavenPress.
28 Kavaratzis, M. (2005) 'Place Branding: A Review of Trends and Conceptual Models', Marketing Review, 5:329-42.
29 Vermuelen M. et al. (2002) City Branding. Image Building & Building Images. Rotterdam: NAI.
30 Evans, G.L. (2014) 'Place branding and Place making through Creative and Cultural Quarters. In: M.Kavaratzis, G.Warnaby and G.J. Ashworth (eds) Rethinking place branding - Critical accounts. Vienna: Springer (forthcoming).
31 Evans, G.L. (2003) 'Hard Branding the Culture City - From Prado to Prada', International Journal of Urban and Regional Research 27(2): 417-440.
32 Florida, R. (2005) Cities and the Creative Class. New York: Routledge.
33 Foord, J. (2013) 'The New Boomtown? Creative CitytoTech CityinEast London', Cities, 33: 51-60.

Heike Derwanz, Metropolitan Culture / HafenCity University Hamburg (HCU)
heike.derwanz@hcu-hamburg.de

Street Artists and Their Careers in Art and Design Markets

A great number of young street artists would love to live off their art. But few of them succeed in making a name for themselves and earning money. How did the careers of these street artists emerge? How did they become producers in the international art and design market? The concept of career helps to systematize different social rules and valuation systems applicable in the street, in the media, and in the art and design market. In every one of those instances new actors come into play who help the artists distribute and promote their work. But especially the art and design market and the system of art history, valorizing art in the longer term, are subject to rules that seem to be opposed to street art as an ephemeral, free and open form of art.

Street Art, Art Market, Career

Introduction

> *"I was an art school punk [...]. To me, the word 'career', next to the word 'artist', automatically meant compromising - selling out. To be fair, even if I wanted to sell out back then, nobody was buying. You had to be in your forties and preferably white and know the right people to get a show in most galleries."* (Dan Witz 2009[1])

The terms artist and career usually conjure up two extremes: the celebrity of world-famous stars such as Pablo Picasso or Salvador Dalí, and the image of the impoverished and misunderstood artist who passionately continues to beaver away without achieving any recognition or earning any money in his or her lifetime, also known as the Van Gogh syndrome. Street artists and their careers in the art and design market expand this collision by another idealizing dimension: they are anonymous, bring their art to the street for free, and customize these works to the specific situation there. The contradiction between their artistic freedom and a career in the arts where it is exactly this remoteness from the market that constitutes art historical significance is highlighted by above quote of street artist Dan Witz, who has been working in New York since 1978. Every career and every network of street artists is unique; there is no training for them and no tenure track. Some of these artists come from graffiti and others from the art world, while still others discovered street art as their art form right from the start. Some street artists started before all the media attention, while others jumped on the bandwagon. Dan Witz debunks the myth of the artist as a genius. Neither his work nor his talent would have enabled his breakthrough, he says, while success can only be reached by social integration. This assessment not only corresponds with a model of the art world developed by Howard S. Becker, but also with his model of a professional career: "The successful career may be viewed as a series of such steps, each one a sequence of sponsorship, successful performance, and the building up of relationships at each new level." (Becker 1997:23). Picking up on his definition of a professional career as various successive steps of production and recognition, I will elaborate it for four social spaces networked by street artists: the street, the media, the design market and the art market.

The careers of street artists are not a new phenomenon and the associated problems were also already present 30 years ago. The New York of the 1980s already featured many ingredients of today's developments: run-down inner city districts, young artists, activist art, the art market with its galleries, buyers and money, and the public space as a favoured area of communication. But the "street art phenomenon" as such has only come about in the 2000s[2]: the development of a worldwide movement where, besides the actual pictures, all manner of dialogues and cultural products are globally circulated in a network comprising hundreds of people. As implied by the name street art, the images are regarded as art and the movement becomes a street art-related art world that is more or less part and parcel of the art world in general. Local authorities, the arts and science, sensitized by the spatial and iconic turn, are increasingly showing an interest in the subject. This attention is not characterized by a concept of powerful players such as a lobby for contemporary art in some ministry or academy, but rather by bottom-up processes in the artistic and publishing practices of hundreds of individual actors in towns and cities around the world. Based on a common interest in the illegal practice in a public space, these actors form the very networks in which the careers of artists (and also the other players) emerge by way of their individual activities - such as creating art, taking photographs of it, exhibiting it, blogging/writing about it, or selling it. These networks and development processes have been traced with the help of ethnographic research methods that, over and above the artists, gallerists and collectors, i.e. the traditional personnel of the Fine Arts and sociology of art, show the actors at work on their careers. This ethnographic approach to street art is most of all methodically based on data gathered during several stays in the field from 2006 to 2010 in London, Stockholm, New York, Barcelona and Leipzig, and on the empirical material generated from them, which was then triangulated with historic theoretical literature. Taking an ethnographic perspective on art means that one has to leave existing and rehearsed ways of thinking behind, turning the dominant scientific approach to art history itself into a field of research with its own field logic. This is because ethnography, with its actor- and activity-centred approach, is predestined to trace the cultural embedding of art forms. Researching visual culture by means of qualitative interviews and participant observation can for example show that field logics and protagonists do not simply constitute an art movement, but only evolve it by the interplay of the actors. The focus on the career of street artists in this essay is meanwhile only one possible actor-centred perspective able to provide decisive insights into the development of specific art phenomena. One of the characteristic categories for street art careers is success in the art market, for example, which in turn has a lot to say about the social and historical significance of street art. This is also discussed by the actors themselves, such as Shepard Fairey in Banksy's film Exit Through the Gift Shop (2010), here summarizing the career of street artist Thierry Guetta:

> *"I do think that the whole phenomenon of Thierry's obsession with street art, becoming a street artist, a lot of suckers buying into his show and him selling a lot of art very quickly - it's an anthropologically, sociologically - it's a fascinating thing to observe and maybe there is some things to be learned from it."* (Fairey 2010)

Street Art or merely Art in the Streets?

Especially urban districts such as East London, Raval in Barcelona, Södermalm in Stockholm, or Williamsburg and SoHo in New York are distinguished by a great visual diversity of street artworks. The result for the viewer are huge spontaneous collages, created on a few square meters from advertising images and building surfaces, street art and graffiti in a host of colours, techniques, styles and motifs, not unlike zapping around on TV. It depends on the legal situation in the country and the atmosphere of the urban district in question whether the places where street artworks join the city's other pictures are freely accessible or hidden away. In the latter case the viewer may be more likely to discover them online, by way of insider information, or on rambles with protagonists of the public space. The legislation in many countries often necessitates that artists quickly leave the place where they put up their work. The street art phenomenon lives off the fact that art is perceived as something special in the public space of the street:

> *"Street art consists of stencils, wheat-pasted paper, stickers, or sculpture installations illegally placed in public places that make one question the urban environment. Street art is ephemeral and disappears over time. It can catch people by surprise, it can make people think differently, and it can bring a smile to your face."* (Wooster Collective, quoted from Blackshaw 2008:169)

Any enquiry into street art will hence have to start in the public space as the first essential point of reference, and also the primary reference for street artists. This is where they install their works in an atmosphere of secrecy and illegality, and this is where their works can then be seen. Describing street art as a location- and situation-related aesthetic practice in the public space is of the essence.

Despite the close dovetailing of street artworks and urban streets, not every artwork has been developed for a specific location. Other ways of appropriating space, such as Shepard Farey's sticker campaign Obey, open up as much geographical space as possible with one (or a few) designs. The impages are developed as posters or stickers for mass production and partly sent out for installation by others. From the perspective of contemporary art and art criticism, artistic concepts of this breed do not permit street art to be generally described as site-specific or on-site. They instead rather resemble "plop sculptures", i.e. examples of art in the public space that have not been specifically tailored to the location by the artist (Büttner 1997:177). One compromise in this regard would be to talk of site-relatedness instead of site-specificity. But these terms have become so dilated and overused in the literature that it appears meaningful to reconcile their application with the characteristics of street art once again.

The English term site-specific first became established in connection with American land art (Krystof 2002:232) and, after Miwon Kwon and Nick Kaye, by way of site-specific art in the minimalist sculpture of the 1960s. Kwon marks it as an anti-idealist and anti-commercial counter-movement that nonetheless ended up being "domesticated by their assimilation into the dominant culture" (Kwon 2004:1). The concept of site-specificity is closely linked with the development of modern sculpture because it was only the mobility and "placelessness" (Butin 2002:149) of the latter in the 1970s that gave rise to the placement of works in spaces outside of art institutions. From the mid-1990s, projects involving community-oriented art in the public sphere that discussed activist and political issues within their surroundings were also created under the umbrella term of New Public Art. Definitions of "site-specific" correspondingly stress the interconnection between the piece and the space in terms of form and content (Krystof 2002:231) as an essential characteristic, which is also highlighted in the following comment by Nick Kaye on Richard Serra's statement that "To move the work is to destroy the work." [(Serra 1994:194)]: "To move the site-specific work is to re-place it to make it something else." (Kaye 2000:2).

There is a whole range of similarities and overlaps with contemporary art forms in public spaces, then. But from the reception perspective of state authorities or members of the art operating system, street art is an anonymous, uncontrolled, unauthorized and unmanageable practice in the public sphere that is not predicated on any kind of political or artistic concept.

Where notions of art are concerned, the street meanwhile points to another contradiction entirely: street art means not showing in a gallery or museum, even. "Street" can be read as an alternative to the art operating system, namely that of working outside the white cube (the prevalent manner of presenting art in the field's spaces), the art market (supply and demand of artworks), the system of public or private assistance, and the rules of the field of art. Amalgamating these connotations, many street artists hence regard the street as the "largest gallery in the world", devoid of elitist entrance requirements. This interpretation most of all reflects the perspective of street art protagonists who wish to draw attention to themselves while simultaneously referring to their works in other art spaces. This marketing-oriented reading is opposed by another that uses the categories of illegality and participation to foreground political motivations, and therefore the street as a place of protest. Two conflicting tropes can be identified here: on the one hand street protest as an element of the appropriated history of the street as a place of public discourse, participation and democracy, and on the other the control and privatization of public urban spaces in recent decades. The latter has led to diverse forms of re-appropriation practices and thereby to various art forms that have been documented for the public and science in a flood of publications (see Lewitzky 2005, Raunig 2005, amongst others).

The authenticity of the actors as derived from their site-specific ties to the street is often referred to as street credibility in the field of popular culture where music, art or fashion are concerned. Klein and Friedrich define street credibility as a form of respect that draws on experiences and activities in the street (2003:42f). Heike Lüken anchors the principle of authenticity that is so central to the street art scene in the legacy of graffiti writing (Lüken 2009:63), Pedro Alonzo in a work ethic:

"In order to succeed, the expression must be authentic. A great part of this authenticity is built as much through hard work in the studio as on the street developing reputation. The commitment of an artist to his or her work is key and most evident in the campaigns these artists have launched around the world through their urban interventions." (Alonzo 2006:8)

Street Artists earn their 'street cred' by keeping up their practice for many years and by their contacts with scene players, passers-by or authorities in the street. As a sub-cultural capital, street credibility can also be forfeited through excessive public dissemination and commercialization, or also withdrawn by important gatekeepers (Currid 2007:145). It unfolds its potency as a currency for the artists by circulation in other social contexts, most of all the art market: "Authenticity is hence no longer only an important principle in the internal perception of the street art scene, but also regarded as a demand-stoking quality criterion for prospective buyers by the established art market." (Lüken 2009:63) For Lüken, successfully authentic career development is here based on a further evolution of artistic contents that addresses the changed spatial and social frame of reference: "What is in a gallery and no longer in the street cannot be street art, but can still successfully refer to it and the public space, thematizing the latter." (Lüken 2009:65). The street meanwhile serves as a dramatic stage and exotic attention-grabber for a certain period of time. But street artists are by no means the first in the field of art whose artistic concepts are defined by their location outside the institutions.

From Books and Magazines to New Media

The myth of the street can only put to good use in the careers of street artists if they can avail themselves of media for initiating the social interaction revolving around them and their artworks, and for establishing a discourse. A pivotal role for the media success of street artists is in this respect played by weblogs. With little in the way of access requirements, street art blogs can promptly describe locally created works for an international readership while simultaneously serving as mediators, transcending geographical, social and cultural spaces by way of the internet. But traditional media such as magazines, books and films also have their part to play in the joint success story of street art protagonists. The operators of the websites depend on the photographs they are being sent, this being the only way how street art from Bucharest, Sao Paulo, Johannesburg and Tokyo can be shown. Countless portals have sprung up that specialize in a particular street art technique, such as Stencil Revolution, Stencilboard and World of Stencils, for example. But besides their print editions, magazines predominantly dedicated to street art or related disciplines such as Modart, Juxtapoz and Overspray naturally also rely on more promptly updatable blogs for presenting interviews with the artists, new exhibitions, editions and the like.

In the terminology of social network analysis, some blogs such as Woostercollective, Ekosystem or Vandalog could be described as super hubs (Barabási 2003:85, 103). This appraisal is based on the view that nodes with many connections are "more powerful" than nodes with only a few (Barabási 2003:221). Super-hubs imply that hierarchies within a network and the world of street art can be deduced from the number of connections (Derwanz 2010b). Connections to other players are hence of key importance for the careers of artists and the existence of galleries and magazines because identical production and commercialization practices will achieve different effects, depending on their interconnectedness.

On the face of it, the mere existence of connections says little about their nature, however. This can be defined by way of their intensity, as Mark Granovetter 1973 has shown with respect to the importance of mostly weak ties for job seekers (Granovetter 1995). But on the other hand they are also being relativized by the lifetimes of networks and steadfastness of their protagonists. While many street art activists specifically try out their artistic work and media success in the street, they will often no longer be seen there once they've become successful. Galleries only exist for one to two years, websites are created and interlinked and given up after a few months. Works of street art and exhibition projects are usually only destined for a lifetime of a few weeks or months.

The artistic practice of the younger generations of street artists includes blogging as much as taking photographs of their works installed in public spaces. This permits them to document the originals that are left in the street, and hence to evanescence. Whether the bloggers most of all present their own work, the street art in their town or a specific selection of global provenience depends on their personal intentions and thematic purview. Exchange and feedback are important data sources and motivators that determine the further development of the blog.

A historic comparison with 1980s New York street art shows that the second generation has successfully managed to enlarge the sphere of influence of their artworks, to be present, in demand, to become relevant, and finally valuable. The Wooster Collective explain this with the development of the internet as a documentation and distribution tool, besides the latter-day provision of cheaper flights, enabling artists to spread their originals all over Europe. It has been a typical feature of subcultures for decades that their magazines start off from a DIY practice, i.e. not from mass culture or a cultural elite. This do-it-yourself principle can on one side be understood as a participation of non-professional players, an appropriation of publicity. But on the other it also engenders professionalization and compliance with the neoliberal maxim of starting your own business (Schwanhäusser 2010). Personal information is foregrounded here, as opposed to the blogs, which often only show and rate photographs. The interview format is one of the most popular ways of demonstrating closeness to the anonymous (underground) artists. The journalists or magazine publishers are important contact persons and act as network nodes between the anonymous artists and anonymous audience. As in the blogs, the anonymity of the street is lifted here by photographs of the artists and background information for the magazine's readership. In the first half of the decade, a variety of different groups have shown an interest in street art images and integrated them in their aesthetics or visual canon. This perspective turns street artists into passive subjects whose images are used by outsiders. But the opposite approach is just as important. Street artists work in advertising, the graphic arts or animation, and in turn rely on the aesthetics of these disciplines in their pictures on the street. Books, as opposed to blogs or magazines, call for longer production periods. This means that months or years can pass between the publication date of a book and its photographs of works in the street, by which time the original may have been destroyed, or the artist ceased to be active. Owing to the short lifespan of street art, books are not nearly as helpful in making street art accessible to passers-by as blogs are, for example. But their strength resides in the fact that they are very long-lived media which will be included in large cultural archives, such as national or university libraries. Having first of all revealed that street art can be found on virtually every continent, it was the books that also identified the cities where it excelled in qualitative and quantitative terms. That their authors were merely mapping their own travel routes and networks is meanwhile not that evident to their viewers/readers. They created a map of the world's centres of street art. This first series of overview books was in 2005 followed by books on street art in individual cities. Like a self-reinforcing cycle, this involved revisiting cities whose street art had already been documented before. Artists travelled there to look at the originals, meet other artists and create new works, which were in turn distributed as photographs, illustrating how much street art there is in the city.

The analysis of geographic accumulations in books such as The Art of Rebellion suggests that the selection cannot be based on quality alone, but rather on the contacts of the authors. Their home towns, travels, favourite magazines and personal interests all shape their decisions about who will be presented in the book. But given the transience of street art, this record nonetheless presents one of the few opportunities for the artists' works and careers to survive. It is not all that surprising that there are no street artists from Stockholm in Beyond the Street. The 100 Leading Figures in Urban Art. They are represented in local blogs, and there are also Swedish books, but artists from New York, London, Los Angeles, Paris, Barcelona and Sao Paolo are still much more likely to make it into an international selection.

Amongst other aspects, the importance of being represented in books such as Beyond the Street is also underlined by the fact that many of the artists shown in it cite it as a reference on their websites. It is certain to be included in art libraries as a standard work, thanks to its size and visual quality, and already serves customers as a reference in galleries and at art fairs such as the 2010 Moniker Art Fair in London. This is highlighted for the generation preceding the street artists of the new millennium by the following quote from a graffiti writer explaining how a small group of New York graffiti artists became successful with the help of the most important books of the 1980s:

> "There are some people in books, magazines and articles that haven't done as much as those who are virtually unknown. And this is fraudulent in the graffiti world: People who get access to the media without paying dues. Subway and Spray Can Art – if you were in those books you were considered well-known, but if you weren't, you weren't considered. Mackie wasn't in it, Futura was." (Currid 2007:136)

Book authors are gatekeepers, then, just like the bloggers. Elizabeth Currid underlines the extent in which ratings by the gatekeepers depend on the social networks of the actors: "Gatekeepers, after all, are human beings, and the very fact that creative goods are subjective makes the relationship between the critic and the cultural producer particularly important to the success of a good [...]." (Currid 2007:137). The relationships established by the authors with the artists while working on their first books therefore serve to strengthen precisely these connections by starting a new book. The first joint venture hence supports the production of further books, providing the artists with space for presenting even more works. The by-products of these exchange transactions are trust and credibility.

Art and Design Market Rules Barring Street Art?

That street art is a well-known discipline today is most of all owed to exhibitions and auction records that have ensured corresponding media reports (Derwanz 2013, 153f). The value of street art in public spaces has been expressly affected by the value of its works in the art market. This market, defined by the reciprocal relationship of supply and demand, has in most cases paid to the anonymity of the artists for their audience, partly because an exchange or transaction has taken place that unmasked them, occasionally also revealing their actual everyday identity, and partly also because the biographical data of an artist have an impact on the value of his or her works within it. First of all, however, the aesthetics of street art were picked out as a trend by the advertising industry, and extensively marketed: "The value lies in establishing a brand. Once there is recognition the advertising agencies start calling." (Alonzo 2006:8). This mass-compatible street art trend had thereby already provided the artists with their first earnings long before their success in the art market. While street art has been thematized as art up to this point, the term design stands for a different concept characterized by adaptation and distribution. The term design, in the sense of drafting an appearance, look or plan, is meanwhile initially only intended to serve as a working concept for summarizing various products with street art motifs or aesthetics. The design jobs could be described as a step on the career ladder of the street art world, providing the artists with valuable experience where their craft, self-management and not least of all their finances are concerned:

> "In many cases, before galleries become part of the equation, the artists here were involved in marketing campaigns for companies that cater to the youth culture lifestyle. Nike, Asics, DC Shoe, skateboard and snowboard manufacturers as well as clothing labels incorporate the art and design of the artists into their product and advertising." (Alonzo 2006:8)

"Flipping the Tortilla. The Aesthetics of Cool and Guerilla Marketing", an introduction by curator Pedro Alonzo to the exhibition Spank the monkey at the Baltic Centre for Contemporary Art in Gateshead in 2006 highlights the rules of the design market, which is unable to bestow the advantages associated with being represented in a gallery that would ideally support an artist's career in the longer term: "The ad agencies and shoe companies don't [fight for the attention of curators and critics] which accounts for a certain lack of knowledge in the art world about this group of artists." (Alonzo 2006:8). As soon as this becomes possible, alas, these careers will be jettisoned in favour of art for art's sake.

If the established research into the history and sociology of art is distinguished by attaching decisive importance to the relationships between artists and gallerists, gallerists and collectors, and possibly also gallerists and critics (Moulin 1987, White 1993), an ethnographic approach will expand these findings by fieldwork data. The rules of this field of street art has meant that artists could only be interviewed about their careers once other actors from their networks had been interposed to get in touch with them. The network I got to know in London most of all included distributors and sellers of street art, many of whom were also street artists themselves. The connections within this local network had initially started out as longstanding friendships, expanded by people one had worked with. Organization in networks is typical for creative project work in the sense of "flexible and contact-based employment relationships" (Loacker 2010:35, 57). While all the people I interviewed within this network professed to knowing Banksy personally, it was understood that I would make no attempt to enquire any further. Besides this I also established contacts to other street art players who formed networks in London by way of other galleries and artists.

Local street art worlds comprise various social networks that either grow closer or further apart over a longer stretch of time, or will never actually meet. The most important actors of local street art worlds besides the known collectors, gallerists and critics have most of all turned out to include bloggers, magazine publishers, festival initiators and printers (works are sold as prints for the art market). While gallerists are generally regarded as gatekeepers in the art operating system (Alemann 1997), and hence represent nodes in these networks, the art world revolving around street art additionally features bloggers who can draw attention to an artist, or pave his or her way to them. The work on projects not only depends on these networks, but also keeps them alive (Schwanhäusser 2010:59). If its artworks are to be sold in galleries, studios, online shops or art fairs such as Moniker or Stroke, 'street art' will first of all need to be turned into an exchangeable and marketable product. The logics of product design and strategies of advertising therefore also need to be applied in quite another way than in the street. The need to turn street art into a different product in purely physical terms becomes especially clear if one considers the following classic description of art in the streets: "There is no commodity involved that can be easily bought or sold. The impermanence and scale of the work discourage the collecting mania." (Sommer 1975:61). Not so today, when works of street art are taken down by restorers, or whole walls cut out.[3] The gap between these two poles, the unmarketable work in the street and the effort of selling a wall bearing a stencil in the international art market, is bridged by incremental stages of feeding street art into a sales mechanism.

Banksy and his gallerist Steve Lazarides hit upon the idea of simply converting stencils into inexpensive prints in the mid-1990s. An employee remembers: "We started selling them [the prints] for 10 pounds. The quality of the prints got better, the paper got better." (Int. HD, London 6:2007). But street artists have also found own ways of reproducing the materiality of their actual works and of their wall designs in indoor spaces. Looking at installations by Jean Michel Basquiat or graffiti artists, one is bound to notice that they worked on picture carriers that were also hung on white walls. Basquiat or John Fekner not only used white canvas, however, but also carriers they had found in the street, as was the case with Swoon or the Finders Keepers Crew 2003 (Dickens 2008:13f). Keith Haring is meanwhile famous for having drawn on anything he could find. Success in the art market already meant that artists would swap their previous glued paper or wooden boards for canvas in the 1980s (Schwartzman 1985: 98-105, Stahl 2009:61, 154-161). Transferring the paintings from trains or walls to mobile picture carriers is one of the key requirements for selling street art or graffiti, just as the mobile panel paintings of the Early Modern period and their detachment from frescoes are a historical precondition for the development of the modern art trade. Street artists nonetheless still often rely on a gallery's walls for painting on directly. This is one of the strategies for referring to the street indoors, and also for breaking with viewing traditions in spaces that are dedicated to art. Another visual reference is the way the pictures are hung. It is reminiscent of the unplanned and associative 'hanging' outdoors, characterized as "open curation" by Luke Dickens (Dickens 2008:19). Street artists use these references to the street in an attempt to distinguish their works from other indoor art forms, to keep the appeal of the unusual alive.

Works of street art have thus been converted from unaccredited artworks in the public sphere into saleable products for the art and design market, as described above. This is where they will be valuated by a group with socially negotiated aesthetic rules, which Howard Becker regards as "characteristic phenomena of collective activity" (Becker 1982:39). Isabelle Graw puts this notion more precisely when she refers to art as a value concept "that consequently harbours an evaluating dimension" (Graw 2010:74). This process always needs to be contextualized historically, as the art ethnologist Maruska Svasek writes:

> "[...] artefacts do not move through local, national and global networks because of inherent aesthetic qualities or innate enchanting powers. These qualities and powers are created in social settings of production, marketing and consumption, and are therefore context-specific and subject to change" (Svasek 2007:121).

All artists are hence torn between satisfying the norms and their freedom, which can end in success or neglect (Becker 1982:34f). Novelty is ensured by challenging and shifting a number of conventions dear to the educated public. Street artists thus play with the rules of the art and design market about what can be sold, and need to maintain their unique selling points as a new trend. One should therefore draw a distinction between two givens at this juncture: a) the players in the street art world recognize the works as art, and b) the protagonists of established art worlds approve of the works. In her study of African art, Maruska Svasek has the following critical comment to make about this:

> "[...] being incorporated in dynamic market settings certain artefacts may gain the power to attract potential customers, but often lose the symbolic meanings and impact they had in the societies in which they were produced. The buyers and owners of such artefacts will mostly use and perceive their new possessions in novel ways." (Svasek 2007:88)

The Schirn Kunsthalle in Frankfurt am Main consequently preferred to opt for the outdoors instead of its gallery space in its Street Art Brazil exhibition in 2013, as the Tate Modern in London had already done in 2008. An editor of the Frankfurter Allgemeine Zeitung commented: "The idea makes immediate sense. No admission fees, no coat check, no waiting at the ticket office, no opening times." (Voss 2013:41) The political context of the Brazilian art was no longer apparent, however. Street artworks from Brazil become tame murals in Germany. And this is actually where a bone of contention is buried in the world of street art itself, but also with the audience and the arts scene.

Career as a Collective Effort

The term career helps me distinguish my deliberations from artists' biographies by placing an explicit focus on their professional development and success in the art operating system. Following Howard Becker, career is here understood as a succession of stations and specific tasks that allows the lives of artists to be looked at without entering into a content-related discussion of their works (Becker 1997:24). Some of these stations for street artists have already been addressed in the previous sections: presence in the street, media distribution, and commissions or the creation of product designs. Career success in the art world, meaning that one is able to earn a living from the proceeds of one's art alone, is meanwhile subject to conventions that shall be addressed below. The initial introduction of street artists to street art is framed in a narration that considers juvenile rebellious tagging as an early phase and then disembogues into an enthusiasm for street art at the beginning of the millennium. This is the standard narrative as legitimized with authenticity by the street art world. That someone was a 'graphic designer before' meanwhile rather serves as a pejorative description of others. Only very few artists I interviewed told me about their entry from other areas or motivations that fail to conform with the 'authentic' standard narrative. Previous training or employment in art and design are two such motivations running counter to this narrative that I would like to briefly introduce here by way of example.

Artist 1 (Int. H.D. New York 9, 2007) applied for a master degree course in the visual arts at a university[4]: "Everyone who goes there comes out with a gallery contract and a show. That's what I wanted. I had really good people around me but I did not get in." Already a visual artist, he had been unable to generate the sales and gallery contacts required to find recognition and financial success. This is the situation in which a colleague introduced him to street art by way of a book: "And I saw the book and I saw what's going on. I was like: Wait. He can get a book and I am struggling as hard as I can to put my foot in any door. And I can do this. We were all talking about this." The new strategy of producing works for the street as a basis for garnering the attention of the media and gaining access to gallerists and exhibitions paid off in the space of a few months already. Artist 2 (Int. H.D. London 1, 2007), in contrast, had trained as a designer and initially worked in this profession:

> *"When you finished college you couldn't just go: Hey, I'm an artist! They were supporting people who could do industrial kinds of jobs. So having trained as a fashion designer, I had a craft I could always fall back on. But about three years ago, when I was really heavily doing street art, a friend of mine, Blek Le Rat said to me: in three years' time you'll be able to make a living just from doing, you know street art, and doing your art."* (Int. HD, London 1, 2007)

The career advice given by the older artist Blek le Rat (born 1951) provided the motivation for expanding artist 2's existing efforts in street art. The idea was to professionalize oneself by way of this art form and see it as a career springboard. Street artist 2 has likewise gained fame in the street art world by means of various activities. His works can be found in important exhibitions and a number of collections. He also stands for a specific style, works under a pseudonym, and has built up a network in Europe and North America that is particularly extensive. My thesis is that the careers of street artists are assembled from two elements: success in the street art world, fame and initial success through street art networks and, after more or less delay, a career in the contemporary art market. In the process, street artists carry with them a specific factor of attention and success that adds a new set of rules and a different (subcultural) capital to the laws governing the art operating system (Reinecke 2007).

Vera L. Zolberg (1990), and later Dagmar Danko (2012), have both introduced art worlds as an essential concept for the sociology of art. In contrast to Sara Thornton's Seven Days in the Art World (2009), where the term 'art world' is applied to all the parties involved in global contemporary art, Zolberg emphasizes that Becker subdivides this into various smaller art worlds: "[...] Becker posits the coexistence of a number of different art worlds, whose actors engage in the process of creating art de novo, by including and excluding works from the category as they define it." (Zolberg 1990:80). It is exactly this aspect that lends street art its identity: a group of actors defines street art, i.e. a particular form of cultural product, as art for itself, and initially against social rules. Becker furthermore introduces a typology featuring four positions for artists: integrated professionals, mavericks, folk artists and naïve artists (Becker 1982). The special status of street artists, or rather the efforts to integrate them in the art operating system, become apparent if one traces the route from one of the first categories through to an integrated professional level. The designation as integrated also highlights the importance of connections to the other actors making up an art world besides the artists: dealers, curators, critics, collectors, or experts in an auction house (Thornton 2009:12) plus engravers and lithographers, publishers or government authorities (Zolberg 1990:132). Although the artists are at the centre of the network, the analysis concerns various people and their tasks (Becker 1982:9, 25).[5] Zolberg and Becker refer to these players as support personnel.

It is this support personnel who create careers in the art worlds by the circulation of artworks, by reproductions, critiques and estimations. Even where street artists maintain their own websites, organize exhibitions, run galleries and write their own texts, their reception, garnering of attention and attribution of value will still ensue in the art worlds. And this is where an entrance problem arises, as Becker points out: "The process is circular: what does not have a good reputation will not be distributed." (Becker

1982:95). Becker understands art careers as processes where artists are called upon to mesh successful production with successful relationship-building (Becker 1997:108). Vera Zolberg lists further requirements for a career to emerge, this time from a sociological perspective:

> "This would show the awareness by sociologists of the fact that artists emerge from the interaction of initial propensities for talent and personality characteristics within the constraints of historically grounded opportunity structures, through changing processes and mechanisms of discovery, recruitment, and socialization." (Zolberg 1990:196)

What is striking here are the categories of talent and personality characteristics, on which the special role of the artist as genius is based in western societies. Looking at general definitions of a professional career such as the one from Oxford Dictionary of Sociology below, however, one becomes aware of the peculiarities that are accentuated by the art world: "A patterned sequence of occupational roles through which individuals move over the course of a working life, implying increased prestige and other rewards, although not excluding downward occupational and social mobility." (Scott 2006). What this implies is a differentiation between a successful career with increasing prestige and rewards and an unsuccessful one, "in whatever terms success is defined within the occupation." (Becker 1997:24). According to Raymonde Moulin, success in the art operating system can be objectively defined by way of the "[...] number of shows, number of works owned by museums and collectors, awards received, prices paid for works." (Moulin 1987:109). But then she introduces two contrary orientations aimed at artistic recognition within established artistic values on the one hand and the preservation of freedom and authenticity on the other (Moulin 1987:109).

Actors, Rules, Careers
Street art or urban art has managed to establish itself as an art movement and label in public discourse, and is slowly gaining recognition in the art operating system as a contemporary art form, thanks to exhibitions in galleries and museums. What appears important in this process now is to nurture what is "different" and "new" in this art form (see Derwanz 2010a:3), in order to introduce it as a novel value in art history. The Association of German Art Historians recognizes the influence of subcultures and, at the 2009 congress of German Art Historians, has shown an interest in how "own art forms and lifestyles [seek to] establish themselves vis-à-vis the respective normative public" (Association of German Art Historians 2009:120). It is not traditionally up to the artists to "inscribe" themselves in art history. This would need to be ensured by the other players now. Jeffrey Deitch has taken a first step in this direction with the historicizing and internationally acclaimed exhibition Art in the Streets at the Museum of Contemporary Art in Los Angeles. But this financial success and recognition in the art market has also served to change the public image of street art: from vandalism to art that is worthy of protection, or to commissioned art in the public sphere. What seems to be important for sustainable careers are three breaks:

First: The careers of street artists are situated in a field of tension that is also characteristic for other artists and designers. They need to weigh their creative and personal freedom against financial gains, the demands of the gatekeepers, and those of the public. The art world of street art meanwhile decides about which forms of work and which forms of distributing them within that group will be accepted as authentic. The topics most frequently discussed by street art protagonists include attention, the city, and social issues, all of which carry political connotations. But it has also emerged that the street artists themselves become part of gentrification processes in the course of all this, or entangled in conflicting relations with the field of advertising. I have shown that the concepts of authenticity or sell-out relied upon by street art's own art world trace demarcations and identity debates within it. These subtle boundaries will no longer be visible in the art market later on, however.

Second: The careers of the artists take place in a field that is incongruent with the art operating system for this very reason. Their careers take off and proceed in a heterogeneous manner and are not based on the teacher-pupil model of art or graffiti writing, for example. Established differentiations dictated by the art education system such as graphic design, product design and fine art become blurred. Although even the named reference examples Andy Warhol or Takashi Murakami successfully merge the spheres of art and business art — from A to B and back again — this classification continues to present problems for street artists. They may be quite naturally inhabiting the multiple roles of entrepreneur, curator and self-marketer, but are still engaged in selling a highly traditional product in the art market. This is rooted in their role as authentic outsiders who, coming from the street, tend to cater to artistic pursuits such as print and painting, and only rarely to concept or media art.

Third: Their roots in street art entail challenges all street artists must face:
a) The greatest challenge is the transition from the street to the galleries. No full-time career will be forthcoming without sacrificing some characteristics of the work in the street.
b) The very term street art becomes brittle as a result, raising questions about its standing in art history, and about the classification of its artists.
c) The character of street art as just one of many movements and fashions in the art market also raises ancillary questions concerning the sustainability of careers. How long can the other, can the outsiders as which they market themselves, remain in fashion? A historical comparison with the artists of the 1980s indicates very short time spans for market success and museum acquisitions. It would therefore appear to be a decisive requirement to expand the presence in the art market into the institutions, and to ensure continued artistic production by means of established recognition mechanisms such as prizes, grants or teaching jobs at the academies. Yet on the other hand art careers call for such an intensive effort in terms of money and time that only few dare embark on them (Plattner 1996:113). Many artists fall by the wayside because they are unable to develop their work any further once it has found recognition, or because a new development in it is not accepted (Röbke 2000:115), for: *"Artists' career trajectories are neither linear nor predictable."* (Jeffri 2005:132).

Notes and References

1 Interview with Ali Gitlow (2009) for Overspray: http://www.danwitz.com/index.php?article_id=5, accessed 10/10/2011.
2 Many books on street art also explore this issue: "[O]ur aim was to try to understand how street art has grown from being an underground, D.I.Y. image-making strategy (at the end of the last century) to become the art world's next big thing, in less than a decade." Blackshaw 2008: 8, Reinecke 2007, Lewisohn 2008 etc.
3 See most recently: Stealing Banksy, April 2014: http://stealingbanksy.com/, accessed 8/5/2014.
4 Especially younger street artists have trained at university or are starting to in parallel to their street art. In keeping with economic studies of other artists (Alpers/Wassall 2006, Towse 1996), I have also been unable to substantiate any direct correlation between a university degree and greater success in the art market here.
5 Becker lists the following players for painting: "Painters thus depend on manufacturers for canvas, stretchers, paint, and brushes; on dealers, collectors, and museum curators for exhibition space and financial support; on critics and aestheticians for the rationale for what they do; on the state for the patronage or even the advantageous tax laws which persuade collectors to buy work and donate them to the public; on members of the public to respond to the work emotionally; and on the other painters, contemporary and past, who created the tradition which makes the backdrop against which their work makes sense." Becker 1982:13.
Alemann, Heine von, 'Galerien als Gatekeeper des Kunstmarktes. Institutionelle Aspekte der Kunstvermittlung', in Jürgen Gerhards (ed.), Soziologie der Kunst. Produzenten, Vermittler und Rezipienten (Opladen: Westdeutscher Verlag, 1997), 211-40.
Alonzo, Pedro, et al., Spank the monkey. On the occasion of the Exhibition Spank the Monkey at Baltic, Centre for Contemporary Art Gateshead, from 27 September, 2006 to 7 January, 2007 (Berlin: Die-Gestalten-Verl., 2006).
Alper, Neil O. und Wassall, Gregory H., 'Artists' careers and their labor markets', in Victor Ginsburgh und David Throsby (eds.), Handbook of the economics of art and culture (Amsterdam: Elsevier, 2006), 813-57.
Banksy, Banksy. Exit through the gift shop (2010).
Barabasi, Albert-Laslo, Linked. How everything is connected to everything else and what it means for business, science, and everyday life (New York: Plume, 2003).
Becker, Howard, Art Worlds (Berkeley, Los Angeles, London: University of California Press, 1982).
Blackshaw, Ric und Farrelly, Liz, The Street Art Book. 60 artists in their own words (New York: Collins, 2008).
Butin Hubertus, 'Kunst im öffentlichen Raum', in Hubertus Butin (eds.), DuMonts Begriffslexikon zur zeitgenössischen Kunst (Köln: DuMont-Literatur-und-Kunst-Verl., 2002) 149-54.
Büttner, Claudia, Art goes public. Von der Gruppenausstellung im Freien zum Projekt im nicht-institutionellen Raum (München: Schreiber, 1997).
Currid, Elizabeth, The Warhol economy. How fashion, art, and music drive New York City (Princeton, Oxford: Princeton University Press, 2007).
Danko, Dagmar, Kunstsoziologie (Bielefeld: Transcript, 2012).
Derwanz, Heike, „Selling work is one thing..." Street Art an der Innenseite der Außenseite der Kunst.', Kunsttexte.de, März 2010a. <http://www.kunsttexte.de/index.php?id=591&idartikel=30735&artaus=3&ausgabe=29377&zu=621.>, Zugriff 8.11.2011.
Derwanz, Heike, „Was es nicht online gibt, gibt es nicht." Tausch und Selektion in Street Art Blogs, in Maik Bierwirth, Oliver Leistert und Renate Wieser (eds.), Ungeplante Strukturen. Tausch und Zirkulation. (Paderborn: Fink, 2010b), 203-220.
Derwanz, Heike, Street Art-Karrieren. Neue Wege in den Kunst- und Designmarkt (Bielefeld: Transcript, 2013).
Dickens-, Luke, „Finders Keepers". Performing the Street, the Gallery and the Spaces In-between', Illuminalities. A Journal of Performance Studies, volume 4 (issue 1, 2008).
Granovetter, Mark, Getting a job. A study of contacts and careers (Chicago u.a.: Univ. of Chicago Press, 1995).
Graw, Isabelle, 'Im Griff des Marktes? Über die relative Heteronomie von Kunst, Kunstwelt und Kunstkritik', in Sighard Neckel (ed.), Kapitalistischer Realismus. Von der Kunstaktion zur Gesellschaftskritik (Frankfurt/Main, u.a.: Campus, 2010), 73-89.
Jeffri, Joan, 'Managing Uncertainties', in Iain Robertson (ed.), Understanding international art markets and management (London u.a. Routledge, 2005).
Kaye, Nick, Site-Specific Art. Performance, place and documentation (London: Routledge, 2000).
Krystof, Doris, 'Ortsspezifität', in Hubertus Butin (ed.), DuMonts Begriffslexikon zur zeitgenössischen Kunst (Köln: DuMont-Literatur-und-Kunst-Verl., 2002), 231-34.
Kwon, Miwon, 'Public Art als Publizität', in Raunig, Gerald, Vera Kockot und Ulf Wuggenig (eds.), Publicum. Theorien der Öffentlichkeit (Wien: Turia + Kant, 2005), 105-11.
Lewisohn, Cedar, Street art (London: Tate Publ., 2008).
Lewitzky, Uwe, Kunst für alle? Kunst im öffentlichen Raum zwischen Partizipation, Intervention und Neuer Urbanität (Bielefeld: Transkript, 2005).
Loacker, Bernadette, Kreativ prekär. Künstlerische Arbeit und Subjektivität im Postfordismus (Bielefeld: Transkript, 2010).
Lüken, Heike, 'Street Art und der etablierte Kunstbetrieb.Szenen einer Entwicklung', in Katrin Klitzke und Christian Schmidt (eds.), Street Art. Legenden zur Straße (Berlin: Archiv der Jugendkulturen, 2009), 58-65.
Moulin, Raymonde, The French art market: A sociological view (Frz. Orig. 1967; New Brunswick, London: Rutger University Press, 1987).
Plattner, Stuart, High art down home. An economic ethnography of a local art market (Chicago: University of Chicago Press, 1998).
Raunig, Gerald, Kockot, Vera und Ulf Wuggenig, Publicum. Theorien der Öffentlichkeit (Wien: Turia + Kant, 2005).
Reinecke, Julia, Street Art - Eine Subkultur zwischen Kunst und Kommerz (Bielefeld: Transkript, 2007).
Schwanhäußer, Anja, Kosmonauten des Underground. Ethnografie einer Berliner Szene (Frankfurt/Main, u.a.: Campus, 2010).
Schwartzman, Allan, Street Art (Garden City N.Y.: Dial Press, 1985).
Scott, John, 'career', in John Scott, Gordon Marshall (eds.) Oxford Dictionary of Sociology. (Oxford University Press, 2005. eNotes.com. 2006.) 4 Nov, 2011 <http://www.enotes.com/oxsoc-encyclopedia/career>.
Sommer, Robert, Street Art (New York: Links, 1975).
Stahl, Sebastian, Wertschöpfung in der zeitgenössischen Kunst. Zur „Young German Art" (Potsdam: Institut für Makroökonomik, Universität Potsdam, 2009).
Svasek, Maruska, Anthropology, Art and Cultural Production (London: Pluto Press, 2007).
Thornton, Sarah, Sieben Tage in der Kunstwelt (Engl. Orig. 2008; Frankfurt/Main: Fischer, 2009).
Towse, Ruth, 'Economics of training artists', in Victor Ginsburgh und Pierre Michel Menger (eds.), Economics of the Arts. Selected Essays (Amsterdam: Elsevier Science, 1996), 303-26.
Voss, Julia, 'Propaganda ohne Auftrag', Frankfurter Allgmeine Zeitung, 12.3.2009.
White, Cynthia A. und White, Harrison C., Canvases and Careers. Institutional change in the French painting world (Orig. 1965 edn.; Chicago: University of Chicago Press, 1993).
Zolberg, Vera L., Constructing a sociology of the arts (Cambridge: Cambridge University Press, 1990).

Interviews
Interview Heike Derwanz, London 6, 2007
Interview Heike Derwanz, New York 9, 2007

Javier Abarca, Universidad Complutense de Madrid
javier@urbanario.es

Revs, the unknown pioneer

The work created by New York graffitist and artist Revs, in particular that produced together as a duo with Cost, also from New York, has been probably the most significant individual force of influence in the development of the history of graffiti and street art. In spite of this, he is mostly unknown, for the academy as well as for the huge audience that nowadays appreciates these forms of art. This text describes his work and the impact of his heritage, and analyzes the artist's difficult relation with graffiti and with institutional art.

street art, graffiti, Revs

Born in 1967 in Brooklyn, New York,[i] Revs started to get involved in graffiti between 1981 and 1982[ii] and took part in the golden age of graffiti on the city's subway, under the name Revlon. But his fame did not take off until, already in the following decade, he started the work that made him become one of the most influential artists in graffiti and street art.

The start of the decade of 1990 marked the end of an era in which both graffiti and street art had had an enormous social and media presence in New York. In the one hand, the very active street art scene leaded by Keith Haring declined with the end of the eighties, and by the start of the nineties it had virtually disappeared. On the other hand, starting in 1986, the subway company was able to renovate and replace its train fleet, and by 1989 every car of every line ran completely clean, for the first time in twenty years. The local government was thus able to win for good what had seemed an impossible battle against the culture of graffiti on the subways, until then so prominent and spectacular that it had become a symbol of the city in the eyes of the whole world.

The cleaning of the subway caused the retirement from the game of practically all graffiti writers. [iii] Only some diehards, mostly European visitors, have kept on writing on the trains. They don't do it any more to see their names run on traffic, which they do very briefly, if ever. The goal is now to obtain photographic evidence of the feat, which is still valuable solely as a tradition. Expelled from the subway, graffiti invaded streets, rooftops and roads. These settings are much more visible and risky than the subway yards, and call for more hasty kinds of work. This caused the complex pieces of the subways to be replaced by faster forms of graffiti, as well as the prevalence of quantity over sophistication.

It was in this scenario of decadence of graffiti and street art where Revs' great project was started. In 1990[iv] he decided to abandon traditional graffiti practices, and began experimenting with materials and approaches beyond those then accepted by the strict codes of the culture[v]. After noticing that Cost, another experienced subway writer who he had met in 1985, was working along similar lines, Revs got in contact with him, and both decided to join forces[vi]. In the following years Revs and Cost developed an extremely intense campaign in the streets of Manhattan, which yielded them an unheard-of level of visual prominence in the city. The campaign, between graffiti and street art, made them become legendary figures of the local popular culture, and got them into the top of the most wanted list of the specialized police department. The artists' work adopted diverse tactics, some of them very innovative. In time, these new methods would become a fundamental part of the toolbox of graffiti and street art.

In their experimentation beyond the canon of graffiti, Revs and Cost produced small-scale figurative pieces, both drawings and paintings, often including texts. These pieces were mostly executed with a brush, whether directly on walls and doors, on pieces of paper that would then be pasted on walls, or on canvases and rigid supports to be installed several meters high, often on the walls of outdoor parking areas. Both artists produced as well at least two rather ambitious bigger-scale figurative murals.

All these tactics had been profusely used in the New York street art scene of the eighties, therefore this activity meant no innovation and did not have important consequences. The work that made the reputation of Revs and Cost was the huge campaign they carried out using posters and rollers, one of the most relentless street art campaigns in history. In 1992 they started the production and mass installation of photocopied posters –about twenty by thirty centimeters in size, approximately a hundred different series in runs between fifty and a thousand copies[vii], which they pasted mostly on the backs of "walk, don't walk" signs. The poster is a means of communication characteristic of punk culture, particularly traditional in New York, which the artists adopted and brought to unprecedented levels of saturation. The campaign made also use of stickers of a smaller size. Posters and stickers had been exceptionally used by some writers in the eighties, although never in such an ambitious way. The work of Revs and Cost was so intense that many testimonies speak of posters on virtually every intersection in Manhattan[viii].

Revs and Cost's posters featured their names set in simple and legible typefaces, together with sentences and words between cryptic and comical, with no apparent meaning beyond plain humor and a desire to intrigue the audience. Some of them included also a telephone number, which the artists used to gather opinions from the audience in an answering machine. The unheard-of campaign caused quite a stir in the city, and in 1993 The New York Times contacted the artists to find the meaning of their work[ix]. In that interview Revs and Cost announced that what had happened so far was just the beginning. And, indeed, that same year they started to produce their spectacular and historic roller pieces.

In 1993 and 1994 the duo created a long series of huge monochromatic signatures, using latex paint and rollers attached to long telescopic painter's poles, something completely unprecedented then in New York street art[x]. Most of the pieces appeared on very centrally located walls, very visible and hazardous – for both physical risk and the possibility of being arrested –, often on rooftops at a height of several stories. The pole and roller approach makes it possible to paint on very high surfaces, unreachable using traditional graffiti tools, but initially does not leave room for the stylistic finesse customary in that culture, therefore the pieces were always extremely simple and crude.

The roller signatures greatly advanced the social impact of the artists. In March 1994 the influential magazine Artforum approached them for an interview[xi], in what appeared to be the beginning of the artists' acceptance into the art system, which did not come to happen. Quite the contrary, the notorious campaign came to an abrupt end shortly after, in December of that year, when Cost was arrested after pasting a sticker on a newspaper box. The graffiti police department had been following him for several days, thanks to a tip given by an informant[xii].

Those years were the most hostile to graffiti and street art in the city of New York up to that date. Rudolph Giuliani had recently been elected Mayor, and was starting to earn his reputation of heavy-handedness against petty crimes, graffiti among them. The second installment of the historic legal battle against Desa, a very active graffiti writer, had just taken place[xiii]. Cost's trial, conducted in 1995, became news, and the punishment was exemplary: two hundred days of cleaning up graffiti, three years' probation, more than two thousand dollars in fines, and psychological counseling[xiv]. After his arrest Cost gave up street art, and did not take it up again until almost twenty years later[xv]. As for Revs, he went for hiding in Alaska for some time[xvi].

By the following year he was back into activity in New York, although since then most of his production has been much more low-key. He started then a new series, as innovative as the previous works, but this time deliberately invisible. Using the knowledge he had gained in his time as a subway graffiti writer, Revs spent five years entering the subway tunnels of New York equipped with a ladder, a roller and a bucket of oil-based paint[xvii]. The artist painted white or yellow patches of several square meters on the upper part of the tunnel walls, and used a black spray can to scribble on them short autobiographic texts that he signed, numbered and dated, as if they were pages of a diary. The tactic was highly hazardous in a system that runs twenty-four hours a day, and in which electricity circulates at floor level, through the so-called third rail.

Few people have seen these inaccessible works, of which only a handful of images are in circulation. Revs called the project a personal mission, and gave little importance to its invisibility[xviii]. A very ambitious mission, with a goal set on writing one page on each one of the tunnels of the huge subway system of New York. The series was cut short in the year 2000 with the arrest of the artist, again due to an informant's tip[xix]. By then the project was nearly finished, and Revs had already painted a page on two hundred and thirty five tunnels[xx].

Revs' arrest marked the end of years of police work. Charges against him included damage and trespassing, and also possession of stolen property: the subway worker's uniform the artist had used to remain unnoticed while working in the tunnels[xxi]. The details of the sentence have not been published. After the trial Revs vanished, and would not reappear until 2004. The work Revs has produced since then consists of sculptures of cut and welded metal, produced at the artist's studio and then installed on the streets, welded or bolted to some existing element, or to the pavement. It is again a mostly unprecedented technique, which the artist had tried out during his experimental phase in the nineties. Most of the sculptures are small, and for the most part they are installed in Brooklyn. They often feature one of the artist's aliases, or some other word, rendered in classic graffiti lettering.

Far from the provocative stance he adopted in his statements in the nineties, Revs now declares that he installs most of his sculptures with permission from the owners of the support[xxii]. In any case, the installation of these pieces involves a very low level of damage, thus keeping the artist below the radar of the police[xxiii]. In 2005 Revs stated he had installed more than a hundred sculptures,[xxiv] and to this date new pieces have not ceased to appear.

Between graffiti and street art

The work of Revs and Cost falls into what is usually considered street art, because it does away with the unintelligible codes of graffiti, which only a small audience is able to understand, and addresses the general public in a loud and clear way. In the words of Revs: "We plan to hit everyone from the five year old kid to the ninety year old woman, so everyone knows our names."[xxv] However, they never got to cut the umbilical cord with the tradition that had been their school. Their statements in the nineties put them in a confusing position. Sometimes they present themselves as graffiti writers who work for the advance of the movement, while in other occasions they vehemently reject graffiti and its community[xxvi].

But the way they most clearly expressed their will to withdraw from graffiti was in their adoption of new tools. The graffiti scene is extremely traditionalist and conservative, and virulently rejects any behavior that falls beyond its narrow codes. One of these rules has historically dictated that graphics should be refined. Thus, the adoption of a tool as crude as the roller meant a veritable provocation. Revs refers to this as a way to inject into graffiti the irreverent and defiant spirit of punk: "The movement is called punk graffiti because it has the attitude of punk rock"[xxvii]. The artist had gotten involved in punk culture by the same years he was starting to do graffiti [xxviii]. Revs' metal sculptures are a sign of this undetermined position, at the same time inside and outside graffiti and its codes. These pieces are, to a large extent, graffiti in metal, an strange mix that implies very strong constraints. The sculptures reproduce the silhouettes of classic graffiti letterforms, very dynamic shapes originated in the lack of friction of the aerosol against the surface being painted, and in the fluid gesture of the body caused by the celerity in the execution. These shapes are doubtlessly uncomfortable in their new incarnation: Revs builds them in a small scale, cutting sheets of metal using a circular saw, with a necessarily stiff and slow movement.

Influence on graffiti and street art

Revs and Cost are among the handful of most influential figures in the history of graffiti and street art. The adoption of the roller as a valid writing tool in graffiti, which has taken place only in the last five to ten years, is a direct, if late, consequence of their work. As we said, the roller is a crude tool, more so when attached to a pole, and does not initially allow for the formal refinement expected in graffiti. This limitation has historically meant the roller has never been used as a writing tool in this culture, but only for the priming of walls, or sometimes to fill-in letters which are later outlined with spray paint of a different color. However, in a graffiti scene every day more competitive and more receptive to crude aesthetics, the huge expansion of reach allowed by the combination of roller and pole has caused the technique to be gradually adopted, and today it is established as one more implement in the toolbox of graffiti. Writers all over the world have become fluent in its use, to the point that it is now not rare to see it used even to produce quite complex and detailed pieces. When considering the conservatism of graffiti culture, whose strict rules have barely evolved since the seventies, one is able to understand the weight of Revs and Cost's heritage, a visionary work which originated one of the most radical changes in the game. Again as a consequence of the work of Revs and Cost, the telescopic pole has also become a fundamental part of the street art toolbox. The italian artist Blu, one of the central figures of the movement since the middle of the past decade, has based his career on that technique. And he has taken it beyond by replacing the roller with a brush, which allows him to outline with detailed strokes his distinctively tall characters, often several meters in height. Following Blu's example, the tactic of producing large-scale murals using rollers and brushes attached to poles has been adopted by a whole school of artists within the street art scene, and has become one of the main identifying features of the culture. Another substantial consequence of the work of Revs and Cost is to be found in the popularization of the poster. The poster has probably been, together with the stencil and the sticker, the most characteristic technique of the current street art scene, particularly during its initial years, around the start of the century. The origin of its adoption lies also, unquestionably, on Revs and Cost. It was their example which made Shepard Fairey use posters as a tool for propagation, and Fairey's work was, in turn, the cause of the generalized adoption of the poster in the street art scene. North American artist Fairey, together with Banksy the most widely known artist in the scene, has built his career around the use of posters. His campaign was initially based on the sticker, a tool he adopted from skate culture, in which he was involved since his teens. But his project really took off starting in 1995, when he greatly increased the intensity of his campaign, and started to use posters. According to Fairey, this shift was inspired by the encounter with the work of Revs and Cost [xxix].

Between graffiti and art

In their statements of the early nineties Revs and Cost adopted an ambivalent position regarding society and the art system. Sometimes they said they wanted to appeal to the public, while others they reveled in the vandalistic quality of their work[xxx]. On the one hand they were worried about setting their work apart from graffiti, and to identify it as contemporary art[xxxi]. An example of this is one of the figurative murals they produced as a duo, which featured their (covered) faces sculpted on the side of Mount Rushmore along those of Andy Warhol and Keith Haring. It seems that, during his campaign with Cost, Revs had hopes of becoming established as a professional artist. In a quote published in 1999, speaking about the time they were close to taking that step, Revs asked himself "How come we didn't blow up?"[xxxii]. Conversely, on the other hand, they defined their production as a form of art set against the art system, and much more authentic than contemporary art[xxxiii].

Today, Revs' stance regarding the art system is no longer equivocal. In these years, when the possibilities of commercialization of artworks from artists linked to graffiti and street art doesn't seem to stop growing, Revs could certainly capitalize, easily and very profitably, on his legendary position in the histories of graffiti and of street art – a double pedigree almost no one else can claim. It is in fact not rare for his sculptures to be taken from the street to later appear for sale online. Even Cost, who reemerged in 2010[xxxiv], has put work up for sale in an auction, commercializes screen-prints, and states his desire to become involved in the art gallery circuit[xxxv]. Revs, however, remains in the shadows. If Cost's figure has regained some presence in the scene, due to the attention he has received from the specialized media in the last two years, Revs continues to be generally unknown for that majority of enthusiasts who have started following street art in the last decade or later. Revs makes his living as an union ironworker, [xxxvi] and his current view of the commercialization of art is made clear in this quote from 2005: "To me, once money changes hands for art, it becomes a fraudulent activity"[xxxvii]. Only once has he offered artworks for sale, in an exhibition held in Philadelphia in 2000 [xxxviii], with the specific goal of raising money for a lawyer in his trial. Revs values his anonymity: "I don't want to become nobody; I just want to do what I do"[xxxix].

Notes and References
According to the second entry of the diary the artist wrote on the walls of the tunnels of the subway of New York. A photograph of the entry is reproduced in Stephen Powers, The Art of Getting Over. (New York: St Martin's Press, 1999), 98.
ii Revs in John Reiss, Bomb it!. (EE.UU, 2007).
iii "Writers" is the term used by the practitioners of graffiti to refer to themselves.
iv Powers, The Art of Getting Over, 98.
v Until relatively recent times, the only tools acceptable in the work of a graffiti writer, in the eyes of his peers, have been wide-tipped permanent markers and spray cans, always used freehand.
vi Glenn O'Brien, "Cream of wheat paste: Cost and Revs", Artforum, March, 1994.
vii Ibid.
viii Ibid.
ix Michael Cooper, "The Straight-Faced Revs and Cost", The New York Times, January 3, 1993.
x The pixação artists of São Paulo were probably already using this technique by that time, although their work was then totally unknown in North America and Europe. It would only get to be widely known about well into the following decade.
xi O'brien, "Cream of wheat paste: Cost and Revs".
xii Zephyr: "NYC's Graffiti Crackdown, 1995: Injustice For All", Ego Trip Magazine, vol. 2, n° 2, 1995.
xiii Belluck, Pam: "Graffiti Maker 'Cost,' a Prankster to Some but a Criminal in the Law's Eyes, Is Sentenced", New York Times, June 29, 1995.
xiv Ibid.
xv J Pablo, "The Return of Cost: The Tag Machine is Back", The Village Voice, vol. LVIII, n° 13, 2013, 9.
xvi Randy Kennedy, "A Graffiti Legend Is Back on the Street", The New York Times, April 18, 2005.
xvii Powers, The Art of Getting Over, 94.
xviii Kennedy: 2005.
xix Bucky Turco and Marina Galperina, "Cost is up", Animal New York, December 11, 2003.
xx Brian Thomas Gallagher, "Act Four. Spray My Name, Spray My Name". In "Cat and Mouse", This American Life, radio program broadcast on 24 February 2005. Chicago Public Media.
xxi Ibid.
xxii Kennedy, "A Graffiti Legend Is Back on the Street".
xxiii Ibid.
xxiv Ibid.
xxv Author uncredited: "Interview with Cost and Revs". Canned Goods n° 1, 1993.
xxvi O'brien, "Cream of wheat paste: Cost and Revs". Author uncredited: "Interview with Cost and Revs".
xxvii Author uncredited: "Interview with Cost and Revs".
xxviii Reiss, Bomb it!.
xxix Shepard Fairey, Obey: Supply and Demand: The Art of Shepard Fairey. (Berkeley: Gingko Press, 2006), 41.
xxx O'brien, "Cream of wheat paste: Cost and Revs".
xxxi Ibid.
xxxii Powers, The Art of Getting Over, 95.
xxxiii O'brien, "Cream of wheat paste: Cost and Revs".
xxxiv Jenn Pelly, "On First Ave., a graffiti artist's return", The Local East Village, New York Times, November 15, 2010.
xxxv Turco and Galperina, "Cost is up".
xxxvi Kennedy, "A Graffiti Legend Is Back on the Street".
xxxvii Ibid.
xxxviii Ibid.
xxxix Ibid.

Minna Valjakka, Art History, Department of Philosophy, History, Culture and Art Studies, University of Helsinki,
minna.valjakka@helsinki.fi

Kaid Ashton: Conflating Streets, Arts, and Charity[1]

Putting up color photographs with captions is a rare trend in urban art images. So is engaging with the less fortunate people from developing countries. Through visual dislocation that highlights the stark juxtaposition of content and the site, Canadian artist Kaid Ashton has managed to raise awareness of social inequalities. Furthermore, by establishing the Home School Project, Ashton has employed art teaching to interact with local communities especially in Manila. In this article, I will examine the art projects of Kaid Ashton to reveal how the multiple forms and levels of interaction between arts, public space and art teaching come together in his oeuvre.

Kaid Ashton, Home School Project, photographic series

Introduction

Growing numbers of creators of urban art images[2] are concerned with the idea of giving something back to society. Rather than vandalism, their actions show caring, sharing, and contributing. I became aware of this form of employing the streets when in the spring of 2012, while starting my new research project, I encountered a sticker on a street sign at the Central in Hong Kong: a young Asian child was pointing a gun at me (Fig. 1).

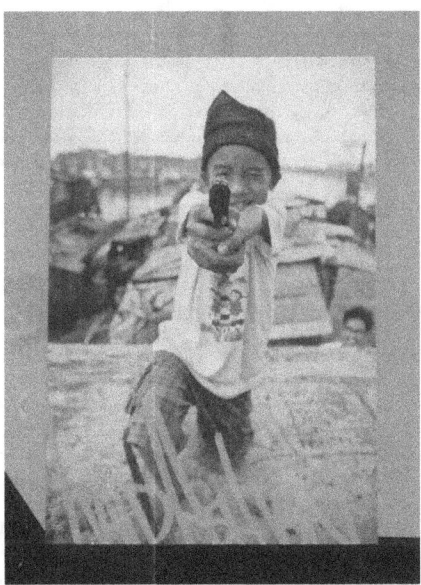

Fig. 1: Kaid Ashton's sticker in Hong Kong, June 2012. Copyright by Minna Valjakka.

In the safe business area of Hong Kong, the image stopped me. Wondering why anyone would put up such a controversial sticker, even with his professional name on it, I came to pay attention to numerous other stickers and wheat-pastes by this artist around Hong Kong. When I got in touch with Kaid Ashton and asked about the photograph that had left me puzzled, he clarified:

> *"The boy with the gun was taken on a rooftop in one of Manila's most notorious slums in the area called Tondo. It was New Year's Eve day and the mood around the slum was quite upbeat. I pasted two photographs on one of the rusty water towers in the community. The boy saw this and as I descended from the tower he approached and I took the shot."[3]*

The reply provoked more questions than it answered. Why would he be in that area? Did it make any sense to be putting up photographs in Asian slums? In order to understand how street art became Ashton's main medium to raise social awareness and how it relates to art teaching, it is beneficial to start with a brief overview of his background.

In the mid-90s Kaid Ashton started to take photographs of urban landscapes, first drawn to contemporary graffiti and train yards.[4] In the university, he took a couple of classes on photography and art and was later able to participate in a photography workshop by American photojournalist Steve McCurry (b. 1950) in New York. Ashton is nevertheless mainly a self-taught photographer who has learned through his encounters with people while traveling.[5]

Ashton's artistic inspiration derives primarily from Steve McCurry and Mexican American photographer and director Estevan Oriol. Ashton appreciates how these two adepts are able to enter any area in the city and capture people in a compelling photograph. The encouragement to engage with the streets comes from graffiti artists Revok (LA), Zes (LA), and Nekst (Houston, d. 2013), whose ability to take risks for their work and pursuit for high quality has been a great inspiration for Ashton to go and put up his works, too. He also enjoys Banksy's ability, through humor and wit, to catch the attention of the world and create awareness for art. In terms of the use of colors, Ashton admires Julie Mehretu's (b. 1970) multilayered color compositions. The warm and welcoming people Ashton meets during his travels are similarly a great inspiration and continuous support from his wife is invaluable.[6]

In 2004, after finishing university, Ashton wanted to see the world. Inspired by the decision of his best friends to move to Taiwan, he decided to join them. While learning to live in another cultural context for three years, he gradually came to be more intrigued by people's ways of living and their individual stories. Since this initial inspiration found in Taiwan, Kaid Ashton's interest in different cultures and people has led him across more than forty countries during the past ten years.[7] During his travels, Ashton became increasingly aware of the prevailing forms of social inequalities, which have an enormous impact on the lives of countless people, especially in the developing countries around the world. With his camera, Ashton started to immortalize the people he met as well as their experiences and life conditions to be shared with the public across the continents.

In 2008, rather than restricting his oeuvre to galleries for commercial purposes or to the social media, Ashton decided to experiment by putting up his photographs in public spaces. The first wheat-paste, a single work itself, went up on a train in Saskatchewan. Satisfied with the results of this "moving gallery,"[8] Ashton was motivated to continue in this direction. He chose to spread his art internationally, to be seen by urbanites in their everyday surroundings—both to enliven the degenerated neighborhoods and to raise people's awareness of their own and others' circumstances in different countries. He hoped to reach audiences who did not have the possibility to visit galleries.[9] As with most creators of urban art images, the physical site for putting up a photograph matters a great deal to Ashton, too. He prefers sites "that provide either a stark contrast or poetic similarity"[10] to the subject matter in the work itself.

In addition to single photographs, working with a series of images on specific themes has become a meaningful method for Ashton. These series have benefited from his travels, and some of them were created simultaneously. The first experimental series of portraits, without any specific title, emerged on the streets of Toronto and Los Angeles during September and October 2010. The main intention was to test the scenes in these large cities and "see how receptive people were before going on to bigger projects internationally."[11]

After gaining this experience, Ashton turned his gaze to Asia. He wanted to humanize the urban space with portraits of individual people, also planning to create visual contrasts between living environments. As a result, starting in 2011, Ashton headed to the slums of Manila equipped with large photographs of the unspoiled nature of Saskatchewan. He ventured on to Sri Lanka, Dhaka and Guangzhou during the next two years with untitled series of nature photographs. So far, creating varying series of works to be discussed in detail in the latter part of this paper, Ashton has spread his works in fifteen cities: Toronto, Vancouver, Los Angeles, Miami, Manila, Hong Kong, Guangzhou, Beijing, Kaohsiung in Taiwan, Tokyo, Dhaka, Cairo, Colombo, Jaffna, and Leon in Nicaragua.[12]

Ashton's two main formats to display photographs in public space are large wheat-pastes and postcard-size stickers. He has pasted around 300 posters and 7,000 stickers, the latter consisting of 30–35 images. Although color images are far more expensive to produce, Ashton personally prefers them because their vibrancy better captures the personality of the people as well as attention on the streets. He also creates black-and-white images if he considers them more suitable for the subject.[13]

To my knowledge, Ashton is one of the very rare artists to put up color photographs in public space and also with such diversified subject matter. At least in Asia, it seems he is still the only one to employ this format. For instance, the French street artist JR, who has also traveled extensively, including Asia, is currently the best-known street artist to employ photographs. However, he focuses on large, black-and-white facial portraits of individuals—or details of them— in his oeuvre on the streets.[14] Occasionally, these images cannot even been seen by the people themselves because they are displayed on rooftops. They are visible only to the media and/or anyone in a helicopter. Another difference between Ashton's and JR's work is that while JR and his crew take and paste portraits of local people, Ashton provides a notion of dislocation: he puts up images of people and sceneries taken outside of the community.

Art for Street Children
The photograph of a child from Tondo holding a gun relates to Ashton's experiences in Manila that left a lasting mark on his life. In January 2011, he was living in Manila, looking for a job, and pasting up his photographs around the city. The main theme he was working on was the creation of a juxtaposition between nature photographs from Canada and the slums of Manila. He was touched by the warm-heartedness and generosity of the people, who were eager to share whatever they had. On one occasion, when local people were helping him to put up a poster, Ashton decided that he needed to give something back to the people—if nothing else, at least his time. In order to show his gratitude as an artist and as a teacher, Ashton promised to return to teach an art class to the children of that neighborhood.[15]

From this promise and idea came the inspiration to develop the Home School Project. In collaboration with the Office of Culture and Design (OCD), a local business promoting socially engaged art practices,[16] Ashton held thirty visual art workshops around varying parts of Manila. Occasionally, volunteers from different backgrounds, such as the local artist Gabby Tiongson, participated in the teaching and organizing. Furthermore, while traveling in 2012, Ashton taught three classes in Sri Lanka and one in Bangladesh. Altogether, he has provided thirty-four workshops on arts with about twenty-five volunteers during the years 2011-2013.[17]

Initially, the aim of the project was to organize art classes for street children in poor neighborhoods where they might have limited access to formal education or their studies are interrupted for different social reasons.[18] However, Ashton's work also caught the attention of a Catholic orphanage, Association de Damas Filipinas (ADDF)[19] and a children's hospital at Taft Avenue, who were interested in having Ashton to give art lessons to the children. In the children's hospital in particular, art activities provided welcome respite from daily troubles and pains.[20] Gradually, thanks to such local volunteers in Manila as Jojo Guballa and the Soulstice break dance crew, the project came to include break dancing and basic education in reading, writing, science, and mathematics to support school studies.[21]

The main idea was to encourage street children through informal art workshops to employ their imagination and creativity to find ways for self-expression.[22] The workshops usually included an assignment, such as transforming and writing one's name as a graffiti style tag, painting one's dreams on a t-shirt, making frames for photographs, developing ideas for sculptures, or creating a collage of one's life wishes as a mood board. First, the assignment was explained and demonstrated and then the children were provided the necessary materials and support—also from their parents—to complete their works of art. The parents were helping to deliver the meals and clean after class too.[23] Teaching was only one of the intentions spelled out by the project. Indeed, giving a chance for the children to nurture some notion of self-esteem became even more important. According to Ashton, it was more "about showing these kids that they are not invisible, that they are worth somebody's time."[24] The importance of sharing time is emphasized also by the OCD:

> "It's about making the time to go for a walk—a purposeful walk—and giving something in return to the people who allow you to trespass their turf. One of the best things you can give to a stranger is your time. We've given lots of it. Fun times for the kids, family time for the parents, community time for the neighbors, and pizza time of course for everyone."[25]

The core inspiration of the whole project was to spread caring and sharing. By initiating collaboration between the parents, the community, and the children, the project ultimately aimed to enhance the interaction and well-being of these underprivileged children—and the whole neighborhood. Furthermore, the project provided meals for the children, their parents, and neighbors in connection with the workshops. Sharing food is an integral component to any Filipino gathering and is an unequivocal sign of respect, peace, and togetherness. It is estimated that more than two thousand people took part in the activities organized by the Home School Project.[26] When the project started, there were no specific plans for the future, but the intention was to get more volunteers and supporters involved and to inspire other people to establish their own similar projects.[27] One of Ashton's personal aspirations was that he could continue developing the project and make it his way of life and his livelihood.[28] Unfortunately, the dreams did not come true. The project's funding was sparse to begin with. It was accomplished mainly by Ashton's own savings and the OCD micro-grants. Fundraising brought generous private donations from numerous Canadians, such as Dylan B, aka the Cameco Kid, and Kelly Rapko. Support also came from the Bonifacio Arts Foundation Inc. (BAFI)[29] and BBDO Guerrero, a local creative agency.[30] Without a continuous funding stream, however, it became difficult to maintain the activities on a scale they had hoped. In late May 2011, Ashton decided to move to Hong Kong for work.

According to the founder of the Office of Culture and Design, Clara Balaguer, the driving force behind the project was the artist's energetic personality and his commitment to explore, interact, and give back to the people he met. Ashton made every child feel special and important. Without him, it was difficult to continue despite their best efforts. For instance, with two other Filipino teachers, Jojo Guballa organized a Sunday Home School class to teach basic reading, mathematics, English, and ethics at Barangay Hall Vitas, in Tondo, from June to December 2011.[31]

Ashton did not give up, either, although he moved away. When he had a chance, he would travel and give a Home School class. Opportunities in new cities arrived in 2012, and in late January , Ashton headed for Sri Lanka, where he taught three art classes: the first in the slums of Colombo, the second in a community which was rebuilding itself after the 2004 tsunami near Uppuveli in Trincomalee, and the third in a refugee camp in Jaffna.[32] The chance to teach a class in Old Dhaka in Bangladesh came in April 2012. In an overcrowded school where 1,200 children take turns to participate in either for morning or afternoon classes, Ashton had 120 enthusiastic students in his arts class.[33] In addition, the OCD has been able to invite Ashton back to Manila to teach on three occasions. The first time he returned on July 30-August 3, 2011 to give a workshop in collaboration with the Bantay Bata 163 program of the ABS-CBN Foundation[34] in Laguna and was able to provide two other workshops during the same visit.[35] The second chance to return to Manila on June 23-24, 2012, was made possible through fundraising in Saskatchewan and by Carmina Panlilio, an American donor. This time two workshops were organized, one on decorating t-shirts in Tayuman and the other based on Ashton's photographs in EDSA.[36]

EDSA is a squatter community of around twelve families underneath the Magallanes SLEX Highway Flyover, close to the Makati commercial center. The original idea for this EDSA workshop was not realizable so instead they decided to work with those of Ashton's photographs that he happened to have along. The assignment was to choose one of the portraits and frame it according to the participants' own wishes. The children were more than happy to interact with Ashton's photographs, creating their own interpretations through colorful frames. In the end, a street gallery of the art works was established with the permission of the photographic shop on its blue wall (Fig 2.).[37]

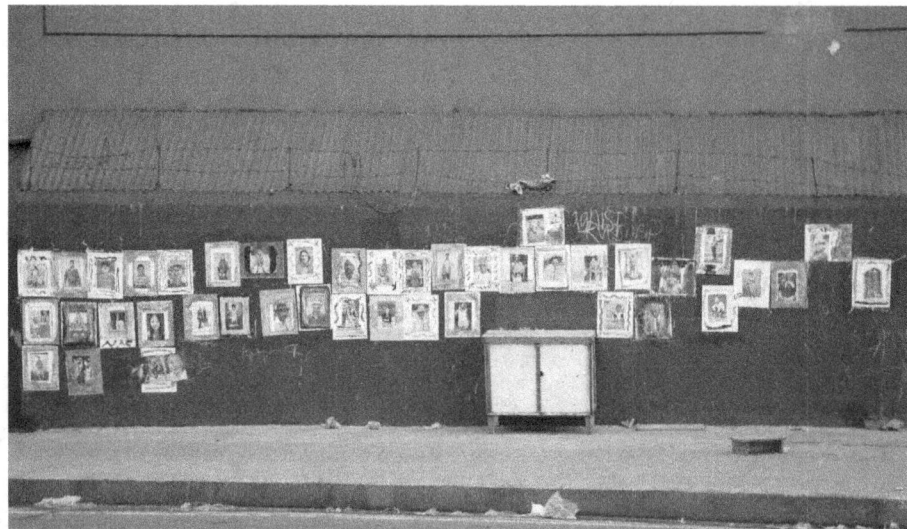

Fig. 2: The framed photographs in the street gallery in EDSA, Manila, 2012. Copyright by Kaid Ashton.

This temporary art exhibition gave children pride, caught the eye of people passing by, and momentarily broke the grayness with color and joyful creation. This was the only time a class was based on Ashton's photographs. It turned out to be his favorite.[38] Unfortunately, the city authorities did not appreciate the outcomes and took the gallery down soon after: "they do not agree that these initiatives (posting artwork) contribute anything to the 'beautification' of the city," wrote Balaguer.[39]

The third time, Ashton came back on December 2, 2012, funded by BAFI. Five workshops were now on the agenda, with a focus on sculptures. First, the children were shown videos of the public art around Bonifacio Global City. The assignment was to draw what kind of alternative uses these sculptures could have if they were located in the children's own neighborhoods. This time too, one of the classes was held in EDSA.[40]

It is often argued that in order to provide any results, community projects should be based on continuity. Even if giving a moment of joy through one workshop was a delightful experience for the children, the possibility to co-operate with the same community and the same children made things easier in the end. In addition, as Balaguer clarified, they understood that no matter how much they did, it would only be a tiny drop of hope. The problem of poverty and its impact on children in Manila is so severe that it would require more long-term efforts by different development programs and government commitment to a massive reform. By returning to give workshops in the same location, the organizers hoped to have some impact. Furthermore, despite the derelict surroundings, the children in EDSA were very enthusiastic to learn and were better-behaved than in some other similar neighborhoods in Manila. Collaboration with the children and the community was easy, especially thanks to the "mother figure" of a thirty-something lady named Esther, who took an interest in the children's well-being and was a mother herself. As a result, the EDSA children came to enjoy four classes on art with Ashton and another four with the Soulstice break dance crew.[41]

It is not easy to verify whether or not the Home School Project has had any long-term benefits to the children and/or to the communities. Balaguer is not entirely happy with the results, believing that much more should have been done to create lasting, long-term impact.[42] However, Ashton is convinced that they truly did see short-term benefits in every class. At least for that brief moment, the children could forget their daily troubles and uncertainties and focus on just being kids and having fun.[43] This is a privilege taken for granted by people in developed countries, but it is not at all as self-evident to children growing up in slums. In addition, it is important to remember that there is a severe lack of possibilities for education in many Asian countries. It could of course be argued that learning art is not a top priority, but if art can be used to teach some basic values or even self-respect, its significance cannot be underestimated.

Ashton himself is satisfied with the project because donations and help from volunteers enabled the organizers to provide a number of classes. Despite this success, the fact that the project ended is a setback. Whether there will be a chance to continue the project in future is still completely open. While the practicalities are a challenge, Ashton would like to continue.[44]

The project taught a lot to Ashton, too. When getting to be accepted by the people and interacting with them through workshops, Ashton was impressed how receptive to the classes the children and the communities. The derelict circumstances did not stand in the way of their engagement. Fundamentally, "everyone just needs an opportunity and someone to believe in them [...] and that lesson can be applied anywhere in the world—it's universal."[45] Ashton also realized that happiness does not depend on money. The whole experience opened his eyes to seeing how the majority of people live with so little. It made him very thankful for everything he has and even for the ability to explore these places.[46] Access to the neighborhoods as a friend, not as a tourist or a reporter, also furthered his photographing and enabled him to take intimate portraits in order to tell the people's stories forward.

Incorporating Livelihoods Between Different Cities

After moving to Hong Kong, Ashton decided to share his experiences of seeing different aspects of the world and of building relationships with some fascinating people. This idea developed into a project entitled People in Poverty, which consisted of thirty portraits of individuals living in the poorest areas in Manila. Through the portraits and short captions in English and in Chinese recounting the protagonists' stories, Ashton wanted to display the severe contrast between lives in Manila and the first world—and especially the contrast to Hong Kong, a global business center.[47] Whether Ashton achieved his aim to remind privileged people of the destitute in the developing countries through individual stories, is hard to tell. However, at least according to the perceptions of a local noodle shop owner in Hong Kong mentioned in the CNN article, Ashton's method of employing individual stories did bring issues of poverty to a far more intimate level and raised the awareness of the viewer.[48]

The ability to approach and interact with people is visible throughout Ashton's oeuvre of portraits, regardless of whether they were taken in conjunction with the Home School project or not. This is seen, for instance, in the series Dignity in Labour, pasted up with bilingual captions in Beijing and in Hong Kong during 2011-2013. The series portrays people from Taiwan, Burma, Jamaica, Laos, Cuba, Oman, Iran as well as from the cities of New York and Los Angeles.[49]

The same relaxed intimacy is visible also in the portraits of the series entitled Women Strong and Confident, created in Hong Kong in 2011. "On any given day the majority of the images we see of women are ones that have been digitally manipulated, 'enhanced' and somewhere along the line that natural beauty is lost," Ashton writes and continues, "[w]ith these photographs, I have tried to capture their confidence and natural beauty while showcasing their strong personalities."[50] The fifteen portraits on women from Burma, Vietnam, Taiwan, Cuba, Philippines, Malaysia, Iran, and the United States were put up around the city with bilingual captions introducing the women's stories and identities. The series was dedicated to Ashton's mother who "showed me what hard work really is and has always encouraged me to believe in myself and keep my spirit free."[51]

One of the portraits which caught my eye in the streets of Hong Kong was of a woman whose smile embraced the world. Her full-body shot was originally part of the above series on women. But this time, Ashton had chosen to put up her facial portrait as a large wheat-paste in the modest, old neighborhood of Tai Hang (Fig. 3). Asked about the story behind this portrait, Ashton replied:

> "The [photograph of the] black lady was taken in LA. She was a recent survivor of breast cancer and full of energy and positive vibes. We talked for a while before I took the photograph and I feel as though I was able to really capture her energy and her soul."[52]

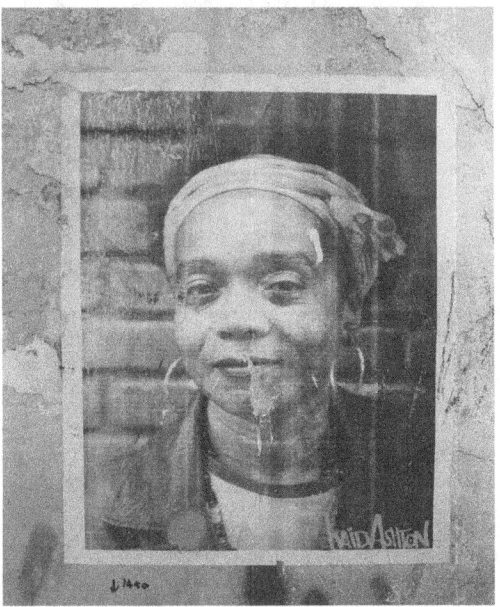

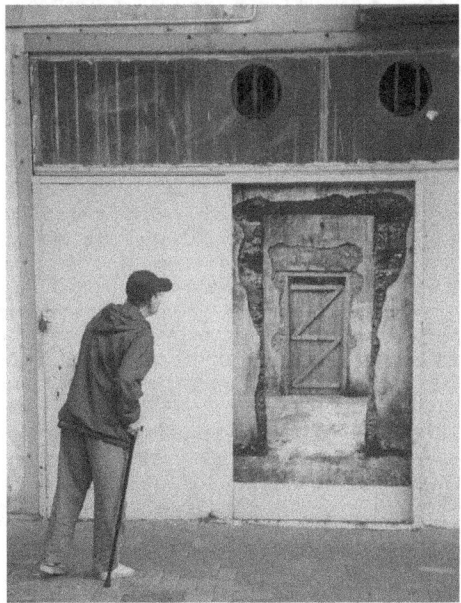

Fig. 3: Wheat-paste of a Los Angeles lady in Hong Kong, April 2013. Copyright by Minna Valjakka.

Fig. 4: A Hongkongnese looking at Kaid Ashton's photograph from the series Through the Doors. The photograph of the door was originally taken in Trincomalee, Sri Lanka. Hong Kong, 2013. Copyright by Kaid Ashton.

Encountering people who were willing to share their stories and to allow Ashton to take their photographs served to make Ashton feel even more strongly that he needed to return something. Occasionally, he would offer them a meal but it would not be adequate enough. Most people he met, for instance, in Manila had barely any access to Internet, not to mention an email address. The Home School Project had been one way of giving back. He now found another: giving the people the portraits he had taken of them—framed. This interaction also inspired a series, Pictures for the People, in Manila in 2011.[53] Ashton saw clearly enough that "[a] framed picture is a small gesture, but I think it can enable people to see themselves in a positive way. I hope it can enhance self-confidence, self-esteem and provide the individual with positive outlook on the next day. Maybe that's all in my mind, but the people here were very happy to receive a picture of themselves."[54]

In addition, to show his gratitude towards his collaborators too, Ashton made a series entitled Inspirational Friends, also put up in Hong Kong in 2012.[55] The series is somewhat exceptional because the seven black-and-white images, except one, are a tribute to artists and musicians in North America.Although the majority of Ashton's oeuvre has focused on people and their portraits, he has also been interested in creating visual contrast through his photographs of urban or natural landscapes. Images of unspoiled nature appear to be readily appreciated by the local people—even in the derelict neighborhoods of Jaffna and Colombo where Ashton continued this series in early 2012. Usually, the local people would welcome Ashton's paste-ups and would want to pose next to them for photographs. However, the surprising reception of the second natural landscape he posted in Jaffna left Ashton deeply touched. The pasting up of the work in the early morning hours did not cause any negative feedback from a group of friendly fishermen returning from their nightly trip, but the photograph was gone when Ashton came back later to take a better image of the work. The locals noticed his disappointment, and when he was leaving they called him back, asking him to follow them to a room where they kept the holy objects for the temple close by. To his amazement, Ashton discovered his photograph on the wall, beside a peacock and a picture of the Gods. This was a very humbling experience.[56]

Ashton found similar positivity in Guangzhou in March 2012, where he was pasting up the remaining photographs of clear skies. The dissimilarity of the images in the industrialized and polluted urban environment of Guangzhou was extreme to say the least. The local people nevertheless liked what they saw. The guard of the industrial area followed Ashton without intervening, and while Ashton was putting up one of the works in a residential area, local people stood up for him when a local army member tried to stop his work.[57] In Ashton's own experience, the majority of the local people's reactions towards his work have been positive regardless of the subject theme of the image. As a rule, the people have been excited about having his photographs in their community, also enjoying the stories behind the photographs.[58] Ashton's works obviously give a chance to connect with and compare experiences from different countries.

Still, the responses have not always been welcoming. In 2013, an uncomfortable incident occurred in Cairo, where Ashton was planning to work on his new series, Through the Doors. This series was initially inspired by the doors and doorways Ashton saw and photographed in Sri Lanka in early 2012.[59] It "was intended," as he wrote in the blog, "to spark the imagination of the viewer and allow them to explore the idea of what lies behind a door and the numerous possibilities that can take place."[60] The original idea was to create this series both in Hong Kong and in Cairo during January–April 2013, but things did not proceed as planned.While pasting up the first piece on a busy street in Cairo, Ashton was ordered to remove it. He went on to do as told, when around thirty aggressive men gathered and inquired about his nationality, what he was doing in Cairo, and what kind of propaganda his works were. The situation grew more hostile with more men gathering and starting to take hold of his belongings and inspecting his camera. To avoid any further trouble, Ashton ran away to his hotel and took care to destroy the posters, stickers and photographs of the incident. Consequently, this series of ten photographs was created only in Hong Kong.[61]

For Ashton, another way of connecting people through images is artistic collaborations. Since 2011, Ashton has experimented with graffiti writers and artists to explore new ways of creation in the streets. One way to work together is based on images exchange: Ashton sends his photograph(s) to a partner in arts who modifies the digital image(s) and sends them back to Ashton to be pasted on the walls. This is how collaboration has worked with the Canadian Luke Ramsey and Huskey Brown from London. The second form of collaboration is interaction through images in the same space: Ashton chose or allowed his partner to choose a photograph that would function as the starting point of the final work. After putting up the photograph, the other artist/writer would then continue interacting with the image and create the piece surrounding it.[62] Naturally, with different companions, the outcomes vary from writing a poem in black in Chinese by Hongkongnese Xeme to multicolored and detailed pieces finished by Kaput from Vancouver.[63]

As with Xeme, the collaborations have usually been short, one-time experiments. This was also the case with American Ewok MSK, KST crew from Manila and a Canadian Rove.[64] With Kaput it was different. Since the first co-created work in July 2012, the artists have worked together for an extended period. From August to December 2013, they were involved in ten collaborations around Vancouver on ten executive Saturdays (Fig. 5). The last piece was made on the walls of the Catalog Gallery in Vancouver for their exhibition "It's a Wacky World!" From twenty photographs Ashton sent to Kaput, he chose ten.[65] After writing his own name around two photographs, Kaput ended up focusing on different words that corresponded with the portraits of people.

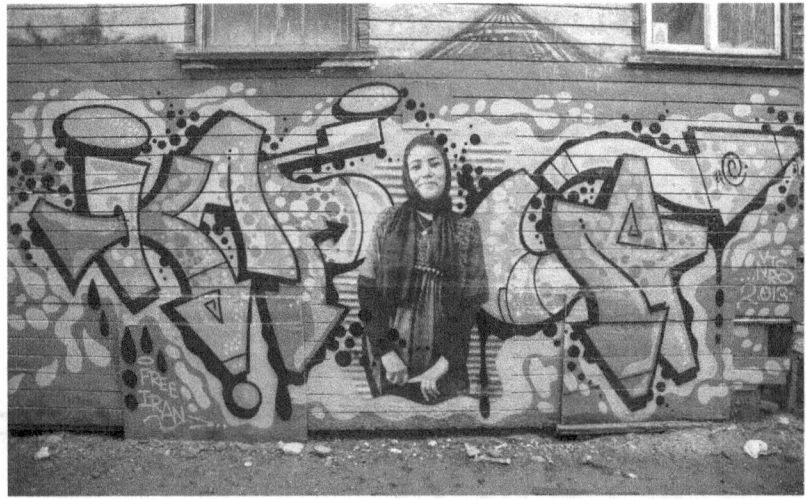

Fig. 5: Kaput-Free Iran, a collaboration by Kaid Ashton and Kaput in 2013. Copyright by Kaid Ashton.

The portrait of this young female artist was taken in Naqsh-e Jahan Square, in Esfahan, Iran. She made an impression on Ashton as "one of few Iranians that spoke openly about how the government suppresses people, particularly women and artists."[66] From Kaput Ashton learned a lot about patience, paying attention to detail, and taking the effort to make the piece as good as it could be. The experiences from the collaborations were "mind-blowing". For Ashton it was very inspirational to see how different artists interpreted and interacted with his photographs. He would definitely want to continue doing this also in future.[67]

Forms of Socially Engaging Urban Art Images
Social activism needs aesthetics. But in our image-dominated world, to catch the attention of passers-by, even for a moment, has become a challenge. Kaid Ashton's blog contains many photographs that show local people keenly examining his photographs. People would stop to show interest, take photographs and even ask questions about the content, meaning and purpose of his work.[68] It is plausible that Ashton's photographs have raised awareness in some circles about social inequality, women's roles and status and the state of the urban environment, although his efforts have not gained much international attention compared to some other celebrities in the urban art scene.[69] His preferred method of visual dislocation, especially through portraits of ordinary people and their private stories in the captions, has nevertheless caught viewers' imagination. Indeed, Ashton's photographs gain aesthetic resonance from the juxtaposition of the content, site and the city's socio-cultural context. In Hong Kong in particular, approachable, human-size portraits are an exception in the public space dominated by glossy and digitally manipulated models.The indexicality of the photographic images is a key starting point for interaction. The interpretations are not, however, fixed but Ashton's work can create a continuum of perceptions depending on the viewer's life experiences, values, self-reflection and defensiveness. The public space of the city serves as a locus of a complex comparison across the boundaries of class, race, and gender, oscillating between notions of joy, curiosity, remorse, and shame.

The captions and sequence numbers of the works, indicating the sequence of the image in the series, transformed the series into a public art exhibition. As Ashton said, "it's a walking tour in the city with an educational purpose to it."[70] He does not regard his actions as criminal because he is only putting up an art show with paper.[71] As I have argued elsewhere in detail, the acceptance and the understanding of the levels of il/legality of the urban art images varies remarkably depending primarily on the content, format, nationality of the creator, and the physical site where the work is put up.[72] The captions besides the images have most likely made them even more acceptable and "legal" to local citizens as a form of urban art images with a message. They have thus enhanced the images' impressiveness.

To raise social awareness or to make socially engaged creative action, art works, and happenings in public space is nothing new. However, socially and/or politically related themes are still clearly a minority among urban art images in mainland Chinese cities, Hong Kong, and Tokyo. Of these, the scene in Hong Kong is the most varied in terms of socially engaged urban art images. For instance, both local and foreign artists reflect on the Tian'anmen Incident, criticize the government, and/or the issues of urban development. One popular way of engaging with the community to improve the living surroundings is to paint the walls.

Even if the urban art images might be able to beautify an area or raise the awareness of a passer-by, how could they initiate people into further actions? Occasionally, the work itself can be related to the development of a social project, as with the South African street artist Faith47 and her latest work the Harvest. Every time the project, Another Light Up, manages to raise enough funding to install a street light, a smaller light is added to the work and lit up.[73] One successful example from Hong Kong is the project of miniature "cage people" by Kwong Chi Kit, his colleagues and two miniature artists in collaboration with the Society for Community Organization (SoCO). In order to make people realize the inhuman living conditions some of them have, three very lifelike miniature people in their "cage homes" made from rat-catching cages were displayed around Hong Kong. Information beside the cages was complemented by a QR code in order for the viewers to send an email petition to the local government for more public estates. Around 10,000 emails were sent.[74]

Without substantial support, it is nonetheless challenging for an individual artist to maintain a long-term socially engaged art project such as the Home School Project by Kaid Ashton. Despite the fact of not being able to continue with the project, Ashton is hopeful about developing further means in the future. He believes that whenever a passer-by stops to look at his work, it has had some sort of impact on the person. And while Ashton has exhibited in ten galleries, he still strongly prefers making his art visible in the public space because this makes it more powerful and creates more interaction with people.[75] Kaid Ashton is an artist-explorer who uses his works to raise awareness, to inspire others, and to travel the world. He admits enjoying the adrenaline rush of the possibility of experiencing the "unknown" city and culture without any specific plans and prejudices. What is more, the chance to interact and connect with people over and above the language barrier by capturing their image through camera is a moment beyond words. Ashton also mentions that every once in a while he still has "the feeling that something positive is going to come out of all this and it already has"—being able to meet amazing people and see the world; all these experiences are invaluable.[76] They are both part of the motivation and the significance of his work.

Notes and References

1   This paper is still work in progress, to be improved based on feedback from the conference. It is part of my three-year postdoctoral research project, "East Asian Urban Images—self-expression through visual images in Hong Kong, Tokyo and Seoul" funded by the Academy of Finland.
2   With urban art images I denote non-institutional creative actions that leave a visible imprint on the public space. They can consist of pictures, text, and numbers, or three-dimensional objects and other materials—or any combination of these. For more detailed information see Minna Valjakka, "Kiinalaisen urbaanin taiteen kulttuurisidonnaisuus." ["The cultural contextuality of Chinese urban art."] Tahiti 1, 2012, http://tahiti.fi/01-2012/tieteelliset-artikkelit/kiinalaisen-urbaanin-taiteen-kulttuurisidonnaisuus/. See also Minna Valjakka, "Contesting the levels of il/legality of urban art images in China," Review of Culture, forthcoming 2014.
3   Kaid Ashton, email message to author, May 14, 2013. See also "Kaid Ashton," on the Home School Project's (HSP) website, accessed May 2, 2014, http://homeschoolproject.wordpress.com/kaid-ashton-2/.
4   Kaid Ashton, email message to author March 1, 2013. See also HSP's website "Kaid Ashton"; Ben Sin, "Signs of the Times," South China Morning Post, December 4, 2011, http://www.scmp.com/article/986717/signs-times.
5   Kaid Ashton, email message to author May 10, 2014.
6   Kaid Ashton, video call interview with the author, May 14, 2014. The earlier perceptions on inspiration were mentioned in Ralph Mendoza, "Take It to the Streets," Rogue, September 2011. Available on Office of Culture and Design's website, http://officeocd.com/news/homesch-rogue-magazine/.
7   Ashton, email message, May 10, 2014. See also HPS's website "Kaid Ashton"; Sin, "Signs of the Times."
8   For some images of the 2010 "moving gallery," see Kaid Ashton's blog, "Whole Car," August 30, 2010, http://kaidashton.blogspot.jp/2010/08/whole-car.html.
9   Ashton, email message, May 10, 2014; Ashton, interview.
10   HPS's website "Kaid Ashton".
11   Kaid Ashton, email message to author, May 12, 2014. For images, see Kaid Ashton's blog, "City of Compton," October 15, 2010, http://kaidashton.blogspot.jp/2010/10/city-of-compton.html and "42 and a half hours in Toronto...", November 7, 2010, "http://kaidashton.blogspot.jp/2010_11_01_archive.html.
12   Ashton, interview; Ashton, email message, May 10, 2014.
13   Ashton, interview.
14   For recent information on JR, see for instance his website, accessed May 14, 2014, http://www.jr-art.net/.
15   Ashton, interview. See also Kaid Ashton's blog, "Homeschool," February 19, 2011, http://kaidashton.blogspot.jp/2011/02/homeschool.html. Postings were usually made afterwards, which is why the dates of the postings do not correspond exactly with the dates of the workshops. See also "Homeschool" on the Office of Culture and Design's (OCD) website, accessed May 4, 2014, http://officeocd.com/projects/homeschool/.
16   The OCD was established in December 2010 by Clara Balaguer as "a platform for artists, designers, writers and projects that investigate solutions for (primarily) developing world issues." In practice, any profits deriving mainly from publications are used to develop future projects. At the moment, to keep the expenses as low as possible, Balaguer has no permanently hired employees or office. Clara Balaguer, video call interview by the author, May 5, 2014. For further information, see also the Office of Culture and Design's website, accessed May 4, 2014, http://officeocd.com/.
17   Ashton, interview; Balaguer, interview. For more information, see OCD's website "Homeschool." See also Home School Project's website, accessed May 14, 2014, http://homeschoolproject.wordpress.com/. For video clips posted by OCD, see "Homeschool 1 EDSA SOUTH SUPER HIGHWAY," accessed May 14, 2014, http://vimeo.com/27368927, and "Homeschool 22 AURORA BULEVARD," accessed May 14, 2014, http://vimeo.com/27369214.
18   Balaguer, interview. See also Kaid Ashton's blog, "Homeschool."
19   "Association De Damas De Filipinas," on the Home School Project's website, accessed May 2, 2014, http://damasphilippines.wordpress.com/visit-us/.
20   Kaid Ashton's blog, "Homeschool x 6 x 7 x 8 - The Orphanage," April 3, 2011, http://kaidashton.blogspot.jp/2011/04/homeschool-x-6-x-7-x-8-orphanage.html; "Homeschool x 18 & 19: The Orphanage and Children's Hospital," July 25, 2011, http://kaidashton.blogspot.jp/2011/07/homeschool-x-18-19-orphanage-and.html. See also "Class #18 Orphanage Class #19 Children's Hospital," on Home School Project's website, accessed May 3, 2014, http://homeschoolproject.wordpress.com/2011/08/04/homeschool-18-19/.
21   Balaguer, interview. See also HSP's website "The Project"; OCD's website "Homeschool."
22   See "The Project," on the Home School Project's website, accessed May 4, 2014, http://homeschoolproject.wordpress.com/. See also Kaid Ashton's interview by Adobo Magazine, "adoboLIVE! Canadian artist Kaid Ashton on the 3-year Home School Project's," published December 6, 2012, http://www.youtube.com/watch?v=69tHXurRDwg.
23   OCD's website "Homeschool."
24   HSP's website "The Project."
25   OCD's website "Homeschool."
26   HSP's website "The Project." See also Adobo Magazine, "adoboLIVE! Canadian artist Kaid Ashton."
27   Balaguer, interview; OCD's website "Homeschool."
28   Balaguer, interview; Ashton, interview.
29   For the Bonifacio Arts Foundation Inc., see their website, accessed May 10, 2014, http://www.artsatbgc.org/.
30   Ashton, interview; HSP's website "The Project." For BBDO Guerro, see their website, accessed May 5, 2014, http://www.bbdoguerrero.com/index.php.
31   Balaguer, interview. See also OCD's "Homeschool."
32   Kaid Ashton's blog, "Homeschool x 24 x The Slums of Colombo," February 6, 2012, http://kaidashton.blogspot.jp/2012/02/homeschool-x-24-x-slums-of-colombo.html; "Homeschool x 25: The Tsunami School," February 15, 2012, http://kaidashton.blogspot.jp/2012/02/homeschool-x-25-tsunami-school.html; "Homeschool x 26: The Refugee Camp," March 10, 2012, http://kaidashton.blogspot.jp/2012/03/homeschool-x-27-refugee-camp.html.
33   Ashton, interview. See also Kaid Ashton's blog, "Homeschool x 27: Dhaka's Tenement Buildings," April 29, 2012, http://kaidashton.blogspot.jp/2012/04/homeschool-x-27-dhakas-tenement.html.
34   For the Bantay Bata 163 program, see their website, accessed May 14, 2014, http://www.abs-cbnfoundation.com/bb163/.
35   Exact dates given by Clara Balaguer, email message to author, May 13, 2014. See also OCD's website "Homeschool" and Kaid Ashton's blog, "Homeschool x 21: Laguna," August 14, 2011, http://kaidashton.blogspot.jp/2011/08/homeschool-x-21-laguna.html; "Homeschool x 22: Back to the Start," August 24, 2011, http://kaidashton.blogspot.jp/2011/08/homeschool-x-22-back-to-start.html; "Homeschool x 23: The Tenements," October 11, 2011, http://kaidashton.blogspot.jp/2011/10/homeschool-x-23-tenements.html.
36   Balaguer, email message. See also OCD's website "Homeschool" and Kaid Ashton's blog, "Homeschool x 28 x Tayuman," July 31, 2012, http://kaidashton.blogspot.jp/2012/07/homeschool-x-28-x-tayuman.html; "Homeschool x 29: The Street Kids of EDSA x Kaid Ashton," September 18, 2012.
37   Ashton, interview; Balaguer, email message. See also Kaid Ashton's blog, "Homeschool x 29: The Street Kids of EDSA x Kaid Ashton," September 18, 2012.
38   Ashton, interview.
39   Balaguer, email message.
40   Balaguer, email message. See also OCD's Tumblr, "HOMESCHOOL COURSE 1 CLASS 24: EDSA MAGALLANES FLYOVER," accessed May 14, 2014, http://officeofcultureanddesign.tumblr.com/post/65358316150 and "HOMESCOOL COURSE 1 CLASS 26: THE CEMETERY TRASHDUMP,

PLUS SOME UNORTHODOX THOUGHTS ON TOURISM," accessed May 14, 2014, http://officeofcultureanddesign.tumblr.com/post/65357482169; Kaid Ashton's blog, "Homeschool x 31: EDSA," January 13, 2013, http://kaidashton.blogspot.jp/2013/01/homeschool-x-31-edsa.html.
41   Balaguer, interview.
42   Ashton, interview.
43   Ashton, interview.
44   Balaguer, interview.
45   Ashton, interview.
46   Ashton, interview.
47   Ashton interview. See also Natalie Robehmed, "Slums to cities: street art's Pied Piper," CNN, July 31, 2011, http://edition.cnn.com/2011/WORLD/asiapcf/07/31/slum.street.art/ and Kaid Ashton's blog, "Poverty Paste: Series 1/3," July 26, 2011, http://kaidashton.blogspot.jp/2011/07/poverty-paste-series-13.html; "People in Poverty: Series 2/3," August 6, 2011, http://kaidashton.blogspot.jp/2011/08/people-in-poverty-series-23.html, "People in Poverty: Series 2/3," August 22, 2011, http://kaidashton.blogspot.jp/2011/08/people-in-poverty-series-33.html.
48   Robehmed, "Slums to cities."
49   Kaid Ashton's blog, "Dignity in Labour: Beijing 1/2," September 15, 2011, http://kaidashton.blogspot.jp/2011/09/dignity-in-labour-beijing-12.html; "Dignity in Labour: Beijing 2/2," September 21, 2011, http://kaidashton.blogspot.jp/2011/09/dignity-in-labour-beijing-22.html.
50   Kaid Ashton's blog, "Women: Strong and Confident 1/3," November 7, 2011, http://kaidashton.blogspot.jp/2011/11/women-strong-and-confident-13.html.
51   Ibid. For the whole series, see also "Women: Strong and Confident 2/3," November 17, 2011, http://kaidashton.blogspot.jp/2011/11/women-strong-and-confident-23.html; "Women: Strong and Confident 3/3," December 6, 2011, http://kaidashton.blogspot.jp/2011/12/women-strong-and-confident-33.html.
52   Kaid Ashton, email message to author, May 14, 2013.
53   Kaid Ashton's blog, "Pictures for the People," April 16, 2011, http://kaidashton.blogspot.jp/2011/04/pictures-for-people.html.
54   Ibid.
55   Kaid Ashton's blog, "Inspirational Friends," October 1, 2011, http://kaidashton.blogspot.jp/2011/10/inspirational-friends.html.
56   Kaid Ashton's blog, "Saskatchewan to Sri Lanka," February 20, 2012, http://kaidashton.blogspot.jp/2012/02/saskatchewan-to-sri-lanka.html.
57   Kaid Ashton's blog, "Saskatchewan Skies to Guangzhou Smog," March 27, 2012, http://kaidashton.blogspot.jp/2012/03/saskatchewan-skies-to-guangzhou-smog.html.
58   Ashton, interview.
59   For some of the original photographs, see Kaid Ashton's blog, "The Doorways of Sri Lanka," March 3, 2012, http://kaidashton.blogspot.jp/2012/03/doorways-of-sri-lanka.html.
60   Kaid Ashton's blog, "Through the Doors," April 16, 2013, http://kaidashton.blogspot.jp/2013_04_01_archive.html.
61   Ashton, interview; Kaid Ashton's blog, "Through the Doors."
62   Ashton, interview.
63   I was personally able to see the collaborations with local Jams and Xeme in Hong Kong in 2013.
64   Ashton, interview. See e.g., Kaid Ashton's blog, "Free Ceschi," September 12, 2013, http://kaidashton.blogspot.jp/2013/09/free-ceschi.html.
65   Ashton, interview. See also, for example, Kaid Ashton's blog, "Kaput and Kaid Ashton Collaborative Series," January 1, 2014, http://kaidashton.blogspot.jp/2014_01_01_archive.html, see also "Kaput x Kaid Ashton collaboration walls," Juxtapoz, December 28, 2013, http://www.juxtapoz.com/graffiti/kaput-x-kaid-ashton-collaboration-walls. The exhibition opened on December 7, 2013.
66   Kaid Ashton's blog, "Kaput and Kaid Ashton Collaborative Series."
67   Ashton, interview.
68   Ashton, interview.
69   Only three articles have been published: Sin, "Signs of the Times"; Mendoza, "Take It to the Streets"; Mitch Moxley, "Artist's mission brightens poor neighborhoods," June 3, 2011, CNN, http://www.cnngo.com/explorations/life/artists-mission-brighten-neighborhoods-446751. For a brief video interview, see Nick P., 'Kaid Ashton In Los Angeles,' published in June 21, 2013, http://www.youtube.com/watch?v=oMvrAayPpQA. A Filipino television company did make a short interview but it was apparently never released (Balaguer, interview). Ashton is not mentioned in either of the two books on graffiti in Hong Kong: Tsan-Kuo Chang and Chung-Linn Kao, 塗鴉香港：公共空間、政治與全球化 Graffiti Hong Kong: Public space, politics and globalization (Hong Kong: City University of Hong Kong Press, 2012); Yingxuan Kuang (ed.) 塗鴉 [Graffiti], (Hong Kong: 上書局 UpPublications, 2011). Nor does he appear in the latest compilations such as Rafael Schacter, The World Atlas of Street Art and Graffiti (New Haven & London: Yale University Press, 2013); Anna Wacławek, Graffiti and Street Art (London: Thames & Hudson, 2011).
70   Ashton, interview.
71   Ashton, interview; Sin, "Signs of the Times."
72   Valjakka, "Contesting the levels of il/legality."
73   Deva Lee, "The story behind Cape Town's newest street mural," April 24, 2014, matador network, http://matadornetwork.com/change/story-behind-cape-towns-newest-street-mural/.
74   Kwong Chi Kit, interview with the author, April 18, 2013, Hong Kong.
75   Ashton, interview.
76   Ashton, interview.

Felipe Carrelli, Ocupe Carrinho Project/Filmmaker
felipecarrelli@gmail.com
Juliana M. M. Soares, Ocupe Carrinho Project/Mastering in Production Engineering
Univesidade Federal de São Carlos – Sorocaba campus
julianammsoares@gmail.com

The Margin in the Center:
the birth of Project Occupy the Car in the Santa Cecilia's district

The urban area of the city of São Paulo was organized to promote the movement operations and the commercial transactions. Today, with a population around 12 million inhabitants, the city faces a serious problem of urban mobility, compounded by lack of urban planning and incentive policies favoring the auto industry in detriment to the public transportation. Thus, a new problem arises: the abandonment of cars. There are more than 1,400 abandoned cars only in the metropolitan region of the city, and dump yards are almost crowded. Hence the cars remain in this patrimonial limbo status (not constituting a private property, they have been abandoned by the owners, nor public, because they remain on public roads even after complaints from residents). The negligence and inefficiency of the government to collect the carcasses is intensified in devalued districts, where some cars arrive to remain stationed for years without any action. Over time, these vehicles end up turning into garbage containers and debris. The abandoned car stimulates the local population a sense of detachment with the space due to the deficiency arose, and therefore the visual pollution generated decrying the landscape and affecting the relationship which the individual sees his own environment. In this context, it created the Ocupe Carrinho (Occupy the Car) project, with the goal of using urban intervention as a tool of redefinition of public spaces. With the participation of the local community, dirty carcass becomes a colorful gardener via cleaning, painting and placement of plants in it. By bringing a ludic alternative to this process, integrating the community through this event, it is proposed a different interaction with the space, to suggest a new attitude towards their own community and its problems. The Occupy Car project was presented as one of the possible ways of exercising that kind of local action, performing over two years and twelve interventions, identifying on the communities a desire to reappropriate the space where they live.

Introduction

In the current brazilian reality, owning a car symbolizes progress, coupled to multiple status values to society. The incentive to production and consumption are part of the strategies of the government to improve the economy, such as the existence of policies that favor the automobile industry since the 1950s. (SANTOS & BURITY, 2002). However, this approach fosters an uncontrolled scene in broad areas, such as environmental, urban and social. Since the continuous extraction of natural resources, increased pollution, overflowing waste on the streets, going to the isolation of individuals in the midst of living under a tangle of traffic, urgently emerges with the need of questioning about the way that the routes in the city are taking, in terms of urban mobility.

The possibility of using the car as artistic medium of expression and creativity of the local culture, to perform a redefinition of the object and its surroundings, as well as an individual medium that travels through the streets for collective expression, appropriate by the streets, and also on the question of the status of junk and gray reality, to the level of artistry filled with colors, ranging from urban nuisance to the object of social inquiry, will be the topics discussed in this article. **São Paulo: The tenuous threshold between chaos and the proliferation of ideas**

> *"(...) The neighborhood is the core where exist the relationships that give rise to the popular. (...)*
> *In the popular neighborhood, traditions, practices, networks and strategies of rural origin are*
> *adapted to the urban context, creating a cultural syncretism. Many of the neighborhoods were*
> *popular culture."* (Ruiz et al., 2013:32)

São Paulo modeled itself over the years according to a known premise of urban literatures, which reports that the contemporary capitalist city became the place of consumption, and consumption of place (ACSERALD, 2013). Urban space was organized to promote circulation operations and transactions of a commercial nature. Over the years, however, the real state speculation has become one of the main economic activities of the city. The neighborhood of Santa Cecilia was one of the first settlements of high class São Paulo, and his story begins around 1860s, when a group of residents asked the city government the permission to the erection of a wooden chapel (Ponciano, 2004). The centrality of the region within the capital and the large lands in the neighborhood were interesting to the construction of the mansions, owned by coffee farmers, which initially occupied the area in a high proportion. However, events such as the Great Depression (crisis of 1929) and a Brazilian political movement known as the Revolution of 1930, reverberated negatively in the region, causing many demolitions of houses, making way for construction of buildings , and thus giving space to such initial speculation. Common was the emergence of precarious collective dwellings, such as pensions and tenements, settling in houses that remained in the neighborhood. Later, from the 1970s , another process would contribute to the collapse of the central municipality: the transfer of offices and business rooms to the area of Paulista Avenue (Wikipedia, 2014), which appears today as a major locations in the city, and also, as one of the most important financial centers in the country.

Policies of Incentive to individual transport present on the 1970s initiated roadworks that potentially qualify the city for such situation of economic strength, such as the construction of the elevated road President Costa e Silva (popularly known as Minhocão), set in the region that covers much of important central avenues (such as São João and General Olympio da Silveira) (Barbosa, 2012). However , the evolutionary decay due to the great social impact arising by this little reflective speech development , was one of the major results generated for regions present in the surroundings of such works.

In the sum of this path, the center underwent a process of gradual abandonment of public power, becoming occupied largely by prostitution activities, illegal trade in electronics, gambling houses, homeless populations and drug traffickers. In this region emerged the Cracolândia, a popular designation for a region where historically developed the intense traffic of drug known as crack, being São Paulo recognized as the first place in Brazil to have records connected with the presence of this type of narcotic (Raupp & Adorno, 2011).

However, the economic depreciation of the region brought itself many cultural groups that began to develop its activities, attracted by the opportunity of financial sustainability, afforded by fixing in these places. In the late 1950's, there the foundation of the Theatre Workshop at the Faculty of Law of São Paulo University, by José Celso Martinez Correa. It was at this place that was launched a major manifesto of Brazilian culture, the tropicalism, a kind of retelling held back in 1960 of the texts of the Oswald de Andrade's anthropophagic movement (Patriota, 2003), exerting strong influence on musicians, poets, among others artists. In the late 1950s, a movement called Marginal Cinema was developed mainly in the region that became known as Boca do Lixo (Mouth of Trash) of São Paulo, next to streets around the subway station called Luz, as well the Vitória and Triunfo streets (Thibis, 2013). The marginal filmmakers denied the dualistic view of a split between Brazil rural and urban. Cities begin to be also portrait of the country, being placed in the scene trivial figures found in these urban landscapes (Ramos, 2005).

These and other movements made explicit the cultural effervescence of the region at the time, concerning of various cultural groups in dialogue with the local reality where they were inserted. The neighborhoods located in downtown São Paulo became to have a national relevance again, but differently the past; such importance appears placed in the cultural, and not more on the economic. These neighborhoods begin to stop being devalued and abandoned sites, starting to be recognized as locals of creative and cultural experiences. This situation has caused more people and projects were trooping over the years, inspired and driven by the success of its predecessors.

However, the artistic and cultural development of the region does not alleviate social inequality produced by the cumulative public abandonment. The many years of neglect have produced an enormous inequality environmental and urban living conditions between richer and poorer areas of the city itself (Rede Nossa São Paulo, 2013). Cleanliness , urbanism and especially basic infrastructure issues, are present in extremely different heights, confronting the realities found in these different neighborhoods .

The abandonment situation is so serious that even social and cultural restoration projects are distanced from the center of the poorest neighborhoods. It can be cited the case of the Virada Cultural event, which is sponsored by the city of São Paulo every year since 2005, with the aim of promoting continuous 24 hours of cultural events in the city (Amorim, 2011), stimulating the rebirth of downtown by bringing paulistanos for the region, which usually empties and becomes a zone of high vulnerability during the night . However , the program does not reach the region known as baixo centro (low- center), located on the outskirts of Minhocão, comprising the districts of Santa Cecília, Vila Buarque, Campos Elísios, Barra Funda and Luz.

The Ocupe Carrinho (Occupy the Car) project
It was like a response to this abandonment that emerged the Festival Baixo Centro (Low-Center Festival) in 2012. With the motto "The Streets Are For Dancing", is born a collaborative street festival that sought to encourage the appropriation of public space by the community precisely in this region. The Baixo Centro sought the occupation of public space by the people who, in fact, belongs, motivating an understanding of that space (Baixocentro, 2013), and greater interaction of people with their everyday traffic areas, work or housing.
A movement of civil occupation that had the proposed to open, hack and dispute the streets. All production steps were made of horizontal, associative, open and free form. There was no institution behind this organization: companies, NGOs or government. The funding was also collective and associative , via crowdfunding and other independent forms of storage (such as auction, raffle and donations). The production of the Festival was to hosted by the Casa de Cultura Digital (House of Digital Culture), a coworking space, where people, ideas and projects circulate daily. Through the stimulus created by the cultural effervescence of the Festival, there was the creation of the Ocupe Carrinho (Occupy the Car) project.
The Occupy the Car Project is an initiative of collective artistic intervention. Initially created by Felipe Carreli, Tobias Rodil and Thiago Carvalhaes, the collective now has fixed integrants (Juliana M. M. Soares and Leila Lobato Graef), as well as non-fixed collaborators. The group started in 2012 and its first action was taken as part of the programming of the Festival Baixo Centro, by the time that an abandoned car that had turned a place for dump was located by the group, near the headquarters of the Casa de Cultura (where the initial three active integrants were working at the time), in the neighborhood of Santa Cecilia. Thus was born the proposed project, occupying the car with the help of the surrounding community. With the participation of some friends and this local community, there was the cleaning, painting and placement of plants in remnants of this car, turning the dirty carcass in a colorful flower pot in the open.
The initial idea was to make only one pontual intervention, but with the success of this first act, new cars abandoned on the city were mapped , and the project was gaining unexpected contours. Currently, Occupy the Car totals up eleven actions, eight in the city of São Paulo (São Paulo – Brazil), one in the city of Brasilia (Distrito Federal – Brazil), one in Manaus (Amazonas – Brazil), and one outside Brazil, made in Buenos Aires, in Argentina.

History of interventions
Carro Jardineira (Dungarees Car)
The first intervention, conducted in 2012, had the participation of over 20 people. The big point of this first activity was to see how participants leave their personal brands in the work through various forms such as painting, plants and even toys. It is noteworthy that children, the elderly, youth and the homeless were united around the action, located in the Santa Cecília neighborhood.

Carro Girafa (Giraffe Car)[1]
Performed one year after the first action, the Carro Girafa was again connected to the Baixo Centro Festival, also in the vicinity of the Santa Cecília district. The work inaugurated an approach linked to the animal figure, a constant intention present on the consequent interventions.

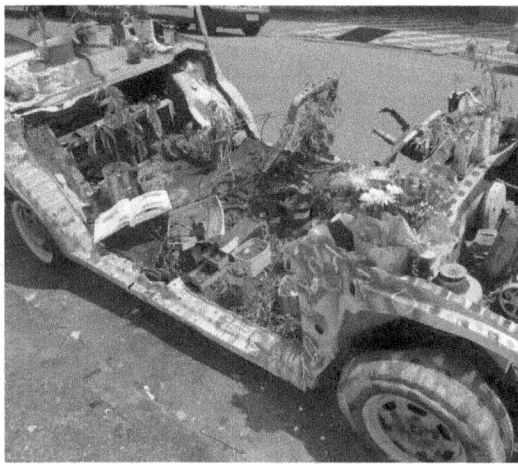

Fig. 1. The first one, Carro Jardineira (Dungarees Car). Source: Felipe Carrelli

Fig. 2. The Carro Girafa (Giraffe Car). Source: Felipe Carrelli

Carro Tartaruga (Turtle Car)[2]
Also part of the second edition of Festival Baixo Centro, the Carro Tartaruga was striking the project, because for the first time there was a big media coverage, through international vehicles (as Inhabitat (USA), Kombini (France), Weibo-i- House (China), Kulturologia (Russia), among others) and national vehicles (e.g. Zupi Land, G1, Globo). The intervention occurred in april 2013, in the Santa Cecília district.

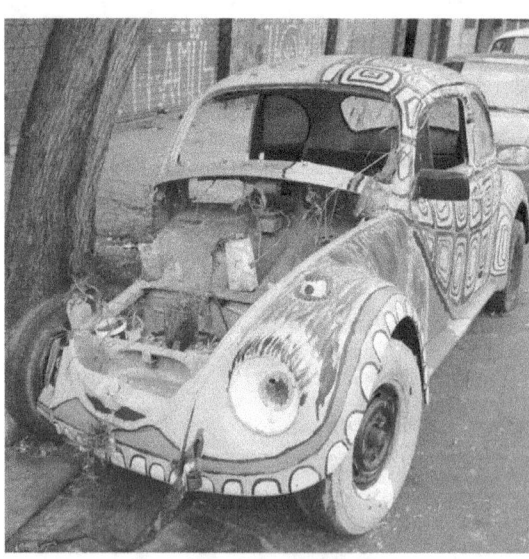

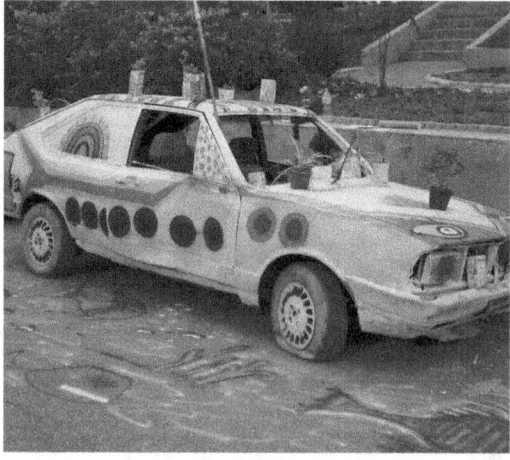

Fig. 4. Carro Submarino (Submarine Car). Source: Felipe Carrelli

Fig. 3. Carro Tartaruga (Turtle Car). Source: Felipe Carrelli

Carro Submarino Amarelo (Yellow Submarine Car)[3]
Held on the eve of International Car-free Day (commemorated in the date of September 22th, 2013), the idea was the dialogue with the Bicicletada Movement, very present in São Paulo, which promotes debates about the rights to city cyclists. The motto of the intervention, occured in São Paulo city, dealt with a playful banter in the absence of the car everyday, being created a slogan referring to the idea: in the International Car-free day, go by submarine.

Carro Boi (Ox Car)[4]

Carro Boi was an intervention carried out in partnership with the "Não Mate" (Do Not Kill) movement, a group of graphic action against speciesism, which promotes debate about Animal Rights through art. The car was located in downtown of São Paulo, and it had been abandoned for about three months. The actvity was performed also with the community collaboration, which hold some plants to their homes at the end of the intervention.

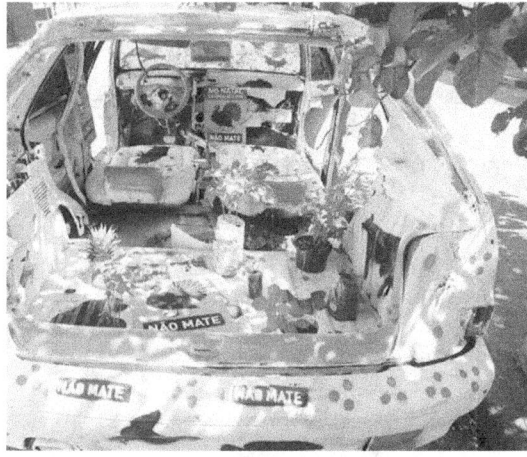
Fig. 5. Carro Boi (Ox Car).
Source: Felipe Carrelli

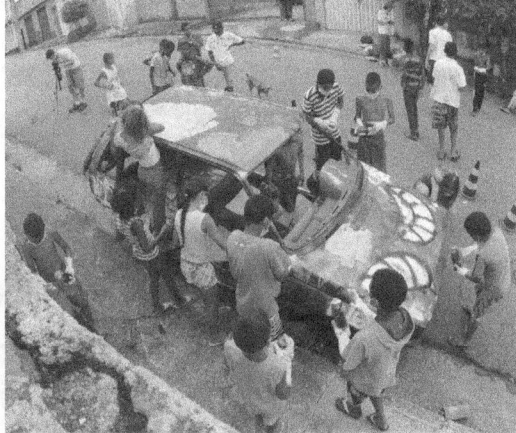
Fig. 6. Carro Tatu Bola (Armadillo Ball Car) and the kids.
Source: Felipe Carrelli

Carro Tatu Bola (Armadillo Ball Car)[5]

The Carro Tatu Bola was an intervention conducted in partnership with the Entretodos Festival of 2014 (6th Festival of Short Films on Human Rights). A workshop was held in a school of the Butantã district of São Paulo, and the action was divided into two parts: at first, a theoretical part, and after, the practical. In the first part, the dialogue on building affective territoriality (the link to the space, a theme of the Festival) and the relationship with our proposed intervention, referrals and documentaries urban of interventions were shown. In the second part of the workshop, an intervention was taken in an abandoned car in the region, with the participation of more than 20 children in the community. The video that recorded all the action was displayed at the opening of the Festival awards ceremony.

Carro Tamanduá (Anteater Car)[6]

As part of the desire to expand the project to other cities and states of Brazil, an intervention outside the city of São Paulo was first made, in 2014. An abandoned car was located in a satellite city of São Sebastião (Distrito Federal - Brazil), and thus occurred the painting of a giant anteater, named after the animal symbol of the cerrado, beyond the placement of native flowers on the vehicle.

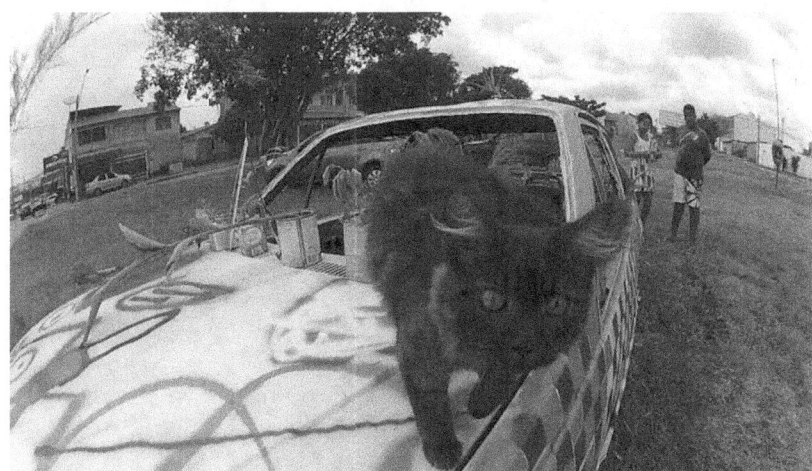
Fig. 7. A cat on the Carro Tamanduá (Anteater Car).
Source: Felipe Carrelli

Carro Galo (Rooster Car)[7]

Carro Galo was inspired by the work of brazilian artist Adriana Varejao, which has grounded its work in very idea of rereading visual elements incorporated into the Brazilian culture by colonization, such as the painting of Portuguese tiles. During this intervention, a resident in doubt about the purpose of the collective action called the military police, claiming that occurred a chop on the vehicle. Two cars and three motorcycles were displaced to the location of the occupation, and about ten police officers were involved. However, there was no assessment or larger implications with regard to work, when they realized that this was an artistic intervention. The artistic act was performed in February 2014, in a central district of the city of São Paulo.

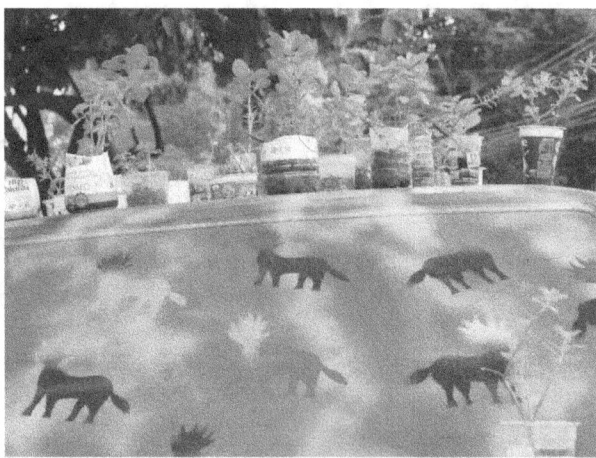

Fig. 9. Some stencils applied on the surface of the Carro Mula (Mule Car).
Source: Felipe Carrelli

Carro Cobra (Snake Car)[8]

The Carro Cobra was made during the workshop on urban art in UNICINE Festival, in march of 2014, held at the State University of Amazonas (UEA). This was the first project contemplated by the Exchange Program and Cultural Diffusion of the Culture Ministry. The workshop was held in collaboration with a local artist, and the chosen animal was influenced by a legend in the region, recited in the video intervention. This art occupation occured in Manaus (Amazonas – Brazil).

Carro Mula (Mule Car)[9]

This intervention was performed in april of 2014, in Butantã District, São Paulo (SP – Brazil), as a workshop for kids of the region. The car was a homage to a brazilian legend, called the legend of headless mule.

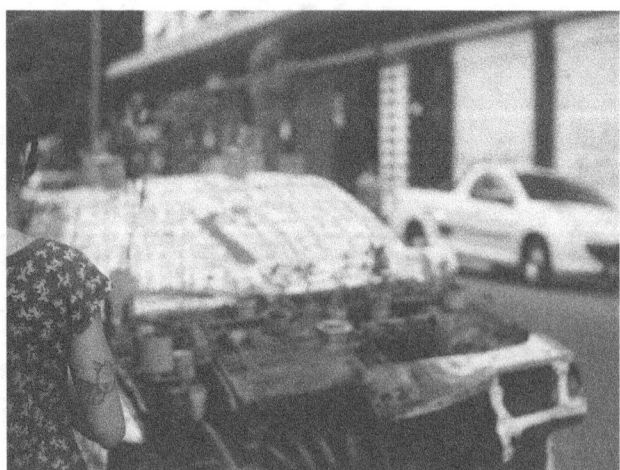

Fig. 8. The blue, red and white Carro Galo (Rooster Car).
Source: Juliana M. M. Soares

Carro Carricho[10]

The Carricho was the first intervention performed outside Brazil, held in Buenos Aires, Argentina. The abandoned car used as plataform for this intervention was located in the La Boca neighborhood, region well known for its vivid colors, which served as inspiration to the art of the car, held in May 2014.

Santa Cecilia: a cradle for orphan cars

The opinion of the community regarding the project was always positive. Besides that, the project managed to reach opposing vehicles of national and international communication. Many alternative media groups (such as environmental movements, urban mobility groups, culture and art websites) reproduced information about the project in their channels. On the other hand the mass media and national television networks, magazines, newspapers and other large internet portals, also divulged the Occupy the Car. It is believed that this unexpected acceptance comes from the fact that we are dealing with an patrimonial limbo. The cars are not private goods because they are abandoned by owners. Nor public because they remain in their places even after numerous complaints from the residents. Thus the project is not labeled as "vandalism", a term commonly used by the more conservative press to describe various types of urban intervention projects.

Moreover, it is remarkable the high incidence of abandoned cars in Sao Paulo. It appears that this problem is even more serious in the Santa Cecilia neighborhood. This fact is importante to understand the importance of the project within the urban context of the city, and in particular, in the neighborhood where the project was born. According to a survey of a news website11, there are over 1400 cars in situations of abandonment only in the metropolitan region of the city, and dump yards are almost crowded, with no capacity for more cars.

> "It turns out, however, that capitalist activity does not just produce sellable goods, but also "no goods" unsaleable; so we have to consider the functional existence of places - in major urban part - not intended for consumer activity, as a forum to launch the accumulation of undesirable products - the so calls sacrifice zones, which receive all sorts of waste, wastewater and gas from the production of goods12. "(Acserald, 2013:241)

During one of our interventions, the Ox Car, three abandoned cars were mapped on the same block. Of the twelve interventions already undertaken by the project to this day, five of these were held in the Santa Cecilia neighborhood. The reason for such a concentration in that particurlar neighborhood can be explained by two reasons.

First, the region presents a wide range of car's workshops. Sometimes the service to fix the vehicle can be more expensive than the resale value of the car itself, causing the abandonment of the owner. The owner of the workshops is exempt from taking legal action, and end up parking the car of their customers in the driveway. An example of such a situation is the fact ocurred with the vehicle of the Turtle Car intervention. According to one neighbor, the car was abandoned for five years in a workshop, and then was parked in the driveway.

The second reason why the region has a high concentration of abandoned vehicles is the fact that it is an economically disadvantaged region, and the policing in this place is quite weak. For several moments cars are found with plates from other cities, and even other states. Hypothetically, it can be supposed that they would be stolen cars abandoned in the region by offering no danger of being tracked, as well by the motive that these cars would be quickly disassembled by homeless people present there (which resell for insignificant values in the surrounding neighborhood). After contact with the prefecture, and also by verbalizations of local citizens, it was discovered that there is a pattern for the removal of cars procedure. To complete the understanding of this process, an information obtained by the spokesperson for of the Municipal Coordinating Subprefectures gave the understanding about the modus operandi of the government.

After an complaint of abandoned car on public roads, a sticker or a paper is placed on the vehicle, stating that it must be removed within five working days, and from that moment, the subprefecture initiates procedures to check the vehicle history, with police and transit departments, and they check if the car is the product of a crime or have some sort of pending litigation. Thus, being no statutory impediment and absence of the owner, after the period of five working days, the subprefecture returns to the street and, if it is found that the vehicle remains in the same place, the team initiates the removal procedure.

If the owner is not found and the vehicle does not have legal disputes, the car shall be considered waste. Also according to Subprefecture, regarding the Law 13.478/02[13], it is forbidden to deposit rubbish, dirt and residues of any kind on public roads. In several cases, in conversations with residents who participated in the intervention, it was found that the abandoned cars remained for two months or more after the request for the removal of the vehicle, like the reported example of a car that was parked on public streets for two years. Often the car ended up turning into dormitory for the homeless people due to this bureaucratic delay. Other end to the car is the sale of parts by the homeless people. Still, it is observed that the rapid action of the city council was taken only in more affluent neighborhoods.

A clear example of this situation of neglect occurred in 2012, one week after the first intervention of Occupy the Car. The BijaRi collective[14] was integrating an exhibition called State of Siege, with its Carro Verde art (Green Car in english, consisted by an old vehicle filled with plants). The car was parked in front of an art gallery, called Choque Cultural, where the exhibition took place, located in Pinheiros, an upscale neighborhood of the city of São Paulo. The vehicle existed since 2009 and was exhibited at International Architecture Biennale 2009, in the Virada Cultural event of 2010, and also in an exhibition of Matilha Cultural in 2011. When the car was not attending exhibitions, the vehicle was parked in front of the headquarter group. The car was arrested by the municipality in just a few days after someone complained. The abandoned cars was taken to the courtyard, and a fee of R$ 12,000 is charged. This rate was imposed to the Carro Verde too, even after explaining the misunderstanding. After much discussion, the group gave up to recover the work.

This position of the São Paulo Municipality regarding urban interventions is not new. The documentary Cidade Cinza, directed by William Valiengo and Marcelo Mesquita, shows that the public policies of the City of Sao Paulo go even against the graffiti movement, erasing with gray paint the work of graffiti artists. This hygienist public policy contradicts itself at the same time enabling and opening panels of graffiti in downtown. The government ignores an entire culture, overlaying it with a layer of gray paint on behalf of an aesthetic bias, as it is observed in all this - except when a media pressure and political burden is negative.

There is still the case occurred in 2013, when the São Paulo Municipality erased a panel made by plastic artists Os Gemeos, internationally renowned exhibitors enshrined in galleries outside of Brazil. After their work was erased, the artists came back and recorded a protest: "Mr. Mayor: In this city there are many serious problems that need results not spend time and money erasing graffiti in the streets".

The experience of Occupy the Car project was not different. It was found that after painting the cars and the consequent dissemination of interventions in media vehicles, the city quickly withdrew the cars. The second intervention of the group, the Carro Girafa, is an example of that. The group discovered an old abandoned car called Opala that was there about three months parked and unclaimed, filthy and filled with rubble and garbage. Just two days after the intervention, the car had been taken to the courtyard. An important and peculiar caveat: the bags with garbage that were removed from the carcass and left near a pole to be collected by the garbage truck, was left behind by the government truck that take the car away.

It is evident the aforementioned contradiction of government: do not remove the abandoned car that accumulate trash and debris, which may become foci of urban pests, but strip away artistic works. It appears then, that there a social consequence such interventions: just paint the vehicles that it will be removed promptly. We realize that besides the ludic side of reframing the car image, there is also another clear meaning behind the project: the protest. This may not necessarily be the primary goal but shows why this work made on the streets is efficient somehow.

Final Thoughts: Urban intervention as a tool for redefinition of public spaces

> "The spaces educate. Creative spaces generate creative people. Our landscape is part of what we are. The city built from a functionalist logic mechanizes the life, without leaving room for creative construction of a free imagination. For spaces that do not oppress, but release and encourage experimentation and experience15." (Popo, 2013:81)

Over those two years, the interventions were performed in different neighborhoods, making contact with people from different social classes, different levels of education and ages. The acceptance of this audience was unanimous. In neither case there were problems with the public and/or the local community authorities. Rather, the active participation of communities and the praise to the project are constants.

This spontaneous activity has several justifications, and it varies in an interindividual way. But we can identify mostly a desire, a need to reclaim the space they live in. The abandoned car stimulates in people a sense of detachment with the space. The accumulation of garbage and the consequent visual pollution detracts from the landscape and affect the relationship with the individual who sees his own half. The public indifference towards this problem discourages further resident. The claim is not effective, then the citizen can do anything, having to accept the abandonment as a form of everyday existence, and that vehicle forgotten as a non-conquest of the landscape where you live. As a way to avoid the hassle, the individual closes itself, by taking a passive way, taking the carcass and turning it into an invisible being, like an annoying neighbor that we have to accept.

It is noteworthy that in a city like São Paulo, this process occurs not only with the car without an owner, but it is a recurring activity in underdeveloped urban environment: we learn to ignore the social problems, violence, congestion, poor condition of public transportation, lack of leisure and entertainment. The individual is influenced, but can not influence. With the pressure of the huge metropolis, this bureaucratic and impersonal organization, he gradually forgets his potential, and gives up its civic role. Slowly becomes more and more passive in relation of his decisions, and feels that your power of influence is increasingly derisive. The attitude becomes to be the blaming of this structure, without even questioning our own responsibility for what criticizes. He becomes the agent of this structure that he, himself, is responsible for his dissatisfaction.

Occupy the Car brings a ludic alternative to this process. This painting is an invitation to childhood and back to our past, when people used to play on the streets. The paint has a very strong power over the individual and collective imaginary. It bothers, attracts, transforms. The ink removes the invisibility of the car. It is now not only a substrate, but an artistic expression of creativity support. A huge panel in the open, unclaimed, waiting to be painted. And with room for everyone.

The main purpose is to interact with the community through this event, propose a different interaction with your space, and thus, suggesting a new community attitude towards itself and its problems. We use urban intervention as a tool for redefinition of public spaces. We present such a tool and returned the decision to the hands of the community, saying that, yes, it can make a decision without asking for that bureaucratic government, that ignores. The community again is responsible for the space itself.

Sure it's just a sparkle, but heading for a potential major change. But still, it may be a begining. The plants that are left in cars have an important symbolic value. Planting a seed, an idea. But it is the community who must care for it, showering – so, that there is germination. This was the case of Yellow Submarine Car. After two years of this intervention, the community had already given up asking the municipality to remove the vehicle. The intervention included the mass participation of the community, especially since the car has been parked in a square, and be a place of passage for many residents of local buildings. Six months after, the car was still there, and according to Veronica Couto (a resident in the area that reported that the group the existence of the car, and also integrated the action): The submarine cart is still here. I think it will continue for another decade! (laughs). They like him, is the ornament of the street... We put water in plants ever!

Notes and References

1 Video of Carro Girafa intervention, retrieved January, 29, 2014, from the World Web Wide: <http://vimeo.com/62217681> 2 Video of Carro Tartaruga intervention, retrieved January, 30, 2014, from the World Web Wide: <http://vimeo.com/63266943>
3 Video of Carro Submarino intervention, retrieved January, 28, 2014, from the World Web Wide: <http://vimeo.com/75145576>
4 Video of Carro Boi intervention, retrieved February, 11, 2014, from the World Web Wide: <http://vimeo.com/80855287>
5 Video of Carro Tatu Bola intervention, retrieved February, 19, 2014, from the World Web Wide: <http://vimeo.com/81520283>
6 Video of Carro Tamanduá intervention, retrieved February, 28, 2014, from the World Web Wide: <http://vimeo.com/83695172>
7 Video of Carro Galo intervention, retrieved May, 22, 2014, from the World Web Wide: <http://vimeo.com/85727433>
8 Video of Carro Cobra intervention, retrieved May, 22, 2014, from the World Web Wide: <http://vimeo.com/90819416>
9 Video of Carro Mula intervention, retrieved May, 22, 2014, from the World Web Wide: <http://vimeo.com/94994357>
10 Video of Carro Carricho intervention, retrieved May, 22, 2014, from the World Web Wide: <http://vimeo.com/96013813>
11This information was available at: http://g1.globo.com/sao-paulo/mapa-carros-abandonados/platb/. Retrieved February, 24, 2014, from the World Web Wide.
12 Translated by the authors. Original text: "Acontece, entretanto, que a atividade capitalista não produz apenas mercadorias vendáveis, mas também "não mercadorias" invendáveis; temos assim de considerar a existência funcional de lugares – em grande parte urbanos – não destinados à atividade de consumo, que servirão de espaço ao lançamento dos produtos indesejáveis da acumulação – as chamadas zonas de sacrifício, que receberão toda sorte de resíduos, efluentes líquidos e gasosos resultantes da produção de mercadorias."\
13 This assertion is contained in chapter VI - Sweeping and cleaning the conservation, Law 13.478/02, of November 30, 2002. Retrieved February, 26, 2014, from the World Web Wide: <Http://ww2.prefeitura.sp.gov.br//arquivos/ secretarias/financas/legislacao/Lei-13478-2002.pdf>
14 The report about this intervention of the BijaRi collective is available at: <http://vilamundo.org.br/2012/03/obra-de-arte-do-coletivo-bijari-e-guinchada-pela-prefeitura/> Retrieved February, 26, 2014, from the World Web Wide.
15 Translated by the authors. Original text: "Os espaços educam. Espaços criativos geram pessoas criativas. Nossa paisagem faz parte do que nós somos. A cidade construída a partir de uma lógica funcionalista mecaniza a vida sem deixar espaço para a construção criativa de um imaginário livre. Por espaços que não oprimam, mas que libertem e estimulem a experiência e a experimentação."
ACSERALD, H. Cidade – Espaço Público? A economia política do consumismo nas e das cidades. Rev. UFMG, Belo Horizonte, v. 20, n.1, p.234-247, jan-jun/2013.
AMORIM, F. C. M. A. Virada Cultural Paulista: promoção e democratização da cultura. In: Biblioteca Latino-Americana de Cultura e Comunicação. 1: Trabalhos de Conclusão de Curso (TCC-CELACC). Universidade de São Paulo (USP). Escola de Comunicações e Artes. 2011. 15 p.
BARBOSA, Eliana Rosa de Queiroz. Minhocão e suas múltiplas interpretações. Arquitextos, São Paulo, ano 13, n. 147.03, Vitruvius, ago/2012.
JORGE, C. De A. Santa Cecília: Contrastes e Confronto. São Paulo: DPH, 2006. 144 p.
MOVIMENTO BAIXOCENTRO. Baixo Centro: O grito dos outros. VIrus, São Carlos, n. 9, 2013. Retrieved February, 15, 2014, from the World Wide Web:<http://www.nomads.usp.br/virus/_virus09/secs/carpet/virus_09_carpet_43_pt.pdf>.
PATRIOTA, R. A cena tropicalista no Teatro Oficina de São Paulo. História, São Paulo, vol. 22 n.1, p. 135-163, 2003.
PONCIANO, L. São Paulo: 450 bairros, 450 anos. São Paulo: Senac, 2004. 358
PORO. Manifesto: por uma cidade lúdica e coletiva, por uma arte pública, crítica e poética. Rev. UFMG, Belo Horizonte, v. 20, n.1, pp.78-89, jan-jun/2013.
RAUPP, L.; ADORNO, R de C. F. Circuitos de uso de crack na região central da cidade de São Paulo (SP - Brasil). Ciência & Saúde Coletiva. Rio de Janeiro. vol. 16, n. 5, p. 2613-2622, 2011.
RAMOS, A. F. Para um estudo das representações da cidade e do campo no cinema brasileiro (1950-1968). Fênix – Revista de História e Estudos Culturais. Vol. 2, y. 2, n. 2. Apr-jun/2005.
REDE NOSSA SÃO PAULO. Quadro da desigualdade em São Paulo. 2013. 93 p. Retrieved February, 10, 2014, from the World Wide Web: <http://www.nossasaopaulo.org.br/portal/arquivos/Quadro-da-Desigualdade-em-Sao-Paulo-2013.pdf>
RUIZ, A. M.; PARK, J. K.; PERUGACHE, D. ¿Quién diseña lo popular? In: VIII Encuentro Latinoamericano de Diseño 2013. Facultad de Diseño y Comunicación. Universidad de Palermo. Actas de Diseño. Acta n.15. Buenos Aires, Argentina.Vol. 15, pp. 31-34. jul/2013.
SANTOS, A. M. M. M.; BURITY, P. O Complexo Automotivo. In: RIBEIRO, A. D. BNDES 50 Anos - Histórias Setoriais: O Complexo Automotivo. 2003.
THIBIS, F. S. O cinema da boca do lixo. In: II Seminário Nacional Cinema em Perspectiva. Proceedings... Vol. 1, N. 1. Curitiba: UNESPAR/FAP, 2013.
WIKIPEDIA. Santa Cecília (bairro de São Paulo). 2014. Retrieved March, 15, 2014, from the World Wide Web: <http://pt.wikipedia.org/wiki/Santa_Cec%C3%ADlia_(bairro_de_S%C3%A3o_Paulo)>

José Guilherme Abreu, Research Center for Science and Technology of the Arts (CITAR)/Catholic University of Portugal, jgabreu@porto.ucp.pt

Laura Castro,Research Center for Science and Technology of the Arts (CITAR))/Catholic University of Portugal, lcastro@porto.ucp.pt

Paredes' Public Art Circuit.
A Public Art and Community Orientated Program

Paredes' Public Art Circuit (PPAC) is the result of an initiative of the Municipality of Paredes which meant to provide the city with an artwork contemporary collection,capable to generate an urban route that would be able to illustrate the aesthetical diversity of contemporary art, and to express different possibilities of intervention in the public space. In order to implement that program two different structures were created: the Board of Curators(BC),meant to conceive and to achieve its curatorial organization, and the Public Art Lab (PAL), meant to indorse community involvement and creativity, through a broad program of sociocultural initiatives.

Public Art, Public Art Lab, Public Sphere

Utopia translates to not place. Utopia is not a destination, but a direction. Steve Lambert, Utopia Letterpress Prints, 2010

Introduction
Public Art Circuit of Paredes (CAPP) is a public art program promoted by local authorities, as part of a process of urban regeneration in this locality in northern Portugal, situated about 30Km from the city of Porto. The initiative of the Municipality of Paredes sought to upgrade and enhance the public space of the city, linking contemporary art practice with the aim of generating an outgoing atmosphere "for the creative design", which was another important area of improvement promoted by the municipality.

The urban regeneration project was launched by the Office of Architecture Belém Lima Architects, under the coordination of architect António Belém Lima, under technical direction of Manuel João Borges.

As the municipality understood it, the public art circuit was a part of the "creative city", dependent on the process of urban regeneration. Through contacts made, it became clear that for the management and implementation of this vast project supported by European funds from the QREN-National Strategic Reference Framework– the establishing of partnerships was the appropriate model for realizing activities of a specific scientific and/or technological nature, which could be found in external research units that would initiate collaborative work with the local authority.

Artistic Program inceptions
Paredes Public Art Circuit was thus implemented by Research Centre for Science and Technology of the Arts (CITAR), R&D unit of School of Arts da Escola das Artes – Catholic University of Portugal, for Paredes' Municipality, through two fundamental instruments, which divided between them the tasks in the areas of curatorship and community involvement. The first was entrusted to the Board of Curators and the second to the Public Art Lab.

The participation of the Research Centre aimed to give implementation of the Circuit the necessary scientific framework and the appropriate technical support for the actions envisaged. It aimed also to encourage the debate of concepts and theories, test innovative proposals, contribute to reference practices and generate knowledge about the role of local authorities in the field of public art commission and its implementation.

The meetings between the two institutions and the first discussions involving CITAR occurred between January and May2011, and led to the establishment of a protocol between the Porto Regional Centre of the Catholic University of Portugal and the Municipality of Paredes, and the signing of a contract between the two entities in August2011.The first half of 2011 may thus be considered as the start-up phase of the project, corresponding to the definition of its conceptual and operational elements. The subsequent phases of development of the CAPP took place between August2011 and June 2013.

During the initial discussions held in the framework of CITAR, it was decided that the artistic interventions in the urban space of Paredes should arise from different ways of mobilizing the artists. Three models were identified for action:

1.A direct invitation to national and international artists for interventions of a permanent nature;
2.The launching of an international competition to select interventions of the same kind;
3. An invitation to artists and artistic educational institutions for submission of interventions of an ephemeral and performative nature.

These different procedures aimed to ensure the presence of artists with a firmly established curriculum and a proven track record in the artistic world (by means of invitation), but also of younger artists or even those unknown in the artistic world and at the beginning of their artistic careers (through the competition process), as well of projects of an experimental nature, led by emergent artists, art collectives or art schools.

The successive forms of action implied a hierarchy in the choice of sites for intervention, with guest artists choosing the locations on which would act, freeing others for the interventions resulting from the competition, with the remaining spaces being available to the invited artists for temporary facilities. This process, of some complexity, occasionally required negotiations with some artists that led, on the one hand, to ensuring that the location proposed was the most suitable–bearing in mind the understanding that the Council had of the whole project– and on the other hand, ensured that the intrinsic intent of the artist's proposal was not undermined in the event that a move was suggested.

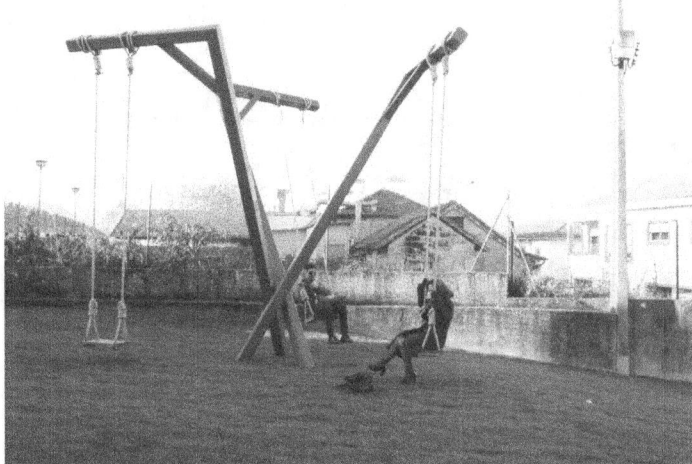

Fig. 1- Didier Fiuza Faustino, Funny Games, 2012, painted iron, wood and rope, Paredes

In no case, were the artists restricted in their field of action, and although this constituted a risky proposition from the point of view of commissioning art for public space, it also seemed the richest, because of the diversity of forms, materials, dimensions, themes and aesthetic models expected.
Decisions would allow the city of Paredes to be provided with eleven permanent artistic installations (seven from invited artists and four selected in the competition); two other permanent installations from students of Education Institutions (School of Arts – Catholic University of Portugal and the Secondary School of Paredes); temporary pieces and performative works made by individual artists, art collectives and students from Faculty of Fine Arts – University of Porto.

Implementation of Paredes Public Art Circuit (CAPP)
Ffrom the very beginning, it was clear to CITAR's team, and also to the municipality, that the implementation of CAPP could not be thought as a mere set ofcontemporary sculptures displayed in the city's public spaces, being one of its goals to organize actions aiming to promote public involvement with the project.
According to Giulio Carlo Argan[1], a city is not an artistic space because it may displayhere and there a few works of art. The city is, first and foremost, in itself, and entirely, a work of art.

And what can turn the city, as a whole, into a successful work of art?
The answer seems obvious to us: the degree of cultural awareness of its inhabitants, and by cultural awareness of the inhabitants we mean the qualitative degree of its collective intervention.
So, whenever the purpose of developing an artistic program is to promote the value of the city as a whole, and not just the value of this or that place or space by means of setting some kind of art work, it becomes imperative to intervene not only in the field of public space, but also to intervene in the public sphere, i.e. to intervene in the realm of interaction with individuals, culminating in the formation of public opinion. Here's how Jürgen Habermas defines the public sphere:

> By "the public sphere" we mean first of all a realm of our social life in which something
> approaching "public opinion" can be formed. Access is guaranteed to all citizens. A portion of
> the public sphere comes into being in every conversation in which private individuals assemble
> to form a public body.[2]

According to Habermas, any intervention in the public sphere is first and foremost an act of citizenship. The central assumption is that the transformation of spaces and the image of the city - urban regeneration - in order to be effective, requires citizen participation, for without their assistance, the goals of rehabilitation become compromised.
The same applies in a more meaningfulway, when the goal is to intervene at the level of the city's image. From a city in which urban structures (such as Squares, Avenues and Gardens); architectural elements (such as Churches, Mansions and Museums); sculptural works (such as Monuments, Statues and Fountains), and street furniture (such as benches, kiosks and street light), compete to embellish the city through a distinction and a clear hierarchy between the utilitarian and decorative functions of informal content, and the symbolic and commemorative records of formal content, there is now an aesthetic dimension in which several layers overlap and relate in a much less differentiated form and, above all, where no clear hierarchy of values is discernible.

For the correct perception of the solutions that are used to produce/upgrade the image of the city, it is therefore crucial to understand and discuss publically the conditions and the means that should engage it, which brings us back to the need to create of a public sphere around these processes. Assured by these notions and premises, we arrived at a model we have called Paredes Public Art Model, which mobilizes and approaches different plans and fields, as shown inthe diagram – fig. 2.

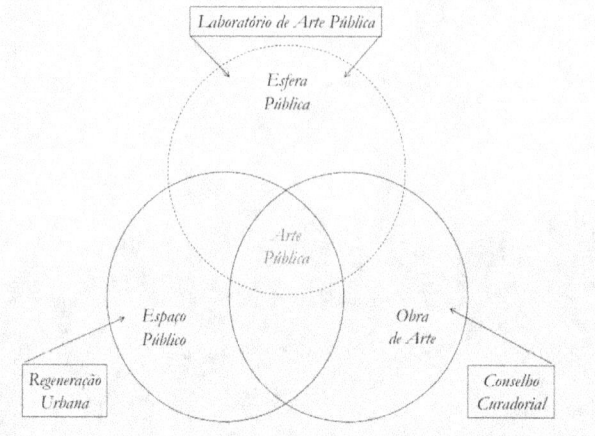

Fig. 2–Paredes Public Art Model

According to this model, we call Public Art to the realm of artistic production formed bythe intersection between the work of art, the public space and the public sphere.

In other words, public art is the field of artistic production in which the artwork is presented and discussed publicly, contributing both to increase the degree of aesthetic consciousness of the citizens, and to indorse of a participatory culture that fosters public appropriation and enjoyment of the artwork, overcoming the difference between public art work and art work in the public space, by the establishment of a public sphere that functions as a mediator in the process of production and reception of the work of art.

Thus, in addition to the operations of adaptation of the public spaces made by the Urban Regeneration team, which intended to create adequate conditions for displaying artistic interventions, and in addition to the work of curators, responsible for the strategies involving the different levels of artistic intervention in the art program (either by direct invitation, or by international tender, conducted by the Board of Curators), it was necessary to create an instrument exclusively devoted to help create a public sphere around the project. That would be the mission of the Paredes Public Art Lab (Laboratório de Arte Pública de Paredes) (LAPP).

Paredes' Public Art Lab Programs

As we have seen, Paredes' Public Art Program had implicit in its conception, a theoretical framework that defines it as a singular and odd study case among public art programming in Portugal, due to the multi-disciplinary and methodological contributions on which it relies, as it was already explained in I Jornadas Internacionales de Investigación Arte y Ciudad[3]:

The theoretical premises [of Paredes Public Art Model] were imposed on us as a strategy to overcome, or rather, to integrate, the a priori unpopular nature of contemporary art, because as already stated, in 1925, by Ortega y Gasset, "All young art is unpopular, and not by chance or accident, but by virtue of its essential purpose."[4]

This is a crucial problem for all public art that purports to be contemporary, and also for all contemporary art that aspires to be public, since both artists and the public, for the most part, are to be found in opposite fields, from the point of view of their cultural references and their aesthetic preferences.

To overcome this dichotomy, we planned a strategy which relied on the theoretic work of art sociologist Nathalie Heinich, in particular her theory of the "Triple Jeu de l'ArtContemporain".

To Nathalie Heinich[5], contemporary art does not represent the totality of today's artistic production, but only a small part, for contemporary art, as she states:

It's an aesthetic category, analogous to what was called in the era of figurative painting a "genre", assuming the fact that what promotes its advancement is a triple play: the playthat sets in motion a chain of reactions: in which the public reacts to the transgressions of the artists, and the critics respond to the public's reactions, where the approval of specialists becomes the acceptance of the institutions, and in turn, the established culture will become, itself, transgressed.[6]

If we accept this theory, we have to realize that the only way to overcome the dichotomy between contemporary art and public reception, is through this very roleplaying between the artists, the public and the specialists, for if anyone tries to prevent, to limit or to stop this role playing, it would only block or distort its dialectics, and in the end would not be able to resolve it or overcome it. That's why, we thought that rather than trying to stop or prevent this play, one should instead be aware that the conflict is the heart and the motor of this dichotomy, and that this conflict should be thought as a legitimate one, equally, in its different facets from the outset, because it is through this play that the very evolution of art pulsates and lives.

The purpose of the Paredes' Public Art Lab was then not to stop this conflict, but to mediate it, opening up new paths and new scenarios for the dialogue and the artistic expression of the Community, through its most active associations and cultural institutions. Through theirteaching, and because theydon't belong to the Contemporary Art System, cultural and artistic associations, can act as instances of mediation between the citizens and Contemporary Art world, and open new channels of dialogue and involvement, since, as Siah Armajani points out:

The ethical dimensions of the arts are mostly gone and only in a newly formed relationship with a non-art audience may the ethical dimensions come back to the arts.[7]

Rooted in these assumptions, we ran a survey of the cultural and artistic institutions in the Municipality of Paredes, and found two academies (one for music and another for dance), ten amateur theatre groups, and seven schools in the 2nd and 3rd cycle of Basic Education, two Secondary Schools, and nearly fifty-four schools of the 1st cycle of Basic Education.

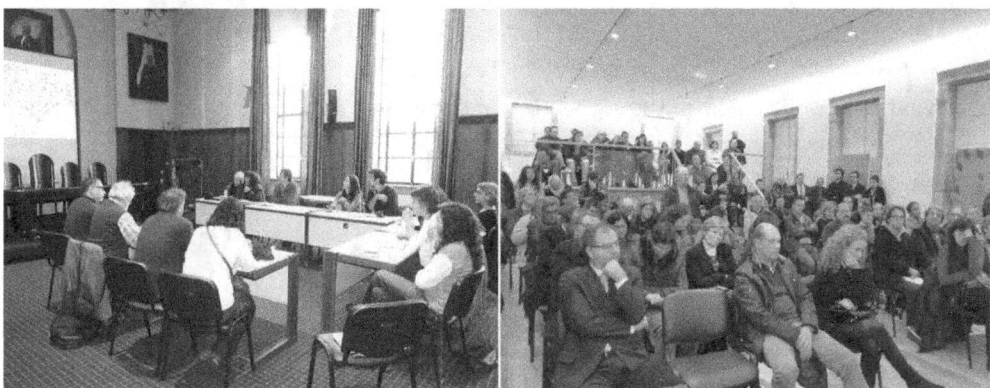

Fig. 3–Paredes Public Art Lab: meeting with Schools; Open Conversation

These institutions were thought as the links of a mediation network, in whichart would operate asa common ground and language among each other, and through their active involvement in the project, between the Public Art Project and the Community too, for our proposal was basically to put members of Community in the role of artists, through temporary and community oriented art programs, which we intended would periodically supplement the Paredes Public Art Circuit, formed by permanent works.

The plan outlined for the year 2012 encompassed a package that included the following programs:
A. Dissemination Activities
B. Involvement of the public schools of Paredes
C. Involvement of artistic and scientific communities
D. Involvement of Municipality Staff
E. Documentation and recording of CAPP
F. Organization of Interpretation Center of CAPP

In describing each of the programs, they breakdown into the following activities:

A. DISSEMINATION ACTIVITIES
Open Conversations – Cycle of public debates to be held at night, one per month - Architecture and the city
Moderator: Tito Couto; Guests: Architect Belém Lima and Architectural Office And-Ré
- Public art and community involvement
Moderator: Tito Couto; Guests: Dr. Celso Ferreira, Architects Belém Lima, José Guilherme Abreu
- Art and the public. Public Art – why and for whom?
Moderator: Susana Marques; Guests: Isabel Campos, Laura Castro
- Art and ideas. What are we discussing when we talk about public art?
Moderator: José Guilherme Abreu; Guests: Delfim Sardo, José Pedro Croft
- Art and its cost. Public art in Paredes. Why? (and why not?)
Moderator: Laura Castro; Guests: Ana Isabel Ribeiro, Álvaro Moreira
- Art and artists. Stories around public art reception in Portugal.
Moderator: José Guilherme Abreu; Guests: Clara Menéres and João Cutileiro[8]
Other meetings: Meetings with local agents in order to present and discuss the project. Meetings addressed religious authorities, art schools such as Dance School and Music Academy, and Theatre groups.
Public Art Days Series of guided toursby members of Public Art Lab.

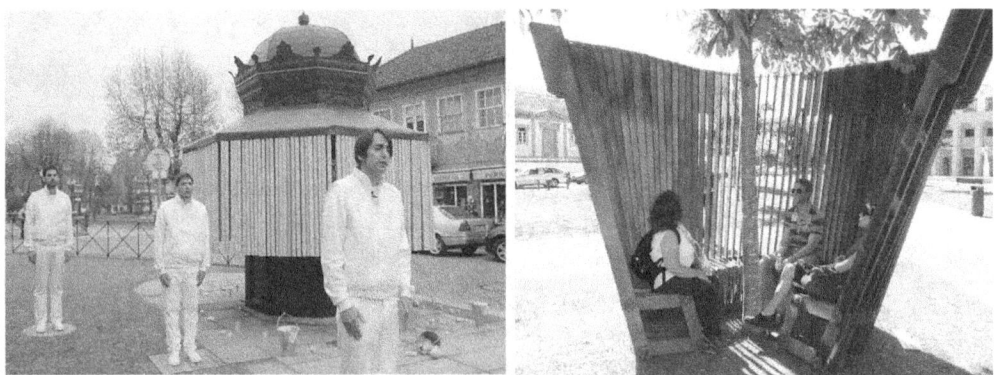
Fig. 4–Paredes Public Art Lab: Public Art Days (OsEspacialistas no Quiosque; Vaso by Artur Fontinha)

B.INVOLVEMENT OF PAREDES' PUBLIC SCHOOLS
Public Art Conferences
The Public Art Conferences were held according to the following schedule:
(Paredes Secondary School)
José Guilherme Abreu: An International case study – SkulpturProjektMünster(1977-)
Álvaro Moreira: A National case study: the International Museum of Contemporary Sculpture in Santo Tirso
Laura Castro and Tito Couto: A Paredes' case study: Circuit + Laboratory + Study Centre
Vasco Carvalho: Music Box. An example of Augmented Reality
Santo Tirso (Abade Pedrosa Museum)
Álvaro Moreira: The Future of the International Museum of Contemporary Sculpture (MIEC)
José Guilherme Abreu: Guided tour of the MIEC
Art in Storefronts Program
Placement in shop windows along the Public Art Circuit, of work done by students, inspired by the artistic expression of artists included in the circuit.
Earth Art Program
This program was aimed at including the learning of art within a philosophy of education for sustainability and the environment, through the cultivation of land as a starting point and in support of arts education. The program was conducted in nine Primary Schools and Secondary Schools in the Municipality of Paredes, and will continue beyond the opening of the CAPP. Beyond its practical results, this program also included the organization of the Art and Earth Conferences, which took place at the Municipal Library of Santo Tirso, with the aim of showing different artwork created with materials from the earth, according to the following schedule: José Guilherme Abreu – Presentation of sculptress Clara Menéres;Clara Menéres –Earth Art ; Paula Reaes Pinto –Salt Art

C.INVOLVEMENT OF ARTISTIC AND SCIENTIFIC COMUNITIES
International Colloquiumon Public Art and Community Involvement
Coordinated by José Guilherme Abreu and Laura Castro. Oct 5-6, 2012
CAPP Presentation by José Guilherme Abreu and Laura Castro in the Workshop La Metodologia del Proyeto, coordinated by Antoni Muntadas at theMuseo de Arte Contemporáneo de León, June 15-16, 2012 Arte em contexto urbano e paisagístico – implicações e propostas tangenciais à conservação preventiva by Laura Castro, Lisbon, Nov. 30, 2012
CAPP. Programación artística e intervención de la Comunidad By José Guilherme Abreu, in I Jornadas Internacionales de Investigación de Arte Y Ciudad,Universidad Complutense, Madrid, 2011.

D.INVOLVEMENT OF MUNICIPALITY STAFF
Public Art Seminar: Organizing a short Seminar on Public Art for Paredes' Municipality technical staff. This training program, was taught by professors from the School of Arts of UCP, and was divided into three sessions of three hours each, the last including the orientation of a route around the CAPP, for training future monitors.
Maintenance Recommendations/Preventive Conservation of CAPP's Artwork and installations
Technical study prepared by conservator-restorer Paulo Pinto, who supervised a visit to CAPP for officials of the Municipality, having a first contact with the pieces, in order to detect early problems to report. This session was attended by the officials of the Municipality department of Gardens and Public Areas.

E.DOCUMENTATION AND RECORDING OF CAPP
Since the beginning of the program, there was a serious concern about registering in book and/or digital media, documental and critical information related to artworks and artists represented in CAPP, as well as on the activities and initiatives developed around it. In the editorial plan, the following materials were posted:
- Catalogue of CAPP, coordinated by Laura Castro playback works with implanted permanently, accompanied by texts by Delfim Sardo, Belém Lima, Laura Castro and José Guilherme Abreu. - Notebook on Temporary and Evolutionary Artistic Interventions of CAPP - Script CAPP, coordinated by LAPP, with the same characteristics. - DVD with documentaries produced by Carlos Ruiz

and Pedro Neves, who recorded the steps of implanting permanent works of art and conversations with the respective artists. - Proceedings of the International Colloquium on Public Art and Community Engagement, coordinated by LAPP

F. ORGANIZATION OF INTERPRETATION CENTER (IC) OF CAPP
Finally, from March 25, 2014, CAPP has in full operation its own Interpretation Centre (IC) which functions as an Interactive Touristic Office too, being the organization of the first planned by LAPP. Its opening show was commissioned by LAPP, and presented the exhibition "The Words of Public Art," which displayed inscribed on the IC's walls a few Public Art definitions, taken from some of the authors and artists of greater relevance in the field of Public Art study and production, such as Malcolm Miles, Antoni Remesar, Vito Acconci, Patricia Phillips and Jonathan Jones, as well as the definition of Public Art given by UNESCO, along with the exposure of a model of Exploratório Visual1.0, which is IC building nearest artwork.

Final notes on CAPP's experience
Completed the implementation of CAPP, the time comes to inform, analyze and critically reflect on the assumptions and strategies developed in this extended public art program.
In a schematic and practice-oriented way, we shall now point the main issues which arise from community involvement and the whole public art program implementation process:
- The processes of public art are inherently long time and long term ones. There is no short length in these processes. The long term, the generational passage of testimony dominate the time of preparing each project. It lacks time for the dissemination and for the involvement, for the embodiment and for the assimilation, as well as for the curiosity, resistance, indifference, acceptance, praise, participation, promotion and integration. Being aware of this temporal gap, allows to the better managing of expectations, aspirations, commitments…, and disappointments.
In this sense, one should:
- Prefer over time spread processes, instead of on short periods focused ones.
- Prioritize flexible procedures capable to respond to project's inherent vicissitudes, in order to prevent to stay attached to solutions that prove to be inadequate.
- Set a framework of artistic plurality, diversity of issues, and generational clash.
- Deal with different and diverse strategies and methods - invitations, open calls, restricted tenders, permanent and temporary interventions...
- Enhance the participation of artists in the working groups that formulate public art programs. The artistic experience such take a consultant part on the conceptual and operational definition of the project.
- Gather multidisciplinary teams promoting the encounter between artists, curators, critics, historians, architects, urban planners, landscape architects, journalists, producers, teachers and students, getting the mobilizing effect of their agendas.
- Gather voices and discourses of different origins – the art world and academia included, so that research, education, and promotion goals can be achieved.
- Relate the running program with other experiences, comprehending both affinities and discrepancies, in order to highlight the identity clipping of the project.
- Value the proximity between the commissioner and the facilitators of the community involvement program, reducing the number of intermediate instances. This proximity accentuates the sense of commitment both to the commissioner, to the curatorial board and to the bodies of the very community. The proliferation of intermediaries tends to hinder and delay the communication, and leads to misunderstandings.
- Multiply visits and discussions with small groups. These actions can perform very relevant reproductive effects, but require patience, persistence and, again, a relatively long time horizon.
These are a few spread and random notes, we think might be useful to consider before the very first steps of commissioning a public or urban art program.
More than beliefs about good practice, the issues listed are conclusions resulting from the experiment described that we think should be shared and discussed.
It is now up to scholars and peers, to analyze the theoretic assumptions, the implementation process and the results achieved critically, in order to provide an assessment of the strengths and limitations of its model.
The future of this public art program is now in the hands of the Municipality, and it is up to the local administration to decide, as CITAR's team had often suggested, if the organization of a future "Public Art Festival" in Paredes, should ensure that CAPP would not become a static public art display, but rather an active and remarkable program, with impact on the cultural life of Paredes (and not only), providing a dynamic agenda, both for the artists and for the public.
Designed as a complement of the curatorial work, bringing community involvement to the project, the model initiated by CITAR's team, can be now applied in other contexts, in order to be tested with in a larger and more reliable basis, so that a rigorous assessment of its merits and its limitations can be performed.

Notes and References
1 Giulio Carlo Argan, A história da arte como história da cidade (São Paulo: Martins Fontes, 1992)
2 Jürgen Habermas, Public Sphere (EncyclopediaBritannica, 1964)
3 José Guilherme Abreu, Proyecto de Arte Público de Paredes (Oporto). Programación artística e intervención de la Comunidad, In, AA.VV, I Jornadas Internacionales de Investigación de Arte Y Ciudad (Madrid: Universidad Complutense de Madrid, 2012), p. 62-63
4 Ortega y Gasset, La deshumanización del arte y otros ensayos de estética, (1925) (Madrid: Alianza Editorial, 1993), p. 11
5 Nathalie Heinich, Le Triple Jeu de l'Art Contemporain (Paris: Éditions du Minuit, 1998), p. 11
6 Nathalie Heinich, Le Triple Jeu de l'Art Contemporain (Paris: Éditions du Minuit, 1998), p. 52
7 Siah Armajani, Manifiesto Escultura Pública en el contexto de la democracia norteamericana, In, AA.VV., Espacios de lectura (Barcelona: MACBA, 1995), p. 36
8 After first having accepted the invitation, João Cutileiro had to decline it, due to health problems.
9 José Guilherme Abreu, Laura Castro, eds., Colóquio Internacional Arte Pública e Envolvimento Comunitário (Porto: UCE/CITAR, 2013)

Ila N. Sheren, Washington University – St. Louis

"The Open-Air Gallery:
A Return to the Revolutionary, or More of the Market?

Introduction

A "gallery without walls," an "open-air museum," an "ephemeral museum:" each of these phrases represents a contradiction in terms. After all, the gallery space is a protected one, and the museum implies permanence, a securing of our cultural patrimony. The question of the street, however, complicates the narrow bounds by which we define these terms. With the growing popularity of street art (an umbrella under which I include muralism, stenciling, wheatpasting, graffiti writing, yarn bombing, guerrilla gardening, and any number of similar practices) in the late twentieth and early twenty-first centuries, it was only natural that the art world rushed to embrace (and market) the cultural phenomenon. The spaces that resulted form a distinct hybrid within the context of outdoor urban display.

If the experience of viewing street art, encountering it in the wild, so to speak, is a defining quality (if not the defining characteristic) of its interpretation and subsequent afterlife, then the open-air museum or gallery space, a legal zone intended to corral high-quality street art (not necessarily 'graffiti') within its borders, presents a conundrum. Is street art created for and viewed within the confines of such establishments truly "street" art, and, more pressing, are the demands of the art establishment culturally and socially incompatible with those of the street art subculture? Can there ever be a natural coexistence of the art world and that of the street? By the early 1980s, graffiti writers in New York had attracted the attention of the art world. As documented in the 1983 films Style Wars and Wild Style, the encounter between these writers, collectors, gallerists and critics was awkward at best and exploitative at worst. In addition, the translation of street style to the indoor spaces of the gallery removed all context. The sense of immediacy, the rush of the urban environment, and the hint of anarchy inherent to graffiti were all neutralized within the walls of the white cube. If the New York City subway system was the first open air gallery, then organized spaces such as São Paulo's Open-Air Museum of Urban Art (Figure 1) and Miami's Wynwood Walls (Figure 2) have sought to re-create the aesthetic, if not the spirit, of those early days. By establishing open-air, outdoor areas for the production of murals, tags, and other pieces, developers and city officials have legitimated street art as a product for public consumption. These open-air galleries become sites for pilgrimage, carefully curated (in the case of Wynwood) and presenting a kind of augmented reality for the art-going public. On the other hand, these spaces still carry the stamp of the art world, and the works within are presented more as high art than street culture. This paper will consider the dynamics of these open air museums in contemporary street art culture, and will explore questions of high and low, public and private, and curated vs. anarchic spaces.

New York Subway Graffiti in the 1970s

The New York City subway system, from the late 1960s until the massive cleanup programs of the early to mid-1980s, constituted the first open-air gallery. Although the graffiti writers of the era did not consciously set out to frame their work as art, and even less so as an organized institution, I would argue that, far from anarchy, subway graffiti of this era constituted a gallery space.

Subway cars traveled throughout the city and the sides of the trains served as billboards, advertising the presence of the artist or writer. Accordingly, the lines exposed to the open were the most coveted.[1] As others have explored, the tags begat a conversation between writers from different groups, different neighborhoods, and different boroughs. Eventually, the conversation spread to other cities and across the Atlantic, when graffiti writers from Europe joined in the cultural exchange. At first, the conversation was a territorial one. Writers claimed space, particularly the transitory space of the train lines, in order to advertise their presence throughout the urban center. Style became the dominant means for communication, with aesthetic qualities eventually surpassing legible content. Style became an authorial gesture akin to (and surpassing) the signature itself.

So how did this scene, an anarchic conversation coupled with a thrilling oneupmanship, constitute a gallery? The very terms seem antithetical at best. After all, a gallery is a serene, curated space, it places its stamp of approval on everything that graces its walls and floors. The New York City subway system in the 1970s and early 1980s, on the other hand, was pure chaos. Images from the time reveal dark, marker and paint-encrusted surfaces, one tag on top of another, on top of another still. The conversation becomes so muddled that it is impossible to understand. It is the exterior of those subway cars, however, that I would argue formed a gallery space for the medium of graffiti.

For example Figure 3 shows Fab 5 Freddy's Soup Train, from 1980. Campbell's soup cans, outlined in black, run down the length of the car. On each label, an identifying tag: Da-da Soup, Pop Soup, Fabulous Soup, Fred Soup. Works such as this one consciously interrogate the status of art and place street art in a lineage of avant-garde, paradigm-shifting moments in the history of art. Dada artists questioned the very nature of art and, by extension, the artist, through use of the readymade. Pop artists equated art with commercial goods, and emphasized our desire to draw distinctions between them. Street art, then, provokes a similar line of questioning into the nature of art and what constitutes an artist. Fab 5 Freddy, then, placed himself as the heir of Duchamp and Warhol, tasked with pushing the boundaries yet again. On the one hand, Soup Train elevates street art, and on the other, it brings the discourse of high and low art down to the level of the street. Work like this could not be taken off the train and into the gallery, because the context determined the stakes of the argument.

The Transition from Subways to Galleries in the 1980s

Although subway art was, by and large, dependent on its location for meaning, the art world soon took up the cause of graffiti. Roger Gastman and Caleb Neelon, in their 2010 study The History of American Graffiti, posit that early subway graffiti began to make its transition to the art world in the early 1970s, with the first book on subway graffiti published in 1972.[2] The collection and publication of photographs of graffiti served both to legitimate the art form and exoticize it for a particular segment of the art-going public. Spaces such as Patti Astor's Fun Gallery opened in 1981, bringing street artists such as Keith Haring into dialogue with the rest of the art world.[3] As documented in the 1983 film Style Wars, the transition from the street to the gallery marked a monumental shift in the way that graffiti writers conceived of their work. While early writers "retired" or left the streets with the advent of more abstract visual style, most prominent writers embraced the gaze of gallerists and collectors alike. The move to the galleries was extremely enticing, after all, most graffiti writers were teenagers who jumped at the idea of getting paid for the work they had been creating all along. The promise of fame - in particular the celebrity status gained by such films as Style Wars and Wild Style - only added to the allure. A scene from Style Wars shows a gallery opening, at which teenage graffiti writers commingle with wealthy art patrons.[4] A woman points out the visual qualities of an aerosol-based painting, claiming that it loses nothing in the transition to canvas (and, ultimately, the gallery space). We, the viewers, are meant to know better. The spray-painted canvases are but a paraphrase of the larger, train-based works. They may appear to inherit the style, but lack the latter's spontaneity and sense of danger.

So why did graffiti artists dilute their work in this manner? The transition from the streets, particularly the subway system, to the gallery space was the result of two major forces. The pull of the commercial market was aided by the push of the New York City government to keep graffiti off the trains. In 1984, Mayor Ed Koch and the New York City Transit Authority initiated a five-year graffiti removal program. Double fences were built around train yards, and by 1989, no spray-painted trains were allowed to run, even if this meant delayed service. Koch was famously quoted as suggesting the double fence be filled with wolves, to add yet another level of security. The disparity between the absurd lengths to which the MTA and the city government went and the relative harmlessness of the crime points to the exaggerated status of graffiti in the popular imagination. Spurred by James Q. Wilson and George R. Kelling's "broken windows" theory (1982)[5] of civic neglect and crime, authorities made graffiti and street art the straw man for every level of urban unrest.

Figure 4, an oil painting by graffiti artist Lady Pink, titled The Death of Graffiti (1982), illustrates the sea change in the mid-1980s graffiti scene. In the painting, a nude figure, presumably the artist herself, stands on a mountain of discarded spray paint cans. She points mournfully at a passing subway train, half its cars graffiti-covered, and the other half a stark white. The advent of the white trains signals the death of graffiti culture as it once existed. A brick wall occupies the lower right quadrant of the painting, and a small patch of spray-painted surface stands, covered by weeds. The juxtaposition of control and neglect, present and past, serves to mark this moment of transition and encapsulate the critical juncture it represented. Graffiti doesn't die, of course, but it moves in two directions: to the margins and into the mainstream.

Miami

Miami's Wynwood Walls is perhaps the most well-known outdoor gallery of street art. Real estate developer Tony Goldman proposed turning portions of the Wynwood Arts District (located between Highway 112 and 20th street and founded in 2003) into a space for legalized graffiti and art galleries specializing in alternative artists. The result is approximately 1.9 square miles (4.9 sq. Km) of walls that read like a street art hall of fame. The gated, curated Wynwood Walls area is much smaller, comprising a single block out of the total area. The official Wynwood Walls gallery stands apart from the street. It is a space intended for pedestrians rather than vehicular traffic. Manicured green lawns flank pathways, leading the viewer through a series of spaces: "Wynwood Walls" and "Wynwood Doors." The walls are set apart with stanchions, keeping the viewing public at bay. In this manner, Wynwood Walls maintains its gallery aesthetic, even within the urban framework.

It is clear from the start that the Wynwood Walls gentrification is a complete reversal of the way graffiti had been regarded in the late twentieth-century. Goldman, quoted on the official site as declaring Wynwood a "giant canvas," helped to bring tourism and increased property values to a virtually abandoned, post-industrial neighborhood.[6] Graffiti, once seen as a sign of urban decay, a symptom of the neglect lamented by the "broken windows theory" proponents, is now a tool for gentrification. The Wynwood graffiti "hall of fame" is first and foremost an art space, organized by star curators and visited by the celebrity patrons of Art Basel Miami and the rest of the Wynwood Arts District.

A tour of Wynwood begins with a brightly colored Futura mural opposite a wall of Shepard Fairey and a work from Faile. The space is dominated by a cafe patio, and the Faile mural's French Bistro aesthetic blends well with the seating area. Beyond this first space, the viewer is led to another space, boasting pieces by Aiko and Ryan McGinness, among others. Beyond this, "Wynwood Doors" beckons, with its murals by Gaia, Vhils, DALeast,, and Miss Van. Around the corner, work by Retna, and through a smaller gate, another space with Maya Hayuk and Nunca. A Ron English mural bleeds into the concrete and over some carefully placed rocks, which in turn are yarn bombed by Olek. Everything coexists in this space, the murals neither overlap one another nor fight for supremacy. There is time and space enough to contemplate each one on its own.

The artworks are carefully labeled. Small, discreet plaques mention the name of the artist and country of origin. This one-size-fits-all system obscures complicated notions of authorship and nationality that have been inherent to street art since the first graffiti writers began tagging. Authorship, in the case of early graffiti, was the entire point of each piece. Subway writers began with their names, after all. But naming was a complicated issue. Initially, the names writers chose were indicative of neighborhood. By including street numbers in their tags, writers invited the public to make all manner of assumptions about where they lived, ethnic or racial identity, and class based on the given neighborhood. The dialogue that emerged with subway tagging, however, crossed those boundaries time and time again, making connections across all parts of the city, with the move to the galleries bridging the largest of those connections. To return to the issue of Wynwood, then, the choice to identify these artists based on national origin seems reductive. After all, Nunca, born and raised in Brazil, has completed murals on almost every continent. His themes adjust to local situations, and his work for Wynwood is merely representative of his signature style. It doesn't necessarily represent "Brazil" or Sao Paulo to the world. The national markers, then, seem more like an allusion to the Venice Biennale, the Olympics, or other relics of nationalism that persist in an international context.

The identification panels also distance this gallery from the earlier spirit of street art. Although tags in that original open-air gallery were identificatory, the advent of Wild Style, among other developments, served to obscure the informational content of a given tag and force the viewer to focus on the technical skill of its maker. Street art moved from a dialogue to a virtuosic display. As mentioned earlier, however, the style itself became the signature, a trait that has continued since those early days, and remains the prime means of attribution for street art today. This is in keeping with the work on display at Wynwood - DALeast, for example, creates energetic figures that appear to be made out of live wires (Figure 5). Handled with expert skill, the lines appear to jump from the wall. The entire composition recalls the work of surrealists such as Rene Magritte and Salvador Dali - two common inspirations for present-day street artists. That technical virtuosity, however, came at the price of clarity. Street art was no longer meant to be identified by name alone, but by a familiarity with a given style, subject matter or oeuvre of a particular artist. The plaques at Wynwood give the game away, and much like the wall text of a traditional indoor gallery, they become the initial focus of the viewer's attention. We seek meaning in the text, rather than in the visual substance of the artworks.

Wynwood also serves to canonize the genre of street art. Much like with traditional museum and gallery settings, the work of creating a hierarchy has been completed in advance. The artists selected to show within Wynwood Walls (and outside as well) represent the top tier of street artists. The work contained within is representative of their styles, but hardly the most challenging versions. Ron English, for example, engages the issue of commodification and consumption of food in Western society, particularly in the United States. His cereal box covers, including one for "Sugar Smack Cereal," depict the cartoon frog mascot from the Kellogg's box shooting heroin. English places these box covers in grocery stores, and encourages the viewing public to do so as well. The fact that this method of working is illegal heightens the impact, but it is not the sole reason for its challenging nature. By equating the consumption of sugary, processed foods with drug use, and by extension, associating this drug abuse with children, English makes a powerful statement about a society of convenience (and pleasure) at any cost. His contribution for Wynwood, on the other hand, reads like a Ron English greatest hits catalogue. The toddler Hulk stands out, along with a number of comic book and corporate logos. The entire piece alludes to the larger issues at play in his other work, but the critique is dulled for its presentation in the gallery. The canon, therefore, becomes a sanitized version of street art. The curators of Wynwood champion technical skill over critical engagement.

Wynwood Walls, by presenting street art with all the trappings of the traditional gallery setting, never allows the viewer to question the works' status as art. One might say that this is a development, an example of how far street art has come since the early days of subway tagging. By presenting these pieces unquestioningly as art, canonizing them into a street art hall of fame, so to speak, the curators take the power out of the hands of the viewers. We enter the gallery space, and rather than interpreting or making our own decisions about the status of these panels, we accept the premise unconditionally. Interpretation is left at the surface level of assessing technical skill, marveling at the works on the walls, but not engaging with the larger questions of the substance of street art. The anarchic spirit of earlier graffiti and street art lay at the intersection of the main questions concerning the genre: its legal status and its status as art. The question of the status of street art was what led to the technical developments and social critique of earlier generations. Innovation was spurred not only by the constraints of the medium (and its illegality) but by a desire to interrogate the very nature of art. When Fab 5 Freddy wrote his name under the Warhol-esque soup cans he painted on the subway car, he wasn't merely trying to elevate himself into the canon, he was shattering the entire notion of one.

São Paulo

São Paulo's contradictions create a fertile ground for street art and urban expression. On the one hand, the anarchist spirit of the city is conducive to all manner of graffiti, street art, and mural painting, but on the other, the social ills of the city detract from the joys of free expression. Vila Madalena, a region of the city located 5.3 miles (8.6 Km) from the downtown core, is home to Batman Alley (Beca de Batman), one of the more well-known avenues of street art. The street, a paved-over river, is narrow and winding, with every square inch covered in paint. Well-known artists such as Eduardo Kobra tag here, as well as undiscovered and yet-to-be discovered artists. Os Gemeos' childhood neighborhood, Cambuci, is also covered in murals by the famous twins, as well as those of their collaborators. The experience of viewing street art in Vila Madalena and Cambuci, however, is far from the serene, controlled ambience of Miami's Wynwood Walls. The streets abound with traffic and energy, and the threat of pickpockets and other petty crime is ever present. That sense of danger, the uncontrolled nature of the area, evokes the early days of graffiti and the subway writers of 1970s New York.

In both of these neighborhoods, street art viewing is precarious. Other than those well-known names, there is no sense of hierarchy or order, and the sense of danger is ever present. In part, this speaks to larger social ills present throughout Sao Paulo (and much of Brazil). Brazil has been one of the beneficiaries of worldwide neoliberal economic policies and the opening up of global markets. Economic inequality, however, has led to one of the widest income gaps in the world.[7] A much-circulated image from Rio de Janeiro, Figure 6 shows the Paradise Towers juxtaposed against the background of a favela. The tower boasts individual balconies that fan out in a spiral, each with its own plunge pool and access to sunlight. The streets of the favela below, in contrast, form a maze of tunnels and alleyways - sunlight must fight its way to street level, and, of course, the water forms fetid cesspools rather than plunge pools.

Still, the plethora of street art and graffiti tags gives these neighborhoods the air of an open-air gallery, one lacking a curatorial eye. Sao Paulo itself reads like an open air museum, albeit one without any observable order. Is the city's establishment of the Open Air Museum of Urban Art then, redundant? At best, the project could be called unnecessary. I would argue, though that it is a combination of the city's social ills and the strength of its street art community that render such a project completely vital to the urban art scene.

São Paulo'sOpen-Air Museum of Urban Art spans thirty-four pillars (with sixty-eight murals) on an elevated rail line in the city's northern area. This stretch, from the metro's Tiete-Portuguesa to Santana stations, is far from the tourist and business centers, but serves as a pilgrimage site for street art viewers, much like the Cambuci and Vila Madalena neighborhoods. The story of the Museum's origin is a simple one. Originally an irresistable site for graffiti writers and muralists alike, the elevated train line became a source of controversy when eleven local street artists were arrested following a graffiti purging campaign.[8] After much agitation, the area between the metro stations was declared a legal street art and graffiti zone, and dubbed the Open-Air Museum of Urban Art. Unlike Miami's Wynwood District, no galleries or art apparatus has sprung up to accompany the work. Instead, the pillars serve as a legal showcase for Sao Paulo's local artists.

One encounters the Open-Air Museum of Urban Art most likely by car. The long, straight divided road runs to either side of the elevated tracks, and the murals are clearly visible from a passing vehicle. In addition, the areas between the pillars house parking lots and sidewalks, although not exactly a pedestrian-friendly space. The murals occupy each pillar, one artist per side. The result is a space that is rigidly directional - looking north tells one story, with one set of images, while looking south reveals another altogether. This linear motion is undermined by a complete lack of narrative or order, but is balanced by the regularity of the artworks. The rhythm is steady, whether to the pedestrian observer or the automobile traffic moving to either side of the divided street. In addition, traffic lights provide natural stopping points along the line. One might say that the open air museum is curated by its traffic patterns and its infrasructure, rather than another organizational method.

The artists of the Open-Air Museum encompass the burgeoning São Paulo street art community. Zezao, Cranio, Tinho, Presto, Whip, Binho Ribeiro, and Nove (among others) are all featured. Because of the uniformity of spaces, no single piece is emphasized over another. Because of the separation of the pillars, no artworks run into each other, overlap, or otherwise compete for attention. Unlike Wynwood, the works here are unlabeled. Of course, most (if not all) are signed by the artist, but street art signatures are not always legible, and in some cases, construction work and street pollution have deteriorated the aerosol paints. Figure 7 shows a pillar painted by Zezão, while Figure 8 shows a work by Whip. The former artist's abstracts can be found throughout the city, and the piece at the Open-Air Museum continues in this manner. Juxtaposed with the scenery (the space was under construction at the time this photograph was taken), it appears that the multicolored, smoke-like form is emerging from a pile of bricks placed against the pillar. In this way, Zezão's contribution works the way the rest of his art does, to augment the urban environment and cause the viewer to re-negotiate his or her surroundings.

Figure 8, the piece attributed to Whip, takes another tactic altogether. The scene is self-referential; the graffiti artist is caught in the act, his arsenal of spray cans is at the ready, with one in his hand. The viewpoint is from above, ostensibly the perspective of the looming figure whose shadow occupies the left side of the composition. The viewer can make out what appears to be a gun in the mysterious figure's hand. Is this shadow a police officer, catching the artist mid-crime? If so, the piece becomes a commentary on the nature of street art, its status as a crime, even in a city positively covered in graffiti and larger pieces. The discrepancy between the spray can, on the one hand, and the gun, on the other, leads the viewer to question the very nature of crime. If the artist's only weapon is a paint can, then why is this gesture met with the threat of violence? In one single composition, Whip reflects on the nature of street art, its supposed criminal nature, and even the recent history that led to the establishment of the Open-Air Museum. Two models for this viewing experience come to mind: the first, spaces such as Chicano Park in San Diego (Figure 9). While attached to a highly-charged and emotional background story, the origin of Chicano Park is beyond the scope of this paper.[9] Chicano Park comprises the junction of Interstate 5 in San Diego with the Coronado Bay Bridge. The resulting entanglement of on- and off-ramps creates a concrete jungle, a cold and alien space. Artists from the local Mexican-American community of Barrio Logan filled these grey surfaces with brightly-colored murals, each depicting moments from Chicano and Mexican history, mythology and the origin of San Diego's community itself. The varied shapes and spaces of Chicano Park, however, give the illusion of walking through a forest of paintings, one occupied by giants, goddesses, and legends of history. Accordingly, this structure create a far different experience than the strict linear regularity of Sao Paulo's Open-Air Museum. On the other hand, Chicano Park's transformation of the structures of transportation into an outdoor gallery clearly set a precedent for all similar interventions that followed.

The other model, of course, is the one with which I began this essay, that of New York's 1970s subway graffiti scene. The connection here is not immediately evident, aside from that between the subway train pillars of Sao Paulo and the subway cars of New York. The Open-Air Museum is stationary rather than mobile, organized rather than chaotic, and, most importantly, legal rather than illegal. These are all key differences that alter the viewing experience, but I argue that, in a sense, the basic underlying principle of competition and one-upmanship remains. Unlike Wynwood, in which curators direct the placement and size of murals, the Open-Air Museum is artist-directed. As a hall of fame (of sorts), only the best, most well-respected artists can gain access to the limited number of pillars. Within each pillar, then, each artist is free to do as he or she wishes, and the competition becomes one of pure style rather than one of spatial presence.

Developments in subway writing in the 1970s led to the formation of ever larger, more colorful and technically complex works of graffiti art. One could argue that technical advancements in street art have peaked since then, and the development of an individual style or social commentary has become the new standard by which street art is judged. In the Open-Air Museum, the identical pillars constrain the size and format of each piece, but in turn allow the artists' individual voices to show through. As such, codes of etiquette pervade the space, keeping errant tags off the showcased pieces, and bringing a tone of civility to the entire enterprise. One might argue that with this focus on style and individualism overshadows the contributions of street art to the social sphere. After all, artists such as Blu and Banksy, among others, create viable social critique outside the purview of institutions. By confining Sao Paulo's premiere artists to the area of the pillars, the Open-Air Museum limits the scale and ingenuity of the message. In many cases, the artists have eschewed representation or legible social commentary altogether. The relatively small murals appear as vignettes within much larger and richer street art practices. If the truly subversive work is to be found outside the purview of this legal space, then what is the role of the such a legalized space?

Conclusions

While far from an ideal method for viewing and displaying street art, the Open-Air Museum concept presents a particularly productive fusion of the art market with alternative culture. When subway graffiti writers made that initial jump to the gallery space, they brought their techniques, their medium, but left their anarchic spirit at the rail yards. Surface was prized over intention, romantic narratives of youth culture over the impact of any given piece.

Wynwood Walls, on the one hand, gives the art world's stamp of approval to the street art scene. The works are monumental; with a glossy sheen lifted from the pages of the latest street art anthology. By protecting and preserving the artworks, creating an outdoor gallery intended as a space of reverence and contemplation, the curators of Wynwood direct the show. Interpretation falls out of the hands of the viewer entirely. The Open-Air Museum of Urban Art, then, presents a kind of middle ground in this discussion, a middle ground but not a compromise. Created and curated by the artists themselves, the stretch of elevated train tracks updates the anarchy of the 1970s for a contemporary viewing public. As with the subway cars, the viewer is left to decide for him- or herself the merits of the work, and, more importantly, its status as art. Competing for attention with the motion of traffic and street commerce, each piece remains wholly integrated with the urban fabric, dependent upon its setting for meaning and significance.

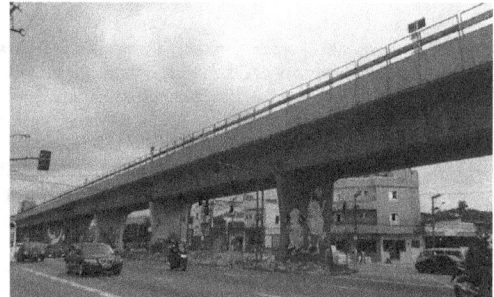

Fig. 1: The Open-Air Museum of urban art, são Paulo

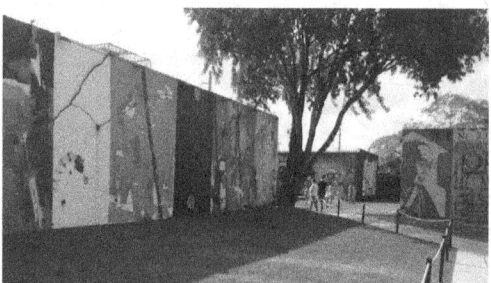

Fig. 2: Wynwood Walls, Miami

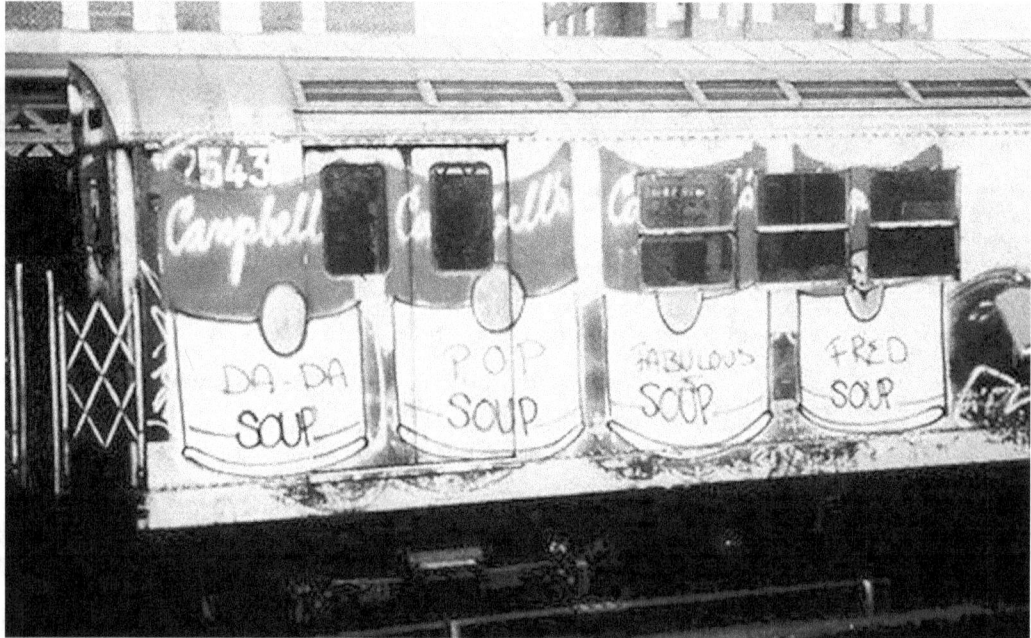

Fig. 3: Fab 5 freddy, soup train (1982)

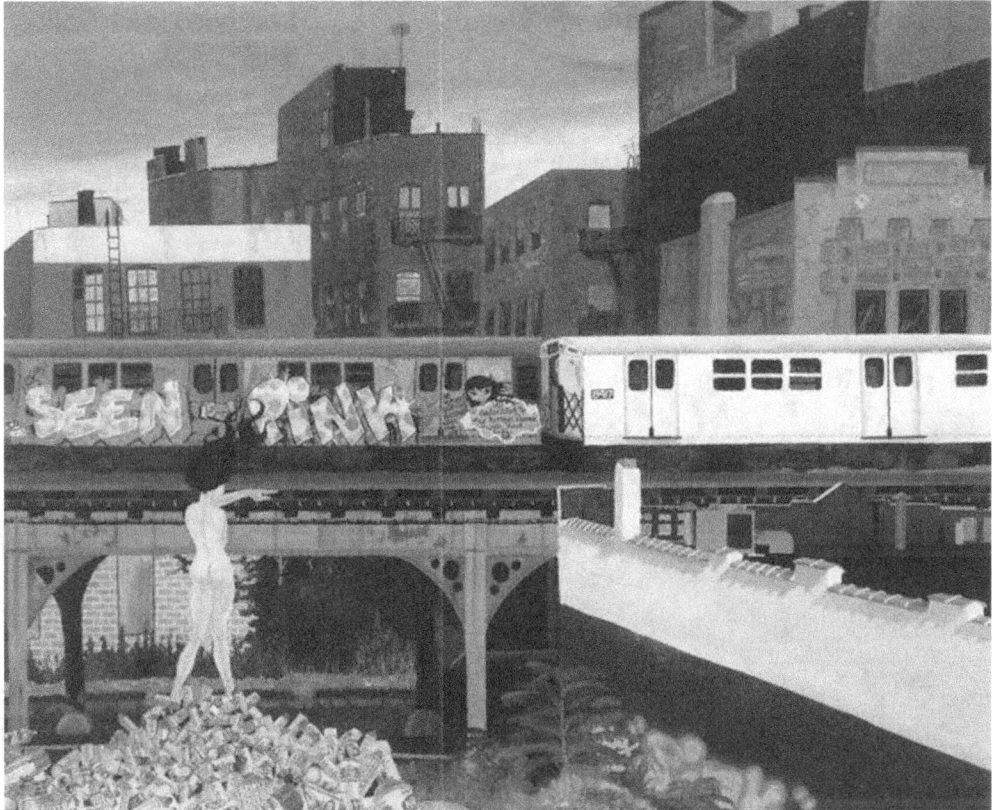

Fig. 4: Lady Pink, The Death of Graffiti (1983)

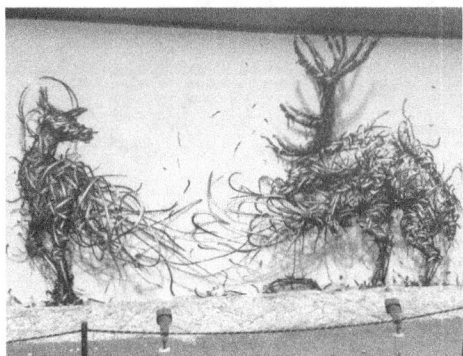

Fig. 5: daleast (Eclipse of the Halo) at wynwood walls

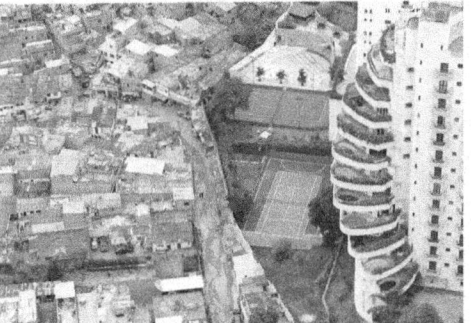

Fig. 6: the paradise towers and favela, rio de janeiro

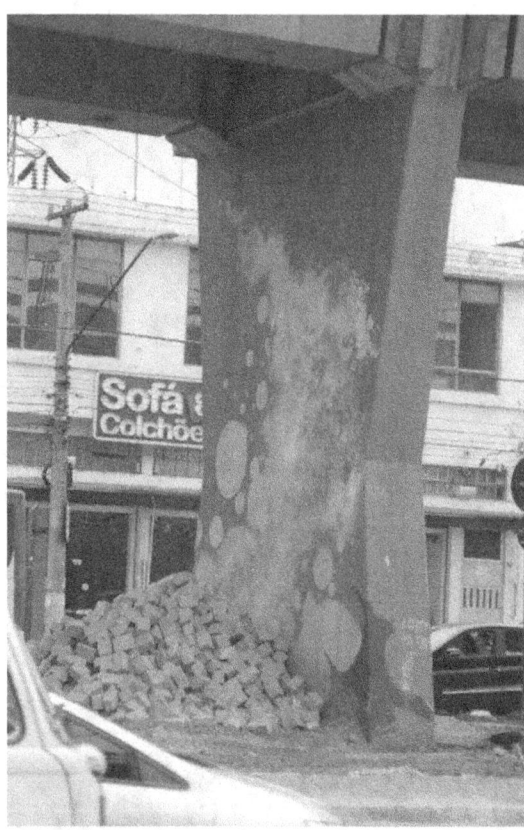

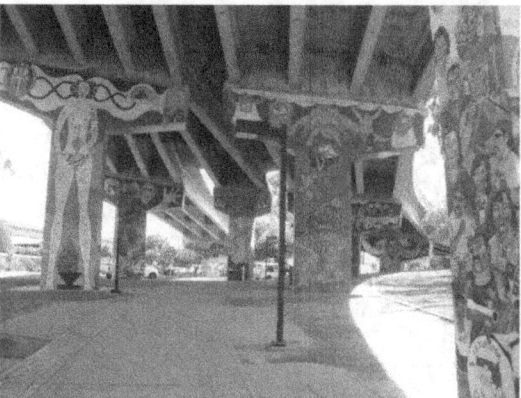

Fig. 8: whip at the open-air museum of urban art, são Paulo

Fig. 7: Zezão at the open-air museum of urban art, são paulo   Fig. 9: Chicano park, San diego, California (established 1973)

Notes and References

1 Roger Gastman and Caleb Neelon, The History of American Graffiti (New York: Harper Design, 2010) 89.
2 Gastman and Neelon, 87.
3 The Fun gallery was short lived, closing in 1985, when the art world's attention moved elsewhere.
4 Charlie Ahearn, Style Wars (1983), documentary film.
5 First published as "Broken Windows: The Police and Public Safety" in The Atlantic Monthly (March 1982).
6 Available online at http://thewynwoodwalls.com/ accessed May 2014.
7 According to the World Bank, the richest quintile receives more than thirty times as much as the poorest. In high-income countries, the ratio is, on average 6:1. See http://www.worldbank.org/depweb/beyond/beyondco/beg_05.pdf, accessed June 2014.
8 The story of the Open Air Museum of Urban Art can be found on several blogs, including http://geostreetart.com/theblog/nove-open-air-museum-urban-art-sao-paulo/ and http://www.insidesaopaulo.com/2011/10/museu-aberto-de-arte-urbana-open-air.html. The museum has no official page or curatorial mission.
9 For details of Chicano Park's founding, see Eva Cockroft's excellent account "The Story of Chicano Park" Aztlán 15 (1) 1984.

Veronica Werckmeister, Artistic Director
Itinerario Muralístico de Vitoria-Gasteiz (IMVG)
veronica@muralismopublico.com

A Case Study in Monumental Contemporary Muralism: Creating Landmarks, Creating Together

Cultural expressions that come from community practice are key <u>indicators</u> of a city's health, social makeup, history and future. Creating monumental community art where there were previously little or no participatory practices requires careful maneuvering. Urban planners, policy makers and artists must be prepared to forego total control so that citizens can experience the power and responsibility of leaving a permanent mark on their own urban landscape. In Vitoria-Gasteiz, Spain, a process was begun in 2005 resulting in an itinerary of monumental murals that are an expression of its citizens.

Mural, Community Art, Collaboration

Introduction

In 2005 an important social and cultural program was initiated in Vitoria-Gasteiz. The single most important aspect of this program was to put the tools and language of artistic creation into the hands of citizens. By using a model of collaborative creativity with roots in American community mural movements of the late 20th century, for the first time citizens of Vitoria-Gasteiz intervene directly in the urban landscape in the heart of their city. They participate actively in their environment, using color to drastically transform cracked and grey walls. The program is part of a plan that goes beyond decorating walls. In fact, it takes into account factors such as the rehabilitation and preparation of facades, use of quality materials, artistic trajectory of workshop coordinators, participation of diverse individuals and organisms in all aspects of the work, support and coordination. This contributes to creating works that withstand the test of time transforming them into monuments and icons of the city. They add value to the urban experience while at the same time producing new cultural patrimony, contemporary works of art that share space and significance with the established cultural patrimony of the city.

The setting

Vitoria-Gasteiz has a population of 240,000, and has an extensive cultural offering that includes a highly recognized international jazz festival, international theater festival, fine arts museum and contemporary art museum as well as prestigious cultural institutions such as Santa Maria Cathedral Foundation, Montehermoso Cultural Center, Museum of Archeology, etc. In this highly developed, but institutionally top-heavy, cultural context we find some independent initiatives that contribute to the cultural make-up of the city. This is the case of Itinerario Muralístico de Vitoria Gasteiz (IMVG) La Ciudad Pintada. (Mural Itinerary of Vitoria-Gasteiz - The Painted City).

> *"Muralism as an organized activity in the city, as part of its collective expression, not only as a reflection of its artistic and cultural capacity, but also of its capability for critical and democratic expression. Muralism regarded and managed as a screen onto which concerns, feelings and ideas are projected, as an interactive tool that changes and renews itself, alive as the city itself and, why not, as a sign of its identity."* –Juan Ignacio Lasagabaster Gómez, Architect Conservator of Patrimony, Director of the Santa Maria Cathedral Foundation, Vitoria-Gasteiz.

The historic medieval quarter, with its patrimonial value, its singular urban layout (almond shaped), its renaissance palaces and medieval squares, is the stage for this new mural movement. It is essential to highlight that the particularity of this project is not only the way in which it is carried out and the cultural heritage it produces, but also the exceptional historic value of the location where the murals are found.

Vitoria-Gasteiz has experimented dramatic demographic changes due to foreign immigration, ageing population, and economic "res-shuffling" towards the end of the 20th century and the beginning of the 21st century. Between 1997 and 2010 the population increased 11.6% while the immigrant population increased 66.4% in the same period. In 2012 10% of the population of the city is foreign born and in the medieval quarter the change is even more significant with 21.3% of the residents being of foreign origin. These statistics are important because the social context is key when utilizing art as a tool for social cohesion, cultural understanding and urban regeneration. Any city or neighborhood can benefit from a program of participatory public art, but a neighborhood in flux benefits exponentially from a program that recognizes and integrates these social realities into its core method. On the one hand it is said that the medieval quarter is in danger of becoming a "shop window" neighborhood due to its patrimonial wealth and touristic interest. On the other hand there is a fear that the neighborhood will become a "ghetto" due to increased levels of immigrant population and aging local population. Neither of the fears is grounded in the reality of the actual residents of the neighborhood. In fact such hypotheses disregard the contributions that the population of the neighborhood make as individuals, associations and active members of society. The murals bring to the surface, quite expressively, the responsibility residents feel and the lengths they are willing to take to participate actively in their streets and in their city. The IMVG is a tool that exemplifies the potential of diversity by creating open spaces of work and common culture that prove that the old city, lives, grows, evolves and becomes new again. In fact the last 20 years has seen an increase in grassroots activity on all levels in the neighborhood.

The tools of artistic creation are put in the hands of the citizens

Generally art has a material nature. The works themselves have individual authors, private or institutional owners or patrons, and monetary value. Community murals have multiple anonymous authors, the ownership belongs to the city and its citizens and their value is intangible. The permanence, quality and central location of the collaborative community murals of Vitoria-Gasteiz is fundamental in understanding their value. The preparation of the surface of the facade, the rehabilitation of damaged structural elements, respect for the architectural structure, use of high quality materials and finally attention to detail, finish and esthetic quality are key components of any successful and long-lasting public art project. When a participatory and social component is added the results are extraordinary. Participants in the workshops embed the process with a sense of civic responsibility, and the importance (in dimension and location) of the work of art motivates the participants to overcome insecurities, work that much harder, taking great care with the process and the result. It is not the same to produce a work of art on the outskirts of town, than to do it at its heart. Creating exterior artwork without adequate surface preparation or using inappropriate materials is quite different from creating a work of art that aspires to a higher level of quality and permanence. It is also not the same to make an isolated piece individually than to create a work of art that is part of a group of similar works, all of which co-exist with important elements of historic and cultural patrimony. When considering the merits and the importance of the murals it is fundamental to look beyond the images themselves and consider the way in which they were created. Artists and non-artists, young and old, men and women, local and foreigners, take on the responsibility of the creation of monumental works of public art together. The opportunity to express oneself in a monumental format, in the center of the urban realm, on quasi-permanent creations, reinforces the creative, critical, constructive and civic sentiment of the participants. In addition, working together with others on a common topic, sharing space and ideas as a team, results in unexpected ideas, and images that are a product of the unique experience.

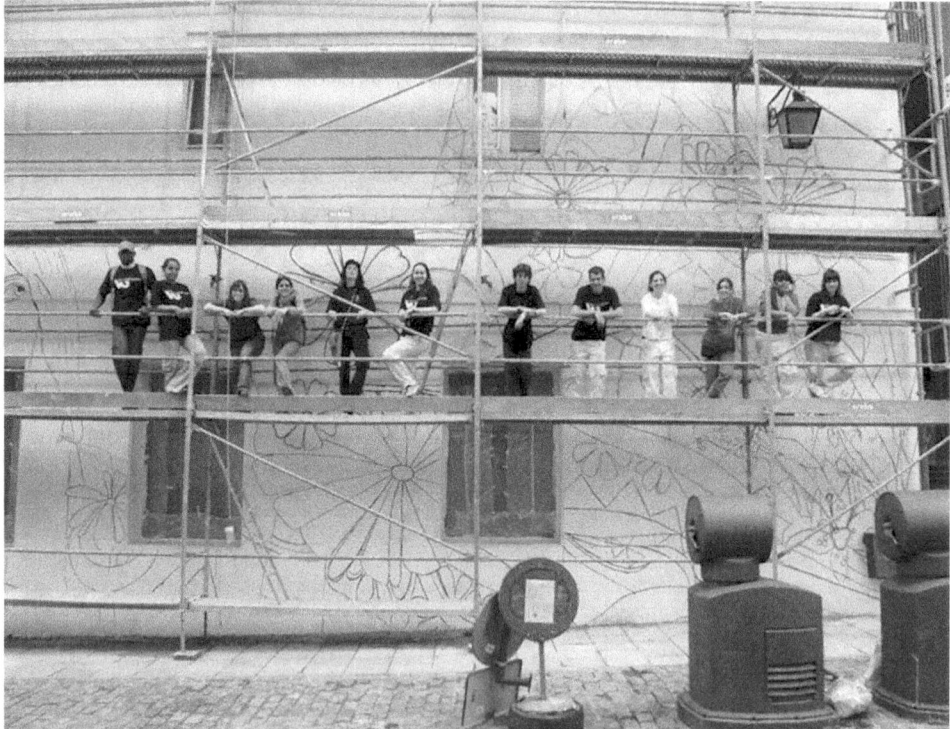

Fig. 1: Volunteer muralists, Vitoria-Gasteiz, 2009 source: IMVG

The opening up of creative channels, facing the imperfection of a non-professional hand, and the loss of control that comes with collaborative creative processes are some of the aspects that make these community murals so important. The current (and historic) conceptual discourse of contemporary cultures restricts artistic practice to an elite, or enigmatic sector of the population. To provide the tools, the canvas, the location and the means of creation to a group of citizens and artists provokes an important alteration in the commonplace disconnect between audience and author. When the process is opened up within a productive context, the artists change, the participants change, the artistic product changes and the audience can interpret the work as product as well as process. It confirms the notion that we can participate actively in our own culture, and it makes us ask the questions: in what other realms of civic life can we take an active role? What limitations are imposed or self-imposed that deny us access to more active ways of participation? What else can we make/create/achieve with the tools of collaborative creativity? *"Art is not a mirror to reflect reality but a hammer with which to shape it."* - Bertolt Brecht

The concept of art as a tool is fundamental in understanding the intention and consequences of a public art program that makes the citizen/artist the main protagonist. It is possible that Brecht, in his famous quote, refers to the content and themes of art as catalysts of social change but one can also interpret his words in another manner. The experience of creating public art collaboratively changes us as a society.

Trust

Trust is one of the most important aspects of this project. In a society full of unspoken rules that are maintained for the sake of coexistence it is essential to re-examine those rules constantly so that such a coexistence is not passive but active. Social norms, behaviors, rules and traditions can be altered and even created to promote a peaceful co-existence and a fulfilling one. The methodology of the IMVG projects require unspoken trust that goes beyond our day to·day. Each mural is designed collaboratively and the design itself is only revealed at the end of this process, days before production begins.

This collaboration entail trust, this is unquestionable. But what other forms of trust are we securing and strengthening with this type of project?

1. Self TRUST- individuals outside the official creative realm must put aside self doubt.
2. Artists must TRUST non-artists.
3. The private citizens who cede their facades for the project must TRUST artists, organizers and their own neighbor participants.
4. The city government must TRUST the citizens, artists and organizers.

How does an IMVG workshop work?

Mural workshops take place in the summer months. The group of 20-25 participants are comprised by:1-2 Lead artists, 1-2 assistant artists, 12-18 citizen volunteers, 6 youth workers (summer employment program for youth ages 16-20). This group dedicates 6 weeks of their summer to the program. The first two weeks the group embarks on the difficult task of ideating and designing the mural. The following 4 weeks the mural is painted by the same group. Organizers coordinate all other aspects of the process, including permissions, licences, surface preparation, scaffold, insurance, materials, accessibility, media, etc.

It is important to highlight that the final image of the mural is not known by anyone until the group has completed the design process. This means that organizers, city officials, neighbors who live and have ceded their facade, neighbors, etc must blindly trust the process of creation set out by the organization. This, in and of itself, is an exercize in social relations and an example of trust.

On some of the projects the group might begin with a pre-established general theme. 3 of the 13 murals created through the IMVG program resulted from pre-established themes. In the other 10 the workshops began without a topic, with a blank page, so to speak. The only requirement for the workshops and their coordinators, is that the processes of creation be open, respecting and taking into account the ideas of all participants, and respecting and even utilizing the urban and social contexts of the locations of the wall in question. Without the need for further guidelines, the participants understand the responsibility they are given, never proposing offensive images or concepts. On the contrary, the groups come up with concepts that contribute to their surroundings, recognizing common history, paying homage to cultural heritage and recognizing the wealth of inspiration that surrounds them in their city.

The murals can also transmit socio-political messages, although this is not essential in developing the connection between citizens and art. The 3 murals that did begin with pre-established topics were proposed not as limitations on creativity, but rather as an opportunity to discuss, analyze and educate by taking on universal themes.

In the first of these thematic murals "The Light of Hope", 2011, the workshop of artists, volunteers and youth workers, began the arduous task of collective creativity with the theme of gender equality. With the mural the group was able to communicate hope and concerns regarding gender inequality, but at the same time they had the opportunity to discuss, learn, think and formulate ideas based on the theme. They shared experiences and emotions with their fellow participants and artists within the workshop and then, through the mural, with the public at large. This mural has become a landmark, and a backdrop for activities relating to gender equality, thus perpetuating its service to society by provoking further discussions surrounding the theme.

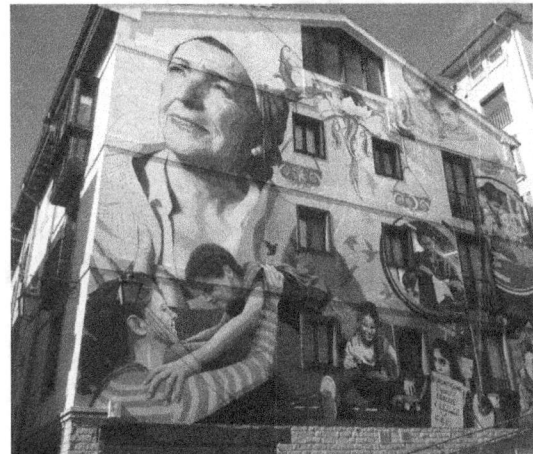 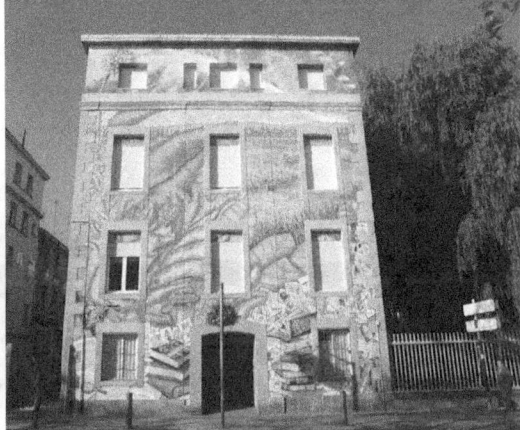

Figure 2: "The Light of Hope", Vitoria-Gasteiz, 2011
Source: IMVG

Figure 3: "What will we do with what we know?", 2011,
Vitoria-Gasteiz Source: IMVG

The second mural based on a pre-established theme was about environmental sustainability. Vitoria-Gasteiz was named European Green Capital in 2011 and because of this accolade the IMVG decided to explore the topic within one of its workshops. The resulting mural explores the notions of knowledge and action, discourse and hypocrisy and other aspects of the environmental debate that affect how our society faces the challenge of environmental sustainability. The mural is titled: "What will we do with what we know?" The title reflects the dilemma that the participants faced as they tried to avoid a purely political or moralistic message, and it illustrates the struggle within our society as it tries to answer the question.

The third mural with a pre-established theme was painted in 2013 and is the first mural to be painted outside of the medieval quarter. This mural is painted in a working class neighborhood just outside the city center, and its location relates directly to its theme. In 1976 police killed 5 striking workers when they participated in a peaceful assembly inside a church. The mural speaks specifically about this event and is located on a private building facing the church where the event took place. The assassination of these workers and the police repression that surrounded the labor struggles of the time had never been dealt with on such a level and certainly not in such public terms. The resulting mural is a monument to the workers struggle and a testament to a people's memory and is titled: "No Present nor Future Without Memory".

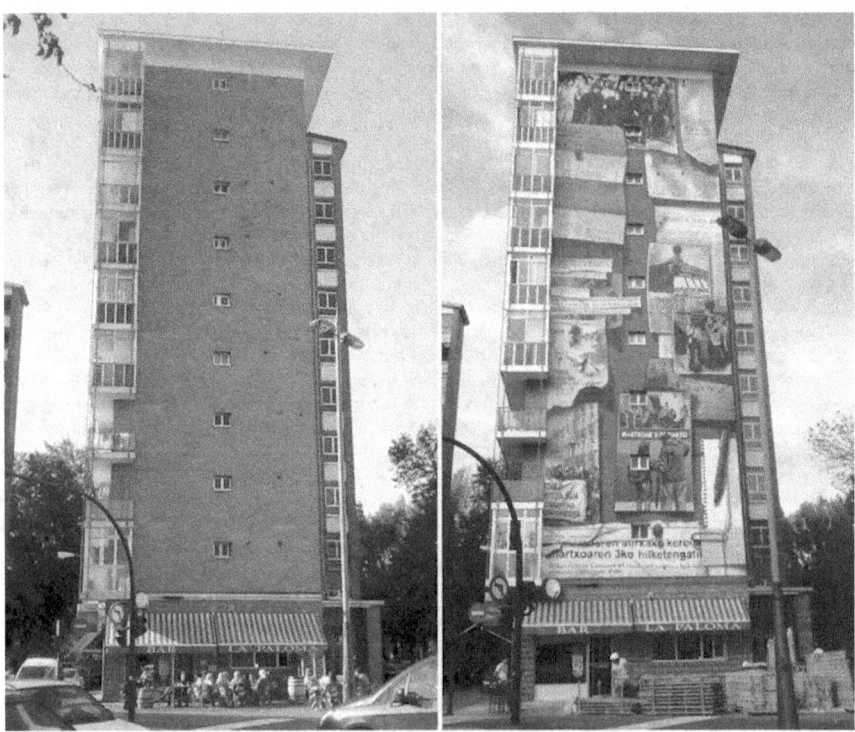

Figure 4: "No Present nor Future Without Memory", Before and After, 2013, Vitoria-Gasteiz Source: IMVG

Empowering citizens
With a pre-established theme or without it we can interpret Brecht's famous quote as an invitation, or indeed an impulse, to use the act of creation as a means of empowering citizens. When a diverse group of individuals comes together with a common goal and is able to create beauty and art where before they were denied that space, the city as a whole perceives the gesture as a victory for its citizens. The mural itself communicates a message, as does the making of it. This active civic participation in the city and culture is the antithesis of the habitual apathy citizens are relegated to by traditional cultural policy that views the citizen as a mere consumer of culture. This is why we believe that the creation of the work has equal if not greater value than the work itself.

Visualizing Participation
Because it is essential to communicate before, during, and after, the way in which the murals were created, the program insists on the importance of recording the development of the workshops. This process of documentation, however, is also subject to the original ideology of participation. Since 2010, the entire process of creating each mural is documented by another workshop, in this case audio-visual. Keeping the format of Artist/Coordinator, citizen volunteers and youth workers, small groups are formed to follow, record and document the mural process. This group functions parallely to the mural making workshop. The result is a short edited documentary, that highlights the indiviuals participating in the mural, the process with which the mural was created and the practical

aspects of creating large format exterior public murals. Each audio visual workshop collaborates in every step, from script writing, to recording, interviews and editing.

The resulting documentaries are projected at the inauguration of the mural itself, during congresses, and conferences about public art, art therapy and urbanism, and they are available permanentlly on the program´s website.The mural program also benefits from a specific media strategy made to highlight the social aspects of community muralism. This strategy has led to the program being features in local, national and international publicactions.

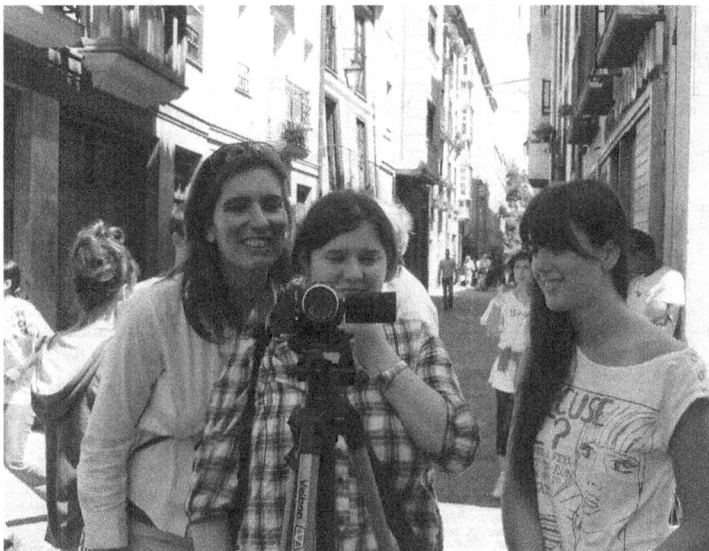
Figure 5: Documentary film workshop, 2010 Source: IMVG

Beyond "Interventionism"
Collaborative muralism has multiple functions. The public nature of the projects imply important alterations in the way our city is constructed. In contrast to urbanistic projects led by institutions and considered public art, citizen initiatives are often referred to as "interventions". This distinction evokes not only differences in the nature of the work itself, but the value, permanence and legitimacy. The IMVG proposes eliminating such distinctions or at the very least viewing partcipatory practices as a contribution to public space rather than an intervention upon it. It is true that municipalities and institutions have a a responsibility in organizing our cities so that they are functional and safe, but who has the responsiblity to humanize these spaces? Will we allow others to express themselves in our name or will we find a way to contribute through collaboration on the processes that regulate our public spaces? Recuperating public space from institutions and corporations empowers citizens in general and as individuals.

Conclusion
Vitoria-Gastiez is changing, not only its outward image, but inwardly as well, through its citizens and through art. It is changing little by little. When we type "Vitoria-Gasteiz" into an internet search engine we can witness how the images found are no longer limited to the medieval stones of its cathedrals and palaces, but include bursts of color. When a visitor strolls within the medieval walls they are surprised not only by the remnants of the past inhabitants but the evidence of the present day neighbors. Once we learn that these colorful images were created by the people of the city we can understand that Vitorians are creative, culturally open, active and generous, and they participate more actively and directly in the city that surrounds them.

Axel Philipps, Leibniz University Hannover / Institute of Sociology;
a.philipps@ish.uni-hannover.de

SergejZerr, Leibniz University Hannover / L3S Research Center; zerr@l3s.de
Eelco Herder, Leibniz University Hannover / L3S Research Center; herder@l3s.de

Chroniclers of Street Art on Flickr

The Internet has become a very effective platform for the circulation of reproductions of digital Street Art. This paper therefore deals with Street Art's chronicling on Flickr and how it contributes to the visibility and reputation of Street Art objects and their creators. We focus on the chronicling behaviour of the general audience, represented by Flickr users who upload photos showing Street Art and how they document them. Our findings challenge the assumption that Internet users are more important to the acknowledgement of street artists than art critics and professionals: most entries on Flickr offer no information on the production context and therefore do not contribute to the visibility or reputation of specific works or artists.

Street Art, documentation, chronicler, visibility, Flickr

Introduction

'Street Art' is a relatively new term that is often used for anonymous interventions on the streets carried out using various media (i.e. stencils, murals, stickers). Some forms of these media have been used for a long time[1], but the term Street Art usually refers to unauthorised artistic creations using these media outside of established art galleries, exhibitions and museums. Consequently, Street Art is usually related to a wide range of art movements ranging from 'post-museum art' (Riggle, 2010) to new avant-garde (Austin, 2010). They also often refer to the history of art and mimic Pop Art, Dada, or Surrealism. Furthermore, street artists often adopt the standards and criteria of producing artists and reproduce the aesthetic ideology of condemning commercialisation (Irvine 2012; Wuggenig, 2009). Last, but not least, like public art, Street Art is accessible to everyone, free of charge (i.e. no exhibition fee), and encourages public debate (Bengtsen, 2013).

In contrast to public art, Street Art seldom appears in exhibition catalogues, review sections of newspapers or travel guides. Often, Street Art objects are visible to pedestrians who casually notice the interventions and may take some time to look at them and think about them. The presence of Street Artin the public realm is often limited in terms of exposure and lifetime, because of their location and decay due to demolition or weathering. By contrast, the appearance of Street Art in printed magazines, books and on Internet websites establishes Street Art as part of both the street scene and recognised art institutions (Irvine, 2012; Snyder, 2009, 2006). Wuggenig (2009) even designates the Internet as the most important promoter for increasing the visibility and reputation of Street Art and its makers. According to Wuggenig, 'there are channels of advancement in artistic status, fame and influence outside those of the central gallery and dealer-critic system of the art field. The Internet and the mass basis for the support of Street Art provide the crucial conditions in this regard' (Wuggenig, 2009). His argument consists of two implicit assumptions. Firstly, the visibility of Street Art depends on how often it is published and discussed on the Internet in general, but less on specific websites dedicated to the advancement of Street Art and its artists. Secondly, art critics and professionals are less important for the recognition and visibility of street artists: more important is the number of Internet users who upload, share and circulate digital reproductions of Street Art objects.

Wuggenig's (2009) study is one of the first to investigate the influence of the Internet on Street Art. However, his assumption is merely based on a Google search for selected (street) artists, when he found more entries for the street artist Banksy than for famous artists such as Robert Rauschenberg, Jackson Pollock or Joàn Miró. His study suffers from several limitations. Firstly, he did not sufficiently indicate possible bias introduced by specifics of the search engine and secondly, he did not control the context of the entries. Hence, he did not sufficiently take into account who distributes digital reproductions of Street Art objects on the Internet. Therefore, this paper specifically focuses onthe attention for Street Art given by regular Internet users who upload such photos. The study concentrates on these regular users and how they contribute to the visibility of Street Art and its makers. What is characteristic about them? How do they document Street Art objects and does this influence its visibility? Instead of using web interfaces such as Google, Bing or Yahoo, this study focused on photographic reproductions of Street Art on www.flickr.com, the largest open photo-sharing platform on the Internet. Photos on Flickr are mainly uploaded by the general audienceand only to a small extent by street artists themselves; rather, Flickr users share an interest in the practice of photography and use it to archive a great variety of images with different themes (Rubenstein/Sluis, 2008; Skageby, 2008; Van House, 2007). Nonetheless, in the field of art and humanities, Flickr's biggest proportion of photos tagged 'art' are often linked to terms such as 'street' and 'graffiti' (Angus et al., 2010). In this paper, photos and further information offered on Flickr are used to examine how Street Art is documented by the users of that platform.

The paper is organised in four parts. Firstly it discusses aspects of documenting graffiti writing and Street Art objects. Street Art is represented in different media such as books, magazines and the Internet but representations vary with the context and contributors. Focusing on Flickr users, the second part describes the methodological approach and material used. Based on the analysis of picture contents and metadata, the third part details the findings. The paper concludes with a discussion of the findings and possible future developments.

Street Art chroniclers

Kimvall (2013) introduced the term 'chroniclers' for graffiti documentarians. Chroniclers are active in various areas related to graffiti writing[2] and Street Art. They are 'collectors of photos of graffiti (both their own photos and photos traded by others), producers of magazines, websites, blogs, books and video-documentaries who interview graffiti writers and reproduce their images and put them in circulation' (Kimvall, 2013: 81). Such chroniclers are a constitutional part of the graffiti writing and Street Art worlds. The chronicling movement started withphotos in self-made magazines and books. Editors selected from their own material and material submitted by writers and street artists. However, these editors were professionals who decided what should be represented and distributed. Often,these editors were acknowledged writers and street artists themselves, or had a professional background in art history, photography or design (Snyder, 2006, 2009). The situation changed with the increasing popularity of the Internet. Nowadays, amateur and professional chroniclers walk through the streets to spot and take photos of graffiti writings and Street Art objects. These digitally reproduced objects are often immediately uploaded to the Internet. Consequently, ephemeral Street Art is archived and globally distributed (Irvine, 2012). According to Ferrell and Weide (2010), digital reproduction transformed the graffiti writing practice even further. At first, graffiti writings appeared on walls but later turned to 'liquid spots' such as subway trains, freight trains, delivery trucks and shutters. With the Internet, 'mediated images and information not only circulate globally, but circle back on their sources in such a way as to melt away any certain distinction between source and simulation' (Ferrell/Weide, 2010: 59). At the same time, writers carefully differentiate between material and digitally-reproduced graffiti, giving less credit to writers who are only present on the Internet. The latter group is disqualified by arguments such as 'cheap fame' (Ferrell/Weide, 2010: 59).

In addition to judgements of insiders, chronicling affects the profile of Street Art. Street Art is most present and globally distributed through the Internet. But how do chroniclers on the Internet contribute to the visibility of Street Art and its makers? How do they document it? Some of those chroniclers are professional magazine and book editors as well as owners of portals such as Art Crimes[3] or the Wooster Collective[4]. They regularly report about Street Art exhibitions, events and artists. The website www.graffiti.org, for example, offers photos from all over the world, informs about new book releases and provides links to current exhibitions and websites of featured artists. The frequent use of hyperlinks allows viewers to relate creations with their makers. Consequently, with the digital circulation of graffiti, the visibility of artists increases. However, there is also a large number of less professional chroniclers who merely contribute to social media and other Internet platforms. They share their photographs but do not create or own websites, magazines or books themselves. This paper focuses on the latter type of chroniclers, represented by Flickr users, and the ways they distribute digital reproductions of Street Art objects. It is postulated that Flickr users approach Street Art professionally, as they use the same specific indicators as art collectors to identify exhibited art or reproductions. Such indicators are often the title, the artist's name, the place and date of production and materials used.

Data and methods

The study focuses on digital reproductions related to Street Art that are published through the photo-sharing Internet platform Flickr, a general-purpose platform for the exchange of pictures. Based on 10,868 digital reproductions related to street art, a randomised sample was created in order to examine the impact of Flickr users as chroniclers. For the study, we used the metadata related to the Flickr users; further, a visual content analysis was employed on the photographic reproductions.

Currently, Flickr hosts over 2.6 million photos[5] with the tag 'street art' (April 2014).These photos cover all uploads since the Internet platform was established in 2004, but the number of photos varies over the years and among Flickr users. It was therefore decided to rely on the basic unit of 10,868 users who uploaded one or more photos with the tag 'streetart' in 2012. This section still contains photos from both less active and very active users, with the consequence that a randomly selected sample would contain more photos from the very active users rather than from less active users. To avoid such imbalances, a basic unit of 10,858 photos was set up by randomly selecting just one photo with the tag 'streetart' for each user. From this basic unit, 1,000 users and their corresponding photos were selected for a manual coding process, using a simple random strategy (with replacement). A representative sample with a level of significance of 1% requires more than 625 cases. Since it was observed that tags sometimes do not refer to photo content (Cox et al., 2008; Liu et al., 2011), it was decided to work with more photos than the minimum.

In addition to the photos, metadata was also collected related to the photos and the Flickr users who uploaded them. For many photos, for example, background information was available about the users and photo-related EXIF-data. Such data provides additional insights, including information extracted from photo titles and descriptions, the number of favourite assignments, the number of views, the number of comments, the camera model used, and the users' places of residence and their gender. Interviews and questionnaires would, of course, have offered a more grounded and comprehensive description of Flickr users and how they represent Street Art. However, by using existing metadata we have been able to analyse a far larger number of Flickr users and their role in documenting Street Art objects.

The analysis was conducted in two stages. Firstly, a manual coding procedure was employed to categorise and count the frequency of the photos' contents (Bell, 2001; Rose, 2012). Two trained coders classified all photos according to pre-defined categories such as Street Art (whether the photo shows the result of a creative intervention or not), identified media, location and artists in the descriptions and tag lists.[6] The agreement among the coders was above 90% for all variables used in the paper.[7] In a second analytical step, correlations between features related to the Flickr users were studied (i.e. gender, number of views, model of camera) and the representation of Street Art objects (i.e. identified media and artists in the photo descriptions and tag lists). Since no statistically significant correlations were found (as discussed in the following section), research concentrated on frequencies to describe the Flickr users who upload digital reproductions of Street Art objects and how they document them. In which part of the world, for example, do the most active contributors live? Do they employ specific categories of the established art world to inform about the artist and the production context? Does Flickr chronicling support Wuggenig's (2009) assumption about the importance of the Internet in recognising Street Art and its makers?

Flickr users and chronicling

In the sample, 957 photos (95.7%) were classified as Street Art reproductions that represent the results of creative interventions by the public. 43 of the photos showed people, animals, and activities unrelated to Street Art. For example, photos showing dogs playing, people in a market, people in front of a pharmacy, people performing as street musicians or as pantomime artists were excluded from the Street Art category and therefore excluded from further analysis. Consequently, the work concentrated only on the photos coded as Street Art by human annotators (n=957).

Flickr users

Continuing with the classified Street Art reproductions, 73.4% (n=702) of the Flickr users disclosed their gender. According to this gender information, more male chroniclers (n=479) circulate Street Art reproductions than female users (31.8%, n=223). Thus, documenting Street Art seems to be a predominantly male activity, although female documentarians do comprise a relevant proportion of the chroniclers. Taking into consideration the fact that, in general, female users are more willing to share photos (Litt/Hargittai, 2014) this does not hold true for pictures showing Street Art objects.

Flickr also asks its users to add their place of residence. 516 users (53.9%)[8] mentioned their hometown, district, state or country, which resulted in a large variety of places from all over the world. As it was difficult to deal with such a multitude of places and the differently used categories, the study therefore reduced and related all places of residence to a continent. Based on continents, it is evident that most Flickr documentarians live in the affluent northern hemisphere (Fig. 2). Users from Europe, together with those from North America, make up 84.1% (n=434) of all Flickr contributors who indicated their place of residence. A reason for this concentration on Europe and North America might be the dominance of Street Art objects in these regions. Based on the frequencies in the tag lists of the sample, the five most prominent cities for Street Art are London (n=68), Paris (n=47), Berlin (n=40), New York (n=32) and Amsterdam (n=28).However, if one would take the size of the total population into account, relatively more Flickr users from Australia uploaded Street Art reproductions than people from Europe or North America. Taking into account the economic situation in these continents, in contrast to South America, Africa or Asia – which had very few Flickr documentarians in relation to their population –, chronicling seems to represent the centre-periphery-differentiation of the global capitalist order. Circulation of Street Art photos via Flickr is more common in wealthy states. Other factors might be restricted Internet access and limited financial resources to afford a camera or mobile device in other parts of the world. Western Europe (including Scandinavia), North America, Australia and Japan demonstrate high access. In contrast, South America, Eastern Europe, Russia, North Africa and parts of Asia constitute zones of medium access (Adams 2009). A further observation is that the camera prices[9] in the sample range from $14.99 to $7,100.00: Flickr users spend on an average $659.28ontheir camera or mobile phone. Although half of the users paid less (median=$469.99), or might have bought a used camera for perhaps a quarter of the original price, they still used cameras that were unaffordable for people in most regions of the world (with an annual income of around $3,300 worldwide in 2006; see Pinkovskiy/Sala-i-Martin, 2009). Thus, one could suggest that Street Art chronicling is limited to financially relatively secure groups. The observation holds true when taking into account the average price of camera models used in different continents (Table 1,) as there is only a small variation among them. In South America, for example, Flickr documentarians of Street Art paid on an average $613.68. This is less than the average price in other regions but still a large proportion of people in South America have anannual average income of around $5,000 (in 2006; see Pinkovskiy/Sala-i-Martin,2009).

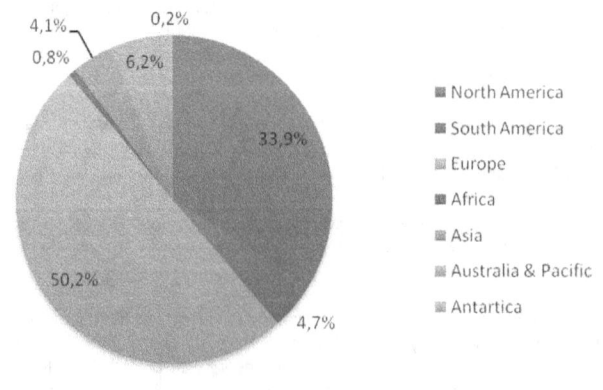

Fig. 2: Percentages of Flickr's Street Art chroniclers from different continents

Continent	Average price for cameras used	Valid cases
North America	$704.19	115
South America	$613.68	16
Europe	$727.84	158
Africa	$229.00	1
Asia	$1.015.39	11
Australia & Pacific	$692.21	18
Antarctica	-	0

Table 1: Average camera prices on different continents (n=319)

Street Art documentation

In cases where Street Art objects appear unexpectedly overnight and disappear after an indefinite period of time, one might expect that most observers spot such interventions by accident. Consequently, the preparation of digital documentation of a Street Art object appears to be an important factor. In the case of an unplanned encounter, for example, chroniclers may use their mobile phones. In contrast, passionate documentarians see it as their task to spot new Street Art objects (Blanché, 2012; Kimvall, 2013) and for this reason they bring their heavy-duty camera, take photos and publish them on the Internet. Based on the number of mobile phones and cameras used in the sample, Street Art documentation seems to be a dedicated activity: most Flickr users took a photo with their photo camera (80.8%, n=497) whereas mobile phones were only used 103 times (16.7%). Additionally, in 15 cases people took the trouble to scan an analogue photo (2.4%) and upload it to Flickr. Hence, most Flickr chroniclers seem be dedicated photographers.

However, it is unclear whether Flickr users put a camera around their neck and go out to find new Street Art objects or rather to capture the next highly appreciated photo in the Flickr community. Flickr, first of all, is a social network and photos are stakes in a game among its users. The goal is 'attention that can be measured in the number of views, commentaries and favouritizations' (Holschbach, 2010: 47). Is this also true for the digital documentation of Street Art objects? A closer look reveals that a Street Art reproduction gains on an average around 62 views (Table 2), whereas half of all uploads in this category only received 29 views or less. 1,123 was the highest number of views for a photo showing a Street Art object. A total of 345 photos of the sample became favourites. Most of these photos gained one to five favourite-assignments (80.4%). Apart from one photo with 107 favourites, the average was 1.7 assignments in the sample. As with favourites, only 231 photos had at least one comment. In contrast to 75.8% uncommented photos (n=723), 6.6% received between one and five comments (n=63). If one compares these indicators of attention with those of the 'World100F'-group[10] in Flickr, it is evident that the documentation of Street Art objects gains only a small amount of attention. The 'World100F'-group represents those Flickr users who have photos with 100 and more favourite-assignments.[11] Focusing on photos incorporated in the group in 2012, a 'World100F'-classified photo received on average 5,600 views, 201 favourite assignments and 384 comments. Flickr's 'interestingness 'algorithm'[12] furthermore determines which uploaded photos are selected for Flickr's portal page (front page). A total number of 166,975 pictures were shown in 2012. Focusing on photos with the tag 'street art', 271 were chosen (0.16%), of which only one photo was included in our sample. Based on these findings, it appears that the investigated Flickr users are primarily interested in the content of the photos – say documenting Street Art objects. Instead of attentiveness, they seem rather to be driven by the idea of contributing to the 'global Web museum' (Irvine, 2012: 242) of Street Art.

Sample	Streetart	World100F
Average views	62.7	5,600.3
Average favourites	1.7	201.7
Average comments	1.2	384.5

Table 2: Average views, favourites and comments on Street Art photos (n=954) and on World100F's photos (n=64) in 2012

The enormous number of photos with the tag 'street art' supports this hypothesis. More and more digital reproductions of Street Art objects are uploaded, although Street Art appears not to be a good topic for gaining popularity within Flickr. However, the study also shows that most photos fail to connect Street Art objects to their context, in contrast to websites such as www.graffiti.orgor www.woostercollective.com, which present digital reproductions of Street Art objects and link them to their creator. The websites of the artists then relate the particular Street Art object to others and give background information on the production context and where to see them. In sharp contrast, this essential information about documented Street Art objects is rarely provided with Flickr uploads: links usually connect a photo with photos on other platforms (e.g. instagram.com, ipernity.com, panoramio.com), to social networks(e.g. Facebook, Twitter)or personal photographers' websites. There are very few links (n=47) to websites of artists or dedicated sites on Street Art like www.endlesscanvas.com, www.snakeoilmagazine.com or www.graffitimundo.com. In line with the kinds of links they provide, Flickr users offer very little background information on artists and the production context (Table 3). They generally mention the place where the photo was taken (80.4%, n=774), as this is a common practice in Flickr. In contrast, more in-depth information on street art is largely missing: the employed medium was identified 299 times (31.2%) and the artist for just 55 photos (5.7%). A closer look at the identified locations discloses some further ambiguity. Instead of detailed specification such as the name of the city, the street and house number, most users just mentioned places such as Berlin, London or New York. Such vagueness, of course, helps to conceal the actual place and who is responsible for the intervention. One could argue it is a practice to protect Street Art objects and artists from removal and prosecution. On the other hand, most street artists use pseudonyms to conceal their identity. Consequently, digital Street Art documents without any connection to such pseudonyms do not contribute to the visibility of street artists and their chances to be recognised. The basic prerequisite for the artists' advancement in status and fame is information about the production context. And this information is practically non-existent in Flickr.

Categories	Dimensions	Frequency	Valid Percent
Identified location			100
	Location	774	80.9
	None	183	19.1
Identified medium			100
	Medium	299	31.2
	None	658	68,8

Table 3: Street Art's production context (n=957)

Discussion and outlook

Various authors have emphasised the importance of the Internet for Street Art and its visibility (Ferrell/Weide, 2010; Irvine, 2012; Snyder, 2006, 2009; Wuggenig, 2009). Wuggenig (2009), in particular, argued that mass dissemination via the Internet was responsible for the prominence of Street Art. He further argued that the reputation of street artists depends less on art critics and professionals: Internet users seem to be more important and their circulation of photos showing Street Art objects.

Concentrating on Flickr users, the findings support the idea of active Street Art chroniclers outside of established art institutions and specialised websites. There are male as well as female documentarians who take photos of Street Art objects and upload them to Flickr. They are active worldwide, with a concentration in the global-capitalist epicentres (Australia, Europe, North America). Together these users keep up a constant chronicling process, which results in a globally accessible Street Art archive. This definitely increases the visibility of Street Art in general, but less its photographers in the Flickr world: Flickr users document Street Art objects, although most of these photos never gain a great community of peers and fans within Flickr.

Nonetheless, the findings also challenge the assumption that Internet users are more important for the recognition and reputation of street artists than art critics and professionals. Art critics, collectors and curators, as well as websites related to Street Art, connect art works with their producers, other creations and contexts. Such information is the precondition for acknowledging the artists and to stipulate their advancement in the art world. In sharp contrast, most entries on Flickr do not offer such connections and information. A Flickr search leads to many Street Art objects, but most of them provide no references or links to their creators and the production context. Consequently, Flickr does not replace or complement (online) galleries, (online) magazines and specialised websites. For this reason, we may conclude that, first and foremost, institutions within the art world increase the visibility and the acknowledgement of street artists. In other words, the advancement of the status of street artists still depends on those organised people who take interviews, post comments and reviews on art works and offer links to personal artists' websites.

Finally, the investigation of Flickr users only sheds some light on Street Art chroniclers. Flickr hosts many digital reproductions of Street Art objects and, as such, is an important constituent of the global Internet archive on Street Art. However, the chronicling process is neither restricted to Flickr nor do Flickr users represent every kind of documentarian. Further research should concentrate on the documentation of Street Art both inside and outside of established art institutions. Street Art is documented in various ways; Street Art objects are exhibited in well-known art museums such as Tate Modern (London), Centre Pompidou (Paris), or MOCA (Los Angeles), in temporary exhibitions and street shows such as The Cans Festival (London, 2008), the iBug (Zwickau, regularly), or the RVA Street Art Festival (Richmond, Virginia, 2012 & 2013), and in many different amateur or more professionally edited books, magazines and websites. Thus,different types of chroniclers with different intentions, backgrounds and practices carry out the documentation of Street Art. And these different types of chroniclers furthermore make use of different online platforms, varying from general-purpose platforms such as Flickr to dedicated websites. These different platforms and their users all contribute to the documentation of Street Art in their own way.

Notes and References
1 According to Pike et al. 2012, Paleolithic hand stencils in Spain are around 37.3 thousand years old.
2 In contrast to most written or scratched messages or icons visible in public, graffiti writing refers to stylish signatures. In the culture of graffiti writing, the style of the letters and the individual mastery of spray painting are pivotal in gaining fame and respect within the graffiti writers' community (Snyder 2009).
3 URL: http://www.graffiti.org
4 URL: http://www.woostercollective.com
5 In 2013 the storage capacity for each Flickr user reached one terabyte.
6 Appendix A offers detailed definitions.
7 A full list of values for agreements and Cohen's kappa for each category is provided in Appendix B.

8 In most cases, the place of residence matches with the time zone. However, some users did not change the default time zone or used fake places such as 'everywhere', 'there should be no borders' or 'Starbuckistan, USA'. The latter cases were excluded from further analysis.
9 Camera prices were retrieved using Google (accessed 18 March 2014). The presented prices, of course, are only approximate values,asit was not known whether people bought new or used cameras, only bought camera bodies, or what additional lenses they had, and so on.
10 The self-defined 'QualityGroup' only invites photos with more than 99 favourites to join the group (see https://www.flickr.com/groups/world100f/).
11 The first rule for this group is: 'World100F presents photos, which are added to the favorites from at least 100 people' (see https://www.flickr.com/groups/world100f/rules/).
12 Flickr writes about the algorithm on http://www.flickr.com/explore/interesting/ (accessed 22 April 2014): 'There are lots of elements that make something 'interesting' (or not) on Flickr. Where the clickthroughs are coming from; who comments on it and when; who marks it as a favorite; its tags and many more things which are constantly changing. Interestingness changes over time, as more and more fantastic content and stories are added to Flickr.'

Adams, P. Geographies of Media and Communication (Hoboken, NJ: Wiley-Blackwell, 2009).
Angus, E., Stuart, D., Thelwall, M. Flickr's potential as an academic image resource: An exploratory study. Journal of Librarianship and Information Science 42/2010, 268–278. DOI: 10.1177/0961000610384656.
Austin, J. More to see than a canvas in a white cube.City: analysis of urban trends, culture, theory, policy, action 14/2010, 1-2, 33–47.
Bell, P. Content analysis of visual images. In T. van Leeuwen, C. Jewitt (Eds.), Handbook of Visual Analysis, pp. 10–34 (London: Sage, 2001).
Bengtsen, P. Beyond the public art machine: A critical examination of street art as public art. Konsthistorisktidskrift/Journal of Art History 82/2013, 63–80. DOI: 10.1080/00233609.2012.762804.
Blanché, U. Konsumkunst.Kultur und KommerzbeiBanksy und Damien Hirst(Bielefeld: Transcript, 2012).
Cox, A.M., Clough, P.D., Marlow, J. Flickr: A first look at user behaviour in the context of photography as serious leisure. Information Research 13/2008, paper 336.
Ferrell, J., Weide, R.D. Spot theory. City: analysis of urban trends, culture, theory, policy, action 14/2010, 1-2, 48–62.
Holschbach, S. Framing (on) Flickr: Modes of channelling an interdisciplinary reservoir of images. PhotoReseacher 14/2010, 46-53.
Irvine, M. The work on the street: Street art and visual culture. In B. Sandywell, I. Heywood (Eds.),The Handbook of Visual Culture, pp. 235–278 (London, New York: Berg, 2012).
Kimvall, J. Towards a conceptual and multi-positional understanding of the project in street and graffiti art. In L. Borriello, C. Ruggiero (Eds.), Inopinatum: The Unexpected Impertinence of Urban Creativity, pp. 79–89 (Rome: Artigrafichebocchia, 2013).
Litt, E., Hargittai, E. Smile, snap, and share? A nuanced approach to privacy and online photo-sharing. Poetics 42/2014, 1, 1-21. DOI: 10.1016/j.poetic.2013.10.002.
Liu, D., Hua, X.-S., Zhang, H.-J. Content-based tag processing for Internet social images. Multimed Tools Appl51/2011, 723–738. DOI: 10.1007/s11042-010-0647-3.
Pike, A. W. G., Hoffmann, D. L., Garcia-Diez, M., Pettitt, P. B., Alcolea, J., Balbin, R. de et al. U-Series Dating of Palaeolithic Art in 11 Caves in Spain. Science336/2012, 6087, 1409–1413.
Pinkovskiy, M., Sala-i-Martin, X. Parametric estimations of the world distribution of income.NBER Working Paper 15433/2009. Available from: http://www.nber.org/papers/w15433.
Riggle, N.A. Street Art: The transfiguration of the commonplace. The Journal of Aesthetics and Art Criticism68/2010, 243–257.
Rose, G. Visual Methodologies. 3rd edition. (London: Sage, 2012).
Rubenstein, D., Sluis, K. A life more photographic. Mapping the networked image. Photographies 1/2008,1, 9-28.
Skageby, J. Semi-public end-user content contributions—A case-study of concerns and intentions in online photo-sharing. International Journal of Human-Computer Studies 66/2008, 287–300. DOI: 10.1016/j.ijhcs.2007.10.010.
Snyder, G.J. Graffiti Lives. Beyond the Tag in New York's Urban Underground (New York, London: New York University Press, 2009).
Snyder, G.J. Graffiti media and the perpetuation of an illegal subculture.Crime Media Culture2/2006, 93–101. DOI: 10.1177/1741659006061716.
Van House, N. Flickr and Public Image-Sharing: Distant Closeness and Photo Exhibition. CHI'07 extended abstracts on Human factors in computing systems. ACM2007, 2717–2722.
Wuggenig, U. The tattooings of cities.Notes on the artistic field and popular art in the city. In Beyes, T., Krempl, S.-T., Deuflhard, A. (Eds.), Parcitypate: Art and Urban Space, no pages (Sulgen: Niggli, 2009).

Appendix A

Street Art: The photographic reproduction shows results of a creative intervention (in public). 'Intervention' means that someone interfered and illicitly transformed a commonplace (or utilitarian object) into something different (e.g. a dustbin into an animal). Pictures presenting no results of a creative intervention were counted as 'others'. Identified location: Flickr photos are often shared along with additional text. In these texts (title, description and tag list), information was sought about the location of the represented Street Art object (location=1, no location=0). This signifies the modest form of context sensitivity.

Identified medium: In the same additional texts, information was also noted about the medium used (medium=1, no medium=0). Identifying the medium indicates familiarity with employed Street Art media.Identified artist: Furthermore, information was sought about artists' names given in additional texts. Names in the texts often refer to the photographer. Therefore, the study concentrated on words and phrases such as 'art by' and 'artist' followed by a name (artist=1, no artist=0). This signifies that users possess knowledge about street artists related to their works.

Appendix B. Intercoders' reliability agreement rates and Cohen's kappa (n=100)

Categories	Agreement rate in Percent	Cohen's kappa
Street Art	99.0	0.795
Identified artists	98.0	0.847
Identified medium	95.0	0.896
Identified location	95.0	0.841

Paulo Barroso, Faculty of Social Sciences and Humanities (FCSH) / Communication
and Language Studies Center (CECL)

Keith Haring's personal visual lexicon and public semiotic-art

The visual-language of Keith Haring (1958-1990) is a semiotic system, exceeding written language and creating a personal visual lexicon, a nonrestrictive language. But, how is it possible to use symbols and produce messages transforming the public space into a communicative display? Looking at his symbolic messages, how can we understand the meaning and the productive mechanism of cultural messages and mythical meanings? What leads us to understand artist's meanings or to recognize his art as an ideological symbol of something else? Is anyone able to create a semiotic lexicon (i.e. symbols, not words) to transmit ideological messages?

Keith Haring, public space, semiotic-art.

Introduction: Keith Haring's personal visual lexicon

Firstly, I do not intend to describe the artistic style of Keith Haring (1958-1990) as an art critic, but to point out the minimum and necessary elements of meaning that make up his work a semiotic system. Secondly, my goal is neither art itself nor art definition or what art is (i.e. the meaning of art), but, on the one hand, the artist Haring who had created political and social art and, on the other hand, the conception of the mentioned semiotic system linked to a communication process.

The idea that art is life and life is art summarizes Haring's life and work, because his life was art and art was his life. It is not only his life that matters in his work, but the human life. Haring's art makes famous and commercial his life. The personality of his life was combined with the social dimension of his art.

Haring's work is one among several allowing the discernment of image as culture and rhetoric, i.e. having two dimensions, a social and a discursive. These social and discursive dimensions compose the two parts of my text. I made this division, but these two dimensions are connected. The reason why I establish these two parts is appropriated to deal with the pictorial image as a means to transmit meanings, connecting two dimensions: image (icons and symbols) and language (semiotics and rhetoric).

These two dimensions, the social and the discursive, reveal the social communicability and the communicational sociability when they are studied together, i.e., both show the logic of sociability and communicability. By studying the art-institution, it is shown that the creation and restoration of social ties depends on a process of generalized symbolic exchange, consisting in sharing. Is this device of sociability that also founds the logic of communication.

Communication is not a product, but a process of generalized symbolic exchange. A process feeding sociability, which generates social ties we have with others, overlying the natural relationships we have with the environment (Rodrigues, 1999: 22). If communication is present in art and if it is a process involving communion and community among its members, therefore communication encourages sociability and contributes to the organization and functioning of society. There are no societies without communication or artistic forms of expression. All societies have spaces or public spheres as one of the fundamental interrelationships between communication and society. The concept of communication is defined by establishing inter-relationships among agents that compose the process. Because it is a way of sharing information and establishing a common situation, communication is characterized by a generalized symbolic exchange, as it is exemplified by art as primitive and social institution, constituting thereby the foundation of sociability. Concerning the meaning, the graffiti is an art produced to manifest two basic principles of semiotics: a system of signification and a communication process. The former has pictorial symbols expressing and conveying knowledge or perspectives; the latter relates people. The system of signification precedes, a priori, any communication process. The meaning is useless without communication, as it happens with the cultural phenomenon of art (Carrere & Saborit, 2000: 71). A system without function or no opportunity to verify the effectiveness of its use is ineffective. As it happens with all cultural phenomena, we don't understand nor define art only by its ability to mean, but also by its implementation in a complex communication process. Therefore, the meaning and communication coexist one because the other.

The role of semiotics in the image is to ensure the relationship between the meaning plan (content plan) and the significant plan (expression plane) (Carrere & Saborit, 2000: 73). In this perspective, an expression is only an expression just because it is an expression of a given content, insofar as a content is only a content just because it is a content of a given expression.

For example, a sign, in general, is the union between a plane of expression (made up by the expression's substance and the expression's form) and a plane of content (made up by the content's substance and content's form). Haring's work presents many symbols and pictorial signs through brush strokes, stains, lines, colors, shapes, etc. which can be described this way, i.e. pictorial signs showing a semic dimension, because they show that something is in place of something to someone, and its material component (the expression) is capable of evoking something else (the content).

From a personal visual lexicon to a social art

The relationship between art and society is necessarily reciprocal, not only because there are influences of the social context in art, which will be the key point for the history of art, but also because the opposite, the influence of art in society. The relationship between art and society is dynamic, complex and socially variable. The work of art is a social product; therefore, it may be a particular interpretation of reality, as the street art, the graffiti.

Haring created simple and mostly symbolic images in the vein of pop art and graffiti art. He disseminates simple truths that don't need exact and developed explanations (Kolossa, 2005: 28). For example, the original drawing of man reaches a vast public and gets their attention when they just flitter by.

If all art is public, speaking about public art is redundant, because we only recognize the art that communicates through certain channels of exposure and expression, as a means of reaching the public (Andrade et. al., 2000: 5). And if all art is public, all art is a public production in which the artist and the public of art communicate. The public art is a more public sort of art, i.e. a sort of art closely articulated to political and cultural citizenship (Andrade et. al., 2000: 14). The transformations of contemporary societies are associated either to risks or to challenges, giving rise to reflections and reformulations also expressed by public art.

When we talk about public art, it is appropriate to distinguish the legitimate art or the art made official by the institutional power from the alternative, marginal or subversive art. Both are public, but the former is legitimately imposed and corresponds presumably to desired canons of power and the latter is privately or illegally imposed (at least until a recent past). The latter art is the marginal public art, typically street art like graffiti from the 1960s in New York subway system. Today, the graffiti is a global social phenomenon working either as stave or as a reflection of trends, fashions and social issues. The graffiti is a specific mode of popular writing, an urban artistic otherness (Andrade et. al., 2000: 54).

Public semiotic-art: iconic language as a visual communication

Some works of Haring were stylized as famous icons through a pictorial language easily accessible and influential, a sort of semiotic mediation between art and social life. The work becomes a testament of time and society, as Andy Warhol, presenting the contemporary society painted as if it were a real iconography insignia of modern civilization.

Haring developed his artistic work based on a peculiar visual-language. He created a sort of semiotic system, in which the symbols carry an idiosyncratic lecture, because the symbols he (the emitter) used express messages following a code, an idiolect or his own language or visual speech. This is the minimum to consider Haring's work an open and public space semiotic system addressed to everyone passing throw the street. According to Nelson Goodman, the symbol is used and interpreted as a very general and neutral term, because it contains letters, words, texts, pictures, diagrams, etc. (Goodman, 2006: 9). It's a basic language of image (iconic language) and text (typographical language), i.e. a "bimedia" language (Costa, 2011: 13). Any message, in this case, as haring's images, is at the same time semantic and aesthetic and it is read in a very complementary and associative manner. The texts are severe about possible meanings; and the images, in its turn, are surface messages (lines, contours, figures, symbols, colors, etc.) by which the eye moves at his pleasure (Costa, 2011: 23).

This pleasure felt by the eye moving over the surface of the image is a process and it includes the iconic and textual perception and the recognition of shapes experienced by the spectator (Costa, 2011: 26), i.e. the eye's freedom to roaming over the represented surface, the aesthetic pleasure deciphered by the mind and the understanding and interpretation of speech (the visual rhetoric of what the image means showing and expressing).

According to Pierre Francastel, the capture of any image by our vision entails the development of a mental activity, simultaneously oriented in two directions: the image and its elements become meaningful when we establish a concerted relationship between materials signs and when we assume that these elements refer to commonly interpreted sets of objects and for a certain group of individuals (Francastel, 1998: 102).

The art is based on the creation of images with meaning and aesthetic value. The image is the principal element for man and social environment interaction. Through the image, we immediately receive, read and interpret a lot of information. An image is an artificial means, because it is a mental and social product; it is created by man as a product of a culture following a process of signification. In the form of drawings or graffiti, an image is always something to give meaning and means anything. The image communicates through the representation, but to represent, an image has to function as a pictorial symbol. The works of art are, in the context of the author and his collection, a language, an aesthetic symbolic system, insofar that neither a work of art nor a symbol work alone in the system or have their own rules.

Haring worked to exceed the limits of the written language and words, creating its personal visual lexicon as a nonrestrictive language to communicate his ideals. He did it to discuss taboo subjects and causes (e.g. AIDS, homosexuality, apartheid, war, freedom, life, birth, death, love, etc.). Therefore, he drew simple graphics and lines to make complex social and political messages. It's very difficult to express emotions through images produced properly to it, but the work of art compels us to see it in a certain right perspective (Wittgenstein, 1998: 7).

There are degrees of content in Haring's work. The communication and understanding of ideas are dependent of such degrees of content scale, which oscillate between the specific and the general, light and dark, equivocal/ambiguous and unequivocal/unambiguous. The drawings in the New York subway system are like this and, therefore, they are also semantically powerful, because they don't say exactly what they mean. The New York subway system was his laboratory and also his showroom.

However, what is the demarcation of Haring's work face to abstract painting? According to Haring, this abstract painting does not have anything to transmit to the world, while his work was focused and concern on communication (the message, the content) than on the aesthetic form (the means, the form), despite its characteristic style (Kolossa, 2005: 19). Art is the only opposition to abstraction and the only freedom expression of what is just thinking, merely ideal and intelligible, pure feeling (Hauser, 1984: 7).

Inspired by the graffiti's power of communication, Haring extended the traditional routes of access to art and culture, i.e. he explored a pansemiotization of lines, contours, figures and symbols to convey social messages. Using non-verbal symbols, Haring created an iconic language exploring the visual communication.

Despite the originality creating lines, contours, figures and symbols as a chaining to produce and transmit messages, the images are easy to read and convey meanings of life, expressing his feelings about it. There are narratives of events or simple expressions of states of mind. He used a monochrome background in which a flowing line extends and a simple shapes repertoire ensures an instant recognition and provokes immediate effects. For this reason and for the graphical painting style, Haring's images reach the icon status.

However, is it possible social recognition without art commercialization? Haring's work was popular due to the artistic community or it was his own merit? The artistic values of Haring's symbols belong to spontaneity (autonomous creation) or convention (external stimuli)?

According to Goodman, all representation is conventional (Goodman, 2006: 41). The creation and implementation of a communication process only becomes understandable when it is submitted to a particular layout and convention, departing from a sphere of private or personal expression and meaning to enter into a sphere of relations between people (Hauser, 1984: 33). To do this, such process must always take into account the content and form of communication which necessarily lose some of their original meanings. Haring's art communicates because of the unique and personal spontaneity of the artist and because the expression conventionality. All art is a language, a way of speaking or expressing which must be recognizable as such and understood by others.

Every expression, every element of meaning, every form of communication and understanding has to decompose forms of indivisible and undifferentiated unity in the experience and assign special labels to it (Hauser, 1984: 41). Art has a voltage between unity and differentiation, spontaneity and mediation, experience and externalization. This is the essence by which art is expressed and becomes more visible.

Artists are social beings, like other people, i.e. they are products and producers of society and its cultural meanings. Generally and paradoxically, the development of artists moves them from a formal and more general language to a more individual language, a language formed by a personal style. The artist departs from the common language and approaches to a more personal mode of expression. It is only possible to decipher the artwork and its human content when we discover the complex reading the whole image features (Huyghe, 1986: 119). All images are signs by which we can find messages.
The appropriation of an artistic style and a system of signs by an artist, on the one hand, and its meanings recognition and reading by the public, on the other hand, are two complementary parts of the same process of creating images, messages or works of art. Haring created a visual code; he stylized a human figure and from then on he drew all human figures according to the same initial style, making his work easily recognizable. Repeating the same signs make these signs recognizable and readable. Therefore, we may compare Haring's signs with pictograms which the main idea is expressed by a single sign understandable by everyone who is familiar with such representation system.

However, we may don't need to be familiar with Haring's work and style to understand the image's message, because the first purpose could be merely expose an colored image with peculiar figures and shapes. The understanding of Haring's art is firstly due to the urban character and exposure of his work. The public art is forcibly and necessarily seen by everyone and Haring makes it happen with his art. In this perspective, it wouldn't make any sense to think art separately from real life. For this reason, we may consider Haring's art production close to the popular art and mass culture.
If the ancient men used to paint rupestral drawings on rocks and in caves as the way to report important facts of everyday life, giving a mystical and artistic meaning or power to the image, Haring conceived a return to the primitive way of representing. The topics of representation are the same for both ancient men and Harring, but the former are contemporary of a mass and capitalist society. Haring's work is a significant example of how art can come out of its ideological and aesthetic field to evoke other territories, namely mass communication and social critique.

With his visual lexicon, Haring proved that ideological messages can be transmitted in the form of art as a simple medium, disrupting and questioning the human condition. Haring claims that his draws provoke public imagination and he insists that art must lead to thinking. Haring's representation of forms or objects on a public surface by means of lines follows an aesthetic simplicity to the creation of artistic pictures. This aesthetic simplicity in his paintings makes us think that these are technically easy to perform, but his style is unique and the symbols acquire a grammatical sense and an ideological message. Haring's artistic mark was his stylistic line, i.e. a continuous and random line formally reduced to the essential. A line first transformed in contour and then in figure and finally in symbol.

At first glance, Haring's images and symbols may seem happy, optimistic and childhood, because the colors used by the artist and the inspiration from fairy tales and cartoons, but they have sexual or even violent content. For example, the figure of Pinocchio, easily identifiable by the long nose and the joints of the limbs, confounds the interpretation of the famous liar with a phallic figure exposing his elongated sex.

Some images are grotesque scenarios, as it is the case of the paintings criticizing the negative effects of technological progress: domineering monsters and robots; headless and small humans (for being obedient, subordinate). Haring's criticism was focused on the technology that replaces the thinking human being in contemporary societies. Therefore, these images become partly absurd. The symbols, which could be explained for being simple and objectively and conventionally a representation of something, are combined in a contradictory way, resulting in an obscure and variable association between signifier and signified.
All composition of symbols, colors, forms and lines follow a stylistic way, establishing a context and a meaning previously nonexistent as a work of art. Haring's style combines a graphic dimension and another imaginative dimension. Normally, the viewer understands at a brief look what there is to see and understand.

The emphasis I intent to show it how is it possible to use symbols and produce messages in murals and subway stations transforming the public space into a communicative display. Haring was familiar with Semiotics theories and authors, namely Roland Barthes and Umberto Eco. Therefore, his visual-language is based on how signs function to produce cultural messages and mythical meanings. Looking at his symbolic messages, how can we understand the meaning and the productive mechanism of cultural messages and mythical meanings? What leads us to understand the artist's meanings or recognize his art as an ideological symbol of something else? Is anyone able to create a semiotic lexicon (i.e. symbols, not words) to transmit ideological messages? No, but Haring worked on his abstract symbols, bright colors, bold lines and simple shapes as a personal visual lexicon to question the messages conveyed and its social-cultural values, playing with dual and modified meanings.

My perspective is that the meanings are visual produced by the conventional use and the artist's style; it is not the symbols itself, because it is not possible to create a sort of a personal code. Such code would be a cryptogram instead of a new shared alphabet. To recognize symbols is the condition sine qua non to communicate. Predominantly in the urban public space, because the place to show a message is strategically studied. If we understand the art-message is because it is not a personal or private code.

Conclusion: ethical implications

The Greeks' belief that beauty is moral goodness (Read 1968: 175) is followed in the nineteenth century, when aesthetics and ethics are considered inseparable by John Ruskin. For Ruskin, beauty and goodness was the same thing. The aim was the perfection of man's life, i.e. a spiritually enriched life. The aesthetic taste was related to the formation of character, constituting an educational aspect that, for Ruskin, was the main social function of art (Furió 2000: 37). From this perspective, Haring's work falls as art letting us discover and understand the relationships between art, in general, and the social environment, on the one hand, and the social conditions that make possible art and influence artistic production, on the other hand. These relationships also point out the material circumstances that influence the production, configuration and evolution of art over time.

In the Tractatus Logico-Philosophicus, Wittgenstein said that ethics and aesthetics are one and the same, because it seems clear that ethics or ethical issues cannot be expressed (Wittgenstein, 1999: 6.421). Ethics is transcendental even when it is expressed in art. However, for Nietzsche, we can only assume the art as a metaphysical possibility, as a way of revealing what it is. Only art reveals the true nature of reality. In his book The Birth of Tragedy, Nietzsche developed what he considered the artist's metaphysics, an interpretation about the universe following art. The art expresses two conflicting trends and art itself becomes a symbol. The Dionysian artist is totally identified with the primary one, with its suffering and its contradiction. The artwork is categorized as repetition or reproduction of the world and reflects this primordial suffering. The world has metaphysics, i.e. there is only an aesthetic phenomenon. The artist is the man who achieves his man condition, the one who liberates the individual will and become the spokesman of reality. Therefore, the purpose of art is not to educate or to improve, but to reveal. This is art-ontology; not art-pedagogy. This art specifies the ontological function of art, allowing the human being be complete and transcendent towards the real world in which he lives.

The artist's metaphysics and the art itself are not homogeneous. Nietzsche pointed out two components of art: the Apollonian (dream) and the Dionysian (drunkenness). These two artistic tendencies, according to Nietzsche, give rise to art. The gradual evolution of art results from the dual character of the Apollonian spirit and the Dionysian spirit. For Nietzsche, only one can speak of art as a synthesis of the Apollonian and the Dionysian. Art is like a cosmic event, a manifestation of two opposing forces of nature; two forces in conflict, but also in harmony. Dionysus is only revealed through Apollo, because only Apollo (the god of the shape and appearance) allows the development of the Dionysian materialized in music or in tragic heroes. In Twilight of the Idols, Nietzsche said the arts are not and cannot be all the same; some allow more transcendence than others, according their creative and immersive possibilities. Concurrently, the association between ethics and aesthetics corresponds to a double production of the good and the beautiful concerning human actions. According to Elisabeth Schellekens, the relationship between aesthetics and moral value aims one of the most important fields of research, an issue highlighted by engaging in reflective and significant terms: the kind of person we pretend to be, the objectives it seeks to achieve and aspire and how to treat other people (Schellekens, 2007: 13).

An example of the functional approach between ethics and aesthetics (i.e. between moral value and art) was proposed by Tolstoy, for whom art is valuable only when it serves moral or religious purposes, i.e. when it allows moral or religious experiences (Tolstoy apud Schellekens, 2007: 38). In this perspective, art must possess moral and religious values beyond a strictly aesthetic value. If Haring's public art became a visual language recognized everywhere, his aesthetics is more than individual, it's universal. Haring is known as "the graffiter" who took the street-art and ghettos-art into art history. Insofar Haring's work is widely recognized and exposed, it has unavoidable ethical implications cause by themes such as the promiscuous sexuality and an assumed homosexuality.

Notes and References

Andrade, Pedro de; Marques, Carlos Almeida; Barros, José da Cunha et al. (2000) Arte Pública e Cidadania – Novas Leituras da Cidade Criativa. Casal de Cambra: Caleidoscópio.
Carrere, Alberto; Saborit, José (2000) Retórica de la Pintura. Madrid: Ediciones Cátedra.
Costa, Joan (2011) Design Para os Olhos: Marca, Cor, Identidade, Sinalética. Lisboa: Dinalivro.
Francastel, Pierre (1998) A Imagem, a Visão e a Imaginação. Lisboa: Edições 70.
Furió, Vicenç (2000) Sociología del Arte. Madrid: Ediciones Cátedra.
Gil, Isabel Capeloa (2011) Literacia Visual: Estudos sobre a Inquietude das Imagens. Lisboa: Edições 70.
Goodman, Nelson (2006) Linguagens da Arte: Uma Abordagem a uma Teoria dos Símbolos. Lisboa: Gradiva
Graham, Gordon (2001) Filosofia das Artes – Introdução à Estética. Lisboa: Edições 70.
Hauser, Arnold (1984) A Arte e a Sociedade. Lisboa: Editorial Presença.
Huyghe, René (1986) O Poder da Imagem. Lisboa: Edições 70.
Kolossa, Alexandra (2005) Haring. Köln: Taschen.
Leão, Delfim; Fialho, Maria do Céu; Silva, Maria de Fátima (coord.) (2005) Mito Clássico no Imaginário Ocidental. Coimbra: Ariadne Editora.
Read, Herbert (1968) O Significado da Arte. Lisboa: Editora Ulisseia.
Rodrigues, Adriano Duarte (1999) Comunicação e Cultura – A Experiência Cultural na Era da Informação. Lisboa: Presença.
Schellekens, Elisabeth (2007) Aesthetics & Morality. London: Continuum.
Wittgenstein, Ludwig (1998) Culture and Value. Oxford: Blackwell.
Wittgenstein, Ludwig (1999) Tractatus Logico-Philosophicus. London: Routledge.

Patricia Kathleen Guiley, Graduate Student of Art History / University of Utah, U.S.A (USA)
patricia@patriciakathleen.com

The World as it is Written on the Wall

When analyzing graffiti it is necessary for the viewer to conceptualize it as a body which can assume two forms, that of text and that of image. In the 21st century, street and graffiti artists sucah as Odeith illustrate how the pedigree of graffiti text is continually expanded upon while artists/writers such as Banksy and Princess Hijabserve to enumerate the intensely controversial social messages that are frequently communicated in graffiti's medium. These works are the platform for uncensored conversations and serve as a form of free speech in many parts of the world, thusly maintaining a unique and sharp historical perspective on political and social climates.

Graffiti, Street Art, Wild Styl

Introduction

Since its inception, graffiti has employed both pictorial depictions (frequently of a human, sub-human, or animal body) and written text to convey complex and controversial social messages. Due to consistent intermingling of words and pictorial subject matter, analyzing graffiti art frequently requires examination of the bodies that are layered within the work. By employing text as a written communicator as well as a kind of pictorial body in its own right, the graffiti artist blends the utility of a written language, capitalizing on the symbolic potential within the piece. The body of graffiti text serves multiple functions, which enable the artist to fold a plethora of information into their work, frequently allowing the viewer a bird's eye view into the pedigree of the artist and their identity. Further, street and graffiti artists frequently use the human body as a kind of malleable platform for political dialogue, generating a diffusive rhetoric within the manipulation of images and the bodies therein. It is by utilizing perceptions of the body, both in text and image, that the graffiti artist illustrates a unique prowess in art history. By placing both text and image under the visual umbrella of a body, one is able to access a crucial pilgrimage that has happened with graffiti text during the 20th and 21st centuries.

Pre-historic graffiti contains both pictorial and text based imagery, while unlinked in their inception, these two forms of communication in graffiti created a formula in which modern day artists have manifested the missing link in the cycle. In some of the oldest examples, illustrating the innate human desire to state one's existence, we find the hand stencil from the Panel de las manos in Spain's El Castillo cave.[1] Dating to at least 37,000 years ago, the simple stencils of what appear to be human hands are argued to be some of the oldest cave stencils in existence. Further, in the ancient ruins of Pompeii, ash from the volcanic eruption preserved one of the oldest civilizations that took to writing on the wall with text. Using a "Vulgar Latin"[2] dialect, the prehistoric graffiti of Pompeii serves to illustrate text based graffiti dating to ~79AD.As many contemporary graffiti works contain both text and image, these graffiti forms will be shown to be more malleable than staunch in their assigned label as picture or text, particularly due to efforts accomplished in street graffiti during the 20th and 21st centuries.

By examining graffiti letters through the lens of a body, one is able to see how the perimeters morph, through a series of abstraction via the advent of new technical styles, as well as transcribe some of the artwork's narrative. After establishing how the body of the text can serve as both a narrative and pictorial body, the analysis of the social narratives enacted by both text and image can be more completely evaluated. Assuming that prehistoric graffiti is tethered to the statement of existence, with the desire to imprint one's body or name on the wall in front of them as a way of instilling history with one's presence, and then the transition from the cave stencils to contemporary graffiti artists becomes rote. As is the case with both the Panel de los manos as well as the Vulgar Latin text in Pompeii, graffiti begins with addressing one's presence. When examining the body of the text in graffiti, this paper proffers that the mutation through which the body of graffiti text undergoes maintains its impetus in a cycle that will here be referred to as the fame-name-game.

Iteration: the Fame-Name-Game

The repeated act of imprinting one's sign or tag in one's environment leads to what can be referred to as the Fame-Name-Game. This term has been created specifically to reference the process whereby graffiti artists become known in their community according to a particular name, tag, or symbol. A graffiti artist's tag is commonly a combination of the artist's identified name, geographical location, and crew or group affiliation. The inception for the Fame-Name-Game, arguably located in childhood, is a universal instinct for civilizations prone to linguistics. Young children are commonly baptized into literacy by being taught to write their name. The impulse to leave a mark of one's presence, manifested by imprinting the walls in front of us, maintains an ironically righteous and universal motive in its inception. Under this assumption it could be argued that all graffiti begins as a natural human instinct. Duplicating one's tag for recognition however, is advancement on simply marking the walls with one's presence, and is a crucial component in the change from a graffiti tagger to a graffiti writer.[3]

The desire to be recognized as notorious is voiced by the prolific amount of tags and/or pieces created by graffiti artists.[4]An iconic example of profuse tagging is the artist known as Taki 183. As a foot messenger based out of the Washington Heights neighborhood of New York City in the early 1980's, Taki 183 epitomized the pursuit of recognition most young graffiti artists on the east coast (of the USA) during this time period would become consumed with.[5] Going "all-city" was an urban term used by graffiti writers that were a part of the New York City graffiti scene in the 1980's. This term referred to getting one's tag or piece up on trains that hit all five of the city's boroughs.[6]Ideally, once a graffiti writer went all-city, their tag (and artistic skill therein) became famous.

Regardless of the motive, the prolific writing of one's name on the walls, from constant repetition grew into an art genre (particularly in the history of graffiti in the U.S.A spanning from the 1950's to current day.)Tagging one's name quickly became a project of creating an art piece with the body of that name. While redefining what the body of text could represent, graffiti writers began making what are referred to as pieces and bombing larger areas with more attention and skill. A noteworthy distinction between tags and pieces is the size, scale, and amount of time required to complete the work. While a "tag" may be done quickly, a "piece" or subsequent "bomb" requires much more attention and forethought in its construction. This concept is not lost on the Graffiti writing social stratum and writers that do more than "tag" are given much more esteem.

Wild Style

With technical ability and artistic agility at the forefront what is required to achieve recognition, the graffiti artist accomplishes more purchase with unique approaches to text and imagery in their work. In addition to the notoriety gained in the "fame-name-game," a pressure to advance in technique accompanies becoming a recognized artist in the graffiti world, particularly as that world is now part of the global contemporary. In conjunction with graffiti and street artists globetrotting, artists can view each other's work around the world within moments of completion. While the worldwide Internet made things accessible, the advent of smartphones, miniscule cameras, and social networking websites made image sharing instantaneous. Because the audience in the global contemporary is the world at large, creating unique and unusual techniques and images is paramount to being esteemed in graffiti art. One of the ways this adeptness is shown is by obscuring the body of the text, thereby increasing the technical difficulty within the letters' construction. In an effort to out-do one another, graffiti lettering began to take on more dramatized and exaggerated lines. This competitive spirit leads to theatrical and oblique representations of letters. Such complex designs are referred to as Wild Style. Wild Style bombs are graffiti works in which the lettering is obscured to the point of making it difficult to decipher where a letter begins and ends.[7] Wild Style pieces infer an elite artistic prowess and skill of the graffiti writer, as its construction requires a prime understanding and adeptness of the medium, spatial techniques, and design. Reading Wild Style text requires an educated understanding of the technique, and sometimes the writer and/or the writer's writing crew to decode the word or message in the work. Here, graffiti leaps from writing text to communicate a simple word, or announce an artist's presence (as can be seen in a simple tag) and enters into a category that is best described as pictorial. Wild Style letters are an artistic subject in their own right, not entirely text and not purely abstract. While the genesis for Wildstyle was arguably born in the 1970's graffiti scene in the U.S.A., various techniques and versions continue to flourish in current day pieces. Lisbon based graffiti artist Odeith has created work that are key examples of recent renditions of Wild Style.

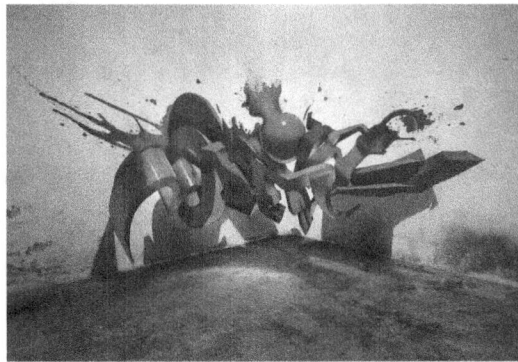 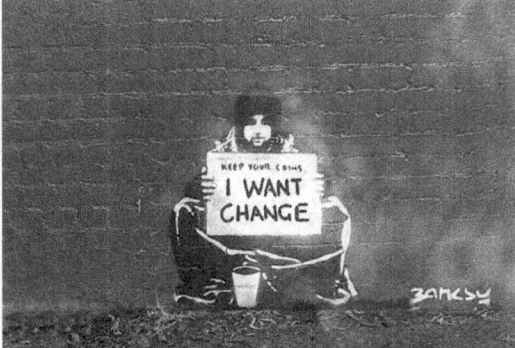

Fig. 1: Untitled, 2014. Odeith, Lisbon Portugal.   Fig. 2: Untitled, 2011. Banksy (allegedly), United Kingdom.

In Figure 1, Odeith creates a new tweak in the Wild Style repertoire, a three dimensional aspect.[8]While Wild Style is built on obscuring a traditional text form, the purpose of asserting presence still serves as one of the endeavors in its construction. Following suit, the imagery in Figure 1 is the artist's name, twisted and turned for the three dimensional affect and garnished with a splattering that conjures images of blood or red liquid spilling out from the upper edges. In addition to the artistic picture created, the name Odeith serves as the thematic purpose of the piece. Within this work the viewer is able to ascertain how Wild Style serves as a bridge between pictorial image and text. By blurring the perception between text and image, Wild Style creates a new platform in which text can carry imagery beyond a letter's lines.

Sociolinguistics: text that serves as both a body and a narrative

In addition to serving as a visual connector between written word and image, graffiti text frequently serves an interpretative or narrative function within the work. Here intensely controversial social messages are communicated in a synergistically artistic manner uniquely found in graffiti's medium. These works introduce the complexity of the relationship the text creates in the work's communication. Figure 2illustrates the intricate complexity text can maintain with regards to the rhetoric of a graffiti piece.

In Figure 2Britain's notorious Banksy creates a political narrative that employs the text of "Keep your coins. I WANT CHANGE" in two distinct ways. Firstly the text is discernable, as a body in its own right. The stark white sign on which the words are written, strongly contrasts with the background of a bricked wall that has been painted a deep blood red, creating a separate visual plane for the sign and the stenciled figure hold it. Secondly the rhetorical message of the text requires an interaction with the body of the figure and a sociolinguistics stereotype associated with both the human figure and the sign in which the figure is carrying.

The body of the text resonates the work's social message only if the viewer maintains an awareness of a vagrant's physical demeanor as well as their traditional signage held up requesting money on behalf of their situation. The work's overarching narrative is exclusively accessed if both the body of the text and the body of the image are recognized for their archetypal symbolism. Once this is achieved, the sentiment becomes a philosophical endeavor in which the viewer considers the socio-economic systems leading to the individual predicament of poverty. Playing on a contemporary colloquialism in which money is referred to as "coins," as well as the multiple definitions of the word "change," text within this piece provides multiple layers of both physical and rhetorical meanings. Ultimately the text furthers the lamentation of the pictorial subject.

Culture Jamming

Interested in a socio-political rhetoric not unlike that of Banksy's, culture jamming street and graffiti artists appropriate images and text located in public spaces in order to communicate a stigmatizing dialogue dealing with social conflict. Culture Jamming is loosely defined as efforts in modifying mass media to convey a conflicting message. Delicately walking a tight rope intertwined with requirements based on a viewer's awareness of advertising images as well as global social conflicts, culture jamming requires that a viewer have knowledge of the original image prior to the artist's appropriation/alteration of it, otherwise the culture jamming work's message, is rendered moot.

Illustrating this concept, contemporary street and graffiti artist Princess Hijab covers parts of an image's body, at once communicating a dense and controversial social message in a visual synergy that calls upon the viewer's prior knowledge of current marketing and global affairs.[9]Locating power in appropriating and reassigning mainstream advertising images of the body, Princess Hijab causes her public to question public space, advertising imagery, and global political conditions within her brief artistic maneuvers. While this technique is referred to as Hijabisation in her work, the term can be analyzed as a form of culture Jamming. Princess Hijab's has implemented her guerrilla niqab art from New York to Vienna, sparking debates about feminism and fundamentalism. Accomplishing new feats with existing depicted bodies that adorn the streets in advertisements; her work appropriates the social narrative in sanctioned public images and swiftly converts that narrative and rhetoric into volatile global socio-cultural issues. As can be seen in figure 3, by clothing previously naked forms, the image's original message is abruptly reassigned a new dialogue at a polar distance from the advertisement's desired sentiment.

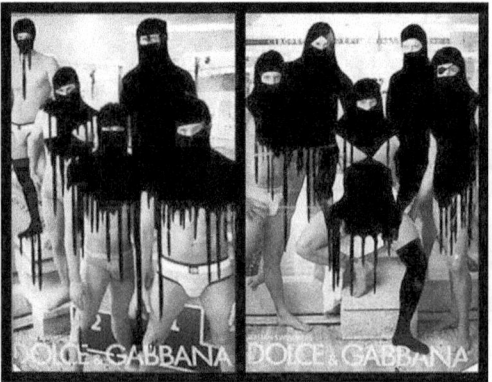

Fig. 3: Dolce (series), 2011. Princess Hijab (allegedly) Paris Metro Station, France.

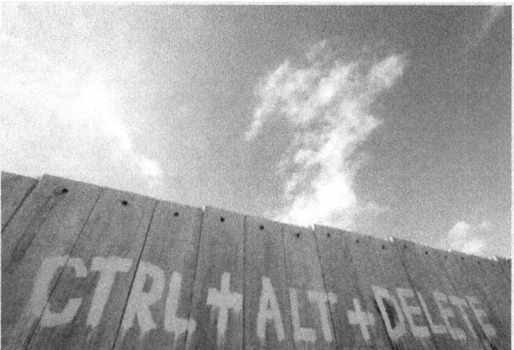

Fig. 4: Anonymous graffiti tag. West bank wall, Palestine 20007.

In this point, the graffiti artist points to the velocity a social narrative can acquire via creating a presence where there was an intended absence. By clothing figures intended to be unclothed, the viewer is immediately confronted with the original assertion of producing an image as naked. This technique uses the human body to ignite immense social messages and thought about one's own culture and how those attributes weigh in on a global scale. In addition to questioning the nakedness of the advertising forms, Princess Hijab's Hijabization simultaneously opens arguments regarding the global climate and stereotypes of the Muslim people and nations in the world. Adding a particularly intense note to the political dialogue is the French government's ban on all face covering articles of clothing put into act in 2010. Princess Hijab's Dolce series at once confronts the French government's apparent consent with nudity (and advertising such notions) while also banning covering one's body. The audience is thusly forced to question issues not only of social law and conduct but the imagery presented by the well-financed advertising industry that presents more visual imagery than any other industry. As is part of many culture jamming artist's motives, questioning the advertising industry and legal governments control over public image display is key to understanding the social ills of society.

Graffiti socio-political messages: free speech

As both a sanctioned and non-sanctioned form of art and communication, graffiti stands as a uniquely universal platform for free speech, thusly maintaining a unique and sharp historical perspective on political and social climates. Anonymity between artist and art is a crucial factor in non-sanctioned graffiti. However, the desire for anonymity is complicated with need to get one's image/message largely witnessed. In this aspect graffiti art offers an ideal vehicle for uncensored conversations and an ideal avenue in many parts of the world in which those who are oppressed can only communicate their voices illegally. Frequently structures that serve to exacerbate a group's civil unrest serve as the physical medium for socio-political graffiti. Like Germany's Berlin wall, Palestine's wall is a central surface on which not only the local people communicate their grievances, but artists from pockets of the globe pilgrimage to in order to communicate their sentiments regarding the socio-political climate in that region. Figure 4 illustrates how socio-political graffiti engages with cultural colloquialisms like culture jamming artists, as well as concepts of the body in order to communicate its dense yet simple social message.

Within the work that created what is referred to as the "Control Alt Delete Wall" on the west bank of the Palestine wall, the viewer is presented with a sentiment deeply connected to the global contemporary. The task for restarting a PC computer is accomplished by pressing down the keys labeled control, alt, and delete at the same time. Doing this, restarts the computer after it has become non-responsive to other keyboard or mouse commands, to use a colloquialism: when it has frozen. The graffiti work here plays on the meaning behind the computer tag in addition to employing the body on which the sentiment is phrased. Representing the political history in which brought the Palestine wall into existence, the piece of the wall in which the words are written on then becomes a symbolic marker for the "frozen" state of the political affairs. The command code for restarting argues that there needs to be a new beginning in the political warfare between the two places. Further the control/alt/delete code communicates a parallel between the two situations, a barrier in which an impasse is experienced. The wall, just like the unresponsive computer screen, indicates a system that is no longer functioning and shutting down; in need of a restart.

The surface of the wall is also used as a physical body compared to that of the sky under which it sits. With letters painted sky blue, the reset command "CTRL + ALT + DELETE" directly calls the viewers' attention to the sky above the wall. This contrasts the unity and globalism of the sky with the finite and dividing nature of the wall. The work employs the body of the letters in order to call attention to the body of the sky. The theoretical communication achieved when comparing the universal and expansive sky to that of the human-made limited wall is dependent on using the body of text to conduct communication beyond simple semiotics, but rather as a body of art in their own right. There are three bodies which enable the viewer to ascertain the full visual and philosophical breadth of figure 4: the body of the wall, the body of the text, and the body of the sky. By perceiving the text as a body in its own right, the viewer is able to make connections unattainable otherwise regarding the work's narrative.

Conclusion

By expanding on the utility and platform of text and image, contemporary graffiti artists have developed a specific genealogy in which a text can emigrate from a written word to a picture. Further, a synergistic rhetoric is discovered while unpacking the various forms of bodies in graffiti art, one in which both text and image are used to supply the viewer with a narrative beyond the sum of its parts.

Notes and References
1 James L. Bischoff, Jose Francisco Garcia, and Lawrence G. Straus, "Uranium-series Isochron Dating at El Castillo Cave (Cantabria, Spain): The "Acheulean"/"Mousterian" Question, "Journal of Archaeological Science 19, no. 1 (January 1992).
2 Vulgar Latin here used as a blanket term covering vernacular dialects of the Latin language spoken from earliest times in Italy until the latest dialects of the western empire.
3 For more expansive definitions on terms and references to graffiti and graffiti technique, see: Snyder, Gregory J. Graffiti Lives: Beyond the Tag in New York's Urban Underground. New York: New York University Press, 2009.
4 Snyder, Graffiti Lives: Beyond the Tag in New York's.
5 For a full biography as well as artist's sentiments and collaborative works being done with Taki 183, see the artists official website, developed in 2009: http://www.taki183.net.
6 The five New York City boroughs necessary to get one's tag on a train that went from the main depot to the borough neighborhoods were: the Bronx, Brooklyn, Manhattan, Queens, and Staten Island. Both the tag's name and numerical assignment refer to the artist's name and home location: Taki was short for the artist's greek name, Demetraki, and 183 is the avenue of the Washington Heights neighborhood where he lived.
7 Gastman, Roger, and Caleb Neelon. The History of American Graffiti. New York, NY: Harper Collins Publisher, 2010.
8 Odeith's interest in 3D images can be fully researched in the artist's biography located on his website: http://www.odeith.com.
9 Veiled herself by anonymity, Princess Hijab is presumed to be a female street artist living and working from a home base in Paris, France. Her art currently centers on veiling the main characters of street and subway advertisements using black paint.

Belting, Hans.The Global Contemporary and the Rise of New Art Worlds. Edited by Andrea Buddensieg and Peter Weibel. Cambridge, MA: MIT Press, 2013.
Bischoff, James L., Jose Francisco Garcia, and Lawrence G. Straus. "Uranium-series Isochron Dating at El Castillo Cave (Cantabria, Spain): The "Acheulean"/"Mousterian" Question." Journal of Archaeological Science 19, no. 1 (January 1992): 49-62.
Bortman, Alan. Year One Rewind: A Survey of Graffiti, Street Art, and Urban Art. San Francisco, CA: Last Gasp, 2009.
Deitch, Jeffrey, Roger Gastman, and Aaron Rose, comps. Art in the Streets. New York, NY: Skira Rizzoli, 2011.
Ferrell, Jeff. Crimes of Style: Urban Graffiti and the Politics of Criminality. Boston, MA: Northeastern University Press, 1996.
Gastman, Roger, and Caleb Neelon. The History of American Graffiti. New York, NY: Harper Collins Publisher, 2010.
Gastman, Roger, Caleb Neelon, and Anthony Smyrski. Street World: Urban Art and Culture from Five Continents. New York, NY: Harry N. Abrams, 2007.
Gonos, George, Virginia Mulkern, and Nicholas Poushinsky. "Anonymous Expression: A Structural View of Graffiti." The Journal of American Folklore 89, no. 351 (Jan - March 1976): 40-48.
Grody, Steve. Graffiti L.A. : Street Styles and Art. New York: Abramsq, 2007.
Iosifidis, Kiriakos. Mural Art: Murals on Huge Public Surfaces around the World: From Graffiti to Trompe L'oeil. Vol. 1. Mainaschaff, Germany: Publikat, 2009.
Mural Art: Murals on Huge Public Surfaces around the World: From Graffiti to Trompe L'oeil. Vol. 2. Mainaschaff, Germany: Publikat, 2009.
McCormick, Carlo, Marc Schiller, and Sara Schiller. Trespass: A History of Uncommissioned Urban Art. Edited by Ethel Seno. Cologne, Germany: Taschen, 2010.
Powers, Stephen. The Art of Getting Over: Graffiti at the Millenium. New York, NY: St. Martin's Press, 1999.
Raychaudhuri, Anindya. "'Just as Good a Place to Publish': Banksy, Graffiti and the Textualisation of the Wall." Rupkatha Journal on Interdisciplinary Studies in Humanities 2, no. 1 (2010): 50-58.
Reisner, Robert George. Graffiti: Two Thousand Years of Wall Writing. New York, NY: Cowles Book, 1971.
Rose, Aaron, Christian Strike, Alex Baker, Arty Nelson, Jocko Weyland, and Mike Mills. Beautiful Losers. 2nd ed. New York, NY: D.A.P./Iconoclast, 2005.
Sliwa, Martyna, and George Cairns. "Exploring Narratives and Antenarratives of Graffiti Artists: Beyond Dichotomies of Commitment and Detachment." Culture and Organization 13, no. 1 (March 2007): 73-82.
Snyder, Gregory J. Graffiti Lives: Beyond the Tag in New York's Urban Underground. New York: New York University Press, 2009.
Wright, Steve. Banksy's Bristol: Home Sweet Home. Bristol, United Kingdom: Tangent Books, 2007.
York, Peter. Style Wars. London: Sidgwick & Jackson, 1983.

Duarte Lobo Antunes, MA Architectural History,
The Bartlett School of Architecture, University College London
duarte.antunes.13@ucl.ac.uk

Desecration, Condensation:
Lisbon's futuristic imagery as a site of urban creativity

Place-specific futuristic urban images are part of a city's heritage: disseminated by virtual and printed media they become part of its inhabitants imaginarium. Historically a result of the Industrial Age's confidence in the future, they are more than mere predictions but actually part of a broader, modern visual culture. By comparing well-known examples from the turn of the 20th century with Lisbon's own treasury of futuristic illustrations and projects, this paper tries to understand the relation between practice and speculation, broad and particular.

Futuristic, Lisbon, Urban

Prologue

"Our imaginary geography is infinitely vaster than the one in the material world. This observation, as banal as it is, allows us to detect the immense generosity of a vital human function: to give life to what cannot be present in the world of volume and weight. As the angelical inhabitants whose hierarchies our ancestors debated, like the unicorn and the manticore, as the concepts of a perfect democracy and the good will towards all men, the imaginary places of the mind don't require materiality to exist in consciousness." [1]
In the 1986 book, "Futuredays, a Nineteenth-Century Vision of the Year 2000", Isaac Asimov, the American scientist and science fiction writer thoroughly analyses "Dans l'aneé 2000", a set of images produced in the early 20th century. These illustrations were created by Jean Marc Coté, an obscure French commercial artist of whom not much is known, for a series of "cigarette-cards" commemorating the 1900 World Exhibition in Paris. The company that commissioned the artwork soon went bankrupt and the images were never published in their supposed format, with only one of the original sets surviving. This didn't stop the propagation of the illustrations themselves that were subsequently issued as postcards, posters, and recently as images in blogs and websites, becoming some of the best-known attempts at a visual description of the future.

Even though there is never an explicit geographic location for the images, given their origin and the fragments of urban depiction, it is safe to assume that they are based in late 19th century French life. As Asimov notes in several passages, Coté's imagination does not spill into the city fabric, which remains strongly within the boundaries of what could be expected at the time. The Eiffel tower, built roughly 11 years earlier for the 1889 World's Fair is vastly more impressive than anything presented in those illustrations.
However, this is not the case in all futuristic images of that time. Some are particularly mindful of the urban settings of their fantasies. Albert Robida's 1882 Illustrated novel "Le Vingtième Siècle" is far more prolific and inventive when it comes to actually reconfiguring the urban backdrop. One of his magnificent drawings, a minute sketch of the "Aerocab station at the Tour Saint-Jacques", shows the tower enveloped by small airships shaped as fishes and topped by a steel-structured platform and a clock.

Both these works explore the idea of urban imagination and refer quite explicitly to a precise future, yet one has the feeling that what is at play here is not a simple attempt at futurism, but a new type of urban visual culture that emerged with modernity and the consciousness of progress.

What is interesting in these representations is not so much their inaccurate futurism, but the fact that they are, in a way, so conservative, so deeply rooted in the signs and meanings of the time they were produced. The effect is necessarily comical, even more so retrospectively: the overlaying of futuristic technologies with outdated forms and costumes, dress and architecture. Asimov rightly points out that futurism relies on the reconnaissance that there is a future that is distinct from the past, which historically has not been self-evident: the notion of change being coupled with the notion of progress is quite a recent invention.
What started as a turn of the century positivist phenomenon fuelled by events like the World Exhibitions has nowadays developed into uncountable images and films continuously propagating urban imagination through the media stream. The public has assimilated these as a separate category (or set of categories) of aesthetic experience, and not necessarily structured predictions.
So if most images of the future are not to be considered, and were never intended to be precise futurism, what is their function? What are the mechanisms that they perpetuate and assure? Furthermore, turning to urban creativity one might also ask: what is the role of the city in visions of the future? How different are the visions created by architects and planners from those created by other cultural agents? Are they useful in the actual design process? How are contemporary urban imaginations related to the ones in the early 20th century and finally, do urban visions of the future posses a pervasive conceptual language that makes it possible to isolate specific categories?

Introduction

Urban creativity is a loose term that is generally perceived to mean the engagement of populations with the physical fabric of the city, whether through the use of existing surfaces as support for visual art, through performances or the production of three-dimensional installations. Its legitimacy as a serious and specific art form that works with typically urban concepts of temporality, decay and transgression has long been establish, as can be attested by passages as the one below:
"In the last four decades, graffiti art has produced a culturally rich visual history that links artists, city spaces, urban audiences and media technologies around the globe. The art form's collectively sustained duration, its historically complex social and institutional development, and its aesthetic sophistication place it among the longest-running, global visual culture movements originating within the 20th century, and perhaps the most important of the last decades." [2]

In this essay I wish to introduce a medium that has not generally been considered as belonging to the same category of urban creativity as graffiti art or street performance, mainly because it doesn't (quite literally) adhere to the same support: representations of future cities, as they are seen in printed and virtual media, postcards, pamphlets, books and illustrations. By bringing together the contents of an imaginary city with those of a real one, a sort of creative overlay occurs that can be considered a legitimate form of urban creativity. I will attempt to understand the nature and function of these illustrations, the way in which they engage the imaginary of the city and its memory, and their desire to actually advance any of its propositions and generate urban renewal. Using Lisbon as an archive and case study, I will mainly analyze examples of this city's imagery and see how they compare to other historical examples. I will argue that, contrary to the quote in epigraph, the "imaginary places of the mind" almost always find a home in the real world by altering or subverting existing material. Not all the cases presented will fit in the same category. The idea is to try to identify the various forms of urban imagination, whether they are conceptual proposals, futuristic illustrations or actual architectural or urban proposals, and to assemble the appropriate theoretical framework to deal with them. In this spirit I chose to compare some of the industrial age futuristic images of cities with a selection of visions centered on Lisbon, mainly journalist and author Fialho de Almeida's "Lisboa Monumental", Manuel Graça Dias's masterplan "Reconversão Urbana do Estaleiro da Margueira", Adalberto Dias's project for an elevator at Poço do Borratém and "Dear Future, Lisbon in 2113", the postcard edition that, together with Caetano de Bragança and Pedro Clarke, I created for the 2013 Lisbon Architecture Triennale.

Desecration, Condensation: The mechanics of urban futurisms
Futuristic urban imagination has been described as a narrative form capable of enriching the connections between places and inhabitants. Natilie Collie, in an article in Futures magazine, argues that futuristic images work against what Michel de Certeau calls the "concept-city", a city imposed from above through elevated views and maps. In her view, renderings of future cities are a non-conventional tool for urban planning, closer to the viewpoint, and easily comprehended by actual users.[3]
In fact urban imagery is rarely preoccupied with its instrumentalization as a planning tool, rather more with establishing believable, coherent narratives and for that it uses every possible angle, every possible framing. Michel de Certeau himself, in his famous essay "Walking in the City"[4] affirms that the desire of seeing from an "un-natural" angle is present in Medieval fictions, predating the technology that actually made it possible, and considering the towers of today merely the materialization of this obsession. In fact, along with other themes that will be explored in this paper, the panorama, the unique unveiling of the city as coherent organism plays a big role in urban futurisms.

There is a rather obscure, but nevertheless vast, scholarly field dedicated to critical explorations of science fiction and futurism. "Science Fiction and the Prediction of the Future: Essays on Foresight and Fallacy" provides an interesting roadbook for those interested in delving deeper into the genre[5]. In the introductory essay Gary Westfahl lays down the fallacies that typically befall these predictions[6], keeping the reader aware that presenting possible narratives of the future is necessarily more of an aesthetic exercise than a reliable source of information. Perhaps the most relevant of these prophetic fallacies to urban visions of the future is what he calls the "Fallacy of Replacement". It consists of the idea that, in the future, new technologies will completely supersede existing ones, as if cohabitation of old and new would become impossible. To justify his opinion that this is not the manner in which technologies evolve, Westfahl gives as an example the fact that all writing technologies that were ever the norm are still in use today, the only change being their relative popularity and specificity. We are still using stone engraving for solemn purposes such as tombstones and regularly use pencils and paper, which essentially have been around for centuries. Word processing software is now the standard for transmitting the written word, but typewriters haven't totally disappeared and are preferred by some professional writers. Technology goes through a process over time and the prevalence of one over the other transforms the landscape, but perhaps the most surprising fact is its additive nature.

The living fabric of cities is the proof that the passage of time rarely eliminates whole ages; quite the contrary – all efforts are made to dig out and reveal artifacts of previous eras and have them commune of the air of the present. In addition to this, buildings are unsurprisingly flexible in their use and can be adapted to suit almost any human activity. The examples from 19th century France mentioned in the prologue are embedded in this notion of symbiosis between new and old, and seem to draw from it their particular strategy of counterpoint. Albert Robida's Illustrations in "Le Vingtième Siècle", the unusual 1882 book that can be called one of the first "graphic novels" and in which the illustration assumes almost equal importance to the text, was to tap into the existing utopian tradition inherited from Verne and as Phillipe Willems puts it: "the realistic portrayal of the estranging 'other', the systematic and rational explanation of these novums, and the dialectical structure of continuous double referentiality offering implicit comparisons with the contemporary state of society and the world. Into this narrative recipe, however, he also boldly introduces the occasional use of unaccounted-for effets de reel, purely connotative elements of a discourse closer to the ludic than to the didactic. [7]

So in which category fall the illustrations that use the existing buildings in novel, even if slightly derogatory ways, as are examples the "Aerocab station at the Tour Saint-Jacques", the "International Hotel on the Arc de Triomphe" or the Central Station sitting atop Paris' most recognizable ancient monument and sacred building, the Notre Dame cathedral? Are they "closer to the ludic than the didactic"? In the section of the text that goes together with this illustration (Fig. 1) Robida writes:

"The old Gothic structure has changed a lot since the end of the Middle Ages, when the great poet Victor Hugo depicted it for posteriority in an admirable novel. Engineers have cleverly improved and modernized it since then. Elevators have replaced the five-hundred-step narrow winding staircases that previously challenged visitors with a laborious climb up the towers. The lateral facades have been rented out to bill posting and advertising companies. And the cathedral's existing towers were used as a base for the construction of Paris's aircraft-omnibus Central Station."[8]

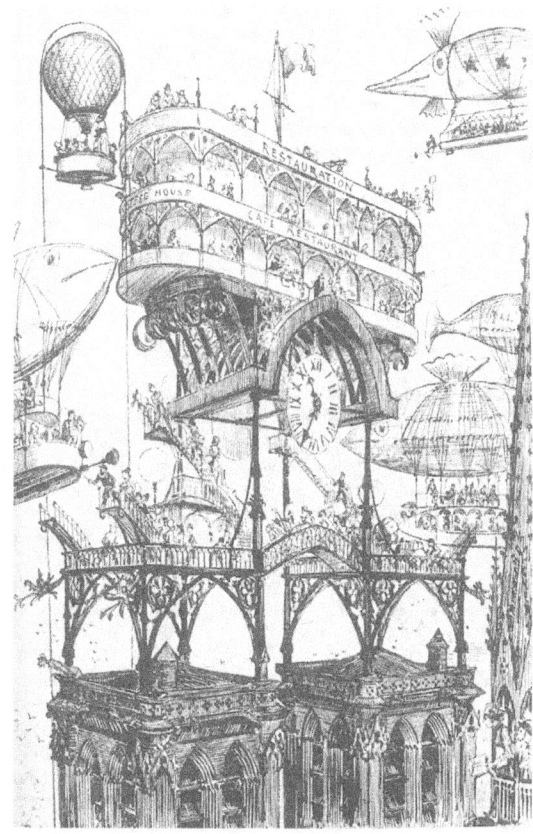

Fig. 1: Central Station atop the Notre Dame cathedral.
Source: Albert Robida, The Twentieth Century, Wesleyan University Press, 2004

Because cities don't easily attract the Fallacy of Replacement, the narrative strategy has to affect the reader's assumption and previous knowledge of what consists an untouchable landmark. By indicating, both verbally and visually, the "improvements" meant to desecrate a precious building the idea is to shock the public into believing real change has been dealt. Its impossibility in the present makes it ludic. The possibility of a future implementation makes it didactic.

It is possible to detect other architectural strategies that are combined in the same examples. One illustration shows the Arc de Triomphe topped by an immense palace with an eclectic architectural composition:

"The Hôtel International was intended to symbolize the international unity of peoples, so its architects sought to blend it into styles from all parts of the world. On the outside, as well as the inside, the international hotel merges architectures from all over the world in one grandiose and harmonious ensemble. The central edifice is European, the left wing is Asian and American, and the right wing is African and Oceanian."[9]

Combining or clustering together several icons produces an urban condenser, a sort of super-icon that instead of replacing the older one uses it as an anchor and extracts meaning and memory from it.

Urban futurisms in Lisbon's imaginarium
As the transformation of an existing fabric, futuristic images deal with the specific obsessions of each city's identity. For Paris it might be the cherished monuments that cut through the low skyline. In Lisbon they most probably deal with key views and panoramas, or it's relationship with the river.

Even if clothed in different circumstances, and some decades later, Lisbon was also touched by the Belle Époque's incessant need to envision future cities.

In 1906, and ostensibly inspired by a visit to the annual architecture exhibition of the School of Fine Arts, Portuguese journalist and writer Fialho de Almeida published a speculative essay on how the city could be transformed. The first decade of Portuguese 20th century was marked by a decline in global political influence and domestic instability that culminated in the authoritarian government of João Franco, the regicide and the implementation of a republic. It is in this context, and considering the tradition of satirical magazines, that one has to read Fialho's highly critical text – Lisbon is portrayed as backwards city that could benefit from some modernizing interventions.

Written in Fialho's ruthlessly ironic style and illustrated by Alonso, nom-de-plume of Joaquim Guilherme Santos Silva, "Lisboa Monumental" appeared in two consecutive issues of the popular current affairs magazine "Illustração Portugueza". It is programmatically different from Albert Robida's graphic novel, but it shares some of the same preoccupations and strategies.

Because of its more propositional nature, Fialho's ideas for Lisbon don't always assume the aura of fantasy of Robida or Coté's illustrations. What is interesting perhaps is that, on the other hand, they are not necessarily feasible or contributing to the modernization of infrastructure or public space. Somehow in between project and speculation, Fialho uses his wit, and more importantly Alonso's skill as an illustrator, to allow readers of a popular magazine to imagine a monumentalized city. Manuel Graça Dias, in an essay dedicated to "Lisboa Monumental"[10] stresses that the proposals should be inserted in the "City Beautiful" movement, which suggested the implementation of ad hoc monuments and large civic buildings, not necessarily taking into account wider planning issues, as a valid tool of urban intervention.

Some of the proposals, especially on the second part of the article, are what any well-intentioned urban planner of the time would suggest. In a city that didn't yet have a physical connection between the two sides of the river, Fialho proposes a steel arch bridge that could join "the two Lisbon's of the future". In a city bereft of decent housing for the working class, the writer imagines a model neighborhood for the families of factory personnel, complete with large playgrounds and leisure spaces, in the spirit of the later Garden Cities.

Fialho's imagination does however sometimes verge towards the iconoclastic. The restricted sense of monumentality apparent in the illustrations is achieved by resourcing to existing typologies (triumphal arch, large infrastructure, crystal palace) scaling them up and inserting them quite shockingly in some of Lisbon's most cherished panoramas, missing Robida's symbiotic capacity of combining past, present and future into condensed imaginary objects. In this sense, they are not obviously futuristic and one misses the airship stations, the rotating house or the telephonoscope. Nonetheless, in proposals like the overpass connecting the belvedere of S.Pedro de Alcantara with Campo Santana above the Avenida da Liberdade, there is more than the desire of creating a convenient connection:

"The bridge above the Avenida and Rua da Palma valleys, connecting S.Pedro de Alcântara with Santana, and this last one with Graça or Monte do Castelo, would be a venture of assured scenographic effect, gigantic and leggy, barring the air in an audacious leap. Beyond the fact that it would establish between peripheral neighborhoods a great circulation, quicker and shorter, it would have the rare predicate of cutting through the monotonous houses of this city without domes or spires, with a magnificent play of artworks."[11]

The most radical image is the one showing Lisbon's castle, the beloved Castelo de São Jorge, overtaken by what appears to be massive domed palace, not so different from the one Robida envisioned in Paris atop the Arc. Here, inhabitants would be able to gamble, watch shows, go to the circus or meet female company, in a "fiery and colossal yashiwara", turning the city's most famous postcard into a pleasure district (Fig. 2).

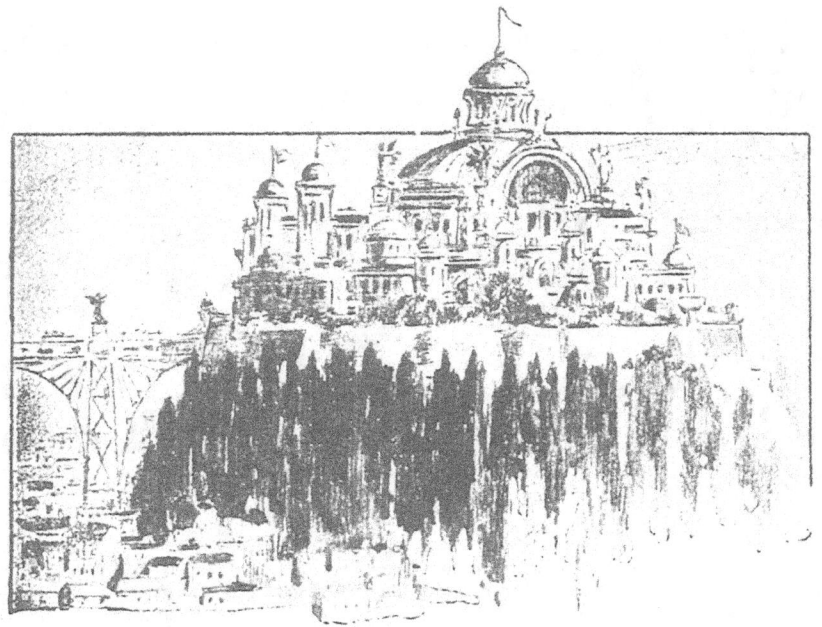

Fig. 2: Palace on the castle hill
Source: Fialho de Almeida, "Lisboa Monumental", in Arte, Arquitectura e Cidade. Lisbon: Parceria A.M. Pereira, 2011

These images are already closer to what can be considered a form of urban art. The aestheticization of the infrastructure and the fact that once again there's the attempt at desecrating cherished views or buildings, disconnected from any real problem solving, give these illustrations a separate quality. The fact that readers would be very familiar with the depicted scenes and would necessarily evaluate them in the light of these new proposals, would allow them to mentally transpose the futuristic visions onto the actual city fabric.

The population's involvement with projects that defy, by their scale or prominence, the consolidated image of the city is a complex subject that involves many political considerations and is certainly not constant over time. The imagery that these projects disseminate can be very close to that of speculative urban imagination, confusing the boundary between entertainment, subversion and actual urban renewal.

The architect Manuel Graça Dias's project for the Margueira shipyards in Cacilhas (1999), across the river from Lisbon and ever-present in the city's panorama, and Adalberto Dias's proposal for an elevator linking the Baixa with the castle (2001) are two examples of actual projects that have generated ample polemic and at the same time have expanded, to this day, the imagination of the city. Graça Dias's project, immediately given the nickname "Manhattan de Cacilhas"[12,] (Fig. 3) was the grafting of a metropolis into a suburb. The scheme was comprised of a network of streets and urban blocks projecting over the riverbank, punctuated by slim towers rising in height towards the east, partially making use of the existing docks. The images that circulated in the media at the time and that are still available, and surprisingly still discussed, in internet forums and blogs, depicts a mass of vertical elements of various heights with subtle variations of proportion anchored to the low-lying terrain. One image specifically shows the composition as fortress in the horizon, its scale disguised by the distance. The project description available in the architect's website is of a semi-poetic nature, closer to Fialho's accounts of his proposals than to the typical architectural summaries:

"an ellipse – with its longer axis over the pontoon of Dock [13] – draws, over the water, a panoramic run that "embraces" the new neighborhood and "holds it" to Almada's side, intertwining, north and south, in the tangle of the city, elevating, flying smoothly and beautifully over the water, over the reflective surface of the water."

Both the images and the lyric language use to describe it do nothing to assail public opinion of the project's serious intentions. It was presented to the responsible ministry and was immediately scraped.

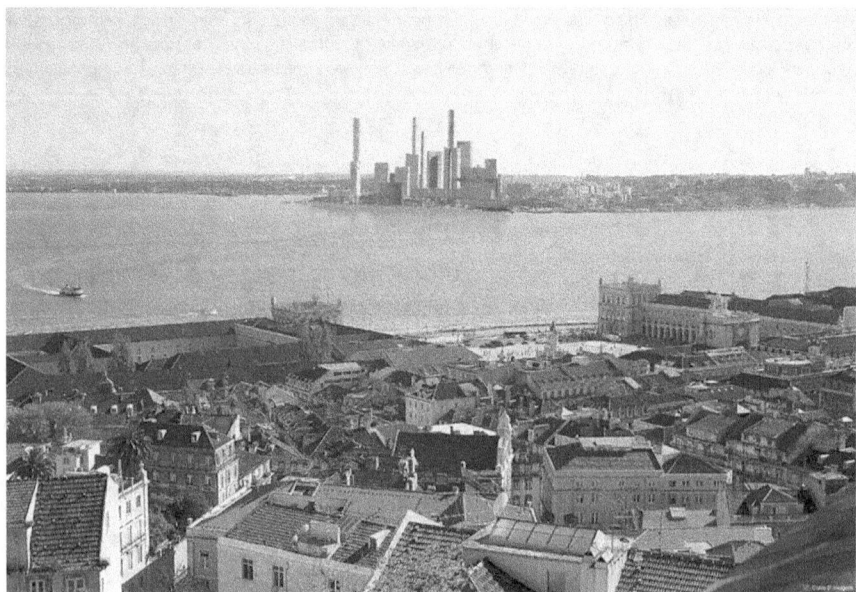

Fig. 3: Manhattan de Cacilhas Source: http://www.contemporanea.com.pt/margueira_01.html
©Manuel Graça Dias / Contemporanea

The elevator at Poço do Borratém was meant to help tourists navigate Lisbon's difficult topography by bringing them up directly to the castle's elevation and shooting across. The images that were made public at the time14 showed the structure emerging from the lower part of the city and drawing a straight angle in the air. The diagrammatic simplicity of the proposal, unlike any other structure in the city, has an oneiric effect, which didn't reduce the public outcry pressuring the local authorities to drop it.
Even though both the reconversion of the Margueira shipyard and the Poço do Borratém elevator were actual proposals, they were received as speculations and have entered the domain of urban imagination. The mediated nature of projects, with architects having to produce convincing images of their designs, ends up only feeding the mediascape.

Dear Future, Lisbon in 2113 a project that I curated together with Caetano de Bragança and Pedro Clarke, was explicitly conceived to be an addition to Lisbon's urban imaginarium. It was produced as a set of 10 postcards designed by young Portuguese architects and illustrators to be part of the official merchandising of the 2013 Lisbon Architecture Triennale, depicting the city one hundred years later. The objective was to create an inexpensive physical support that would allow the images to be propagated by mail, creating an exhibition par avion of uncertain end and destination. With the set came also a blank card with the address of the Fundação Arpad Szenes – Vieira da Silva pre-filled, meant for the public to resend with their own visions of the future.

The city, support format and target date for the visions was the only available brief, with each author being free to develop their own graphic language and conceptual approach. Not having accompanying texts, it was for the images to allow the audience to deduce, or otherwise invent, a narrative context.
Two of the commissioned illustrations are especially representative of the themes I have explored in this essay: Caetano de Bragança's view of Basilica da Estrela and Ana Aragão's illustration merging Lisbon's icons into one superstructure.

It is unusual for urban visions of the future to venture into representations of interior space. The view of the Basilica da Estrela by Caetano de Bragança (Fig. 4), even tough it is from within a building, is thematically linked to Robida's illustrations of the Notre Dame cathedral: from a raised point of view it shows two tennis players on a court that occupies the nave of one of Lisbon's main religious sites. It appears on a first reading that the author is trying to achieve an immediate shock effect with the profanation of a sacred building, but subtleties in the composition tells us that there is more complex and ambitious program in the image. The use of a central perspective and the way the light is entering the space seem to preserve the hierarchy of the church's architectural structure, as does the perfect placement of the tennis court, lodged in the main nave. Above the playing field is a mysterious reflective platform, for which no explanation is given – three figures are standing on it, apparently oblivious to the match below. There is no audience for the match, apart from these three figures.

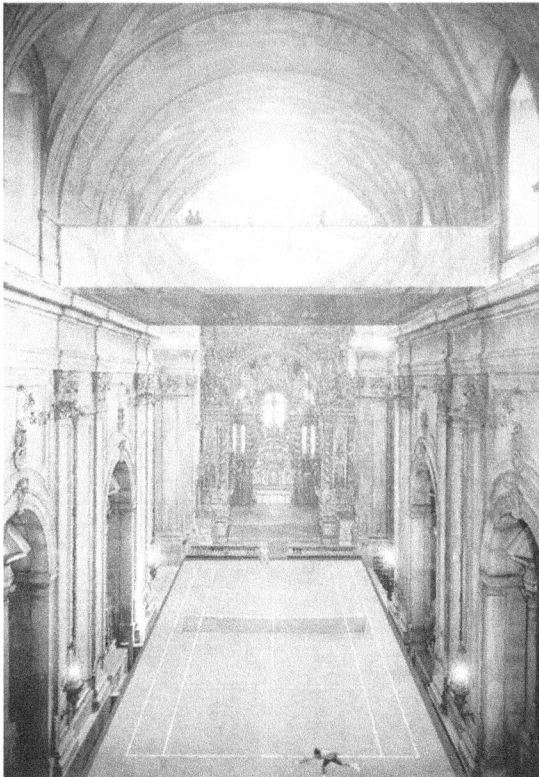 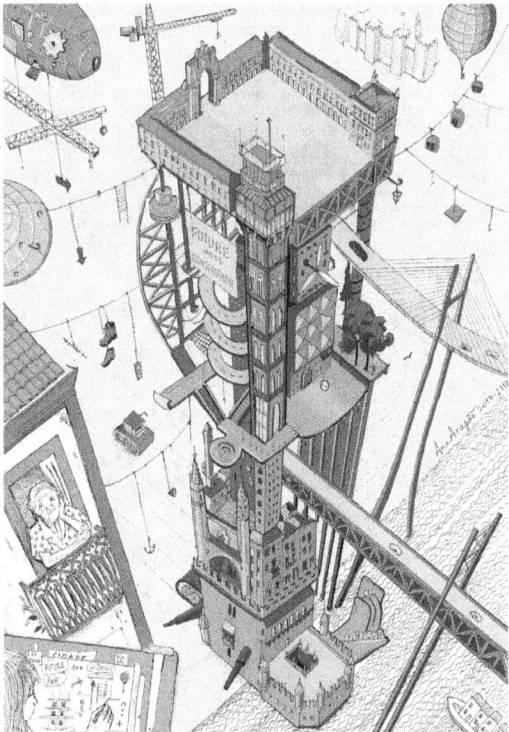

Fig 4: View of Basilica da Estrela. ©Caetano de Bragança   Fig 5: View of Lisbon from Above. ©Ana Aragão

Even though desecration might remain the theme, especially when seen by our 21st century eyes, the image's serenity and respectfulness points to a substitution (or perhaps an evolution) in what might be considered sacred. This is reinforced by the collage of the main altar from Oporto's São Francisco church that is brought into the centre of the composition. The space has not lost its sacred aspect by the addition of the tennis court; it has managed to surprise us by elevating the activity to the level of reverence and with it generating a narrative cue to what this specific future might be like.

In the image "Lisbon From Above" Ana Aragão plays with the established iconography of futuristic images.

Her illustrations are typically intricate, maze-like hand sketches of cities and architectural structure that make use of drafting conventions (hatches, sections) and play with the idea of buildings as objects or textures.

For "Dear Future" Aragão portraits Lisbon as an amalgam of monuments scaled to fit in a tower-like structure (Fig. 5). Zeppelins and balloons hover close to the edge of the buildings in a clear reference to the nostalgia of past futures. The background is a pale colored surface leadings the viewer to think that all of the city has been condensed, contracted into one singular structure, as if cities could be analogous to machines with not contact with topography.

Epilogue

Existing literature on the subject of futuristic imagery takes most of its examples from film, rarely looking at older popular sources, and the approach is seldom to look at urban imagination as a transformation of an actual fabric and an existing iconography.

Both graffiti art and urban futuristic imagery use the city as a support and both are characterized by questions of value, either by, in the case of graffiti, accentuating and consecrating a surface or a view, or in the case of futuristic imagery playing with our assumptions regarding the life of monuments. Both try to condense meaning, to radically shift it from one part of the city to another. In this essay I tried to relate some examples of Lisbon's catalogue of futuristic visions with their counterparts in the turn of the 20th century. Even though focusing on different scenarios, they share strategies and partake in the same visual culture brought about by modernity. The pervasiveness of futuristic representations of the city is such that their strategy of desecration and condensation, especially when applied at the same time, can convince architects and urban planners to make use of them, not always to the public satisfaction.

My idea was not to present a unifying theory, rather to get closer to the nature of this type of image and to test it against the notion of "urban creativity". Futuristic images of a city are a real, living, but so often invisible, heritage.

Acknowledgments: I would like to especially thank Prof. José Sarmento de Matos for his insights and by calling to my attention the treasure trove of Lisbon's futuristic images. I would also like to thank the invaluable collaboration of Pedro Clarke and Caetano de Bragança in the production and curation of "Dear Future, Lisbon in 2113" as well as all the authors that accepted our challenge.

Notes and References

1 A nossa geografia imaginária é infinitamente mais vasta do que a do mundo material. Esta observação, por muito banal que seja, permite-nos detectar a generosidade imensa de uma função humana vital: a de dar vida ao que não pode reclamar presença no mundo do volume e do peso. Como os habitantes angélicos cujas hierarquias os nossos antepassados debatiam, como o unicórnio e a manticora, como os conceitos de democracia perfeita e de boa vontade para com todos os homens, os lugares imaginários da mente não carecem de materialidade para existir na consciência." Alberto Manguiel and Gianni Guadalupi, Dicionário de Lugares Imaginários (Lisboa: Tinta da China, 2013), xii.
2 Joe Austin, "More to see than a canvas in a white cube: for an art in the streets". City: analysis of urban trends, culture, theory, policy, action. 14:1-2 (2010): 35
3 Natalie Collie, "Cities of imagination: Science fiction, urban space, and community engagement in urban planning". Futures 43 (2011) 424-431
4 Michel de Certeau, The Practice of Everyday Life (Berkeley & Los Angeles: University of California Press, 1984)
5 Gary Westfahl, "Pitfalls of Prophecy: Why Science Fiction So Often Fails to Predict the Future" in Science Fiction and the Prediction of the Future: Essays on Foresight and Fallacy, ed. Gary Westfahl et al. (Jefferson, NC: McFarland, 2011), 9-22
6 The full list of predictory fallacies might be useful: the Fallacy of Universal Wealth, the assumption that in the future all will be able to afford any technological advances, the Fallacy of Inevitable Technology, positing the notion that all new technologies will in fact be used, the Fallacy of Extrapolation, that assumes that current trends can only be amplified in the future, the Fallacy of Analogy, stating the belief that a use of new technology will be analogous to the one that preceded it, the Fallacy of Universal Stupidity, the assumes that future societies will be unable to deal with the consequences of their new technologies, The Fallacy of Drama, assuming that change will come in a catastrophic event or led by a single individual and the Fallacy of Replacement, which stipulates that new inventions or forms will completely substitute old ones.
7 Philippe Willems, introduction to The Twentieth Century, by Albert Robida (Middletown, CT: Wesleyan University Press, 2004), xiii-lxii
8 Albert Robida, The Twentieth Century (Middletown, CT: Wesleyan University Press, 2004), 78
9 Robida, The Twentieth Century, 38
10 Manuel Graça Dias, "Arte, Arquitectura e Cidade, A propósito de 'Lisboa Monumental' de Fialho de Almeida" in Arte, Arquitectura e Cidade (Lisbon: Parceria A.M. Pereira, 2011), side B
11 Fialho de Almeida, "Lisboa Monumental", in Arte, Arquitectura e Cidade (Lisbon: Parceria A.M. Pereira, 2011), side A, 16
12 This expression is even funnier to a Portuguese by the abysm of scale and prestige of the two words Manhattan and Cacilhas.
13 Manuel Graça Dias, http://www.contemporanea.com.pt/margueira_06.html
14 It is strangely rather difficult to find the original images online. They seem to have been deleted from the city hall's website.
Austin, Joe "More to see than a canvas in a white cube: for an art in the streets". City: analysis of urban trends, culture, theory, policy, action. 14:1-2 (2010): 33-47.
Manguiel, Alberto and Guadalupi, Gianni, Dicionário de Lugares Imaginários. Lisboa: Tinta da China, 2013
Westfahl, Gary, Kin Yuen, Wong & Kit-Sze Chan, Amy ed., Science Fiction and the Prediction of the Future: Essays on Foresight and Fallacy. Jefferson, NC: McFarland, 2011
Graça Dias, Manuel, Arte, Arquitectura e Cidade. Lisbon: Parceria A.M. Pereira, 2011
Certeau, Michel, The Practice of Everyday Life. Berkeley & Los Angeles: University of California Press, 1984
Robida, Albert, The Twentieth Century. Middletown, CT: Wesleyan University Press, 2004
Collie, Natalie, "Cities of imagination: Science fiction, urban space, and community engagement in urban planning". Futures 43 (2011): 424-431

Giada Pellicari, Editor in Chief www.streetartattack.com,
giadapell@hotmail.it

Graffiti and New Media
The Correlations between the two cultures

This essay aims to study the correlations between Graffiti and New Media cultures in order to create a field of research in which they are analysed together. It begins with the idea of Graffiti as a relational medium in the urban public space and its translation into the online one. It proceeds to develop parallelisms between hacker culture, tactical media and graffiti regarding the way they hack space against capitalism and private property. The final part discusses some examples of projects regarding graffiti and technology, where the last one is not only a tool but a fundamental part of the whole process.

Space, Hacker, Technology

Introduction

This essay about the correlations between Graffiti and New Media should be considered as a work in progress, since it is based on very few existing bibliographies; most of what I wrote derives from my experience as a curator and art critic of Graffiti and New Media, which in this case are meant to be considered as "cultures" that have overlapping thresholds. This study, therefore, is an attempt to create a cohesive field of research in which these two disciplines are analysed together, particularly in cases where they are both created by the same people, or derived from the collaborations between artists who stand in the middle of them. Despite the few existing essays about this topic, the fact which gave me the reason to proceed into this research is that there are lots of case studies that can be considered interesting and innovative with regard to such a relationship, especially when the graffiti writer is also a new media practitioner.

What first emerges when dealing with New Media and Graffiti Writing cultures is that both are aspects of the contemporary world that are difficult to understand from all points of view, meaning that their definition, development and thresholds elude a closed, defined configuration. This is because both are connected to what is considered as the contemporary space: a category that encloses the urban space and the online one, where the social sphere exists, constantly evolves and has the ability to change its formation.
For many reasons these disciplines must be considered as formed by closed groups of people that are selective towards new arrivals or people who try to follow them, because they have the characteristic of being comprehended only by those who know "the code" and the so called "non-written rules".

For this essay I will also focus on hacker culture, Tactical Media and projects that touch on the relationship between technology and graffiti, such as cases where projectors, 3D Mapping and lasers are used. It is because of these different kinds of technologies and relationships that for the title of this essay I used the term "New Media," because it has to be considered as a kind of cauldron that contains both cultural aspects and technological ones. New media is defined by the well-known new media theorist Lev Manovich as: "consisting from two distinct layers: the "cultural layer" and the "computer layer"[1] and "an old media which has been digitized"[2]. This essay is divided up into different paragraphs that propose a visualization of these correlations through a kind of path: I will start with an analysis of the urban space, passing through the translation of graffiti into the online space in which it becomes digital, the correlations between hacker culture, tactical media and graffiti, and the latest developments with some case studies of projects that involve both graffiti and new media. In order to write the last part of this paper I have done field research, meaning speaking on several occasions with writers, artists and new media practitioners that deal with both areas in order to understand the different opinions and points of view through the use of an interdisciplinary approach.

Graffiti as a relational medium within the urban space

The city and the urban space have usually been considered, particularly in contemporary times, as places characterised by many contradictions, because of the fact that they appear to be affected by capitalist dynamics and the presence of a social sphere which is constantly evolving.

For instance, according to the sociologist and urbanist Henri Lefebvre, from Modernism to the present day there has been a feeling that the social space is something closely related to the forces of production, where the relationships that take place in the urban space are related to them[3]. The urban environment, in fact, stands as a social space where actions occur, and the city therefore becomes a space formed and invested in by social activities during a well-defined temporality.
Graffiti itself is usually understood in relation to the city, and even the graffiti writer himself moves within this assumption, considering the public space and its commodification as one of the key triggers of his work, but also those whom he opposes by painting graffiti. In this sense, very often, graffiti becomes a way to recapture the public space through the objectification of the sign on the wall, developing itself as a practice characterized by its visualization into an artistic form.
What is worth noting for us regarding the relationship with the urban space is that graffiti can become a relational medium within either the urban space or the online one. In the case of the urban space, graffiti, by being something that could catch the attention of the contemporary passerby, meaning a kind of flaneur, has the capability to create a triangular relationship between the place-the work-and the passerby. In this case the concept of the flaneur is taken into account as a historical reference to elucidate the relationship with the passerby, in the form of a theoretical assumption in order to link the urban space to what is considered as that of the traveler.

Along with this discourse, it is important to say that the traveler's space has become the archetype of the much better known "non-places"[4] theorized by the anthropologist Marc Augé, which are spaces that are not anthropological and are not integrated with spaces understood in a historical sense.

If we look at the theories discussed so far, we see how the art project or in this case, graffiti, can become a kind of medium within the urban environment, because it can be seen as something that really creates a triangular relationship between the place, the work of art and the passerby, by forming a moment of focused attention. This means that the fruition and the encounter with the artwork creates a moment of stillness that makes the place relational, which is to say that the space becomes a place, as defined in Augé's categories, that is relational, historical and connected with identity. The city that could be seen as a non-place (meaning not relational, not historical, and therefore not an "anthropological place"[7]), because of the continuity of peoples' movement inside of it, according to Michel De Certau, for whom "space is a frequented place"[8] is now seen as a relational place because of the fruition of the artwork in this settlement. New relations between the variables of space, time and public dimension are determined, as in this case the art possesses the peculiarity of auto-determination[9] of the space and has the ability to transform a public space into a place of art, resulting in a form of relatedness with the place. In this way, therefore, graffiti becomes a landmark, by constituting itself as that moment of pause that turns a place into a space of art.

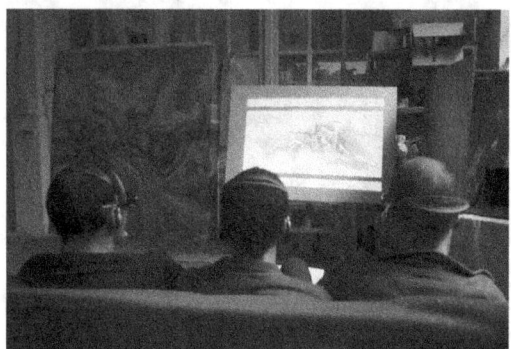

Fig. 1: Apparati Effimeri and Peeta, Le Ecrit Animé, 2012.
Courtesy © Apparati Effimeri

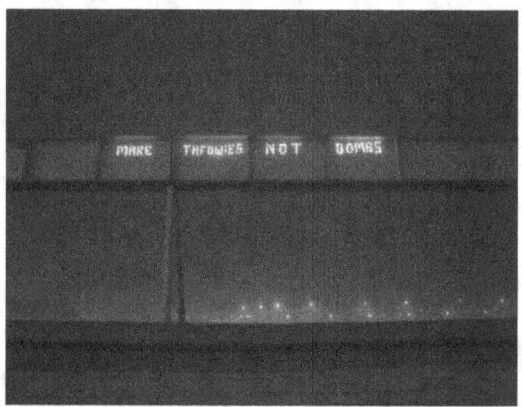

Fig. 2: Graffiti Research Lab, Make Trowies not Bombs, 2007. CC Common License 2.0, available online at: https://www.flickr.com/photos/urban_data/380295510/in/pool-graffitiresearchlab/

Graffiti becomes digital

I would argue that the function of Graffiti during these last years has changed. If at the beginning of its own history it was experienced along the streets and developed in close contact with the urban landscape, with the advent of the internet the whole phenomenon has undergone a process of evolution towards a different perception, due to the fact that now, more than ever, it tends to move between two different spaces: the effective public – meant as what can be considered as the "cultural landscape", which is offline; and the intangible one – which is the one that occurs on the web, the online world, and through a total translation into it.

The correlation between graffiti and what is considered the "cultural landscape" is something that has always been bound together, for the cultural landscape "expresses the values of the society, the city in its morphology being a medium through which these attributes are transmitted"[10]. This fact appeared in the development of graffiti because of the launching of some websites about the topic beginning in the mid-nineties, such as Artcrimes which is one of the best known, and since then graffiti writers themselves have realized that the Internet and especially social networks could give more visibility to their pieces and to their notoriety.

In fact, the graffiti writer has always lived with the desire to see his name written everywhere, in the highest places, the biggest walls and most popular spots, thus hyper-branding his name through his tag and his own style, due to this obsession with the repetition of his name. The perception of space, therefore, has changed for the graffiti writers but also for the potential users and audience, making the web a sort of extension of the urban space.

A writer in a private conversation has stated: " Graffiti writers are no longer doing the pieces to put them on the street, but to post them on Facebook ", a claim that not only arises as a critique of this last phenomenon, but that also stands as a consideration having the capability to define an effective practice by graffiti writers and street artists at the present time. Actually, in the beginning of what can be considered as the Graffiti movement, writers used to "send trains" from one city to another in order to see what was happening and to show the evolution of their styles. Other places to look at graffiti were the fanzines and the blackbooks, an important heritage that was rarely seen by anyone outside of the inner circle of writers.

Now, however, these types of approaches are diminishing in favor of the online world, in which the pieces are posted every day, thus determining an emancipation of the whole phenomenon, an emergence to a mainstream level of the culture and, most importantly, a new methodology of self- statement within the closed environment.

This is a very important transformation for understanding the evolution of graffiti styles, which are no longer closely tied to local visual culture; consequently, new generations of writers are at an advantage as far as their technical development thanks to the greater availability of information. At the same time, the whole phenomenon of what can be considered as the visual documentation of the piece by the writers themselves, whether in the form of video or photography, assumes some functions that are completely different: these means are no longer seen simply as documentation for their own sake, for personal use or for fanzines, but more as visual memes to be exported within social networks and as a means of self-assertion and demonstration to the peer group of what they are capable of doing. It is worth noting, then, that through websites graffiti, which is by its nature ephemeral, is frozen and represented in this way as an eternal, digital present, consequently preempting their decline with the passage of time. This new expansion of graffiti writing into the online world has brought about a de-territorialisation of the phenomenon, as the theorist Lachlan MacDowall explains:

> In spatial terms, this process can also describe graffiti's de-territorialisation, in which images and styles of graffiti circulate beyond their original sites and become embedded, re-territorialised, in new contexts. These processes continue to affect graffiti production itself, as practitioners adapt to the increasing circulation of images. [11]

Very recently an interesting new book came out that was written and edited by a young blogger who is editor in chief of Vandalog, one of the most well-known website about graffiti and street art. The book, called Viral Art, was an attempt to analyse how the internet and social networks have affected the way that graffiti and street art have spread all over the world, by suggesting that:

> ... the internet is the new frontier for the kind of public engagement that street art and graffiti are about. Viral art is my term for art that takes advantage of this new environment, but I differentiate between viral art that spreads naturally as it gets shared and viral art than invades digital space like street art and graffiti invade physical space.[12]

In fact, if graffiti has a transient nature, we can think about how digital documentation in reality can change either its duration in time, or its fruition, and furthermore determining its global nature. The piece that by its nature must be considered site-specific, through the photographic image and the internet is extracted from its original place and is decontextualized. In this sense the fact of being site-specific has to be seen in a broader way, since while it is true that it is formed in a given context, it is also true that the user is no longer just the passerby but also the public network.

Wi-Fi, in this case, is an important invention that has modified how culture spreads, because it has totally changed the relationship between space and the internet and has enabled a continuous exchange between space on and off line, even making it possible to easily share online graffiti pieces in real time, either in the moment in which they are being made, or when they have already been completed. If we take Facebook and Twitter as the latest examples of this time-flexible category, we can think of them as spaces of communication, where everyone can "post" thoughts and share files, in the case of graffiti sharing the pieces.

The internet could also been described as an ephemeral city: in this sense it takes on the connotation of an informational city[13], meaning a space of contemporaneity; that is to say, a coming together of different times which can be considered as a "place of flows"[14], referring to the technological and organizational possibility of practising simultaneity without contiguity. The idea of the identity and self-establishment which is one of the most important characteristics of graffiti, therefore, has to be considered, for space, through the use of the internet. It has acquired fragmented dimensions, where the on-line identity allows a simultaneous presence in various spaces and contexts, a constant "reproduction" of the self sans body, an identity characterized by "multiplicity, heterogeneity and fragmentation"[15]. The identity of the graffiti writer, therefore, now has to be considered in close connection with the use of social networks and websites, where the assertion of one's name is no longer connected to an urban phenomenon, but has undergone a massive extension characterized by its coexistence in many different places at the same time.

My conclusion is that if the internet is a new kind of public space, and if art has the capability to turn a place into a space of art, even the internet can become a place to see and experience graffiti, of course in a new way, which is interesting for the fact that the whole culture is undergoing an important shift, by demonstrating that new media technologies have the capability to affect the way graffiti writers are doing graffiti.

Graffiti, Hacker Culture and Tactical Media

It is a kind of challenge to write about the correlations between hacker culture and graffiti realm, because they could be considered as two very different currents in the world. They are usually understood to be two practices that belong to the "out-law" way of life and are seen unjustly only in a "dark" way, not considering, instead, that they have the capability to challenge the space in which we are living. My attempt to address the hacker movement is not only with the premise to talk about political implications and protests that, in any case, underlie this phenomenon, but rather to investigate the existence of a sort of internal unwritten code of ethics to be respected within hacker culture. Moreover, hacking entails a specific use of online space, denoted by aspects of "invasion" and reappropriation, similar to what graffiti does with the urban landscape.

If we look at both the urban space and the internet, we know that they are characterized by the use of advertising and the existence of commercial interests. Whether we are walking down the street or surfing online, we face the fact that we are bombarded by marketing and viral media through emails and websites.

The artist and researcher Evan Roth, for instance, has already been able to create a correlation between the two spaces and between graffiti and hacker culture, by saying that both the internet and public space are "uncured spaces"[16]:

> *... it's one of those places where you truly have uncurated free speech. It's like there's no moderator removing comments from the comment thread. There's no curator allowing work into the exhibition. It's just what someone said, and it's gonna stay there until somebody cleans it off[17].*

Through this declaration he gives a sort of analysis of internet space, thinking about it as a free space to work with. However, it is worth noting that the internet is not actually a real free space, because it is affected by capitalism and digital capitalism dynamics, two themes for which there is a link between hacker and graffiti culture. Graffiti, actually, has always been considered as a way to re-appropriate the public space and often as something that collides with private property and is contrary to capitalism. Since its onset the Internet has been privatized, a fact that made web space subject to corporations and private interest, becoming itself a demonstration of its limitation. The academic Dan Schiller has explained what happened to the web through the term "Digital Capitalism", which "has involved radical social, as well as technological, changes"[18]. The sociologist Manuel Castells argues too that our society is subjected to capitalism and that, through the advent of internet capitalism and informational technologies, network space has changed:

> *The information technology revolution was instrumental in allowing the implementation of a fundamental process of restructuring of the capitalist system from the 1980s onwards. In the process, this technological revolution was itself shaped, in its development and manifestations, by the logic and interests of advanced capitalism, without being reducible to the expression of such interests.[19]*

But a way to counteract these dynamics is actually what Evan Roth has proposed with the idea of "hack" the space, by giving this definition of the term hack: " ...a hack alters a system's intended purpose and turns it into something new. In this sense, it can be applied to many things outside of the world of software development"[20] and because of this he considers graffiti writers as hackers: "Graffiti writers hacked the subway system to move art around New York City (and later the world)"[21] .
I would argue that Tactical Media are very close to the Hacker Culture and Graffiti modes of hacking space, because even if they have political implications and protest methodologies, they are also characterized by a strong artistic component, which is why they are interesting with regard to this theme. The most interesting aspect of Tactical Media is that they are able to effectively unify media activism and involvement with the creativity of the artist using new technology.

When Geert Lovink and David Garcia wrote the manifesto of Tactical Media they already thought of the graffiti writer as a person denoted by a tactical mentality, saying that "Tactical media are media of crisis, criticism and opposition that involves people like: the activist, the nomadic warrior, the hacker and the writer"[22].

The Hacker Manifesto, therefore, is treated at this point in order to understand in depth what the hacker culture is and the use that it makes of online space. Even in this case there are unwritten rules among the community of hackers, an essential aspect of the culture that is evident in the same way as when one gets closer to the world of Graffiti Writing.

Written by McKenzie Wark, the Hacker Manifesto was actually conceived in close collaboration with other hackers, who have been involved with him for a shared production of the contents, a point illustrated by the list of thanks at the end of the book. It is also a kind of ethical guidance that helps to understand the hacker world, a book that appears to be very logical and rational, more so because it is written through the use of points, like a real manifesto. The structure itself is very interesting because it does not have numbers on the pages, only paragraphs, and is divided into different topics such as: hacking, history, information and production. According to this book one of the definitions of hacker is as follows:

> *Hackers come to struggle against the particular forms in which abstraction is commodified and turned into the private property of the vectoralist class. Hackers come as a class to recognize their class interest is best expressed through the struggle to free the production of abstraction, not just from the particular fetters of this or that form of property, but to abstract the form of property itself[23].*

The similarities between New Media and Graffiti also lie in the use of some terms such as "tag", something that was already underlined by the writer Matt Mason:

> *"Tags" are already used in search engines: you get the results you want by searching for tags or keywords. Tags are attached to sites to give information visibility and make it accessible, and they will be even more important in the Internet of things. When people begin virtually annotating real space, the nature of privacy, the public domain, and the role of graffiti suddenly changes. Who will and who will not have the right to tag the virtual environment? "[24]*

At this point it is important to look at one of the most important manifestos in the history of graffiti writing, which is the one written in 1979 by the famous graffiti writer and guru of the hip hop world Rammellzee called "Ionic Treatise Gothic Futurism Assassins Knowledge of the Remanipulated Point One to 720". It was equipped with a logical structure and an ethical dimension, in which all the styles were analysed in points and all the ideas regarding Ikonoklast Panzerism explained and analyzed[25]. All the letters are described in this list, in a form of a code that should be respected. Written thus as a discourse between master and disciple, it illustrates how the methodology of writing and the way of approaching the explication of an argument is very similar.

Towards a new field of research between Graffiti and Technology

In this last section of the essay I will talk about some examples of the correlations existing between graffiti and technology, mainly focusing on the discourse about what Visual Mapping is intended to be, digital painting and the use of lasers. This parallelism has started because both Graffiti Writing and these uses of technology are strongly correlated to the relationship with the architecture of pre-existing buildings, through a contextualization of the works that take shape developing on the wall of the façade. Another important issue is time: both graffiti and visual mapping are characterized by ephemerality, a certain period of time which is represented by the contingence of a moment and what is considered as a performative act.

3D videomapping consists in creating a site-specific creation on the walls of a pre-existing architecture, developing a sort of redesign of the space through the use of programs such as cinema4D, After Effects and visualization with high quality projectors. In order to write this paragraph, I have done field research and spoken about my idea on several occasions with graffiti writers, new media artists, gallerists and people who deal with both aspects in order to understand their different opinions and points of view.
Some well-known examples are the artists Evan Roth, and the Italians Verbo, Asker and the collective Apparati Effimeri who produced a project in collaboration with the graffiti writer Peeta, which can be considered one of the first examples of interaction between Mapping 3D and Graffiti Writing.

By starting from the research done by the artist and thinker Evan Roth, who explicated his thesis well, and was subsequently published in Geek Graffiti which is free to download[26], we can understand how he created an interesting bridge between New Media and Writing, thanks to the invention of a digital software that had the ability to study and analyze the gestures of movement in the creation of a tag and bombing, creating a Graffiti Taxonomy.

Evan Roth is a key figure for my research because in addition to dealing with graffiti and New Media, he is also one of the creators of two interesting collectives that work closely with technologies and whose practices are related to Tactical Media and Graffiti, through which they are able to hack space through the use of technology: Free Art and Technology and Graffiti Research Lab. They are closely interconnected and can be an important example of how technologies, critical elements, graffiti and hacking the space can function as works of critical thinking. One example of this could be the performance "Make Throwies Not Bombs"[27] (Fig.02) realized with LEDs on a high wall, turning the space into something new, in a tautology in which the work itself talks about graffiti and is graffiti at the same time, in a short circuit where the visual aspect is also important.

Among the technologies invented by GRL is the Laser Tag, which is fundamental to this research, because it was the one that gave me the impetus to investigate a relationship between visual mapping and graffiti, becoming the first small step in this analysis. It is actually a work that is capable of commissioning existing walls, an intervention that belongs of course to the world of Graffiti writing, much like tags, but also to that of technology.

With this project, Graffiti Research Lab was also invited to exhibit in Venice by the cultural association of graffiti writers called Urban Code, during the first edition of Headlines. Highlights from the bottom, in 2009. The project realized was called Tagging Pinault, which became an art project connected to a form of social protest, by reclaiming space and giving visibility to the problems existing in Venice between big institutions and citizens.

At that time, Punta della Dogana and Palazzo Grassi weren't yet opened to the public and the intervention of Urban Code, in collaboration with Sale Docks, took place during an evening in front of these places symbolic of culture and its contradictions. Actually, they have a connotation of places of power within the art world, but for the most part they are presented as being a foreign reality settled in Venice that bring to the place a vision from outside without taking into account the local one.
I invited Urban Code to be part of a series of lectures that I curated in 2012 at IUAV University in Venice, called On Writing. Talking about Graffiti and Aerosol Art, in which we had the chance to talk about this project and Cyros, a graffiti writer that belongs to Urban Code said:

> We did this initiative called Tagging Pinault, in which we made tags on Palazzo Grassi and Punta della Dogana, not bringing any harm to the structure but just making a theoretical discourse. We know how much is invested in Venice in monetary terms and also speculation in contemporary art. At the same time we know how difficult it is to have the space for working from the bottom or at least to get to take advantage of the ' immense capital invested[28].

If we look, however, at the methodological approach of Urban Code, it is easy to understand that a form of protest usually underlies it. In fact, the association was born as a result of a difficult period where the police had carried out lots of investigations and gotten several graffiti writers from Venice into trouble. In response, they formed themselves into a group in order to give legitimacy to their movement and to explain what the discipline of Graffiti Writing was about. In this sense this project is important because it is an example of the relationship between graffiti and hackers, giving weight to the theory of "hacking the space" as explained by Evan Roth, because the technology that had been used was the one invented by GRL. This point stands as an important step toward elucidating the existing correlations between graffiti and new media, which finds critical support through an analysis done by the researcher Lachlan MacDowall, who has identified a relationship between new media, graffiti and the urban space, saying that:

"... the complex relationship between graffiti, new media and urban spaces, beginning with graffiti's shift from a marginal cultural practice to a highly visible, global phenomenon across the twentieth century. Secondly, it examines the similarities in the contemporary uses of new media by a range of graffiti stakeholders across three related fields: tagging, archiving and mapping urban space."[29]

The terms site-specific and ephemeral are therefore key words for the correlations between the two practices: what differentiates graffiti from videomapping is that the former is site specific and ephemeral in an unconscious way, whereas in the case of the latter, there is a rigid premeditated design with the building. The real difference, then, is connoted by the dichotomy between legality / illegality, a reflection that emerges from a private dialogue between me and Fabio Paris, one of the co-founders of the Link Art Center of the Information Age in Brescia. According to him the discriminating factor that differentiates the two disciplines is the notion of illegality, because graffiti is born in an illegal manner, whereas videomapping must be forcedly legal, due to the fact that it needs a long period of premeditation and time to obtain permissions. But what happens when instead of tags, throw ups and illegal pieces the writer approaches the halls of fame, or even more complex projects of urban muralism? The relation in this case turns upside down, in the sense that the legal part becomes common between them, time becomes less constrained, and consequently there is a loss of the instinctual part. Moreover, in some cases of huge walls technologies are used in order to contextualize the piece on the wall, by using some specific programs to arrive at a tridimensional aspect. In this legal case, however, graffiti falls short of its function of hacking the space, becoming a normalization of the phenomenon itself and a rejection of the gestuality of the movement that characterizes tags, throw ups and pieces on trains. Even the re-appropriation of space is no longer a characterization of this way of doing graffiti, since it becomes accomplice of governments and social welfare. The researcher Liz Kinnamon has noted that: "Where it is illegal and therefore confrontational, graffiti is a direct rejection of power structures, an effective "Fuck the Police." But where it begs permission, the subversive premise is debased."[30]

In these specific cases, the technology is not just subjected to the achievement of the piece, but becomes a creative aspect in the execution of the work, exactly the same thing that happens in videomapping.

Another peculiar case study for the correlations between Graffiti and New Media is the graffiti writer Asker, from Milan, who works with graffiti, interactive design, visual mapping and digital painting. In an interview that I conducted with him, he made a clear distinction between graffiti and mapping, because to him graffiti stands more as a culture, whereas mapping 3D is considered to be a tool. The reflection that he explained on the idea of time is very interesting:

The fact that mapping also acts on architecture and on large dimensions is definitely the factor that has most of all attracted many graffiti writers … I find the meeting between graffiti-mapping very intriguing, the writers are now playing with the dimension of time-animation that can make their letters" living " while staying, however, in their urban environment. There will also be a sort of reversal of time: before you acted at night to be visible during the day, now you work to be visible at night (or in the dark).[31]

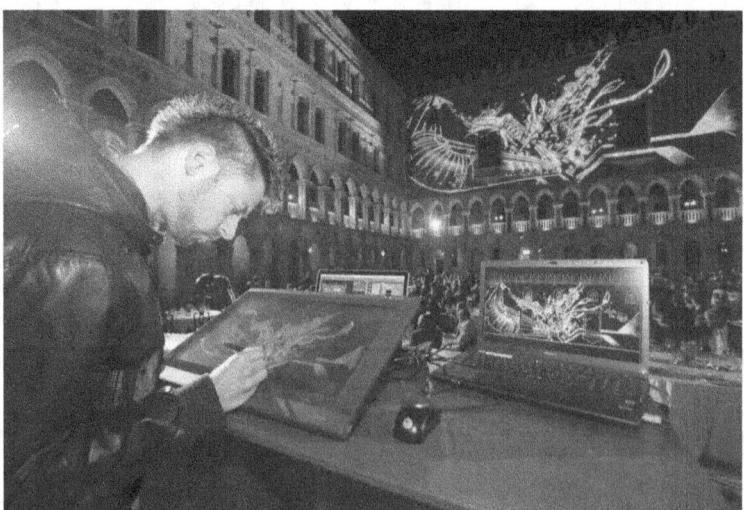

Fig.3: Davide Asker, Giochi di Luce, Palazzo Ducale, Venezia, 2013. Client: Snam technical equipment;
Courtesy © Davide Asker

The fact that Asker makes the distinction between culture and method, in the sense that Writing is a culture whereas mapping is a method, is partly true, because with this opinion he is likely to diminish mapping as an art form and new media as a culture, by seeing it only as a tool of expression and a technological way of creating displays. This is a contradiction that sometimes happens in the case of 3D mapping with regard to studies of visual design, because it is usually used as a display for events, whereas it is in all effect an art form.

In some specific cases such as that of the Apparati Effimeri a collective from Bologna, their work is divided up among different sectors and, when they do an art project, they produce it looking only at the artistic and critical parts, whereas when they collaborate with other agencies they change their approach somewhat. Their name was born out of the fact that they have always had an idea of the spectacle of the moment and have always conceived of parties as social time, taking inspiration from the scenographers of the seventeenth century. They usually intervene on architecture and consequently in the urban space, creating 3D mapping with the idea of working visually by re-creating the images without doing any damage.

During an interview that I conducted with the collective by asking some questions regarding my theory of a correlation between the two cultures, they said:

> *Ephemeral means everything that is short-term and some of the greatest masterpieces of Street Art are now lost. For other reasons instead it is the concept of duration that separates them, Architectural Mapping in fact is ephemeral in advance. The intent not to invade begins mainly by the short duration of the visual and the fact that you can experiment with endless creative solutions. In this way we learn to understand the true nature dynamics of the urban context.*[32]

One of their lasts project is particularly interesting because it is a collaboration with the world-famous graffiti writer Peeta, who is particularly inclined to graffiti writing 3D style. Together they developed one of the first projects regarding the relationship between graffiti and 3D mapping, and thus they are interesting in this context, because they open up a new field of research where new media and graffiti are conceived of jointly and where the container and the content are the same thing. Marco Grassivaro, one of the members of the collective, has known Peeta for a long time, because both of them were from Padova and spent time in the area of the banks, a place where all graffiti writers from the town used to meet, in particular the crew of the EAD, of which Peeta is part. In the case of this project, titled Le Ecrit Animé, Apparati Effimeri intervene on a piece painted by Peeta on a wall through the use of 3D mapping and stereoscopic effects, beginning a series of works regarding the connections between mapping and graffiti.

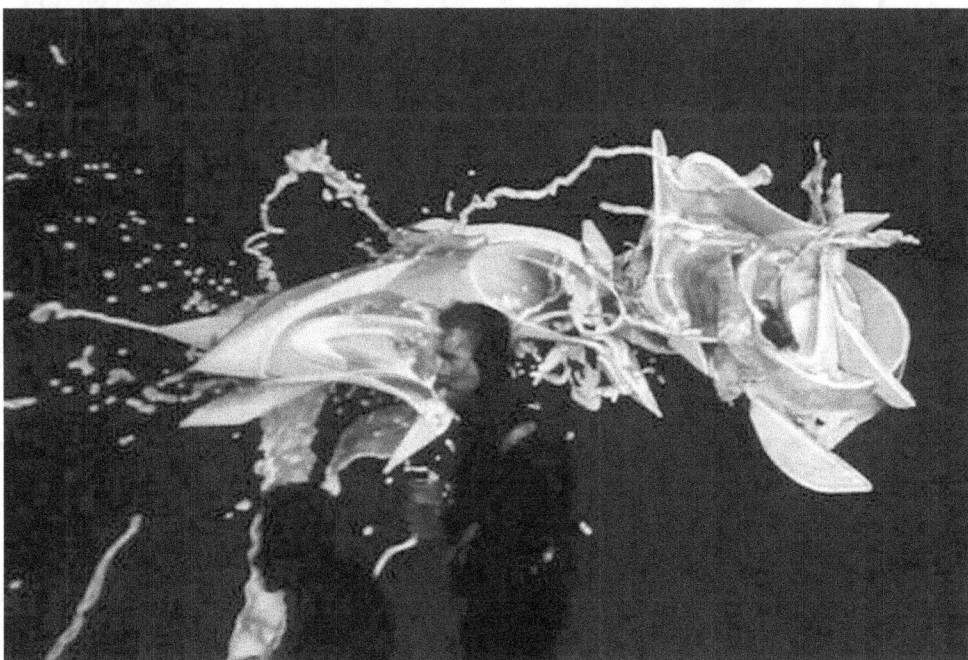

Fig.4: Apparati Effimeri and Peeta, Le Ecrit Animé, 2012, Venezia. Courtesy © Apparati Effimeri

The same thing has been done on a smaller scale, during a performance attended in Peeta's studio (Fig.01), reproducing it on canvas and watching it using glasses. Regarding this project Apparati Effimeri has said:

> *The relationship with Peeta derives from the analysis of his work, in particular, we were interested in the extremely innovative way with which his works related in both lighting and structural terms*

with the space that welcomed them. From this relationship L'Ecrit Animé was born, which is a project still going on. The relationship can work if the writer wants to give continuity to the forms, but in the field of this current the needs are different, so we believe that it is a matter of poetic rather than a technical approach.

It is worth noting that this interdisciplinary approach towards a new field of graffiti, new media and the specific case of visual mapping, has been opened up further from writers that were already doing graffiti in a European style, connected to the 3D technique. This is because this style itself regards a third dimension of the development of the piece, and most of the time has led those who approach this technique to the creation of sculptures, installations, and the use of technological programs, such as CAD.

My attempt, therefore, has been to focus attention on a new way of thinking about graffiti, in which technology is not just a tool but an important part of the whole process of its conception. A new field of research should be started, in which the interdisciplinary approach is key to understanding these works and both fields, which now, more than ever, are connected.

Notes and References

1 See, Lev Manovich, The Language of New Media, 2001, available online, accessed November, 8, 2013, http://www.academia.edu/542739/The_language_of_new_media, 63.
2 Ivi, 65.
3 See, Henri Lefebvre, The Production of Space, trans. Donald Nicholson-Smith (Oxford, UK: Blackwell Publishers, 1991), 70-4.
4 See Marc Augé, Non-Places - Introduction to an Anthropology of Supermodernity, trans. John Howe, (London: Verso, 2009), 86.
5 Ivi, 78.
6 Ivi, 77-81.
7 Ivi, 87.
8 Ivi, 79
9 See Peter Osborne, "Non-Places and the Spaces of Art", The Journal of Architecture, 6 (2001): 191.
10 Alexandru Calcatinge, " Visions of the Real in Contemporary City", International Journal of Art and Sciences, 3 (2010): 321.
11 Lachlan MacDowall, The Graffiti Archive and the Digital City, in Place: Local Knowledge and New Media Practice, ed. D. BUTT, J. BYWATER, N. PAUL (Newcastle: Cambridge Scholars Publishing 2008), 138.
12 RJ Rushmore, Viral Art - How the internet has shaped street art and graffiti, web accessed December 6, 2013, http://viralart.vandalog.com/read, 4.
13 Peter Osborne, "Non-Places and the Spaces of Art", The Journal of Architecture, 6 (2001): 191.
14 Ivi, 190.
15 Christian Paul, Stream of Consciousness: Info-Narratives in Networked Art, in Reframing Consciousness. Art, Mind and Technology, ed. Roy Ascott, (Portland: Intellect Books,1999), 161-62.
16 Evan Roth, Lecture at the University of Mariland, web accessed November 2, 2013, watch the video: https://www.youtube.com/watch?v=KcAM6Riw2BM
17 Hahzem Fahmy, Evan Roth Challenges Intellectual Property In New Exhibition, web accessed February 26, 2014, http://wesleyanargus.com/2014/02/06/evan-roth-intellectual-property-donor/
18 Dan Schiller, Digital Capitalism. Networking the Global Market System, (Cambridge Mass.:MIT Press, 1999), 3.
19 Manuel Castells, The Rise of the Network Society, (Hoboken: Wiley-Blackewell, 2010), 13.
20 Evan Roth, Artist Hacker: From Free Software to Fine Art, in F.A.T The Manual, ed. Domenico Quaranta, Jeraldine Juarez, (Brescia: Link Editions, 2013), p. 16.
21 Ivi, p. 17.
22 Geert Lovink, Tactical Media. The Second Decade, 2005, web accessed March 8, 2012, available online: http://laudanum.net/geert/files/112972 4590/
23 Wark McKenzie, A Hacker Manifesto, (Cambridge Mass.: Harvard University Press, 2004), n.22.
24 Matt Mason, The Pirate's Dilemma. How Youth Culture is Reinventing Capitalism, (New York: Free Press, 2008), 132.
25 See Rammellzee, Ionic Treatise Gothic Futurism Assassins Knowledge of the Remanipulated Point One to 720, 1979, web accessed December 18, 2013, https://post.thing.net/node/3086
26 Evan Roth, Geek Graffiti. A study in Computation, Gesture and Graffiti Analysis, 2009, web accessed, August 10, 2011, http://www.ni9e.com/graffiti_analysis/graffiti_analysis_09.pdf
27 See Graffiti Research Lab Website, web accessed August 10, 2011, http://www.graffitiresearchlab.com/blog/projects/make-throwies-not-bombs/
28 Giada Pellicari, On Writing. Talking about Graffiti and Aerosol Art – The associations and the Meeting of Styles, IUAV University, Venice, 2012, Watch the video, accessed December 4, 2013, http://www.youtube.com/watch?feature=player_embedded&v=8JX_n2CBDWY
29 Lachlan MacDowall, The Graffiti Archive and the Digital City, in Place: Local Knowledge and New Media Practice, ed. D. BUTT, J. BYWATER, N. PAUL (Newcastle: Cambridge Scholars Publishing 2008), p. 135.
30 Liz Kinnamon, "London Riots, Living Walls: Questions of Resistance in Late Capitalism", in Rhizomes 25 (2013): 6.
31 Giada Pellicari, Intervista ad Asker, trans. Mine, web accessed November 18, 2013, http://streetartattack.blogspot.it/2013/02/intervista-ad-asker.html
32 Giada Pellicari, Mapping e Graffiti – Intervista agli Apparati Effimeri, trans. Mine, accessed November 18, 2013, http://streetartattack.blogspot.it/2013/02/mapping-e-graffiti-intervista-agli_26.html
33 Ibidem.

Augé, Marc, Non-Places - Introduction to an Anthropology of Supermodernity, trans. John Howe. (London: Verso, 2009).
Brighenti, M. Alessandro, "At The Wall: Graffiti Writers, Urban Territoriality and the Public Domain", Space and Culture 13 (2010).
Jean Baudrillard, Symbolic Exchange and Death. London: Sage, 1993.
Calcatinge, Alexandru, " Visions of the Real in Contemporary City", International Journal of Art and Sciences, 3 (2010).
Caputo, Alessandro, ed.by, All City Writers, Bagnolet: Kitchen 93, 2009.
Careri, Francesco, Walkscapes. Camminare come pratica estetica. Torino: Einaudi, 2006.
Castells, Mauel, The Rise of the Network Society. Hoboken: Wiley-Blackewell, 2010.
Critical Art Ensemble, Digital Resistance. Explorations in Tactical Media. New York: Autonomedia, 2001.
Daigneault, Ginette, "Space and Time. For a Spatiotemporal Sensititvity", in Reframing Consciousness. Art, Mind and Technology, ed.by Roy Ascott. Portland: Intellect, 1999.
Deitch, Jeffrey, et. Al, Art in the Streets. Los Angeles: Rizzoli, 2011.
Fahmy, Hahzem, Evan Roth Challenges Intellectual Property In New Exhibition, web accessed February 26, 2014, http://wesleyanargus.com/2014/02/06/evan-roth-intellectual-property-donor/
Finkelpearl, Tom, Dialogues in Public Art. Cambridge MA: MIT Press, 2001.
Grau, Oliver, Virtual Art. From Illusion to Immersion. Cambridge MA: MIT Press, 2003.
Hebdige, Dick, Subculture. The Meaning of Style. London and New York: Routledge, 2002.
Kinnamon, Liz "London Riots, Living Walls: Questions of Resistance in Late Capitalism", in Rhizomes 25 (2013).

Kwon, Miwon, One Place After Another. Site-Specific Art and Locational Identity. Cambridge MA: MIT Press, 2004 (2002).

Lefebvre, Henri, The Production of Space, trans. Donald Nicholson-Smith (Oxford, UK: Blackwell Publishers, 1991).

Lefebvre, Henri, Writings on Cities. Oxford: Blackwell, 2000 (1905).

Lovink, Geert, Dark Fiber. Tracking Critical Internet Culture. Cambridge MA: MIT Press, 2002.

Lovink, Geert, Zero Comments. Blogging and Critical Internet Culture. New York: Routledge, 2008.

Macdonald, Nancy, The Graffiti Subculture. Youth, Masculinity and Identity in London and New York. New York: Palgrave Macmillian, 2001.

MacDowall, Lachlan, The Graffiti Archive and the Digital City, in Place: Local Knowledge and New Media Practice, ed. D. Butt, J. Bywater, N. Paul, Newcastle: Cambridge Scholars Publishing 2008.

Manovich, Lev, The Language of New Media, 2001, available online, accessed November, 8, 2013, http://www.academia.edu/542739/The_language_of_new_media

Mason, Matt, The Pirate's Dilemma. How Youth Culture is Reinventing Capitalism. New York: Free Press, 2008.

McKenzie,Wark, A Hacker Manifesto. Cambridge MA.: Harvard University Press, 2004.

Miles, Malcolm, Art, Space and the City. Public Art and urban futures. London: Routledge, 1997.

Miles, Malcolm, Hall, Thomans (ed.by), Urban Futures. Critical Commentaries on Shaping the City. London: Routledge, 2003.

Osborne, Peter, "Non-Places and the Spaces of Art", The Journal of Architecture, 6 (2001).

Lovink, Geert, Tactical Media. The Second Decade, 2005, web accessed March 8, 2012, available online: http://laudanum.net/geert/files/112972 4590/

Paul, Christian, Stream of Consciousness: Info-Narratives in Networked Art, in Reframing Consciousness. Art, Mind and Technology, ed. Roy Ascott. Portland: Intellect Books,1999.

Pellicari, Giada, On Writing. Talking about Graffiti and Aerosol Art. Venezia: Edizioni Luckyshoes, 2012.

Pellicari, Giada Intervista ad Asker, web accessed November 18, 2013, http://streetartattack.blogspot.it/2013/02/intervista-ad-asker.html

Pellicari, Giada, Mapping e Graffiti – Intervista agli Apparati Effimeri, accessed November 18, 2013, http://streetartattack.blogspot.it/2013/02/mapping-e-graffiti-intervista-agli_26.html

Raley, Rita, Tactical Media. Minneapolis: University of Minnesota Press, 2009.

Rammellzee, Ionic Treatise Gothic Futurism Assassins Knowledge of the Remanipulated Point One to 720, 1979, web accessed December 18, 2013, https://post.thing.net/node/3086

Evan Roth, Artist Hacker: From Free Software to Fine Art, in F.A.T The Manual, ed. Domenico Quaranta, Jeraldine Juarez. Brescia: Link Editions, 2013.

Evan Roth, Geek Graffiti. A study in Computation, Gesture and Graffiti Analysis, 2009, web accessed, August 10, 2011, http://www.ni9e.com/graffiti_analysis/graffiti_analysis_09.pdf

RJ Rushmore, Viral Art - How the internet has shaped street art and graffiti, web accessed December 6, 2013, http://viralart.vandalog.com/read

Dan Schiller, Digital Capitalism. Networking the Global Market System. Cambridge MA:MIT Press, 1999.

Terranova, Tiziana, Network Culture. Politics for the Information Age. London: Pluto Press, 2004.

Julio Da Cruz Paulos, University of Paris 8, ETH Zurich
jdcpaulos@gmail.com

Agata Walny
agata.walny@gmail.com

The Art of Pragmatic Action

The increasing and integrative 'urban production' (cultural, economic, political and architectural) results in a re-structuring of the city and thus alters the spirit of time: spatiality and temporalities of public places, the collective social identities and the disappearance of the line between the public and the private realm have been substantially modified. The possibility of a wide global scape is causing physical space to become obsolete in favor of virtual space, giving the possibility of a wider audience. This paper addresses the issue of virtual space (ethnoscape) as the new canvas for urban art/social movements. Contestations on mobility have been a recent phenomenon arising in many cities across the globe underpinning this reflection - namely 'Freeriding'. The aim of this paper will be to understand a new form of resistance, currently emerging, which will be defined as pragmatic

body culture; biopolitics; supermodernity;

Introduction

> "In the classical world, however, simple natural life is excluded from the polis in the strict sense, and remains confined – as merely reproductive life – to the sphere of the oikos, "home" "
> (Agamben, 1995)

Since the beginnings of urbanization, there has been a division of power - who rules, who owns, who is obeys. This was in a sense justified with the need for a certain order, which paradoxically made it easier to enforce power - which was in the greater form the ability to divide and distribute the space within the city between its inabitants. This brings up the questions however, who can have this power to divide space? Who can "own" space in order to have the right to divide it? Should it not be that those who use the space decide what to do with it - and not by those who have no emotional - or even physical- understanding of the space and what affect it has on those within it? How has and does society culture - and in this the division of space - construct our knowledge and view of the urban? How does it conceptualize what is valuable, and what should be discarded or hidden from view ultimately leading towards an urban cultural purification of sorts?

The structure of cities has in a sense been formed by the idea of efficiency - make the "best" use of the space with the least effort. This, although is a good concept - is not efficient when dealing with humans - people who become attached, and grow alongside their surroundings. Learning and absorbing ideas and information from your surroundings is the process of life - it is how we evolve and how we push things forward. There is a need for citizens to take back space - physical or not - in order to reclaim a right to the city. As true democracy is an obsolete idea - the power of how to use the city should be given to those who actually use it on a daily basis.

One way to reclaim space is to reclaim the right to transportation - a simple idea, however not always enforced. We need to get from one place to another, to or jobs, to school, to visit others - and the fact that it is given to citizens more in the sense a of a 'privilege' rather than a right shows that fighting back, and increasing the integrative 'urban production' - in this cultural, economic, political and integrative - can result in a restructuring of the city and thus alters the spirit of time. This can causes a shift in the spatiality and temporalities of public spaces, the collective social identities and between the public and private realm one example of this is the increasingly popular 'freeriding' movement. Freeriding - defined in its simplest form - the use of resources provided without the adequate remuneration in return.

The particular movement discussed in this paper shows how it can be used as a statement against the current status quo, and show how the space of a city can be reclaimed by the citizens, even with the scarcity of physical space, a more futuristic idea that physical space is not necessary in order to create a 'physical' and very present movement. The new emergence of virtual space - moveable space - space that is present, but cannot be seen, therefore it can't be taken away. Space that borders on being an idea - the "imaginary" way in which we wish the physical space could be used. The topic will be discussed further in three sections: (1) Body Culture: in which a more detailed explanation of the ideas of modernity, supermodernity and biopolitics will transition into (2) the restructuring of the city scape through the ideas of the virtual realm, global and ethnoscape, and ultimately ending in the discussion of (3) social movements - infrapolitics and freeriding. These sections follow closely the ideas of Agamben, Augé, Blok, Derrida, Foucault, Kärrholm, Latour, Negri, Scott: and follow the structure of (1) the present/ the absent, (2) the imaginary, and (3) the discourse, respectively.

BACKGROUND: Body culture, Modernism and Supermodernity
Body Culture
What is the cultural implication of what is excluded from our view of the city? How does the control of our space create a constant struggle that has been around from the beginnings of time to present day? Everyone wants to be in control, but the problem is not to have the power, it is what is done with the power. Control of space has been a changing topic in its form due to changes in ideals, in policies, laws, and ideals that have been progressing along with society, although the topic spatiality has always been a key topic surrounding the power struggle. Who gets what? Who has the right to decide this? Space is a very individual topic, yet it involves

everything, as everything that has a physicality, takes up space.

Body culture deals with this topic, on a more human level. This ideas has been studied in detail through the lenses of Michel Foucault, Pierre Bourdieu, and many others. The main ideas stating that the body, being a physical entity always creates space. Space in the sense of physical, and also in the socio-physical sense. The space that you cannot see, but in a sense you can feel it. It is what you intend to do with the space - it is how one reads their surroundings, and how they decide it can be used. It is the freedom to do with the surrounding space what you please - without having someone enforce their ideal upon it. It is more in a sense a blank slate, a physical 'silence', however it does differ from the modern approach in that rather the minimum, everything is disposable and to be made use of. Nothing is added, nothing is taken away. It is not superimposed on the ideal, it is morphed through the preferred ideal. It is a difficult topic to find a solution to- as through this mentality, everyone has the possibility to do with the space that surrounds them what they please - to use it in the best way possible that meets their own personal needs. To study this topic through the lens of social movements - and more specifically freeriding - will give a depth and scale of importance to the problem at hand, and also provide a real time example of how the virtual (or third) realm is being utilized in order to fight back against the trend of dividing and annexing space by those who do not have a first hand experience with it.

Modernism

How do systems of classification construct our knowledge? This question is the basis of everything that we experience within the city. The way in which things are classified give us people a formed hierarchy of what should for us be important. However, the main question that has to be answered for this is, who has the power to decide what should or should not be important for us? This hierarchical classification system led to the belief that efficiency, automobiles and zoning was the 'best' way to construct the city. However, a brief investigation of the consequences into modernism shows that it led society towards social "purification" - a social homogeneity - the idea that if everything is the same, it will run smoothly and more efficiently. In the imaginary world this works well - however reality proves different. Modernist urban planning and its stress on efficiency led to a loss of important 'details'. Changes in urban form led to a different use of space that created more zoning and natural exclusion of people from certain areas. Now there is a task of how to reclaim space that was 'taken' away? How can we the people find a way to use the space that is around us with the utmost efficiency, in a way that will enrich all those who use it, and also opening the door to different forms of use for it.

Around the beginning of the nineteenth century modernism in urban planning began to take a hold. There was a trend to minimize and create more efficient utilization of spaces within the city. Along this thread, modernism became a way to transform the transportation networks in cities - with a lean towards a city made for the automobile. It was the futurization ideal. The city of the future would no longer be human scale. With the designs of Le Corbusier becoming the "poster designs" for modernist planning, it very quickly became clear that this type of design does not meet the needs of the people who use them on a daily basis. This idea goes together with almost all aspects of power and rule. Those who decide what is to be done usually do not have to deal with the consequences of their ideas. According to Foucault, a society's "threshold of biological modernity" is situated at the point at which the species and the individual as a simple living body become what is at stake in a society's political strategies (9) (Agamben, 1995). This stress on the individual having the power to make changes in society, and the individuals being able to come together to create a mass capable of high scale changes led to the level up from modernism.

The idea of supermodernity was the effect of the deepening intensification of modernism. People began to take charge of their power to change the space around them. The increasing use of technology that was being introduced into the "imaginary realm" would quickly create a reality out of it. The addition of technologies to let us build how and when we wanted, the ability to travel across miles at speeds not known to man earlier - this would all lead to a more privileged society, a society that evolved physically, but can be said failed to evolve "psychologically". The new generation may be born with new ideas, however it was and is still the older generation that rules. Their ideas are bred into them, and create a wall between the new and old. This clash of ideas becomes one of the reasons for the emergence of the study of 'biopolitics' - the idea that, in the words of Michel Foucault (1981), "Society must be defended". The illustration of theoretical insights the transition from modernity's mass culture for the subject of 'supermodernity' (Augé, 1995) - studied through the lens of biopolitics - in order to shed some light on how the contemporary self is objectified through a process of formation

> "Man remained what he was for Aristotle: a living animal with the additional capacity for political existence; modern man is an animal whose politics calls his existence as a living being into question" (Foucault, 1981).

According to Foucault the "threshold of modernity" was reached with the transition from sovereign power to biopower, in which the "new political subject" of the population became the target of a regime of power that operates through governance of the vicissitudes of biological life itself.

Biopolitics

> Jameson associates postmodern aesthetic and cultural movements with the psychoanalytic category of schizophrenia. Borrowing from Lacan, Jameson defines schizophrenia as "the failure of the infant to accede fully into the realm of speech and language". The schizoid neonate fails to fully acquire language, and as a result cannot individuate, because the infant must enter into a social/linguistic field to develop an ego. Jameson writes that: "schizophrenic experience is an experience of isolated, disconnected, discontinuous material signifiers which fail to link up into a coherent sequence. The schizophrenic thus does not know personal identity in our sense,

since our feeling of identity depends on our sense of the persistence of the "I" and the "me"
over time" (Peretti).

The defense of society is not defending the current status quo - it is the defense to bring forth and make a reality the ideas upon which the current society was structured upon. The ideas that got lost in translation, that have created strain the thread in which society runs. In order to be able to pragmatically defend out society we must be aware that there are things that are hidden from us - processes that go on without any acknowledgement of their existence. How does the exclusion of these processes from the common knowledge affect our view and our experience of how we view the city? To answer this question one has to look at the subject in a pragmatic way. In a sense it is the return to the modernist principle - efficiency. However it goes further beyond. It does not strip away layers - it builds upon them, and creates new ones. It has the ability to read between the lines - and ultimately create a new line in between.
One's task becomes to make the invisible visible. To create a window to the new realm, and build and enrich the city life through it. In order to do this it is important to understand the concept of excess and its relation to the formation of the "archive" - the historical processes that catalogue the path that society has took and is taking - the significance of reintroducing heterogeneity into the modern social aspect shows that it is a key that can lead to social movements that signify a shift and change in society, a society made for the majority of people, rather than the miniscule amount that are in power. According to Foucault, a society's "threshold of biological modernity" is situated at the point at which the species and the individual as a simple living body become what is at stake in a society's political strategies (Agamben, 1995)

RESTRUCTURING THE CITY SCAPE: Virtual realm and global scape

> *One of the most persistent features of Foucault's work is its decisive abandonment of the*
> *traditional approach to the problem of power, which is based on juridico-institutional models*
> *(the definition of sovereignty, the theory of the State), in favor of an unprejudiced analysis of the*
> *concrete ways in which power penetrates subjects' very bodies and forms of life.* (Agamben,
> 1995)

In order to begin a restructuring of space, first the question to answer is what is hidden in society? What does the society culture exclude from the physically visible urban realm? Looking back to the consequences of 'modernist purification' - the simplification and processes that arise from it mask the complexity of problems, leaving the underlying causes hidden and unanswered - like physical space - we only see the surface, while with the virtual space we can see the processes at hand. Because of the creation of a 'hidden urban realm' (non-places) how is this in turn making physically visible space obsolete in the sense of artistic/social movements? Latour writes of "a combination of technicians, machines and apparatuses, which together are capable of transforming a substance into a kind of visual display that can become part of a scientific article" (Blok, 2001). "facts exist only in and through networks of actors and material objects" (Blok, 2001) Kärrholm (2012) discussed spatial rhythms: (1) settled/pre-settled (waiting for a scheduled event - this can be thought of as the physical urban art we see in cities - it has been pre-arranged - we see it because someone decided to put it there - we are just waiting for it to appear), (2) the unsettled (waiting for the solution to an unintentional circumstance. The non-settled is the virtual. This idea blends closely with Lacan's definition of the self.

This idea according to Jacques Lacan (2004) (the other, the imaginary, the symbolic) shows how society projects itself to the outside world - we are not the real roots of the society, but the imaginary, the symbolic and the other - "we" the outsiders see what others want us to see, it seems everything that is visible is somehow "staged" - we don't see what goes on backstage - we only see what the final product is - everything that is visible is somehow allowed to be that way by society, so in a way it is already not a real depiction of the truth - it has already been analyzed and specified and shaped for the audience.

Society is divided between what is seen and unseen. The unseen is taking over the 'virtual space' and becoming present not physically but more the ideas are spreading quickly throughout the world - more and more people are becoming aware - they don't see, but they hear. They take part together and support each other through spreading the idea rather than making physically present art movements or physical statements. The virtual realm is a tricky topic. Alain Badiou (2009) asks the questions: how can we make use of that which can not be discerned? How can we reclaim this "lost" information and "space"? If we cannot claim physical space, how are we able to claim the "virtual" space? The answer is simple to state, but difficult to process - through widespread social movement. The formation of a new reality in which it is easier to get ideas across and in a way an invisible platform of resistance that is constantly on the move. The change from a physically visible and static art "window shop" to a present but yet constantly changing movement of ideas - that you see if you know where to look - when working with virtual space the constraints are limited to the surroundings that are available - and the amount of people that are willing to take part and spread the movement - it seems that the only constraint is the possibility of how many people can be reached. The more people that are reached through the fluid movement - the less spatial constraint there is. It becomes a sort of tessellation - although in the end it is possible for overlaps to occur in the reach-out availability. Latour (1993) attempts to answer this through his investigation of the emergence of hybrid spaces (not physical, but not completely virtual). This is central to Latour's critique of modernity—understood at an academic viewpoint stemming from "a separation between Nature and Society" (Blok, 2011).

> *The "ordering of space" that is, according to Schmitt, constitutive of the sovereign nomos is therefore*
> *not only a "taking of land" (Landesnahme) – the determination of a juridical and a territorial ordering (of an*
> *Ordnung and an Ortung) – but above all a "taking of the outside,"* (Agamben, 1995).

Mobile, flexible capital is capable of inserting itself into any cultural milieu (Harvey 1989 via Peretti). It does not have an "I", an ego, or a unified identity. It works instead as a polymorphous destroyer of codes. It continually breaks down the cultural, symbolic, and linguistic barriers that create territories and limit exchange (Peretti). Virtual space is a quick way to reach the masses, spread ideas - and in a sense retrieve the physical space that modernism 'unintentionally' took away from us. The possibility of a wide globalscape is causing physical space to become more and more obsolete in favour of virtual space, giving the possibility of a wider audience. The significant task here is how to pragmatically outgo the imposed morality. One answer lies in infrapolitics, the invisible resentment, and the result of oppressive policies and harsh penalties for disobedience or open criticism. The virtual space is a possibility to create a resistance in an 'invisible realm' therefore less adept to blocking from third parties - but nonetheless just as strong as a traditionally physical resistance - if not stronger due to its unconventional form. Scott (1987) sees infrapolitics and this resistance as a pragmatically covert and anonymous reaction differing from resistance in the traditional sense because it is rarely open and done as a group, but more as a platform upon which normal resistance can grow.

SOCIAL MOVEMENTS: Infrapolitics

How is the discarded and/or hidden information being reclaimed through social movements within the 'invisible urban realm'? How do they account for what is hidden and /or excluded? This prerogative of the social movements of the 1990s is still very present in recent struggles, evidenced by the Occupy [Wall Street] movements. But aside from these collective movements and media, a new form of infrapolitics is emerging in the interstices of freedom left by the power, but the horizon is more vague and sometimes non-existent in its claims. Without the mutual realm, the original practice established seem to be part of a new insurrection, latent and «underground».Operating on the basis of their history and heritage, conscious or not the practice offers an effective alternative to power and its current neoliberalism. The concept of infrapolitics borrowed from James C. Scott (1987) was developed from the analysis of situations of individual and collective interactions of extreme domination. Without doubt definitions of words such as resistance or domination do not completely coincide. In current political literature, the term infrapolitics proved to be the most appropriate term to define this new form of resistance in the underground opposition to the rule justly, and its designation of a hidden practice dominated directly under the gaze of the dominant.

The research conducted between November 2013 and January 2014 on freeriding collectives in the Paris region is based on interviews and observations, but also theoretical and historical research. Attendance at monthly meeting of the original collectives, with time allowed a network to build with other dodger collectives. Observations at meetings as well as evenings discussions and support for the economic survival of a mutual gave a in depth first hand experience of how these collectives com together to bring back the space of a city - in the virtual realm. The collectives use public transportation without paying their tickets, either because they can't or because they assume that the prices are too high. Members pool together a monthly fee that allows them to pay for fines levied in their individual and group commuting.

Originally this first freeride collective was issued from the Réseau d'Abolition des Transports Payants (Abolition of Paid Transport Network), called so by analogy to the RATP Régie Autonome des Transports Parisiens (Autonoumous management of parisian transports). The association was founded in 2001 and claimed free transport for all, with the first collective established in 2005. It was part of a protest nebula of fifteen activist communities in France: the broad criticism varied among the diverse associations including denunciation against nuclear energy, as well as advertising or CCTV cameras. The "fight" for free transport was inserted in a social and ecological critique. However, due to the shortness of this movement in early 2005, a few activists chose not only to claim free transport but to make it effective in creating a freeride collective. This idea came after learning of the creation of dodger collectives in Sweden in 2001. Resuming their practice and organization, the Parisian collectives were inspired by the political grammar of the worker associations of the late nineteenth century. The main idea was to develop an economic, insurance- assistance to meet a daily problem. Daily trips for work, job search, education or leisure, are then considered a necessity for all, and therefore, free.

Today there are a dozen groups in Ile-de-France. Their existence is discreet, but political will for some, and fear of accusation of fraud call for other collectives. Their invisibility is also a consequence of how they are created , that is to say, simply on the basis of a few motivated friends. Principle is the same: to be sufficiently large so that everyone, stopping to pay for travel and paying the monthly fee can move freely on a daily basis and without fear of economic repression carried out by the fines. The claims may differ: the original collective inserts it in a practice of free-for-all and is an association part of a Bakunian working class principle inherited from the 1800. Another collective is only there to meet the high cost of travel, without further developing social or political criticism. Others oppose the capitalist system and refuse to enter its game through not paying the rates charged by the transport authority. Finally, some justify their existence by the mere fact of doing otherwise what the system requires, without wanting to change the policy practiced in mobility. Despite these differences, the collectives converge on certain points such as the establishment of a daily assistance or ending of a public transport system contribution that generates inequalities and in the service of security policies to control and exclude.

The operation is also summarily common, although the conduction may differ. That is to say, once a month, the collective meets, pays fines levied by its members and receive contributions. Then it comes to discuss the practice, fraud, technical details how to avoid controllers, passing turnstiles, fear that invades the freeloader before passing it, or even difficulties how to pass behind regularly paying users. Sometimes, discussions turn into substantive debate, denouncing the oppressor state. Publicizing their practice is not required, although some members have already agreed to contact the media, anonymously. Willingness to federalize among the different collectives is not asserted. Attempts have occurred but without concrete results. These factions are minimally present on the internet and are absent on social networks - maybe due to lack of time, but also the will to remain manageable. Meetings are announced by mail to members, through a mailing list. Less commonly discussions sometimes take place by e-mail exchanges.

Freeriders do not dream of a better future by claiming suppression of the paid public transport system. They are neither radicals nor revolutionaries. But this act, this tactic they develop in small groups is more than a directory of action. There is strength in action. This practice is then pragmatic in the sense that the mean coincides with the end. Those without tickets would like to see their disputes and claims as they develop. They do not expect a recognition from the decision-making bodies. They do not count on a sufficient number of members for their "action" to have an impact in public media. Put simply, they cheat, and improve their personal situations. This act is not an act of resistance. There is no external enemy to incarnate power. The power is against new individuals and cultural practices, because it is precisely biopolitics. In describing this new form of protest of infrapolitics is just what biopolitical nature wants to emphasize - through managing a relevant political opposition.

The timing of the fraud is individual. The freerider is alone when he decides to jump over the turnstile, sharing the ticket with someone else with him through the entrance doors, not asking for permission. The dodger is alone the day he realizes that all electronic technologies - embodied in the Navigo chip, the beep of the authorized crossing , CCTV cameras or the new billboards - act upon him a way of being and thinking, even consuming . It is also in daily practice he learned that dodging is "criminalized ". For this reason the practice is sub- political. Refusing to submit his body to technical coercive power is evident in the daily practice of fraud. Between tactics and strategies , dodgers are not passive - on the contrary. They play, model, create, structure, criticize , in the free space left between them and the "coercion devices". Free riders reclaim the constraints imposed on them by transforming the object of their domination: the turnstile, but the discourse that marginalizes them . They use the rule, which is a " power game ", not a state, and its own production mechanism into a freedom to be and to do otherwise. They do not act outside of power but from within it.

The individuality of the action, and generating free riding freedom pushes the limits established by the neoliberal government between the public and private sphere. Practicing new ways of being in the public space blurs the limits of privatization, and pushes the liberalism. Freedom then becomes policy in changing a normally perceived as internalized and apolitical behavior. This is also why most of these riders are against a highlighting of the individuality and the practice. It is in the anonymity they develop a critical practice as de-subjectivization leading to a politicization of existence. The double pragmatic nature of this infrapolitics should be stressed: it exists within the act, which becomes an end in itself, and behavioral decolonization by those it operates. It is not under a common project. The belief of re- politicization of existence through the growth of rhizomes protesters. As noted above, these rhizomes are collective and take the form of mutual funds, giving individuals the practical ability to undermine the bottom unfair devices. This is the invention of new ways of being and the development of new ways of a consistent opposition to of biopolitics begins to take shape.

Freeriding is like a metaphor for the processes going on 'beneath the city', while the physical art we see on the surface is like a band-aid for urban social problems. The division of space shows how society is becoming more and more separated and torn apart - there are ideas from the 'underground' that are emerging and they are creating a polarity of society - there is now more and more a sense of two societies emerging: one that is the physical and visual, yet 'unreal' society, and the second is the virtual (seemingly unreal) but more psychologically physical and true. As stated by Derrida (2001), spaces are becoming more deconstructed - we are now able to tear apart what we see and come closer to the core - not just see the symptoms but the cause. Because of the creation of a 'hidden urban realm' (non-places) how is this in turn making physically visible space obsolete in the sense of artistic/social movements? Marc Augé (1995) answers this through the idea of places of transience -places that do not hold enough significance to be called 'places'. The virtual is not a place - but it is one of the greatest tools we have today to get the truth out. Because it is not a real place it is hard to track down and much harder to destroy. Social movements, like freeriding, that make their way into the virtual - even though they are not making a physical imprint they are technically more permanent than if they were drawn or painted out physically in out cities and in front of our eyes. Because the ideas are traveling so fast, and constantly mobile, they are able to make more of a permanent impact.

JC Scott discussed how subaltern people resist dominance: "All identities, without exception have been socially constructed" (Scott, 1987). Alluding to Antonio Negri's (2009) concept of multitude - when we are part of a social movement our identities are being socially constructed at that moment - and parallel to this - they are being linked with others. In a way even those who have nothing in common are brought together in multitude 'fighting for a cause' - but it can be said that this is a temporary commonality as once the movement is over, people return to the previous state. Although they are always linked through [this] movement, they are in the future not sharing ongoing commonalities. Freeriding can be looked at as a temporary social unification movement. It temporarily brings a homogeneity to a heterogenous population, to bring forth - in a sort of hipcritical way - a way for a more heterogenous society. Freeriding - as a social movement - is a playing on the canvas of the city, and the people are the 'brush strokes'. It is a moving canvas - and therefore in a sense an example of this 'virtuality'. It is physically not physical. It doesn't take up space per se - but it takes up a mental capacity. It is visible - yet invisible. You see it - but if you are not aware of it, it becomes invisible.

Conclusion

> "The paradox of sovereignty consists in the fact the sovereign is, at the same time, outside and inside the juridical order. If the sovereign is truly the one to whom the juridical order grants the power of proclaiming a state of exception and, therefore, of suspending the orders own validity, then "the sovereign stands outside the juridical order and, nevertheless, belongs to it, since it is up to him to decide if the constitution is to be suspended in toto" (Agamben 1995).

218

Freeriding is a good example of social critique, and how it helps uncover what is happening underneath the cities virtual space layers. It is a virtual canvas that is most effective in exposing and making a permanent impact on the world. What we see in cities today is in a sense 'art' is so subjective, and mostly a way for society to impose on us the status quo. We seemingly have the choice of what to think - but its all staged - we don't see the processes of how things got into their physical place in the city, while with the virtual we are able to go along with each stage, because there is no physical 'recordings' of it, we have to be there at the time - we have to experience it - it is like an experience art form.

Space is a broad concept - always having been on the radar. It is the most important thing that drives the city - it is more and more becoming a scarce entity - so how do we reclaim it? Who has the right to it? Can the city be "owned"? Movements like freeriding are in a sense a cry against the social constructs that have been built around for centuries, but more so it is a cry to reclaim what is in your right.

Do not command what you cannot enforce - Sophocles

Notes and References

Agamben, G. (1995) Homo Sacer: Sovereign Power and Bare Life. tr. Daniel Heller-Roazen, Stanford University Press, Stanford, 1998; Homo sacer: Il potere sovrano e la nuda vita, Giulio Einuadi.
Appadurai, A. (1990) Disjuncture and Difference in the Global Cultural Economy.
Augé, M.: Non-places (1995): Introduction to an Anthropology of Supermodernity. Verso. London, New York. 1995.
Badiou, A. (2009) "Jacques Lacan." Pocket Pantheon. Trans. David Macey. London: Verso
Bataille, G. Base Materialism and Gnosticism. Visions of Excess:
Blok, A & Elgaard Jensen, T, Bruno Latour. (2011). Hybrid Thoughts in a Hybrid World', Routledge..
Derrida, J. (2001). Deconstruction Engaged: The Sydney Seminars. Sydney: Power Publications.
Foucault, M.(1981). History of Sexuality, Volume 1: An Introduction, tr. R. Hurley, Penguin, London:
Kärrholm, M. (2012). Retailising Space: Architecture, Retail and the Territorialisation of Public Space. Ashgate Publishing Ltd..
Lacan, J. (2004) The Four Fundamental Concepts of Psycho-Analysis. Karnac Books.
Latour, B. (2007). Reassembling the Social: An Introduction to Actor-Network Theory. Oxford University Press, USA
Latour, B. & Porter, C. (1993). We Have Never Been Modern. Harvard University Press 1st Edition.
Latour, B. & Porter, C. (2004). Politics of Nature: How to Bring the Sciences Into Democracy. Harvard University PRess.
Negri, A. & Hardt, M. (2009). Multitude: War and Democracy in the Age of Empire. Penguin Books.
Peretti, J. Capitalism and Schizophrenia Contemporary Visual Culture and the Acceleration of Identity Formation/Dissolution
Scott, J.C. (1987). Weapons of the Weak: Everyday Forms of Peasant Resistance. Yale University Press.

Panizza Allmark, Associate Professor Edith Cowan University Perth, Western Australia

Statues, Subversive actions and Surveillance

This paper provides an overview of the undressed body in public art in Perth Western Australia. Of particular focus is the statue of female swimmer, Eliza Since her unveiling in 2007 there have been numerous pranksters dressing her in various outfits. In acts of guerrilla art Eliza's body has been stripped and restripped. This form of guerrilla art may be seen as creative, playful and irreverent. The subversive element of dressing the body could be seen as a means to reclaim public space, but also in consideration that this is a statue of a young woman's body there is a sense that gender performance and body politics are subtly at work.

Statues, Gender, Public Art

Introduction

Near the banks of the Swan River in Perth, Western Australia, the larger than life statue of Eliza stands poised with her arms out stretched, ready to dive into the waters. The statue, by sculptors Tony Jones and Ben Jones and commissioned by the Perth City Council commemorates the Crawley Baths, which for fifty years from 1914-1964, was the premier swimming area in Perth. It is interesting to note, that in 1914 there was some strong opposition to the Crawley area being used for the public baths. "It was argued that visitors walking the terraces on nearby Mt Eliza could look down on swimmers and those dressing" (Bathing, State Library of Western Australia). Nevertheless, the area became a very popular swimming area and thus the statue of the female swimmer was erected in 2007, to acknowledge this popular community site.

The bronze female statue is dressed in tightly fitting swimming attire, indicative of the 1940s. By situating the statue of Eliza in the river, she is placed in a site, which for pedestrians is inaccessible. There isn't an intimacy to gauge her texture up close. Essentially, she is to be viewed from a distance of about fifteen metres, from the walkway and cycle way on the banks of the river. She is also to be surveyed by the many motorists that drive past on the adjacent main road. Although Eliza is not presented as a conventionally erotic figure, her muscular toned appearance is larger than life by today's beauty standards.

The statue as a female gendered body, moreover as a woman, is the object of the gaze. The gaze maintains a relationship of controlled proximity and distance. Standing forthright with the backdrop of the azure waters of the river, Eliza is a spectacle. Cher Knight in her work on public art and populism states "spectacle is enchanting, seductive, engaging, memorable, invigorating, sensual, provocative, and powerful" (Knight 2008, 157). The statue of Eliza seems to engage with all of these attributes. Eliza also supports and plays up to the historical concerns relating to the Crawley Baths of bathers being looked upon. The position of Eliza invites the gaze. As a statue looking is promoted and with the understanding that the statue is of a woman this may follow John Berger's seminal work, Ways of Seeing, in which her femininity "is surveyed" (1972, 55).

Harriet F. Senie argues that in the reframing of public art "an attractive site elicits more positive responses" (2003, 187). Certainly, the Swan River presents a picturesque vantage of Eliza. It also follows the tradition of the female figure in the landscape which is at the core of traditional western pictorial conventions and still persists today in popular culture. It is important to consider the reasoning behind the choice of a female swimmer, rather than a male figure for the statue commemorating the baths. The body of a man poised diving into the water, may not draw as much attention from the public in terms of the engagement with the statue. The figure, of a scantily clad female statue in a highly picturesque setting elicits the gaze. Furthermore, her near nakedness in a very public location and the subsequent dressing of her by the public follows the cultural understanding that woman's bodies are subject to 'improvement' or being dressed or fashioned.

From a feminist standpoint Eliza is positioned for the pleasure of viewing, or in psychoanalytic terms Eliza evokes scopophilia, the pleasure of the gaze or "the overwhelming desire to look" (Homer 2005, 30). This reading can be particularly enriched through the notion that this female statue is constantly being dressed and re-dressed in various outfits. Following this perspective, importantly, her swimsuit maybe considered undergarments. Her clothing changes every few days and marks special occasions. At Christmas she is adorned with tinsel or a Santa Claus suit. Other times of the year she is spotted wearing a school uniform, a bikini, football scarves, designer dresses and so on. In acts of guerrilla art Eliza's body has been stripped and re-stripped. This form of guerrilla art may be seen as creative, playful and irreverent. The subversive element of dressing the body could be seen as a means to reclaim public space, but also in consideration that this is a statue of a young woman's body there is a sense that gender performance and body politics are subtly at work. Fashioning the female body could be seen as a means to exert symbolic power, by various disparate community groups of Perth

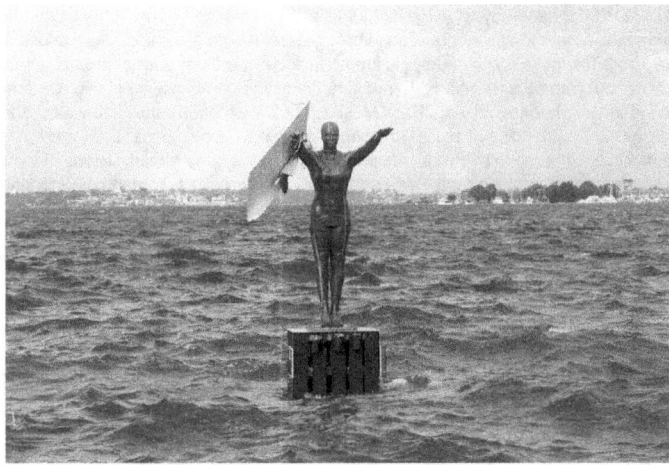

Fig. 1: The Eliza Statue, photograph by Panizza Allmark

Eliza was unveiled on October 15, 2007. Within weeks of her unveiling she was dressed and re-dressed, and has continually been refashioned in its seven year history. Her placement near one of Perth's busiest thoroughfares, Mounts Bay Road, is also within the proximity of the University of Western Australia. It has been assumed that university pranksters are responsible for her fashion makeovers. However, very few have taken claim for dressing her, though there are many suspects due to the affiliation of certain clothing to various groups in the community, such as various football and rowing team supporters as well as high schools, birthday celebrations etc. Defacing public property is illegal and this form of guerrilla art, which would involve swimming or rowing out to the statue under the cover of night, or early hours of the morning "has joined coincidentally with heritage commemoration to give back to Perth a version of the social value associated with the Crawley Baths that were once an important part of Perth life" (Harris 2009, 5). "Urban public art is often used as a way of mythologising...a city's historical, social and cultural development...In doing so, it 'naturalises socially constructed narratives" (Gonçalves & Thomas 2012, 331-332). The statue conjures the memory of the site as being central to the leisure and sporting activities of Perth. Harris, who has documented the heritage value of Eliza, emphasizes that "community play with Eliza has not damaged the statue or altered it permanently, it seemed wise to conceptualise it as guerilla art", as it is not deemed as antisocial, yet is still subversive (2009, 6). She further asserts

"it can be seen to support heritage ideals because, in the larrikin spirit of unsanctioned activity and its collision with a government-installed monument, there is reactivation of the social value of the baths. The witty playfulness elicits smiles, community connection and social value in a way that the statue alone could not." (Harris, 2009)

There is indeed a sense of playfulness in dressing Eliza. By referring to the 'larrikin spirit' Harris is using a term that dates back to the early history of Australian identity. John Rickard in his work on the 'lovable larrikins' asserts "that it was their brazenness in taking control of public spaces (as if they owned them!) which was galling to bourgeois society" (1988, 79). The term was used in the 19th century press. For example, from the 1870s it was reported that there was a need to establish bathing facilities in the Swan River to prevent "the nude bathing and larrikin behaviour that was taking place off the town jetties and at Mill point and the foot of Mt Eliza" (Bathing, State Library of Western Australia). It seems that the dressing and undressing of the statue of Eliza can be read as reflecting a subversion of middle-class values by the deliberate altering of public property. Interestingly, Eliza is named after Mount Eliza. Mount Eliza (now known as Kings Park) was named allegedly after the wife of a former governor of New South Wales. Hence, the act of guerrilla art could also be read as an affront to social hierarchy and class through covertly dressing and un-dressing the 'governor's wife''s namesake.

In popular Australian culture the larrikin is someone who humourously breaks tradition or rules (Bellanta, 2012). The term is used affectionately for a person who has a disdain of propriety and this seems an apt way to describe the practice of guerrilla art, with the dressing and un-dressing of this statue. Notably, though defacing public property is illegal the authorities have not prosecuted anyone for the antics surrounding the statue and this lack of prosecution reinforces the acknowledgement of the 'larrikin' spirit, which is embedded and accepted within Australian culture. Harris further notes the significance of the statue as public art monument that engages the community. She states: "In the space of Eliza, the land traffic flows by while the water traffic moves around it and people clamber up. The public has made the space its own as both artist and audience" (Harris 2009, 14).

Femininity and Eliza

The Eliza monument is more than just a statue commemorating the Crawley Baths. It has taken on a life, albeit a gendered one. Through the community engagement, or guerilla art, she is anthropomorphised. The adornment of this statue has stimulated public discussion and there are more than a dozen websites dedicated to Eliza. There is also a Facebook page, titled 'Eliza the Swan River Statue'. Eliza's physical presence is matched with an online life in which she is the topic of much commentary about her physical appearance. As previously stated her femininity is 'surveyed'. Interestingly, Marina Warner, whose work has examined the allegory of the female form in monuments, asserts that a symbolized female presence both gives and takes values and meaning in relation to actual women (Warner 1995, xx). This point is commonly illustrated in social media discussion boards in which the statue is referred to not just in a gendered form, but also as a woman with traditional feminine personality aspects. On a flickr site, titled the 'Many moods of Eliza' there is very gendered commentary such as "Must ask boating friends if they know Eliza and suggest they contribute costumes to the lady's wardrobe :-)" "she now has a skirt and some lovely new accessories" and "Will this woman ever make up her mind what to wear!". The title itself referring to the 'many moods' also conveys constructed notions of femininity in which women in western cultural history are considered more emotional and unpredictable, as well as women being focused on fashion or outward appearances.

Eliza's femininity is on display and her fashion or the dressing up of the statue is significant. Fashion, as Elizabeth Wilson discusses, is at a core of a culture expressing something genuine about it (Wilson 1990, 209). Malcolm expands this idea in "acknowledging that fashionable clothing is used in western capitalist societies to affirm both membership of various social and cultural groups, and individual personal identity" (2002, 12). In the dressing of Eliza and in the many community commentaries about the statue it seems that she is indeed given a personal identity. This makes her part of the community and also makes her a unique public art statue in Perth. The dressing of Eliza could also be seen as a political act in which pranksters dress her in outfits that commemorate, celebrate and engage with popular media events, such as Valentine's Day, the football grand finals and the Tour de France. But it should also be noted that Eliza has also been used for personal and political purposes with the assistance of authorities. For example, Eliza was used to raise awareness for social and health issues. Ovarian Cancer Australia director Steph Alvarez recalls assisting Karin Margolius, who was diagnosed with ovarian cancer and "who was determined to raise awareness of the disease" stating

> "I still remember the Sunday morning when Karin, her husband Ron, my husband John and I dressed Eliza the statue in the Swan River. The water police helped Karin out there and she was determined to climb up and dress the statue in teal, the international colour of ovarian cancer. We even had a sign made saying, 'If in doubt rule your ovaries out'." (cited in Cahill 2010)

Through the dressing of Eliza and her online presence she is somewhat of a fashion celebrity. The opening statement of a web site titled 'Eliza's ensembles' is as follows:

> Residing in the Swan River along Mounts Bay Road, Perth's Eliza statue is frequently clothed by Perth residents. From simple tee-shirts to complex and thematic outfits, Western Australia's capital city expresses itself through Eliza's clothing. This blog follows the various outfits of the city's best dressed statue and attempts to understand what the city of Perth is trying to express through her.

The blogger, Erica Boyne, goes on to tell us that for a year she will be "recording and commenting on the various outfits of Perth's leading fashionista". Notably, Boyne depicts Eliza as a woman who 'resides' in the Swan River rather than as a statue that has been placed in the Swan river. Eliza is further depicted in life-like reality, has a privileged status of waterfront views and in Perth is on an expensive area of real-estate, befitting 'Perth's leading fashionista'. The web site has various photographs of Eliza in different outfits, and as highlighted earlier the pictorial conventions of a solitary woman in a picturesque landscape prevail. Like the majority of websites dedicated to Eliza, photography plays an integral role in picturing her many styles. The 'Eliza's Ensembles' website, set up as a fashion blog, documents Eliza's different attire and alongside the images are various short commentaries such as.

> "After a long period of nakedness, a citizen of Perth has dressed the Eliza statue in a white drape with no other distinguishable markings. Appearing to be a long sheet with a circle cut through the center, the piece of cloth has been place over the statue's head and hangs around it's front and back"

and

> "Eliza must have has a late night and slept through her alarm, as she didn't' quite get her blue polo shirt on correctly in her rush out the door."

The first descriptive statement is written in the manner of a fashion commentary referring to the 'nakedness' and then way the statue is styled, despite that Eliza is clothed in a swimming outfit. The other commentary is an example of the anthromorphism of this statue. Her personification is exemplified in the notion of that she was in a 'hurry to get dressed', rather than referring to Eliza as an inert statue. Another website 'Observing Perth' follows this trajectory in its reference to Eliza's 'dignity', in the process of being dressed and un-dressed. In the online commentary of the statue of Eliza she is personified. She is depicted as possessing moods, dignity and charisma.

As previously described the Eliza statue is larger than life. The bronze statue is 2.2 meters tall and conveys a feminine figure that could be considered robust as she is muscular toned and does not reflect the dominant fashion model's appearance of thinness. Yet, she is embraced as a fashion icon in the community. Eliza is depicted as a capable woman in her action of solitary diving into the waters. This follows the notion that the semi-clad female figure in western thought "expresses strength and freedom" (Warner 1995, 77). Nevertheless, the strength and freedom is imbued not just by the statue, but by those who have dressed her and through the public discourse about her. The pleasure and power of dressing the statue is aptly described in the following statement on one of the blogs which describes Eliza as "Our statue of many costumes, Barbie for grown ups." (The Many Moods of Eliza) The use of the term 'our' conveys a sense of belonging and ownership. Describing the statue as 'Barbie' also relates to power and 'god' like agency in which the Barbie doll is dressed up. Furthermore, pleasure is derived in the act of dressing another, which entails expressiveness and creativity. This is further enhanced with the knowledge that the dressing and undressing of Eliza is an illicit activity.

The dressing of Eliza is also a tourist spectacle that engages the community through humour, curiosity and entertainment. The many photographs of Eliza on various web sites document her fashion, but may also serve the purpose of sharing a touristic encounter. For tourists, visiting public art is considered a photo opportunity. "It is an acknowledgement of its function as a place marker, the perpetual appeal of a souvenir that says I was here" (2003, 188.). But as the statue is situated in the river, there are problems with accessibility and it is very difficult to be photographed up close with Eliza. As such, being photographed with the statue is not as important as communicating the acts of guerrilla art or the fashion styles of Eliza. The numerous photographs of Eliza that permeate the web on various blogs suggest that these images may serve as a shared tourist's photo album which also offers the possibility of further contributions from others. John Urry in his notable work on the tourist gaze asserts that "Photography is evidently central to the tourist gaze…" and furthermore "with Web 2.0 tourists increasingly produce and consume ordinary photographs placed on 'public display'"(2008, 186-187). The photographs that capture Eliza's fashion styles serve to further popularise the statue as a form of public art that engages the community and serves as a tourist site. Eliza is a spectacle not just as a statue, but through her presence in photography. Knight (2008, 162) asserts "spectacles are sensory: they require us to react and enact and experience rather than passively receive".

One of the most controversial images taken with Eliza captures the planking trend of 2011. Planking involves being photographed lying face down with the body rigid and motionless across structures in public areas. The photographs are then shared online. Interestingly, Facebook has revealed that in 2011 the horizontal art of planking topped Australia's status trends (Blight, 2011). It was more popular than the death of Osama Bin Laden. The overwhelming popularity of planking within Australia, most likely entails the notion of larrikinism which, as described earlier, is embedded in the culture.

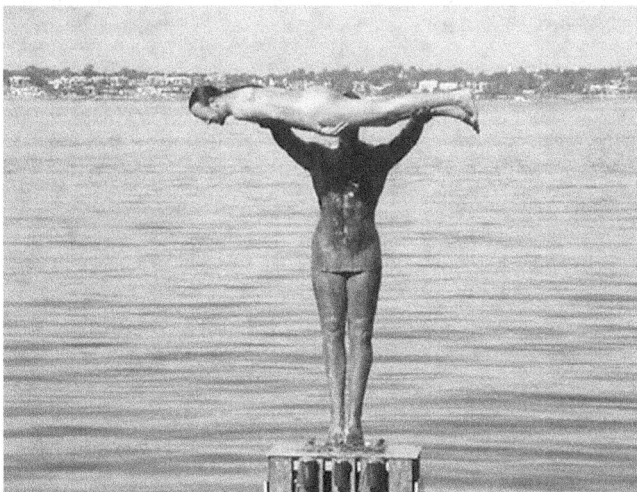

Fig. 2: Simon "Spuddy" Carville in the arms of Eliza. Picture: Facebook. Source: PerthNow

Lying face down, naked, across the outstretched arms of Eliza, Perth resident Simon 'Spuddy' Carville was photographed and this image became an internet sensation. It achieved international exposure for Eliza and was the topic of a number of news articles across the world. The online version of the UK Daily Mail describes his 'naked ambition' and cites him stating "I think this has gained me a fair bit of respect among people in my age group and that, of course, includes the ladies" (25 May 2011). Interestingly, gender politics come into play in the act of a male person lying naked in the arms of a female statue. "Spuddy said he walked out to Eliza, in chest deep water, before using her ankles to lift himself up her 'smooth, slippery' body and into her arms." (Perth Now, 2011). The statue is described in sensuous terms and notably is anthropomorphised and sexualised. This also follows Urry's assertion that: "Locals and tourists also, from time to time, exercise power, performing and picturing against or bending the 'scripts' of those of tourism organisations and wider discourses. (2008, 188).

It seems that the statue of Eliza has very positive connotations, albeit as a feminine sensuous spectacle within the community. She has been embraced as public art. Public art is art, which has as its goal a desire to engage with its audiences and to create spaces—whether material, virtual or imagined—within which people can identify themselves, perhaps by creating a renewed reflection on community, on the uses of public spaces or on our behaviour within them. (Sharp et al., 2005, 1003-1004)

The community behaviour surrounding the statue of Eliza seems to venerate her presence. The acts of guerrilla graffiti art celebrate her feminine status.

Yagan and Heirisson Island

This reception of Eliza is however in stark contrast to that of the life-like statue of Yagan which also is also situated near the Swan River, on Heirisson Island near the eastern corridor of Perth. In terms of geographic layout "Heirisson Island has been described as a "gateway to Perth" (Mckenzie 2011, 117, Stratton 2013, 285). This term could also be used to describe Mounts Bay road where Eliza is situated on Perth's western strip. Nevertheless, unlike the manicured riverfront of Crawley, Heirrison Island remains undeveloped from a western aesthetic tradition of displaying mastery over the environment in that it does not display the design of a formal landscape. Interestingly, the surrounding area of the eastern gateway presents a "postmodern Perth of consumerism and recreation -emphasising the fruits of the long resource development boom" (Stratton 2013, 285). In relation to Heirrison Island Fiona McKenzie states that "tourists have no encouragement to go there, it is simply a piece of land to be traversed to get to the city center, even though it has a statue of a significant Aboriginal man, Yagan, the hero of resistance to the white colonial invaders" (2003, 117). The statue of Yagan is situated in the southern enclosure of the Island on the rise of slight hill on the island facing the river. His slightly elevated position gives him prominence in the landscape. Surrounding the statue of Yagan is grassed land, native shrubbery and kangaroos. Notably, there is only pedestrian access to the site and as such one can view Yagan in quiet contemplation. This public reserve is unlike the busy thoroughfare in Crawley where Eliza is situated.

Plans to develop the area of Heirisson into a major tourist attraction have met with protests from the traditional owners of the land. The construction of a Tent Embassy in 2012, and media reporting of this further fuelled the divide between the government, the mainstream media attitudes and the local Aboriginal Nyoongar community. "Heirisson Island has been a site of the public demonstration of Aboriginal Sovereignty", documented since 1978 (Kerr and Cox 2013, 12). The local Nyoongar activists claim that Heirisson Island, whose original name is Matagarup, is sacred to traditional owners and was a traditional crossing. The land is also said to be a former birthing ground for Indigenous women. Local community Elder, Hubert Bropho asserts that: "The government has been ignoring our concerns about the desecration of our sacred sites" (WAtoday, May 16 2013). It is important to consider that "the Noongar Tent Embassy was (and remains) an essentially peaceful affirmation of native title of Nyoongar country and a legitimate Aboriginal use of a state-registered Nyoongar heritage site (Cox and Kerr 2013, 18). In terms of town planning, the Western Australian Police Headquarters is built in a position to have a clear vantage over the gateway to city of Perth. Jon Stratton in his article about 'surveillance power and the authoritarian State' asserts "that situating the Nyoongar tent embassy highlights the links between the "Nyoongar population the police and the government" (Cox and Kerr, 2013, 89). In a significant discussion of Perth media reportage of the Tent Embassy titled 'Setting up the Nyoongar Tent Embassy', "which is based on 104 media texts produced by the electronic and print media in February and March 2012", the findings conclude that "media reports, with few notable exceptions, positioned the Tent Embassy as a law breaking, menacing, 'Aboriginal protest camp' despite "members' demonstrated commitment to non-violent discussion and negotiation"(Kerr & Cox, 2013, 5, i).

It is important to note the comparison between the two sites of Crawley and Heirisson. The site of the Eliza statue is an expression of the dominant western aesthetics associated with a 20th Century history of use of the space by the white middle-class, whereas Heirisson island or Matagurup predates this by thousands of years and is used as a traditional area by the local Nyoongar community[1]. Furthermore popular reporting and government views see Heirisson Island as land that needs to be redeveloped. The media reporting of the two sites are also in remarkable contrasts. As described earlier there are very positive accounts about Eliza's site but very disturbing racist reporting about Heirisson Island, the site in which the statue of Yagan is placed.

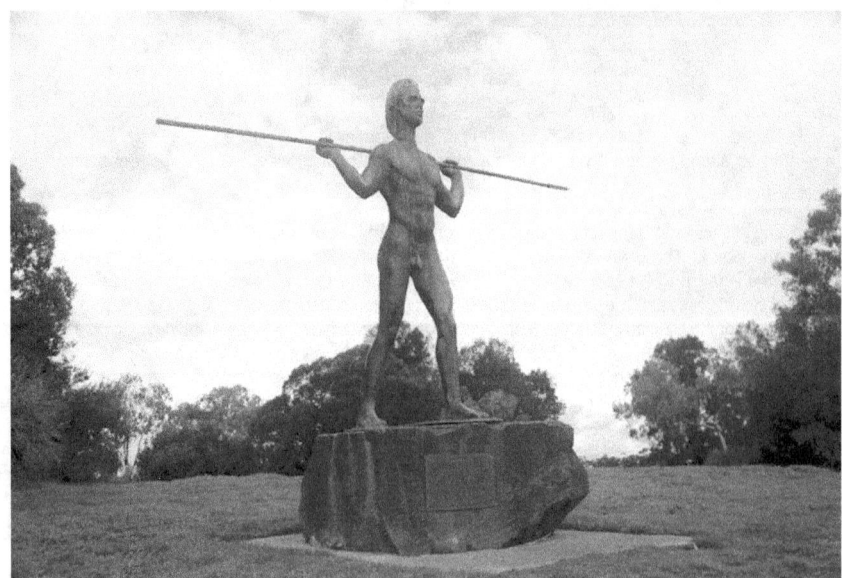

Fig. 3. The Statue of Yagan. Photograph by Panizza Allmark

Yagan was an "early resistance leader for the Nyoongar people of southwest Western Australia" (Martin, 2007, 312). For more than a decade the Nyoongar community lobbied the government for a memorial to Yagan. Finally, in 1984 a life-like bronze statue, by sculptor Robert Hitchcock was erected on Heirisson Island. The statue commemorates Yagan's important role in Nyoongar history and it has wide resonances within the indigenous community. Furthermore, the statue recalls a neglected collective history of indigenous resistance in Western Australia. Yagan is notable for leading the first significant indigenous resistance in 1831, just two years after White settlement of Perth in 1829. Yagan's history represents the history of many colonised people who have experienced violence and denigration. Yagan, however, reached notoriety for his involvement in a series of conflicts with white settlers. He was declared an outlaw and there was a reward for his capture, dead or alive. Yagan was shot and murdered by two white teenage brothers in 1833. "His head was cut off in accordance with the barbaric English colonial practice of the time and then sent to England where it was displayed in various fairs and sideshows" as an anthropological curiosity (McGlade 1998, 246). "Yagan's cranial remains were lost to his people for the next one-hundred-and-fifty years..." (Martin 2007, 313). In 1997, after many years of lobbying for repatriation of the skull Yagan was returned to the Nooyngar elders and later formally buried in a private ceremony in 2010. "The story of Yagan is an extremely powerful story: it is a story of invasion, of early contact between two cultures, of colonialism and its racist, bloody nature" (McGlade 1998, 252), This history is integral in term of the statue of Yagan as public art.

In 1997, shortly after Yagan's head was returned, his memorial statue on Heirrison Island was decapitated with an angle grinder. A replacement head was constructed. However, within nine weeks Yagan was beheaded for a second time. It was reported that "An Aboriginal elder appealed for calm after the bronze head was stolen but said he feared an attack on European statues around Perth, including one of Queen Victoria." (Irish Times, 8 September 2007). However, no further attacks were undertaken on any other statues around Perth. There were no signs of retaliation from the Nyoongar community on other statues that represent colonialism. Significantly, in Western Australia "the historical monuments (with the exception of the Yagan Statue near the Causeway) are focused on the people who were primarily responsible for that dispossession." (Dowding 1997, 96). The beheading of Yagan seems a deliberate political act of racist violence, apparently committed by an anonymous British loyalist. Notably, as discussed earlier, Heirrison Island is in the eastern gateway to Perth and as one blogger, the Lazy Aussie, from the website the 'Worst of Perth' states "I don't think the reasons were really discovered, or the severed heads and, as far as I know, the head choppers were never caught. Oddly the best view of the crimes would have been from Police Headquarters" (3 February, 2008). Also to consider is that the act of decapitation, with an angle grinder, would take a considerable time. The removal of Yagan's head was not a swift act.

Though there may be surveillance of Heirisson Island from the vantage point of the police headquarters, this act of violent vandalism seems not to have been witnessed. Furthermore, no-one has been prosecuted for the actions. David Martin in his work on monuments and masks asserts that the act "speaks not only to the continuance of white settler racism, but also to the power of mimesis to invigorate our modern memorials and monuments with a life of their own" (2007, 316). Of importance is that:

> Urban public art is often used as a way of mythologising, in a Barthes (1987 [1957]) sense, a city's historical, social and cultural development. It presents dominant ideologies in a simplified way that makes the world intelligible. In doing so, it 'naturalises' some socially constructed narratives...(Gonçalves & Thomas 2012, 331-332)

Yagan and Eliza

The Yagan statue as public art stands naked and has been violated in contrast to that of Eliza who is embraced and dressed as 'our Barbie'. Dominant discourses around gender and race prevail. In the act of beheading, the male native body is emasculated. The proud and austere look of Yagan is removed whereas in the dressing of Eliza her femininity is enhanced and celebrated. The narratives around the two statues in Perth convey the social inclusion of Eliza as a woman, and the social exclusion of Yagan as an indigenous male. There is the difference of veneration versus denigration of the two public art statues on the Swan River. This seems to follow that "public art that is developed through the effort of local governments" and other agencies "does not necessarily turn out the way that was intended, alternative meanings and practices might emerge" (Sharp et Al 2005, 1015). Importantly in very different ways, the statues of Yagan and Eliza have enticed community engagement and the reclaiming of public space to display hegemonic attitudes.

I would like to acknowledge the support of CREATEC (the Center for Research in Entertainment, Arts, Technology, Education and Communications) at Edith Cowan University, Perth, Western Australia.

Notes and References

[i] "Archaeological evidence from Perth and Albany suggests that the Noongar people have lived in the area for at least 45,000 years. South West Aboriginal Land and Sea Council)
"Anger in Perth over Heirisson Island plans" Watoday. Last update May 16, 2013
http://www.watoday.com.au/wa-news/anger-in-perth-over-heirisson-island-plans-20130516-2jo2m.html#ixzz33vlLkXmW
Barnard, Malcolm. 2002. Fashion as Communication Second Edition. New York: Routledge
Bellanta, Mellisa. 2012. Larrikins: A History. Brisbane: University of Queensland Press.
Blight, David. 2011. "Planking Dominates Facebook trends" Adnews. Last updated 8 December.
http://www.adnews.com.au/adnews/planking-dominates-facebook-trends
Cahill, Denise Sharon. 2010. "Karin's cancer battle continues to inspire", Western Suburbs Weekly, September 7. http://eastern.inmycommunity.com.au/news-and-views/local-heroes/Karins-cancer-battle-continues-to-inspire/7568507/
Daily Mail Reporter. 2011 "Is this the best planking stunt yet? Naked man stretches out on statue in the middle of a river" Last updated 25 May. http://www.dailymail.co.uk/news/article-1390085/Planking-Naked-man-stretches-arms-statue-internet-craze.html
Dowding, Peter. 1997. "Eddie Mabo's Legacy" Australian Planner, 34:2, 96-99.
"Eliza Ensembles" http://elizasensembles.blogspot.com.au/
"Eliza Statue" http://observingperth.wordpress.com/2013/03/27/eliza-statue/
Fforde, Cressida. 2002, "Yagan" edited by Cressida Fforde, Jane Hubert, and Paul Turnbull, 229-241. The Dead and Their Possessions: Repatriation in Principle, Policy and Practice, London: Routledge.
Gonçalves Ana & Thomas Huw, 2012. Waterfront tourism and public art in Cardiff Bay and Lisbon's Park of Nations, Journal of Policy Research in Tourism, Leisure and Events, 4:3, 327-352.

Harris, Jenifer. 2009. "Eliza: Guerilla Art Supports Heritage Value." In National State of Australian Cities Conference, Nov 24, 2009, Perth: Promaco.
http://soac.fbe.unsw.edu.au/2009/PDF/Harris%20Jennifer.pdf
Homer, Sean. 2005. Jacque Lacan. New York: Routledge.
Kerr, Thor and Cox, Shaphan. 2013. Setting Up the Nyoongar Tent Embassy: A Report on Perth Media. Edited by Robert Briggs, Niall Lucy and Steve Mickler. Perth: Ctrl-Z Press: Perth
http://www.ctrl-z.net.au/wp-content/uploads/2013/08/Setting-Up-the-Tent-Embassy-Kerr-Cox.pdf
Knight, Cher Krause. 2008. Public Art: Theory Practice and Populism.
The Lazy Aussie. 2008. "Long Lens on Yagan" The Worst of Perth. Posted on February 3. http://theworstofperth.com/2008/02/03/long-lens-on-yagan/
"The Many Moods of Eliza" https://www.flickr.com/groups/perth_photo/discuss/72157603622763465/
Martin, David L. 2007. "Of monuments and masks: historiography in the time of
curiosity's ruin", Postcolonial Studies, 10:3, 311-320.
McGlade, H., The repatriation of Yagan : A story of manufacturing dissent, Law Text Culture, 4(1), 1998, 245-255. Available at:http://ro.uow.edu.au/ltc/vol4/iss1/15.
McKenzie, Fiona Haslam. 2011. "The Swan River: Look But Do Not Touch", in, Water policy, tourism and recreation: Lessons from Australia edited by Lin Crase and Sue O'Keefe, 115-131. USA: Taylor & Francis.
Rickard, John. 1998. "Lovable larrikins and awful ockers", Journal of Australian Studies, 22:56, 78-85.
Senie, Harriet. F. 2003. Reframing Public Art: Audiences Uses and Appreciation Art in Its Publics: Museum Studies at the Millennium edited by Andrew McLellan, 185-200. Oxford: Blackwell
"Simon Carville comes forward as naked planker pictured with Perth icon" Last updated May 23, 2011. http://www.news.com.au/travel/travel-updates/naked-planker-simon-carville-just-wants-to-have-fun/story-e6frfq80-1226061333539
Sharp, Joane, Pollock, Venda and Paddison, Ronan. 2005. "Just Art for a Just City: Public Art and Social Inclusion in Urban Regeneration" Urban Studies, 42: 5/6, 1001–1023.
State Library of Western Australia "Bathing"
http://slwa.wa.gov.au/swan_river/living_with_the_land/bathing
South West Aboriginal land and sea council, The Nyoongar people
http://www.noongar.org.au/noongar-people-history.php
Stratton, Jon. 2013. "The Western Australian Police Headquarters Building Surveillance, Power and the Authoritarian State" Cultural Studies Review. 19 (2): 261–89.
"Vandals cut off head of warrior's statue". 1997. Irish Times p.15, 8 September.

Carolyn Loeb, Residential College in the Arts and Humanities/Michigan State University
loeb@msu.edu

Reimagining the City: West Berlin Murals and the Right to the City

This paper proposes that the almost 250 murals created in West Berlin in the 1970s and 1980s contributed to contemporary efforts by citizen-activists to reimagine the city and claim their "right to the city." Unlike earlier influential precedents from the 1930s that asserted people's claim to the state, West Berlin wall paintings introduced a new position for murals in relation to the public and to the design and experience of specifically urban space. This paper provides an overview of legal (official) and illegal (unofficial) murals and their connections with activist political, social, and urban planning cultures as a basis for this argument.

Murals, West Berlin, right to the city

Introduction
Almost 250 wall paintings were created in West Berlin between around 1974 and 1989[1] Little-remembered today beyond their local sites, they nevertheless constitute a valuable chapter in the history of mural-making and of public art. Among other insights into the contemporary moment that they provide, they allow us to notice a historical shift in the focus of mural painters. Works by earlier leaders of the mural movement in the 1930s in Mexico and the United States had contributed to the project of constructing national identity. By the 1970s, we can see the emergence of mural practices that focus, instead, on urban space, neighborhood sites, and on the project of reimagining the design and experience of the city in relation to citizens' claim to the "right to the city." This paper charts this shift.

To foreground the context in which I wish to consider these murals, the first section of the paper presents the culture of urban development in West Berlin at the time these murals were created. The second section discusses the nature of the modern mural tradition, locates other, more contemporary influences on West Berlin murals, and proposes a new perspective on late twentieth-century murals that regards them through the lens of citizens' claim to the right to the city. The final section presents an overview and examples of these West Berlin murals that anchor the preceding analysis in works on the ground.

Citizen-activists and the culture of urban development in West Berlin
The murals that are our subject were executed at the same time that West Berlin saw the rise of an unusually animated urban planning culture. Seventy percent of Berlin's buildings had been destroyed or severely damaged by the end of the Second World War. As the pace of rebuilding quickened in the 1960s, mainstream planners targeted the demolition of many remaining older structures in favor of large-scale new construction and highway development, following the model for urban renewal that was widely promoted at the time in West Germany, Western Europe, and the US. By the early 1970s, however, a shift in wider social and political attitudes had occurred that affected how the built environment was viewed. This shift took place in West Berlin as the younger, postwar generation began in the late 1960s to break the silence that surrounded the Nazi past. Their inquiries involved not only opening frank discussions about that past with their elders, but also tracing history's material remains in the streetscapes and structures of the city.[2] The experience that young architects, planners, historians, and citizen-activists gained by organizing workshops and study groups to research the physical forms that embodied the past and, more importantly, their concomitant recognition that remaining urban forms help tell the story of the past, fed a growing resistance to dominant urban renewal schemes. As one observer noted, it was not until a younger generation "saw urban development with critical eyes," that dissatisfaction with prevailing practices and plans for the cityscape arose.[3] Instead of demolition, activist citizens and critical architects and planners began to argue for preservation and renovation of existing older buildings, street patterns, public spaces, and neighborhoods.

The challenge to mainstream planning schemes and the development of alternative proposals took two, often overlapping forms. Building occupations occurred when landlords neglected structures that were slated for demolition. Occupiers contested the hegemonic power of property relations through their own active use and physical reclamation of buildings. Occupations were often part of larger programs for social and political change that included introducing experimental living arrangements and alternative educational models, and demonstrating against nuclear power locally, oppressive regimes elsewhere in the world, such as in Chile and Iran, and militarism, among other issues. Whether it was due to their threat to property relations alone, or to the multifaceted package of unconventional and oppositional ideas that squatters represented, occupations frequently met with harsh police actions. Occupations occurred in many West Berlin districts, but the most intense site of activity and the one with which the squatters' movement became most identified was Kreuzberg, a center for both alternative and dissident culture.[4]

Citizens' initiatives constituted the other form that opposition to dominant planning practices took. These political interventions challenged existing plans for particular neighborhoods by introducing alternative proposals. Often growing out of or supplementing actions such as occupations and street protests, citizens' initiatives were based on the historical and architectural study and analysis of their neighborhoods. They were informed by earlier texts that addressed the loss of urban culture and also by critiques of the impact of contemporary planning ideas, including Jane Jacobs' 1961 The Death and Life of Great American Cities.[5]

These initiatives successfully blocked new highway construction and resulted inmaintaining aspects of local spatial and architectural design that defined particular neighborhoods and encouraged social interaction. Such interventions led to the preservation and renovation of areas such as KlausenerPlatz in Charlottenburg[6] and Chamissoplatz in Kreuzberg, and eventually to municipal adoption of preservation practices that came to be called "cautious urban renewal."[7] These practices were also promoted in the 1980s

International Building Exhibition that showcased local architectural traditions through both preservation and new construction throughout West Berlin.[8] The research that the IBA drew on and promoted has been acknowledged by one architectural and planning practitioner as contributing to the awareness of "the buildings that were on a particular site" that marks the culture of Berlin.[9]

While occupations could create social conflict, they often resulted in the course of the 1980s and into the 1990s in the legal transfer of property ownership to the squatters, who were able then to more systematically renovate their buildings. Similarly, citizens' initiatives transformed the city's urban planning practices and thus affected the character of future redevelopment. These movements, in other words, were effective in changing local discourse about urban form, and they did this in part by introducing new participants into the arenas of discussion and decision-making. Murals contributed to the processes that led to these achievements.

The modern mural tradition and its supersession

Just as important as the urban, political, and social activist context was for the West Berlin muralists of the 1970s and 1980s was the modern tradition of mural-making. There was widespread awareness of the works by Mexico's Los TresGrandes– Diego Rivera, JoséClemente Orozco, and David Alfaro Siquieros – and of the New Deal murals created in the United States.[10] The populist character of this tradition typically originated in its subject matter, which addressed an audience of non-elite viewers, and in the location of murals in public institutions that were designed to construct and serve this audience. Modern murals depicted historical events as they affected the nation's citizens, whose experiences had usually been left out of the history texts, and local stories that celebrated regional contributions to national identity. They were located predominantly in buildings erected by the state to serve its citizens, from the Ministry of Education in Mexico City to post offices in small towns throughout the US.

The project of 1930s murals that were created in Mexico and the US can be described as asserting people's claim to the state. Muralists in both countries depicted the broad masses of their societies, including the oppressed and still-disenfranchised, as citizens whose stories contributed to the nation's history and identity. The murals themselves and the sites where they were painted were claimed and celebrated as "public property,"[11] belonging, as did the state itself – at least nominally – to those depicted on these walls. The circumstances characterizing murals created in West Berlin in the 1970s and 1980s were very different, whether they were official, legal murals or unofficial and illegal ones. The initiative for their creation often came from local residents of neighborhoods in which the murals were to be located; their sites were not public buildings.[12] They used as their support and thus drew a new kind of attention to structural elements – firewalls exposed by wartime bombs or older buildings' façades – that on their own told a story about the city'shistory. There was a range of levels of local participation, of skill levels, of professionalization, and of involvement by local government, but even when municipal programs underwrote murals, they were often a response to what had already been initiated within a local community. The difference between traditional modern murals and those created in West Berlin registers in subject matter as well. Here, too, there is a wide range, but the vast majority of murals created in West Berlin address the quality of urban life, often by protesting specific urban or environmental changes or projecting alternative cityscapes.

As aware of the modern mural tradition as West Berlin wall-painters were, they also cited as inspirations more contemporary international mural-making trends developing in places such as Bologna, Sardinia, Portugal, Mexico, and Chile, places where murals were being used as a means of direct political expression.[13] Perhaps more surprising and an important, if subtle, indicator of the cultural ties between West Berlin and the US at the time, was the exhibition held as early as 1974 at Amerika Haus Berlin, the US State Department's cultural center within the still-occupied city, entitled Street Art: Public Wall Painting in the USA. The majority of the images were of murals in Los Angeles, Santa Monica, Venice (California), San Francisco, and Berkeley, but Detroit, New York, and Chicago were represented as well. All had been painted since 1967. The exhibition divided the images into four sections:"Advertising as Wall Cosmetics: Examples of New Advertising Paintings" (24 images), "Individual Wall Paintings: The Extension of Architecture through Fantasy" (21 images),"Public Painting Projects at Schools: Sign of Active Art Education" (19 images), and "Political Wall Paintings: Collective Wall Paintings in City Districts of Political Minorities" (30 images).[14]

Helga Retzer's brief catalogue introduction places these contemporary US murals against the backdrop of Mexican and US mural production in the 1930s and highlights features of the contemporary "Renaissance in wall painting in the USA" that, she argues, sustain George Biddle's claim to President Roosevelt from decades earlier that young American painters wanted to realize in permanent form their awareness of social revolution.[15] She emphasizes the heterogeneity of American society, the omnipresence of visual media, especially large-scale vehicles such as billboards, and the collective nature of wall painting projects in the urban ghettos of ethnic minorities, where churches and schools helped to support these efforts. Retzer singles out the roles played by the Wall of Respect in Chicago, muralist Mark Rogovin and the Mural Manual, published in 1973, and the creative appropriation of public space by the Los Angeles Fine Arts Squad for their surreal visions of alternative realities. All of these ideas and precedents would be reflected in West Berlin murals.

An activist climate that focused on new ways of living in and shaping the city, along with new approaches to mural painting as public art, created a new framework for muralists working in West Berlin. As we will see in greater detail in the next section, murals in West Berlin became a vehicle for citizens to contribute to the discourse of urban development by challenging mainstream practices, creating solidarity, redefining citizens' place in the urban community, and reimagining the design and experience of the city. Using urban structures to intervene in the processes that were defining urban experience became a way in which the broader community claimed a role in shaping the city. As specific urban constituencies faced new social, political, and urban challenges, they seized the walls for commentary as a way to assert their ideas about as well as embody their vision of new urban practices. Rather than affirming peoples'identity as citizens of the nation, as had the works of the modern muralists, West Berlin murals made the claim to citizens' "right to the city."

The concept of the right to the city derives from the work of French urban theorist Henri Lefebvre, who argued that "the city is an oeuvre – a work in which all its citizens participate."[16] However, as geographer Don Mitchell notes, increasingly "the spaces of the modern city are being produced for rather than by us."[17] David Harvey, an urban geographer and social theorist whose work draws on Lefebvre's framework, observes that "the right to the city is far more than the individual liberty to access urban resources: it is a right to change ourselves by changing the city."[18]Lefebvre studied the active construction of space; the processes of its production and the nature of the created space, he argued, yield new possibilities or constraints for social life. In modern times, abstract space prevails, a space shaped by and in turn organizing the universalizing, homogenizing social relations of capitalism. Today, for example, the interests of developers and multi-national corporations may be seen as imposing their imprint on the form that cities take; this accounts for the placelessness of many developments. Differentiated space, as Lefebvre called it, recognizes and is a product of particularity and heterogeneity and can only be created by means of social struggle. Particular, heterogeneous needs and desires are made known through their representation, which occurs in and thereby creates public space. Lefebvre saw the city, then, as a shifting embodiment of the play of these dialectical encounters through which people struggle for their human right to the city or, in Harvey's terms,to "the freedom to make and remake our cities and ourselves."[19]

The shift in mural art to neighborhood locations and participation and to themes addressing local urban and wider political issues suggests a new role for public art, a new position for murals in relation to public space. It was a shift, moreover, that seems to have been occurring internationally. In the US, community residents'"demonstrations to save the Wall [of Respect in Chicago, painted in 1967] held back Urban Renewal in that area for three years."[20] John Weber, one of its creators, asserted that the role of the public artist was "to speak as a citizen in society."[21]The editor of the 1973 Mural Manual, mentioned above, recognizing that social struggle is bound up with and shapes the space in which it occurs, observed that contemporary murals "are not merely painted on walls, but speak of the walls, of the community, and its people, and demand justice and human dignity."[22]In Paris, where the events of 1968 were influenced by and in turn inspired Lefebvre, such slogans as "under the paving stones, the beach,"and "beauty is in the streets,"similarly situated social struggle in contested urban space.[23]It may be the case that in retrospect we can identify a new, international paradigm for public art in the late twentieth-century that, while still inspired by earlier precedents, shifted the discourse from nation-building to an urban focus.[24] Further investigation of diverse locales would be needed to assess how widespread a new emphasis on site, community activism, and urban development was and how insistently the public art, including murals, that embodied these asserted the right to the city. But these were, indeed, the emphases that shaped West Berlin murals in the 1970s and 1980s as they contributed to the struggle there for the right to the city.

West Berlin murals

With these contexts and concepts in mind, then, we turn to a necessarily brief overview of West Berlin murals created in the 1970s and 1980s.

Ben Wagin's 1975 World Tree I – Green is Life is recognized as having been the first mural painted in West Berlin.[25] Wagin, a Polish-born freelance artist, gallerist, and environmentalist who settled in Berlin in 1955 when he was 25, chose as the site for his work a typically dreary firewall that had been exposed during Allied bombardments of the city. Located around the corner from Wagin's gallery, this wall was particularly apt, since it faced a rapid-transit (S-Bahn) station and a major entrance to the central city park, the Tiergarten. Wagin was assisted by four other artists and had the support of the city administrator for building and housing along with permission from the building owner, who could not afford to restore the wall. These factors mark his mural as an example of officially-sanctioned public art.

World Tree depicts a massive exhaust pipe on the right, which expels gases that force a shriek of pain from the tree that dominates the image on the left. A steamship closes the composition at the top, firmly echoing the wall's horizontal roof-line as it plies the seas to deliver new trees from afar. The mural is still visible, although it is in very deteriorated and faded condition.

Ecological themes recurred in many other murals, principally in those painted by activist groups. Their work was mainly unofficial, created outside the frameworks of municipal administration and institutional support whose development is discussed further below. Activist groups were allied, instead, with the protest movement that focused on such issues as energy production, especially opposition to nuclear energy, housing provision, and urban redevelopment, including opposition to highway construction, of the sort discussed earlier. By the mid-1970s, protestors added the creation of community murals to demonstrations, leafleting, street festivals, and other activities as one more aspect of their political practice. Risking police harassment and arrest for painting on walls illegally, activists yet hoped that "more people and/or groups decide to pick up brushes and colors to paint their fears, despair, and utopias on the gray walls" and extend this activity as a means of struggle.[26]

As integral, influential, and numerous as activist murals were, they were also often ephemeral, though not necessarily by choice. Working with fewer financial resources, the materials at the artists' disposal were often poor and subject to relatively rapid deterioration. Unofficial murals were also more vulnerable to destruction by police and building owners. They were often produced in response to immediate situations by participants with little training who had only a sketchy sense of mural-painting practices and, because they were illicit, were frequently painted in haste and without the proper preparation of the underlying wall. All of these factors contributed to their short lifespan. Their disappearance skews the historical record; as early as 1983, when the Amerika-Gedenkbibliothekat the Berlin Central Library in Kreuzberg exhibited photographs of contemporary Berlin wall paintings, few spontaneous activist murals were in good enough condition to be documented.[27]

Three activist murals from the 1970s provide a sense of the varied histories found in this arena of public art. All are large-scale works designed to endure; two survive today. The other had a checkered existence that reflects the contentiousness of the period. By 1978, activist artists had painted two massive firewalls on the Kreuzberg Art and Cultural Center, known as KuKuCK, an abbreviation of its name in German. A center of the squatters' movement – the Center was itself illegally occupying a commercial building that had stood empty – this institution was "a thorn in the eye of the [West Berlin] Senate."[28]

KuKuCK was evicted from the building in 1984 and the walls were painted over and replastered.[29] To protest this destruction, images inspired by one of the murals were integrated into a new wall painting at the Tommy-Weisbecker-Haus, a self-managed living collective for youth located in the same district (Fig. 1).

The title of the KuKuCK mural was German Model, referring to West Germany's postwar economic reorganization, which was celebrated for creating what was often cited as an "economic miracle" of prosperity in the 1960s. Using this term ironically, the mural's outlook was, instead, far more critical: destruction of the environment, the ticking time-bomb of nuclear power, and inhumane housing conditions were some of the themes it depicted, colorfully and through the use of gently expressionist exaggerations and distortions of form.

The other surviving activist mural is much simpler and less skillfully painted. A bold tree form with bright green, spreading foliage covers the façade, anchored by a reddish-brown central trunk (Fig. 2). The colors now are faded, but the yellow banner painted above the first-floor windows is still visible, along with the slogan, "we're staying put;" originally, this was accompanied by the words, "we have sunk roots," in the middle of the trunk. Also located in the district of Kreuzberg, this building was in an area slated for widespread demolition. When their lease ended in early 1975, the people living there decided to fight eviction. Their first act was to paint the mural and thus to create awareness of their intentions throughout the neighborhood. Not long thereafter, the building was sold to someone who honored the community form of living they had established; it was saved from destruction, while many buildings around it were razed. As one participant noted, "One kept a finger, but forgot to take the whole hand."[30]

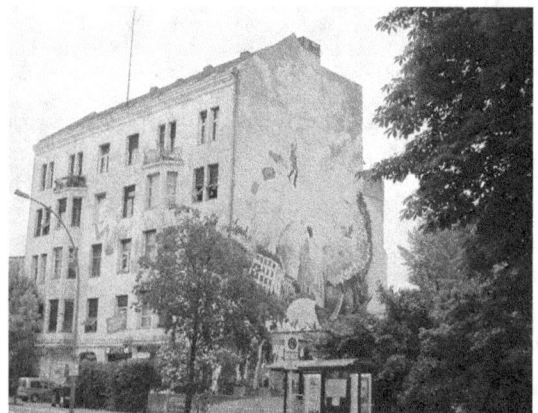

Fig. 1. Andreas Dornbusch, Tommy-Weisbecker-Haus, Kreuzberg, 1984. (Source: Author, 2014)

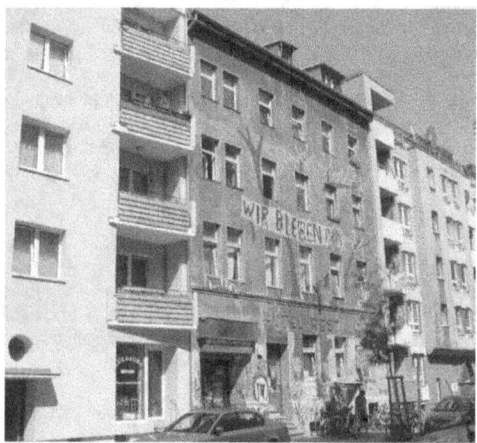

Fig. 2. Wirbleibendrin, Kreuzberg, 1975. (Source: Author, 2012)

Official murals were ones that received municipal support channeled through district government, were commissioned by the building owner or a local business, or had won a local competition. Programs to underwrite artwork by making use of a dedicated percentage of building costs had existed in Germany since the 1920s, but in 1973 the city of Bremen introduced a broader program to sponsor art in public spaces; it was not limited to new construction and it promoted what was seen as a more democratic selection process.[31] This was widely influential; even the [West] German Association of Cities recognized at this time a need to create livable cities and connections between citizens and their city by involving the creative arts in city planning proposals.[32] The West Berlin Senate adopted a program in the mid-1970s, entitled "Color in the Cityscape," to support mural painting, and published a handbook for building owners in 1979. Artists' and architects' professional organizations, the local newspaper Morgenpost, and other city institutions collaborated with the Senate in their encouragement of mural exhibitions and competitions. One writer described such support in this period as starting a "colorful wave" throughout the city.[33]

In 1989, it was reported that there were almost 250 wall paintings in West Berlin;[34] vacant lots from war damage were still widespread throughout the city. Since then, as a result of post-reunification redevelopment that has occurred in every district and neighborhood, the greatest threats to official murals painted before that date have come from the construction of new infill buildings in the vacant spaces adjacent to the firewalls on which they are painted, and from the razing of the entire building on which they appeared. Some have been lost due to overpainting. Some are very faded, while others have been preserved through repainting, signaling the high regard in which they are held in their neighborhoods and by building owners and residents.

One of the early wall paintings to enjoy this esteem is Gert Neuhaus' 1979 Zipper in the district of Charlottenburg. Neuhaus, a Berliner born in 1939, studied at the fine arts university there and was working as a freelance artist, exhibition designer, and gallerist when he began to paint large-scale murals in 1976. This piece, commissioned by the building owner, underwent a significant modification in design in order to keep costs down. As originally conceived, the entire wall would have been covered with an illusionistic painting of a Wilhelmine building façade; a zipper running down the center would have opened to reveal a small section of the firewall behind it.[35] To avoid the cost of painting the whole wall, Neuhaus'swife suggested reversing the images: now, the unpainted firewall is bisected by the painted zipper to reveal a glimpse of the Wilhelmine building. Fortuitous though this change was, it prefigured the edge that fantasy or the depiction of an alternative reality would typically have over the literal in Berlin murals in this period. While both conceptions playfully manipulate illusions, the first idea would have frankly uncovered the firewall that actually exists behind the painted illusion. As created, that actual wall incredibly opens to expose the pristine façade that it seemingly hides. Neuhaus, a prolific muralist, went on to paint many that embody a fanciful, illusionistic approach that plays with the theme of Berlin architecture. Zipper achieved a special renown, however, when it was used on posters to promote the city, accompanied by the slogan "Berlin feels good."[36]

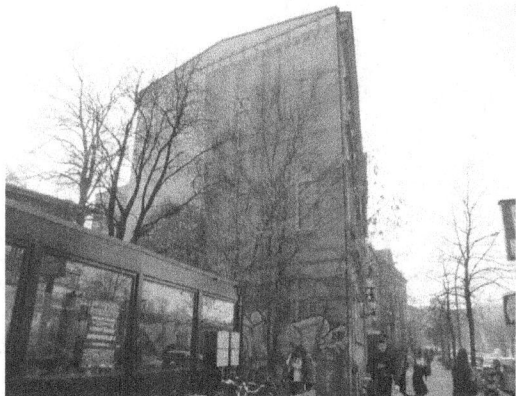 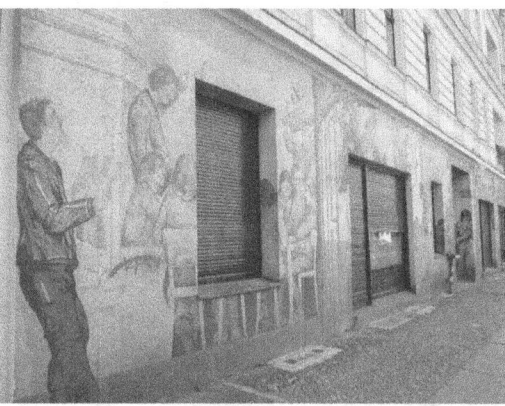

Fig. 3. Irene Niepel, Kreuzberg, 1981. (Source: Author, 2014   Fig. 4. Ratgeb Artists Group, Kreuzberg, 1982. (Source: Author, 2012)

A similarly Magritte-like sense of surreal architectural transformation characterizes Irene Niepel's 1981 mural on the firewall of a teachers' residence in Kreuzberg (Fig. 3). Niepel was still a student at the fine arts university in Berlin when she won a district competition with this design. Her painting continues the façade of the building along its side wall, but here the façade takes the form of an illusionistic curtain seen hanging from a rod and opening at the other end of the wall to reveal a green landscape against an intense blue sky. The mural remains intact despite the restoration of the building, although trees have grown up in front of it that make it difficult to view except in winter.

On Admiralstrasse in Kreuzberg, artists Christian Rothmann and Jürgen Wäldrich, working with three others, used a variety of visual vocabularies in their 1986 mural, which was also selected on the basis of a district competition. At street level, they painted an illusionistic shop-front, incorporating surviving architectural elements, including a jagged piece of broken wall, into their depiction of a window display, signage, and passersby. Above, spilling across the wall of the façade, the intact building of the past is shown in explosive fragments. The firewall side of the mural presents figures isolated in abstract, room-like compartments, engaged in disparate activities, dominated by a large TV set. The mural's title is What's left of Admiral Street?[37]

The activist Ratgeb Artists Group created a number of murals in Berlin between 1979 and 1986. They took their name from the sixteenth-century painter JergRatgeb, whose murals in the Frankfurt Carmelite monastery were the largest at the time to be painted north of the Alps; only fragments survived bombardments of the city in 1944. JergRatgeb was publicly executed as a traitor in 1526 for his diplomatic and political work on behalf of peasants during the Peasants' War. For the Berlin muralists, JergRatgeb represented the union of wall painting and social engagement. The Ratgeb Artists Group collaborated with and shared their knowledge of mural painting with building occupiers, children, youth, and the incarcerated, but their own work was usually produced with official support.[38]

A 1979 mural that the city commissioned from the Ratgeb Artists Group was titled The Civilization-damaged Tree of Redevelopment Breaks through Moabit's Historical Landscape. Luxuriant fronds at the street level of the firewall break through an illusionistic canvas and turn into a tree with distorted members that towers over a placid historical view of the bucolic area. Bonds and cables fetter the tree; others seem to hold the canvas in place. These perhaps allude to the human bondage found in the institution that is dwarfed by the tree and that is actually located a block away, the Moabit hall of justice and prison. Urban redevelopment, environmental depredation, judicial rehabilitation, and even the remodeling represented by mural painting seem to be equally implicated in the imposition of constraints on human and natural development. The Ratgeb Artists Group also executed a mural in 1982 that stretched along the ground floor and framed the door and shop-window openings of a workers' training center in Kreuzberg (Fig. 4). A painted legend states that the center was founded in 1979 "to realize self-directed work and shared living in this building." The mural, it notes, was painted following occupation of the building. Using a style clearly influenced by 1930s social-realist murals, it depicts workers in the carpentry, electrical, and heating and sanitation installation trades. Men and women work together in all three, reading schematics, developing plans, and dynamically interacting along wooden and metal grids in active poses. The mural adds layers of spatial illusionism to the bland streetscape, playing off areas of three-dimensionality against the planar, rectilinear choreography of pipes and lumber that echo elements of the building's façade. Representatives of West Berlin's immigrant communities contributed to the production of murals, including artists from Chile and Iran as well as German-Turkish painters. Iranian-born artist Akbar Behkalam studied in Tabriz and Istanbul and, after working in several European capitals and a stay in Iran, settled in Berlin in 1976. His 1980 city-sponsored mural in Kreuzberg asymmetrically juxtaposes a loose crowd of delicately painted figures with a lone tree (Fig. 5). It is accompanied by a poem by the celebrated modern, communist.

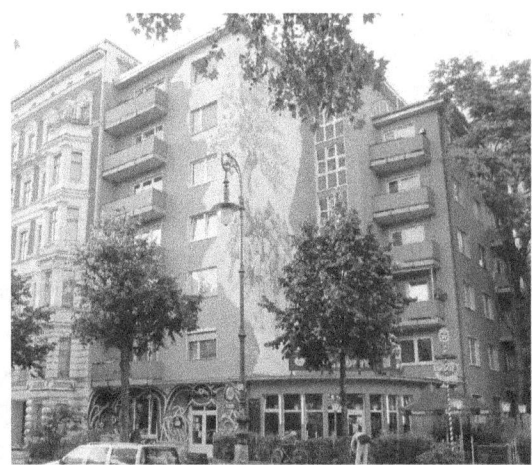

Fig. 5. Akbar Behkalam, Kreuzberg, 1980. (Source: Author, 2012)

Turkish poet NazimHikmet that reads,"To live/ alone and free/ like a tree/ and brotherly/ as a forest/ is our longing."[39] Despite the different visual character and cultural references of this work, Behkalam'sfocus on the poles of the individual and human solidarity and of nature and human longing connects his work to the social and environmental themes that mark many other murals in this period. Also notable is the way Behkalam wrapped the mural around the harshly jutting edge of this projecting part of the building to soften its urbanistic effect. This overview of a small selection of murals provides some sense of the variety as well as the consistency of certain themes and the range of visual forms deployed in both official and activist works. The architecture of the buildings and walls on which the murals were painted, the cityscape past, present, and future, the spaces of the city as arenas for struggles over social definition, and the fragility of nature and the threats it faces are some of the recurring themes. What also emerges is a sense of a particular social environment in which these murals were created, one that fostered collective decision-making and action, identification with local community, and attention to the built forms of the city. By articulating the ideas and ideals of various social groups, the murals created sites for discussion and interaction that promoted mutual understanding and, often, mutual support.[40] They contributed, in other words, to the discourse of the right to the city.

Conclusion

Considering the broader West Berlin context, discussed in the first section, of avid engagement with urban development, which took both illegal and parliamentary forms, it is difficult not to see the equally intense activity of muralists in the 1970s and 1980s as participating in the same discourse in which citizens struggled to define the character of the city. Muralists' identification of the plentiful firewalls that pocked the city as appealing surfaces for their works had the effect of revaluing the walls and reintegrating them into their social, spatial, and architectural sites, transforming them from dreary, blighted pockets into neighborhood landmarks. This helped to strengthen the solidarity among squatters and the larger community of protestors, and it paralleled the achievements of citizen-activists in winning support for policies that encouraged preservation and renovation. Municipally-backed programs, such as "Color in the Cityscape," competitions, and exhibitions that were created to support the development of wall-painting, recognized and endorsed the contributions that community-based murals made to strengthening local identity as well as to promoting more administrative goals such as marketing the city. Thematically, four types of West Berlin murals can be seen as contributing to the discourse of the right to the city. One type, which was not represented in the above overview because none of its examples seem to be extant, consists of contemporary city and architectural views and historical street plans. The latter were especially important instruments in neighborhood preservation struggles. A 1986 mural in Charlottenburg, for example, addressed the protests over a renewal project, depicting citizens and nature bursting through an illusionistic schematic drawing of the neighborhood.[41]Images of the past, such as that executed in 1979 by the Ratgeb Artists Group in Moabit, discussed above, compose a second thematic type. Early nineteenth-century district views, illusionistic depictions of neighborhood shops, a Baroque estate that had once occupied the site of the building on which the mural is painted, and specific historical events are some of the subjects that situated contemporary communities within the narrative of the city's development.[42]A third thematic type addresses environmental issues, which, as we saw earlier, concerned both official and unofficial muralists and their communities. These could represent vistas of bucolic or wooded landscapes, often painted as imaginative illusions, or they could be sharply critical of the depredations stemming from the contemporary indifference to nature and the threats posed by current public policies.[43]

The fourth thematic type is the most numerous. It consists of fantastic, visionary, or utopian images, which usually focus on architectural or urban elements. Irene Niepel's and Gert Neuhaus' murals, both discussed above, present examples of how illusionistic depictions dissolve walls to create alternative worlds. This was (and remains) a specialty of Neuhaus' work; he was very active in these years, painting 26 walls in a 12-year period. One feature that recurs in the works of many muralists who depict such fantastic scenes is the way in which the wall is explicitly shown as shattered or broken to reveal the visionary world that lies beyond it. In a city that was itself enclosed by the Wall, it is tempting to understand such scenes as referring not only to the potential to remake the urban environment but also to the dream of some West Berliners of ending the division of the city.[44]In this connection, the desire that was expressed by building owners who commissioned murals to see a representation of "an intact world" suggests that their goal was not merely beautification in a cosmetic sense but rather as a token of a profound reconstitution of the city both physically and socially.[45]Other commentators noted at the time that to conceive of alternatives to existing functionalist architectural regimes, people needed the space to imagine that murals of fantastic cityscapes offered.[46]These possibilities were ones that the critical, alternative, and oppositional constituencies of the mural movement in West Berlin would have endorsed. What we find, then, is that a characteristic feature of West Berlin in the 1970s and 1980s was the breadth of its mural movement and its consistency in articulating, in various ways, the right of diverse neighborhood residents to the city. Over a roughly 15-year period, both unofficial, activist murals and official projects that received support from the local administration and building owners were created in residential areas. Despite the differences we have noted, murals executed in both arenas addressed significant social and political issues, very frequently posing them in relation to the built environment. Moreover, mural painting contributed to wider movements for social change that transformed urban development practices; occupations were in some cases legitimized, saving traditional neighborhood structures and leading to building renovations, and citizens' initiatives influenced the development of "cautious urban renewal" that achieved the same ends. By representing the critical positions of heterogeneous communities through their wall-paintings, West Berlin muralists produced differentiated, social, public spaces that supported people's on-going efforts to shape the city and their lives within it.

Notes and References

1 An earlier version of this paper, "West Berlin Walls: Public Art and the Right to the City," appears in Public Art Dialogue 4:1 (2014), pp. 100-120.
2 This applied to buried remains as well, as in the excavations that exposed the Topography of Terror. See Karen E. Till, The New Berlin: Memory, Politics, Place(Minneapolis: University of Minnesota Press, 2005). I must also note that while my focus here is on the impact of these critical historical and political studies on urban awareness, such work was directed as well to the War in Vietnam, imperialism, militarism, feminism, and other political, social, and economic issues.
3 GritaHesse, Gemaltelllusionen: Wandbilder in Berlin(Dortmund: Harenberg, 1983), p. 9.All translations are by the author unless otherwise indicated.
4 For the protest movement in Kreuzberg, see Roger Karapin, Protest Politics in Germany: Movements on the Left and Right Since the 1960s (University Park, PA: Pennsylvania State University, 2007), especially chapter 2, "Urban Renewal Conflicts in Hanover and West Berlin," pp. 61-116. The wider social context includes an influx of youth drawn to the exceptional environment of Walled-in West Berlin – including substantial numbers of young men seeking exemption from military/civil service – as well as immigrants, especially "guest-workers" from Turkey. For similar oppositional activities in other German cities see, for example, Manfred Wegner and Ingrid Scherf, Wemgehört die Stadt? (Munich: UlenspiegelDruck, 2013), the catalogue for a MünchenStadtmuseum exhibition that documented actions in Munich in the 1970s.
5 Significant texts that addressed specifically Germany and Berlin were Alexander Mitscherlich'sDie UnwirtlichkeitunsererStädte (The Inhospitableness of Our Cities, 1965) and Wolf JobstSiedler, Die gemordeteStadt (The Murdered City, 1964), cited in Norbert and Melanie Martins, HauswändestattLeinwände(Berlin: Norbert Martins, 2012), p. 9.
6 Josef Paul Kleiheus, Versuchsgebiet Charlottenburg (Berlin: Der Senator fürBau- und Wohnungswesen, 1973).
7 For an introductory overview, see Herbert Schwenk, Lexikon der Berliner Stadtentwicklung (Berlin: Haude&Spener, 2002), pp. 309-310.
8 See Hardt-WaltherrHämer and Josef Paul Kleihues, eds. Idee, Prozess, Ergebnis: Die Reparatur und Rekonstruktion der Stadt (Berlin: Frölich und Kaufmann, 1984).
9 Philip Broadbent and Sabine Hake, "Interview with Barbara Hoidn," in Broadbent and Hake, eds. Berlin: Divided City (1945-1989) (New York and Oxford: Berghahn Books, 2010), p.198.
10 The literature for both is extensive and continues to grow. See, for example, Alejandro Anreus, Robin Adèle Greeley, and Leonard Folgarait, eds. Mexican Muralism: A Critical History (Berkeley: University of California Press, 2012).
11 "Manifesto of the Syndicate of Technical Workers, Painters and Sculptors" (1924), in Mexican Muralism: A Critical History, p. 320.
12 It is worth noting that West Berlin had district town halls, schools, theaters, etc., but no major civic buildings. These were concentrated in the old city center that was located in East Berlin.
13 Hauswände, p. 10; Wandmalereien und Texte, (Berlin: Karin Kramer Verlag), 1979, p. 37.
14 Street Art: ÖffentlicheWandmalereien in den USA (Berlin: Amerikahaus, 1974).
15 Helga Retzer, "Einleitung," in Street Art, n.p.
16 Don Mitchell, The Right to the City: Social Justice and the Fight for Public Space (New York: The Guilford Press, 2003), p. 17. See also Henri Lefebvre, The Production of Space, trans. N. Donaldson-Smith (Oxford: Blackwell, 1991) and "The Right to the City," in Writings on Cities, trans. E. Kofman and E. Lebas (Oxford: Blackwell, 1996).
17 Mitchell, p. 18.
18 David Harvey, "The Right to the City," New Left Review, 53 (Sep./Oct. 2008): p. 23. Republished in slightly altered form in Rebel Cities (London and New York: Verso, 2012).
19 Harvey, p. 23.
20 John Weber, "Murals as Peoples Art," Liberation 16:4 (Sep. 1971): p. 44.
21 Weber, p. 45.
22 Tim Drescher, "The U.S. Mural Movement," in Mark Rogovin, Marie Burton, and Holly Highfill, Mural Manual (Boston: Beacon Press, 1973), p. 105.
23 See Johan Kugelberg and Philippe Vermès, eds. Beauty is in the Street (London: Four Corner Books, 2011).
24 For the struggle to recognize the evolution of the modern mural tradition, see Bruce Campbell, "An Unauthorized History of Post-Mexican School Muralism," in Mexican Muralism: A Critical History, pp. 263-279.
25 This seems to be an honorary recognition stemming from the prominence of the site and Wagin's on-going actions to keep peace and nature in the forefront of Berliners' consciousness, as in the Parliament of Trees Against War and Violence (originally 1990) in the government quarter. A handful of murals predate his World Tree. It also needs to be emphasized that unofficial, illegal, activist murals also predate Wagin's work. For a photograph of this mural, see Hauswände, p.69. Aside from this source, which carries Norbert Martins' documentation of murals to the present, and my own exploration of extant murals in situ, I am relying on documents from the period, as cited in these notes, for information about and photographs of original murals. I have located no substantive subsequent research on them.
26 "BeijederAktionsteheneinpaarLeuteSchmiere," Zitty 15: 1978, in Wandmalereien, p. 36.
27 Hesse, p. 11.
28 Hauswände, p. 33.
29 See Hauswände, p. 33, for this history and photographs. Following reunification, the building was torn down.
30 Wandmalereien, p. 125.
31 Wandmalereien, p. 136.
32 Hauswände, p. 9.33 Norbert Martins, Giebelphantasien (Berlin: HetSteinVerlag, 1989), p. 7.
34 Giebelphantasien, p. 9.
35 Hauswände, p. 29.
36 Giebelphantasien , p. 11. No date is provided.
37 This is the author's translation of Woist die Admiralstrasse geblieben?
38 Giebelphantasien, p. 10; Hesse, p. 11.
39 The German and Turkish texts can be found in Giebelphantasien, p. 75.
40 Hesse, p. 10-11.
41 Giebelphantasien, p. 61; see pp. 21, 26, 29 for other examples.
42 Giebelphantasien, pp. 20, 22, 31, 36, 41, 53, 54, 78, 79, 97, 107, 116.
43 Giebelphantasien, pp. 100, 105, 106, 111.
44 Giebelphantasien, pp. 18, 19, 30, 42, 50, 52, 59, 109, 112, 120.
45 Wandmalereien, p. 137; the phrase that is used is die heile Welt.
46 Hesse, p. 10.

Laura Iannelli, Department of Political Science, Communication Science and Information Engineering, University of Sassari, Postal Address: University Square 11, 07100 Sassari (Italy), Telephone number: + 39 347 5418597, email: liannelli@uniss.it

Lorenza Parisi· Department of Political Science, Communication Science and Information Engineering, University of Sassari, email: lorenza.parisi@gmail.com

To Govern artfully. Linking public art to political participation towards new forms of urban governance

The study considers relational public art as a form of political participation and reflects on the relationships between the models of "projectual citizenship" proposed by artists and the participatory urban governance. The analysis triangulates information gathered through mixed-methods. It is based on a quantitative mapping of 85 Italian artistic projects produced about the political problems of urbanity and a qualitative focus on Sardinian cases. The paper argues that these artistic practices share several characteristics with contemporary forms of collective actions. Moreover, artists perceived their works as effective in transforming the city by looking at "performative" and "interpretative" audiences. Finally, the observed relational public artworks suggest creative models of information, consultation, deliberation, and mobilization in urban settings.

relational public art, political participation,cultural processes

Analysing contemporary political participation through relational public art

Communication is a political process, a site of conflict where power and counter-power are constantly interacting in order to buildsocial reality (Castells 2009). The symbolic power of communication is the power to build representations and interpretations of thosebeliefs, values, and norms (shared cultures)that influence social actions and shape social organisation. The communication processis significant for participatory politics because of its potentials to buildcitizens' knowledge, opinions, and attitudes,thus orienting their behavioursas well (such as attempts to influence political ideas, votes, protests). Therefore, the relationship between communication and political participation has always appeared to be a central theme onthe public agenda and the academic debate, involving sociologists, cultural studies scholars, and political scientists.

Nevertheless, as Carpentier (2011) also noted, one limit of the scientificdebate on communication processes, culture and participatory politics is that it often depletes itself in the media field. In the pre-web age, according to Carey (1989), the study of communication was narrowed to products explicitly produced by and delivered via mass media, and therefore "generally isolated from the study of literature and art, on the one hand, and from the expressive and ritual forms of everyday life – religion, conversation, sport – on the other" (1989: 32). The diffusion of "new" media has fostered this dominant approach to the relationship between communication, culture and political participation: numerous studiesfocus on participatory technologies used to understandcontemporary political practices.

In this study, we lookinstead at the relationship between political participation, culture and communication focusing on the art field, wherein audio-visual and interactive media represent one of thespacesof representation/interpretation of politics that may (or may not) be usedduring the artistic communication processes.

The relationship between artistic communication, culture and political participationhas been studiedthrough different theoretical and methodological approaches. Literature reviews show the development, in the last three decades, of two main veins: the first approach emphasizes an institutional perspective and third sector actors (voluntary and non-profit organizations) in contexts wherein public funding for art is declining; the secondapproach focuses on the use of art in contentious politics and social movements.

In the first approach, we include the seminal research of DiMaggio (1986) on new institutionalism,and Crane (1992) on cultural production, but also the cultural statistics produced by national and international research institutes, where the citizens' participation in the art is considered as the catalysts for democratic citizenship, an essential component of human rights, and – as such – a general policy concern (UIS 2012; Laaksonen 2010).In these cultural statistics, participation in "high" and "popular" arts is measured for an institutional understanding of the social differences in the access to culture and to orient cultural policies. However, as shown in the UNESCO Framework for Cultural Statistics (UIS 2012), only some of these statistics are able to distinguish between creative and receptive participation in art, describing – in the first case – the involvement as volunteers in cultural institutions and the donation of money, the participation in art classes, clubs and groups, the show of personal work in exhibitions and/or on the Internet, and – in the second case – the ownership of artworks or the attendance of individuals at museums, heritage sites, theatres, concerts, dance performances, crafts, design and creative services (measured in terms of frequency, time spent, satisfaction,motivation, and expenditure).

Research on art in social movements has been fostered by the "cultural turn" in the social sciences and humanities, a turn toward cultural processes as analytical focus (Johnston, Klandermans 1995; Melucci 1996; Johnston 2009). The symbolicstruggle of contemporary movements has been studied for the last three decades through this cultural approach, that has tried to explain how social movements come into being and develop, focusing on narratives, texts, speeches, metaphors, rituals, actors, artifacts and performances. In particular, "cultural" scholars from art criticism and literary studies analysed speeches, texts and performancesin the visual and performing artsin (and around) feminist protests (Roth 1983), AIDS activism (Crimp 1988; Roman 1998), the anti-apartheid movement (Marsh 1985), and other cause-based activism (Lippard 1984). Music has been the most widely studied artistic form, seen as a resource forpolitical struggles, a way to build identity and to bring people to participate in the movements.Cultural studies scholars studied the central role of music in punk subculture(Hall, Jefferson 1976). From the perspective of political science (Mattern 1998; Street, Hague & Savigny 1998), music was studied in its functions to support the different forms of organization of political action. From a sociological perspective, music was interpretedas a form of knowledge, a "cognitive practice", oriented to articulate a collective memory (Eyerman, Jamison 1998), and as a "specific cultural project" subject to dispute, with a focus on the relationships between folk-music genres and movements related to race issues(Roy 2010).

Despite the increaseofparticipatory artisticforms (activated by artists and practiced by the public) around social and political issues, our analysis of this scholarship on social movement and art that adopts a cultural approach, spanning different disciplines, revealed a smaller body of research oriented toward investigating artists as actors of the contentious politics on their own, which activates collective actions in order to obtain social and political change: art is instead considered mainly as one of the repertories that activists choose among others. Only in some analyses, artists and artistic organizations are studied as acting in ways resembling social movements (Baumann 2007; Reeds 2005; Cockcroft, Barnet-Sanchez 1990), with rare (but interesting) attention on how different artists', experts' and lay citizens' beliefs about the value of art may hinder contemporary collective actions (Lee, Long Lingo 2011); some scholars studied conflicts in artistic professional unions, strikes, and militant communist parties (Glynn 2000; Browarnik, Benadiba 2007; Yankovskaya 2006).

Our analysis of the scholarship oncultural statistics and institutional perspectivesshowed that this approach also struggles to portraythe increasing complexity ofthe cultural processes activated in contemporary participatory artsto obtain social and political change. Volunteering in cultural institutions and the frequency/satisfaction of attending an art group or class do not reflect the complexity of the "creative participationin art". The "attendance/receiving" activities measured by cultural statistics are not able to describe the overall experiences of the citizens engaged in the artistic actions (at least as co-authors). Despite its aims to direct cultural policy through surveys and administrative data, the approach of cultural statistics neglects the complexity of those "creative communities" that are committed in social and political problems.
As the European Union itself acknowledges, referring to the strategies of Horizon 2020: "the contribution that cultural and creative sectors can bring to social and economic development in the EUis still not fully recognised" (EU 2012).

These considerations encouraged our choice to focus on the contemporary forms of participatory arts that deal withpolitical issues, looking at them as forms of contentious politics in themselves, analysing the models of citizens' participation they aim to activate, and reflecting on their relationship with institutional politics and policy.

In particular, our study focuses on the so-called "relational public art" (also defined by artistic criticism as "dialogic art", "community art", "contextual art", or "processual art").

In the 1990s, relational public art wasseen as a"new genre" of artistic intervention that defined a new canon in public art, political as well as esthetic (Lacy 1995). Artistic criticism considers Mary Jacob's artistic project in Chicago, "Culture in Action" (1993), as one of the first interventions of the new, relational, public art (Jacob et al. 1995). In this project, a network of women worked with Suzanne Lacy to identify 100 other women who had contributed to Chicago public life; they then situated 100 rocks to remember them, in a city where no monument was dedicated to women.Other projects included Christopher Sperandio and Simon Grennan involvingNestle workers in the realization of an artwork that celebrated their job in the historical chocolate factory, and Manglano and Ovalle engagingadolescents of a street gang in a multimedia artwork, creating a space for sociability within an environment of everyday violence (Miles 1997).

Going beyond these historical experiences, art-in-the-public-interesthas been aimed,for the last twenty years,at socially engaging the public space and encouraging community involvement (Know 2004). Unlike traditionalpublic art, the relational artworks claim anautonomous projectual space in the existing urban architecture (Detheridge 2010), and imagined publics of relational public art are no more the passive audiencesof museum art, the sum of single viewers with cultural skills and interests, but active actors engaged in dialogical and connective aesthetics (Kester 2000, 2005; Gablik 1992). This new genre of public art activatesa relational process between production and consumption of artworks in urban spaces: artists prioritise citizens' experience of the place andthe traditional monologue of the individual artist changes into anopen conversation that produces unanticipated collaborative knowledge about the place. Artists involve other citizens in collective actions that aim to transform (often temporarily) physical urban spaces, to create new relations with and within the places where they live, and to build a shared and alternative representation of these places and their conflicts.

Focusing our analysis on relational public art as a form of contentious politics in itself, we aim to increasesociologicalknowledge about the transformation of contemporary collective actions, that literature describes in terms of "subpolitical" and "lifestyle" forms of resistance, oriented to trigger more democratic processes, and based on an affective sense of belonging (Beck 1986; Giddens 1991, 1994; Micheletti 2003; Snow 2004; Van Dyke, Soule, Taylor 2004; Armstrong, Bernstein 2008; Bennett, Segerber 2012; Castells 2012).
Moreover, we aim to explore the multiple models of citizen participationin urban problems that relational public artists propose. The processual and relational nature of these models of civic involvementin and though the art makes them"unpredictable";they cannot

be found in an "artistic toolbox", nor are there manuals that order them in standardized methodologies (unlike participatory methods used in architecture and urban planning, such as town meetings and other consensus-building techniques).

Exploring these participatory modelsproposed by artists (both during and after the activation of artistic actions), we aim to connect them to the most general processes of participation analysed in the literature about the "active", "perfomative", and "empowered" audiences of (political)communication (Abercombrie, Longhurst 1998; Jenkins 2006b; Castells 2009, Dahlgren 2009),and to the forms of engagement activated in participatoryurban governance and spatial planning (Arnstein 1969; Healey 2003;Lane 2005), without losing the richness of differences among these experiments of democracy,andtrying to imagine a different urban politics and policy that can be "revitalized" by these artistic participatory actions.

Contexts, research questions, cases,and methods
Our study started at the end of 2013, funded by the Sardinia Region. We entitled it "To Govern Artfully", and it is atwo-year research programme that involves sociologists of culture, communication scholars, and architects with the aim of analysingboth the contemporary forms of participation activated through relational public artand the relationship between this genre of participatory art and the institutional politics and policy within Italy and focusing on Sardinia.

Like other contemporary democratic systems, Italy is indeed experiencing a profound crisis in traditional forms of political participation. Statistical data show a stable decline of electoral participation, a low level ofengagement in the parties,and a slight presence during demonstrations,while there is an increase of antipolitical sentiments and distrust in politics; only the discussion about politics and the access to political information remain a "vital" trend (Istat 2013). Sardiniareflects and "exasperates" this national scenario of crisis in the traditional "manifest" forms of participation and the persistent centrality of "latent" participation (Ibidem) in those (often mediated) communication processes wherein citizens build their knowledge, opinions, and attitudes toward social and political issues.
This statistical scenario partly justifiedour choice to focus on Italy and Sardinia. The available dataand the missing information on the broader forms of political participation in the cultural sphere fosteredboth ourexplorationof contemporary artistic communication processes as a field of participatory politicsandour in-depth analysis of the collective actions activated by public relational art, entirely neglected in the official statisticsonsocial and political participation.

The focus on public relational art in Italy and Sardinia was alsosuggested by another trend that these contexts share with other democraticcountries: a gradual change in the models of territory governance and spatial planning, becoming increasingly "participatory" models, as a result of EU recommendationsand national/locallegislative initiatives (Lane 2005).
Unlike other European countries, such as France (where approval from urban residents is required for any work planned in their neighbourhood)and the UK (where statutory public participation in planning was introduced in 1968) (Querrien 2005; Culling, Nadin 2002), in Italy there is no national legal framework about participation in the field of spatial planning.

At the regional level,Toscana, Emilia Romagna are two exemplary (and unique) cases, with their laws (issued respectively in 2007, 2010)of promotingcitizen participation in regional and local public policies, to enforce the quality of consensus, to reduce conflicts, and to increase the efficacy ofthe representatives' decisions. During Sardinia's last legislature, the "Regional Landscape Planning"(a very problematic topic, influencing the former Governor's resignation) was supported by some consulting roundtables and an online blog involving experts, stakeholders and local representatives, despite the absence of a general legal framework about participation in public policies.

In this "participatory turn" of the Italian regions' territory governance, the most serious risksare the exclusionof many "non-expert" citizens from the roundtables and theimpoverishment of participatory processes, imagined only in terms of consultations, designedto create a consensus that justifies the experts'decisions, rather then a "shared knowledge" aboutthe places(Mazzette 2013;Ciaffi, Mela 2006; Tidore 2009). Moreover, theseItalian regional models of participatory territory policies neglectthe opportunities opened, by art and creativity,to citizen participation in the transformation of urbanspaces.

We look at urban municipalities to find primarycases of participatory public policies that take into accountart and creativityinthe transformation of public spaces (Titolo 2008;Birozzi, Pugliese 2007). In 2014, for example, the Municipality of Bolognaadopted a legal framework on the "collaboration between citizens and public administration for the care and the regeneration of common urban goods".With theserules, the Municipality supports active citizens that adopt participatory methods in projects of urban requalification, by considering creativity, arts, and artistic education as one of the fundamental tools to value their territory and create social cohesion. In Sardinia in 2012, the Municipality of Cagliari publishedguidelines for its cultural policy, identifying in art, creativity and culture "a driving force in the urban, social, and economic relations of the city". The project "Possible Worlds. Re-inventing the city", based on relational public art, is part of this cultural planning. The commitment of the Sardinian Municipality of Sassari to projects of public relational art is maybe less systematic but still interesting in its "effervescence" (Coccia 2014); here, projectssuch as "StreetArt" and "Habitat Immaginari"have been funded by the Culture Department.
Our choice to focus on Italy,Sardinia, and particularlyon their urban scenarios, drew on thisbackground analysis of boththe statistics aboutpolitical participation and theparticipatory models of urban governance. In thesenational and local contexts, we exploredrelational public art,considering it as a form of political participation in itself, and reflecting on the relationships activated (or achievable) by the models of "projectual citizenship" proposed by artists and the participatory models of urban governance.

In more detail, we aimed to analyse (RQ1),thecharacteristics of these artistic actions comparing them withcontemporary collective actions whose traits have been described by sociological literature and communication studies (the use of participatory technologies, a broader cultural and social target than instituzionalized politics, the increasing request of more democratic processes, and an individualised sense of belonging to a collective cause). Moreover, our study aims to explore the different forms of citizen participation that relational artists propose, analysing (RQ2) the artists' beliefs about the different levels of citizen engagement described by literature on communication and political participation, and thereby what effects artists think they are achievingwith their actions. Finally, we aim to reflect about(RQ3): if and how thesemodels of citizen engagement proposed by relational public artistscan "revitalize" the forms of participatory urban governance and spatial planning, updating the traditional categories of information, consultation, deliberation and mobilization, and exploring the relations between artists and public administrations.

In order to answerthese research questions, we identified the most important Italian art projects that make use of public art to activate civic participation in order to transform urban spaces and to modify citizens' relations within and toward the public places where they live. We selected only those artistic projects that dealt with political issues concerning the development of the territory (e.g. social conflicts, ethnic and cultural minorities, environmental issues, abandoned industrial areas, lack of historical memory, etc.). Moreover we decided to include in the mapping the projects activated since 2000, in order to follow their development in relation to some events that had marked the participation processes during this long temporal window (for example, the diffusion of web 2.0, the explosion of the economic crisis, and the relative intensity of"indignant"movementsthat ask to be included indemocratic processes).

The national cases have beenselected through a literature review (referring mainlyto art criticism and art history), national and international databasesbuilt by artists themselves (in particular, the web archive edited by Anna Detheridge), and interviews with art critics and curators, "key informants" of the processes we were analysing (Payne, Payne 2004).
In order to analyse the selected case, we adopted a mixed-method approach that combines standard and non-standard techniques (Craswell, Plano Clark 2010).
First, we mapped these projects of relational public art through a semi-structured questionnaire gathering information that artists left on their websites, online newspapers, Facebook pages, etc. about five macro-issues: project's author/sand date; organizational structures of artists (single, duo, group/collective/association, network of groups); the commission and funding of projects; spatial and social characteristics of the contexts where the projectstook place; (sub)political agendas of relational artworks in public spaces; involved audiences and participative methodologies adopted in the projects. We stored this information in a databasewhichis routinely updated, and whichwill be translated in a geolocalized map during the second year of the research programme.

For the Sardinian case studies, we also produced in-depth interviews with the artists involved in the mapped projects. The interviews with the artists cover the following macro-issues: artistic education and other experiences outside Sardinia; definitions used to describe the artistic projects; beliefs aboutthe value of art, its effects on the territory and on the different levels of audience engagement; proposed models of citizens' participation;motivation for adopting specific communication strategies in order to involve citizens; relations with public institutions, and opinions about their role into supporting art in public spaces. In-depthinterviews with artists – suitable when trying to develop a detailed description of an unexplored process –were then transcribed, analyzed by using a process of "thematic coding", and triangulated with information drawn from the quantitative mapping (Flick 2009).

Through these two different methodological tools (semi-structured sheet and qualitative interview), we aim to gather information on what types of things artistsdoin the observed participatory communication processesand what types of things artists say in relation to the other actors of theseprocesses, thus referring to the "practice-based approach"suggested by Couldry (2004, 2010, 2012) forsociological-oriented media studies. Despite its emphasis on mediated processes, Couldry's practiceapproach is indeed useful to go beyond the dominant cultural analysis of collective actionscentered on activist texts(pamphlets, manifestos, slogans,etc.) and on the media's framing of activist actions. The "practiceapproach" allows translation of theincreasing attention to the "artistic culture"ofcollective actions into concrete questions related to the perspectives of those involved in these artisticsocial actions and the "anchoring" of these artistic practices to othercommunication processesdeveloped in different social contexts. Couldry indeed suggests a theoretical and empirical attention to the relation between the different reflexivities and the contexts of symbols, texts and meaning about where individuals live.
In this article, we provide an analysis that is based on the mapping of 85 cases in Italy and on qualitative interviews with 10artists who worked in Sardinia on 15 artistic projects.It is a subset of the data that we are collecting during the two-year research programme, but it is relevant to the questions addressed above.

Analysis
In order to explore the relationships between the contemporary forms of political participation and participatory urban governance and the collective actions activated by relational public art, we triangulated information gathered through different sources (the descriptionsleft online by artists, collected through a semi-structured questionnaire,and what they said during face to face in-depth interviews, as descripted above).

Referring to data collected since 2000, we found that 53 out 85 observed cases took place between 2010 and 2014. The development of these projects in the last years seems scarcely related to the diffusion of participatory technologies, that in Italy can be indentified after 2008, in the "post-Facebook age". Indeed only eightcases(fairly distributed over the course of time from 2004) used the different environments of web 2.0 for adding collaborative spacesfor citizen engagement in public art projects. Even if not related to the rise of participatory technologies (unlike other contemporary collective actions), the development of these projects in Italy, in the last years,followedover timethe increase ofcollective actions that (wordwide) came from indignant and oppositional sentiments,asking for changes indemocratic processes and building an affective sense of belonging to different (sub)political causes.
To explore this relation, we analysedinformation about the organizational forms of artists in the Italian cases we mapped, the (sub)

political agenda of thesecases,the Sardinian artists' beliefs aboutthe aims, the political values, and the effects of their actions on the territory and on the different levels of audience engagement.

In 60 outof the 85 observed projects, artists worked as collectives or networks of groups. This is also the case of the ten Sardinian artists we interviewed, belonging to three (open, often redesigned) collectives(aliment(e)azione, Az.Namusn.Art, Teatre en vol), whorealized 15 projects (almost all after 2010). During the individual interviews,artists referred to the considerable efforts required in the organization of a collective, but at the same time they defendedthis choice in aesthetic and political terms.
As we described in the introduction, relational public art is indeed based on the new paradigm of "connective aesthetics": authors must exchange soliloquy, individualism, and self-referentiality for dialog, an interdependent self, polyphonic narration, open conversation, and listening. In the words ofElisa (Aliment(e)azione), "Each member has to take his or her specific personality and artistic imagination away, in order to foster the rise of a cooperative artwork".
"Our art consists of meetings," added Antonio, a member of the same group.He describes his sense of belonging to the collective, "What I find more interesting is to give up one's own name, to drop the self-satisfaction of accomplishing an artistic work.... I mean, I think that this has great value, even political value."

This idea of collective, cooperative,artistic research emerged in the words of all interviewed artists, but it does not concern only the organizational forms of artistic projects. During the interviews, artists explicitly attributeda political valueto the collective actions they activated.Their aims areto activate more democratic processes and to suggest cultural changes which involve other citizens in an artistic process that makes a statement about the problems of urbanity.
Antonio explained that aliment(e)azione"carries out a sort of political and a civic function;" itsartistic projects aim to "let the people talk;" it "encourages citizens to use a critical point of view, a critical conscience toward their surrounding."
In this idea, he was supported by Andrea D., another member of the collective, "We give a microphone to people, people who cannot speak, who aren't able to speak and were born under conditions which prevent them to speak [...] Their answer is our aim."Also Teresa (aliment(e)azione) wants "to highlight a problem" thorughrelational public art. Michéle (Teatre en vol) referred again to her collective's"civic and political function";theirartworks aim to "express an idea, a vision" in order to "elicit a different point of view, another possible world," and "to increase citizens' knowledge."The political role of relational public art also emerged clearly in Riccardo's words(Az.Namusn.Art), "We politically make artin Sardinia, that symbolically encompasses the contradictions of the capitalistic mode of production and the inequalities that globalization produces."

Like Az.Namusn.Art projectsin Porto Torres, a small town in northen Sardinia, whose citizens were divided on the question of a petrochemical factory, 29 out of the 85 Italian mapped projects work on environmental and ecological issues.These projects aim to renew (or create) public places, mainly in dismissed or abandoned urban areas, to denounce ecological problemsand related conflicts (i.e. air pollution, chemical waste, lack of green areas),and to ask for public initiatives in order to promote sustainability, ecological lifestyles or alternative means of transportation.
Similar to this specific ecological agenda, we found that artistsworked aroundmore general social and political issues (N=79), with the aim to re-semanticize the spaces, to find an alternative vision about the future of neighborhoods (against property speculation),to publicly represent citizens' memories about the place, and to foster an intercultural dialogue. A few projects (N=7) were specifically dedicated to value local activities, such as handicrafts or organizing courses for the unemployed youths. working classes and youths.

Youths represent, for the relational public artists, a broadly engaged audience: 21 out of 85 observed projects are specifically designed to involve this targetgeneration in the realization of artworks(in particular, students and scholastic communities). Yet, regarding the engaged audience of these artistic actions, we have to make an analytical distinction between (1) the citizensinvolved directly in the project, (2) the city pedestrians that observe, interpret and (sometimes) comment on the evolution of the project, and (3) a third audience, less "performative" but equally "active" in the cultural process of interpretation,that look at the mediated worksrealized (photos and video) for public exhibitions or websites (23 out of the 85 observed artistic actionsrealized these mediated post-productions).

This representation of a progressive scale of citizen involvement (from the collaboration in the production of public artworks to the mediated interaction after the project) emerges also in the words of interviewed artists. In particular it comes to light through the words ofthe members of Aliment(e)azione who work mainly in theurban area of Sassari, with a historical city center recently and partially regenerated and an extensive industrial suburb. They speak of citizen engagement andcitizens' reactions and feedback, which are expressedeither during or after the project in the public space. "Without an audience reaction, there would not be any artistic work," (Teresa)."Audience feedback is the artwork," (Edoardo)."The turnout of a project relies on the collective answer we receive from the public," (Andrea D.)."Our artistic process includes communication, too," (Antonio). But, at the same time, they acknowledge that the reactions they observeduring the projectsare only a part of the effects artistic actions can (or cannot) have over time on citizens' perceptions of urban problems and their relative behaviours."We have no instruments to evaluate the process over the time" (Elisa), "We should visit again the places where aliment(e)azione projects occurred in order to redesign the artworks (...) I think several projects would benefit from a new creative step, otherwise they will just appear as single inputs," (Andrea D.).
The aliment(e)azione'sproject "Vedi tu" ("Take a look" 2012) clearly illustrates how the first and the second level of audience engagement can interact over the time, after the artists have left their work to the community. In this project, alimente(a)azione distributed stickers to Sassari citizens and asked them to paste these stickers on abandoned areas of the town(the stickers claimed: "This is an abandoned area, claim it back and repair it"). After two years,stickers are still pasted around town, and they can draw attention to specific urban places. Moreover,they have also been "ri-mediated"by a political candidate running for office, who used the same image to support his campaign based on urban care.

This is just one example of the many "unpredictable" effects that relational public art can achieve, involving different (more or less performative) audiences, during the realization of the projectsand over time. Even if the artwork is a temporary collective action (N=63), only sometimesdesigned to permanently transform the physical space (N=25), and rarely included in a recurring(and then recognizable) event (N=13),the artistic communication processesare able to work beyondthe first moment of collaborative productiondirectly involvingonly a small number of citizens. Moreover, the mostperformative audiencesseem to have a central role ininvolving other citizens in the artistic communication process, as Michélle (Teatre en vol) pointed out, "Those citizens that are engaged by artists in the artwork interact with the most uninterestedcitizens."The procedural and relational nature of these collective actions,developed in and though the art in public spaces, makes the short and long-term effects "unpredictable".

The models of citizens' involvement are also procedural and relational "by default" (as required by the connective aesthetics), and,for this reason, they cannot be "planned" or inspired by an "art manual". Nevertheless, when an artistic action is "concluded", artists can say what they did to activate citizen engagement and how citizens (re)acted (at least, the most "performative" audience). This kind of information (left online by artists and expressed during the in-depth interviews) allowed our analysis to connect participatory models proposed by the artists with the traditional patterns of engagement activated in participatory urban governance and spatial planning.

In this way, we found that most of the observed artistic practices"mobilized" citizens (N=52), fostering them to actions that changed public urban spaces (even if only temporarily) and the relations within these spaces, such as furniture building or tapestry creating, a collective crossword puzzle, or the transformation of a psychiatric clinic to a "museum" opened to neighborhoods. Another model of citizen participation activated in the observed artistic practices is the "consultation" (N=38).Artists used creative ways to listen to the citizens' voices, such as contests, collections of postcards, para-sociological questionnaires, psycho-geographical walks à la Debord, selfmapping, etc. The "deliberative" model has been used in almost one-third of observed artistic practices (N=26); artists promoted different points of view and public debates concerning urban space via outdoor roundtables (sometimes organizednext to the building painted by streetartists), picnics in central squares and in abandoned areas, and by placing domestic couches in the street. Some projects engaged citizens in the realization of video, music, and handicrafts to represent the place they live in, after some courses to teach them how to use a specific artistic language, thus activating an "informal learning" model (N=20).

A few projects generated (in addition to other strategies) an "information" model (N=9), using leaflets, images, and artistic kits, to give more information about thehistorical memoryof a specific place or about a social, cultural or political issue. In some, interesting cases, "fake" information was given to "shake" citizens' perceptions of urban problems and to critically reflect on them. An example of this "fake information" model is "Pac Corporation", whereinan imaginary corporation informed citizens thatsome urban green area would be removed and the historical trees would be used to produce "green plastic". As the artists explained, "People look at these trees everyday, they look at the trees without seeing them; if we ask, 'How many trees are in that street?' I think nobody could answer that question." Because the artists saw the citizens' indifference to environmental issues as a problem, they created a project combining pre-existing language (slogans, symbols, formats, etc.) but subverted their meaning.These "tactical" practiceswere also used in other projects realized in Northen Sardinia, an area distressed by the petrolchemical industry.

Despite the antagonistic nature of these projects (denouncing industrial capitalism and the political choices that encourage it), some of themhave been supported by local public administrations."Pac Corporation" waspart of the project "StreetArt", funded by the Municipality of Sassari.Also, "Anarcheology" – with its unauthorized collective walk in the industrial area of Porto Torres – was included in the institutional programme "Open Monuments".

Outside Sardinia, data gathered in our mapping of public relational art in Italy show a relation between the industrial history of the placeswhere these actions have been produced and the public and privateinvestment in these creative communities. The observed projects concentrated onthe area called the "industrial triangle" (Milan, Turin, Genoa), industrial districts that started to invest in culture and creative industries in order to renovate their own production. Among these projects in the North of Italy(N=44),we found a relatively strong presence of projects founded by a public institution or a private company (N=25). Another variable is related to the public and private supportfor the observed Italian projects. Most of the funded projects (48 out of 50) were carried out by artists who live or work in the same place where the projects are located.At first glance, this relation seems to describean easier access to local funds by local artists anda better connectionbetween local artistic andlocal administrations and companies. However, the words of Sardinian artists reveal ambivalentbeliefs of this relationship with public administrations, and thesedifferent perceptions concern members of the same collective.

On one side, artists are very proud when they produce their zero-budget artworks because they do not need any financial support from any public institution. Antonio (aliment(e)azione) clearly illustrated this topic, "I believe that to apply for public funding limits my artistic vein, using a romantic expression; moreover, I think it could even be risky for us, in some ways it can even turn against us and affect the public opinion of our work."Also Teresa (aliment(e)azione) claimed that workingwith public institutions reduced her creativity; artists have to spend a lot of time carrying out bureaucratic procedures,In addition, they cannot realize a project illegally, and they have to carefully describe to the administration a performance before they are going to put into practice. On the contrary, Andrea D. (aliment(e)azione) said that he liked "working with public funding to create culture", and he defined the relationship with the public administration as an arena that citizens have to "dig" in order to obtain some satisfactory results. Andrea also harshly criticized inactive citizens who complain about the lack of cultural initiatives and considered those people the main cause of the laziness of institutions.Like other artists we interviewed (in particular the members of Teatre en vole and Az.Namusn.Art), he asked for better-trained and up-to-date public administrators and for more audacious public institutions that are able to effectively support and encourage relational public art projects.

Discussion and conclusions

Our study explored relational public art considering it a form of political participation in itself, and reflecting on the relationships created (or achievable) between the models of "projectual citizenship" proposed by artists and the participatory models of urban governance. Triangulating information gathered through mixed-methods and different sources, the analysis showed that the development of Italian relational public art projects in recent years (from 2010) is scarcely related to the diffusion of participatory technologies. In Italy, this "digitally enhanced" relational public art has not been a significant fieldrecently, despite its increase in international contexts (Broeckmann 2004) due to the fact that relational public art and web 2.0 share the same collaborative and participatory logic. Although not related to the rise of participatory technologies (unlike other contemporary collective actions), the recent development of these projects in Italy followed, over time, the growth of the economic/democratic crisis and the relative forms of protest. Moreover, we argued that these artistic actions share some other characteristics (RQ1) with these contemporary forms of protest. They targeted a broad range of cultural and social issues, from collective identity to ecology, finding in urban "scenes" a site of (sub)political and "lifestyle" resistance (Beck 1986; Giddens 1991; Snow 2004; Van Dyke, Soule, Taylor 2004; Armstrong, Bernstein 2008). As much as in the recent movements of "indignant" citizens (Castells 2012), the activists-artists we interviewed triggered a more democratic political process. With public artworks, interviewed artists aimed to activate a relational process, involving other citizens, as "required" by contemporary aesthetics rules, around the problems of urbanity. But they also defined "politically" their choice to be part of an artistic collective (the wider organizational form among the 85 mapped cases).In their words, we see a shared belief about the importance of the individual artist's participation in a collaborative and democratic idea phase. In a contest of crisis for the traditional forms of participation (as shown by statistics considered above), the observed artistic actions represent cultural fields where artists are, still, able to build a "we" that acts for social and political change. The participation these artistic practices generated within the collectives and among citizens is no more ideologically driven, but rather "process-driven".Artists and artistic groups combine and re-combine in different collectives and networks fordifferent projects, but they believe in the importance of the relational and democratic process they bring about in each project. We can consider these artistic practices as forms of "individualized collective actions" (Micheletti 2003; Bennett 2012): "individualized" because they are based on individual beliefs (and not mass ideologies), but at the same time "collective" in their aims.

Referring to RQ2, our study showed that the interviewed artists shared a common belief about a progressive scale of citizen involvement which they are able to activate. They achieved "reactions" from the most "performative" audiences (Abercrombie, Longhurst 1998) and,once they left the artwork to the community, they expected"re-mediation" processes (Bolter, Grusin 1999) and long term effects on "interpretative" audiences of their post-production mediated public artworks (Jenkins 2006b; Castells 2009). With their words, Sardinian artists gave voice to the numbers of the mappingthat described asignificant diffusion, in Italy, oftemporary relational public art projects. In fact, even if urban settings had not been physically and permanently transformed, artistsperceivedtheir results mostly bylooking at theparticipatory processesthat public relational art activates, and they believedthat they involve different audiences in these processes(more or less active, with their "interpretative" powers, exercised in the short and long period). Therefore, temporary relational public artworkswere perceived as "effective"in transforming the city, looking at the reactions of the most "performative" audiences and at the "interpretations" of the most spectatorial audiences.Yet,the artistsacknowledged that they are not able to follow these long-term effects, and some of them think that these participatory processes should be re-activatedover time or included into a recurring (and then recognizable) event.

Our study also connected the forms of citizen engagement proposed by the observed artistic projects with the traditional patterns of engagement used in participatory urban governance and spatial planning, "revitalizing" these traditional processes (information, consultation, deliberation, mobilization) with creative examples (RQ3). These artistic models of citizen engagement referred, in particular, to mobilization processes, but the analysis also showed interesting information processes that weregenerated on environmental issues and that can be defined as "tactical" practices, moving in on 'the other's' terrain (in these cases the terrain of multinational corporation and the commercial advertising) (De Certau 1980; Jenkins 2006a; Cammaerts 2007). Additionally, among these antagonistic practices, we observed a significant presence of projects funded by public administrations or private companies. However, the words of Sardinian activist-artists revealed different beliefs and competing ideasregarding this relationship with public administrations. Within the same collective, some artists defended their independence from politicians and bureaucracy, others evoked the inherent responsibility of public institutions in art and culture. As shown by Johnston (2009), the inner conflict of collective actions can be a source of innovation, experimentation, and opposition, while other scholarship identified tensions some non-conventional organizations faced in integrating artistic expression and political goals (Chen, O'Mahony 2009). However,the interviewed artists shared the request for better trained, up-to-date, and audacious public administrators.These actors, together with the citizens involved in public artworks, are the two keyactors of the broad and overlapping processes we are analysing.For this reason, in the next year, the research programmewill focus both on public administrators that supported these artistic actions in Sardinia and on the citizenswho will be involved in the artistic projects planned for the next months(and identified byresearchers during the interviews). The city is not only a site of struggle between artists and administrators, but also between artists and citizens that interpret artistic communication about urban problems. Different beliefs about the value of art and participation and differentlegitimations of the artists (by public administrators and by "non-expert" citizens) can demobilize the results artists think they have achieved, as shown by some movements' scholarship (Roy, Down 2010; Lee, Long Lingo 2011). However, this informationabout the failures of relational public art is important to understand the potential of art in participatory politicsas much as the information on its positive results.

Acknowledgments

The project "Governare ad arte" was funded by the Sardinia Region (Regional Law 7/2007, "Promotion of the scientific research and technological innovation in Sardinia", year 2012). Scientific Coordinator: Laura Iannelli (University of Sassari).

Notes and References

Abercrombie N., & Longhurst B. J. (1998). Audiences: A Sociological Theory of Performance and Imagination. London: Sage

Armstrong, E.A., Bernstein, M. (2008). Culture, power, and institutions: a multi-institutional politics approach to social movements. Sociological Theory 26, 74–99

Arnstein, S.R. (1969). 'A Ladder of Citizen Participation', Journal of the American Planning Association35 (4): 216–224\

a.Titolo (ed) (2008). Nuovi Committenti. Arte contemporanea, società e spazio pubblico. Cinisello Balsamo: Silvana Editoriale

Baumann, S. (2007). A general theory of artistic legitimation: how art worlds are like social movements. Poetics 35, 47–65.

Beck, U. (1986). Risikogesellschaft. Auf dem Weg in eine andere Moderne. Frankfurt: Suhrkamp

Bennett, L., Segerber A. (2012). The Logic of Connective Action: Digital Media and the Personalization of Contentious Politics. Information, Communication & Society, 15 (5): 739-768

Birozzi, C., Pugliese, M. (2007). L'arte pubblica nello spazio urbano. Committenti, artisti, fruitori. Milano: Bruno Mondadori

Bolter, J. D., Grusin R. (1999). Remediation: Understanding New Media. Cambridge, MA: The MIT Press

Broeckmann, A. (2004). Public Spheres. Public Spheres and Network Interfaces. In Graham, S. (ed), The Cybercity Reader. New York: Routledge, 379-

Browarnik, G., Benadiba, L., (2007). Militant artists of the Argentine Communist Party. Historia, Antropologia y Fuentes Orales, 37, 89–99

Carey, J. W. (1989). Communication as Culture. Essays on Media and Society (ed. Adam G. S.). NewYork, NY: Routledge

Carpentier, N. (2011). Media and participation. A site of ideological-democratic struggle. Bristol, UK: Intellectual

Castells, M. (2009). Communication Power. Oxford: Oxford University Press

Castells, M. (2012). Networks of Outrage and Hope: Social Movements in the Internet Age. Cambridge: Polity Press

Chen, K., O'Mahony, S. (2009). Differentiating organizational boundaries. Research in the Sociology of Organizations, 26, 183–220

Ciaffi, D., Mela A. (2006). La partecipazione. Dimensioni, spazi e strumenti. Roma: Carocci

Coccia, M. (2014) Una rivoluzione non richiesta. Modelli di arte inclusiva dal nord Sardegna. Roma: Aracne Editrice

Cockcroft, E.S., Barnet-Sanchez, H. (eds.) (1990). Signs from the Heart: California Chicano Murals. Albuquerque, NM: University of New Mexico Press

Couldry, N. (2004). Theorising Media as Practice. Social Semiotics, 14(2), 115-132.

Couldry, N. (2010). Why Voice Matters Culture and Politics After Neoliberalism. London: Sage

Couldry, N. (2012). Media, Society, World. Social Theory and Digital Media Practice. Cambridge: Polity Press

Creswell, J., Plano Clark V. (2010). Designing and Conducting Mixed Methods Research. Thousand Oaks, CA: Sage

Crimp, D. (Ed.), 1988. AIDS: Cultural Analysis/Cultural Activism. MIT Press, Cambridge, MA. Culling, Nadin 2002

Cammaerts, B. (2007). Jamming the Political: Beyond Counter-hegemonic Practices. Continuum: Journal of Media & Cultural Studies, 21(1), 71-90

Comune di Bologna (2014), Regolamento sulla collaborazione tra cittadini e amministrazione per la cura e la rigenerazione dei beni comuni urbani, Bologna, 22.02.2014, available at http://www.labsus.org

Connecting Culture. online database Artplaces, available online athttp://www.artplaces.org/artplaces/

Crane, D. (1992). The Production of Culture. Media and the urban Arts. Newbury Park, CA: Sage

Dahlgren, P. (2009). Media and Political Engagement. Citizens, Communication and Democracy.Cambridge, MA: Cambridge University Press

de Certeau M., (1980). L'invention du quotidien. Arts de faire, Union Générale D'éditions, Paris

Detheridge, A. (2010). La nuova arte nella sfera pubblica, Territorio, 53, 39-43

DiMaggio, P. (ed) (1986). Nonprofit enterprise in the arts: Studies in mission and constraint. New York, NY: Oxford University Press

European Union (2012). Promoting cultural and creative sectors for growth and jobs in the EU. Communication from the Commission to the European Parliament, the Council, the European Economic and Social Committee and the Committee of the Regions. Available at http://www.europarl.europa.eu/registre/docs_autres_institutions/commission_europeenne/com/2012/0537/COM_COM%282012%290537_EN.pdf

Eyerman, R., Jamison, A. (1998). Music and Social Movements: Mobilizing Traditions in the Twentieth Century. New York: Cambridge University Press

Flick, U. (2009). An Introduction to Qualitative Research. London: Sage

Gablik, S. (1992). Connective aesthetics. American Art, 6(2), 2-7

Giddens, A. (1991). Modernity and Self-identity: Self and Society in the late modern age. Cambridge: Polity Press

Glynn, M.A. (2000). When cymbals become symbols: conflict over organizational identity within a symphony orchestra. Org. Science ,11, 285–298

Hall, S. e Jefferson, T. (eds) (1976). Resistance Through Rituals: Youth Suculture in Post-War Britain. London: Hutchinson

Healey, P. (2003). The Communicative Turn in Planning Theory and its Implications for Spatial Strategy Formation. In Campbell S., Fainstein S. (eds.), Readings in Planning Theory. Malden: Wiley-Blackwell, 237-256

Istat (Italian National Institute of Statistics) (2013). Aspetti della vita quotidiana. Available at http://www.istat.it/it/archivio/4630

Jacob, M. J., Brenson, M., Olson, E. M., (1995). Culture in action: A public art program of sculpture in Chicago. Seattle: Bay Press.

Jenkins, H. (2006a). Fans, Bloggers, and Gamers. Exploring Participatory Culture, New York University Press, New York

Jenkins, H. (2006b) Convergence Culture. Where Old and New Media Collide. New York, NY: New York University

Johnston, H. (2009). Culture, Social Movements, and Protest. Aldershot UK: Ashgate Publishers.

Johnston, H., Klandermans, B. (eds.) (1995). Social Movements and Culture. University of Minnesota Press, Minneapolis, MN.

Kester, G. (2000). Dialogical aesthetics: A critical framework for littoral ar, Varient 9

Kester, G. (2005). Conversation Pieces. The Role of Dialogue in Socially Engaged Art. In: Kucor Z., Leung S. (eds), Theory in Contemporary Art since 1985. Oxford: Blackwell, 76-88

Kwon, M. (2004). One place after another: Site-specific art and locational identity. Cambridge, MA:MIT press

Laaksonen, A. (2010). Making Culture Accessible: Access, Participation in Cultural Life and Cultural Provision in the Context of Cultural Rights in Europe. Strasbourg: Council of Europe Publishing

Lacy, S. (ed.) (1995). Mapping the terrain: New genre public art. Seattle, Washington: Bay Press

Lane, M., B. (2005). Public Participation in Planning. An Intellectual History. Australian Geographer, 36 (3), 283-299

Lee, C. W., Long Lingo, E. (2011). The "Got Art?" paradox: Questioning the value of art in collective action. Poetics, 39, 316–335

Lippard, L.R. (1984). Get the Message? A Decade of Art for Social Change. New York: E.P. Dutton

Marsh, D. (ed.) (1985). Sun City. Penguin Books, New York

Mattern, M. (1998). Acting in Concert: Music, Community, and Political Action. New Brunswick NJ: Rutgers University Press

Mazzette, A. (ed) (2013). Pratiche sociali di città pubblica. Roma-Bari:

Melucci, A. (1996). Challenging Codes: Collective Action in the Information Age. Cambridge, UK: Cambridge University Press

Micheletti, M. (2003). Political Virtue and Shopping. Individuals, Consumerism, and Collective Action. New York: Palgrave MacMillan

Miles, M. (1997). Art, space and the city. London:Routledge

Payne, G., Payne, J. (2004). Key Concepts in Social Research. London: Sage

Querrien, A. (2005). How Inhabitants Can Become Collective Developers: France 1968-2000. In Jones P., Petrescu D., Till J. (eds) Architecture and Participation, London: Spon, 105-115

Reeds, T. V. (2005). The Art of Protest. Culture and Activism from the Civil Rights Movement to the Streets of Seattle, Minneapolis/London: University of Minnesota Press

Regione Toscana (Legge 69/2007). Norme sulla promozione della partecipazione alla elaborazione delle politiche regionali e locali.Bollettino Ufficiale n. 1, parte prima, 3 gennaio 2008

Regione Toscana (Legge 46/2013). Dibattito pubblico regionale e promozione della partecipazione alla elaborazione delle politiche regionali e locali. Bollettino Ufficiale n. 39, parte prima, 7 agosto 2013 and the updated version of the law: Regione Emilia-Romagna (Legge regionale 3/2010, deliberazione legislativa n. 115/2010 del 4 febbraio 2010). Norme per la definizione, riordino e promozione delle procedure di consultazione e partecipazione alla elaborazione delle politiche regionali e locali

Roman, D., 1988. Acts of Intervention: Performance, Gay Culture, and AIDS. Bloomington, IN: Indian University Press

Roth, M. (ed.) (1983). The Amazing Decade: Women and Performance Art in America. Los Angeles: Astro Artz

Roy, W.G. (2010). Reds, Whites, and Blues: Social Movements, Folk Music, and Race in the United States. Princeton, NJ: Princeton University Press

Roy, W.G., Dowd, T.J. (2010). What is sociological about music? Annual Review of Sociology, 36, 183–203

Snow, D.A., 2004. Social movements as challenges to authority: resistance to an emerging conceptual hegemony. In: Meyers, D.J., Cress, D.M. (eds.), Authority in Contention: Research in Social Movements, Conflict, and Change. New York: Elsevier, 3–25

Street, J., Hague, S., Savigny, H. (1998) Playing to the Crowd: The Role of Music and Musicians in Political Participation. Political Studies Association BJPIR, 2008, 10(2), 269-285

Tidore, C. (2009). Processi partecipativi nel governo del territorio. Metodi per conoscere e decidere. Roma: Franco Angeli

UIS (UNESCO Institute for Statistics) (2012). Misuring Cultural Participation, available at http://www.uis.unesco.org/culture/Documents/fcs-handbook-2-cultural-participation-en.pdf

Van Dyke, N., Soule, S.A., Taylor, V. (2004). The targets of social movements: beyond a focus on the state. Research in Social Movements, Conflict, and Change 25, 27–51

Yankovskaya, G., 2006. The economic dimensions of art in the Stalinist era: artists' cooperatives in the grip of ideology and the plan. Slavic Review, 65, 769–791

Dr Cecilia Dinardi, Department of Culture and Creative Industries, City University London, United Kingdom,
Cecilia.Dinardi.1@city.ac.uk

Urban creativity from below: Exploring the value of grassroots cultural interventions to creative cities

While official culture-led urban regeneration has been widely documented, urban revitalization from below has been overlooked in academic and policy debates. This paper engages with the question of urban creativity in Latin American cities by examining how grassroots interventions shape public culture in Buenos Aires and Rio de Janeiro. Through desk-based research on the conversion of industrial factories into cultural venues, the paper argues for the value of informal grassroots interventions for developing inclusive creative cities. By bringing to the fore alternatives to exclusionary strategies for urban renewal, the paper seeks to de-centralise the production of knowledge about creative cities.

Culture-led urban regeneration, grassroots creativity, Latin American cities

Introduction

Over the last few years there has been a rise of urban creativity and a fascination with creative city policies. Creative cities have been put at the centre of urban policy through different initiatives, such as the creation of city indexes; governmental support projects and regional networks; experience-exchange platforms, blogs and national digital portals; reports, handbooks and countless papers; new postgraduate courses; and a plethora of consultancies offering toolkits and mapping assessments, among others. Examples of these initiatives can be found around the world, from Europe and North America, to Asia and more recently, African and Latin American cities. In particular, creative city policies have ranged from supporting the cultural and creative industries locally, to launching creative industries observatories and cultural industry markets, and implementing flagship cultural developments. Clearly, there is a strong policy, academic and economic interest in developing, understanding and selling creative cities, respectively.

However, little is known about the ways in which grassroots cultural groups develop forms of urban creativity from a bottom-up, rather than a top-down perspective. Grassroots initiatives express the inherently political nature of cultural activities and their potential for social change. They 'challenge prevailing cultural values and political institutions, by refusing some spatial forms, by asking for public services, and by exploring new social meanings for cities' (Castells, 1983:15). The work of grassroots cultural groups constitutes an alternative to mainstream cultural and creative projects: their conceptions of culture, creativity and the city tend to be closely associated with social transformation through active citizenship, social inclusion and solidarity. This suggests a different view of the role of culture in the city, when compared to an official policy narrative that invokes culture as a panacea (Dinardi, 2012) for place-making, city marketing and urban regeneration. These two types of cultural and urban imaginations – grassroots and official – tend to be researched separately from each other as if one exerts no influence over the other. Yet grassroots projects often develop in response to official policy-making; thus, it is necessary to put them in dialogue to both research the existing tensions that often accompany the realm of cultural policymaking and assess the prospects for future collaboration between policy and practice.

The aim of this paper is to reflect on how grassroots cultural initiatives shape forms of public culture in the city and contribute, in an informal manner, to the development of inclusive creative cities. It will examine one main question: In what ways do grassroots cultural initiatives contribute to urban revitalisation? This is of interest because grassroots cultural groups' work represents alternative forms of culture-led urban regeneration, ways of enhancing city areas through cultural activities. Their work often goes unnoticed by local authorities, who are more concerned with investing in high-impact capital projects or organising festivals that will attract media coverage. Informal cultural groups work in spaces that are often self-managed, with limited resources, run on collaboration and are environmentally friendly. They are regenerating the city through culture – in its re-signification of abandoned spaces, its transformation into active cultural venues, its practices of public participation. In doing so, they are creating a public culture – a culture that is not regulated by a market logic but one geared towards social transformation.

Based on a review of relevant literature and desk-based research into cultural groups' initiatives, the paper is divided into three sections. The first discusses the concept of grassroots culture; the second examines two case studies, one in Buenos Aires and one in Rio de Janeiro, involving recovered factories through cultural use. Finally, the third section brings the theoretical discussion and the empirical analysis together in order to open up a space to think urban creativity differently. The paper concludes by arguing that in an international context in which urban cultures are mostly studied from a prevalent economic perspective, it is time for urban planning to look at the grassroots to inform the making of cultural and creative city policies, in a way that reflects more closely the everyday experiences, views and needs of those working in the city's cultural sector.

Methods

This paper is based on exploratory research as part of a new postdoctoral qualitative research project. While fieldwork for this project in Rio de Janeiro and Buenos Aires has not taken place yet, the context of an international conference such as Lisbon Street Art & Urban Creativity represents an opportunity to test ideas through critical debate with other experts in the field. Given the early stage of this project, this conference presentation is based on secondary research into the selected grassroots cultural initiatives, particularly an analysis of the information contained on the groups' official websites, and the media coverage of their work. It will be followed up by in-depth interviews with artists and other cultural workers as well as on-site observations later this year.

I have chosen two case studies for this paper: Fabrica Bhering in Rio de Janeiro, Brazil, and IMPA Ciudad Cultural in Buenos Aires,

Argentina. These cases have been selected as they illustrate bottom-up process of revitalisation of abandoned urban infrastructure (factories) through culture and the arts, and are on-going interventions. Equally, they represent alternatives to widespread top-down strategies of culture-led urban regeneration. The focus on cultural grassroots projects responds to their progressive political nature, social goals and capacity to imagine alternative models of society and national identity. My previous research into the ways culture shapes urban imaginations and city branding (Dinardi, 2007) showed that grassroots initiatives indeed offer alternative understandings of culture, citizenship and the future of the city, to those of the local policy-makers who are often concerned with culture insofar as it contributes to tourism, place-making, and economic development.

The research is of comparative nature. It compares grassroots cultural and creative development initiatives with a visible impact on urban space. The choice of this unit of analysis responds to the project's specific aim to identify ways of imagining cultural and creative initiatives which are socially progressive, inclusionary, community-led and successful according to those who developed and implemented them. In view of the existence of a vast array of research on top-down, large-scale urban development projects, often led by governmental organisations in partnership with the private sector and/or driven by real estate interests, this research will shed light onto a much less examined area of cultural and creative urban development involving bottom-up processes of material transformation. These questions become more urgent in view of the existing need for comparative research across different urban experiences, in particular with a focus on those cities which have been ignored by the academic literature, with the aim of developing 'an international and post-colonial approach to urban studies (Robinson, 2011:2). Although located in specific cities and situated within particular historical and political contexts, the transformation of the built environment through cultural and creative public policies, private projects and community initiatives cannot be understood detached from a global phenomenon of urban transformation and creative economy growth which is rapidly expanding across the globe.

The role of the grassroots in culture-led urban regeneration

The grassroots is a constituent part of urban life. From a conceptual perspective, grassroots cultural interventions refer to the activities organised, developed and implemented by amateur, participatory, activist, voluntary, independent, community, informal or non-commercial groups. This vast and heterogeneous sector comprises myriad cultural forms, ranging from community radio, activist theatre, experimental poetry and squatted arts factories, to social movements' cultural festivals, social circus, street performers, arts collectives, informal crafts fairs and improvised music venues. The grassroots, then, functions as an umbrella term that encompasses a range of different initiatives that often share a common attitude (reluctance to become part of the mainstream), a similar work logic (non-for-profit) and the same organisational dynamic (collaborative, self-managed, horizontally-run).

Grassroots cultural interventions have been researched from different disciplines and perspectives, from the study of activism and social movements in sociology and political science, to the analysis of community development and empowerment in urban studies, anthropology and social psychology, and the emergence of oppositional subcultures and political resistance through the arts in cultural studies. In terms of what concerns this paper – the way these groups contribute to urban revitalisation – several policy reports and academic publications agree on the existence of a significant knowledge gap in how grassroots cultural groups contribute to society.

From a policy perspective, there has been growing interest in the grassroots cultural sector. A recent publication by the Arts Council England (2014) compiled the limited empirical evidence on the benefits of culture and the arts to health, economy, and community life, stating that there are important gaps in the evidence-base on the economic impact of grassroots and amateur arts activities. Similarly, in its extensive report on the current state of the creative economy in cities, UNDP and UNESCO (2013) expressed great interest in the grassroots sector, particularly community-based creativity, pointing out that informality shapes the creative economy in so-called developing countries. A main issue considered in the report is how to build creative economies from the grassroots level, based on 'whatever materials and resources are available' (p.98). The challenge is how to map existing local assets - cultural, economic, institutional and physical - that enable policy development (UNDP and UNESCO, 2013:109). In a similar way, the World Cities Culture Forum, a collaborative platform of cultural policymaking, in first updated report (2013), which contains comparative cultural statistics and profiles about twenty one cities, stressed how the dynamism, vitality and diversity of world cities are expressed in their growing informal cultural scenes. The report reveals the notable lack of statistics about informal culture, despite being an important economic and social attraction in cities. It identifies the work dynamics and potential contribution of informal culture as an area of growing policy interest where further research and data would be most valuable.

From an academic perspective, within the vast research on culture-led urban regeneration, some studies have shown interest on the role of the grassroots. Research has focused on the extent to which artists accompany urban strategies (Zebracki and Smulders, 2012); how self-managed community cultural projects can lead to collective action and empowerment (Matarasso, 2007); the need to resort to local cultural resources and community mobilisation for successful urban regeneration (Lin and Hsing, 2009); and the ways public art can facilitate social inclusion in the city (Sharp, Pollock and Paddison, 2005), among many others. In studying and measuring the contribution of culture to regeneration, Evans and Shaw (2004) have identified three models involving the deployment of cultural activities, one of which would include the grassroots as a key player in shaping regeneration outcomes. The first model, what they term 'culture-led regeneration', is based upon high-profile flagship architecture as the main driver for regeneration through the construction or re-use of buildings for cultural purposes. In the second type, 'cultural regeneration', cultural activities constitute an integral part of urban policies and the arts are more deeply integrated throughout the policy process. Finally, in 'culture and regeneration' cultural interventions result from a less planned, more organic process initiated by local residents or organisations with the aim of re-using redundant buildings in their neighbourhoods – grassroots cultural interventions would be included under this third model.

There have been several efforts to engage with bottom-up cultural practices in the city. For example, analysing Dutch cities, Zebracki and Smulders (2012) comparatively examine cases of urban regeneration which have been 'accompanied by' artists. They look at two cases: one in Utrecht, where artists were offered buildings for cheap rent in exchange of a financial contribution towards cultural activities in public space involving the local community; and another in Rotterdam, where artists were offered affordable work and living spaces through a partnership between housing corporations, the city district and other civil-society organisations. In this analysis, housing corporations occupy a space perceived as left vacant by the local government as a result of its insufficient service provision. While the authors point out that 'bottom-up, grassroots artists-accompanied urban regeneration may spur sustainability in cultural planning' (p.622) and acknowledge that rarely culture represents a goal in itself in the planning of urban public space, these cases are examples of housing corporations-led process of urban regeneration, rather than processes initiated by artists themselves.

Another example is that of Lin and Hsing (2009)'s study of community participation in culture-led urban regeneration in Asian cities. They argue for the need to mobilise existing cultural resources through the active involvement of local communities in festivals and heritage renewal projects, which stress the need to move beyond the instrumentalisation of culture through flagship cultural developments. A third example is the study of public art, which has also looked at its various impacts on the city. However, the use of public art can be deployed both for inclusionary and exclusionary purposes as part of wider urban strategies (Sharp, Pollock and Paddison, 2005). Despite its contribution to urban creativity and revitalisation, the use of public art, often commissioned by local authorities, is commonly seen as 'the lipstick on the gorilla or as sticking plaster for a broken back' (Evans and Shaw, 2004:14).

The scoping study conducted by Ramsden at al. (2011) showed that participation in community arts activities produced impacts of different sorts, such as improving participant's mental health and wellbeing, helping to secure paid jobs in the creative industries, enhancing educational achievements and work performance. These activities also contribute to the economy through the hire of resources locally. The growing number of amateur arts groups in England, for example, which currently account for over 49,000, shows the importance of a sector which nonetheless remains largely overlooked as research is limited and fragmented (Ramsden et al., 2011). Despite increasing interest in the grassroots in studies of urban cultures, these activities remain largely invisible to policy and their scope, difficult to define.

Case studies from Latin American cities
Fabrica Bhering, Rio de Janeiro, Brazil

Originally a chocolates and sweets factory, Fabrica Bhering is today a large centre for arts production located in Santo Cristo, in the port area of Rio de Janeiro. Its 20,000 sq metres provide workspaces to 70 artists and 20 small creative enterprises, working across various cultural fields, from sculpture, fine arts, and photography, to video art, design, restoration, and multimedia. There is also gallery space, a book publisher and a recently open cafe.

Built in 1934, the factory used to employ over a thousand workers in the making of sweets, until 2003 when it had to close down due to economic problems. The company owners (the Barreto family) began to let factory spaces to artists who, from 2010, started to move spontaneously into the building. The Barreto family had a tax debt of R$150,000 with the federal government, which led to a judicial auction in 2011. An offer of R$ 3,2 million was made by a real estate company (Syn-Brasil Empreendimentos) which finally bought the building to the federal government, without informing of the existence of artists-tenants in the factory. The factory owners, in turn, contested the value with which the building was sold as well as the judicial auction, since they claimed they were already paying back their debt. The artists-tenants, unaware of the auction, received eviction notices to leave the factory within thirty days, which they challenged by organising an online campaign to save what had become an 'arts factory'. The judge who authorised the judicial auction is being investigated in view of various irregularities in the action process.

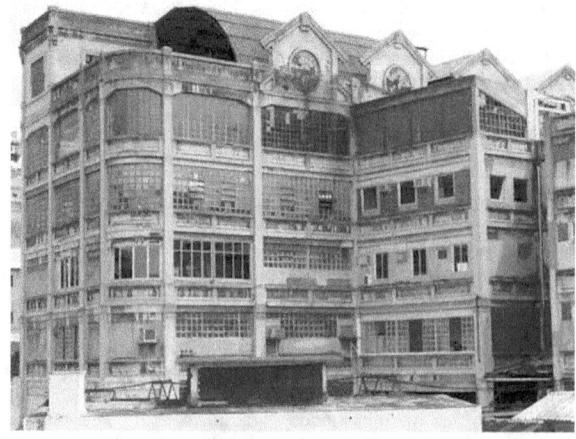

Fig. 1. Fabrica Bhering.
Source: Carlos Ivan / Agência O Globo

Surprisingly, the municipal government announced the expropriation of the building by rapidly issuing an official decree which declared it part of the city's heritage in view of its architectural value and importance for the urban landscape. It will have to pay the indemnification for expropriating the building; however, it is not clear to whom yet, whether the family who owns the factory or the real estate company which bought the building at the auction. Rio de Janeiro Mayor, Eduardo Paes, expressed his support to the fifty artists occuping Bhering in his twitter account (30/07/2012):

> 'The eviction of various art spaces in the old Bhering Factory in the port area makes no sense, even considering the small amount for which the building was taken to auction. We will act to stop this nonsense. It is precisely that function that we want the area to perform' [original in Portuguese[1], author's translation]

It is important to note that Santo Cristo, adjacent to the Gamboa and Saude districts in the centre of Rio de Janeiro, is part of what is termed the city's port area, currently undergoing dramatic transformations in light of the preparations for the 2016 Olympic Games. The municipal government's large urban operation, Porto Maravilha (Wonderful Port), seeks to revitalise Rio's decayed port region and boost its economic development through a number of high-impact interventions in public space, transport, urban infrastructure, culture and heritage, and property development (mostly for commercial, residential and institutional use). The operation is supported by the state's and federal's governments and managed by a new company created for the region's urban development (CDURP), which works under municipal control. In terms of cultural development, initiatives include the creation of new infrastructure (Museu de Arte do Rio de Janeiro and Museu do Amanhã), restoration of heritage buildings, and a series of events, festivals and entrepreneurial activities, which result from the Porto Maravilha Cultural awards. This competition has recently awarded 35 cultural projects to revitalise heritage and foster cultural development in the port area.

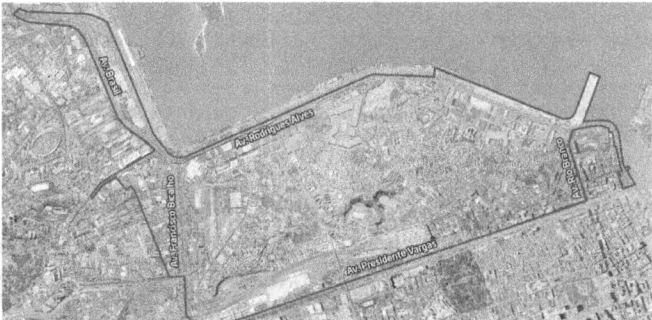

Fig. 2: Rio de Janeiro's 5 million sq mts region of the Porto Maravilha programme. The red spot shows the location of Fabrica Bhering [author's composition]. Source: Porto Maravilha's official website.

While Brazil has experienced continuous economic growth over the last years, inequality, corruption and violent crime persist in cities like Rio de Janeiro. The series of massive protests that took to the streets in Rio last and this year illustrate the generalised social discontent with the government, the existence of structural problems such as political corruption and an inefficient provision of public services. In this context, the organisation of international sporting events in Brazil - the 2014 World Cup and the 2016 Olympic Games - has triggered both urban redevelopment programmes and resistance to the displacement of poor residents from the port area.

It is interesting in this case, apart from the material transformation and re-signification of abandoned industrial space, the changing relationship between the artists and the local government. Today the factory functions as an intermediary between the local residents and the newly transformed port area led by the local government. The planned transformations for the port area have spurred resistance from residents, many of whom were evicted to give way to the new developments. The artists created a civil association (Associação Civil Criativa Orestes 28, aka ACO28) whose mission is to work along three axes: strengthening the links among the factory workers, establishing cultural partnerships and professional relations in the field, and improving the experiences of those visiting or living in the area (ACO28, official website). By creating this association Bhering artists successfully applied for government funding (Porto Maravilha Cultural awards) to implement the on-going event En Torno da Fabrica. It aims to strengthen the relationship between local residents and the factory's artists by offering temporary arts workspace for free to local residents, and includes exhibitions, open ateliers and performances.

The transformation in the life of this factory exemplifies wider socio-economic and urban processes taking place on a global scale. 'The history of Bhering is the very history of the development of the occupation of Rio de Janeiro city', as the businessman Rui Barreto stated in an interview. Fabrica Bhering, far from being an invisible underground initiative, is today listed in Mapa de Cultura, a state government's online platform and has appeared in the Time Out magazine too. Perhaps the future development of Bhering will also reflect the recent changes Rio de Janeiro's port area is going through.

IMPA Ciudad Cultural, Buenos Aires, Argentina
Before examining the emergence of IMPA it is necessary to give a brief account of the context out of which it was born. In 2001

Argentina experienced a profound crisis of multiple forms. The implementation of a series of neo-liberal policies, particularly during the 1990s, created a context of economic instability with substantial foreign debt, the privatisation of key public services, spending cuts suggested by the International Monetary Fund, long recession (between 1998-2001) and increasing social exclusion with high unemployment rates and incessant strikes. In such a context, the devaluation of the national currency in a highly dollarized economy and the governmental restriction to access and withdraw personal savings in banks sparked social protests across the country, including riots and supermarket looting. On 19th December President De La Rua imposed martial law. But pot-banging protests (cacerolazos) took to the streets demanding 'throw all politicians out!' (que se vayan todos!). The Economy Minister resigned. Protests were violently repressed and left over 25 people dead and over 400 injured. They finally led to the resignation of President De La Rua, who abandoned the Government's House in helicopter. Three temporary presidents followed, until Eduardo Duhalde took over the national government in January 2002. Over a period of two weeks, Argentina had five different presidents.

In the aftermath of this financial, social, political and institutional crisis, Argentina witnessed the return of barter clubs and alternative currencies, the emergence of new political actors such picket organisers and spontaneous neighbourhood-based public assemblies, and an explosion of the 'recovered factories' (fabricas recuperadas) phenomenon across the country, which accounted for 170 factories between 2001-2003 (Micheletto, 2003). IMPA was the first factory to be taken by workers. Founded in 1910 with German investment, IMPA produced aluminium and plastic packaging in three industrial plants in Buenos Aires, being the one in the Almagro neighbourhood the only that persists to the present day. In the 1940s the company was nationalised and from 1961 was run by a cooperative. The 1990s were tough economic times for IMPA and many other national factories with widespread unemployment, labour precariousness and interrupted production; its administrators sought to declare bankruptcy due to a substantial debt. However, in 1998 workers occupied the factory and managed to re-negotiate the debt. They began to work in the factory, despite receiving little or no salary, through a self-managed cooperative and with limited financial and infrastructural resources.

Apart from producing aluminium packaging, a year later the factory started to produce cultural activities. An open cultural centre was created, IMPA Ciudad Cultural, and began to offer community workshops across a range of areas, ranging from popular music, theatre, puppetry and dance, to circus, capoeira, mask-making, tango and many more. There is also a theatre, a radio and a TV channel, a free health centre, a university, a popular education college, and an adults' school. Recently a factory museum was inaugurated, recovering the factory's social memory through a photographs and objects exhibition and a film-based debate. In 2000 the factory hosted 70 performances, and in 2001 it was declared 'site of cultural interest' by the municipal government, which described it as the city's most creative and valuable experience, born out of the recent crisis (GCBA, 2001). In 2012 IMPA was one of the venues of the Shakespeare International Festival. According to its website, approximately 20,000 people attend annually the various activities offered at the factory.

Despite working at times with no light or electricity as a result of service-cuts, the factory cultural centre 'has managed to offer productions and expressions of great artistic quality, demonstrating that it is possible to produce valuable cultural facts without large budgets or logics rulled by commercial success' (Bokser, 2010:7). It runs on collaboration, voluntary work, financial contributions from the workers, and the self-management of technical equipment. Bokser (2010) argues that it is precisely in the problems cultural and industrial workers face on a daily basis that bonds are strengthened among them and between them and the building. This, he notes, leads to the erasure of hierarchical distinctions between audiences, workers and artists, as each of them share a common experience: that of being in a factory with very limited resources which in turn allows for the emergence of innovative and collaborative practices.

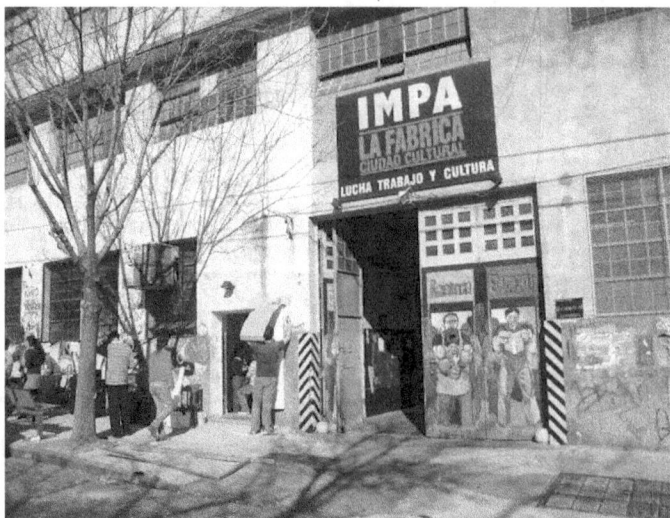

Fig. 3. IMPA's facade. Source: Diego Adrian Fernandez (2013), caminandobaires.com

After a few years of being occupied and run by its workers through assemblies, IMPA became the target of legal disputes with the creditors. Investors were also attracted to the factory and tensions arose with the workers, who were going through economic problems. In 2005 the factory had a critical moment – its cultural centre and college closed down. In 2008 workers were evicted from the premises and a series of protests were violently repressed by the police. Finally, after camping and resisting the eviction, the workers managed to successfully occupy the factory. A new law was also passed by the city's legislature to expropriate the factory in the favour of its workers.

Despite the expropriation law which gave the works the right to stay in the factory, legal disputes with former cooperative members led to the annulation of the law on the grounds of unconstitutionality and a subsequent order to evict the workers from the factory. In turn, an appeal requested to re-consider the annulation but was not given attention. Today IMPA demands the definitive expropriation of the factory. The factory workers' success in self-management has led to the emergence of what has been termed the IMPA's method - an open factory based on the slogan 'occupy, resist, produce'. IMPA's self-managed industrial production has inspired other social organisations' political struggles, cooperative efforts and squaring methods. The case of IMPA Ciudad Cultural is important as it illustrates successful grassroots urban revitalisation through culture and the arts, based on collaboration, self-management and political resistance in times of economic crisis. The initiative has managed to produce metallurgic goods as well as cultural activities, engaged local residents in the new life of the factory, convert an industrial area into a venue for diverse forms of cultural production. While the re-appropriation of IMPA started over a decade ago, its study is still relevant in showing the need to obtain political support via legal recognition of the building's new use, the uncertain future of this type of initiatives, and the extraordinary success in creating a highly innovative cultural space organically, from below, and with limited resources. Although IMPA pioneered the recovered factory movement, other cases such as the BAUEN Hotel which, after declaring bankruptcy in 2003, was occupied and recovered by its workers, epitomised innovative workers-led initiatives that combine self-managed industrial work with creative arts and cultural production.

A comparison of grassroots urban creativity

American urban sociologist Sharon Zukin famously described public culture as a result of a social construction that takes place at a micro, rather than a macro, level:

> 'It is produced by the many social encounters that make up daily life in the streets, shops, and parks – the spaces in which we experience public life in cities. The right to be in these spaces, to use them in certain ways, to invest them with a sense of our selves and our communities – to claim them as ours and to be claimed in turn by them – make up a constantly changing public culture. People with economic and political power have the greatest opportunity to shape public culture by controlling the building of the city's public spaces in stone and concrete. Yet public space is inherently democratic. The question of who can occupy public space, and so define an image of the city, is open-ended' (Zukin, 1995:11)

The dimension of the everyday, that is the repetition and re-production of views, practices and beliefs, is a key element in the making of a public culture. Grassroots cultural groups enact values such as solidarity and collaboration and produce culture in creative ways through their social encounters with the others in the recovered industrial buildings. In fact, 'notions of solidarity, mutuality, and voluntary altruism constitute prime rationales of nonprofit activity' (Toepler, 2003:237). These cultural workers contribute to the reproduction of public life in the city by opening the doors of the factory to local residents, organising a diverse cultural programme collaboratively, and striving to obtain official political support for the sustainable development of their grassroots projects. In what follows I provide a preliminary comparison between the two cases, focusing on four analytical dimensions: the relationship between the grassroots cultural groups and the local authorities, urban transformation, cultural offer and audiences, and future prospects.

Relationship with the local authorities

The relationship between grassroots and official practices is complex, varies across cases and defies easy demarcation, resisting simple categorisations between the formal and the informal. The IMPA cultural centre applied for state funding without success, for not meeting the city government's safety and licensing requirements for cultural venues (Bokser, 2010), which became stricter after the tragedy of Cromañón in 2004, a music venue in which almost 200 young people were killed in a fire, in a nightclub which had blocked emergency exits and no fire extinguishers despite the government's permission to operate. Unlike IMPA, Bhering artists have recently been awarded municipal government's funding for one of their initiatives involving strengthening the relationship with local residents. It is important to note, thought, that Rio de Janeiro's port area is currently the target of wide urban regeneration programmes, and Bhering has become an un-official partner in delivering such programme.

Urban transformation

While the occupation of Bhering was initiated by one individual visual artist – Vivian Caccuri – who liked the place and then invited her friends to join her; IMPA, in contrast, was occupied by a group of industrial workers who used to work in the premises and wanted to preserve their jobs in a context of tough economic crisis. The factory interior space, in both cases, maintain its industrial features and decay, and was re-signified through arts interventions –creative objects, new colours and unusual materials. This enables the survival of the traces of past industrial uses, maintaining some of the factory memoires alive. Likewise, these traces enable a remembering of the industrial past of the cities and reveal the struggles faced by industrial production of manufactured goods. The exterior space of IMPA, in contrast, has been modified: art murals decorate the factory entrance, whose name has been changed to IMPA, 'cultural city'. Bhering maintained its original façade and name, although, 'creation centre' was added to its name on the factory website. The ways the conversion of industrial factories into cultural venues transform the urban fabric go beyond the physical transformation of space, to encompass urban revitalisation through new perceptions of place, new uses of buildings, the inclusion of new venues into existing cultural circuits – both mainstream and alternative –, and the recovery of derelict infrastructure by grassroots initiatives which fill the vacuum left by the public/private sector.

Cultural offer and audiences

IMPA offers a very diverse offer of activities, which could be grouped under the category of popular culture. Bhering's cultural work, in contrast, concentrates on the arts and the creative industries. While in IMPA a wide diversity of non-commercial cultural and arts activities unusually co-exist in a factory setting with metallurgic workers, in Bhering artists pay rent to use workspace in the factory. IMPA attracts a mix of audiences that bring together adult students, party goers, artists, militants, local residents, and members of other workers' movements and social organisations. Both Bhering and IMPA have established links with organisations which are external to the work made in the factories – from other alternative cultural groups to official arts circuits, such as Rio de Janeiro's Art Festival or Buenos Aires' Museums Night. On the one hand, this represents alternative forms of cultural production in the city. On the other, it highlights the existing interest in the mainstream cultural sector to liaise with alternative initiatives and showcase examples of grassroots creativity in their booklets. Likewise, this integration into formal cultural circuits in the city helps the factories widen and diversify their audiences.

While Bhering artists have come together to create a civil association through which they applied for governmental funding for creative initiatives with local residents, in IMPA cultural resistance and political contestation shape the cultural programme on offer. The potential of cultural activities, such as theatre, to imagine more just societies through collaborative practices, has been invoked by IMPA's cultural workers, when trying to resist the power of large corporations often in charge of capitalist cultural industries (Bokser, 2010). In this sense, a decentralised and horizontal management of cultural activities as well an ad hoc planning and informal decision-making at IMPA allowed for cultural development based on experimentation and the creation of alternative spaces of socialisation which widen social inclusion networks (De Felice, 2007).

Future prospects

Because IMPA has pioneered the recovered factories movement in Argentina, it has accumulated several years of experience in conflict management, receiving support from other social movements and political organisations. Bhering, in contrast, is a fairly recent initiative currently in its early stages. In fact, its early development reminds traditional processes of artists-led urban regeneration contributing to gentrification, a rise in properties and a displacement of local populations, exemplified internationally. As Evans and Shaw (2004:17) state: 'This cycle is now familiar in artist zones in regenerated areas of cities from Berlin, New York and Toronto, to London, e.g. Tate Modern, Southwark and Clerkenwell and Hoxton, in the "City Fringe".' Extreme caution might prevent Bhering artists from becoming part of exclusionary gentrification-led interventions in a much disputed area of Rio de Janeiro. Although the definitive transfer of property ownership to the workers has not yet been accomplished in the cases examined here, it is still the object of legal processes and incessant political struggles.

Conclusion: Towards informal creative cities?

In a global context where culture-led urban regeneration is predominantly examined from a top-down, policy perspective, this paper has sought to explore cases of grassroots urban creativity in two Latin American cities, Buenos Aires and Rio de Janeiro. The analysis has shown how grassroots cultural initiatives have appropriated derelict industrial heritage in those cities and re-signified it through the arts. In so doing, they have contributed to create novel forms of urban creativity. Such creativity is expressed in the creative and spontaneous process through which industrial architecture was appropriated, as well as in the content of what is creatively produced in the factories today.

The analysis of the case studies - Fabrica Bhering and IMPA - has highlighted the ways in which grassroots cultural interventions shape the city's public culture. They do it in myriad ways, from their views of culture as a tool for social transformation and participatory decision-making, to their collaborative practices with others, the self-managed nature of the cultural venues, and the spontaneous recovery of derelict buildings in the city. Overall, the cultural offer of these art factories as well as the organic ways in which they impact on the urban fabric – for instance, by keeping rather than erasing the traces of the building's industrial memories – constitute alternatives to mainstream cultural policies for urban regeneration.

So what are these case studies telling us about urban creativity? At least three important lessons can be drawn. First, that creativity is a contested process, rather than one exclusive to official urban cultural policy interventions. Civil society can mobilise resources, organise itself and have the necessary motivation, born out of direct need, required to take the initiative to find workspace, produce culture, attract audiences and secure support from similarly minded organisations. Second, that grassroots creativity is an open-ended process with uncertain future. The difficulties in predicting the evolution of the projects lies in the complex contexts they are immersed, where political factors, economic capitalist forces, private sector interests, global urban trends, and local circumstances are intermingled. Third, that the creative process of producing arts and cultural activities in recycled spaces finds the freedom of not being attached to particular funding requirements or political constraints under a self-managed model; creativity develops and gives way to a diversity of art and cultural forms, expressed in the varied cultural programme of the factories, especially IMPA. Last but not least, apart from art and cultural forms, strong bonds and new social relations among cultural workers are created in their everyday encounters in the factory, producing and reproducing solidarity, collaboration, and self-organisation, in times of extreme individualisation. This in turn shapes the content and method with which culture is produced, contributing to the survival of public culture in the city.

Several factors currently threaten the future development of bottom-up culture-led urban revitalisation projects, namely, lack of resources, unpaid voluntary work, eviction threats, safety issues, limited technical infrastructure. This signals an area where cultural policy action could be of utmost help while at the same time providing a platform for experimentation in participatory policy design. In this sense, it is necessary to bear in mind what Jenkins (2014:271) stated in reference to a 'participatory turn' in cultural theory and politics:

> *'In some of these cases, the call for participation is largely rhetorical, with mechanisms offering only limited and mostly meaningless ways of entering the process, whereas in others, significant shifts are occurring which are providing the people greater voice and influence in the decisions that impact their everyday lives. It becomes more and more urgent to develop a more refined vocabulary that allows us to better distinguish between different models of participation and to evaluate where and how power shifts may be taking place'.*

In this sense, targeted support programmes could open up new spaces for collaboration between formal cultural policymaking and grassroots cultural practices, and in doing so create an alternative foundation for the development of inclusive creative cities.

Acknowledgements

The author would like to thank the Urban Studies Foundation for funding the research upon which this paper is based through a three-year postdoctoral fellowship (2013-2016) based at City University London.

Notes and references

Arts Council England (2014) The value of arts and culture to people and society. An evidence review. Manchester: Arts Council England.
Bokser, J. (2010) 'Tensiones de la autogestión cultural: el Centro Cultural de IMPA', conference paper presented at the II Jornadas Internacionales de Problemas Latinoamericanos, Universidad Nacional de Córdoba, 19-20 November 2010. Available online at: http://fisyp.org.ar/media/uploads/autogestion.pdf#page=5 [Accessed 20 May]
Bop Consulting (2013) World Cities Culture Forum Report, London: Bop Consulting.
Cheng-Yi Lin and Woan-Chiau Hsing (2009) Culture-led Urban Regeneration and Community Mobilisation: The Case of the Taipei Bao-an Temple Area, Taiwan, Urban Studies, 46 (7), pp. 1317–1342.
De Felice, A. (2007) 'La fábrica cultural, otra forma de producción simbólica', Reflexión Académica en Diseño y Comunicación, 8 (8), pp. 85-94.
Evans, G. and Shaw, P. (2004) The Contribution of Culture to Regeneration in The UK: A Report to the DCMS, London: LondonMet.
Gobierno de la Ciudad de Buenos Aires, GCBA (2001) 'Sitios de Interés Cultural', available online: http://www.buenosaires.gob.ar/areas/cultura/cpphc/sitios/?menu_id=14928 [Accessed 15 May 2014]
IMPA, la fábrica (2014) 'Historia', available online at: http://impalafabrica.org.ar/historia/ [Accessed 15 May 2014]
Jenkins, H. (2014) 'Rethinking 'Rethinking Convergence/Culture'', Cultural Studies, 28 (2), pp. 267-297.
Matarasso, F. (2007) 'Common ground: cultural action as a route to community development', Community Development Journal, 42 (4), pp. 449-458.
Micheletto, K. (2003) 'Rescate a puro candombe', Pagina 12, 20/12/2003, available online: http://www.pagina12.com.ar/diario/espectaculos/6-29498-2003-12-20.html [Accessed 15 May 2014].
Ramsden, H. et al. (2011) The role of grassroots arts activities in communities: a scoping study. Working Paper. University of Birmingham, Birmingham, UK. http://epapers.bham.ac.uk/1555/
Sharp, J., Pollock, V. and Paddison, R. (2005) 'Just Art for a Just City: Public Art and Social Inclusion in Urban Regeneration', Urban Studies, 42 (5/6), pp. 1001–1023.
Toepler, S. (2003) 'Grassroots Associations Versus Larger Nonprofits: New Evidence from a Community Case Study in Arts and Culture', Nonprofit and Voluntary Sector Quarterly, 32 (2), pp. 236-251.
UNDP and UNESCO (2013) Creative economy report 2013 special edition: Widening local development pathways, Paris: UNDP and UNESCO.
Zebracki, Martin and Smulders, L. (2012) 'Artists-accompanied urban regeneration', Tijdschrift voor economische en sociale geografie (0040-747X), 103 (5), p. 615-623.
Zukin, S. (1995) The Cultures of Cities. Cambridge, MA: Blackwell.

Gabriela Vaz-Pinheiro

No passage should go unnoticed:
a case for a critical stance in temporary public art interventions

In 1995 Sara Selwoood, taking the United Kingdom as an example, in her publication "The benefits of Public Art", has debated how permanent public works of art may impact on audiences and public spaces. This book has brought into question the well-doing effects with which many policy makers have attempted to defend permanent works of art in the public realm. However, an analysis of the correspondent impacts and public engagement that temporary works and interventions may trigger still needs to be made.

Since 1995 a lot has happened, and since issues of representation and expression of the political power are less visible in these forms of art, and since what is at stake with temporary processes in the public realm is much more difficult to measure, much more fragile to be granted expression, it may be useful to debate that temporary forms of art in the public space are also, often, very impactful in the contexts where they take place because they may give rise to immaterial and critical processes that should not be overlooked. I will present some thoughts around these issues, thoughts that are in a constant state of fluidity, as they should, and that I hope this text will help take a bit further. These thoughts mainly refer to interventions in which scale and time are inversely proportional to their critical potential, attempting to demonstrate that, the space we live in public, is a shared territory of political tensions, but also a space onto which individual pulsions are projected.

Starting from previous thoughts, expressed in other conferences and publications, thoughts on site, on the idea of the local (which I prefer to call proximity) and on the impact that art practice can have on and withdraw from them, I would like to reiterate that my interests and continuous investigation all started from a dissatisfaction, I believe this is known.

Site-specificity, radicalized mainly by Richard Serra's "Tilted Arc", increasingly became a term that could not be applied to many forms of art practice that were still being called as such. Personally I felt that it did not apply to my practice and that a radical thinking that seemed to make sense in late 70's and a good part of the 80's, did not make sense anymore. This is how I started a PhD and a series of art interventions in different places and contexts.

I will draw from some past writing[1] in an attempt to update this paper with some current and relevant critical thinking on this matter. I have said, on a few occasions before, that I find that the term site-specificity has been too widely used to define forms of working that take their placement as part of their conception. For a number of years now, I have been attempting to explore forms for the definition of the very idea of transference, of transferability, as I will explain later, of the trajective, which are embedded in the connection between art and space.

For the purpose of this paper, and although this will mean to re-take a few steps back from other moments of reflection on these issues, I would like to briefly do a quick analysis of the term site-specificity. The triad of "work of art – observer – site" proposed by Michael Fried stills helps making sense of the terms in question. In this triad the observer and site are made and defined to the image of the work of art, with a Minimalist and abstract root, that is: they are abstract entities as well. This is why this model is not adequate to speak for the work that today is produced from places.
If we change the terms, in line with the progression of critical thinking, the observer becomes a multiple subject expressing the actual condition of the ways in which we position ourselves in the world and if site is considered as place: a locus of experience, memory, dissent. The work of art made to the image of the multiple observers and of site as place therefore becomes of a different kind altogether. In other words, in more recent forms of working the terms in question become multiple in characters, and it is the work of art that is made to the image of the observer as multiple subjects and of the site as place. But I am interested in adding here another direction of relations, because this text is less intended to update the Minimalist triad than in fact it is in reflecting upon the mutual influence between subjects and places.

Miwon Kwon has used the term site-oriented. Her critique of site-specific practices also signals the crisis rose from the fact that works and their site are inseparable, indicating a more flexible approach than theoreticians before her, by privileging an analysis of the new models of public art such as the so-called new genre public art and community based art. In line with Kwon's thinking, we could also proceed by questioning the universal character of the models of representation presented by art institutions themselves even, and more often than not, those supporting art in the public space.[2]
I have also been very interested in what James Meyer[3] calls the literal and the functional sites. And the key point to retain from his notions for us today is that artists may actually reinvent the functions of places, (which may even not be a physical place at all) and map out movements and crossings, fluidities and transferences, recurrences and analogies, anecdotes and minutia, or otherwise blocks of stories that make local histories (histories of proximity) and ultimately how these contribute to the making of History, thus reinventing the functions of the work as well. Perhaps even the functions of History with a capital letter. But I am being too optimistic here.

We know the functions of the work of art have constantly been reinvented across the centuries. From religious to celebrating, from commodity to enlightenment or contemplation, it is perhaps through the changing functions that both the art system and artists attribute to the work of art at a particular time, that new modes of production develop. Differences in function determine differences in out-put and in outcome. All along the last Century, we have witnessed artists moving their focus from outcome to process, from object to event, and although these changes in focus may be followed from developments rooted in performance art, happenings, and generally art that favour time and action over object and contemplation, we may consider major differences.

Forms of public art that privilege place and fluidity will very likely have a strong performative character and an accent on process. In fact, unlike more traditional forms of art, process identifies them perhaps more than outcome. And it is never superflus to draw attention to the dangers presented here… Outcomes sometimes create what I have called before, temporary closures of meaning.[4] They instigate moments in which the audience comes into contact with them but are then carried through to another stage/space. To another possibility of existence. I am extremely interested in forms of art that take in effect a movement of people (what I called earlier the multiple subject: that is, on the one hand, artists; and on the other, audiences, both as witnesses to the work and often as participants) (later we may come back to the hyper rated idea of participation if you like). So I am very interested in the movement of people and of works of art through different kinds of spaces.

James Clifford speaks of what he calls the Art-Culture System[5], trying to demonstrate how objects move through different categories and status. In simple terms, within this System, an object could be produced in a given continent as an everyday tool or icon. Once decontextualized by a field scientist e.g., it could become an ethnographical object, be incorporated into the ethnographical museum and transformed, by means of this institutional conversion, into what we tend to consider a "work of art"; only to move on to be reproduced for sale as a tourist commodity (key ring or a postcard) and thus return into the everyday. It is obviously not the object itself and I am taking a risk here by seeming to be overlapping object and image, image and space, but at their root objects, images and spaces are part of and are inserted into the production of meaning(s) to which I will come back a bit further.

James Clifford's model may help us understand the sort of mobility I have been referring to in the previous paragraphs. It illustrates the differences in function that an object may have throughout the validation processes put in place by the Art and the Museum systems, and it can perhaps be reshaped to fulfil our concerns today with regards to public space and urban interventions. The methodologies from the social sciences help to explain these movements in more detail and artists and creative practitioners may learn from and invent new functions for those methodologies and put them to the use of the work of art[6]. It is crucial for us today to try to understand how these methodologies have influenced the work of art not only in what concerns the character of its modes of production, but also in what concerns the character of its modes of presentification, in which mobility seems to be important. The character of its outcomes, however, tending to seek a status of non-closure does not generate an appeased status…

John Law argues of the social sciences that they can never catch a dimension of life that slides out of the disciplinary methods. In fact neither can history nor can definitions of culture or of society.[7]

He says: "(…) the world is (…) textured in quite different ways. My argument is that academic methods of inquiry don't really catch these. (…) Pains and pleasures, hopes and horrors, intuitions and apprehensions, losses and redemptions, mundanities and visions, angels and demons, things that slip and slide, or appear and disappear, change shape or don't have much form at all, unpredictabilities, these are just a few of the phenomena that are hardly caught by the social science methods."[8] And possibly, that large part of the world left out by other knowledge domains, is bequeathed to art to grasp, address or redress.

Despite Hal Foster's claims made from Walter Benjamin's "The Author as Producer", for an intervening artist in society, to a more current "(…) object of contestation"[9], that is, "the bourgeois-capitalist institution of art (the museum, the academy, the market, and the media), its exclusionary definitions of art and artist, identity and community"[10], claims that justify for him the so-called ethnographic turn at the end of last century; despite those claims, I was saying, we are ever more aware that neither to base knowledge in ethnography, history or statistics will produce a reliable account of the world, nor a truly post-autonomous art will ever prove and sustain its existence without acknowledging there is no solid and permanent terrain for its very definition. For better and for worse.

Foster continues: "(…) the subject of association has changed: it is the cultural and/or ethnic other in whose name the committed artist most often struggles" (Foster, 1996, p.173), to which I would like to add that, in such a struggle, it is the very nature of artistic practice that comes, as I hope to demonstrate, to be questioned and reformulated.

From Jacques Rancière, and in the follow up by Claire Bishop, recent art is constantly shifting between the condition of autonomy, considered as indispensable for the delivery of aesthetic freedom, and authoring license and heteronomy. The complete quote reads as follows: "Rancière argues that the system of art as we have understood it since the Enlightenment—a system he calls 'the aesthetic regime of art'—is predicated on a tension and confusion between autonomy (the desire for art to be at one remove from means-end relationship) and "heteronomy (that is, the blurring of art and life)".[11]

It seems that art is constantly aiming for an uncontaminated condition, promise laid void by a failed Modernism but still holding a strong grip for the sake of artistic freedom, at the same time that it dreams of a sense of a total experience, the immersion of both art and life in each other, that feeds from the notion of a "total art" defended by Kaprow in his famous Essays.

This deep contradiction leaves artistic practice stranded at the limbo of formal externalisation[12] as opposed to allowing for a ground in which the aesthetic would move into its inherent political consequences, as Rancière suggests, a condition that would, in extremis, let go of any formalisation, since the political is an acted becoming. And this begs the question: What is the form of the political? A question that I hope will remain in our critical space for a while longer!

The argument for an art that refuses the placidity of pure contemplation but does not want to be ideological; an art that rejects aestheticization but demands for mechanisms through which it is able of conveying the aesthetic experience; an art that will drink from the source of the history of art but will open itself to the readings and contributions of ordinary or uneducated people; the argument becomes insoluble if we are to seek for a point of appeasement. And I refer to Claire Bishop again:

> "(…) I would argue that unease, discomfort or frustration – along with fear, contradiction, exhilaration and absurdity- can be crucial to any work's artistic impact." (Bishop, 2012, p.26).

This uneasiness is absolutely key if we want to give clarity to the unfounded but generalised hopes that art, particularly the socially engaged type, as well as temporary forms of art in the public space, are meant to bring a better life to those touched by it, hopes that foster romanticised notions of community/ies and expect a resolution of any alleged social issues the projects may be addressing. Socially engaged processes are not happy, nor bring them a bright future to those involved, but instead they may enable for critical processes to be started. They induce awareness, and the discomfort Claire Bishop is talking about is very often a means for a process of disclosure of one's own position in society, and that is, in itself, a valuable tool for a more empowered social condition. Bruno Latour, paraphrasing Souriau, says *"(...) without activity, without worries, and without craftsmanship there would be no work, no being."* (Latour 2011, p.10).

I am very interested in how art projects can move through all those categories, through all these different spaces. I am very interested in what happens to meaning in this process. How it is shaped, perceived and constructed, and how the system that enables art works to be considered as such, can actually participate in this construction at the same time that it is somehow tricked into validating objects or actions that would not otherwise enter it.

I am very interested in how art projects raise and reflect upon questions such as: what is there, in art made in response to a particular place that may actually be transferable? What is there that artists may detect (with their very distracted or visionary eyes) under the surface of what we call reality, that can be reinvented within new functions for a place? Perhaps even, what is there, in the mundane and harsh realities brought about by technocracy and a complex and not always just society that artists may approach critically or creatively?

I suppose there are no clear cut answers to these questions, nor is there a unique and universal way of working with them. One of the points made by these ways of working is that art is no longer considered to be a universal given, but it can perhaps speak across differences. Or it can try. Perhaps.

I often ask why, in that broad picture we have become used to call global, artists often chose to work more and more locally? Or in proximity, a word I prefer. I am very interested in this apparent contradiction. That the more our world becomes a vessel with no boundaries; the higher number of artists seems to chose to work geographically and in a detailed manner. I suppose the answer to this is more in the transferable nature with which I have attempted to define these forms of thinking and working, than it is in some form of specificity a place an artist chooses to work from may have, so we need to revise the term specify as well. And I do not believe it is by antithesis, (between local and global, close and farther, and so on) nor it is by antinomy, but by fluidity.

Can we reflect upon the map of a locality in proximity to our neighbourhood, our city, our country - and make something that could enable us to navigate a different world? How are the mappings of our own worlds of importance to others? And ultimately, in what ways does it matter where we are in the world?

How can we be aware of the permeable character of our everyday life and, consequently, our thinking and our artistic work, and still resist grabbing the cultural recurrences of the everyday to feed the work we do as if they were buoyants of identity or markers of specificity?

In this sense, specificity would only be at the service of cultural allegories, amongst which the so-called universal character of art can be considered. As artists and thinkers, we are left with the great difficulty of trying to negotiate private (or local if you prefer) meaning, with the transversal aspiration of the resonance of the work of art, its communicative and consequently less private (or less local if you prefer) function. Because the true universal character of the work of art can only be that we are able of imprinting onto it something that will allow it to speak from the particular and resonate to others. So we move from specificity to an idea of transferability.[13]

Paul Virilio speaks of the notion of trajectivity. Besides objectivity and subjectivity as means to "know" the world, the notion of the trajective adds a sense of motion and fluidity to our knowledge of the world and how we position ourselves in it. In fact, we know the world because we move through it, and movement may not necessarily have a purely physical dimension, and because the here and now is sometimes indistinguishable or contains in it itself the there and then.

To describe this Kenji Nishitani uses the concept of sunyata, roughly translated to 'becoming', in which any given being is simultaneously what it was, is and will be (become).[14] If we consider culture (and cultures) to be a permanently remade territory and I believe we agree on this notion of culture, if there is no appeased frame for a stable definition of the present, then we must at least attempt to understand our positioning in the world in relation to that sense of becoming. Temporary interventions act on a level of becoming that is so difficult to consolidate, they shake up certain aspects of a public stability that may not necessarily express a sense of simultaneity and progress to an idealised cultural condition of a society, and this is why they tend to be undervalued. I have recently written that we need monuments that represent the fluidity of our experiences, the sensitivity for the living, and the detail of that which is susceptible.

So how does experience avoid annihilation when it becomes an object of observation or reflection? How does a collective experience avoid becoming a frozen narrative? A dilapidated representation of sorts? How can multiplicity be expressed in a single image or object? And how can the passage of people, time and narratives be materialised in such a way that it may be experienced by others? To measure the true character and impact of the experience of a temporary work of art in the public space becomes a hard task, when, more often than not, questions of entertainment or embellishment come to the fore. And when the expectation of an audience is not the driving force of something taking place in public, again more often than not, a critical process triggered by a temporary project tends to install discomfort, (Bishop, 2012).

In spite of that discomfort, and if we consider the public domain as one in which the passage from subjectivity to a notion of simultaneity of singularities takes place, what could allow public space to become a space of expression of singularities? The audience's and the artist's?

Malcolm Miles once brought to my attention Anna Arendt's idea in which, "for her, publicity (that is making public) means the condition in which identity formation is enabled amid the perceptions of others, and only amid such perception." So that the visible, or better, making visible, enables existence... oblivion or under-exposure, equals annihilation.

I would not like to think that there is a redemptive drive in art practices that invest in this territory. Singularity is not a resolved matter, nor it is necessarily and always a positive thing. And I do not believe in an appeased form of simultaneity.

I wish I could appease you by saying that the answer is a (perfect) balance between a socially driven art practice and one which entails the artist's individual expression. But I do not hold the key to this balance. I have tried to produce some projects and curate some groups of people (artists and others) in an attempt to experiment possibilities for this equilibrium, or at least to come closer to believing in it. And I can tell you I have come closer to believing in that balance. I have come to believe that sometimes an individual life story, a critical positioning or a simple private gesture may instigate a rather dynamic process of re-evaluation of the very notion of public, of the notion of the public.

Post autonomous art may help to move away from colonising forms art practice, often "too site-specific", too unconcerned with negotiation, but also often insufficiently authorial. Minimalist practice from which radical site-specificity developed, on the one hand celebrated forms of industrial signature, as it would, but at the same time, they stimulated forms of authorial hegemony. Richard Serra's work from the 80's onwards is, for this, the most radical example!

But later, context driven practices have so intensely attempted to annihilate the author (and the idea of an author) that they have become indistinct from either policy or pamphlet... so this does not seem to be the way forward. I believe that authorship should be defended even if in a non-hierarchical mode. I explain - something that could perhaps be called transversal (less vertical) authorship. To summarise, the idea of inside or outside is obsolete, every museum or every gallery space are a public space because they work towards a public (an audience) and towards a political commitment (a choice).

The notion of transferability (although an unsteady fabrication of mine) is presented, in this course of argument, as a means to try to position meaning, interpretation and visuality in a process that allows for their transference between different modes, moments and spaces. And temporary forms of intervening in public (or other type of) spaces seem to convoke our deepest sense fluidity, an awareness of the transitory that we fear, but that we know is our only true condition, as biological and as cultural beings.

How is the notion of the "temporary", the fluidity of human experience, sewn together with the built environment? And how is the built environment made to make sense with the fluidity, chaos and complexity of human experience? I believe that there is a space here that artists and spatial practitioners may grab and grasp critically.

Notes and References

1 Part of this writing has been redone from Gabriela Vaz-Pinheiro, Curating the Local, Some Approaches to Practice and Critique, (Bilingual edition) (Torres Vedras and London, ArtInSite, 2006).
2 Miwon Kwon, One Place After Another – Site-specific Art and Locational Identity, MIT, 2002.
3 James Meyer, "The Functional Site; or The Transformation of Site Specificity" in Erika Suderburg (Ed.), Space, Site, Intervention – Situating Installation Art, University of Minnesota Press, 2000, pp. 23-37.
4 For more on this issue see for example: Gabriela Vaz-Pinheiro, "Beyond site: towards a definition of place-specificity" in Point - Art and Design Research Journal - Framing the Future, N.12, Aut/Win 2001; or the Portuguese version in Margens e Confluências Vol 3, A Ideia de Paisagem, Dec 2001.
5 James Clifford, The Predicament of Culture – Twentieth-Century Ethnography, Literature and Art, Harvard, 1999 (1988).
6 For a more detailed analysis of this turn to the social sciences methodologies see Hal Foster, "The Artist as Ethnographer" in The Return of The Real: The Avant-garde at the end of the century, Cambridge, Mass. MIT, 1996, pps 171-204.
7 Parts of this text also appeared in Gabriela Vaz-Pinheiro, "Contextual practice and beyond, some reflections on ReaKt" in ReaKt - Views and Processes / Olhares e Processos, Project Catalogue, Guimarães 2012, Fundação Cidade de Guimarães, 2013 (Bilingual edition / Versão bilingue), pps 4-11.
8 John Law, After method, Mess in Social Science Research, (London and New York, Routledge, 2004, p.2).
9 In other versions of this text Foster uses the term "autonomous art".
10 Hal Foster, "The artist as Ethnographer", in Hal Foster, The Return of the Real, (Cambridge Mass and London, MIT Press, October Books, 1996, p.173).
11 Claire Bishop, Artificial Hells, Participatory Art and the Politics of Spectatorship, (London and New York, Verso, 2012, p.27). See also Jacques Rancière, The Emancipated Spectator. (Tran. Gregory Elliott) (London, Verso, 2009) and Dissensus: On Politics and Aesthetics. (Tran. Steven Corcoran) (London and New York, Continuum. 2010).
12 Kaprow himself says: "We ourselves are shapes (though we are not often conscious of this fact)". Allan Kaprow, Essays on the Blurring of Art and Life, (Jeff Kelley Ed.) (Berkeley, LA and London, Uni California Press, 1993, p.11).
13 See Gabriela Vaz-Pinheiro, "Da especificidade à transferabilidade: debatendo práticas artísticas place-specific" published online in Boletim da Associação Portuguesa dos Historiadores de Arte, nº 1 (Dez. 2003) and, in bilingual version, "From specificity to transferability: debating 'place-specific' art practices" in ArtInSite - Arte vs Local, Vol1, summer 2004, (Torres Vedras, Transforma ac).
14 See Hal Foster (Ed.), Vision and Visuality, Bay Press, 1988, p.96.

Bishop, Claire, Artificial Hells, Participatory Art and the Politics of Spectatorship, (London and New York, Verso, 2012).
Clifford, James, The Predicament of Culture – Twentieth-Century Ethnography, Literature and Art, (Harvard, 1999 [1988])
Foster, Hal (Ed.), Vision and Visuality, (Bay Press, 1988)
— "The Artist as Ethnographer" in The Return of The Real: The Avant-garde at the end of the century, (Cambridge, Mass. MIT, 1996)
Kaprow, Allan, Essays on the Blurring of Art and Life, (Jeff Kelley Ed.) (Berkeley, LA and London, Uni California Press, 1993)
Law, John, After method, Mess in Social Science Research, (London and New York, Routledge, 2004)
Meyer, James, "The Functional Site; or The Transformation of Site Specificity" in Erika Suderburg (Ed.), Space, Site, Intervention – Situating Installation Art, (University of Minnesota Press, 2000, pp. 23-37)
Miwon Kwon, One Place After Another – Site-specific Art and Locational Identity, (MIT, 2002)
Rancière, Jacques, Dissensus: On Politics and Aesthetics. (Tran. Steven Corcoran) (London and New York, Continuum. 2010)
— The Emancipated Spectator. (Tran. Gregory Elliott) (London, Verso, 2009)
Vaz-Pinheiro, Gabriela, "Beyond site: towards a definition of place-specificity" in Point - Art and Design Research Journal - Framing the Future, (N.12, Aut/Win 2001); Portuguese version in Margens e Confluências Vol 3, A Ideia de Paisagem, Dec 2001
— "Contextual practice and beyond, some reflections on ReaKt" in ReaKt - Views and Processes / Olhares e Processos, (Project Catalogue, Guimarães 2012, Fundação Cidade de Guimarães, 2013 (Bilingual edition / Versão bilingue), pps 4-11)
— "From specificity to transferability: debating 'place-specific' art practices" in ArtInSite - Arte vs Local, Vol1, Summer 2004, (Torres Vedras, Transforma ac)
— Curating the Local, Some Approaches to Practice and Critique, (Bilingual edition) (Torres Vedras and London, ArtInSite, 2006)

Victor Correia, Ma. in Art Philosophy and Aesthetics Mestre em Estética em Filosofia da Arte, Faculty of Letras, University of Lisbon. PhD in Political Philosophy, Sorbonne, Paris. Post-Doctoral researcher at the Faculty of Social Sciences and Humanities, NOVA University of Lisbon

Public Art: a Conceptual Problem

There are many different meanings and interpretations of the concept of public art, which lend themselves to great ambiguity, and that we analyzed here. Alternatively, other names have been proposed, which also we reviewed here, and that we believe are also ambiguous. The main contestation to the concept of public art consists of the statement that all art is public, so there isn't sense to talk about public art. The main reason of the dispute is the confusion between fact judgment and value judgment. Given that with the concept of public art we make a fact judgment, according to which public art is the art placed in the public space, so only some art may be regarded as public.

Art, public space, ambiguity, fact judgment, value judgment

MEANINGS OF THE CONCEPT OF PUBLIC ART

There are different meanings and a plurality of interpretations about the concept of public art. For example, in 1950 Gilbert Seldes created the concept of public arts to speak about radio, film and television,[1] but this meaning isn't the meaning in which is usually to employ the concept of public art, and that is the meaning used by us : the art situated in the public space, in the spatial sense (its territorial framework).

An important difficulty in understanding the concept of public art, comes from the parallelism with other domains also designated as public, such as public school, or public health (for example). According the Administrative Law, as Marcelo Caetano says, "(...) are proprietary directors the things belonging to a person of public law, which due their natural or functional destination produce direct and necessarily public utility (...), so that a thing has a public utility when only plays its particular role serving the use of everybody, or constitutes the goal of a public service or securing directly a goal of the State ".[2] So, this is the things produced by the State, or kept under his management, which is lawful to everybody use individually or collectively, with the restrictions imposed by the law or by the administrative regulations. In legal terms the enjoyment, the use of public things, is their intrinsic function, so that or are used for all or for the benefit of all. Public utility means the public use.

But, what relationship can be established with the art? It's possible to speak about public domain in art as we do the same whit other areas? These areas are for example, as we have said, public education, and public health. In the case of public education or public health, or health education for all, intending it to mean that everyone can, respectively, be taught, or be treated medically, and everyone can enjoy these public services. However, we can't say this in relation to art, not even in relation to the so-called public art, that although placed in public space is spatially but not culturally near everybody, especially the contemporary art, due to the plurality of aesthetic languages in general, and due to the complexity of some of them in particular, facing more for specific publics.

The public art is the art of all, understanding the meaning of the word of all as property? It's possible said that a public school and a public hospital belongs to everybody, but in the case of art, while certain work of art acquired in a gallery belongs only to your buyer, or a particular work of art that exists in the Church belongs to the Church, in the case of a work of art that is part of a building which is public property, in this sense this work of art also belongs to all, so in this sense this is public art. The art situated in a public building can considered as public art The art situated is in a public building can considered as public art . However, this isn't the meaning of the concept of public art, which refers to the art that is placed in the public space. One thing is the art which is placed inside a public building, and another thing is the art that is placed and highlighted in the public space (in the physical and territorial meaning), and that's why so-called styling as public art.

But the title of art as public can have other meanings, due to which there is a contestation. According this contestation, the art is always public; the art is always a product of the public and for the public (public as synonym of society). As a product of the public, this means that the political, economic, social context, etc., determine the artistic production, the art feeds on ideals and values that aren't born by spontaneous generation in the soul of the artist, and that art can't be reduced to a mere manifestation of feelings, ways of being and concessions of each artist, because it found a supra-individual dimension, the art is always a reflection of the public domain, of the society, which directly or indirectly determines the art.

As a product to the public, it means that the art has a character of commitment, conveying values such as religious, political, moral, the art is a form of criticism and complaint, education or indoctrination, and constitutes an act of social intervention, or even of rebellion. The art has a goal fundamentally public, because the art transforms the society, and this goal can be presented in terms of explicit confession (confession of beliefs, doctrines, direct advertising), or in terms of perspective tacitly assumed in the works of art which at first sight seem devoid of any social reference. In short, and as Mikel Dufrenne says, "we can see that society intervenes in the different moments of the process of creation: it's the art that, through the public, asks the creator.(...) It's the art that proposes or imposes on the creator certain intellectual and technical resources developed within system of thought and values, artistic codes, and styles. Is the art that forwards these goods for several circuits and offers consumers. Is the art that judges through those who invest the power to judge ".[3]

Another meaning of the conception of art as public, has to do with their publicity, as something intrinsic to it as art, and in this case it can be said that, as Umberto Eco notes, "Every artist aspires to be read. There isn't private correspondence of any artist (...) that don't demonstrate how this author, even though he knew that it was against the horizon of expectations of the common and current reader itself, aspired to form a future reader, able to understand, and to appreciate, a sign that he was orchestrating his work as instructions for a Model Reader able to realize, to appreciate and love him. There is no author who wishes to be garbled or unreachable ".[4] This conception meets the conception of open work, defended also by this author, according to which the artwork is completed by the public, being "open to a virtually infinite range of possible readings".[5]This means that from the moment when the artist does the work she is of all, she becomes of all, the public takes ownership of it and recreates it.

The conception of Umberto Eco is similar whit the conception in an another author, Jacques Rancière, who contest the opposition between the look and the act, arguing that to look is already an action (the action of observing, selecting, comparing, translating, interpreting, creating an original idea of what is observed). According to Rancière, the reader "composes his own poem with the elements of the poem that he has in front of him," [6] as the actors, the playwrights, and the directors. Refusing the logic of reduced spectator to be passive and dopey, changes the relationship of the theater with the public, making him an emancipated community, which is for Rancière "a community of accountants and translators in which all individuals are active in the construction of the artistic and aesthetic significance of the show".[7] So, there isn't inequality but a fusion of subject in the experience of the artistic experience, in which creativity is also in the side of the public.

On the other hand, the art is public, of the public and for the public, due to the fact that in the spectator she constitute an act of sociability and socialization in frequentation for example of a show or an exhibition of paintings, coming up to the point of these events sometimes being almost in themselves, and so the frequency of the public while subject due more to the public event itself. Even in a public meeting more spontaneous, especially in the context of today's urban society, the works of art (a movie, a song, etc.) are subject of conversation, and the arts acquire an increasingly important presence. The american sociologist Paul DiMaggio, based on various empirical studies conducted in Europe and the United States of America, argues that once people invested in their houses, on television, in the refrigerator, as a form of prestige to show visitors; Today, with changes of sociality, must have capital more mobile, most topics of conversation which can serve to establish relations, bridges with other people.[8] Taking into account the meanings presented, speak in public art would be a kind of redundancy, as with the expression: public spectacle, because all the art is public, and the whole show is public.

However, there is a difference between the spectacle and the art: while for example the theatrical representation to be spectacle has to be public since it is what comes before an audience, the same isn't the case in other art forms. The artistic act in itself (painting, sculpting, etc.) can be done without the public, the artist don't have to have spectators in front of him. On the other hand, the theatre, for example, takes place in front of the public, is something that requires spectators, the act of representing happens along the public. As says Frank Smith, referring to the cct of painting or sculpting, "artists don't need ratings. They can enjoy them, at certain times, and possibly depend on your support or sponsorship by psychological reasons or practices, but the first, the primary and often sole audience of an artist, is the artist himself. The artists create to express themselves, please and satisfy themselves (although they are not necessarily the most pleased or satisfied with their creations)."[9]

In the spirit of this conception, it is necessary to highlight the creative freedom of the artist, whereby the artist in its creation should not be subordinate to public criteria, or other criteria, such as religious, moral or political, by precepts, even if they are aesthetic precepts, and that should not even be limited by the actual objects and the principle of imitation, and should be moved more by the principle of the invention than the social reproduction. In accordance with the principle of the invention in the act of creation, in the art always remains something behind or beyond the public dimension, and is out of the public requirements and out of the spatial and timeline determinism: the act of creation is fundamentally something inside, due to the inspiration, as advocate some authors, of which one of the classical authors most representative is Plato, that presents as an example the poetry: "it isn't mercy of an art (techné) who the poets make works of poetry and say beautiful things about the subjects they are talking (...) but for a divine privilege, and each one can only successfully composed in the genus in which the Muse inspires the poet",[10] a transcendent sense, a mystery, a don't-know-what, according to another classic author, a spanish author of the XVII and XVIII centuries, who says :" in the productions of all the arts there is this don't-know-what. The painters were recognized in his own art, under the name of way, a word that as they understand it, means the same and in the same way confused that the don't-know-what." [11]This means that the art is not unveiling completely, and although the opening to various interpretations, and even with the more objective of discussions, or more explicit content, always remains something unfathomable, ineffable, unconscious, and that the psychology of depths makes the artist's personality reduce: "the artist is at the same time an introvert that touches the neurosis (...) possesses the power to model certain materials to become faithful image of the existing representation on your costume, and connecting to this representation of your unconscious fantasy a amount of pleasure enough to mask or suppress, at least provisionally, the psychological repression".[12]

On the other hand, there are works of art that were intended to be for the public. For example, the famous Portuguese Letters that Soror Mariana Alcoforado wrote to his french lover, not meant to be published, but today are widely appreciated for its literary value. We can perfectly imagine that the nun just intended to give wings to your imagination, and that this lover didn't even exist, keeping to themselves, in the greatest of secrets, the result of their romantic reveries. If that had happened, and the fact we did discover the letters, they would no longer have artistic interest? We don't see reason to deny them the status of a work of art. Therefore, it is perfectly possible to have artists whose works of art are created without having in mind the public.

You can also object to the concept according to which that all art is public, that the concept of public does not constitute a specific attribute characteristic of art, including the so-called public art, since one can use the concept of public to designate the status of public extensible to all individuals, and across all social groups (the population, the people in General), or to give an account of the number of spectators who develop practices of frequentation of events and artistic productions. However, in the case of art does not exist exactly the public but a diversity of publics (in the dances, in the theaters, in the movies, in the classical music, etc.), the art is something from groups and for groups, the art constitutes a reign of differentiation and even segregation, because the art need sensitivities and knowledge to be understood, so the art isn't the public domain, the art isn't for everyone, even the so-called public art, so in practice the art is public only to some people. Even if this situation doesn't happen only with the art, understanding the word public in the meaning of something for everyone, the art is the thing less public that exist, because in the art there is many subjectivity, individuality, and disparity of opinions and tastes, that is more evident in the contemporary art, which directly or indirectly is more directed for a stringent public.

So, everything depends of the uses of the concept of public, which may mean on the one hand the society, the people in general, or on the other hand the number of people who watch a certain show, or who attend a particular cultural event, such as a painting exhibition. The discussion around the question of the art be or not be public is resolved if we understand what is for the artist your audience, not public as a quantitative entity (what belongs to all and for all), but rather the public of a particular artist or of a particular art form, and therefore each art can be considered as public. We arrived to a contradictory situation, which consists in the fact that art that is considered as public (the public art), can be considered as the least public of all arts, because while for example the classical music, the folk art, the ballet, or other forms of art have their audience, though restricted, and only in this sense they are public, the public art on the one hand is an art for everybody (in the sense of placement and visibility in public space), and on the other hand isn't directed to anyone in particular, because this art is not sought or frequented by certain public, this art has a public uncertain, vague and undefined, and therefore doesn't really have any public, this is a public in the abstract sense.

However, if we think about the world of art galleries and in the respective market, as a form of privatization of art, and if you understand the concept of private as opposed to public, so the art present in the private space of the galleries, despite having your audience, is the less public, whereas the called public art, which don't belongs to the art market, and the scope of private collections, is the more public art, directed to the entire audience, on the one hand because it is an art that belongs to all (not is neither a collector nor any institution in particular), and on the other side because it's in the space that belongs to all in the sense of use : the public space. Not only through the galleries, but also through the churches, palaces, and museums, the art is traditionally referred to a private status and segregationist, which decreases or even denies the public meaning (considering as public that it is something for everyone), and as a consequence we can put the emphasis on the public nature of the so-called public art, and defend that this art is really the public art, unlike the art of institutions.

On the other hand, the public nature of the art is something not only about the space but also historically constituted, that grows and changes, the art is something open to different and even conflicting usages that differ with different contexts, because the concept of public, in the sense that today we give her, isn't apply to the ancient and medieval art, because in these times was used a code that everyone understood, and public was all the public community, and there wasn't the notion of the artist as creative individuality. The artist, as today is understood, only appeared with the Renaissance, and is also from Renaissance which the public unit is broken. From now on, the art use codes that are accessible only to certain groups or social classes, the art becomes an aristocratic fact, an idle and solitary cultivation, of an individuality that is stated and opposes to the crowd, this art hit by classes, with their own leisure to devote themselves to the art. The Aestheticism was one of the basic theoretical elements for the emergence of Romanticism, which rejected the utilitarianism of the art and gave a principal value for the creativity, the intuition, the freedom and individual vision of the artist. According to the conception of Aestheticism, advocate of art for art, the art was an end in itself, removing the art from claims to have a public function, social and democratic.

The democratization of art, the extending of the schooling and university education, and technical possibilities of production and reproduction of oeuvres (the press, the screen printing, the audiovisual, etc.), changed in our time this situation, because the art became more accessible to everyone (from the point of view of artistic creation, and from the point of view of the public as spectator). The media made this access a reality, because we can see for example a painting on TV, in a magazine, or on the Internet, which shows the conquest of public space for art, their democratisation, a process that was not always the same throughout the ages.[13\]

As Walter Benjamin says, with the reproduction technique of the work of art, the photography, the television, the radio, the print media, the book fairs, the multiplication of exhibitions, cinemas, theaters, and concerts, the art has become, little by little, something for all. So, as in other areas (public education, public health, etc.), the art has become increasingly public, everyone has been able to have access to art, she has passed increasingly to be something for everyone, in the sense of the possibility of viewing and listening of works of art. On the other hand, there is also the possibility of a greater number of people being artists, both men and women, both rich and poor, and its generalization to all as subjects of creativity, has been advocated by some authors, and even by some artists, that Joseph Beuys is one of the best examples. Beuys intends to put an end to the idea of art as an isolated practice, defending before an expanded concept of art, opening the horizon of artistic creativity and not only beyond the ghetto of art. There are, according to him, a continuity between art and life, putting the art in freedom and free movement. Thus, the works of art abandoned the museums and the galleries to act directly on reality, because as Beuys says, "each man's artist."[14]

The conceptions about the art as public, can be summed up so the three following aspects : every art is public; the art isn't a public thing; only some art is public. The conception according which every art is public, on the one hand has to do with the context and the social purpose of art, and on the other hand has to do with your display and your publicity. The conception according to which the isn't a public thing, has to do with the emphasis on the inner and individual world of the artist, and his inspiration, seeing for instance the art as something ineffable and transcendent, and taking this concept to the extreme, does the artist a be on the fringes of society, especially the genius. For its part, the conception according to which only some art is public refers to a peculiarity of the art, in this case the fact of being placed in the public space (the public art).

However, we can't easily make these separations, that are too reductives. If we limit to the public and the social dimension of art, we fell in the sociologies, if we see the uniqueness of the creator act, the inner world and the personality of the artist, we fell in the psychologies, and if we valuing only the artwork, forgetting the audience and the creator, we fell in a kind of aestheticism. All these approaches are only partly true, but they forget always aspects and fundamental dimensions of the artistic phenomenon, because only the vision of the totality of the artistic reality allows us to understand the multiple interactions between all its elements.

SPATIAL MEANING

The controversy about the concept of public art, presented in the previous chapter, is a consequence of the confusion between fact judgments and value judgments. The fact judgments are judgments that relate to reality, judgments that described only, they merely express certain facts, they result from a finding, they are true or false depending on whether or not to adjust real, they are empirically verified and are subject to consensus, as for example when we say: "much of the Tagus river is located in Portuguese territory". In contrast, the value judgments concerning the quality of the things and of the facts, the appreciation and value that assigns them, these judgment aren't true nor false but positive or negative, aren't checked empirically and don't obtains easily a consensus, as for example when a person make the following affirmation: "Picasso's painting is beautiful".

However, it isn't always easy to make the distinction between fact judgments and values judgments, distinguish between the descriptive use and the value use, as happens for example when we use the word art and the word work of art, because how do you remember Casey D'orey, "these words are ambiguous, because both may serve to designate the kind, class or category of goods to which an object belongs (descriptive use) – how to assign value or artistic merit to an object (use value). And thus the question 'what is art? 'Or ' what is a masterpiece? 'Can both be inquire what objects are classified under ' art ' or ' art ' as be to inquire what objects are good or have artistic value".[15]

   In the case of public art, can be a descriptive use of the term public, or a value use. But the descriptive use and value use can be sometimes mixed. Just as in the concept of art can be a descriptive use or value use, meaning the concept of art an artifact produced by someone, or something with a special quality (artistic), assigning it a value, also the concept of public art can be referring to art placed in public space, simply this fact, or we may be saying that is a good thing (the fact that is placed in the public space). There is an interrelationship between these judgments, and regarding to the two judgments can succeed sometimes a confusion between them, because if we speak about public art saying that is the art located in the public space, and if on the one hand what is in the public space is what is for everyone, and on the other hand if this is regarded as something positive, can then make a value judgment.

The controversy comes from, as we have already said, to make a use value of the term public, wanting with this usage to mean the meanings of the concept of public art seen in the previous chapter, that have to do with the nature and the value of art, leading sometimes to contest the designation of public art, contestation according which all art is public, and don't make sense using the word public. However, the position in which we are to refer to public art is that only some art is public, because with the word public we refer not to the nature or the value of the art, but a fact, because if the public art is located in the public space, and if only some art located on the public space, then just some art is public. So, we employ this concept in the descriptive meaning and not in the axiological meaning (we make a fact judgment, not a value judgment).

In order to avoid the ambiguity of the designation of public art, and according to our meaning (that is consider the art having regard to the place where it is inserted), could be used other designations, for example environmental art, outdoor art, art in public space, situ art, landscape art, street art, urban art, etc. However, also these designations aren't free from ambiguity, also they are vague or little far-reaching, and not express effectively what we intended when we speak about public art.

The fundamental criterion of public art has to do with its accessibility in physical terms, the general public, so the outdoor spaces as spaces where there is the public art. However, saying that public art is one that is accessible to the general public due to the fact that if you find placed outdoors, isn't also correct, because there are works of art placed outdoors that are not easily accessible to the general public, in particular the land art, because although placed outdoors is often distant, placed for example on a mountain, on a plain, on a lake, etc., as for example the Robert Smithson Spiral, in the Great Salt Lake of Utah, in the United States of America.

An appropriate designation might street art, due to the fact that the public art meet on the street. However, the designation of street art isn't also the most appropriate, because there are many public art works that aren't' only in the streets, but also in squares and roundabouts. On the other hand, the designation of street arts usually employed for certain artistic events as contortion, acrobatics, animal tricks or with cards, ventriloquism, clowns, dances, presentations of music, poetry recitals, living statues, etc., who are on the streets without transit of large cities (for example Las Ramblas in Barcelona, or the Rua Augusta in Lisbon). Sometimes the public art is also called urban art. However, it is fair to say that public art is urban art, on the one hand because the urban art includes other artistic expressions, and on the other hand although the public art is a phenomenon more characteristic of the urban areas, particularly the cities, also exists or can exist public art in villages and even in the middle of nature (in the mountain, on the plain, on the beach, etc.), or still in service areas of the highways. Among the various designations, the best alternative would be the art in public space, due to the fact that fit better to a fact judgment, and not a value judgment as one who can lead the designation of public art, and also because is a more comprehensive designation. However, to simply say public space is also not susceptible of clarity, because the concept of public space itself raises too many ambiguities.

Clarifying the meaning with which we employ the concept of public space (squares, roundabouts, streets, boulevards, public gardens, etc.), allow us to employ the expression art in public space, but between the two possibilities (public art , or art in public space), and having determined that the designation of public art has underlying the concept of public space in the spatial sense (being so indifferent employ one or other designation), we opted for the designation of public art, due to the fact that this is the most commonly used designation for the type of art we're talking about.

It is difficult to identify the author who had initiated the designation of public art; however she only appears in the second half of the 20th century, about the contemporary public art. While one can consider that there is already public art in the 19th century, with the commemorative statuary (due to the fundamental criterion here followed: their individualized placement outdoors), his contemporaries referred to him using generally the designation of monuments, since there wasn't the conception of public art, as we understand it today. Also some authors today refer to her with the designation of monuments, preferring the designation of public art for the art placed in public space in our days, not because they don't consider the monuments as art, but precisely because these authors, through the designation public art are doing, not a fact judgment (the fact of being placed in the public space), but a value judgment. One of these authors is for example Siah Armanjani, which states: "the public art is non-monumental. Is downstairs, common and near to the people. It is an anomaly in a democracy to celebrate with monuments. A real democracy should not look for heroes ".[16]

It is true that there are differences between one and another, that's why we distinguish (the traditional public art and contemporary public art), but if the criteria established to consider art as public art is not topological but axiological (its placing in the public space in the territorial sense), then the designation of public art can be for the traditional public art and for the contemporary public art. Although the specificity of the traditional public art is the fact that she is a monument, before there were already works of art placed in public spaces, which weren't monuments, and on the other hand today there are also many works of public art that are monuments. So, according our definition, is correct to apply the expression public art to the art placed in the public space in other times (notably the nineteenth century), as to actually.
The difficulty in identifying the public art also comes from the difficulty in identifying the art itself, given that throughout the History the art has obeyed the radically different definitions, through the various theories: essentialist theories, aesthetic-psychological theories, theories of blurring of art, institutional theories or theories of symbolic functioning, among others, that are restrictive and narrowing definitions, irreducible to a common notion, constantly changing what is considered as art, the boundaries between the various kinds of art, and its relations with the remaining social productions.
Thus, in order to avoid the difficulty and the impasse arising on these theories, we don't enter in the technical criteria that establish that a particular object is considered as sculpture, a certain scenic representation is regarded as theater, or a certain sound is considered music, and we don't enter also on the criteria to be considered as a good work of art. We depart from a consensus, which is the criterion of the theater or the music being considered as art, designating with the word art, the category to which they belong (we do a descriptive use of the concept), even if some specific examples may not be considered as theater or as music, or as good theater or as good music.

Other art forms such as theatre and music, due the fact that sometimes happens in the public space, could also be regarded as public art. However, the key criterion that here we present, for that particular work of art be considered as public art, is the common uses of the word art, that are the so-called fine arts, because when it makes use of the words theater and music is in reference to these forms of art, while making use of the term art is generally as reference to the painting and the sculpture. However, also regarding the expression fine arts, don't enter in this expression some forms of contemporary public art, as for example the video For this reason sometimes is used the designation of visual arts, but that also is not satisfactory, since this designation includes other forms of art, such as the cinema.

So, our emphasis goes mainly for the sculpture and the painting, in our concept of public art. Of course, there are also here some ambiguities, because in the public space there are many sculptural elements, pictorial, and urban design, artistically worked, whose borders sometimes aren't easy to establish from what is meant or what we can understand as public art. In fact, we can find in the public space elements of very diverse nature: historical symbols of the place, and religious elements (cruises); elements of utility character (fountains, lighting columns, signage, telephone booths, mail bottles, benches for people to sit, exhibitors, protective railings, irons to hold bicycles, garbage cans, hose taps in case of fire, iron barriers for cars parking, parking meters, etc.); elements of playful character (gazebos, for example); elements of a non-commercial nature (billboards, kiosks, etc.); aesthetic elements (flowerbeds); elements of artistic character as itself (sculptures, ceramic panels, wall paintings, graffiti).

Regarding to these elements in the public space, some of them may sometimes be considered as public art, although they have another purpose: we refer especially to the utility and commercial character, aimed at purposes such as citizens ' guidance on the public highway, safety, comfort, sale, or use pure and simple, and in this case, as in other criterion to distinguish what is art and what isn't art would be the fact that they have utility, and so another purpose other than artistic.
However, there are many objects of the past, today considered as works of art, whose function was the usefulness: Persian or Greek vases, or certain pieces of furniture as an armchair Voltaire or a dresser Louis XV. One could say that today it no longer has this function, and today may be considered as works of art, while many objects of the public space, such as the street furniture, currently have utility, and in consequence these objects can't be considered as art. However, even today there are objects that despite its usefulness are considered as forms of art, such as jewelry design, design, and fashion. Citing Dorfles, we can say that "if we accept the fact that we can't make a clear hierarchical distinction between applied art and pure art, if we consider art to modern architecture (which often approaches visibly of industrial design, especially in the case of prefabricated elements) will also have to consider art, at least partially, the industrial object."[17]

Therefore, the idea of usefulness by itself does don't constitute a criterion sufficient to prevent the user to consider eventually as public art for example before the sidewalk-mosaic, or currently certain banks which are placed on the street, for people to sit, because although they have a utility function, contain a predominance of artistic elements, and which are sometimes very well-crafted from the artistic point of view. On the other hand, even in the works regarded as artistic works in the strictest sense of the term, there is sometimes some use, as is the case, for example, the public sculpture (rehabilitation, qualification and urban planning, etc.). Even if the usefulness of sculpture isn't the most common meaning of the concept of usefulness, the sculpture is used with a certain purpose, aiming at something through it, so this sculpture also has a utility, despite being art. The sidewalk-mosaic, despite its usefulness as a sidewalk, can be considered a work of art (not referring to the entire sidewalk-mosaic, but a few examples). On the other hand, it should be noted also that some contemporary public artworks include benches for people to sit, and have to be seen as a whole. Therefore, if looking for works that have only an artistic function, which are only art, or aimed only to be art, in the strict sense of the term, one falls in the demand of the so-called art for art, in a kind of aestheticism, forgetting that art isn't an innocent activity, purely gratuitous, closed in itself, but is implicated with the everyday life of the people.

However, although we must consider the field of public art as something large and comprehensive, as happens with art in general, in order to our conceptual reference, and according to the criterion behind established (according to which we rely on the common use of the term art, in particular the reference to the fine arts), consider how public art fundamentally the following forms of artistic expression: sculpture, ceramic panels, murals, graffiti. Some of these artistic expressions, such as sculpture or ceramic panels per se aren't public art, which gives them the category of public art is the fact that they are placed in the public space, and therefore intended to the public in undifferentiated quantity and quality, the unwitting public, because it is an art that isn't wanted, unlike with a painting exhibition, with the theatre, the ballet, the cinema, or with other art forms.

There are other forms of art in the public space, such as installations, photographic panels, collages, works in neon, video, and similar artistic expressions, that are ephemeral, and which can also be regarded as public art. However, our selection in our concept of public art will for the permanent works of art, given that they give identity to the place, and become an integral part of it (the in situ art), that were made expressly for it, lacking its sense (while public art) if they are removed, transferred, or that although haven't been created expressly for a given location; these works became part of a location over the years: giving identity and symbolism to a public space.

Notes and References

1 Gilbert SELDES, The public arts , New York, Ed. Simon and Schoester , 1956.
2 Marcelo CAETANO, Manual de Direito Administrativo, Lisboa, Empresa Universidade Editora, 1937, p. 20.
3 Mikel DUFRENNE, A Estética e as Ciências da Arte, 2°. Vol., Lisbon, Ed. Livraria Bertand, 1982, p. 45.
4 Umberto ECO, Sobre os espelhos e outros escritos, Lisbon, Ed. Difel, 1989, p. 121.
5 IDEM, A obra aberta, Lisbon, Ed. Difel, 1989, p. 92.
6 Jacques RANCIÈRE, O espetador emancipado, Lisbon, Ed. Orfeu Negro, 2010. P. 32.
7 IDEM, p. 35.
8 Paul DIMAGGIO, "Classification in art", in American Sociological Review, New York, vol. 52, Ag., 1987.
9 Frank SMITH, Pensar, Lisboa, Ed. Instituto Piaget, 1994, pp. 133-134.
10 PLATO, íon, Lisboa, Ed. Inquérito, 1992, pp. 533-d-534-e.
11 Benito FEIJÓO, Um não-sei-quê, Lisboa, Ed. Veja, 1998, p. 10.
12 Sigmund FREUD, "Théorie générale des nevroses", Introduction à la psychanalyse, Paris, Ed. Payot, 1932, pp. 354-355.
13 Cf. Walter BENJAMIN, "A obra de arte na era da sua reprodutibilidade técnica", in Sobre Arte, Técnica, Linguagem e Política, Lisbon, Ed. Relógio d'Água, 1992, pp. 71-113.
14 Joseph BEUYS, "Cada hombre , un artista", in Documenta 5-1972, Madrid, Ed. Visor, 1995.
15 Carmo d'OREY, "O que é arte" ? ou "Quando há arte" ?, Lisboa, Análise, n°. 14, 1990, p. 67.
16 In DIAMONSEN, Diálogos sobre a arquitetura, Barcelona, Ed. Gustavo Gili, 1976, p. 20.
17 G.DORFLES, As oscilações do gosto, Lisbon, Ed. Livros Horizonte, 1989, p. 126.
BENJAMIN, Walter, "A obra de arte na era da sua reprodutibilidade técnica", in Sobre Arte, Técnica, Linguagem e Política, Lisbon, Ed. Relógio d'Água, 1992.
BEUYS, Joseph, "Cada hombre , un artista", in Documenta 5-1972, Madrid, Ed. Visor, 1995.
CAETANO, Marcello, Manual de Direito Administrativo, Lisbon, Ed. Empresa Universidade Editora, 1937.
DIMAGGIO, Paul, "Classification in art", American Sociological Review, New York, vol. 52, Ag., 1987
DIAMONSEN, Diálogos sobre a arquitectura, Barcelona, Ed. Gustavo Gili, 1976.
D'OREY, Carmo, "O que é arte" ? ou "Quando há arte ?" , Lisbon, Análise, n°. 14.
DORFLES, G., As oscilações do gosto , Lisbon, Ed. Livros Horizonte, 1989
DUFRENNE, Mikel, A Estética e as Ciências da Arte, 2°. Vol., Lisbon, Ed. Livraria Bertrand, 1982.
ECO, Umberto, A obra aberta , Lisbon, Ed. Difel, 1989.
IDEM, Sobre os espelhos e outros escritos , Lisbon, Ed. Difel, 1989.
FEIÓO, Benito, Um não sei quê , Lisbon, Ed. Veja, 1998.
FREUD. Sigmund, "Théorie générale des nevroses", Introduction à la psychanalyse, Paris, Ed. Payot.
PLATÃO, Íon, Lisbon, Ed. Inquérito, 1992.
RANCIÈRE, Jacques, O espetador emancipado, Lisbon, Ed. Orfeu Negro, 2010.
SELDES, Gilbert, The public arts , New York, Ed. Simon and Schoester, 1956.
SMITH, Frank, Pensar , Lisbon, Ed. Instituto Piaget, 1994.

Hoppe,
Institute of Art and Visual History / Humboldt-Universität zu Berlin;
ilaria.hoppe@culture.hu-berlin.de

Urban Art as Countervisuality?*

As cultural techniques within the urban environment, Graffiti and Street Art are investigated by many disciplines. Mostly art historical studies have explored the contradictory relationship between Street Art and the art market. My research is inspired by the approaches of Visual Culture Studies and their critique of the central perspective; furthermore by Mirzoeffs concept of 'neovisuality' describing actual fields of power constituting themselves in a permanent crisis that demands and legitimizes control and surveillance. The analysis applies these issues as methods for finding new ways of seeing and discussing Graffiti and Street Art in form and content, also questioning their potential as a countervisuality.

Keywords: street art, central perspective, drones

Introduction

The motivation to ask, if Urban Art is a form of 'countervisuality' derives from the critique that started with the beginning of scientific research on the topic. Many positions seem to enhance the contradictory aspects like the involvement of Urban Art in processes of gentrification, sell-out to the art market or advertising business.[1] The critique of these phenomena is of course very important, but it also reduces the potential of a worldwide movement of artists and activists on the streets. So I would like to highlight again the more subversive aspects of Urban Art, and add criteria for a better understanding of the movement's success and for the artistic choices being made.[2] Before I proceed with my formal analysis, I would like to clarify the two main terms 'Urban Art' and 'countervisuality'.

In my understanding, Urban Art implies Graffiti, Street Art and all visual expressions on the streets or related within the art system of galleries and museums. I am aware of the Anglophone notion of Urban Art as being the less valuable indoor Street Art.[3] But in the non-Anglo-American languages Urban Art is used as an umbrella term for many forms that rely on the notion of contemporary urbanity. The idiom allows nevertheless stylistic differentiations between Graffiti, Writing, Street Art, Urban Knitting, Guerilla Gardening and so forth.

The term 'countervisuality' was coined by Nicholas Mirzoeff in his book The right to look. A counterhistory of visuality from 2011.[4] He traces back the term 'visuality' to the 19th century and the representation of history that implies not only images, but also texts and, moreover, the authority to produce meaning and to install a dominant discourse.[5] As 'countervisuality' he acknowledges any form or image that is at the same time linked and opposed to this normative truth, as a subculture strategy "the attempt to reconfigure visuality as a whole."[6] Following Mirzoeff, we are now living in the era of Neovisuality that "(…) is a doctrine for the preservation of authority by means of permanent surveillance of all realms of life, a Gesamtkunstwerk of necropolitics."[7] Several characteristic of today's Urban Art react to these forms of visuality. The formal analysis of selected works will show how Urban Art undermines traditional ways of seeing, and how it works as a subversive strategy opposed to the neoliberal urban development and the policies of surveillance and control.

Visuality and the central perspective

One of the main criteria to discuss visuality is linked to the central perspective as a visual construction of a power relation in Western tradition. Besides Panofsky's seminal study, the discussion was revived in the Sixties and Seventies with the Marxist critique about the architecture of medieval castles, Renaissance villas and Baroque gardens, showing how these structures allowed a dominant view from above for the ruler, serving as instruments of control.[8] Mirzoeff applies these figurations on the colonial plantations of slavery. Again this system allowed the dominant view for an overseer in order to surveil the slaves as subordinated subjects.[9] In images, it is traditionally the central perspective that puts the beholder in the dominant position. A famous example for this tradition, developed in the Renaissance, is illustrated in Albrecht Dürer's Treatise on Measurement published in the second edition 1538 (1st edition 1525).[10] The text is an advice for artists on how to construct, among other things, a central perspective and a perfect illusionistic space in which objects and bodies can be positioned. The example chosen here shows the construction for a nude in Venetian manner with the female body lying within an architecture and before a landscape (Fig. 1). The underlying power relation spans here between the white, male artist and the female body positioned behind the frame of the visual apparatus. The result would be a picture that can suggest spatiality and puts the beholder in the same dominant position as the artist-creator.[11]

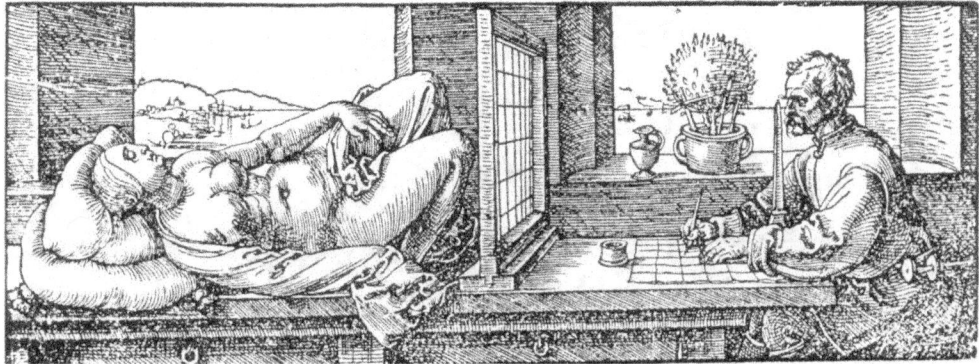

Fig. 1: Albrecht Dürer, Treatise for measurement, 3rd book: Of the bodies, 2nd edtion 1538 (Bonnet 2001, 58)

Mostly authors from visual culture studies have put forward the critique on central perspective as a 'scopic regime' and have shown how it found its effects in contemporary media like television, photography, video camera, computer, satellites and most recently in the techniques of the drones.[12] Used as instruments of control and surveillance, these technologies seem to generate objective evidence and serve to construct and maintain a hegemonic discourse of power and legitimacy, in Mirzoeffs words 'visuality', also because they are accompanied by a discourse on how we are supposed to understand the images they produce.[13] The instruments are used globally for counterinsurgency and the so-called 'war on terror', but it should not be forgotten that these techniques are transposed on our everyday life within the city. Thus, the argument of Mirzoeff is that the system of surveillance of the colonial plantation was first brought to what he calls the "metropole", that is the modern city as an agglomeration of powerful networks and institutions figuring as the nation-state, and then spread out globally in a post-panoptic visuality, where the divine eye of the drone or the satellite sees everything without being seen themselves.[14]

Kool Killer and the Drones

The appearance of American Graffiti in the modern city can be described as a true subversive visual practice that spread around the world and is still going on until today.[15] The graffiti piece consists in a written name (pseudonym), put on the wall in a variety of styles, sometimes readable and sometimes not. At last with the 3D-style the letters began to show a visual depth, but only within the written name or an additive character. The writing itself is not set in the rectangular frame of central perspective and therefore disturbs our habitual way of seeing. Moreover, the strongly coded significance of graffiti is not open to a generic meaning and does irritate the public, as Jean Baudrillard has already argued in his essay Kool Killer.[16] While graffiti developed further in a variety of styles and found its way even into the art market, it is perceived at the same time as vandalism and therefore severely prosecuted. In fact it does not only show the 'arty side' of technical skills, but is often acted out as aggression towards society, as the graffiti slang itself shows by using terms like 'bombing the city'. In his article, The wars on graffiti and the new military urbanism, Kurt Iveson has shown how the 'war on graffiti' has "contributed to the diffusion of military technologies and operational techniques into the realm of urban policy and policing" and how the 'war on terror' has both gained advantage of and reinforced these strategies.[17] This militarization of the urban includes razor wires, mobile surveillance cameras sending alert and real time images to smartphones of security agents, acoustic sensors able to detect the frequencies emitted by spray cans, GPS locators, smell sensors, intelligence and counterintelligence operations.[18] Since last year the German police and Railway Company are testing the use of drones to prosecute graffiti-sprayers.[19] Following Mirzoeff's argument of neovisuality – "the preservation of authority by means of permanent surveillance" – then the use of drones and the technologies listed by Iveson indicate that graffiti can still be seen as a subversive strategy within the urban space. To reverse this practice the New York based KATSU – who calls himself vandal, artist and hacker – experiments with the technical possibilities of the drone for painting.[20] So instead of using the drone to control sprayers, KATSU thinks about using this technical device for graffiti in areas which are out of reach and difficult to access. To sum up, graffiti is perceived as a chaotic threat for the security of the city – and that means for society in general – like a guerilla tactic that has to be controlled.

Street Art and the lack of perspective

If we turn to Street Art, which has its roots in the Seventies and Eighties, but was widely spread after the turn of the millennium, we see that most of the images do not show a perspective either. The form that has become emblematic for Street Art is the cutout figure drawn, painted or pasted up directly onto the city walls, which functions as its visual background. Though it is often treated three-dimensionally in itself, so that we can visually grasp the form of a body, it is not set in a frame with a perspective view. The beholder's eye is attracted by the cutout forms and he or she has to arrange it actively within the environment, because we are used to order things within space. The most interesting pieces are therefore those, who show carefully chosen positions and an interaction with the architecture of the city.[21] These settings allow a playfulness with our perception: the girl with the fly agaric by Dolk for example was positioned right onto the wall of an old and abandoned brewery in Berlin, in order to turn the courtyard of the building into a bewitched forest (Fig. 2). Those pieces interact with the urban environment, but their spatiality has to be produced by the beholder.

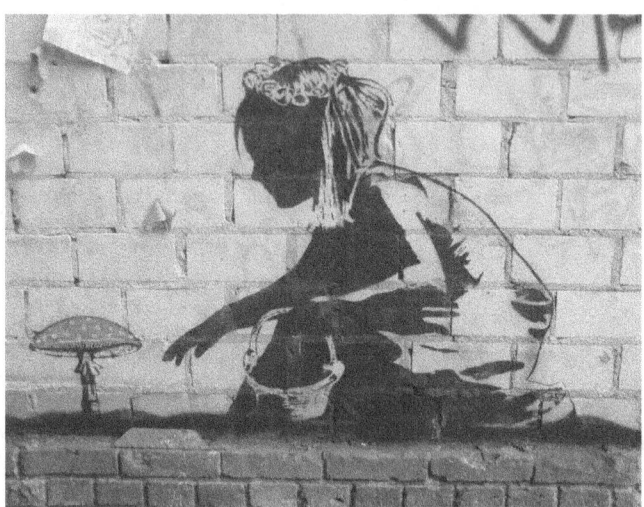
Fig. 2: DOLK, Berlin 2008, exhibition Urban Affairs in the former brewery building Friedrichshöhe (IH)

Thus, the reception of Urban Art needs a participatory involvement because of its situation within the urban environment that is experienced mostly through the movement of the body. We need to move around the city to discover Street Art as the artists are moving around looking for suitable places.[22] One such artist who has referred directly to this performative aspect of Street Art is Swoon.[23] Her playing children are only to be seen entirely while moving onwards down the street (Fig. 3). At the same time, the architecture functions visually as a playground. So I would argue that one of the most striking features of Street Art is the active participation of the passerby. His/Her physically engagement in the visual reception turns him/her into an active subject, even when this moment may last only a few seconds.

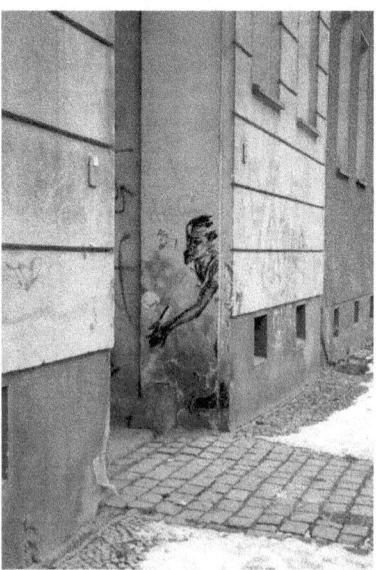
Fig. 3: Swoon, Berlin 2007 (IH)

This form of perception differs significantly from the main visual systems in the city, which are mostly traffic signs and advertising. In the first case, the signs order the traffic and are often redesigned by urban artists. In the second case, advertising campaigns are maybe the most dominant images within cities. More than traffic signs, they can be regarded as a form of 'visuality'. They make use of traditionally composed pictures with a central perspective, in which bodies and consumer goods establish a normative discourse of the real and common, on how we should look, and what we should buy and so forth. Since the Seventies, these images are the target of political movements like Culture Jamming and Ad-Busting, which are significant parts of today's Urban Art.[24]

Street Art and video surveillance

The next system of order that especially Street Art deals with extensively, is the video control of urban environments (Fig. 4). It is not surprising that this issue is so widely spread among Street Artists, because through their activity of spot searching they gain a deep and detailed knowledge about of the urban fabric.[25] They really pay attention to the realm of everyday life and actually see where and how many cameras are installed, which the average passer by does not notice. With these pieces we find an explicit reaction to what Mirzoeff has described as 'neovisuality', namely the continuous surveillance of our everyday life, without knowing, who actually sees these images, how they are used or to what end they are really made for. Here Urban Art refers directly and often ironically to the mechanism of urban surveillance. By doing so, Urban Art overtly addresses the politics of the 'scopic regime', of controlling the city.

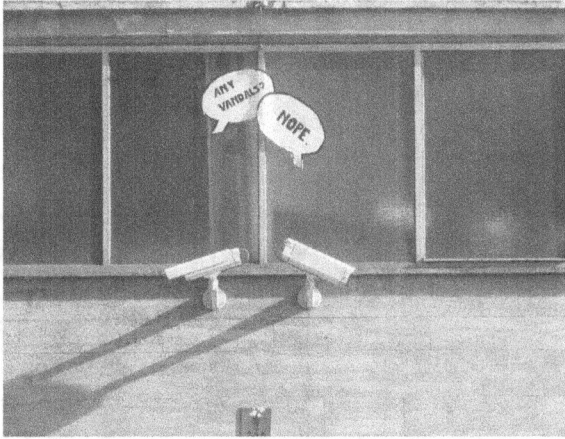

Fig. 4: Aachen 2011 (Maik Glatki)

Street Art looks back

Another example of a subversive visual strategy can be seen in the photo installations of JR, which very often show people looking back at the viewer, questioning again 'visuality' as a normative system. One of his first campaigns took place between 2004 and 2006 and is called 28 Millimeters, Portrait of a Generation.[ ] The artist took portraits of young people of the Cité des Bosquets and La Forestière in Clichy-sous-Bois, where the 2005 riots started in the French suburbs. Afterwards these portraits appeared in the city center of Paris. The images did not only show the segregated and underprivileged, but individuals that defiantly look back. The black-and-white photographed heads almost fill the complete space of huge posters. Though the format shows the usual rectangular frame, the heads do not leave any space beneath or behind so that they look very similar to cut out figures. Moreover the portrayed faces are grimacing and show a perspective distortion, maybe caused by using a fisheye lens. These formal choices lead to alternative photographic portraits with an additional sense of humor. JR's work realizes with a tacit understanding the right to look that "claims autonomy, not individualism or voyeurism, but the claim to a political subjectivity and collectivity."[26]

As many other artists, JR expanded his work across the borders of his city and now works globally. Nevertheless, he adheres to his style and the question of who has the power to see or not, as in the case of the Israeli separation barrier.[27] In this work, he dealt again with how the power of the gaze may have far reaching and severe consequences in the ways in which we perceive each other. In his campaign Women are Heroes, carried out in different slums worldwide, JR attempts an even larger scale by placing huge images on houses and rooftops.[28] Here again those most haunted by poverty and violence are constituted as individuals via the image that is a close-up adhering to the architecture in a typical Street Art manner. But in contrast to the smaller dimensions within the city, here the eyes of the women are looking back at the panoptical eye as these pictures are big enough to be seen from high above, from helicopter, satellites and drones. Inspired by this campaign, a group of artists and the Reprieve/Foundation for Fundamental Rights installed a huge portrait of a young girl in Kyber Pukhtoonkhwa region of Pakistan, who according to FFR, lost both her parents and two siblings in a drone attack.[29] Again the image is big enough to be seen from high above and it is intended to raise awareness of the civilian victims in drone military operations. It was released in the internet under notabugsplat, referring to the military slang of drone operators, who see human bodies merely as little spots moving on their screens, and describe them as "bugs being crushed". In this case, the huge portrait image is addressed directly to the military complex.

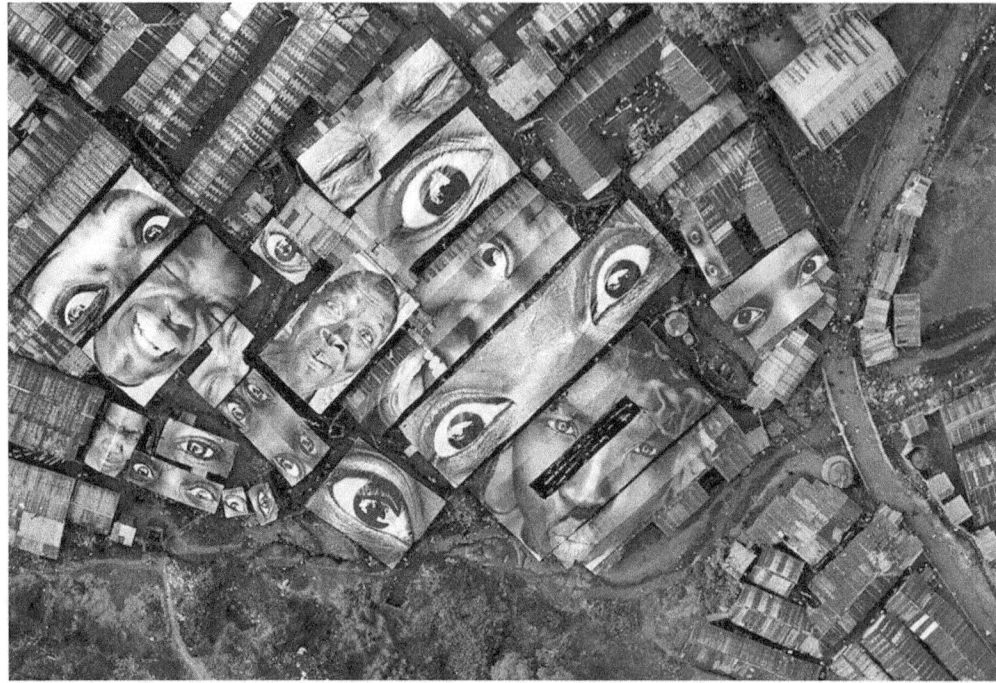

Fig. 5: JR, Woman are Heroes, Kibera, Kenia, 2009 (jr-art.net)

In sum, the campaigns by JR and his staff clearly constitute subjectivity and the claim to look and to be seen as a metaphor for autonomy and human rights. But as in the Dürer picture mentioned in the beginning, we do see these images from the same perspective as the 'scopic regime'. It seems that the underlying power relation did not change in the last five centuries. Therefore, are these images of women and children only reinforcing their status of 'victims' in the neovisual order? Are only the weak to be seen, because to have control over the scopic regime means to possess real – unseen – power? As these questions remain at stake, from a formal point view we can describe these images as a contemporary way of portraiture. The faces are shown as fragments and are not situated in a frame of spatial illusion. At least these images are not imitating the scopic regime.

Urban Art as popular culture

In the end I am not sure, wether Mirzoeff would acknowledge Urban art as a form of 'Countervisuality' and of course not every single position of Urban Art claims to be political. But if we think of it as swarm intelligence with its distinct features and topics that I have shown here, it clearly challenges the authority of visuality.[] In the last chapter of his book, Mirzoeff refers to Antonio Gramsci's writings and his concept of a resilient popular culture:

> „Gramsci argued that one of the reasons that the subaltern classes could not be fully absorbed into the dominant hegemony, and thus retained the potential for revolution, was their folklore. Folklore maintained an "unstable and fluctuating" element in the nation-state that provided the potential for a spontaneous uprising, the "great 'undoing.'"[30]

So if we no longer struggle anymore to show that Urban Art is a form of contemporary fine art, but treat it as a less restricted form of popular culture, the modern way of an urban folklore, then we can assign a subversive potential to it. The "unstable and fluctuating" sides of Urban Art belong to the reasons, why it has proven to be such a powerful and interesting movement.

Notes and References
1 *This paper is part of my larger project on Urban Art: Urbanity as aesthetic experience. I would like to thank Julia Ahmad for proofreading it.
Julia Reinecke, Street-Art. A subculture between art and commerce (Bielefeld: Transcript, 2007); different entries in Katrin Klitzke and Christian Schmidt, eds. Street Art: Legends to the street (Berlin: Archiv der Jugendkulturen, 2009); Claudia Willms, Sprayer in the White Cube. Streetart between everyday culture and commercial art (Marburg: Tectum, 2010); Ulrich Blanché, Consumer Art. Culture and commerce by Banksy and Damien Hirst (Bielefeld: transcript, 2012); Heike Derwanz, Street-Art-Careers. New Ways into the art and design market (Bielefeld: transcript, 2013); Peter Bengtsen, The Street Art World (Lund: Peter Bengtsen and Almendros de Granada Press, 2014), esp. 65-128, with further refernces (all my translation).
2 For similar approaches see e.g. Ulrich Blanché, Something to s(pr)ay: The Street Artivist Banksy. An arthistorical analysis (Marburg: Tectum, 2010; my translation) and Rafael Schacter, Ornament and Order. Graffiti, Street Art and the Parergon (Aldershot: Ashgate, 2014).
3 Compare Bengtsen, The Street Art World, 67-69 and Schacter, Ornament and Order, xix, introducing the term 'Independent Public Art' for "all forms of autonomously produced aesthetic production in the public sphere."
4 Nicholas Mirzoeff, The right to look. A counterhistory of visuality (Durham/London: Duke University Press, 2011).
5 See also his summary on the "Keyword Visuality" in Nicholas Mirzoeff, An Introduction to Visual Culture, 2nd edn (New York: Routledge, 2009), 89-93.
6 Mirzoeff, The Right to Look, 24.
7 Mirzoeff, The Right to Look, 34.
8 Erwin Panofsky, Perspective as symbolic form, transl. Christopher S. Wood (New York: Zone Books, 1991 [German edition 1927]); Reinhard Bentmann and Michael Müller, The villa as architecture of governance. An arthistorical and sociohistorical analysis

(Frankfurt on the Main: Suhrkamp, 1970); Stanislaus von Moos, Tower and Bastion. Contributions for a political iconography of Italian Renaissance architecture (Zurich: Atlantis-Verlag, 1974; all my translation).
9 Mirzoeff, The Right to Look, 48-76.
10 Albrecht Dürer, Woodcuts and Wood Blocks, ed. Walter L. Strauss (New York: Abaris Books, 1979/1980), 579-80; Joanne G. Bernstein, "The Female Model and the Renaissance Nude: Dürer, Giorgione, and Raphael," Artibus et Historiae 13 (1992): 49-63, here 60.
11 For the discussion of the interrelations between gender, space and gaze see esp. for this example Svetlana Alpers, "Art History and Its Exclusions: The Example of Dutch Art," in Feminism and art history: Questioning the litany, ed. Norma Broude and Mary D. Garrard (New York: Harper and Row, 1982), 180-199, here 184-185; Irene Nierhaus, Arch⁶. Space, gender, architecture (Vienna: Sonderzahl, 1999), 48-54; Anne-Marie Bonnet, The 'Nude' by Dürer (Köln: König, 2001), 58 with earlier references (my translation).
12 In summery first by Hal Foster, ed. Vision and Visuality (Seattle: Bay Press, 1988).
13 Mirzoeff, Visual Culture, 1-30.
14 Mirzoeff, The Right to Look, 19. For an overview on the vast discussions about the politics of surveillance I used the introduction to "Regimes of visibility. Control, safety and privateness in 21st century", ed. Leon Hempel et al. Special edition of Leviathan. Zeitschrift für Sozialwissenschaft, 25 (2010/2011), 7-24 (my translation).
15 For the latest approaches towards an analysis and history of Graffiti see the special issue of City: analysis of urban trends, culture, theory, policy, action, 14:1-2 (2010); Ralf Beuthan and Pierre Smolarski eds., What is Graffiti? (Würzbug: Königshausen und Neumann, 2011; my translation); Blanché, Something to s(pr)ay, 17-29; Roger Gastman, The history of American graffiti (New York: Harper Design, 2011); Anna Wacławek, Graffiti and Street Art (London: Thames & Hudson, 2011), 10-28; Schacter, Ornament and Order, 2014.
16 Jean Baudrillard, "Kool Killer, or The Insurrection of Signs," in Symbolic Exchange and Death, trans. Iain Hamilton Grant (London: Sage Publications, 1993 [French edition 1975]), 76-86.
17 Kurt Iveson, "The wars on graffiti and the new military urbanism," in City: analysis of urban trends, culture, theory, policy, action, 14:1-2 (2010): 115-134.
18 Iveson, "The wars on graffiti," 118-122.
19 Klaus Jansen, "Deutsche Bahn plans to use drones to catch graffiti artists", DW, March 3, 2013. Accessed October 23, 2014. http://dw.de/p/18ife.
20Oliver Wainright, "Spraycopter: the drone that does graffiti", theguardian, April 21, 2014. Accessed October 23, 2014. http://www.theguardian.com/artanddesign/architecture-design-blog/2014/apr/21/drone-does-graffiti-street-art.
21 See also Wacławek, Graffiti and Street Art, 139-146; Peter Bengtsen, "Site Specifity and Street Art," in Theorizing visual studies. Writing through the discipline, ed. James Elkins et al. (New York: Routledge, 2013), 250-253.
22 For the aspect of walking in the city as a practice that constitutes the perception of the urban fabric and urban art see Robert Behrendt and Katrin Klitzke, "Mind walks," in Klitzke and Schmidt, Legenden, 146-161 (my translation) and Jeff Ferrel and Robert D. Weide, "Spot theory," in City: analysis of urban trends, culture, theory, policy, action, 14:1-2 (2010): 48-62.
23 For the performativity of Street Art and Swoon particularly see also Wacławek, Graffiti and Street Art, 96-102.
24 A critical insight to these forms gives Hagen Schölzel, Guerillacommunication. A genealogy of a political form of conflict (Bielefeld: transcript, 2013; my translation); see also Blanché, Something to s(pr)ay, 39-41.
25 Ferrel and Weide, "Spot theory."
26 JR, Marco Berrebi and Ladj Li, JR 28 mm (Paris: editions Alternatives, 2011); http://www.jr-art.net/projects/portrait-of-a-generation. Accessed October 28, 2014.
27 Mirzoeff, The Right to Look, 1.
28 For the documentation of this campaign see Marco and JR, Face 2 Face (Paris: editions Alternatives, 2007); Wacławek, Graffiti and Street Art, 139-141.
29 For the documentation see JR and Marc Berrebi, Women are Heroes. A Global Project by JR (New York: Abrams, 2012) and the film Women are Heroes. Un film de JR (France: Studio 37 and 27.11 production, 2011); Wacławek, Graffiti and Street Art, 139-141.
30 http://notabugsplat.com/. Accessed October 29, 2014.
31 For the comparison of Writers to 'swarm' after the Hardt and Negri concept of 'Multitude' see also Iveson, "The wars on graffiti," 130; compare also Wacławek's chapter on "Urban visual culture," Graffiti and Street Art, 157-195 and Schacter, Ornament and Order.
32 Mirzoeff, The Right to Look, 275.

Alpers, Svetlana. "Art History and Its Exclusions: The Example of Dutch Art," in Feminism and art history: Questioning the litany, edited by Norma Broude and Mary D. Garrard (New York: Harper and Row, 1982), 180-199.
Baudrillard, Jean. "Kool Killer, or The Insurrection of Signs," in Symbolic Exchange and Death. Jean Baudrillard. Translated by Iain Hamilton Grant. London: Sage Publications, 1993 (French edition 1975), 76-86.
Bengtsen, Peter. "Site Specifity and Street Art," in Theorizing visual studies. Writing through the discipline, edited by James Elkins et al. New York: Routledge, 2013, 250-253.
Bengtsen, Peter. The Street Art World. Lund: Peter Bengtsen and Almendros de Granada Press, 2014.
Bentmann, Reinhard and Michael Müller. Die Villa als Herrschaftsarchitektur. Eine kunst- und sozialgeschichtliche Analyse. Frankfurt on the Main: Suhrkamp, 1970.
Bernstein, Joanne G. "The Female Model and the Renaissance Nude: Dürer, Giorgione, and Raphael," Artibus et Historiae 13 (1992): 49-63.
Beuthan, Ralf and Pierre Smolarski, editors. Was ist Graffiti? Würzbug: Königshausen und Neumann, 2011.
Blanché, Ulrich. Something to s(p)ray: The Street Artivist Banksy. An arthistorical analysis. Marburg: Tectum, 2010.
Blanché, Ulrich. Konsumkunst. Kultur und Kommerz bei Banksy und Damien Hirst. Bielefeld: transcript, 2012.
Bonnet, Anne-Marie. „Akt" bei Dürer. Köln: König, 2001.
Derwanz, Heike. Street Art-Karrieren. Neue Wege in den Kunst- und Designmarkt. Bielefeld: transcript, 2013.
Dürer, Albrecht. Woodcuts and Wood Blocks, edited by Walter L. Strauss. New York: Abaris Books, 1979/1980.
Ferrel, Jeff and Robert D. Weide, "Spot theory." City: analysis of urban trends, culture, theory, policy, action, 14:1-2 (2010): 48-62.
Foster, Hal, ed. Vision and Visuality. Seattle: Bay Press, 1988.
Gastman, Roger. The history of American graffiti. New York: Harper Design, 2011.
Hempel, Leon, Susanne Krasman and Ulrich Bröckling, editors. "Regimes of visibility. Control, safety and privateness in 21st century", Special edition of Leviathan. Zeitschrift für Sozialwissenschaft, 25 (2010/2011).
Iveson, Kurt. "The wars on graffiti and the new military urbanism." City: analysis of urban trends, culture, theory, policy, action, 14:1-2 (2010): 115-134.
JR. Women are Heroes. Un film de JR. France: Studio 37 and 27.11 production, 2011.
JR, Marco Berrebi and Ladj Li. JR 28 mm. Paris: editions Alternatives, 2011.
JR and Marc Berrebi. Women are Heroes. A Global Project by JR. New York: Abrams Inc, 2012.
Klitzke, Katrin, and Christian Schmidt, editors. Street Art: Legenden zur Strasse. Berlin: Archiv der Jugendkulturen, 2009.
Marco and JR. Face 2 Face. Paris: editions Alternatives, 2007.
Mirzoeff, Nicholas. An Introduction to Visual Culture. 2nd edn, New York: Routledge, 2009.
Mirzoeff, Nicholas. The Right to Look: A Counterhistory of Visuality. Durham/London: Duke University Press, 2011.
Moos, Stanislaus von. Turm und Bollwerk: Beiträge zu einer politischen Ikonographie der italienischen Renaissancearchitektur. Zurich: Atlantis-Verlag, 1974.
Nierhaus, Irene: Arch⁶. Space, gender, architecture. Vienna: Sonderzahl, 1999.
Panofsky, Erwin. Perspective as symbolic form. Translated by Christopher S. Wood. New York: Zone Books, 1991 (German edition 1927).
Reinecke, Julia. Street-Art. Eine Subkultur zwischen Kunst und Kommerz. Bielefeld: transcript, 2007.
Schacter, Rafael. Ornament and Order. Graffiti, Street Art and the Parergon. Aldershot: Ashagte, 2014.
Schölzel, Hagen. Guerillakommunikation. Genealogie einer politischen Konfliktform. Bielefeld: transcript, 2013.
Wacławek, Anna. Graffiti and Street Art. London: Thames & Hudson, 2011.
Willms, Claudia. Sprayer im White Cube. Streetart zwischen Alltagskultur und kommerzieller Kunst. Marburg: Tectum, 2010.

Luisa Santos, Humboldt-Viadrina School of Governance / CCCPM, Berlin
With the support of Fundação para a Ciência e Tecnologia (FCT / BD)

Public Art Projects - Towards a Critical Discourse on Urban Aesthetics: Row Houses; Morrinho

Urban art expressions are present in various forms and contexts and are increasingly becoming regarded as projects with social change aims. But how can an urban art project contribute to social change for the better in a specific urban community? This paper intends on understanding and describing how the combination and integration of existing cultural references with urban art and project management, in multidisciplinary approaches, can increase the economical sustainability and social change in a community. The research will look into obstacles and achievements using Row Houses (USA) and Morrinho (Brazil), as examples of urban art projects for social change in different contexts.

Culture-led regeneration, urban art, project management, multidisciplinary.

Introduction

There is an enormous variety of urban art projects showing a sustained interest in impact, in social and political terms presenting critical points of view that range from passing a message to asking for participation which, in some cases, means taking real political action (Lind, 2011). Nevertheless, it seems that most art projects fail in producing social change, and this is how the main question of this research arose: how can an urban art project contribute to social change for the better in a specific urban community?

Inevitably the combination of art and social change relates to Luhmann's idea of art as a social system (1995). This sheds light onto the main research question. In keeping with his larger project, the specific semantic theme of art is the relationship between the non-social domain of conscious perception and the social domain of communication. The function of art would thus consist in integrating what is in principle incommunicable - namely, perception - into the communication network.

Perception is an idea that came up in the critical analysis of Project Morrinho and Project Row Houses, projects with a strong art focus but that involve other disciplines and might be regarded as multidisciplinary: both projects aim to change the preconceived ideas (or perceptions) of what their communities (a favela – in the case of Morrinho; and a so-called problematic neighbourhood, in the case of Row Houses) might mean. When critically looking at these projects, through observation, interviews, the understanding of its existing cultural references, it was interesting to see that multidisciplinary projects fighting preconceived ideas, mainly through art, show themselves preconceived ideas. Narrative methods (Boje, 2000) were of utmost importance as a methodology to answer the research question, as, through the stories of the projects analysed, it was possible not only to understand what are possible crucial disciplines in a project for social change but also to understand that there are alternative narratives to the grand narratives of the same disciplines.

The disciplines identified and analysed as important in urban art projects for social change were cultural studies, as the understanding and integration of existing cultural references is fundamental, and project management, which is of utmost importance in the planning and understanding of the steps of a project. It seems that art, as a discipline, fears that scientific disciplines, as project management, take away the creative spark of a project. On another hand, it also seems that scientific disciplines look at art as a discipline incapable to work with specific goals and within a structured thought in tasks as analysis of cultural references.

An understanding of the true meanings – in opposition to preconceived ideas – of each discipline will, potentially, lead to results for the development of the execution of projects for effective social change. We are still far from a broader discourse of multidisciplinary and future projects for social change can develop this approach. Such multidisciplinary approach understands the importance of planning and strategy without dismissing creativity and the power of the individual.

Art as social system

In the Manifesto for an Independent Revolutionary Art André Breton and Diego Rivera (1938)[1] argued that art can only have an effect in society and be revolutionary if it becomes independent of any social constructs: "True art, which is not content to play variations on ready-made models but rather insists on expressing the inner needs of man and of mankind in its time –true art is unable not to be revolutionary, not to aspire to a complete and radical reconstruction of society" (Breton and Rivera, 1938)[2]. Breton's concept of the independence of art commented on the role of art and culture in class society. It reflected the idea that art can only have a social role if it is free from the logic of domination. Only in this way, according to the Manifesto, it could contribute to a free society that shows an activist response towards exploitation and domination and where individuals can freely associate themselves and determine themselves. This was a clear denounce to fascism and Stalinism, two dictatorships suffocating artistic expression as they were drowning workers' opposition but it was also a comment on the role of art and culture in the social realm. The manifesto opposed the abstract idea that art could somehow be neutral in a class-based society.

Some researchers and academics argue that certain social systems regulate form and content of art. According to this approach, art is reduced to a certain part or state of society. In such approaches art might be considered as an automated echo of the state of the economy, or of the state of the political system. Lukács argues that reality exists objectively and independently of consciousness, and, therefore, cognition would be a reflection of reality. In the same way, art would have to be a factual reflection of the totality of reality, providing an image of reality where the opposition between essence and appearance of reality is given in a natural unity. Each artwork would have to be a closed universe that advances a more complete and livelier reflection of reality than the recipients have, it would have to seize the shiftiness and inexhaustibility of reality. For doing so art's role would not be to portray individual persons and situations, but representative characters under representative social and cultural contexts. Art would have to convey a rich expression of the experiences of life, for doing so it would require a propaganda character (Lukács, 1954) and would have to educate the masses, as in Stalinism line of thought.

Traditional objective theories of art (as the 18th Century views of Baumgarten and Herder), presented a different approach. These have seen art as the Ideal of Beauty that it is its aim and it represents divinity and hence is everlasting, intrinsically autonomous and aspiring for perfection in the sense that Beauty is an endless value that is independent of changing human values, everyday life, human practice, and human interests: Baumgarten writes that "The aim of aesthetics is the perfection of sensible cognition as such, that is, beauty, while its imperfection as such, that is, ugliness, is to be avoided" (Baumgarten, 1750 / 1961). In Herder's view, visual art must aim at beauty because only in that way can it overcome the essential conflict between its own spatial, static character and the incessantly changing, transitory character of everything in nature (Herder, 1993). In these traditional art theories, art is seen as a system representing unlimited values that surpass society, being considered as a system with a high position in relation to other social systems (Fuchs & Holzner, 2000).

Other approach in terms of looking at art as a social system, considers that society is a social system and defended the existence of various subsystems and each one is always autonomous and with one unique function in society (Luhmann, 1995). Therefore, one social system would never do the same as other social system. To Niklas Luhmann (1995), who developed the idea of social systems theory, art is considered a functioning closed system and would work autonomously from other social systems. According to Luhmann, the function of art, as a system, in modern society would be, through perception and communication, to show a reality that can be observed (Luhmann, 1995).

Whereas Breton and Rivera see the autonomy of art as crucial for its role revolutionary role in society, for Luhmann the question of autonomy is one of operational functions, not one that sees art as a specific system that has a role of looking critically at society. According to Luhmann, art is a social system that shows how reality is, not as it could be. For Luhmann the autonomy of art is not specific to art as a social system as, to him, autonomy is not critical and it is a characteristic inherent to all systems in modern society (Luhmann, 1995).

While for Adorno the autonomy of art resides in the production of the work of art, not specifically in the aesthetic judgments of the subject, an autonomy from society within capitalist society by making its function not having a specific function: "the autonomy of art lies in the work of art, in its production, not specifically in the aesthetic judgments of the subject" (Adorno, 1958), for Luhmann the autonomy of art is a functional autonomy within society that is not different from the autonomy of the other subsystems of modern society.

Whereas for Marcuse, the advantage of art lies in the perception it gives on society by showing what it could be, more than portraying it in realistic terms (Marcuse, 1978), for Luhmann, art would be inherently ambiguous (Luhmann, 1995). In this view, artworks would show advices for observation, but this would not be particularly relevant as observers could interpret them in various ways. Different forms of art would be coherent in the way that all make observations that encourage other observations. Luhmann considers art is anything that is communicated as being art. Here, is important to mention that for Luhmann, social systems are based in communication: "While living systems reproduce themselves on the basis of life, social systems reproduce themselves on the basis of communication and psychic systems on the basis of consciousness or thoughts, their elements are not physical substances but elements of meaning" (Luhmann, 1995).

In his production, Luhmann defends that art is self-referential and based on second-degree observations and in communication on the ideas of art and art's meaning. Art would not play roles of other social systems but only its one and only role, of presenting observations of reality. These observations would then be subject to other observations putting the focus of art in the realm of perception, which is a crucial domain in the following projects analysed.

Project Morrinho: a multidisciplinary project fighting a grand narrative
Socio-cultural context of the Favela: a grand-narrative

In current discourse, when one says the word favela, commonly, the assumptions made are with social problems, segregation and urban violence. A historical reading shows however that the favela has been a topic of debate for at least a century, concurrent to a chain of images and representations that diverge from the social constructions that politicians, writers and social scientists have built up over the years in dealing with this particular social and urban phenomenon (Valladares, 2009). Looking at the origin of the word favela, it was first cited in 19th century Portuguese dictionaries, and it meant favela tree, which was commonly found in Bahia[3].

After the Guerra de Canudos (Canudos War) in Bahia, between 1895 and 1896, government soldiers, who had lived amongst favela trees[4], trailed to Rio de Janeiro to get their expected payment for war service. They settled on one of Rio's hills and gave it the name "Morro da Favela" because of the tree that prospered in the location of their victory against the rebels of Canudos War. They waited for their payment but it never came, so they decided not to leave the Morro da Favela, which became the first favela in history.

Many descriptions of the favela in the first half of the 20th century appeared in the form of journalistic or historical writing. Euclides da Cunha's well-known book Os Sertões (1902) covers the Canudos War and describes the coast versus the back lands as the opposition between cultured and uncultured, making a comparison to explain the difference between the favela and the city. The history of the favelas is thus one of land invasion by poverty-stricken migrants, impoverished soldiers.

In essays of architects, social workers, and doctors that entered the communities in the beginning of the 20th century, the favela was described as the wrong way, poor and dirty. This period was highly significant because it created the image of favela as the habitat of the poor (Perlman, 1977), an idea that still prevails in popular representations and people's mind during the 20th and 21st century.

As Brazil's civil society expanded, growing attention and research for the favela both from academics and politicians led to NGOs increasingly entering these communities, setting up programs and doing their own research, adding to the growing body of literature and knowledge, as well as changing the perception of what a favela might really mean. In 2007, President Lula announced the Programa de Aceleração do Crescimento (Program for Acceleration and Growth), a four-year investment plan, which includes the promotion of urban development for the favelas. There have been public policies from local governments specially directed at the favelas. In Rio de Janeiro, programs such as the Favela-Bairro[5] and Rio Cidade[6] have attempted to mitigate the problem of poverty and weak development within the favelas. The problem with these programs is that people living outside make these programs, who come up with solutions of what they think might be the problems to solve. Usually, this leads to little participation and short-time change.

In order to truly change this perception of what a favela might mean, a first step would be, probably, to refer to its true-form, understanding and integrating the existing cultural references. The people living in favelas, maybe due to the lack of resources, possess a "do-it-yourself" spirit and a "build-your-own" mentality. These were the founding characteristics of Project Morrinho, a project which aim for change is based in changing the dogmatic perception of the favelas. Nelcirlan Souza de Oliveira, a 14-year-old boy who had recently moved to Rio de Janeiro, created Project Morrinho in 1998.

Small stories of Favela do Pereirão through Project Morrinho

As a 14-year old boy, Oliveira was impressed with the architecture and style of life in the favela and decided to playfully reproduce this reality in his own backyard with bricks and paint leftover from his father's construction work. This diversion caught the attention of seven other local children, and what was once just a game turned into their reality and routine. In a short time, a miniature favela of 350 square meters took shape. Within the miniature urban world of Morrinho, they acted out a role-playing game with the numerous Lego-block avatars that inhabit the model, recreating life in this Rio's favela, with samba performances and gangs co-habiting in the same place. Currently, more than twenty teenagers are following the example of the founding members.

The project was never planned as a work of art but it was a very natural step to change itself from play to art. In 2001, the encounter between filmmakers and producers Fábio Gavião and Marco Oliveira with the young creators of the model was crucial for what is today Project Morrinho. The idea of Fábio Gavião and Marco Oliveira, when they climbed the hill of Pereira da Silva and first saw Morrinho, which was then not more than a visually beautiful play made by a lot of children, was to create a collaborative documentary with the young people from the community. As a proof of trust, but also as a means of producing a documentary as natural and collaborative as it could be, they left a digital camera and the group began recording their plays. These recordings turned into short films and were used to the documentary Deus sabe de tudo mas não é x9 (God knows everything but is not a snitch). By giving the cameras to the children, and trusting them, the filmmakers contributed to the main aim of what became Project Morrinho: to change the negative perception of what a favela might be.

Robert Storr got to know about Morrinho through the work of the artist and photographer Paula Trope, who presented a photographic exhibition in partnership with Morrinho artists at the São Paulo Biennial in 2006. Storr simply showed up in the community and said he wanted the young creators to reproduce a model of Morrinho at the Venice Biennial. Robert Storr wrote a very interesting piece about Morrinho, where he makes a parallel to the concept of social sculpture that was advocated by the conceptual artist and social activist Joseph Beuys. It is a very interesting parallel, as the community as a whole can be regarded as one great work of art to which each young creator contributes creatively.

The project has been able to use the attention it attracts to evolve, more than as a work of art, into an organisation with aspiration for social change. The creation of an NGO assured the authorial rights of the work and helped in communicating the project to get more resources for further development. Today, Morrinho is formed by four initiatives encompassing various disciplines, interests, and knowledge: TV Morrinho, Tourism at Morrinho, Expo Morrinho and Morrinho Social. Each initiative play an important role in showing the vision of Project Morrinho and help directly, contributing to the social, cultural and economic development of the surrounding areas.

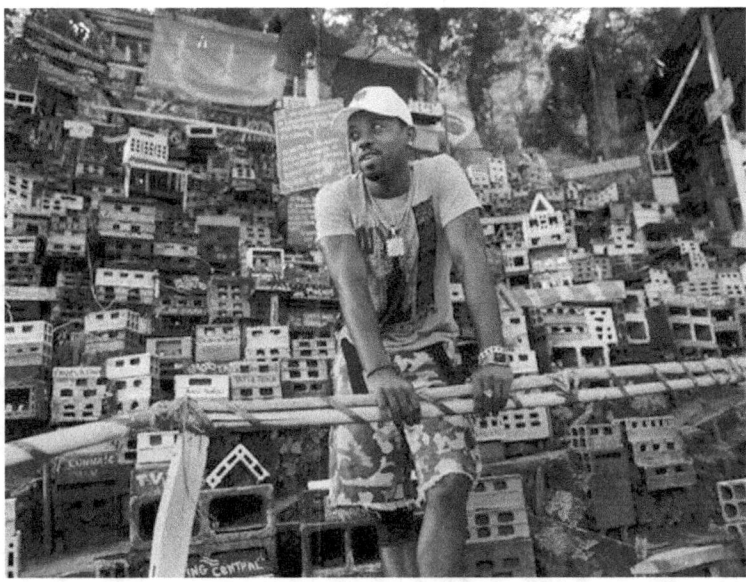

Fig. 1: Project Morrinho. © Project Morrinho

Multidisciplinary as a motor to achieve social change

It is not that Project Morrinho presents itself as multidisciplinary project. It is the choice of this thesis to describe it as such describing its success through the combination of disciplines, all with the same level of importance for the Project, and collaborative practice within its four initiatives that make what is today an NGO, and, in the words of its creators, an organisation aspiring social change: "In the first years of the NGO, between 2006 and 2008, we had resources from companies through Laws of Culture Incentive and more than half of the people working at the Morrinho were living in the community. The artists who initiated Morrinho had a radical change in their lives: in their self-esteem, in their way of speaking and believing in themselves. Above all, it's a leisure space in the middle of community, created not by the public power or private enterprises but by its inhabitants. It's a magical space, a micro-universe inside the universe of Brazilian favelas" (Serra & Oliveira, 2012). The multidisciplinary vision goes beyond the exact sciences and demands dialogue with the humanities and the social sciences, as well as with art, literature, and poetry.

Beyond teaching local youth the craft of constructing the model of Morrinho and how to use the space for various forms of play, Morrinho Social also attends to various kinds of popular education that NGOs offer in the communities. These programs include classes in citizenship education, youth leadership, and media arts education. Under the motto "Initiating a small revolution", Morrinho sets its goals in offering an educational component: art-education, social conscience, and economic development. In both formal and informal level, these values make use of disciplines as art, education, sociology, psychology, and economy.

Multidisciplinary is very important in Project Morrinho, with its various initiatives, as it makes part of the key for its success. Project Morrinho is a community-based organisation, and collaboration is one of the keywords in the community as well as in the volunteers: each individual shares a different knowledge in the different initiatives (from TV production to exhibitions and guided tours to tourism). Multidisciplinary contributes to a better involvement of the community making the project more appealing and sustainable, even if facing difficulties, because when one part of the project does not work, as it should, there is always another part of the project that supports it. This diversity of interests represents a moving away from the academia, the introversion of modernism and the belief of "art for the sake of art". It is remaking networks and realigning narratives to make contact with the pulse of wider social, disciplinary and cultural change and not simply formal innovation. The work at Project Morrinho has drawn its team into the areas of urban regeneration and planning. At the moment, Project Morrinho has more in common with members of tenants and action groups, radical planners and cultural geographers, than it does with artists as it did in its early steps. From the point of view of Cultural Studies, Morrinho emerged out of the favelas and target favela publics but have expanded well beyond favela boundaries to reach national and international partners. Morrinho is political and openly own an ideology.

Even though Morrinho's leaders and participants are not afraid to engage with markets and make money so that they can be financially independent from sponsors and the state, they look at outsiders with fear and would not trust someone outside the community to play the role of a project manager, not only because of being an outsider to the community but also because project management is not seen as something essential by the authors. They seem to think that art is in the centre of the project and that there is not a need to plan too much as that is not understood as creative. This is an observation that is not only applicable to Project Morrinho but to Arts as a discipline. Art projects seem to fear that involving scientific disciplines in the process takes away the creative spark of the project. Although, if we look to the history of scientific disciplines as Project Management, we find that chaos, creativity and complexity are in their core. Interestingly, Project Management also shows a preconceived idea of Arts. According to professional project managers, art projects and projects initiated in NGOs are incapable of understanding and dealing with planning and structure (PM4NGOs 2011; Cropper 2013). It might be true that a lot of art projects look chaotic but there are serious attempts to plan and many succeed in finding ways to find stakeholders and fundraisers even if the process is not the same as of project management and if there is a lot to be improved.

Analysis of the characteristics, methods and actions of Morrinho shows that they are sui generis and innovative showing an alternative to the grand narrative of project management. Their explicit aims are the recognition of the culture and rich potential of favela life-worlds, the demolition of urban barriers and the dialogical crossings that can produce transformative changes both in the public sphere and in social and individual subjectivities. They openly compete with the drug trade for influence in the routes of socialisation open to young favela people and work as mediators of conflict in disputes between the drug factions, the police and favela dwellers. Their range of actions is extensive, engaging both favela communities and the larger public sphere of the city. They put emphasis on the regeneration of the built environment of favelas, on the construction of spaces for positive sociability and conviviality and on psychosocial interventions that aim to foster self-esteem, self-control and awareness for the transformation of individual and collective trajectories.

The structuring of everyday life takes a central role in the communities' perception and is seen as vital for avoiding criminality and engaging people in meaningful activity. Participants explicitly say that Project Morrinho give them something to do, something to commit to, an opportunity to be responsible. Project Morrinho's motto "a small revolution" proves, then, to be true. It is a small revolution because it is a local revolution within a specific community. But it seems to have the potential to contribute to change the grand-narrative of the favela and this is not such a small change (revolution).

Project Row Houses: a multidisciplinary project fighting a grand narrative
Socio-cultural context of the Third Ward: a grand-narrative
The Third Ward is a neighbourhood in Houston that was historically populated by African-Americans. When Rick Lowe initiated Project Row Houses, the Third Ward's neighbourhood was then characterized by a large number of rundown, abandoned houses and lack of a viable private enterprise which ended up in a high unemployment rate and its associated problems as poverty, crime, deteriorating housing and poor health care for the community's citizens, seen by outsiders with fear who avoid to enter or pass by the neighbourhood. The History of the neighbourhood tells a different story to these associations.
By the 1880s, approximately twenty-five per cent of Black households in Third Ward were owner occupied. The homes built in the Third Ward followed a number of vernacular styles, including some that were hybrids—an innovation brought about by the advent of house catalogues, which allowed homeowners to pick the style of house they wanted to build and add on details from other styles listed.

This resulted in the diffusion of regional styles on a national level, including one commonly found in Houston's Black communities: the shotgun house. Receiving this name because a shotgun shell fired at the front door would travel through the house and out the back door without hitting anything, shotgun houses were one room wide, one story tall, with the rooms arranged in a row without hallways, and doors at opposite ends of the facade. Though some relate the style to the New York brownstone, the shotgun is believed to have travelled from New Orleans, where such houses date back to about 1800. Others believe it originated in West African house building traditions, or that the shotgun represents a New World Euro-American hybrid style that came to New Orleans via Haiti (Vlach, 1976). Even as transformed over the years and influences, the shotgun house expresses the enduring social values and cultural traditions of African-Americans. For newly freed African Americans, the shotgun was not only a symbol of freedom but also a means of defining themselves as a united community outside of the confines of slavery.
The shotgun form grew out of the value traditional African society placed on the continuity of the extended family and a reverence for one's ancestors. The lives of family and clan members were so interwoven with each other that the boundaries between self, family and community were ambiguous. The architecture of the Yoruba[7] compound reflected the lack of importance Africans gave to individuals in opposition to the praise of the collective in family and community terms. This architecture and importance are kept in Project Row Houses.

Small stories of the Third Ward through Project Row Houses
After studying the architecture of the houses and their history in social and cultural terms, which reflected diverse self-contained African American communities, Rick Lowe decided to refurbish them as a new form of art, cultural and social action among the community. The assumption of Lowe was that the site could provide both a powerful and accessible material link to the African-American past and a setting within which the work of contemporary African-America artists could be produced and accessible to the African-American community of The Third Ward.

Ultimately, the houses were transformed into affordable homes for single mothers and artists in residence, while maintaining their architectural integrity. In this way, Lowe has rewritten the traditional narrative of urban redevelopment by locating the shotgun houses as a focal point of the Third Ward, an element to be celebrated and linked to cultural traditions in the face of processes that seek to remove poor and working-class residents.
Since their inception, Project Row Houses has grown both in spatial and activities terms: from the original one and a half to six blocks, and from twenty-two to forty houses. In the beginning, it was assumed that changing the aesthetics would be enough but this proved to be wrong as what was pointed as a real need (by the community) were jobs. Although, to create jobs, it was important to first change the perception of outsiders to the community and this could be, partially, done through the aesthetics of the place, making it look safer and showing its true stories and History. These include twelve artist exhibition and artist in residency spaces, seven houses for young mothers (Young Mothers Residential Program at Project Row Houses provides housing and counselling on

personal growth and parenting skills), office spaces, a community gallery, a park, low-income residential and commercial spaces. Project Row Houses can be described today as a public urban art project, which encourages art production but also "art and cultural education, historic preservation, neighbourhood revitalization and community service." (Tucker, 1995)

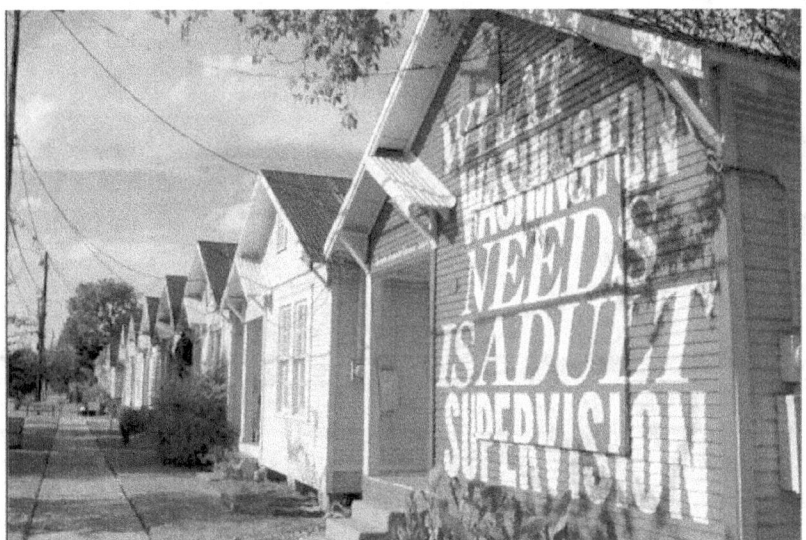

Fig. 2: Project Row Houses. © Project Row Houses

In 2003, Project Row Houses established the Row House Community Development Corporation as a separate corporation. It was created with the aim of broadening the project's focus to preserve community, and addresses housing and related community and economic development needs by providing low-income rental housing.

In 2012, Project Row Houses was in the mist of developing its 10-year plan. According to Rick Lowe (2012), the plan had two parts: local, and national and international activities. On the local level, the plan was described as a "continuation of growing impact within the 40 block area by building additional houses, preserving architecture, both houses and commercial buildings, adding new cultural and social service facilities, and nurturing small business development." On the national level, Project Row Houses defined their methodology and, in 2013, began a process of selecting sites to expand the project in similar social and cultural contexts.

Multidisciplinary as a motor to achieve social change

Project Row Houses exists comfortably between the worlds of art, culture and project management: "The multi-layering of the different ways of seeing, i.e., artists, architects, community members, historians, arts administrators, developers, etc., gave the project a complexity that was more natural than if it was developed strictly by artists or architects. If it was not for the multiple interests in the project, I'm not sure if it would have been sustainable or on going. It's expected for artists or architects to think about the "final" product of their work, but when community interest, i.e., residents, city government, historian, administrators, etc., are truly connected to the project, the vitality of the project becomes creatively responding to the issues and challenges brought forth by the community. Not in the refinement of the final product." (Lowe, 2012). Rick Lowe started the project in 1993 having in mind the artistic, cultural and economical development of The Third Ward. His idea to create temporary public urban art installations in The Third Wards neighbourhood grew out of discussions about how African-American in Houston could make their work more accessible to the African-American community.

Rick Lowe, the artist who initiated Project Row Houses, is highly influenced by the concept of social-sculpture, a philosophy coined by German artist Joseph Beuys (1921 – 1986) and by artist John Biggers (1924 – 2001), who was born in a shotgun house. Project Row Houses is founded on the principle that art creates a community, in a social activity, and that can be the foundation for revitalising depressed inner-city neighbourhoods. In this way, Project Row Houses can be compared to the idea of social-sculpture or sculpture as an art form and a social activity where every individual can be an artist. The mission of Project Row Houses is to create community through the celebration of art, African American history and culture.

Project Row Houses' central mission is to establish a forum for dialogue between artists and the Third Ward community within the context of its African-American culture and history, putting the focus on the understanding and integration of the existing cultural references. During a residency, an artist is required to conduct workshops with community members where they discuss their installations in the houses or give instruction on small art projects. The art produced and exhibited within these characteristics of participation and collaboration express a framework of cultural self-definition and collective identity which is inherently bound up with the traditions, history and social values of the African-American community. The project challenges each artist to interweave his personal vision with the community and the unique space of the shotgun house – echoing the traditional African artisan's creative process of melding collective values and personal visions (Willett, 1971).

In Project Row Houses, the leadership of the project endeavour spans from a generalist role for all aspects of design and delivery including cost control and time management to responsibility for identifying stakeholders, presenting a strategy and raising funds. This approach can be more identified with an early concept of project management, prior to the modern project management or complex project management, and lacks a thorough understanding of what Project Management truly means and its potential in terms of taking a project to a successful outcome. This was observed in many art projects. Project Management is increasingly becoming a claimed discipline in the Arts. Museums recruit art managers but they lack an understanding of what the discipline means as a profession. This can be seen in the description of the roles of an art project manager, which corresponds more to the role of a curator than to the one of a project manager. As observed in Project Morrinho, it seems that the role of a project manager is put as a role of the artists and project's authors for reasons as the fear of losing control of the project and loosing the creativity inherent to art and not identified in scientific disciplines, which shows that experts in a field have very little knowledge of other fields.

Conclusion: finding a broader discourse of multidisciplinary in urban art projects

This research started with the goal of exploring the idea of art projects producing social change and answering the question how can an urban art project contribute to social change for the better in a specific urban community? Along the research path, observing various art projects and understanding the history of art in relation to social change, it became clear that art alone might not be able to produce effective social change.

In the case of Project Row Houses, the authors began with the assumption that changing the aesthetics of the neighbourhood would be enough to make outsiders feel safe and this would produce change. The programmes and activities at Project Row Houses advocate that art and creativity should be viewed as an integral part of life, exemplified in African cultural traditions wherein art is interwoven into the very fabric of life through rituals and ceremony activities. Even though the art aspect in this project was always considered as important and it can be concluded that it does play a very relevant role through its activities and solutions proposed, the community members pointed the main problem of the lack of jobs and it was observed by the authors that they were not very interested in arts itself but in what they could do with it in a more informal and natural way, through the creative creation of jobs. Here, three facts became clear: the crucial importance of understanding the existing cultural references; the need to understand that art can play a role but alone, might not be enough in producing social change; and, finally, the need to make a plan for implementing a sustainable project.

The need of planning was exactly what seemed to fail in Project Morrinho, which strongest point showed to be simultaneously the weakest point. Project Morrinho did not start as a project and had no intention to change a thing in the community where it was implemented. With all its activities and branches it was quickly named as a project. Created within the community, it naturally respected, understood and integrated all existing cultural references, which is something unique in a project. Although, the artistic, DIY and spontaneous-anarchic characteristics that made the project so interesting also put it in danger many times. The project leaders and members show some resistance to have outsiders in the project, besides the sporadic intervention of volunteers from outside the community.

In the case of Project Row Houses, Rick Lowe started the project in 1993 with long-term goals and project management strategies were applied, in an informal level, from the very start with contributions from professional art managers, administrators, community members, historians, and developers. The strategies of Project Management identified in Project Row Houses share a common preoccupation with routine, day-to-day maintenance of the work processes and people for whom they are responsible. Even though the project did not hire a professional project manager, the multidisciplinary team managed to follow project management phases and steps and identified stakeholders. This identification from an early phase made possible to sustain the project and make it evolve to an organisation that programmes and plans for each five years. It can be concluded here that the use of project management is of utmost importance in this project in special for the planning and the identification of stakeholders in order to keep the organisation alive and sustainable.

Project Morrinho lacked planning and dismissed the professional use of project management, which they only used in such an empirical level that they did not acknowledge. As observed before, the artistic, chaotic and creative aspects that make the project work in many ways put it at risk many times and it seems that it would benefit tremendously from the use and contribution of professional project management. For a project which main goal is changing the perception that the general people have towards the inhabitants of a favela, this would be a great achievement.

The third concluding remark is linked to the possibility of using multidisciplinary as a motor for achieving social change in linking different disciplines. At first sight, the proposal of combining and integrating such apparently different disciplines in a multidisciplinary approach might sound odd. A common mistaken assumption is that Art is a discipline praising chaos, creativity and refusing organisational methods. This might be partially true, in special when looking at traditional art academia but if we look into contemporary art and the field of arts management this proves to be a wrong assumption as there is a clear need for organisational, communication and management skills. To someone with little knowledge in Project Management, it would be easy to assume that this discipline is very structured, pragmatic but that it also dismisses creativity. It does not take a very deep study to prove this assumption wrong as, in Modern Project Management, creativity is highly regarded. The way the same concepts are seen under each discipline shows various differences. This might be one of the reasons why the combination of the scientific disciplines and art is still rather problematic and needs further study. The concluding remark lies exactly in this need for further study in the combination and integration of the different ideas towards the same concepts by each discipline. Each discipline shows its specific narratives towards social change but, alone, each of them show problems in being successful. Integrating the knowledge of Art, Cultural Studies and

Project Management in a Multidisciplinary approach to the primary research question is to be seen as one possibility among others. Multidisciplinary implies the integration and combination of knowledge, narratives and experiences from different disciplines at various stages of the project.

Finally, it is possible to observe that the lessons learned point to a possible conclusion of this study, which remains open for future research focusing on the importance of the role of multidisciplinary in linking Art, Cultural Studies and Project Management in projects for social change. Common assumptions and preconceived ideas about what each discipline might encompass may be the reason why art projects claiming to be multidisciplinary are, in fact, multidisciplinary only within creative and similar disciplines. If the assumptions and preconceived ideas about disciplines and their different notions about the same concepts would be clarified, we might be able to successfully integrate very different disciplines in the same project in a broader discourse of multidisciplinary.

Notes and References

1 It is believed that Trotsky and André Breton wrote the Manifesto, although Rivera and Breton signed it.

2 Herbert Marcuse in his letters to the Chicago Surrealists (Marcuse 2000, pp. 109-128) cited this passage of the Manifesto (Marcuse, 2000, p. 123) to clarify is position arguing that art is not revolutionary by making calls to the working class and bringing the masses together to manifest in the streets. To him, in a one-dimensional capitalist society the working class would always be manipulated, and therefore, the revolutionary would be the role of the form of artworks as they could subvert instrumental reality and empower imagination. In other writings Marcuse argues that revolutionary literature cannot be democratic in a society where the proletarians have no interest in the revolutionary (Marcuse, 1972, p. 121) and that art is not revolutionary if it is made for the working class, but that revolutionary art is oriented on the form of art itself (Marcuse, 1977, p. 197).

3 Valladares, Licia. Social sciences representations of favelas in Rio de Janeiro: A Historical perspective. 2009.

4 Favela trees are a typical plant of the Caatinga region, in Bahia, resistant to the long dry period to which they are submitted.

5 "Inter-American Development Bank funded this US$180 million "slum to neighborhood" project in 1995 in which it sought to integrate existing favelas into the fabric of the city through infrastructure upgrading and service increases. The project involves 253,000 residents in 73 communities. Key to the success of this large project was a committed and flexible city government and the use of intra- and extra-institutional partnerships with NGOs, the private sector, churches, and the general population. Especially instrumental was the use of grass-roots level infrastructure upgrading experts as project managers who could work easily with both the government and with the community members." Source http://web.mit.edu/urbanupgrading/upgrading/case-examples/ce-BL-fav.html (August 2012)

6 "Rio Cidade Project was part of an urban intervention established in Rio, between 1995 and 2000, following the 90s urban investments, with strong influence from the politics applied at American and European cities, like Barcelona. "Rio Cidade" was part of one of the projects included in Rio de Janeiro's City Strategy, under the subtitle "the urbanism is back to the city". This plan was worked out on Cesar Maia's council administration (1993-1996) and it was concluded in September, 1995." Source http://www.ub.edu/geocrit/-xcol/338.htm (August 2012)

7 The shotgun was introduced to the U.S. by free Haitians who, in essence, reconnected African-Americans with the socially intimate housing space that many historians believe evolved form the one-room units of the Yoruba compound in West-Africa – where most slaves brought to America were captured.

Willett, Frank. African Art: An Introduction. New York: Thames and Hudson, 1971.
Valladares, Licia. Social sciences representations of favelas in Rio de Janeiro: A Historical perspective. Lille: Lanic Etext Collection, 2009.
Vlach, John Michael. "The Shotgun House: An African. Architectural Legacy." In Common Places: Readings in American Vernacular Architecture, by Dell Upton and John Michael Vlach, 58-77. Athens, Georgia: University of Georgia Press, 1976.
Adorno, Theodor W. Aesthetic Theory. Translated by Christian Lenhardt. London: Routledge and Kegan Paul, 1958.
Baumgarten, Alexander Gottlieb. Aesthetica. Hildesheim. G. Olms., 1750 / 1961.
Bourdieu, P., and A. Darbel. The Love of Art : European art museums and their public. . Translated by Caroline and Merriman, Nick. Beattie. Cambridge: Polity Press, 1969.
Bourdieu, Pierre. Distinction: A Social Critique of the Judgement of Taste. Cambridge: Harvard University Press, 1984.
Breton, André, and Diego Rivera. Manifesto for an Independent Revolutionary Art. 1938. http://www.marxists.org/subject/art/lit_crit/works/rivera/manifesto.htm (accessed October 28, 2011).
Cropper, John, interview by Luisa Santos. personal communication (June 3, 2013).
Fuchs, Christian, and Franziska Holzner. Art as a Complex, Dynamic System. INTAS-research project "Human Strategies in Complexity"., 2000.
Herder, Johann Gottfried. Kritische Wälder, oder Betrachtungen, die Wissenschaft und Kunst des Schönen betreffend ("Groves of Criticism, or Considerations concerning the Science and Art of the Beautiful"). Edited by Gunter E. Grimm. Frankfurt am Main: Deutscher Klassiker Verlag, 1993.
Luhmann, N. Social Systems. Stanford, CA: Stanford University Press, 1995.
Luhmann, Niklas. "World Art." In Unobservable world of art and architecture., by N. Luhmann / F. Bunsen / D. Baecker, 7-46. Bielefeld: Haux, 1990.
Lukács, Georg. Art and Objective Truth. London: Merlin, 1954.
Lind, Maria. "Returning on Bikes: Notes on social practice." In Living as Form: Socially Engaged Art from 1991-2011, by Nato Thomson, 46-56. New York: The MIT Press, 2011.
Lowe, Rick, interview by Luisa Santos. Project Row Houses - interview with Rick lowe in the frame of There is no knife without roses (September 25, 2012).
Marcuse, Herbert. The Aesthetic Dimension: Toward a Critique of Marxist Aesthetics. Boston: Beacon Press., 1978.
Perlman, Janice. O Mito da Marginalidade: favelas e política no Rio de Janeiro. Rio de Janeiro: Paz e Terra, 1977.
PM4NGOs. "PM4NGOs - Pro guide." PM4NGOs . 2011. http://www.pm4ngos.org/ (accessed June 11, 2012).
Serra, Chico, and Cilan Oliveira, interview by Luisa Santos. Project Morrinho: interview in the frame of There is no knife without roses (September 10, 2012).
Tucker, Sheryl G. "Reinnovating the African-American Shotgun House [Roots]." Places Journal, no. 10 (January 1995): 64-71.

Leticia Carmo, Luca Pattaroni, Mischa Piraud, Yves Pedrazzini
Laboratory of Urban Sociology, EPFL, Switzerland

Creativity without critique
An inquiry into the aesthetization of the alternative culture

The category of "creative city" is far from neutral. Indeed, it can be linked to very contrasted – and even opposed – practices and urban worlds. In order to grasp those differences, we need to take a closer look at what is entailed in the concepts of "creativity" and "art", analysing in particular their political dimension. In this paper we defend the idea that it is the ambiguous polysemy of the notion of creativity – especially under the influence of the work of Florida (2002, 2012) – that is the cause of many problems in the contemporary analysis of urban dynamics. Among other, contemporary conceptions of creativity tend to underestimate its potentially subversive dimension in order to accentuate its compatibility with economic imperatives. A striking illustration of this "creativity without critique" is given by the aesthetic register of the « alternative culture » – characterized by recycling practices, urban wastelands – which nowadays tends to become devoid of its political implication and be used as a commercial niche (a process we call « aesthetization »). To illustrate this question, we analyse various examples found in cultural places in Lisbon, Geneva and Ljubljana.

For the contemporary tourist – guided by his Easy Jet magazine – it is nowadays quite normal to visit in European cities arty squats or have a drink in bars full of graffiti and recycled chairs. Usually those places are nowadays only loosely linked to what used to be called "alternative culture", based on a radical critique of the capitalist society. In other words, they appear more as the aesthetic scene of new consumption niche than places of an enacted critique of the established order (Pattaroni, 2014) In this paper we will attempt to account for this transformation, that is the partial removal of the subversive dimension of the aesthetics of the alternative culture. How was it possible to turn it into a mere "motif" detached from its initial political context and applied as a decorative design in other areas. More fundamentally, at stake beyond what we propose to call here the aesthetization of the alternative culture is a relative de-politicization of the central notion of creativity, shying it away from it longstanding critical tradition. Indeed creativity went, in 40 years, from one of the central category of the critique of capitalism to one of the core concept of the "cognitive capitalism" (Moulier-Boutang, 2007). This is not an anecdotic shift, as the critical dimension of creativity is almost one of its constitutive features.

Creativity, Productivity and the Art: Subversion and the City
« De la création d'art – rare, exceptionnelle – et de sa divulgation, il en est comme de ces îles désertes dont la sauvagerie, qui en fait l'attrait, cesse sitôt que la propagande hôtelière y amène des touristes. N'y reste plus alors qu'une feinte sauvagerie rebutante et les amateurs de sites rares exceptionnels, cherchent un autre lieu où planter leur tente » (Dubuffet : 43).

The critical stance of creativity
As it is well known, art isn't intrinsically linked to the idea of creativity. It is only around the 18th century, and its subjectivist turn, that it begins to supersede a system based on imitation. Indeed, up to that time, art was thought of fundamentally as a mimesis, an imitation of the world where beauty is truth (Genard, 2003). On the contrary, creativity was at the centre of a conception of art as a subjective act of the artist seen as a "demiurge". The new "vocational" status of the artist that came along this art system based on an ideal of creativity and innovation (Heinich, 1996) expanded rapidly throughout the 19th and 20th centuries to the point of becoming in the last decades the model of the worker (Menger, 2002) and of neo-management (Chiapello, 1998). A central step in this evolution is the constitution of the romantic ideal of the 19th century – along the notion of bohème – that gave creativity its full critical dimension. Indeed, this model of a creative and unconventional artist became the explicit counter-model to the "ponderous, inhibited, hypocritical bourgeois who is incapable of innovation, wrapped up in convention, in calculation" (Genard). During the last part of the 19th century an "artist critique" of capitalism emerged – intertwined with its "social critique" (among others the Marxist one) – based on a denunciation of the oppressing and dehumanization effect of the capitalist system (Boltanski and Chiapello, 1999).

It is nevertheless only in the early 20th Century that this critical and political dimension of creativity took its full dimension within the modernist avant-garde where the subversive individuality of the artist and the political figure of the citizen came together in their common refusal of austere bourgeois productivism. By the mid-century, various artists and intellectuals gave it its full theoretical meaning. Thus, for Dubuffet the value of a work of art is measured by the gap that separates it from the establishment: i.e. the value of art is directly linked to its potential for subversion (Dubuffet, 1986 : 99). This opposition between art and establishment is systematized in particular in the work of T. W. Adorno. Indeed for Adorno, art as a principle of non-identity is deeply subversive with regards to the establishment and, as a result, incompatible with a bourgeois order and even more so with the market. Therefore, it doesn't only concern "engaged art" that carries a manifest message with a critical aim, but, more fundamentally, the displacement undertaken by art and new realities that it produces. We can link this to Deleuze and Guattari's idea of art opening a "ligne de fuite". Art is subversive as such by breaking with an oppressive reality's identity principle, not because it suggests other ways of perceiving the world.

This critique of an asphyxiating order – and the new intertwining of art and the political that it entails – was enacted in particular in the "Events of May 68" that established a new political commitment as much as an artistic commitment of the political. Under the influence of the situationnists among other, the emergence of the New Left thus signalled a new relationship between art and the political: on the one hand, politics are no longer restricted to the limits of political institutions but take form in "everyday life"; and on the other hand the different "artistic worlds" open up post-May 68 and extend beyond the official "cultured-culture". As Genard states it, this encounter contributed to a real democratization of the figure of the artist as a creator which is also the start of it later "recuperation" (Genard, 2003).

If creativity and art took a crucial role it is because the critique had to be enacted in everyday life, questioning not only an abstract system but also the "partage du sensible"[1], i.e., the functionalist shaping of the space (standardization, zoning, and so on) that was at the root of (re)production of the capitalist urban order (Lefebvre, 1974; Cogato, Pattaroni, Piraud and Tirone, 2013, Pattaroni, 2014) The "alternative culture" was born in this new political perspective, moving away from the traditional and "authoritarian" left – who was in general suspicious toward the subjectivity of artists. As we were able to study it in the history of urban struggle in Geneva (Cogato et al., Pattaroni, 2014), it is more precisely product of an encounter between new leftist movement (Maoist, amongst others) and situationnist perspectives (along with movements such as the living theatre).

During the European urban struggles of the 1970's a double split – vis-à-vis both institutional "democracy" and revolutionary institutions – put into question the entire political and police framework that had been established at the end of the 19th century. This political framework of "organized modernity" is based upon the development of mass political parties, the rationalization of the State and its means of intervention (statistics, planning, etc.) as well as of means of production (Fordism) (Wagner, 1996). The result was a generalized rejection of all the entities that participate in this reality, whether they were in power or contesting it (the communist movements in particular, shared the major presuppositions regarding an organization of the society based on mass representation and rationalization of the production and state apparatus). In terms of the division of perception, this police order was based in particular on an array of territorial measures aiming to manage the salaried masses, standardized social housing, zoning, development of road systems (Du Pasquier & Marco, 2009). From then on, criticism with regards to the living environment and life in general was taken up, both in Geneva and elsewhere in Europe, by a "New Left" – a multitude of small political groups with wide-ranging ideological orientations, struggling for various causes – against atomic energy, for the Women's Liberation Movement, pacifist movements, neighbourhood associations, etc. (Duvanel and Levy, 1984; Gros, 1987).

Accordingly the political discourses and practices of this New Left – fed from the double sources of "self-managed" Marxism (i.e. Trotskyism and Maoism) and "psycho analytic theories of the personality and human interaction" (that we find in the writings of Marcuse for example) (Duvanel and Levy, 1984: 119) – constitutes an "alternative culture" marked in particular by a reorientation, a transition from the democratization of culture to cultural democracy – i.e. from the circulation to the greatest number of a legitimate body of work to the establishment as culture of the creations of the largest number of people. In other words, creativity (which in this perspective means "the capability of each one") was not anymore a side activity but it contributed directly to the perceptual and material critique of the established order. In this perspective, "the aesthetics of the alternative culture" was an intrinsic part of its political project. Before we turn to the "aesthetization" process, we have to describe more in detail the perceptual characteristics of the "alternative culture" and the way they corresponded to a critique of the capitalist order. A first step is to better understand the ambiguity of the notion of alternative.

The political dimension of the Alternative culture and its ambiguities

Alternative isn't necessarily connected with a marginal or peripheral kind of world. The word "alternative" comes from "alter", which in Latin means "other", another possibility. In this fundamental sense, alternative is about opening new possibilities, therefore about hope and empowering (Nishat Awan, 2011, p. 27). Nevertheless, as we suggested before, the historical opposing reference – the alter – is the "mainstream culture", the dominant one, making the alternative an opposition. Thierry Paquot et al. (2012) describes this link between the search for experimental lifestyles, the ideological and the physical opposition to norms : an alternative person "would be someone who refuses to conform to the norm", "one that is non-conformist as well as experimental"; alternative groups "endeavour to live, to produce, to consume, to educate and to love differently… their paths…[marking]…a divergence from the pervading conformism" and "they offer an aside from what is imposed, normed, prescribed and standardized"; alternative movements are "an act of political protest, a stance against the establishment".

The already classical work of Raymond Williams is probably the most insightful attempt to clarify those ambiguities. Indeed, in his famous article "Base and Superstructure in Marxist Cultural Theory" (1973), Raymond Williams opposes the gramscian notion of "cultural hegemony" to the notion of "alternative culture". The former, understood to be "a core system of practices, meanings and values that can be considered to be dominant and effective", doesn't imply any idea of worth but depends principally on its centrality (Williams, 2006: 136). According to him, hegemony isn't the product of "simple opinion or simple manipulation" but rather the results from an "entire body of practices and expectations – the focus of our energy, our basic understanding of human nature and the world around us (ibid). In other words, understood as such, an hegemonic culture can be compared to what Bourdieu called the "practical sense", something along the lines of a widely shared sense of reality: "the sense of reality that is absolute because it is well-tried, it is very difficult for most members of society to go beyond it, in most areas of life" (ibid).

Williams distinguishes the alternative elements and oppositional elements, and this shift allows us to analyse more subtly the emergence of contemporary urban practices:

« There is a simple theoretical distinction between alternative and oppositional, that is to say between someone who simply finds a different way to live and wishes to be left alone with it, and someone who finds a different way to live and wants to change the society in its light. This is usually the difference between individual and small-group solutions to social crisis and those solutions which properly belong to political and ultimately revolutionary practice. But it is often a very narrow line, in reality, between alternative and oppositional. A meaning or a practice may be tolerated as a deviation, and yet still be seen only as another particular way to live. But as the necessary area of effective dominance extends, the same meanings and practices can be seen by the dominant culture, not merely as disregarding or despising it, but as challenging it. » (Williams, 2006 : 138). As suggested here by Williams, the narrow line between alternative and oppositional depends not only on the attitude or will of the actors but also on the range of authorized differences a given order allow for. What happens in reality is the fact that the mere attempt to invent and practice alternative ways of life usually confronts the established urban order and its normative ascription of a restricted range of authorized and legitimized lifestyles (Pattaroni, 2007). It is exactly what happened when people in the 70's and 80's started to live – in various squats across Europe – according to the major principles of the raising "alternative culture".

In our earlier work we have been able to identify some of the major principles governing the squatter's alternative culture (Pattaroni, 2007; Breviglieri, 2009). We believe that those principles were largely shared by the all movements and it is easy also to show that they have been embedded in the actual ideology of the urban sustainable development which can be seen partly as a result of the penetration of the ideals of the urban struggles and the institutionalization of their actors. Briefly stated, the "grammar of the alternative culture" – drawing the "good" ways to organize and live together – was based on 4 major principles : Self-determination (self-management, participation and autonomy against authoritarian systems), Solidarity (sharing, collectivization of goods against private property), Hospitality (conviviality, inclusion against individualization process and exclusion), Creativity (Do-it-Yourself (DiY) and subjective expression against standardization and automation process). Those principles weren't an abstract ideology but, as we suggested with the idea of an enacted critique, they actively contributed to a social and spatial transformation of the built environment. When a vacant building is first occupied, the squatters will set about making the place inhabitable. This activity is undertaken in accordance with the shared principles of the "alternative culture". Walls are demolished in squatted houses in order to allow for shared spaces enabling political and festive assemblies. Objects are collectivized and houses are painted and manually transformed in order to appropriate them and mark their difference within the urban order. Each different coat of paint is the trace of non-standardized human activity where different coloured door frames indicate reused pots of paint. Aesthetics, in this perspective, is an outcome – or more a coproduction – of the implementation of this enacted or embedded critique, opening up alternative possibilities of living together.

Indeed, this horizontal organization of work leaves "traces" on the physical aspect of the place – frequently without work share. C.S. Peirce (1978) would describe this mark of horizontality and liberation of desire as an "index". These traces form a set of percepts and tangible elements that indicate that the work has not been standardized, is not "professional" and has not tried to erase all the traces of the work required for this type of do-it-yourself renovation. The mosaic that adorns the floor of the toilettes of the Image #1, for instance, illustrates this desire to live differently – political orientation is inscribed physically on the place.

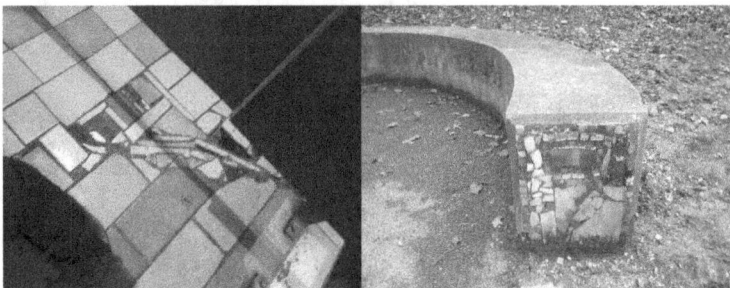

Image #1 – Wc mosaic, Menza Pri Koritu, Metelkova, Ljubljana | Bench mosaic, Théatre Galpon, Geneva, Switzerland (photos by Letícia Carmo, 2014)

Let's see now in detail these perceptual elements.

The aesthetics of the alternative culture
As we just suggested, alternative culture builds upon an intimate link between politics and aesthetics. Therefore, an alternative experience implies the production of specific places, which tend to group certain spatial and aesthetic characteristics. In the following table (Table #1), we can see examples of cultural spaces (in some European cities like Berlin, Ljubljana, Geneva or Paris, and approximately in a timeframe that considers the last 20 years), that join together some common elements of what we call "the aesthetics of the alternative culture", supported by an architectural structure; working as a whole, this provokes a scenographic effect on this sort of places, which is based on artists' and craftsmen's interventions, on recycling practices of construction, rearrangement and decoration and also on a spontaneous, participative, organic action. This way of transforming and appropriating the space in this way enhances the sense of unity of these places, in what concerns its aesthetics, and it also gives them a specific identity. Some of the elements we can identify on these images are:

- the use of street walls as canvas: painted murals, graffiti, tags, stencils, posters, paste-up's, etc;
- political, poetic and spiritual manifest messages (usually having a strong symbolic character, being present on walls, but also on flags, for instance);
- occupation of old, abandoned or degraded buildings (mainly factories, barracks, storage pavilions, palaces…) and construction of new precarious buildings;
- coloured façades and other particular architectural elements, such as windows, for example;
- use of natural materials, such as wood, and metal handcrafted structures, urban furniture, sculpture or other objects;

- recycled objects and construction materials, which are used also for the previously mentioned cases (old bicycles, hanged old shoes, etc);
- untidy and chaotic environment given by old and ruined elements, such as broken tiles, ceramics and glass, raw and rough details, unfinished work or overlapped interventions;
- wild" vegetation and gardening.

This aesthetics of the "alternative culture" is intrinsically related to artistic and political practices that tend to work together. It seems to us that Street Art follow the same line – of what we could call "expressive politic" – and is a particular good example of the way art can be constitutive of a political stance. Indeed street art was – and still is to a certain extent – an expression of a rupture with the standard ways of living and a critique of the urban space.

If we focus on this wish for rupture and resistance vis-à-vis the standard, we realise that there exists in contemporary settings a clear contrast between the dominant and the alternative, which is constantly present in the examples we gave. Nevertheless, this dissimilarity is, sometimes, not totally clear-cut. If we explore this issue in a more concrete way, through the analysis of some examples in the city of Lisbon (Table #2), we realise that this aesthetics of the alternative culture that we mention is a more complex thing than we might have thought in the beginning. It is probably due to the fact we are in a situation where this aesthetics has already largely been legitimized as part of the ordinary landscapes of contemporary cities. In Table #2, we observe some examples of street art and urban creativity that vary in accordance with the adopted technique, the material support or the contents. Some of the walls belong to the streets and some others to inner environments. Nevertheless, they all belong to urban environments and we might agree that they display an alternative kind of aesthetics; yet, their contents definitely vary, the examples presented on the left side of the table clearly being distinct from those on the right side.

So what remains from the subversive dimension of, Street art and more broadly of the creative dimension of alternative culture? We may notice that, as we move from the left to the right side of the previously mentioned table of images, the political and social commitment and the critical contents of the examples decrease. We realise as well that, as far as we go to the right of the table, the exposed artistic interventions benefit more and more from institutional support, municipal or private (a factor that is intrinsically related with "creative cities" strategies of the development of the city – Florida, 2012 & Landry, 2003). On the other hand, as we go to the left on this table, the interventions are more spontaneous and critique; therefore more ephemeral. Many of those last examples are "popular appropriations" of small fragments of the city, representing interesting forms of a lively usage of the common space producing stimulating affordances enabling a more intense urban experience and eventual feelings of belonging. The Image #19 of the Table # 2 is exemplary of this micro-scale re-appropriation of the city. It acts over just a small detail but it is powerful, because it reinvests the city in order to transform it into a non-ordinary place. It is at this level of action, that we can find a parallelism with the Situationist approaches when they invite us to consider the city as the place "of a revolutionary transformation of the existence, achieved through the participation of the citizens and the reintegration of the poetic into the ordinary life"[2] (Simay, 2008).

What we call "aesthetization of the alternative culture" – against its aesthetics – is precisely when the percepts of this culture starts loosing the link with the project of everyday appropriation of the urban environment. More broadly, this "aesthetization" closes practical alternative possibilities to the capitalist dominant urban order. Once aestheticized, the perceptual affordances loose their role of support for re-appropriation (and their emancipatory situationnist potential), playing only a visual and consumerist role, as if the "alternative" had become a decorative motif, an architectural style (as gothic, or baroque, for example). In other words, the link between the significant and the signifier is broken, and the visual aesthetics of the alternative culture functions as a "floating signifier". In order to understand this process we need to go back to the history of capitalism and the relation between the "alternative" world and the ideology of the "creative cities".

Aesthetization of the alternative culture: creativity within the market

Following the reorganizations of the Seventies, a third age of capitalism emerged which we can call "late" or "cognitive". In this new capitalist era the share of the production of knowledge, and more widely "the production of man by man", has risen dramatically. (Moulier-Boutang, 2007). The theories on the "creative economy" constitute a hybrid attempt to describe these transformations and testify the reorganization of social structures around this notion of "creativity". These theories are hybrid in the sense that they function within a system they describe and that they claim to criticize, at the same time promoting a "creative city" brand (http://charleslandry.com/; www.creativeclass.com). These theories generally oppose the people who generate income through a creative activity to those who don't. Yet this re-identifies creativity and productivity. Indeed seeing how the capital has established any form of externality within itself, these authors equate the lexical field of creativity with that of an innovation as part of the process of capitalist production. In the previous methods of production – Fordism – cities served as "infrastructural hubs" favouring business (Sassen). However this new "creative economy" integrates cities as merchandise and a means of production. Cities are no longer outside the process of production but an integral part of it. Thus, the semantic field of creativity is reduced to creativity-productivity, leaving out the non-capitalist aspect of creation.

It is this ambiguous polysemy of the notion of "creativity" – especially under the influence of the work of Richard Florida (2002, 2012) – that is the cause of many problems in the contemporary analysis of urban dynamics. Among others, those contemporary conceptions of "creativity" tend to underestimate its "élan vital", or "vital impetus" (Bergson, 1907, Deleuze, 1966) and, as we argued, their historical subversive dimension. This intended underestimation tends to create a compatibility with economical imperatives. To compensate for this ambiguity we should probably distinguish Florida-Landry's creativity-productivity (2002-2012; 2000) from a Bergson-inspired "vital creativity" in which creativity consists more generally in the act of creating virtual differences through a vital impetus (Deleuze 1966; Kisukidi, 2013). Indeed, in his Manifeste différentialiste published in 1970, Henri Lefebvre used the terms of "creativity" and "productivity" to distinguish creative activities from those that are involved in the process of capitalist production. From this perspective, "creativity" sides with "use value" and therefore can be opposed to the "exchange value". This dimension of "creativity", with regards to capitalist productivity, is generally present in the Marxist conception of art.

We believe that this distinction is very important to understand the transformations of the relation between dominant and alternative culture (Image #2 and Image #3), and more specifically the way « alternative culture » tend to become a mere aesthetic motif of the contemporary « creative city » loosing its subversive dimension. This shift is not only a matter of ideological transformation: it plays out in the way alternative culture and the various artistic practices have been institutionalized (towards a productive-creativity).

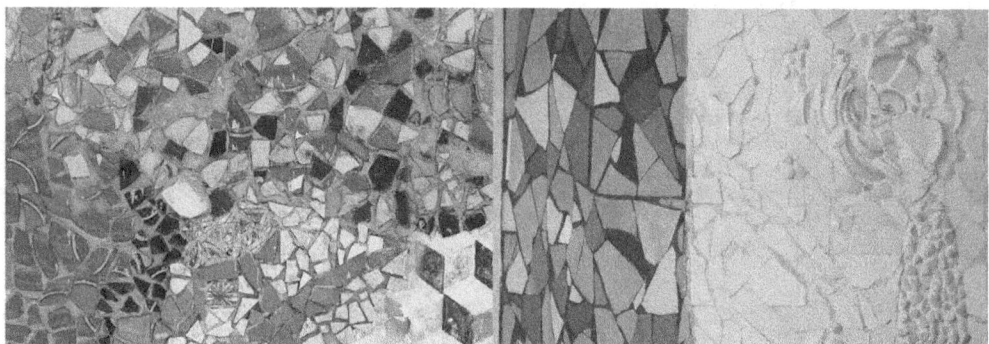

Image #2 – Walls's ceramics covering mosaic, at Metelkova, Ljubljana. On the image on the left we can see the grassroots' technique, made up with broken tiles, plates, etc, while on the image on the right we can see the wall of the youth hostel Celica, decorated by the artists' group Sestava and run by the students' organization ŠOU. (photos by Letícia Carmo, 2014)

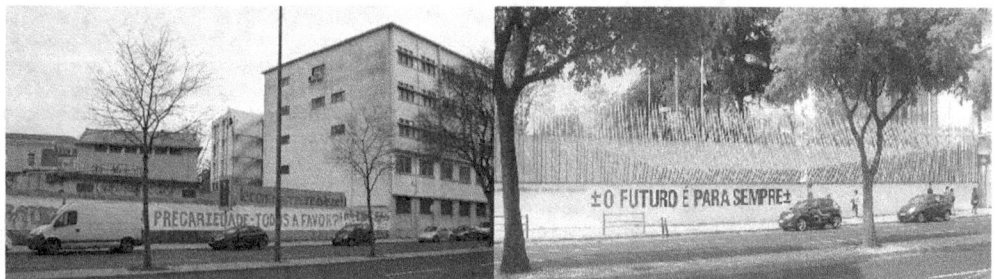

Image #3 – Walls of Avenida de Berna, in Lisbon, interventions done side by side – second one by the artist +- (photos by Letícia Carmo, 2013, and Mischa Piraud, 2014)

For instance, Street art as an underground and grassroots movements was at first mostly non-professionalized. But slowly, along its recognition as a legitimate art and an interesting input for the quality of urban environment (as a form of urban creativity), street art has evolved and become more and more professionalized and institutionalized to the point that its techniques are nowadays part of the academic formation.

In order to analyse more in detail those transformations, and open up the concept of institutionalization, it is interesting to distinguish three levels of action within the universe of urban creativity,: 1) grassroots and popular; 2) artistic (professionalized); 3) business. The trend is clearly from 1 towards 2 and 3. It is both a professionalization of alternative artistic expression and more fundamentally, as we suggested with the idea of cognitive capitalism, an integration of creativity within the core of capitalist process (creative management).

Just like Boltanksi and Chiapello enlighten about the integration of the "artistic critique" in the neoliberal system (Boltanski & Chiapello, 1999), there has been an integration of the "alternative universe" in the market and in city development strategies sustained by the concept of "creative cities". And this process occurs mainly through the recycling of the aesthetics, by creating an image, just as if alternative had become a slogan, or one more brand in the competitive worldwide market taking advantage of the process in order to make profit with it. In other words in this context of advanced capitalism, the term "alternative" seems to have become autonomous from its original signified form and functions as a "floating signifier" (Lévi-Strauss, 1950). The term is distanced from its original meaning and evolves away from its depart point. "Alternative" therefore no longer designates a non-hegemonic cultural system, but just a style that can be commodified.

In other words, the percepts of the traces of DiY that were at the roots of the aesthetics of alternative culture have now blossomed in many different places – more or less institutional ones or with a mercantile purpose – mostly removed from alternative principles, modes of organization and ways of life. In this way, this register of perception detached from its "signified" becomes the autonomous register of "hip" and "trendy", but also of "sustainable development" and "creative cities". In Geneva, the café La Petite Reine (just behind the central station) resorts to a whole series of "alternative" symbols, as we can see on the Image # 4. La Fureur de Lire hired interior designers to decorate it in a "squat style". In Lisbon, similar processes happen, like for instance in places as Pensão Amor, Lx Factory or Casa Independente (Image #4). Pensão Amor used to be a brothel existing in an underground street of Lisbon, and when it was transformed into an alternative cultural (night) place, the designers and the architects responsible for the new project decided to recover those underground memories in the new decoration of the place (Table #3). In this commodification of the aesthetics of the alternative culture, it can be argued that the creativity's subversive potential has waned.

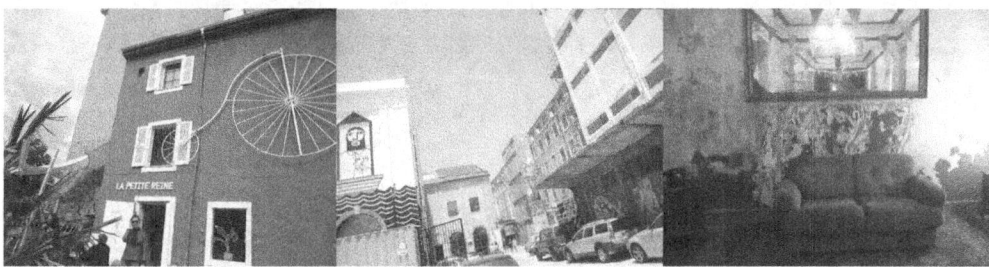

Image #4 – La Petite Reine, in Geneva, and Lx Factory and Casa Independente, in Lisbon
(photos by Letícia Carmo, 2012, 2014)

Under this ideology, and its counterpart of the sustainable urban development, Lefebvre's "the right to the city" (Lefebvre, 1968) has become a slogan that is conveniently used at any time, being easily found amongst the wide offer of graffiti that decorate the walls of the cities (Paquot, 2012, p. 269). Participation is not anymore the outcome of urban struggles and of occupied spaces but it is now registered in the texts of law[3] (Collectif Etc, 2012, p. 178). It is within such broader transformations of urban policies that the aesthetization of alternative culture takes its full political meaning, as an essential part of the larger process of producing the contemporary "guaranteed" and "attractive" urban environment.

Alternative as a trademark
Just as the participative process is gradually being framed by institutional authorities, so is the space of the city. This space is becoming more and more controlled, and reorganised under certain rules and obeying to particular laws, standards and regulations. As for this matter, the sociologist Marc Breviglieri draws on a guaranteed city ("la ville garantie"), where the urban environment is becoming more and more framed and "functionally normalised" and where spontaneity is disappearing and everything becomes safely predictable[4]. Such process of normalisation may lead to different kinds of consequences, such as:

- the control of one's behaviour, which can be made through the design of objects, urban furniture and environments, thus preventing people from acting in undesired ways (sometimes, actually, resulting in a very "unpleasant design"[5], just like, for instance, is elaborated by Savić and Savićić (Savićić & Savić, 2013));
- pre-defined and "convenient" ambiences created for a specific place.

Street art has a big influence in this matter of the creation of controlled ambiances, as if its purpose was the creation of huge scenographic panels at the scale of the city, thus becoming the stage for the expected actions of their actors (the inhabitants). In the case of Lisbon, for example, institutional (municipal) agents like GAU (Galeria de Arte Urbana) define which walls are or are not authorised for painting, in order to fight "vandalism", according to GAU's official Sílvia Câmara (in (Masboungi, 2013, p. 116). Consequently, spontaneous artistic action in the city is being controlled. A dilemma nevertheless results from this, since in 2013 a new law[6] was enacted that punishes illegal graffiti as a crime, the institutional context appearing in this way as contradictory: one institution protecting street art (GAU), while the other is punishing it (the national law). Being aware of the role assumed, GAU states that "urban art makes obviously part of the attracting power that Lisbon has over tourists or young creatives" (notice that Sílvia Câmara mention "urban art" and not "street art"). Nevertheless, it is interesting to see that they are also aware of the limits of their program: « The institutionalization of protest and independent forms is often accused of political appropriation of a popular expression that resists to the idea of "framing""[7] (Sílvia Câmara, in (Masboungi, 2013, p. 118).

Also the creative clusters (or creative industries) have a similar role on this process. Fábrica do Braço de Prata, Lx Factory[8], or more recently Village Underground Lisbon[9] are good examples, in Lisbon, of spaces that promote street art artists. But then, once again, these are controlled spaces for art production (the word "cluster" itself is already a sign of that), where – just like those "authorised walls" – places are available for urban art rather than street art (considering that street art has necessarily a spontaneous and free character, and that urban art works through curatorship processes and commissions, generally speaking). Hardly will subversive dimension be present in these walls now considered as works of art.

At this point, we would like to enlighten the importance of 3-dimensional space in relation to the graffiti and urban art, and the alternative culture. Not only walls have the role of supporting this kind of art, as we have already seen through some examples presented in the table of images #2, but also some architectural structures do have that role. One of the best examples is the Village

Underground (Table #4), that represents most of the main issues we have discussed on this paper:

- graffiti painting as a 'work of art', and scenography of the overall scene (by Corleone, as part of the outside exhibition of the Underdogs gallery);
- labyrinth 3-dymension structure, calling to explore its non-linear path within an adventurous spirit and an appealing sensible approach;
- semi-vacant post-industrial wasteland as the chosen place for territorial occupation (inside a delimited area of Carris, the public transportation company);
- containers as the architectural support, representative of the latest years' fashion of recycled ready-made architectures of rusty, unfinished and raw materials;
- normalised details: necessary safety objects, clean and finished construction details, uniformed and designed fancy furniture, sponsoring panels.

The combination of urban art, design, architecture and urban wastelands seems to be a formula of success to attract young creatives, supported by a "total design" that now also includes "creative management". This is obviously not the world of the counter-culture, but it is nevertheless based on alternative aesthetics, as we have seen. In the counter-cultural architectural experiences, the political and the subversive dimension of creativity play together in the everyday life environment. These total spaces are at the same time places to sleep, to encounter the other, to party, to create and to meet politically, and tend to disappear due to strict delimitation of functions (linked with security and market logics). What remains are places which look like squats but do serve for capitalist compatible creative activities.

Nevertheless places like Lx Factory. a nearby creative cluster in a former industrial compound, not only look alternative but they also embed part of the principles of the alternative culture (as they were integrated in the urban policies, new management principles and more broadly sustainable development ideology). The situation is therefore complicated and we should avoid raising a simplistic critique of the aesthetization of the alternative culture. Prior actors of that culture are now the producers of the guaranteed urban order), trying to promote creative places and participatory process (and even self-management within the institutions). The limit between critique and reinforcement of the established order is very thin and blurred. Artists themselves tend to oscillate between mere animators of the city (producers of its various ambiances) and actors of new critical intervention with the inhabitants. Theories of art reflect those new ambiguities, as it is shown by the movement "les nouveaux commanditaires" who attempt to remove art from capitalism – undoing what happened it the last decades (Hers & Douroux, 2011). The ambiguity of the treatment of street art – at the same time recognized and criminalized – is another indicator of this complexity. We believe that a detailed description and theorization of those processes of institutionalization – the "anesthetization" of alternative culture being only a part of the story, as is shown in the example of the Village Underground – is central in order to renew the possibility of artistic, social and political critique.

Notes and References
1 We use here Ranciere's concept which invite us to reflect on the material and aesthetic dimension of the political (Rancière, 1998, 2000 ; Dikeç, 2012)
2 Our translation of : « le lieu (…) d'une transformation révolutionnaire de l'existence, à travers la participation des citadins et la réintégration du poétique dans l'ordinaire. »
3 Our translation of : "Nous sommes arrivés à une situation étonnante: l'impérative participation des habitants à la fabrique de la ville est actée, inscrite dans les textes de la loi!"
4 "L'environnement urbain contemporain subit une normalisation fonctionnelle, il est désormais comme entièrement recouvert par un espace de références conventionnelles facilitant la prévisibilité de l'utilisation normale qu'on peut en faire » (Brevigleri, 2013, p. 218)
5 http://unpleasant.pravi.me/
6 Lei n.º 61/2013 de 23 de Agosto (http://dre.pt/pdf1sdip/2013/08/16200/0509005092.pdf)
7 Our translation : « L'institutionnalisation de formes essentiellement contestataires et irréductiblement indépendantes est souvent taxée de récupération politique d'une expression populaire qui résiste à toute idée de "cadrage". »
8 In collaboration with Wool (http://www.woolfest.org/about/wool-the-name/)
9 Associated with Underdogs gallery (http://www.under-dogs.net/)

Adorno T.W. (1978), Dialectique négative, Paris, Payot & Rivages Bergson H. (1907), L'évolution créatrice, Paris, PUF   Boltanski, L., & Chiapello, È. (1999). Le nouvel esprit du capitalisme. Paris, Gallimard.
Brevigleri, M. (2009), «Les habitations d'un genre nouveau : Le squat urbain et la possibilité du "conflit négocié" sur la qualité de vie», in L. Pattaroni, V. Kaufmann et A. Rabinovich (éds), Habitat en devenir, Lausanne, PPUR
Brevigleri, M. (2013) «Une brèche critique dans la «ville garantie» ? Espaces intercalaires et architectures d'usage» In Cogato-Lanza et al., De la différence urbaine. Le quartier des Grottes / Genève (pp. 213–236). Genève, MétisPresses.
Charbonneau, J.-P. (2012). «Eloge de la simplicité et du recyclage». In AlterArchitectures Manifesto (pp. 173–175). Gollion, CH: Eterotopia/ Infolio.
Chiapello E. (1998), Artistes versus managers: le management culturel face à la critique artiste, Paris, Metaillié
Cogato-Lanza E., Pattaroni L., Piraud M. & Tirone B. (2013), De la différence urbaine. Le quartier des Grottes / Genève, Genève, MétisPresses.
Collectif Etc. (2012), «Des architectes ordinaires" In AlterArchitectures Manifesto (pp. 173–175). Gollion, CH: Eterotopia/ Infolio.
Deleuze G. (1966), Le bergsonisme, Paris, PUF
Dikeç M. (2012), «Immigrants, Banlieues, and Dangerous Things: Ideology as an Aesthetic Affair», Antipode Vol. 45 No. 1, pp 23–42
Dubuffet J. (1986), Asphyxiante culture, Paris, Ed. de Minuit.
Du Pasquier J.-N. et Marco D. (2009), «Le rapport territorial: essai de définition», Paris, 3ᵉ forum de la régulation.
Duvanel, L. et Levy, R. (1984), Politique en rase-mottes. Mouvements et contestation suisses. 1945- 1978, Lausanne, Réalités sociales.
Florida R. (2012), The rise of the creative class : and how it's transforming work, leisure, community and everyday life. New York, Basic Books.
Glass P. (2012), « Doing scene: Identity, Space and the Interactional Accomplishment of Youth Culture », in Journal of Contemporary Ethnography, 41(6), 695–716.
Gros D. (1987), Dissidents du quotidien: la scène alternative genevoise, 1968-1987. Editions d'en Bas
Heinich N. (1996), Etre artiste, Klincksieck, Etudes, Paris
Hers F. & Douroux X. (2011), L'art sans le capitalisme, Paris, Les Presses du Réel
Kisukidi N. Y. (2013), Bergson ou l'humanité créatrice, Paris, CNRS Ed.
Landry C. (2003), The Creative City : A Toolkit for urban Innovators, London, Earthscan
Lefebvre, H. (1968). Le droit à la ville, Paris, Anthropos.
Lefebvre H. (1970), Le manifeste différentialiste, Paris, Gallimard
Lefebvre H. (1974), La production de l'espace, Paris, Anthropos
Lévi-Strauss, C., (1950), Sociologie et anthropologie, Paris, Presses universitaires de France.

Masboungi, A. (2013), Le projet urbain en temps de crise : l'exemple de Lisbonne, Paris, Le Moniteur.
Nishat A. (2011), Spatial agency : other ways of doing architecture. London: Routledge.
Moulier-Boutang Y. (2007), Le capitalisme cognitif. La nouvelle grande transformation, Paris, Amsterdam
Paquot T. (2012), « Le droit à la ville et à l'urbain », In AlterArchitectures Manifesto (pp. 173–175). Gollion, CH: Eterotopia/ Infolio.
Paquot T., Masson-Zanussi Y., Stathopoulos M. (eds.). (2012), AlterArchitectures Manifesto. Gollion, CH: Eterotopia/ Infolio.
Pattaroni L. (2007), «La ville plurielle: quand les squatteurs ébranlent l'ordre urbain», In M. Bassand, V. Kaufmann et D. Joye (éds), Enjeux de la sociologie urbaine, 2 éd., Lausanne, PPUR, pp. 283-314.
Pattaroni L. (2012), « Les friches du possible. Petite plongée dans l'histoire et le quotidien des squats genevois », In. Gregorio Julien, Squats, Genève, Labor & Fides
Pattaroni L. (2014), «The fallow lands of the possible an inquiry into the enacted critic of capitalism in Geneva' squats», in Cattaneo C., Martinez M., Squatting Europe Kollective,(ed.), 2014, The squatters' movement in europe : Everyday Commons and Autonomy as Alternatives to Capitalism, Londres, Pluto Press, 60-80
Peirce C.S. (1978), Ecrits sur le signe, Seuil, Paris
RAAC – Rassemblement des artistes et acteurs culturels (2009), Art, culture et création. Propositions en faveur d'une politique culturelle à Genève, Genève, Labor et Fides
Rancière, J. (1998), Aux bords du politique, Paris, Éditions La Fabrique.
Rancière, J. (2000), Le Partage du sensible, Paris, Éditions La Fabrique
Savićić G., & Savić S. (2013), Unpleasant Design. Belgrade: G.L.O.R.I.A. Retrieved from http://unpleasant.pravi.me/
Simay P. (2008), « Une autre ville pour une autre vie. Henri Lefebvre et les situationnistes ». Metropoles, (4).
Wagner P. (1996), Liberté et discipline: les deux crises de la modernité, Paris, Métailié.
Williams R. (2006), « Base and Superstructure in Marxist Cultural Theory », In Durham Meenakshi Gigi and Kellner Douglas M.(Ed.), Media and cultural studies : keyworks / edited by. Blackwell Publishing, pp. 130-143

Helena Maria da Silva Santana, Departamento de Comunicação e Arte,
Universidade de Aveiro, hsantana@ua.pt

Maria do Rosário da Silva Santana, Escola Superior de Educação,
Comunicação e Desporto, Instituto Politécnico da Guarda, rosariosantana@ipg.pt

Flash Mob as a moment of creation and human intervention on urban spaces

Currently a Flash Mob is a sudden gathering of people in a public space in order to Perform. Given the growing interest in these actions, we want to understand how they serve the public and urban spaces to build an artistic object while enhancing a specific social intervention. We also want to characterize their constituents, particularly its musical component. At the same time we want to understand the development and the importance of this artistic and social movement in Portugal in order to determine which way it is contextualized in the urban spaces, thus determining new art spaces and objects.

Flash Mob, Music, New Art Spaces.

Introduction

Although the expression Flashmob appeared only in 2003, the expression Flash Mob (or flash mob) dates to the XIX century. However in 1800 it did not have the connotation it is given nowadays. The word was firstly used to describe a protest of a group of prisoners in Tasmania that used a special language to communicate called flash language (Trindade, Figueiredo, Santos, Mangan, Constante 2012: 26). Their action was that of producing, in 1844, a revolt in the prison they were in. The action, in which approximately 300 hundred people have participated, ended in a riot where the prisoners, back to the local reverend, to the governor and the first lady, pulled up their clothes showing their intimate parts and doing, at the same time, a strong noise with their hands. The word flash mob came up after this situation being used to refer to what was happening after a collective action of a group using flash language to communicate[1].

The flash mob as a happening, in its current configuration, happens preferably in the city and has as main characteristic a determined and exclusive focus, clear objective, function, timetable, duration, style of the event and participants (in number, gender etc). Historically, there is information that the north-american journalist Bill Wasik designed it for the first time, in this context. The author organized, for the first time in 2003, via email, a mobilization in Manhattan, New YorK, United States of America[2]. During 2003, mainly in the centre of big cities, not only American but also European and all over the world, there were many mobilizations having in common the way they were organized, the speed at which they build the space of the city, and the means they used to bring it to public à posteriori (Schieck 2005). The speed and the efficient mobilization of the people and facilities in the city intending to have a quick action, made them known as flash mob[3] . On the other hand, as they were not politically marked, the manifestations spread all over the world with a mark that shows, according to the situations, the social, political and behavioural specifications of each community. We note that the city while screen rebuilds continuously, being that "the city with its billboards, street signs, storefronts and billboards, transforms and renews itself, then, as a place of symbolic exchange unity, city, region, country, culture and social and urban spaces where they are made. Ideally, the flash mob consists of an action that is quickly made, using the technological means and the internet, allowing assembling a huge number of people in a certain location and time in order to perform a free action and intervention in the city space (considering space and non-space in the concept of Marc Augé) to be dismissed as fast as it started. To Marc Augé the non-places can be considered not only as in-flight, road or train means but also as "the cable or wireless nets that mobilize the extraterritorial space to a communication so weird that, often, only connects the individual to an image of himself " (Augé 2003: 75)[4]. The format of the event to be held, sent primarily by e-mail is disclosed on a website where, those who are interested in participating, are previously enrolled. In the realization of the event there are several elements that are created, and/or chosen, by the one who triggers the action, the mobber, according to the objectives and to the social, political, artistic, cultural or environmental scope it aspires to. From the artistic point of view, the flash mob serves the material and immaterial spaces of the places in which it is developed, and to which it is overlapped, other layers of meaning not only material but also immaterial, directly related to the function and objectives of the event. Thus, in the light of its objectives and nature, the elements may differ widely as "the relation between space and time is centred, as the city, in the precise moment of the experiences [...], is made the place crossed by two kinds of spaces: the physical and the cyberspace. [We can see that] the flash mob is a movement created in cyberspace and materialized in a personal contact that when it fades ends up by returning to he cyberspace, mainly in blogs, twitters and videos. In other words, a flash mob is born from virtual organization in the form of interaction in social network on the Internet and it is perpetuated in virtual, but only has its raison d ' être for their action / intervention in the physical/ present state " (Trindade, Figueiredo, Santos, Mangan, Constante 2012: 36)[5].

Flash Mob as a space of creation and human intervention

As we have referred, the first flash mob in current contexts happened in 2003 in the centre of Manhattan, New York, as an event where "nearly a hundred people were invited by an email sent by "Bill" – anchored to the site "The Mob Project" –, to meet in the 9th floor of Macy's, [and to] stay enjoying the carpets for a few moments and afterwards to ask the assistant for the love rug and, so, as they appeared they should fade away in the crowd " (Schieck 2005: 4)[6]. Strange for that period, the event had immediate consequences, as actions were immediately taken in other parts of the world. In Portugal these events are newer not possessing the expansion nor the dimension of those constructed in other countries, not only in Europe, as in the rest of the world. While text that fits within the city, this space that is defined as logical and apparently stabilized, the flash mob is established and characterized by the social and discursive mode of its different structures of information not only material but also immaterial, namely the sources of social, intellectual, moral and cultural of their participants. In this sense, the urban space, together with new technologies, show us a new way of being in the collective, and another notion of space and time. It is shown a means of community mobilization for the realization of various social awareness actions, dominated, often by "environmental awareness actions, cultural creative actions (such as dance and fine arts), actions against racism and social inclusion actions, actions of cultural preservation and heritage (buildings and monument) [...]. They are flash mobs with social concerns, this is, with impact in citizenship " (Trindade, Figueiredo, Santos, Mangan, Constante 2012: 35)[7].

However, the events which we have seen and analyzed have predominantly a playful function, although there is also an intervention and sometimes political function. As some authors say, notably André Lemos (2006), the flash mobs are apolitical and recreational actions, because he considers them one of the possible forms of smarts mobs. According to him, "they emerge from the synergy between mobile communication, portable computing, wireless telematics networks and the various forms of collective" (Lemos 2006: 73)[8]. For the author, the mobilization and expansion of citizenship actions relating to social, cultural and urban events, considered essential for the development and awareness of contemporary societies, computerized or not, and among which we highlight the environmental awareness, cultural and creative against racism, exclusion or social inclusion, environmental preservation, patrimonial or cultural, are the purpose of many of the events called flash mobs (Lemos 2006)[9]. There are some clear consciousness actions, like that which took place in Quebec, Canada, which reflected on an environmental issue and which manifested itself inside a shopping mall. This action was proposed within a shopping centre starting when one of the actors leaves an empty plastic bottle next to a recycling container and everyone expects someone to put it in there. We realized that before this happened; many of the participants in the action are already in the space of action expecting the gesture that will start it. All the participants of the flashmob are already in the physical space where it is built and are in the crowd waiting for the course of action. We also see that there are many passersby who, while possible actors, do nothing. The duration of the flash mob is so unpredictable, as well as the sound that surrounds it. When someone finally gets in the bottle and places it in the Recycle Bin, all actors get up, put on a Red Hat, and applaud the fact effusively.

Having been proposed by Greenpeace, this Organization made use of this resource as a way of fighting against the waste and not recycling potentially dangerous products to the environment looking for a stimulation of our environmental awareness. Other actions are regularly promoted by this organization aiming at, for example, the fight against the use of nuclear energy. Using a proposal where the dancing and the music mix, a performance, Greenpeace made use of musical success Gangnam Style, in 2012, to draw attention to this cause[10].

The lightness of contents and purposes is lost when the events marked admit an imprint of social, environmental, cultural awareness or another, that is, when they support issues that have impact on the level of human existence. In this sense, the event takes on not only the role of playful, artistic and social event, but also a role of educator and trainer of new consciousness, establishing new types of interaction and occupation of spaces, ecological, technological and social and urban. Through the use of information and technological communication means, those allow new forms of communication and information, these actions, by being the subject of media attention, and disclosed almost immediately on the Internet, allow high visibility to concerns of various kinds in an almost instantaneous. A quick social awareness, politics, aesthetic, social and environmental development, is done with great rapidity, efficiency and at greatly reduced costs (Andrade 2010). In these events, the mobilization capacity is directly proportional to the capacity of individual identification with the event. Being the invitation sent by the Internet, only those that have access (more or less free), as well as those that are available to integrate social groups and are enrolled in determined sites, will have, initially, access to information related to the event. However, the citizen who is not in these communities can always integrate the event spontaneously when it is happening or when he is asked to do so, as "the interesting thing is to understand the capacity of mobilization, that relies on the identification of the person willing to participate" with the mobber's intention (Trindade, Figueiredo, Santos, Mangan, Constante 2012: 35)[11]. In this construction, the urban space, in conjunction with the new technologies, will generate a new collective way of being and, in a moment where all relationships are perceived as quick and ephemeral, we question why we abandon routines to intervene, for a few minutes, a public city space. Is it a position towards the individual / collective boredom that has settled in society and in the city? Is it the result of a lack of political, cultural and social goals in life?

By analyzing various testimonies of individuals who participate in this type of actions we have concluded that both choices come true, the boredom and the lack of goals. Its analysis shows us that both the hassle as the lack of objectives produce a feeling of "permanent dissatisfaction which finds, in satisfaction of the sensations, the main anchor for the constitution of their identities" (Salem 2004: 153)[12]. So the immediate sense of pleasure produced, not only on an individual basis, as a collective, is one of the great driving forces of this type of actions. The feeling of belonging to a group on the one hand, the manifestation of an ideal on the other, associated with the defiance and provocation, come up in these actions that are made of many individual but that, having no face, are, in essence, anonymous. At the same time, a certain fascination, and the will to act, to make a difference is shown, as facing the numerous possibilities of choice and in the absence of a more robust social and political positioning, individuals end up satisfied in immediate realization of desires and, consequently, in actions in which the immediate and the transitory prevail.

Apart from its political or apolitical character, the mobilization via the Internet or mobile phone, allows the construction of these actions, sometimes, at a world level. The Internet and mobile communication establish a culture that is in possession of the youngest, and that, increasingly, is for everyone. Free from any boundary, the ties that these communities built are experienced instantly without the commitment to constitute an obligation. In this way of acting, "What fascinates is the unusual, participate in some movement – without political or social connotation – which is organized with the simple goal of causing some surprise at some point in the city. We are so accustomed to our routine that we are interested in doing something that totally breaks it".[13] Thus, the city and society determines and evolves.

Because they are social phenomena with a format of mobilization and performance that is almost the same, it would be unwise not to mention the smarts mobs. The question is how can we distinguish a flash mob from a smart mob. We distinguish them by purposes. The smarts mobs are always related to a political activism; the flash mobs are organized exclusively for entertainment (Schieck 2005:7)[14]. In this paper, we use the concept of flash mob as manifestations/ mobilizations which take place in a very quick, apolitical way, constituting itself as a happening or a performance, which is organized using the new media and communication technologies, such as emails, blogs and social networking sites, bringing together citizens who, very often, do not know each other, in public places. This fact does not necessarily cause any weirdness and perplexity when the event breaks out in the crowd and in the physical and material space of the city. In this context, the flash mobs do not just single out a form of contemporary event, referring also to an emerging form of experience in urban space. Shafiq (2006) argues that the current experiences of co-presence, of which the flash mobs are here considered examples, refer to sensitive dimension of social links. According to him, these events are anchored in the affectation of technological experience, and in the way the esthetical experience (dimension of the sensitive) is related, more and more, to the reality lived every day. A possible way to approach the flash mobs in the context of these concerns is to perceive them as a possible way to construct an aesthetic experience, catalyzed by a first action, disseminated over the internet, and consolidated, in the urban space, by a group of individuals, that settle a community. The formation of these communities, in essence heterogeneous, and the objects which they produced, the flash mobs, return to the network into smaller documents almost instantaneously, and which are accessible, not only to those belonging to this group, but the whole virtual community.

Given the growing interest in these actions we want to understand how they serve the public and urban spaces to be built while boosting social intervention artistic objects specific (political or other), as well as characterize its constituents, including its musical component. We also intend to understand the development and importance of this artistic and social movement in Portugal, in order to determine in what way it contextualizes in urban space, determining new spaces of art.

Charactering the musical component of a Flash Mob
The analysis of different flash mobs shows us that the subject that mobilizes in these actions cannot be identified with that who commonly goes to acts of claim or public manifestation, be they of a political, social, cultural, environmental character or other. The participant wants to be mistaken for the common citizen, understood as that who is touched by the initiative and the need to communicate something together, collectively, identifying himself or herself only there [15]. The flash mob is an instant event, unexpected and made from a previous organized work. At this stage, the objective is disclosed in the expectation of being significant enough to produce identification and, thus, produce a number for its realization. While cultural and musical action, their objectives are often to honour a group or celebrity. In this sense, we find several actions that are tributes to musicians or groups of modern times (XX and XXI century) . In this context we find several tributes to Michael Jackson (broadcasted on the 29 April 2010, Cebu, Filipinas[16]; or other events over the years [17], for example), the Abba (broadcasted on the 1 st June 2010, Swedish Medical Center celebrated the hundredth anniversary interpreting the music Dancing Queen[18]; broadcasted on the 31 May2011, Shopping Vila Olímpia – Brazil, interpreting the music Mamma Mia[19], for example), Madonna (broadcasted on 29 October 2011, dance Flashmob Madonna, Warsaw, Poland [20], for example), Lady Gaga (broadcasted on 12 November 2013, byLittle Monsters of Argentina, to celebrate the arrival of Artpop[21], for example), Beyoncé (broadcasted on 19 January 2012, Recife, Brazil project End of Time[22], for example), or others.

As a tribute to a certain film, character or producer, we highlight the performance of the song "Do, Re, Mi", fundamental element of the movie The sound of music[23]. One of the flashmob it originated happened in the Central Station of Antuerpia, Belgium (broadcasted on 16 November 2010, A Belgian commercial for VTM. Do Re Mi... Let your body move!, 2009[24]). In these cases, defined the hour, place in which the event will take place, and after some previous encounters where choreography is rehearsed, (generally the reproduction is adapted to a choreography originally made by the celebrity), the participants go to the place in a random order, simulating that chance brought them together. In the beginning of the music, one of the participants is a professional dancer, who begins and conducts the execution of the performance. At this stage, the objective is disclosed in the expectation of being significant enough to produce identification and, thus, produce a quota for its realization. While cultural and musical action, their objectives are often to honour a group or celebrity etc (Augé 2003). The Internet summons the organization of these events and that has two stages. The first, the one who, the mobber, suggests a theme and makes an appeal by setting the goal of action, time, location and duration of the event. The second is when the interventions return to the Internet in the form of audiovisual records[25].

As the flash mobs create new types of interaction and use of urban spaces, as already mentioned, the use of digital media and technology that enable new forms of communication and information, we find that these events /actions are configured as ways of escaping that briefly interfere in the urban landscape.

"The flash mob happens, in this way, as the city movement lapse: the (un)predictable that there erupts. In the midst of continuous traffic of people circling in their roads, people ordered in their various places and locations, the performance of the flash mob configures itself as something that distinguishes itself in the linearity that is ideologically worked as logically stabilized and determined of the way the city space conforms. There are apparently audience and spectacle. To fall apart, however, the performance of the flash mob points to the dispersion: the individuals who were momentarily "ordinary dancers" get confused with the crowd and his movement is absorbed in the flow of the city, of its linearity rebuilt. The effects of the senses and the possible interpretations that the event may raise stay" (Rodrigues 2011: s.p.)[26].

By interfering like this, they completely destabilize the city space momentarily emphasising something that is proper. An urban intervention of type flash mob transforms the scenario where the human being develops enabling their rights and their duties. In the case of actions that act at different levels and in different ways, the flash mobs are heading to an audience but at the same time; serve that audience while constituent of work of art. The city as physical element and material deconstructs itself, by building another in the course of the action. The city as a crowd, transforms from passive and apathetic to active, eyeliner and creator of new symbols, establishing a dialogue where the viewer interacts with the art and the art spaces. This intervention wants attention, purpose and sensitivity towards what is, what this represents, creates, develops and dissolves while the subject material and especially immaterial. We note that the city while screen is continually rebuilt, being that "the city with its billboards, street signs, storefronts and billboards, transforms and renews itself, then, as a place of symbolic exchange" (Mazetti 2006: 5)[27]. Here art is born, reflecting as a spec of art. Here the relation between space and place get the central role, as the city, in the precise moment of these quick experiences, is made as place a crossed by two kinds of space that are: the physical and the virtual. This happens because the flash mob is a movement that starts and creates in the virtual space, materializes in the personal contact, physical and material, to dissipate, returns to the virtual [28].

On the other hand the flash mobs have degrees of randomness, of indeterminacy, which we sense on several levels, from the moment of its activation and proliferation on the Internet. Analyzing various examples of flash mobs, as well as their creative and compositional dynamics, we notice that the flash mob has creative background the use not only of indeterminacy, as the construction of various happenings and performances from the mid-20th century. From the use of indeterminacy works are born whose subject, an unstable support, becomes future movement. There are works that are not closed, fixed, but able to be carried, under construction, coming from the apparent movement, a real movement. To dare the non-determination in the creation and interpretation of a work implies the presence of certain determinations. This duality allows confronting the deterministic elements, present in the game instructions and paths that the interpreters and intervenient make every time they act, and the elements, present of non-deterministic construction work and, also, of the action. The indeterminacy develops into a work of art that is not closed nor girt herself in rigidity of determinism, but open to all elements at our disposal, including the sounds of nature and the environment, on which we cannot act, as well as the spaces of the city and the actors who move in this precise space of city, in the precise space of art. This fact leads to building of a new world, open, mobile. Is not the same in a flash mob?

In a general way, noise is a sound that disturbs, made up of an infinite number of components with amplitude features, phase and frequency randomly distributed. In Physics the noises are described by variables such as strength, the spectrum and spatial distribution. In noise we ca not determine its height precisely because, the irregularity of the vibrations which constitute it, make it impossible. A noise disturbs, a sound does not. However, we can consider a sound like a noise from the moment this becomes stranger, when it has no meaning, thus we can consider a noise, sound, when it gains meaning. Is not the same with the sounds of physical spaces in cities and in the world we live in? Are not spaces full of sounds that are just waiting for a meaning from our side? On the other hand, an attitude that makes us feel the urban space as a sound in potential fruition, does it not propose us a vision of a musical masterpiece? A masterpiece where the sound becomes music?

In this context emerges this great innovative thinking of the American composer and musician John Cage who proposes not only a new sound world, as a new way to structure and signify the artwork. In a context of a more scholar creation of musical work, who asserts "the interpretation of an indeterminate sheet of music (and we include action), about the strict interpretation plan is unique because there is no repetition. Each new interpretation is necessarily different. So, nothing is done because the work cannot be seized temporarily as the subject. The register of the work, working as a postcard, searches for the knowledge of something that already existed even though the knowledge of action that defines the work hasn't happened yet" (Cage 1970: 39)[29]. In the flash mob case we believe that these suggest us the same line of thinking, in the sense that they come true while unique unrepeatable actions, which are built as a result of the action and development of their players against a proposal for action that conveys via the Internet as a game of art. Does not this proposal suggest that the music sheet determines the way the flash mob will be conceived, the object of art? Does it not fulfil as an object of art in interaction with the public and the physical ad material space where it is located? Does it not crystallize the art in an object that is unique and irreplaceable? Is not that the flash mob?

Thus, the work, open to any kind of sounds while is projected within the city, emerges as a receptacle, a listening space of the sound world that surrounds us, forcing us to introspection, to gather, to reflection and to hearing a new sound world, often overlooked or not heard, which, filled with other sounds, represents the work of art[30]. In some cases, like those in which the action determines that those involved should stay anywhere in a static, or non-place, one day and hour marked, without moving nor producing any sound during a predetermined period of time, thus giving the opportunity to the public to hear the silence, we find ourselves in the presence of a representative of those places sound world and non-places of physical space, material and immaterial of cities. We know that depending on the location, time and spaces in use, the sound component is distinct and sometimes radical. The same action in different spaces, cities and architectures is built differently. The same action in spaces, architectures and cities alike, at different times may result in a work of art completely distinct. So it is important to understand and reflect upon immaterial spaces. Throughout the immaterial art competes for the material; no flash mob is, in our view, essential. On the other hand, silence, being a primordial element in musical creation, has the possibility of being itself, and the music, to exist without the intervention of the author. Allowing us to act in the context of creation, the mobber gives us the possibility of, as interpreters, intervene in the urban space and art, leading others to question themselves, to question us, and wondering about themselves, each other, and the material and immaterial spaces that involve it. In this questioning the unusual shape spaces are realized and built, and sometimes unusual, being that the work is determined by itself, and for itself, within itself, the city and the world. Crystallized in a postcard that is your recording, appears to be the illustration depicted for posterity, bounded and crystallized, in what was and it will never be, a record of work, a register of art. If for John Cage the composer should let the desire control the sound, retrieve his spirit from the music, and promote means of discovery that allow sounds to be themselves and not the vehicle of theories made by men or the expression of human feelings, in our opinion, the mobber should leave his desire to control the processed action, retrieving his spirit after the broadcast, promoting the interaction and the social mobilization with a view to a new art space, and the involvement with a certain public and space of the city. For Cage, the silence becomes the vehicle of sound, which consists, in this context "on a set of unorganized noise, not dominated as a result of the compositional act" (Bosseur, 1993: 37)[31]. Associated with the ninth Indiana emotion, tranquillity, silence has "the quality of transparency, not obstruction" (Bosseur, 1993: 24)[32]. Within the city the silence does not exist. Simultaneously, the consciousness that we possess of the sound of urban spaces is rare. The mobber can use this reality, or build other sound spaces that overlap the non-physical silence, but above all by non-emotional and intangible silence of cities[33].

Simultaneously, we find the use of non-places to determine spaces of art that are flash mobs. In Portugal, specifically, we confirm the use of some non-places such as the Lisbon Airport or the Airport of Ponta Delgada, for example, malls, hospitals, gardens, where the actions are built not only in an entertaining manner but also, as conscious actions. Here, the action is often trying to draw attention to social causes, environmental or specific health. So, remember those conducted to stress the importance of donating blood or bone marrow, propagating a social conscience and huge human value and citizenship. As examples, we refer that made in Lisbon, intending to sign out the National Blood Donator Day. In this Flash mob, under the slogan "red is fashion", the organization urged that all players wore red and entered the Santa Maria Hospital in Lisbon to donate blood. In a statement, it was stated that the Hospital of Santa Maria would perform a set of initiatives that would enable "the public awakening to the importance of blood donation. Thus, The 11:0 of the day March 27 was scheduled a flash mob, organized by the School of Dance, in which participated Lx dancers and Athletes. It was also scheduled the performance of Carlos Alberto Moniz, at 15h.[and] confirmed the presence of several public figures related to music, theatre, television, sports and fashion, like: Simone de Oliveira, actress and singer, Paula Teixeira, singer and gestural language interpreter, Ricardo Vilão, humorist, Carla Matadinho, model, Quimbé, actor, Valéria Carvalho, actress and singer, Sabri Lucas, actor, Susana Cacela, actress and Lena Coelho. The organization asked to come dressed in red so that they would be associated to the cause and framed in the spirit of share on that day."[34]

While citizenship action we can still refer those where actors call attention to the city's green spaces, including the built in space of Parque das Nações in Lisbon[35]. In this case the musical part arises in two ways: appears as sound construction where, in addition to the ambient sound of the physical, architectural and urban space chosen, overlaps the one chosen as the initiator element of the performance. We often find a musical band allocated instantaneously s to a feeling, an emotion, an experience, having a strong impact on the public that experience this same space. Sometimes we build up in the space of sound that only space itself and the vibrations that arise from the performance space. Sometimes, it comes as a support for a physical, emotional, conceptual, social and experiential action an intention of appropriation of the other, their attention and excitement for itself, and for the community and the cause that moves us.

Final Considerations

A work, which is based on the non-determination, is characterized by the absence of fixity, which, together with the variability, is a principle of creation and an end in itself creating works that are always unique and singular. The autonomy of the artwork, the flash mob in this case, its sound, its constituents, its creation, its spaces and spaces, contribute to the creation of plural art worlds that are in continuous transformation by the multiplicity of forms and contents that provide the spectator of art spaces in certain areas of the city, whether they are spaces or non-places. The enjoyment of a flash mob, an action determined on the indeterminacy of the subject and the spaces of the city, will always be the reflection of an action, a willingness, the creator's domain, be it the web surfer, the mobber, ordinary people, which responds to the request of mobilization or the citizen-interpreter. In the case of Portugal we see that as art space using the city space, it constructs in physical and architectural spaces that reveal being, according to Marc Augé concept, non-places. Flash mobs aim to reach as many people as possible and, therefore, are carried out in days and hours of traffic, particularly in the case of the use of physical spaces such as airports and malls. On the other hand they are probably connected, preferably, to humanitarian causes. So we see the construction of these events on dates of strong emotional impact as the dates of celebration of birthdays, Christmas, etc. They are also allocated to registers of strong manifestation of citizenship actions. The audience they reach is immense in terms of age, gender, social status, formation, ideologies, etc.; actors and agents also. The musical component tries to capture the attention of a wide layer of the population in the places where they are erected. Alongside the musical component, the flash mob shows a strong dramatic component enough allocated to dancing and dramatization. As proactive and integrative action of spaces, of intent, of art, it takes the city to define itself as another, showing it richer, more human and more social.

Notes and References
1 Yet this time, the term flashmob was used to designate a segment of society, not showing any other similarities to the modern term or events described by him today.
2 https://www.youtube.com/playlist?list=PL713AA1F9D0F9D273 accessed April 10, 2014
3 In New York they emerged and continue to arise various actions/instant mobilizations of people. In example we remember the manifestation that happened in Central Station, a major railway station in New York. A crowd gathered quickly and efficiently, clapped for fifteen seconds and disappeared so suddenly as it came (Trindade, Figueiredo, Santos, Mangan, Constante 2012: 32).
4 "as redes de cabo ou sem fio que mobilizam o espaço extraterrestre para uma comunicação tão estranha que, muitas vezes, só põe o indivíduo em contacto com uma outra imagem de si mesmo" (Augé 2003: 75).
5 "a relação entre espaço e lugar ganha centralidade, na medida em que a cidade, no exato momento dessas experiências [...], constituiu-se em "lugar" atravessado por dois tipos de espaço: o espaço físico e o ciberespaço. [Verificamos assim, que] O flash mob é um movimento que se cria no ciberespaço, se materializa em um contato pessoal, e ao se dissipar, acaba retornando ao ciberespaço, principalmente a partir de registos em blogs, twitters e vídeos. Em outras palavras, um flash mob surge pela organização virtual na forma de interação em rede social na Internet e se perpetua no virtual, mas só tem sua razão de ser pela sua ação/intervenção no plano físico/presencial" (Trindade, Figueiredo, Santos, Mangan, Constante 2012: 36).
6 "onde cerca de cem pessoas foram convidadas, através de um e-mail enviado por "Bill" – ancorado no site "The Mob Project" –, a se encontrarem no nono andar da loja do departamento Macy's, [e a] ficarem apreciando os tapetes expostos por alguns minutos, em seguida pedirem aos vendedores o tapete do amor (love rug) e, assim como surgiram, deveriam se dispersar na multidão" (Schieck 2005: 4)

7 "ações de conscientização ambientais, ações culturais criativas (como a dança e artes plásticas), ações contra o racismo e ações de inclusão social, ações memorialistas de preservação cultural e patrimonial (prédios e monumentos depredados) [...]. São flash mobs com objectivos sociais, isto é, que têm impacto de cidadania" (Trindade, Figueiredo, Santos, Mangan, Constante 2012: 35)

8 "emergem da sinergia entre a comunicação móvel, a computação portátil, as redes telemáticas sem fio e as diversas formas de ação coletiva" (Lemos 2006: 73)

9 In this sense, these actions are built with social objectives by developing basic notions of citizenship and of interest to many fundamental questions of human existence.

10 This event took place on September 22, 2012. https://www.youtube.com/watch?v=0rOBxWtGcvA accessed May 13, 2014

11 "o interessante é perceber a capacidade de mobilização, que conta muito com a identificação de cada pessoa que se dispõe a participar" com a proposta do mobber (Trindade, Figueiredo, Santos, Mangan, Constante 2012: 35)

12 "insatisfação permanente que encontra, na satisfação das sensações, a principal âncora para a constituição de suas identidades." (Salem 2004: 153)

13 "O que fascina [...] é o inusitado, participar de algum movimento – sem conotação política ou social – que é organizado com o simples objetivo de causar alguma surpresa em algum ponto da cidade. Estamos tão acostumados com nossa rotina que [ficamos interessados] em fazer algo que quebre totalmente isso". http://flashmobs.blig.ig.com.br-.url accessed October 2, 2003

14 In this sense, the author André Lemos (2006) differentiates the smarts mobs, connoting them with specific events not only of political action, as well as social action, professional or artistic events. Flashmobs of playfulness, they remind happenings and performances by middle of the previous century.

15 Regularity in this movement is the fact that participants dress in the most discreet way possible. This seems like a feature that structures the flashmob, it is a fact in most objects constructed. If any special clothing is required, it appears at the time of the outbreak of the event or in the course of it. Until then discretion is the main rule.

Uma regularidade nesse movimento é o facto dos participantes se vestirem de forma o mais discreta possível. Esta parece ser uma característica que estrutura o flashmob, pois é um facto na maioria dos objetos construídos. Se alguma indumentária especial é necessária, ela surge no momento de eclosão do evento ou no decorrer do mesmo. Até esse momento a discrição é a regra.

16 https://www.youtube.com/watch?v=dpxzvc8ehBQ accessed May 10, 2014

17 http://globalgrind.com/2011/06/24/top-michael-jackson-flash-mobs/ accessed May 8, 2014

18 https://www.youtube.com/watch?v=eDW0QlFFvvc accessed May 8, 2014

19 https://www.youtube.com/watch?v=q-M0WjdR9P0 accessed April 3, 2014

20 https://www.youtube.com/watch?v=hcDR64OUgqo accessed April 3, 2014

21 https://www.youtube.com/watch?v=Qs1kXWN_HUg accessed March 3, 2014

22 https://www.youtube.com/watch?v=lGm_VsuXeTl accessed May 14, 2014

23 The sound of music is an American film based on the musical of the same name. Was done by Robert Wise in 1965 and contains several songs composed by various authors. The songs Sound of Music and, above all, Do, Re, Mi, are the best known.

24 https://www.youtube.com/watch?v=bQLCZOG202k accessed May 14, 2014

25 In this sense we can give as many examples flashmobs organized at Lisbon Airport (broadcast on 28 December 2009, held on 23 December to celebrate Christmas http://www.youtube.com/watch?v=EzOH6sSpsCY accessed May 13, 2014); spread the April 3, 2010, to celebrate the 70th anniversary of KLM (accessed May 13, 2014). The basic characteristic of the flashmob is speed not only the organization, such as the completion and dissemination of results, supported by the use of the internet.

26 "O flashmob acontece, dessa maneira, como lapso no movimento da cidade: o (im)previsível que aí irrompe. Em meio de tráfego contínuo de pessoas circulando por suas vias, pessoas ordenadas em seus diversos pontos e localidades, a performance do flashmob configura-se como algo que se distingue na linearidade do que é trabalhado ideologicamente como logicamente estabilizado e determinante do modo como o espaço da cidade se conforma. Formam-se aí aparentemente plateia e espetáculo. Ao se desfazer, contudo, a performance do flashmob aponta para a dispersão: os sujeitos momentaneamente "bailarinos ordinários" se confundem com a multidão e seu movimento é absorvido no fluxo da cidade, de sua linearidade reconstruída. Ficam os efeitos de sentido, as interpretações possíveis que o acontecimento pode suscitar" (Rodrigues 2011: s.p.).

27 "A cidade, com seus cartazes, placas de trânsito, fachadas de lojas e outdoors, transforma-se e renova-se, então, como lugar de troca simbólica" (Mazetti 2006: 5)

28 A flash mob comes in the virtual space, perpetuating itself there too, materializing in an action/intervention on physical presence plan.

Ou seja, um flashmob surge no espaço virtual, perpetuando-se também aí, materializando-se na ação/intervenção no plano físico/presencial.

29 "a interpretação de uma partitura indeterminada [e nos incluímos ação,] sobre o estrito plano da interpretação é único pois não existe repetição. Cada nova interpretação resulta necessariamente diferente. Assim, nada se encontra acabado pois a obra não pode ser apreendida temporalmente como objecto. O registo da obra, funcionando como um postal, procura o conhecimento de qualquer coisa que já existiu mesmo que o conhecimento da ação que define a obra ainda não tenha acontecido" (Cage 1970: 39)

30 Not so with the first hearing of 4 '33" John Cage? The first hearing of the work took place in the Maverick Concert Hall, a room that allows sound from abroad, particularly from the surrounding forest. That sound flood the space of the concert hall making, in this case, the sound material of the work.

31 "no conjunto dos ruídos não organizados, não dominados na sequência do ato compositivo" (Bosseur, 1993: 37)

32 "a qualidade da transparência, da não obstrução" (Bosseur, 1993: 24)

33 It should be noted that, when that silence is not obvious, it is the will that mobber shows too realizing it.

34 "ao público despertar para a importância da dádiva de sangue". [Assim,] Às 11h [do dia 27 de março foi] agendada a realização de um flashmob, organizado pela Escola Lx Dance, no qual [participaram] bailarinos e atletas de alta competição. [Esteve] também prevista a atuação de Carlos Alberto Moniz, às 15h.[e] confirmadas as presenças de várias figuras públicas ligadas à música, teatro, televisão, desporto e moda, entre elas: Simone de Oliveira, atriz e cantora, Paula Teixeira, cantora e intérprete de língua gestual portuguesa, Ricardo Vilão, humorista, Carla Matadinho, modelo, Quimbé, ator, Valéria Carvalho, atriz e cantora, Sabri Lucas, ator, Susana Cacela, atriz e Lena Coelho. A organização [apelou] aos lisboetas para que, neste dia, [vestissem] uma peça vermelha antes de saírem de casa, para que se [associassem] à efeméride e para que [estivessem] enquadrados no espírito solidário que se pretende neste dia." http://www.justnews.pt/agenda/hospital-de-santa-maria-assinala-dia-nacional-do-dador-de-sangue#.U3Hn2Shtt-w accessed May 13, 2014

35 Flashmob performed in the Park of Nations in 2012, Lisbon, Portugal. http://www.youtube.com/watch?v=nFvDX1fpTyg accessed May 13, 2014

Lígia de Oliveira Trindade, Ewerton Luís Faverzani Figueiredo, Nádia Maria Weber Santos, Patrícia Kayser Vargas Mangan, Robson da Silva Constante, Multiculturalismo Urbano: o fenómeno Flash Mob. (Florianópolis, v.8, nª1, p. 25-39, Jan./jul. 2012)

André Lemos, Mídias locativas e territórios informacionais. In: Lúcia Santaella; Priscila Abrantes (orgs). Estéticas tecnológicas – novos modos de sentir (São Paulo: Editora PUC SP, 2007)

Henrique Moreira Mazetti, Intervenção urbana: representação e subjetivação na cidade. In: Anais do Congresso Brasileiro de Ciências da Comunicação. (São Paulo: Intercom, 2006)

Eduardo Alves Rodrigues, Uma leitura da cena contemporânea: o flasmob como metráfora da relação entre silêncio e linguagem. V SEAD (Porto Alegre: UFRGS, 2011)

Jean-Yves BOSSEUR, John Cage, ([s.l.]: Minerva, 1993.

John Cage, Silence – discours et écrits, coleção Les Lettres Nouvelles. (Paris: Minerva, 1970)

Marc Augé, Não-lugares – Introdução a uma antropologia da supermodernidade. (Campinas, SP : Papirus, 2003)

Muniz Sodré, As estratégias sensíveis – afeto, mídia e política. (Petrópolis: Editora Vozes, 1998).

Pedro Salem, Do Luxo ao Fardo – Um estudo histórico sobre o tédio. (Rio de Janeiro: Relume Dumará, Conexões, v.21, 2004)

Renato Andrade, Flash mob: a união faz a força. Grupo Foco: comunicação, cotidiano, marketing. 2010. Disponível em <http://www.toptalent.com.br/index.php/2010/11/29/flash-mob-a-uniao-faz-a-forca/>. Acedido em 17 de março de 2011.

Zygmunt Bauman, Comunidade – a busca por segurança no mundo real. (Rio de Janeiro, ed. Jorge Zahar, 2003)

Ana Vilar Bravo, Faculdade de Letras da Universidade de Lisboa
ana_vilar_bravo@hotmail.com

Participatory Urban Art

This paper focuses on the definition of participatory urban art's concept and is also introducing the guidelines of a participatory urban art project. We will also try to address some questions concerning participatory urban art itself and outline the projects planning and its intentions. Weaim at measuringto what extent should we go in the participatory dimension assigned to a projectsuch as this onewhose purpose is empowering the users, giving them a sense of ownership and co-responsibility for the space and the art therein. The study will guide us through the observation of the project's development and will focus mainly on how the "participatory" aspect affects its outcome and the all agents involved.

Urban art, participation, collaboration.

Short Introduction

The main objective of this paper is to address the subject of participatory urban art. Firstly, we will attempt to define the concept of participatory urban art, in the context of urban art and urban intervention, within the contemporary city. We will also introduce a particular artistic project that will take place, in the near future, at a specific urban public space, in the city of Lisbon. This participatory urban art project is mainly oriented towards perceiving and studying some different situations: the users' relation to the space and their response to an artistic project's call; the interaction and the collaboration between the artists and the community; the extent of local authorities' support; the cultural patronage and sponsorship. There are also some important questions we will try to answer: should this project have its foundations in the structured analysis of the place itself? Should the artistic teams take into consideration the community's desires and to what degree can/should the community interfere in the creative process? What can be the role of the cultural manager as the corner stone in the management processes and the projects' implementation in the urban intervention domain? And, how do we manage the collaboration process between all the agents included - the artistic teams, the residents and the users' community to whom this participatory urban art project is addressed.

Contextualization

To begin with, participatory urban art has already proven to be a very challenging study subject and fertile ground for experiments in the social field. Social and cultural inclusion are the main ensigns of participatory art projects, but these kind of programs are also fertile as far as community, participation and collaboration concepts are concerned. Usually, participatory urban art claims the credits for inclusion strategies and social empowerment methodologies, in an attempt to reach a broader public that, otherwise, would be left out of any kind of art process or project. Often, the intention underneath this kind of project is more dialogic and performative rather than object-based. What really matters here is the creative process, the collaboration methods applied, the actual interaction and the effective cultural and social sharing, and not the artwork itself. We are at the beginning of our studies in these theoretical issues domain and we are, also, at the same time, starting the actual implementation of a participatory urban art project. One of our main goals is to promote the involvement and the inclusion of the community in the project itself and manage the interaction between the public and the artists - this collaboration will be preponderant and the users' participation will be indispensable throughout the whole project. Being the main objective of this paper to address participatory urban art's subject, we will attempt to define this concept in itself, and in the context of urban art and urban intervention within the contemporary city, and we will also list a group of activities and processes that we already have identified as being crucial to the project and its implementation.

This project, which is now in its early stages, will, hopefully, be a testing-ground for different models of staging participatory urban art projects. It will encompass different interventions and we aim at defining different collaboration structures, based on both the invited artistic community and the resident and usufructuary community preferences. Our proposal is to cover interventions both in the street art and graffiti domains, but not only. We will also be inviting artists from other artistic disciplines, such as painting, architecture, sculpture, illustration and crafts, just to name a few. This urban art project will take place along of the largest gardens in the city of Lisbon – Parque da Quinta das Conchas e dos Lilases - and has already confirmed the institutional support from some public institutions, including: GAU – Galeria de Arte Urbana, Departamento de Património Cultural, Câmara Municipal de Lisboa; Junta de Freguesia of the neighborhood that will host the project; During one of the first stages of this project, we will try to reach a wide audience. The target community ranges from the local community, i.e. the residents of the neighborhood in question, to frequent users or occasional visitors from other parts of the city and beyond and even tourists. We will also attempt to join some of these individuals in groups, target each group by the appropriate means, for example, by meetings with local associations, in order to promote their participation. For non-locals, for example, we will try to get in touch with them by using questionnaires. For all groups of users, inhabitants, locals, visitors and usufructuary, we will try also a more trendy, easy and technological approach, by enticing them to follow the project online, via Facebook, for example, or even other platforms, and participate, also remotely, in the decision-making process. One of the main goals in our list is to have a long term involvement of a large physical and virtual community in an urban art project such as this one. The involvement can go from voting on sub-projects to be adopted, to choose from numerous art project's proposals, and, ultimately, to participate in the actual execution, depending on the artist and the community preferences. All this should be accomplished respecting both the artists and the public wishes and needs.

Participatory urban art definition attempt and the concept application (in) to a specific art project

We will start off with the attempt to define participatory urban art. Participatory urban art is the kind of art that does not exist without the interactive process and the close collaboration between the author and the recipient(s). Participatory art is based on the assumption that recipients will be given the opportunity to be involved and actually intervene in a particular work of art, since its conceptualization process until the elaboration/construction/installation of the piece of art itself. That is to say that participatory art consists essentially in the engagement and the empowerment[1] of the target recipient(s). It is our firm intention that the community's empowerment becomes the heart of the whole collaboration process. This concept, above all, will empower, socially and culturally, the members of the invited groups that have already been marginalized or put aside, experienced social discrimination and were excluded from all decision-making processes within community life. Empowerment will be used also as a methodology and applied in its strong educational nature and pedagogical label throughout the whole project. Recipients will be required to actively collaborate throughout the whole creative process, and will be allowed to become co-authors, therefore dividing the authorship with the artist. Urban is the adjective that places this kind of participatory art that we have just defined. The participatory urban art exists and reaches its full meaning because it happens within the cosmopolitan and contemporary city. As far as urban intervention is concerned, we stress the set of artistic practices that can be developed and be applied, having in mind social consciousness and never putting aside issues such as locational identity, sense of community, built(-in) environment, and physical, structural and emotional weight of that specific public place. Though only graffiti and street art are properly and often associated to the urban art concept (Hoppe 2009), here we will try to convey the idea that a wider group of artistic disciplines can and should be enhanced and strengthen such a restrict concept.

Urban art is a statement and a reality within the contemporary city all over the world. The walls of every cosmopolitan urbe are already stage for illegal fine samples (Sackman 2006) and legal extraordinary examples of urban art. Engaged art projects are flourishing within the capital cities around the world. Urban art is, definitely, trendy. Many urban art projects have recently led to some interesting experiments in Europe and urban art events are increasingly happening within the city of Lisbon also. Most of them are not participatory art projects, that is to say that, most of the time these projects are meant for the community but the community, here, is seen as a target, much more than an agent of the whole process. As far as we know, in Portugal, there is only one project which we can include in the participative public art designation - Monumento à Multiculturalidade, which happened in Almada, between 2011 and 2013 (Gato et al. 2013). Using a similar approach and parallel strategies, applied to our project we will try to reach and involve a specific audience – the community of residents and the users of the specific urban public space in which the project will happen. So, our approach has to go beyond the art world alone and aim for social and artistic exchange, always taking into account the needs and the interests of the audience(s) we are trying to reach out and making them the most important piece in/of this whole game.

Now, in a more practical approach, we will try to enumerate the most important aspects of the already mentioned project and its implementation. First of all, the users' relation to the specific urban public space where this participatory urban art project will take place and the user's response to the artistic project's call are two huge stages of the whole process. It is crucial for us to acknowledge the importance of this space for the city, in general, and for the usufructuary community, in particular. It is also fundamental for us to observe how the community will host this idea of an artistic urban intervention in a physical domain that has been, at least until now, exclusively theirs[2]. Secondly, we have the very important task to question the artistic community. Broadly speaking, artists, in defense of the work of art itself and the creative process are not often very fond of this type of project. The artistic community is, sometimes, reluctant to accept to participate in this sort of projects. Legitimately, we understand, the predisposition and willingness to share their work of art's elaboration and implementation is not much, but above all, the conception itself, we believe, is the most difficult stage of the whole art process to share. The truth is that, opposed to the usual single authorship to build a public monument or to paint a wall, here, the artists have to let go of, at least some, of their artistic individuality, in order to meet the wishes of both the local and the usufructuary communities, at the same time as they will try not to lose their own identity and brand[3]. Thirdly, it will be necessary to evaluate the population's acceptation, as far as the artists and their works of art are concerned. What kind of welcome, reception and hosting will happen and how this relationship unfolds, both in a physical as well as emotional place that the residents and users understand as being theirs. That is, probably, one of the moments throughout the project where the executive committee's role can be critical, but also, decisive and crucial. This is the stage in which we will have to emphasize the importance of the collaborative purpose and function of the primal idea underlying the whole project.

The interaction between the artists and the community, and this collaborative outcome, is another important aspect issue in the project. The ways in which the community will, in fact, be invited to participate are also very significant. We will begin to implement several strategies to get in touch with the community and start the consultation process: first of all, by spreading the information, by mail and e-mail, about the project and our intentions with it, trying to reach numerous groups and associations within the community and other networked groups. These same groups and associations will be asked to spread the information among the citizens, and disseminate the project's fundamentals. Then, to apply and enforce public consultation, a virtual/digital platform will be operating. Therein the community will be able to express its opinion and so participate in the decision process. In an early stage, the community will be asked to help to choose, from a list of artists, the artists to invite. They will also be invited to help to choose the drafts, the sketches and the proposals of the art pieces that the artistic community will submit to the community's appreciation. But, more importantly, the users will also be asked to join the artists chosen and participate in the work of art's creation and conception, and then, in the elaboration, implementation and installation process. Above all, the community will be invited to be permanently in touch with the project's organization team and its executive committee, during all the phases, following all the steps, throughout the whole process. All these strategies will facilitate and promote the adequate partnership(s) between the artists and specific groups within the community.

Another very important aspect will be the extent of the local authorities' involvement and support. The parish council and the city council's support will be crucial. In the first place, we sounded the parish council's interest in this project and the answer could not be more positive. They accepted to support the project. Then, we confirmed the parish council true interest with formalization meetings with the institutions involved. And finally, we guaranteed their support with the hosting of an internship of a post-graduate student. Logistic, production and press release support will also be needed and asked. But, the most important and perhaps the most difficult kind of support to get will be, we suspect, the financial one. In this moment of economic crisis in which the country is plunged in, we know that we will have to be very wise and astute to work out the project's added values, in order to seduce the potential stakeholders. The project's innovative character, its artistic, cultural and social significance, and the importance of bringing this project to this specific community, will be enforced so that we can and collect every aid and support we can possibly get and manage to raise. Cultural patronage and private sponsorship are also two very important ways to get the much needed financial support within this kind of participatory urban art project. Unfortunately, nowadays, patronage is most commonly decreasing, and we find it very difficult to get the attention of potential individual sponsors for this kind of intervention. Even with the local authorities' precious help and boost, we find no easy task in the attempt to collect, at least, a small part of the total budget. On the one hand, this urban art project is, in fact, a case study, and its academic nature, content and scope, does not provide us any financial support. Currently, the University, in general, but also the Faculty, in particular, lacks the financial means to support this kind of initiative. That is to say that, we have a hard task ahead of us. The ability to get cultural patronage and private sponsorship will be another tough challenge to overcome. In the first place, we will try to invite local small and medium entities and local private enterprises to support our project, but then we will move forward and try to reach both national and multinational enterprises, non-governmental organizations and social organizations also. We strongly believe that the event itself, the project's climax after all, has to have some big names and major brands supporting it and we will try to get it. Until the actual observation, in the follow-up stage of the project, we will not be able to evaluate if projects with greater community involvement are easier to sponsor, or if the sponsors rely more on the artist's talent to capture non-participant consumer's attention, rather than on the members within the community that would first-hand acknowledge the fruits of the patronage itself.

To answer the question if this project should have its foundations in the structured analysis of the place itself, we believe it should. In fact, what we are trying to do is, above all, to create an even more intimate relation between the user and the place itself. We strongly believe that this relation can only be established by means of an accurate study of the place in which we want to intervene. How can the structure of the space contribute to the projects' conception is another question that we propose to answer. We believe that it is very important to take in consideration the physical structure of the space, the architectural elements and their implementation in the field, not forgetting the involvement with the surroundings. All elements are important to observe: the technical cabinets; the walls; the benches; etc. The projects' conception can only be successful if thought and developed around all the relevant elements of that specific place. Should the artistic teams take into consideration the community's desires, and to what extent should they go, as far as the works of art are concerned and to what level should the community interfere in the creation process? Well, this might be, by far, the most difficult, controversial and fracturing question to address in this paper. It is neither a simple nor consensual issue. If on the one hand, most of the authors give primacy to the work of art itself and the conceptual process of creation, and strongly believe that the space and its publics and audiences are secondary. And that is to say that, publics and audiences should accept, embrace, enjoy and appreciate whatever work of art is given to them. On the other hand, there are some artists and scholars that defend the idea that the community must be heard about the interventions on the spaces that are effectively theirs. This faction understands that collaboration is essential in the work of art creative process, from the conceptualization to the actual execution. We will aim also at making some contributions to this discussion, by experimenting different types of collaboration and studying not only its results, but also the reaction of potential sponsors to these kinds of projects. To answer the question about the role of the cultural manager as the corner stone in the management processes and the projects' implementation in the urban intervention domain we have to consider some important questions. The cultural manager's role is to promote the planning and execution of the project, respecting the author's creative freedom as well as the public's will. This is a delicate and very thin edge which requires diplomacy and the ability to concentrate the attentions in the essential values of the project's primal goal. The management of the collaborations between all the agents included and involved - the artistic teams, the residents and the users' community to whom this Participatory Urban Art project is addressed – will be no easy task. Another assignment for the cultural manager to deal with will be to guide and manage several agents - the local authorities, the artists, the numerous groups and associations, and the inhabitants. Social dialogue will be the foundation of the cultural manager's main tasks during the whole process. Above all, the cultural mediator will have to be updated, each and every step of the project, intervening as little as possible and discreetly moderating and facilitating the collaboration processes, smoothing the differences between the agents involved.

Conclusion
We expect the final result to be diverse yet integrated. As far at the community is concerned, the main subject will be the empowerment in the decision-making process and the collaboration throughout the whole process. As to the artists, the most important issue will be the sharing – embrace other agents' participation in the whole artistic process without losing its individual identity and branding. Both the artists' ideas and the public's opinion should count and be taken into consideration equally. This whole participatory urban art project should culminate in the observation of good practices, pedagogic approaches for the several communities involved. One of the final conclusions should allow us to acknowledge what this new form of urban art projects represents for the populations and the city itself. Ultimately, we will be able to find that we have accomplished some of our many goals with the implementation of this participatory urban art project and others. Other goals may not be achieved, and those should be a matter of study as well. Maybe, we will conclude that our project left its mark and that will indelibly not be forgotten by the community.

Short Planning
2014; from June to December; Characterization and study of Lumiar, both as a place and a community. Characterization of Parque da Quinta das Conchas e dos Lilases; Place Manual; Logo; Corporate Identity; Communication Plan; Auscultation of the Community; Invitations and interviews with the Artists; 2015 –January: Call for artists; February: Jury's Panel constitution; March and April: Applications; May: Applications' evaluation and selection; Early June Results release; Mid June: Press Release; Late June and early July: Event; September to December: Follow –up and clipping.

Future Work

This participatory urban art project will be under evaluation and further analyzed. Several issues will arise from this whole experience, and the experiment will, surely, bring out questions such as: Did this participatory urban art project represent an added value for the agents involved (being the agents, mostly, the artistic community and the resident and usufructuary community)? Which kind of art projects did the participants wished for? To what extent did the artistic community gave in to the local community's wishes? Were the communities' expectations and their collective imaginary cherished, respected and reached? What social benefit did the artistic community and their collaborators draw from these kind art practices? Was this project a success in terms of social practice in art and culture? These are some of the questions we will try to answer, after the end of the projects and the follow-up phase, once we have the distance and the clarity required to analyze and evaluate the whole project as impartially as we can. Finally, we strongly believe that there will be further work(s) and studies to perform within these domains and, since this project is a replicable model, luckily, we will be able to re-implement it and test other paths, new methodologies and different approaches. This project does not end only in this initiative and in one single event. There is already a plan for a series of initiatives in the same context, which will be implemented only after the end of the project. We believed that this type of project is replicable in other places and other cities, and so, with the appropriate adjustments, and the specificities of each community taken into account, we will try to implement it again.

Notes and References

[1]The historical path that nurtured the empowerment concept seeks the individuals' release from institutional structures, cultural contexts and social practices which already proved to be unjust, oppressive and discriminatory. Empowerment advocates often assume that marginalized and discriminated groups in society suffer from a lack of power and that this situation prevents them from fighting for their rights and take any advantage of social benefits. It is almost always vetoed to some minorities to participate in the decision-making processes such as political, social and cultural. We strongly believe that too change this situation it is necessary that these groups increase their skills and their power by being challenged to participate in its community's social as well as cultural life. This empowerment will be the result of the actual application of the concepts of the individual's autonomy and responsibility. We will try to provide the community with a greater awareness of its power and importance by completely rejecting any kind of discrimination and exclusion that society have eventually and somehow already generated.

[2] To prevent the community's rejection of such a project, the development and physic changes proposed by our plans must be based on the local identity, both of the space and of the individuals. There will be multiple paths to adopt but none of them must forget the community for which we are working. We will try to put great emphasis on every group and association own identity and seek to discover what similarities we find in each of them, in order to help to build a stronger sense of belonging and collective identity. Indeed. This stronger sense of belonging and the collective social and cultural identity as a cohesive group will provide the basis for the deconstruction of the any ideological hegemony of the so called urban local elites.

[3]Brand, the most valuable asset of the artist's identity and value, can be put in danger as far as the idea underneath this participatory urban art project is concerned. The collaboration aspect we defend and will foment may be understood as a pinch in the artistic personality. However, we truly believe that identity, name and brand can be preserved and survive to the participative nature of the project. The challenge for the artists will be to maintain uniqueness and authenticity although immersed in the collaborative content of the project's fundamentals. Individual contributions may be effectively reinforced with the participation process and the authors' artistic legacy may prevail nevertheless.

AAVV (2010), Teoria e Critica de Arquitectura - Século XX. Lisboa: Caleidoscópio.
Águas, Sofia (2012), Do Design ao Co-Design: umaoportunidade de design participativo na transformação do espaçopúblico. Barcelona: On theW@terfront.
Aguilera, Fernando G. (2004), Arte, Ciudadanía y EspacioPúblico. Barcelona: On theW@terfront.
Appadurai, Arjun (1986), The Social Life of Things: Commodities in culturalperspective. Cambridge: Cambridge University Press.
Artus, Diana (2007), Die Zeichen auf der Tass. Read in 21-01-2014. In: http://jungle-world.com/artikel/2007/30/20030.html
Ascher, François (2010), Novos Princípios do Urbanismo. Seguidos dos Novos CompromissosUrbanos. Um Léxico. Lisboa: Livros Horizonte.
Augé, Marc (1994), Nãolugares, Introdução a umaAntropologia da Sobremodernidade. Lisboa: Bertrand Editora.
Baudrillard, Jean (1973), Ó Sistema dos Objectos. São Paulo: Perspectiva.
Bauman, Zigmunt (1998), Work, consumerismandthenewpoor. Buckingham: Open University Press.
Bauman,Zigmunt (2007), Consuminglife. Cambridge: Polity Press.
Benko, Georges (1999), A Ciência Regional. Oeiras: Celta.
Bishop, Claire (2010), Artificialhells :participatoryartandthepoliticsofspectatorship. Read in: 19-04-2014. In: http://selforganizedseminar.files.wordpress.com/2011/08/bishop-claire-artificial-hells-participatory-art-and-politics-spectatorship.pdf
Boyer, M.Christine (1994), The City of Collective Memory. Massachusetts: MIT.
Campos, Cristian (2012), The Graffiti Wall – Street Art FromAroundthe World. Barcelona: Promopress.
Choay, Françoise (1965), L'urbanisme, utopies et réalités. Paris: Seuil.
Clarke, David B. (2003), The Consumer Society andthe Postmodern City.London: Routledge.
Collings, Matthew (2008), Banksy'sideashavethevalueof a joke. Read in 20-01-2014. In: http://michaelleonardphoto.blogspot.pt/2008/01/banksys-ideas-have-value-of-joke-by.html
Danysz, M.and Dana, M. N.(2011), From Style Writing to Art: A Street Art Anthology. Rome: Drago.
Deitch, J.,Gastman, R. and Rose, A. (2011), Art in thestreets. Los Angeles: MOCA.
Fortuna, Carlos(1997), Cidade, cultura e globalização. Oeiras: Celta.
Gastman, R. andNeelon, C. (2007), Street World: Urban Art and Culture fromFiveContinents. London: Thames& Hudson.
Gato, M., Ramalhete, F. and Vicente, S. (2013), "Hoje somos nós os escultores!" Agencialidade e arte pública participada em Almada. Read in: 27-04-2014. In: http://www.portalseer.ufba.br/index.php/cadernosaa/article/view/6723
Gato, M., Ramalhete, F., Vicente, S. and Esteves, José (2012), Arte Pública Participada: O Monumento à Multiculturalidade no Parque Urbano do Fróis. Read in: 03-12-2013. In: http://www.aps.pt/vii_congresso/papers/finais/PAP0992_ed.pdf
Gottdiener, M.andHutchinson, R. (2006), The New Urban Sociology. Colorado: Westview Press.
Hoppe, Ilaria (2009), Street Art und, Die Kunst im öffentlichen Raum, Read in 26-12-2013. In: http://edoc.hu-berlin.de/kunsttexte/2009-1/hoppe-ilaria-6/PDF/hoppe.pdf
Jaine, Mark (2005), Cities andConsumption. London: Routledge.
Ket (2011), Street Art: The Best Urban Art fromAroundthe World. London: Michael O'Mara Books.
Klanten, R. and Hübner, M. (2010), Urban Interventions - Personal Projects in Public Spaces. Berlin: Gestalten.
Landry, Charles (2000), The Creative City: A toolkitfor urban innovators. London: Earthscan Publications.
Lewisohn, Cedar (2011), Abstract graffiti. New York: Merrell.

Lopes, A. S. (1995), Desenvolvimento Regional: Problemática, Teoria, Modelos. Lisboa: FundaçãoCalousteGulbenkian.
Lopes, Raul (2001), Competitividade, Inovação e Território. Oeiras: Celta.
McCormick, C., Schiller, M.and Schiller, S.(2010), Trespass: A HistoryofUncommissioned Urban Art. Köln: Taschen.
Miles, M.and Miles, S. (2004),Consuming Cities. New York: Macmillan.
Miller, Daniel (1987), Material Culture andMassConsumption. Oxford: Basil Blackwell.
Nguyen, P.andMacKenzie, S.(2010), Beyondthe Street: The 100 LeadingFigures in Urban Art. Berlin: Gestalten.
Paddison, Ronan(2001), Handbook of Urban Studies. London: Sage Publications.
Pólese, Mario (1998), EconomiaUrbana e Regional. Coimbra: APDR.
Ransome, Paul (2005), Work, consumptionandculture - affluenceandsocialchange in thetwenty-first century. London: Sage.
Rodrigues, Walter (2010), CidadeemTransição. Lisboa: CeltaEditora.
Sackmann , Reinhold (2006), Graffiti zwischen Kunst und Ärgernis – Empirische Studien zu einem städtischen Problem. Read in 28-02-2014. In: http://www.soziologie.uni-halle.de/publikationen/pdf/0601.pdf
Sacramento, N.andBispo, M. (2010-2011),Manual do Lugar: Observatório das Idiossincrasias dos Lugares, Conceito, Propósito e Metodologia. Lisboa: ARTIS – Revista do Instituto de História da Arte da Faculdade de Letras de Lisboa.
Salgueiro, Teresa (1992), A Cidadeem Portugal: UmaGeografiaUrbana.Porto: EdiçõesAfrontamento.
Scott,A. J.(2000),The Cultural Economy of Cities. London: Sage.
Short, John (2006), Urban Theory: a criticalassessment. New York: Palgrave.
Silvano, Filomena (1997). Territórios da Identidade. Oeiras: Celta.
Thorns, David C. (2002), The Transformation of Cities. New York: Palgrave.
Vartanian, Hrag (2010), The Emergenceof Real Pop Art: Jeffrey Deitch& Street Art. Read in 25-04-2014. In: http://hyperallergic.com/2108/jeffrey-deitch-street-art/
Waclaveck, Anna (2011), Graffiti and Street Art. London: Thames& Hudson.
Zukin, Sharon(1995),The Culturesof Cities. Oxford: Blackwell.

Filipa Ramalhete, CEACT/UAL and e-GEO/FCSH,
framalhete@netcabo.pt

Maria Assunção Gato, DINÂMIA'CET,
magoo@iscte.pt

Sérgio Vicente, CIEBA, Faculdade de Belas Artes da Universidade de Lisboa (FBAUL),
ateliersergiovicente@gmail.com

Gerber tVerheij, CIEBA – Centro de Estudos em Belas Artes, Faculdade de Belas Artes da Universidade de Lisboa / CRPolis,
Universitat de Barcelona, gerbertverheij@vfemail.net

A Participatory public Art Process in Almada – Agents and Values

The impact of public art on the territory has an undeniable cultural dimension since it creates new sensorial and visual agents, with potential social interactivity. In this paper we present and discuss a Portuguese case-study of participated public art, developed for the Caparica Civic Centre (Almada, Portugal) by a team that includes artists (sculptors), anthropologists, local associations and inhabitants. The territory and the community were the main pillars for the conception of a three piece monument, built in a multicultural neighborhood,through a progressive and interactive working methodology, between 2011 and 2013.

participatory public art, public space, Almada

Introduction

The impact of public art on the territory has an undeniable cultural dimension since it creates new sensorial and visual agents, with potential social interactivity. The many, at times contradictory, opinions on public art have, however, given rise to much debate on its nature, goals and effectiveness. Public art is a complex concept, involving two ambiguous domains, art and the public, not necessarily resulting from the simple intersection of both. As Remesar (2003) says, the artist, when working in public space, cannot act as a demiurge sovereignly imposing his or her art on the public space, advocating instead a conception of public art as a means of citizen control over the aesthetics of their own environment. In this context the role of public art participatory processes (in opposition to traditional authorship processes) has led to recent interesting experiences, such as the ones held in Barcelona(Remesar, 2003; Remesar and Vidal, 2003; Aguilera, 2004; Ricart, 2009, Águas, 2012). In fact, there is increasing recognition of the importance of public participation as a way to social cohesion and community empowerment, supplying tools that enhance the full exercise of citizenship, while providing better effectiveness of public interventions(Remesar et al, 2012; Seixas; Albet, 2010; Gomes, 2010).By facing knowledge as a shared resource (Hess;Ostrom, 2007), participation opens up a whole new range of possibilities regarding finding new solutions for old dilemmas such as the construction of more inclusive territories.In this context projects of public space are particularly relevant (Brandão, 2008) as mediators between the inhabitant'srepresentations and their everyday experiences (Gato et al, 2012), asthey may reinforce the relationship between populations and their territories, by creating pieces that may be, simultaneously, a reference to the past and a starting point for the future.

In this paper we present and discuss a Portuguese case-study of participated public art, developed for the Caparica Civic Centre (Almada, Portugal) by a team that includes artists (sculptors), anthropologists, local associations and inhabitants between 2011 and 2013. The fact that we're in the presence of a multicultural neighborhood with a strong social and cultural diversity - where the resident population has generally low incomes and ismainly composed by people who came from Portuguese rural areas, immigrants from several African countries and Gypsies - led to the construction of a monument inspired in the concept of multiculturality. The territory and the community were the main pillars for the conception of a three piece monument, built through a progressive and interactive working methodology, having the Barcelona experiences as a reference, combined with the use of methodologies for the promotion of public participation in regional planning (Vasconcelos; Baptista 2002; Vassalo;Farinha, 2010). During the process, the Barcelona experiences in participated public designwere adapted with new methodologies for the promotion of public participation in regional planning.Beyond the concept, this presentation proposes to discuss the different agents (which includes, besides the team,local associations, the municipality and inhabitants)and values implied in participatory public art processes

The Monument to multiculturality project: objectives and methodology

The monument arose from a municipal initiative for the new green space (Fróis Urban Park, later integrated in the Monte de Caparica Civic Centre) and the team's proposal to make a participatory art project in Almada. Asmulticulturality is one of the main social characteristics of that neighborhood, the challenge was to build a monument to multiculturality through a collaborative art process. Thegoal was to build an artworkresulting fromthe active participation of the neighborhood residents, from its conceptualization to the effective modeling of the object.This implied a participated process the final result of which should reflect local identity values and have the potential to be a future landmark for that territory. Local agents were thus essential for the process, right from its conception and methodological design. The main partners were the local municipality (Junta de Freguesia) and the Clube Recreativo União Raposense, a local association whose headquarter is located precisely in the park area. This association supplied their facilities for the workshops and also a precious view and opinion on the neighborhood and on the participative process. The Monument to Multiculturality was developed over a two-year period (July 2011–July 2013) in seven public workshops. Average attendance was about forty individuals, some of them returning to each workshop, others participating in just one or two. While participation was not statistically representative of Monte de Caparica residents, the average number proved to be adequate to the methodologies used.

In fact, previous analysis of the territory and its communities had indicated that participation would be characterized less by the quantity of participants as by the diversity of their cultural references and their wealth of life experiences.

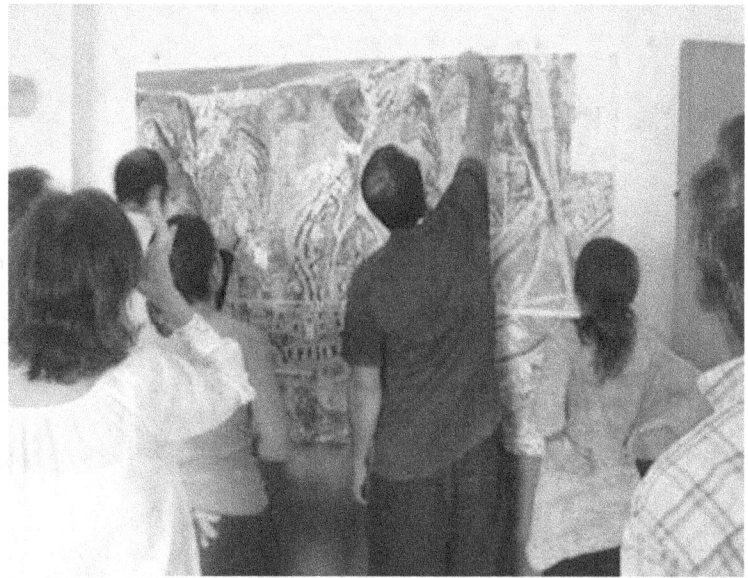

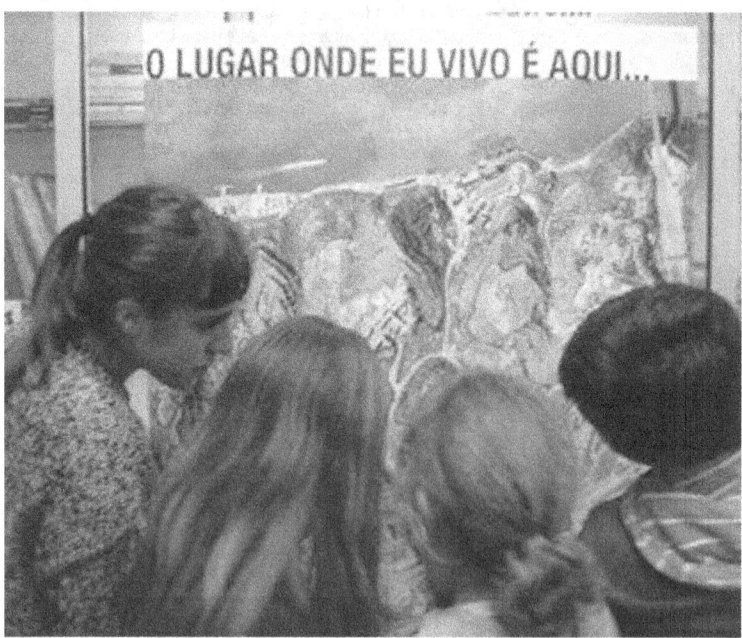

Fig. 1 and 2: Territorial approach to the neighborhood

The first three workshops were dedicated to the collective production and discussion of spatial perceptions, memories and speechesabout the experience of sharing a common territory, which resulted in a consensual list of synthetic ideas about the community's territory (Fig. 1 and 2). This list included the community's social diversity, the intercultural universe of the local school community, the large presence of teenagers and the reflection of this presence and their actions (not always perceived as positive) in public spaces; the general environment of insecurity felt by the community and the lack of places of sharing and collective experiences; and the importance of exchanging values related to the area's material heritage, spatial memories and sociocultural diversity. Groups of participants were then challenged to transform these ideas into three keywords which, transformed in a narrative sequence, would translate their spatial and social reality.

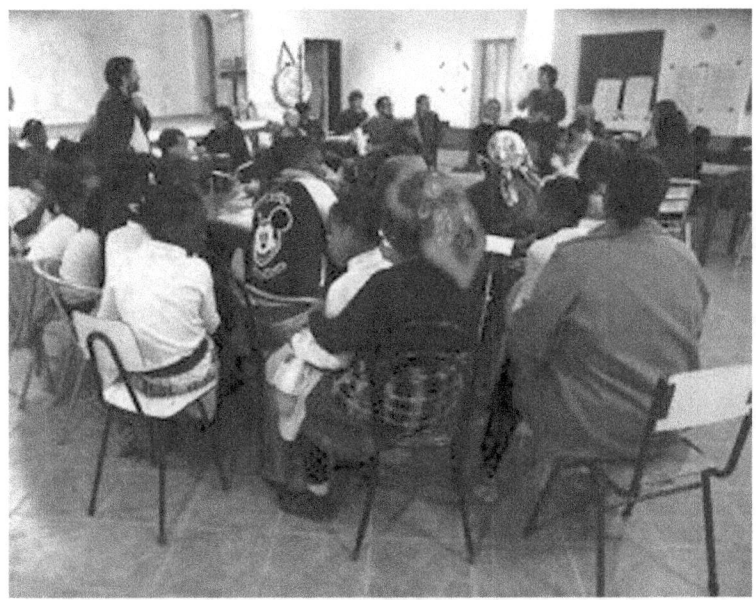

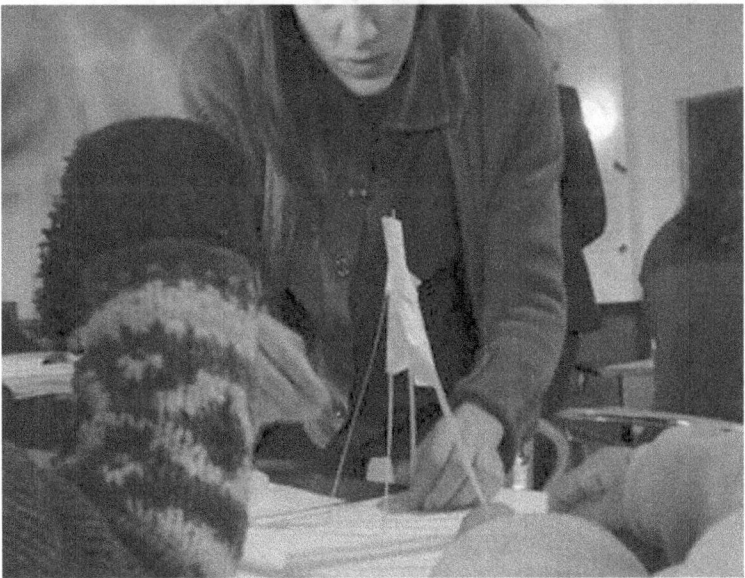

Fig. 3 – Discussing concepts.Fig. 4 – Making proposals

In the following workshops, these references were used as a starting point for the formal conception of a proposal for the monument (Fig. 3 and 4). A worktable with different materials invited the participants to start developing models in groups. At the end, rather than simply alluding to or representing cultural diversity, the models began to proliferate into various places of "meeting" and "sharing" which aimed at reinforcing the already existing diversity. These models, each explained by a group representative, passed in the following sessions through a process of selection, ending with three models, which had also gone through a formal synthesisand rethinking in terms of scale, materials and construction by participating sculptors and students (Fig. 5 and 6).

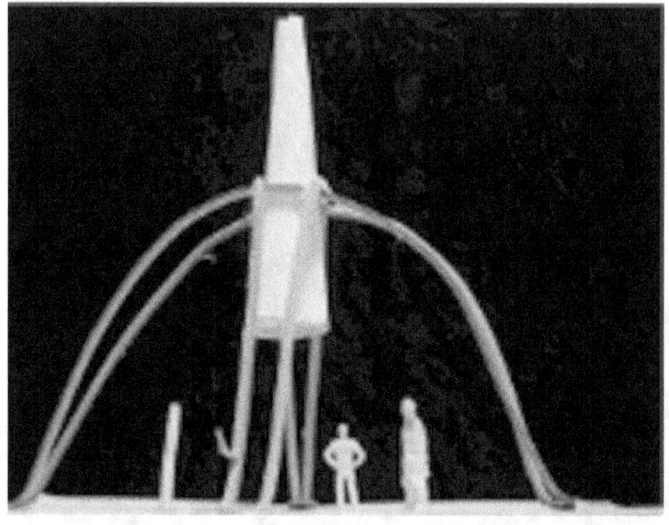

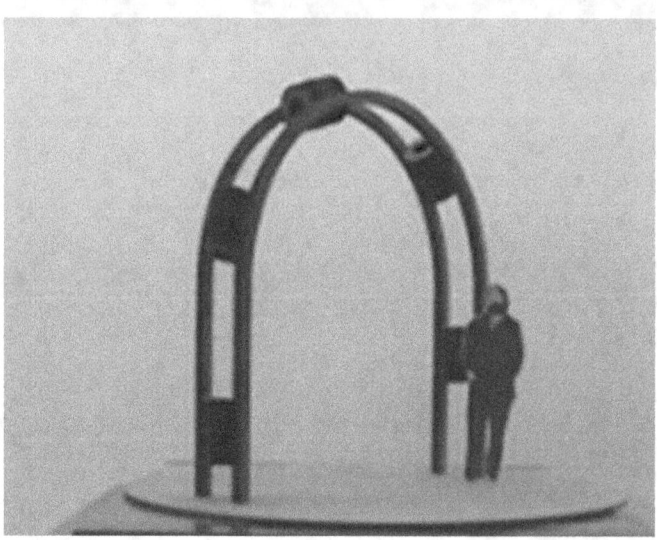

Fig. 5 – A proposal for the monument. Fig. 6 – One of the proposals exhibited in the municipal museum

One of the most interesting aspects of this process was that each group had produced more than one model, but during the workshops several were abandoned, mainly because the concepts were present in models built by other groups. The participants were thus willingly to abdicatetheir proposals in favor of others, revealing a strong capacity of negotiation and reaching spontaneous consensus.In agreementwith the Almada Council, it was decided to execute three models, which together would compose the "monument". The interest and involvement of participants, the diversity of the presented proposals, and the interest of the Municipality can be credited for this multiplication. The last workshop)Fig. 7 and 8) consisted in the presentation and collective discussion of the three sculptures, to which the participants added a word (estamos[we are], fazemos[we do] and sentimos[we feel]) and colors (red, blue and yellow) as visual, symbolical and territorial enhancement. These were chosen in relation to the ideas each sculpture symbolizes and the active role participants desired the works would have. It was hoped they would not only be material and symbolic witnesses, but also places by themselves: a "meeting place" where dialogue among cultures could happen; a "place of reflexion" and of shared memories; and a "place of observation" of the surrounding reality, in order to actively enact and enhance existing cultural diversity.

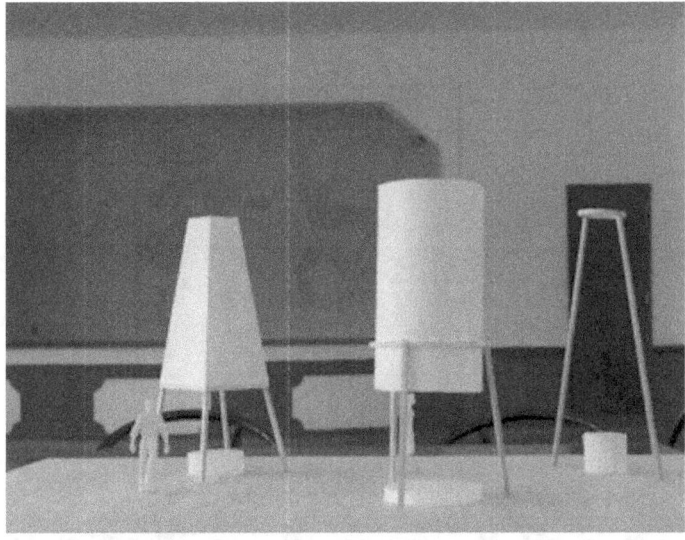

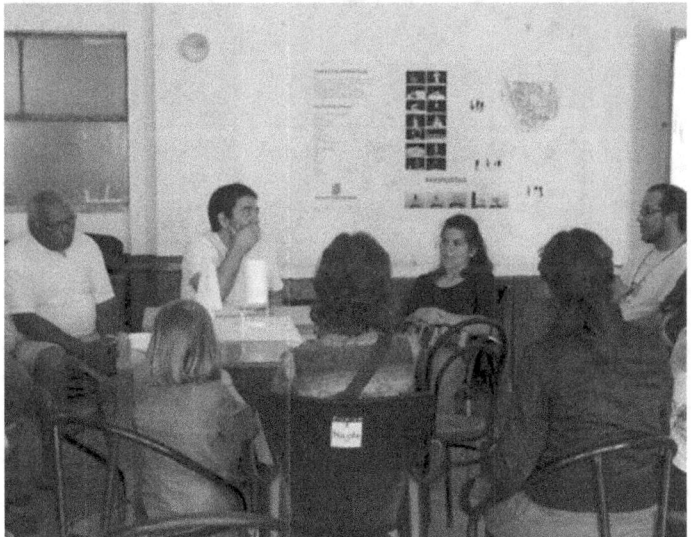

Fig. 7 – Final models.Fig. 8 – Discussing and proposing around the final model

Results and conclusions

The Monument to Multiculturality was inaugurated on the 27th April 2013 in the Monte de Caparica Civic Centre (this space includes the new Raposense headquarter, a swimming pool, a library, and the green area where the sculptures are located). Meant to be a gathering point for the different agents in the community, reinforced with the written message "we are, we do, we feel", the monument reflects a participated proposal and the values of the agents involved in the process. However, it is also a testimony of the local capacity and will analyze and conceptualize memories regarding the territory, proposing future solutions based on them, executing models for the proposals and discuss them, in an iterative and reflexive collective creation process.

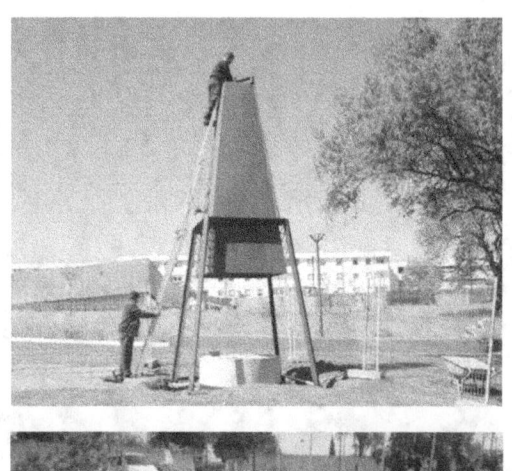

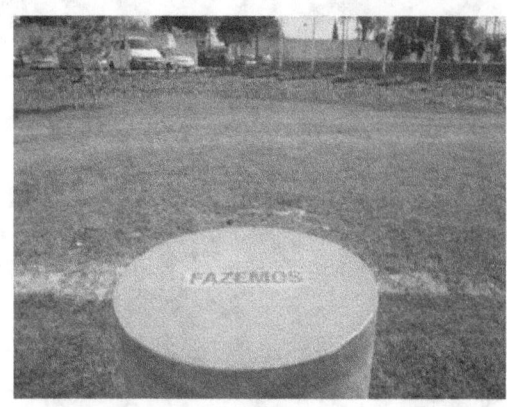

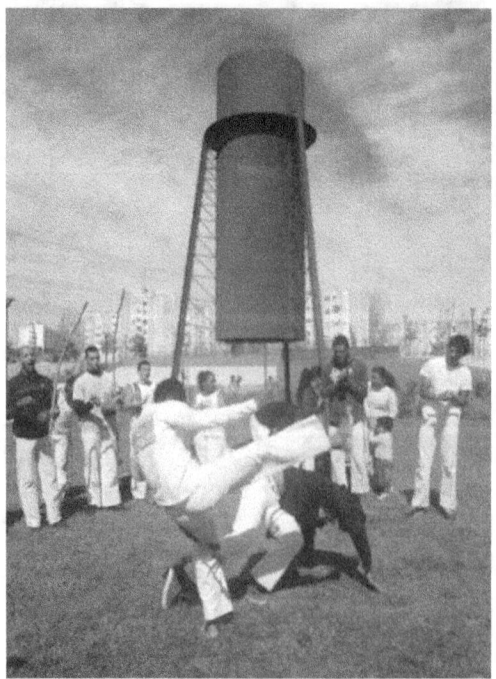

Fig. 9 – Monument construction.Fig. 10 – "We do". Fig 11 – Inauguration day

The complexity of multicultural suburban territories representsa challenge to societies and territories. Normally, these neighborhoods are the result of public housing policies, which may partially explainthe low levels of formal education, high unemployment and social disarticulation and social and territorial segregation. Within these contexts, the use of dynamic and innovative tools for territorial construction and management contribute to improve the urban quality of life, by helping to meet the community needs, interests and expectations.

This participatory process is currently under evaluation and three main questions arise: does this participatory public art process represent an added value for the agents and participants who were involved? Which kind of values did the participants wish for? Were the prime expectations converted in real benefits? The data already gathered show that all the partners involved feel strongly about the monument and have, to some extent, gained something with the participative process. The final goal of building a collaborative artwork was accomplished and new projects and are now necessary, in order to continue the dynamics created.

Notes and References
Águas, S., Do Design ao Co-Design: uma oportunidade de design participativo na transformação do espaço público (On the W@terfront, 22, 2012, 57-70).
Available at: http://www.raco.cat/index.php/Waterfront/article/view/252044/338393
Aguilera, Fernando Gómez, Arte, Ciudadanía y Espacio Público (Onthew@terfront, Barcelona:Universitat de Barcelona,5, 2004, 36-51).
Available at: http://www.raco.cat/index.php/Waterfront/article/view/214757
Brandão, Pedro, A identidade dos lugares e a sua representação colectiva. Base de orientação para a concepção, qualificação e gestão do espaço público (Lisboa: DGOTDU. Série Política de Cidades. 2008). Available at:
http://politicadecidades.dgotdu.pt/docs_ref/Documents/Pol%C3%ADtica%20de%20Cidades/S%C3%A9rie%20Pol%C3%ADtica%20de%20Cidades/serie_politica_de_cidades-3.pdf
Gato, Maria Assunção; Ramalhete, Filipa; Vicente, Sérgio, "Hoje somos nós os escultores!" Agencialidade e Arte Pública Participada em Almada (Cadernos de Arte e Antropologia, 1/2013, 53-71).Available at: http://www.portalseer.ufba.br/index.php/cadernosaa/article/view/6723/4870
Gato, Maria Assunção; Ramalhete, Filipa; Vicente, Sérgio; Esteves, José,Arte pública participada: o monumento à multiculturalidade no parque urbano do fróis (Porto: VII Congresso de Sociologia, 2012). Available at: http://www.aps.pt/vii_congresso/papers/finais/PAP0992_ed.pdf
Gomes, Carla Patrícia Rocha, A integração do princípio da coesão sócio-territorial no processo de reabilitação urbana: o caso da Baixa Pombalina (Lisboa: Universidade Nova de Lisboa, Dissertação de mestrado em Ordenamento do Território e Planeamento Ambiental, 2010).
Hess, Charlotte;Ostrom, Elinor,Understanding Knowledge as a Commons:From Theory to Practice(Massachusetts:Massachusetts Institute of Technology,2007).
Pinto, Ana Júlia, Espaço Público e Coesão Territorial – O Caso da "Rambla de La Mina" (Onthew@terfront, 12, Barcelona:Universitat de Barcelona, 2009, 149-163).
Availilable at: http://www.raco.cat/index.php/Waterfront/article/view/218898/299218
Remesar, Antoni, Arte e espaço público. Singularidades e incapacidades da linguagem escultórica para o projecto urbano(in Pedro Brandão andAntoniRemesar, Design do espaço público. Deslocação e proximidade, Lisboa: Centro Português do Design, 2003, 26–40).
Remesar, Antoni; Salas, Xavi; Padilla, Samuel; Esparza, Diana, 2012, Inclusion and empowerment in public art and urban design(On the w@terfront, 24, Barcelona:Universitat de Barcelona, 3–32).
vailable at: www.raco.cat/index.php/Waterfront/article/view/259235
Remesar, A.; Vidal, T., Metodologias Creativas Para la Participación - documento de trabajo (Doctorado Espacio público y Espacio Urbano: arte y sociedad, Barcelona: Universidad de Barcelona, 2003).
Ricart, Núria,ArtPúblic, Regeneració Urbana i Participació. El ProjecteCartografies de la Mina (Onthew@terfront, Barcelona:Universitat de Barcelona, 12, 172-186, 2009).
Available at: http://www.raco.cat/index.php/waterfront/article/view/218900
Seixas, João; Albet, Abel, Urban Governance in the South of Europe.Cultural identitiesand global dilemas(Análise SocialVol. XLV (3.°). 197 (2010) 771-787, Lisboa: Instituto de CiênciasSociais).
Vasconcelos, Lia T.; Baptista, IdalinaEvaluating participation at local level – results for implementing sustainability (Paper presented at the ACSP Conference - Planning and Regional Issues in the Border Regions. Baltimore, Maryland (USA), 2002).Vassalo, P.L.; Farinha, João M. Critérios de avaliação para áreas urbanas sustentáveis(Conferência apresentada no PLURIS 2010 Thechallengesofplanning in a web widewold – 4° Congresso Luso-brasileiro para o planeamento urbano, regional, integrado, sustentável, Faro: Portugal, 2010)

Conference Committees

Honour Committee

Prof. Dr. Fernando António Baptista Pereira, Faculty of Fine Arts, Lisbon University;
Prof. Dr.ª Raquel Henriques da Silva,
Faculty of Social Sciences and Humanities, NOVA University of Lisbon;
Prof. Dr.ª Teresa Valsassina Heitor, Instituto Superior Técnico, Lisbon University;
Prof. Dr.ª Maria João Gamito, Faculty of Fine Arts, Lisbon University;
Prof. Dr.ª Margarida Brito Alves,
Faculty of Social Sciences and Humanities, NOVA University of Lisbon;
Prof. Dr. Nick Dunn, Lancaster University;
Prof. Dr. Javier Abarca, Universidad Complutense de Madrid;
Prof. Dr. Lachlan MacDowall, University of Melbourne;
Dr. Luca Borriello, Phd., Inopinatum, Sapienza - University of Rome.

Scientific Committee

Prof. Dr.ª Ana Tomé (IST-UL / ICIST)
Dr. Bruno Marques (FCSH-UNL / IHA-CASt)
Prof. Dr. Cristovão Pereira (FBA-UL / CIEBA)
Prof. Dra. Giulia Lamoni (FCSH-UNL / IHA-CASt)
Dr Lachlan MacDowall, University of Melbourne, Australia
Dr.ª Lígia Ferro (ISCTE-IUL / CIES)
Prof. Dr. Javier Abarca, Universidad Complutense de Madrid
Dr. José Pedro Regatão (FBA-UL / CIEBA)
Prof. Dr. Jorge dos Reis (FBA-UL / CIEBA)
Prof. Dr. João Castro Silva (FBA-UL / CIEBA)
Prof. Dr.ª Margarida Brito Alves (FCSH-UNL / IHA-CASt)
Prof. Dr.ª Maria Rosália da Palma Guerreiro (ISCTE-IUL / CIES)
Dr.ª Marta Traquino (FBA-UL / CIEBA)
Prof. Dr. Nick Dunn, Professor of Urban Design at Lancaster University
Prof. Dr. Pedro António Janeiro (FA-UL / CIAUD)
Prof. Dr. Pedro Costa (ISCTE-IUL / DINAMIA'CET)
Dr. Ricardo Campos (UA / CEMRI)

Executive Committee

Pedro Soares Neves - FBAUL / CIEBA, IST-UL
Daniela V. de Freitas Simões - FCSH-UNL / IHA-CASt

Secretariat during the Conference

Ana Celeste Glória - FCSH-UNL / IHA
Véronique van Grieken - FCSH-UNL
Catarina Diz de Almeida - ISCTE-IUL / DINÂMIA'CET // FA-UL

This conference was institutionally framed by the Art History Institute/line of Contemporary Art Studies (IHA/CASt) of The Faculty of Social Sciences and Humanities – NOVA University of Lisbon; and the Artistic Studies Research Centre (CIEBA) of the Faculty of Fine Arts, University of Lisbon.

3rd of July – Thursday

08h00 – 09h00: Registry of Delegates and General Public
09h00 – 10h00: Welcome Session by Pedro Soares Neves and Daniela V. de Freitas Simões
Prof. Fernando António Baptista Pereira (CIEBA/FBA)
Prof. Margarida Brito Alves (IHA/FCSH)
Dra. Catarina Vaz Pinto (Lisbon's Councilwoman for Culture – CML)
Guest Speaker: Prof. Helena Barranha (IST-UL/IHA-FCSH)

10h00 – 10h30: Keynote Speaker: Cedar Lewisohn
10h30 – 11h00: Coffee Break

11h00 – 12h15: Art Institutions // Chairman: Helena Barranha (IST/IHA-FCSH)
Ema Rocha, 'Musealizar por aí'. Graffiti – The street as exhibit
Sofia Ponte, How does street artworks survive in museums?
Ulrich Blanché, Banksy vs. Bristol Museum - Street Art or street "flavored" art?
Alice Nogueira Alves, Emerging issues of Street Art valuation as Cultural Heritage

12h15 – 13h30: Lunch

13h30 – 14h45: Cultural assets // Chairman: Rute Figueiredo (IHA-FCSH / ETH Zurich)
Helena Elias,Inês Marques, Susana Leonor, Recent public art interventions in the context of the luso-brazilian cultural relationship: street murals of Os Gémeos in Lisbon and Vhils in Rio de Janeiro
Ronald Kramer, "The thing about walls is they became big murals": The rise of legal graffiti writing cultures
Daniel D'Amico, Lessons from Mardi Gras: Fostered Culture Between New Orleans and an Online Learning Community

14h45 – 15h15: Keynote Speaker: NUART Festival intervention
15h15 – 15h30: Coffee Break

15h30 – 17h00: Tactical Urbanism // Chairman: Mário Alves
Carlos Alcobia, Largo da Batata Video Mapping and São Paulo's forthcoming arenas of protest
Maria Domenica Arcuri, Utopia on Walls: The Collective Political Artworking of Felice Pignataro
Kris Murray, Rethinking political subjectivity in the urban context through the lens of graffiti and street art
Luis Menor Ruiz, Street Art and Urban Space. A problem or an opportunity for local governments? Barcelona as a case study
Manuel García y Ruiz van Hoben, Art(s) in the City. Chronicles of a Spray Can

17h00 – 18h15: Community and Historiography actions // Chairman: Cristóvão Pereira (CIEBA/FBA)
Maria do Mar Fazenda, Urban Acupuncture, artistic interventions in a deactivated shop window in Lisbon
Lara Seixo Rodrigues, The Wool – Covilhã Urban Art Festival as an instrument of (community) transformation
Jacob Kimvall, Mapping an Institutional Story of Graffiti and Street Art
Susan Phillips, Bomb the Canon: Re-Writing the History of Graffiti in Los Angeles

 19h00: André Saraiva's Exhibition inauguration at MUDE
around 21h00: Dinner at Bellalisa Elevador Restaurant (previous Registration Required!)

4th of July – Friday

09h00 – 10h15: Public Space vrs. Urban Creativity // Chairman: Margarida Brito Alves (IHA-FCSH)
Julia Tulke, Aesthetics of Crisis. Street Art, Austerity Urbanism and the Right to the City
Susan Hansen, Danny Flynn, "This is not a Banksy!": Street art and the transformation of public space
Ágata Sequeira, Out in the streets: The possibilities and implications of making art in the city's public space
Theodore Kuttner, Os Gémeos & São Paulo: Reappropriating Public Space in a "City of Walls"

10h15 – 10h30: Coffee Break

10h30 – 12h00: City-branding, Economy and Urban Art // Chairman: Daniela V. de Freitas Simões (IHA-FCSH)
Graeme Evans, Graffiti, Art and the City: from pariah to place-making
Christian Omodeo, Graffiti: between public art and entrepreneurial cities
Heike Derwanz, Street Artists and their careers in Art and Design Markets
Pedro Costa, Ricardo Lopes, Is street art institutionalizable? Challenges to an alternative urban policy in Lisbon

12h00 – 13h30: Lunch

13h30 – 14h15: Authors // Chairman: Marcus Willcocks (UAL/CSM)
Javier Abarca, Revs, the unknown pioneer
Minna Valjakka, Kaid Ashton: conflating Streets, Arts and Charity
Juliana M. M. Soares, Felipe Carrelli, The Margin in the Center: the birth of Project Occupy the Car in the Santa Cecilia's

14h15 – 15h30: Open air and market // Chairman: Giulia Lamoni (IHA-FCSH)
Laura Castro, José Guilherme Abreu, Paredes' Public Art Circuit. A Public Art and Community Orientated Program
Ila N. Sheren, The Open-air Gallery: A Return to the Revolutionary, or More of the Market?
Peter Bengtsen, Stealing from the public: on the removal of street art from the street
Veronica Werckmeister, A Case study in Monumental Street Art: Creating Landmarks, Creating Together

15h30 – 15h45: Coffee Break

15h45 – 16h15: Keynote Speaker: Marcus Willcocks

16h15 – 17h45: Semiotics, Visual Arts and Media // Chairman: Rogério Taveira (CIEBA/FBA)
Axel Philipps, Eelco Herder, Sergej Zerr, Chroniclers of Street Art on Flickr
Paulo Barroso, Keith Haring's personal visual lexicon and public semiotic-art
Patricia Guiley, The World as it is Written on the Wall
Duarte Lobo Antunes, Desecration, Condensation: Lisbon's futuristic imagery as a site of urban creativity
Giada Pellicari, Graffiti and New Media: the correlations between the two cultures

19h30: Alexandro Farto aka Vhils' 'Dissection' Exhibition inauguration at EDP Foundation

5th of July - Saturday

09h00 – 10h15: Contradictions // Chairman: Javier Abarca (UCM)
Julio da Cruz Paulos, Agata Walny, The art of pragmatic action
Panizza Allmark, Statues, Subversive actions and Surveillance
Carolyn Loeb, Reimagining the City: West Berlin Murals and the Right to the City

10h15 – 10h45: Keynote Speaker: Dra. Graça Fonseca (CML)

10h45 – 11h00: Coffee Break

11h00 – 12h15: Urban Creativity and Innovation // Chairman: Pedro Soares Neves (CIEBA/FBA-IST)
Laura Iannelli, Lorenza Parisi, To Govern artfully. Linking relational public art to urban governance toward new forms of civic participation
Cecilia Dinardi, Urban creativity from below: grassroots cultural interventions, politics and informal creative cities
Gabriela Vaz Pinheiro, No passage should go unnoticed: a case for a critical stance in temporary public art interventions

12h15 – 13h30: Lunch

13h30 – 14h45: In Theory // Chairman: Daniela V. de Freitas Simões (IHA-FCSH)
Victor Correia, Public Art: a conceptual problematic
Ilaria Hoppe, Urban Art as Countervisuality?
Luísa Santos Silva, Public Art Projects - Towards a Critical Discourse on Urban Aesthetics
Mischa Piraud, Luca Pattaroni, Yves Pedrazzini, Leticia Carmo, Creativity without critic. An inquiry into the aesthetization of alternative culture

14h45 – 15h15: Tactical Urbanism (book launch),
Mário Alves, João Seixas and Pedro Campos Costa
15h15 - 15h30: Coffee Break

15h30 – 16h30: Participation // Chairman: Lígia Ferro (ISCTE-IUL/CIES)
Helena Maria Santana, Maria do Rosário Santana, Flash Mob as a moment of creation and human intervention on urban spaces
Ana Vilar Bravo, Participatory Urban Art
Filipa Ramalhete, Maria Assunção Gato, Sérgio Vicente, A Participatory Public Art Process in Almada – Agents and Values

16h30 – 17h00: Closing Session

Website: Urbancreativity.org

Contact:
info@urbancreativity.org
conference.urbancreativity@gmail.com

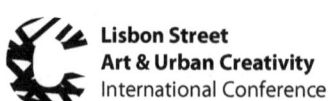

**Lisbon Street
Art & Urban Creativity**
International Conference

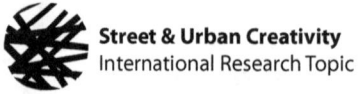

Street & Urban Creativity
International Research Topic

Urbancreatvity.org